Füsun Onur
Once upon a time…

59th International Art Exhibition
La Biennale di Venezia
Pavilion of Turkey

Curator: Bige Örer

La Biennale di Venezia
59. Esposizione Internazionale d'Arte
Partecipazioni Nazionali

Mousse Publishing

TABLE OF CONTENT

Curatorial Statement by Bige Örer

> The meaning of life also gives meaning to
> the world
> it is only by giving meaning to the world that
> life can have meaning
> because the world and life are identical in
> their meaning:
> your world is your life; your meaningful life,
> your world.
> —Oruç Aruoba, *Long Since*[1]

Over more than half a century of artistic practice, Füsun Onur has become a leading name in Turkish contemporary and conceptual art, commanding a language beyond time. Since the 1970s, she has pushed the limits of sculpture and even painting by transforming how they are understood; at every opportunity she invites renewed reflection on and discussion of their fundamental elements. Through her reinterpretations of forms and concepts, she has ensured that terms like 'installation' and 'assemblage' have entered into the local lexicon, becoming in the process a preeminent figure in the art history of Turkey. One of the artist's most significant interventions has been to offer new forms that remove sculpture from its static position and spatialise it in order to interactively incorporate the viewer.

Onur reconstructs and transforms her own world in every work. Rather than choosing the permanent materials of traditional sculptural works, she prefers to use provisional readymade objects that come from everyday life and are easy to procure. In some of her pieces she leaves these objects as they are, building relationships among them; in others she will intervene by altering them. For Onur, their forms are as important as their meanings. Similarly, the geometry of the spaces and objects is as important as their spirit. By staging relationships between different objects, and by creating contrasts and repetitions among them, she calls attention to their mathematical, poetic and musical rhythms. An indispensable feature in her works is the way in which they conjure silent rhythms and melodies, equating to musical notes.

Amongst the first generation to test, through her own subjectivity, the limits of the modern, Onur was

1. Oruç Aruoba, *Olmayalı* [Long Since], (Istanbul: Metis Publications, 2003), 75.

part of a group of artists considered to be leaders in conceptual art in the 1970s, including Altan Gürman, Sarkis, Nil Yalter, Cengiz Çekil, İsmail Saray and The Definition of Art Group (Sanat Tanımı Topluluğu, or STT). Though this era might not have provided an environment for radical art, each of these artists nonetheless produced works that interrogated what was present and that generated alternative languages, forms and discourses. Onur's works in the 1970s called into question the Minimalist art that came to prominence across the world at that time by combining abstractionism with narrative form.

Onur's early works, made while still at primary school, were small clay objects based on scenes from films and concerts. She experimented with baking these objects, and remembers crying when some of them burst in the oven. She painted the intact ones to add to her collection. These pieces, which became a universe of miniatures, exhibit parallels with the fundamental elements of the installation she has produced for the Venice Biennale. Similar in size to trinkets made of porcelain, glass and other materials that ornament the home, all of these objects are imbued with life by Onur. Some of them are still hidden in a cabinet in the home in Kuzguncuk where she lived as a child and which she uses as her studio and home.

Along with her father, whom she lost at a young age, her mother was supportive of her desire to make art. When friends expressed their admiration for Onur's figurines, her mother encouraged her to make new versions to give to them as gifts, and Onur did so to please her. But when she examined the copies, she saw a significant difference from her first figurines: the copies were lacking in spirit and emotion, she found, and she understood then that she would never make art to order or for money.

Onur's sister İlhan, has been her constant companion since their childhood, and occupies a place all her own. She has searched for materials with Füsun, shared her ideas with her during production, helped to create some pieces, offered guidance in spaces during exhibitions, photographed works, produced an archive, and saved works from being tossed into the sea or thrown in the trash. In addition to her endless love for Füsun, the respect, care and dedication she feels for her sister's work has allowed them both to lovingly embrace the world they have built together over the years. Ponpon, Tekir, Zorba and Lolita, their cats and dear companions who have joined them on this journey, frequently appear in Onur's creations. Zorba, who forced himself on them by lurking for days outside their window before ensconcing himself in the house, has become one of the main characters in the work she produced for Venice. Onur's relationship with creatures has shaped the animistic nature of her art, with cats, birds, elephants, and butterflies appearing in works such as *From Outside In From Inside Out* (1976), *Stories for Grown-Ups* (1977), *Bird* (1984), *Impromptu* (2003), *Elegy for Tekir* (2009–12), *Dance of the Crows* (2012), and *Miracle* (2013).

At the 59th Venice Biennale, Onur exhibits a new installation titled *Once upon a time…*, in which she has created different characters and scenes by bending and shaping metal wire. *Once upon a time…* is the story of an artist who gives meaning to the world. It is as much a portrait of a time filled with anxiety, fear, and ambivalence as it is of the feelings of solidarity, love and the joy of life that Onur has harboured over the course of her career.

The tale unravels over clouds spread throughout the space. Each scene can be interpreted on its own, but when they come together, they form a narrative on which Onur has worked for the past two years, never leaving the house due to the pandemic. The main characters of this fable, which looks back on the present from several centuries in the future, are mice and cats. When the mice learn about the pandemic from newspapers delivered by children outside of a school, they discuss what they can do to overcome the plague, which threatens the future of the world. They decide to join forces with cats in a common struggle against the manmade disaster. This solidarity between animals will protect the world from the disastrous human-driven approach that the pandemic makes visible. When the cats and mice begin working together, one mouse embarks on a journey to Venice, his curiosity piqued by the praise his artist friends in Istanbul have given to the city. The home of the friend receiving him there is in the exhibition space, and the following morning, they go exploring the city together. Encountering a festival in Venice, the mouse gets carried away by the magic of silent music and falls in love there. As the musicians perform their lively concert, the audience joins in by dancing around them. The transformative and dizzying power of the mouse's love – love not just for another mouse, but for art, life, and the city in which he lives – sets the course of the story.

For each scene, Onur gives straightforward notes that concisely narrate the story with poetic language. Narrative does not supersede the world experienced in the exhibition space; it merely accompanies the viewer, offering keys to enter into the fable. The ending is left to the viewer;

it invites many possibilities and encourages us to imagine different narratives, adding new meanings to the exhibition by viewing it through our own relationship to the world, to art, and to Venice.

'Wherever I go, I take Istanbul with me,' Onur has said, and in this work she imagines the first part of the story in Istanbul where she was born and raised, an Istanbul present in many of her works. She allows unexpected encounters and coincidences to shape her work; for instance, when she turns on the radio in the evening and hears the lyrics 'If the heart doesn't love Istanbul, what does it know of love, what does it know of love?' from Münir Nurettin Selçuk's song 'We Come to Kalamış for a Little Peace of Mind,' she brings those lyrics silently into her work as a reflection of her relationship with the world. The love she has for the world and for the city in which she lives reveals its presence in the character who finds love in Venice after the most difficult of times. Once again, Onur points us to the strength of art to give hope, to open up another perspective on the world, to access our emotions and instincts.

One of the signature features of Onur's artistic practice is her choice of materials. Working with those that best suit what she wants to express, she incorporates everyday things such as paper, cardboard, rope, cloth, sponge, plastic, beads and lace into her work. By selecting fragile, rippable, destructible materials, she embraces the ephemerality of art. She devised her story by drawing designs in the margins of newspapers and other papers that have passed through her hands. She then transformed them into three-dimensional forms. With the easily procurable thin metal wires she has bent and shaped by hand in this work, she was able to give the characters many different movements and feelings. The delicateness and permeability of the wires converges with the fragility of our own bodies. The wires vary in thickness and colour, and have been embellished with ping-pong balls and coloured crepe paper. Ordinary objects like pillows, blankets, chairs, books, rugs and curtains, musical instruments, and the vehicles like boats and cars that accompany the characters on their journey, are amongst the many elements that feature in this miniature world.

Space itself is a crucial aspect of this work. As the basic elements of the narrative, the small-scale objects stand in contrast to the emptiness of the exhibition room. Onur has mostly preferred to remain close to the ground when installing her works, without taking a vertical relationship to the gallery, without trying to occupy it, but rather, punctuating it with empty spaces and stopping points. In this exhibition, the sequential scenes of the story have been placed on clouds at different heights, strengthening the works' relationship with the floor and allowing the viewer to enter into a performative relationship with them. By removing sculpture from its pedestal, Onur opens up an arena of freedom for her objects, introducing lightness and transparency. Sometimes the clouds rise up in the space; sometimes they invite the viewer to kneel or sit down in order to look closely. The rhythm they create ignites a synesthetic experience in which spatial compositions and colour turn into music.

Onur has strived for the development of conceptual art in Turkey, and has served as a highly influential reference point for subsequent generations. In addition to her solo exhibitions in Turkey, and five editions of the Istanbul Biennale, she has exhibited works in international group exhibitions. But despite this international presence, she has been underrecognised in the global art world. Never separating her private life from her practice and using traditional and domestic forms such as weaving and textiles, she can be considered in the context of feminist art history. It is of great significance that her current work is exhibited in the Pavilion of Turkey at the 59th Venice Biennale, and that her creative practice, along with her poetic and candid language, will be followed, reread, reinterpreted and circulated in the international art world. Casting aside all expectations of large scale exhibitions such as the Venice Biennale, however, one of the most important meeting points for the art world, she sets her own rules by taking a stance that avoids monumentalism.

In a critical time like ours, in which art practices and forms of working are being interrogated and undergoing radical transformation, questions regarding what art is, and why making art matters are more important than ever. The fabulous world that Onur creates with her boundless imagination and creativity, nurtured by philosophy, literature and music, stages a poetic relationship between life and art that characterises not just her works, but her lifestyle and creative preferences. *Once upon a time…* is a masterwork that has meaningful things to say for the age in which we live, opening the door for careful eyes to see into a new and exciting world, producing new languages, and learning from nonhumans, loving and living together.

POSTSCRIPT: The exhibition and the publication were made over two years during difficult times thanks to solid bonds and the collective efforts of many – first of all, Füsun Onur, who has taken me into her inner world and shared her imagination, intuition, artistic excellence and love of life with me; İlhan Onur who has inspired me with her dedication to her sister's work and shared her albums and stories; Zorba and Lolita for their tenderness and joy. Then, of course, the supporters, all the contributors to the publication, the exhibition and publication team, mainly Selen, Yelta, Duygu, Marcello, Ilaria, my meticulous co-editor, Nilüfer, my beloved companions İnci, İz and Elif. I wish to thank them all. In particular, I would like to thank Bilge Uğurlar and Fulya Erdemci for their friendship and wisdom, as well as Timuçin and Ceyla for their devotion and support.

This text grew out of my conversations with Füsun Onur between March 2020 and March 2022. Throughout this process I benefited from the monograph *For Careful Eyes* (2007), published by Yapı Kredi Publications, which includes the translation of the original text Margrit Brehm wrote for Onur's exhibition catalogue for *From Far Away So Close* (2001), held at the Staatliche Kunsthalle Baden-Baden. I have also benefited from the book *Füsun Onur*, published as part of dOCUMENTA (13), the catalogue accompanying Onur's 2014 retrospective exhibition *Through the Looking Glass* at Arter, other texts written by Onur, and additional research conducted for the chronology included in this book.

Once upon a time…

59th International Art Exhibition
La Biennale di Venezia
Pavilion of Turkey

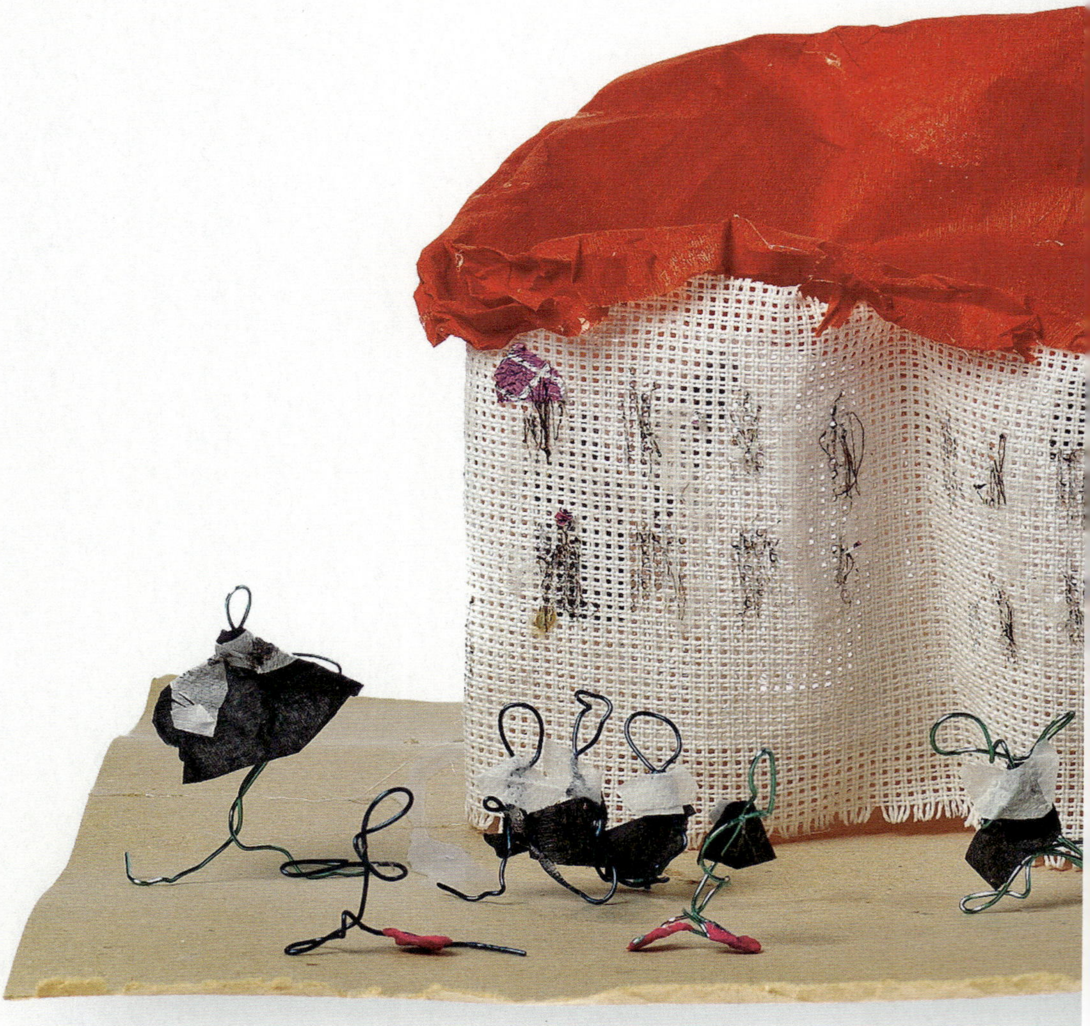

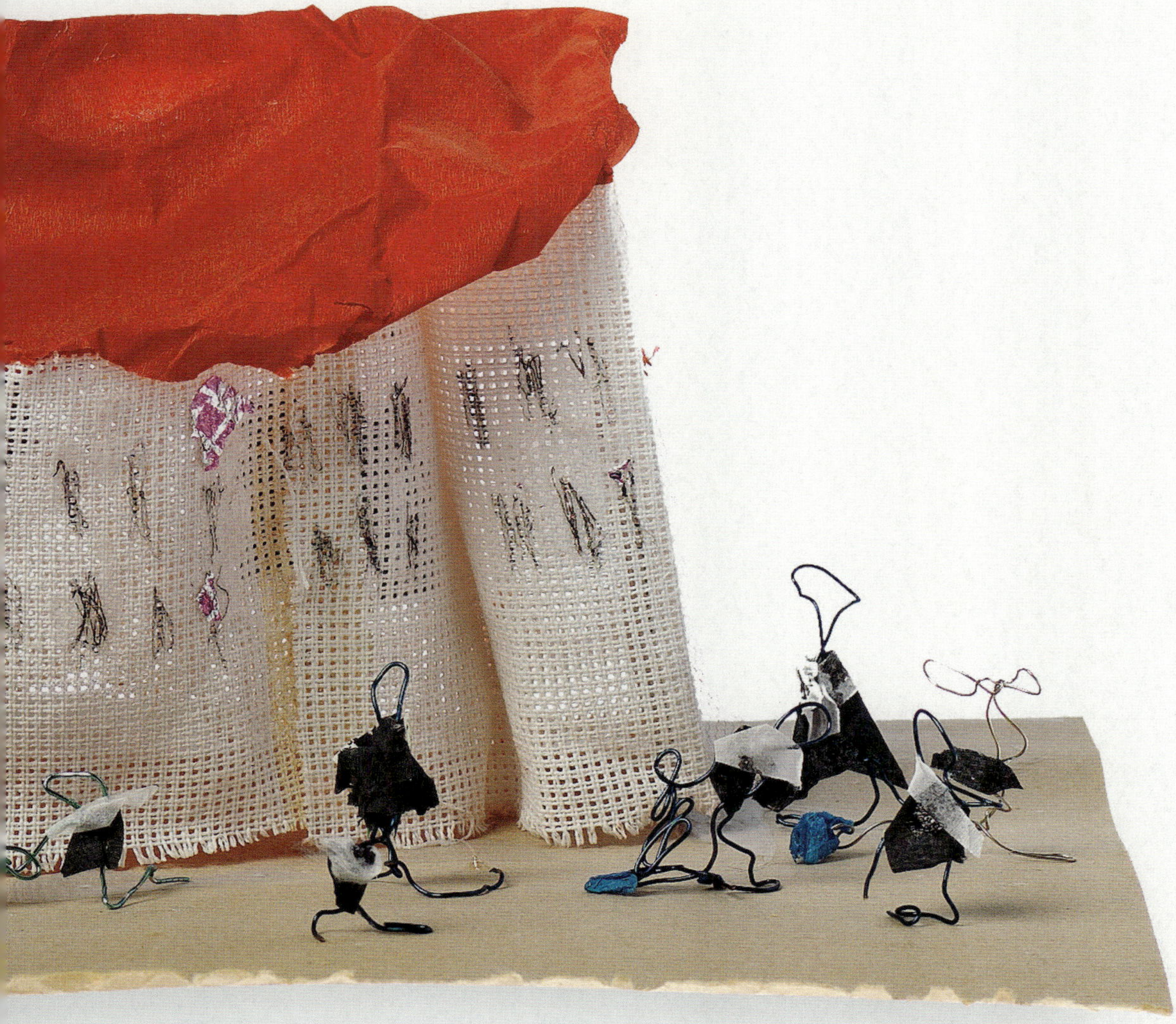

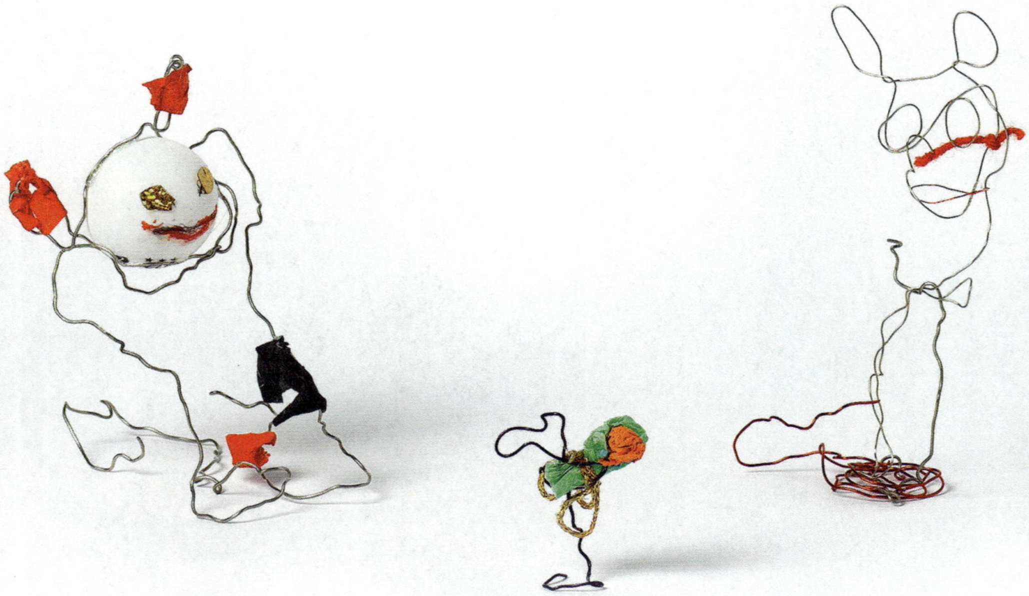

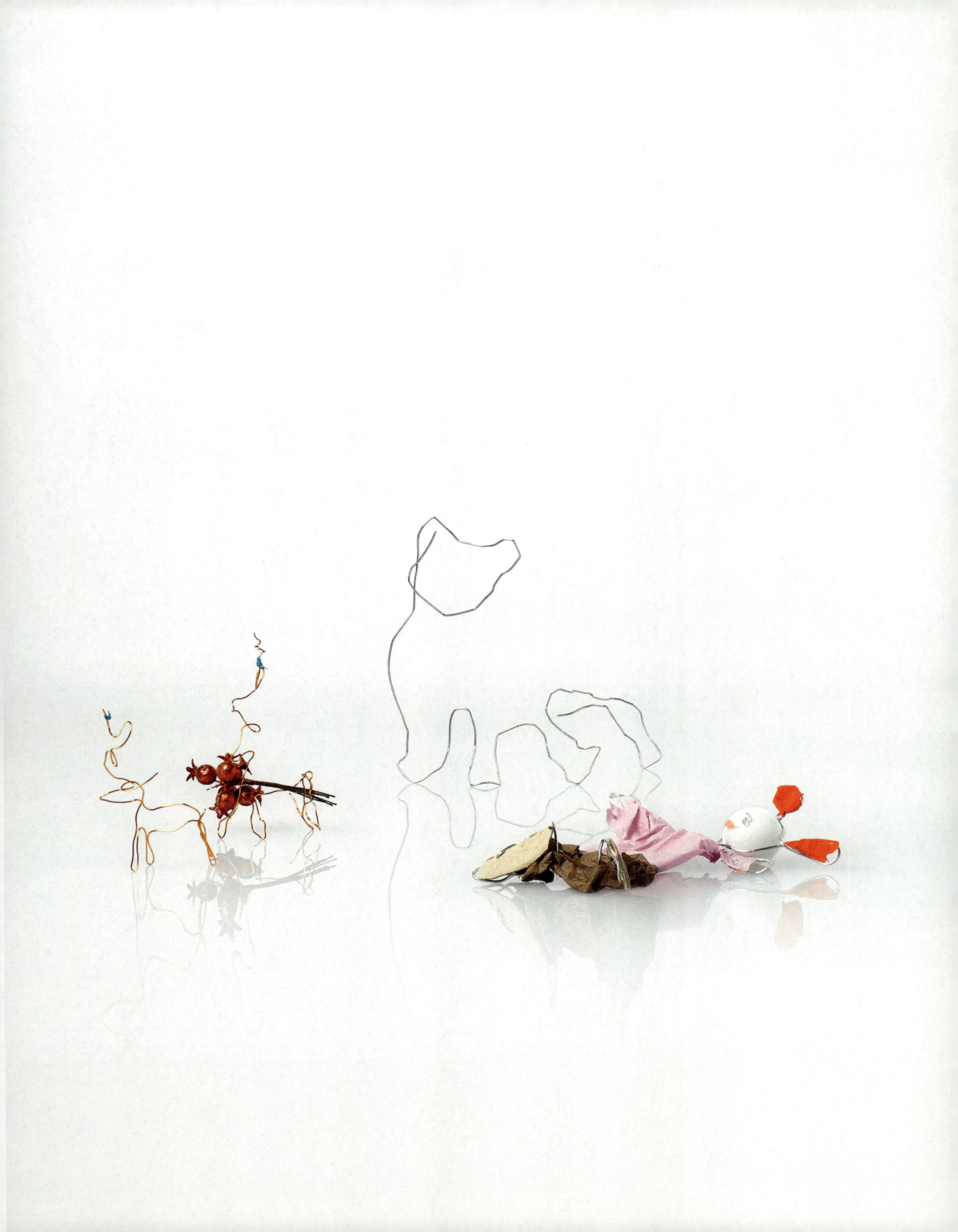

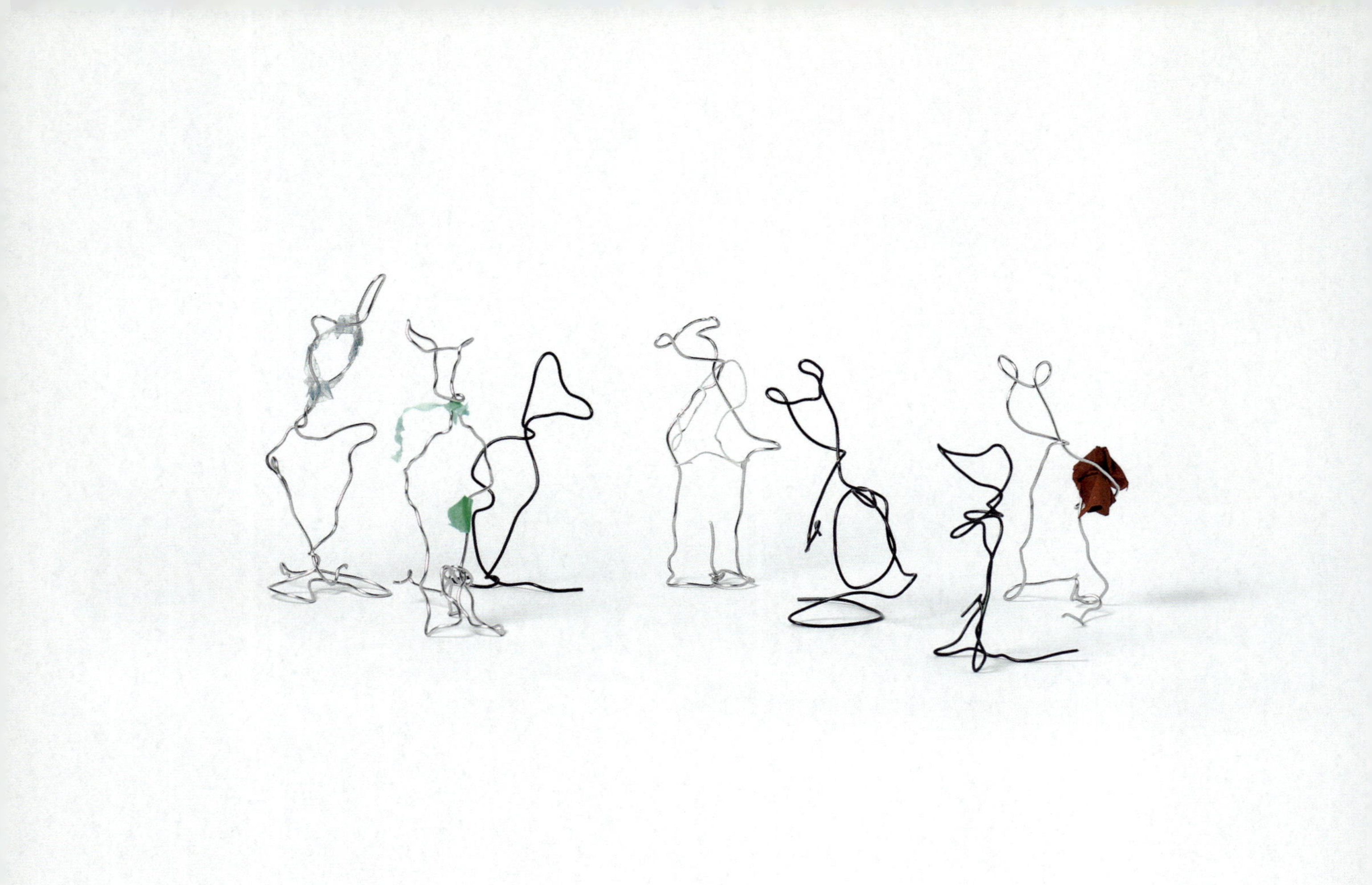

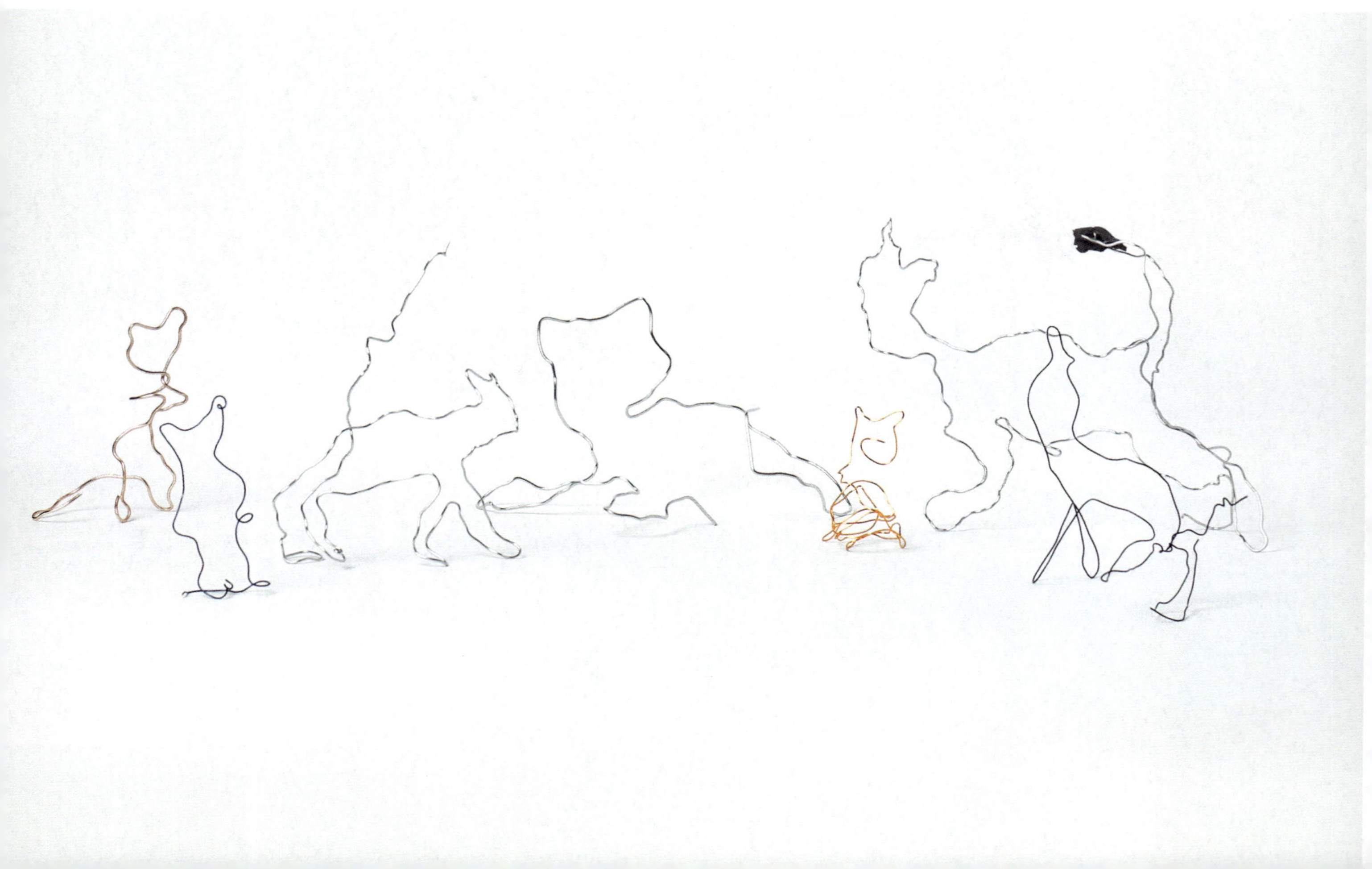

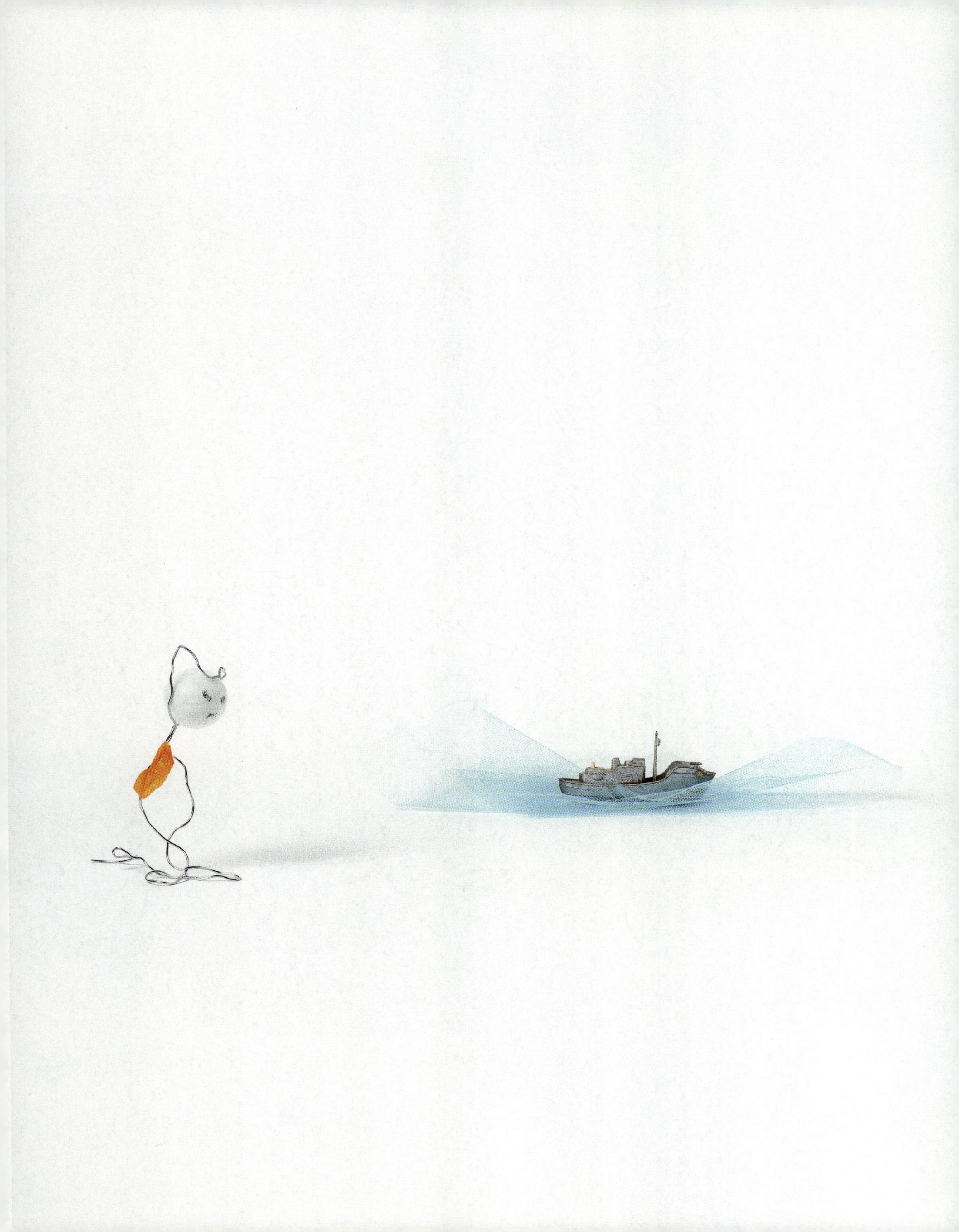

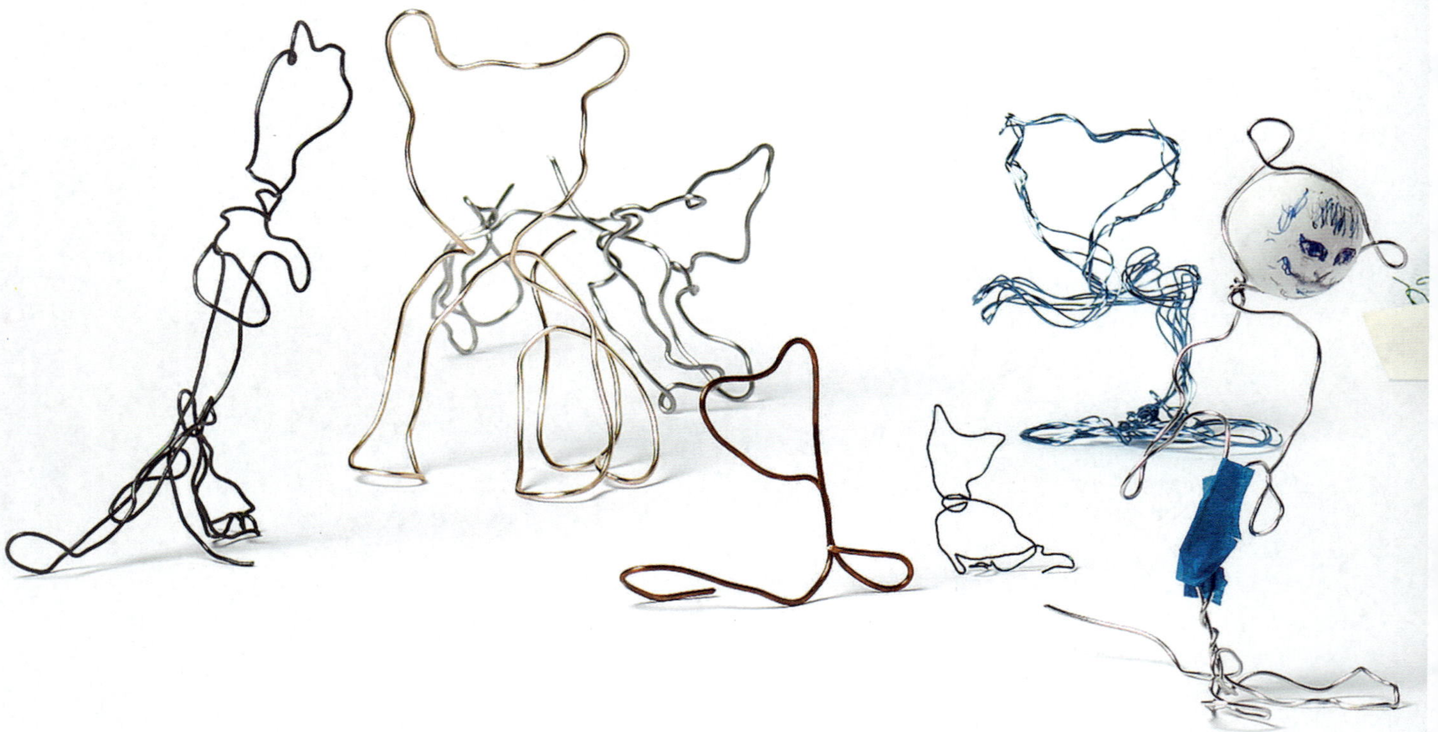

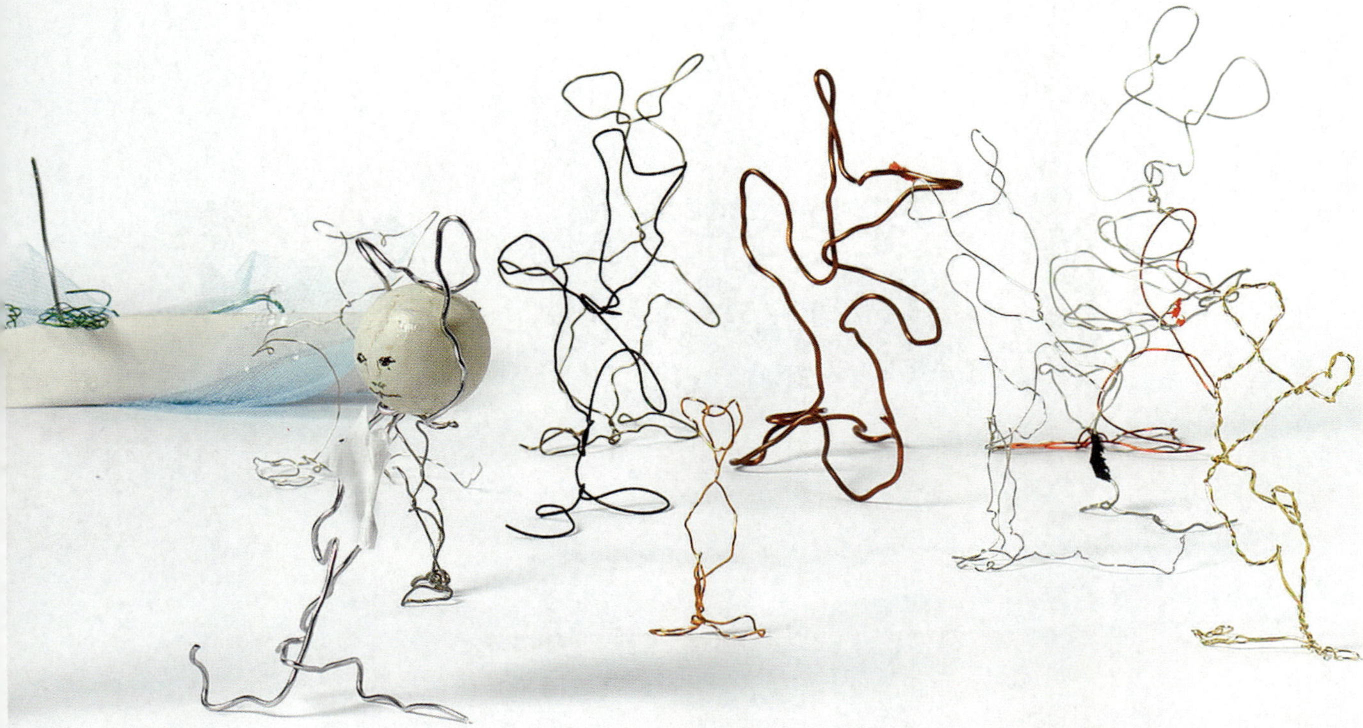

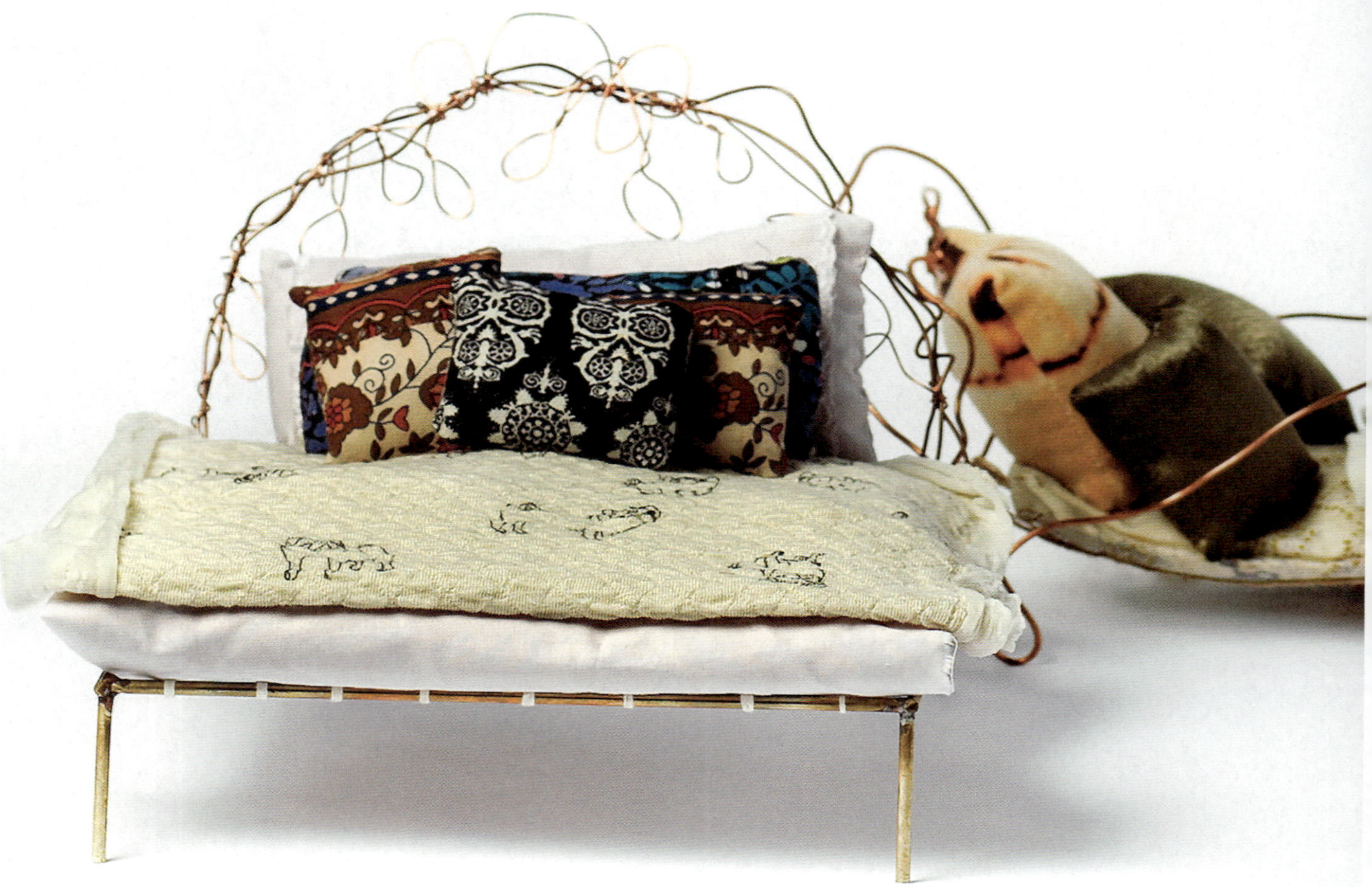

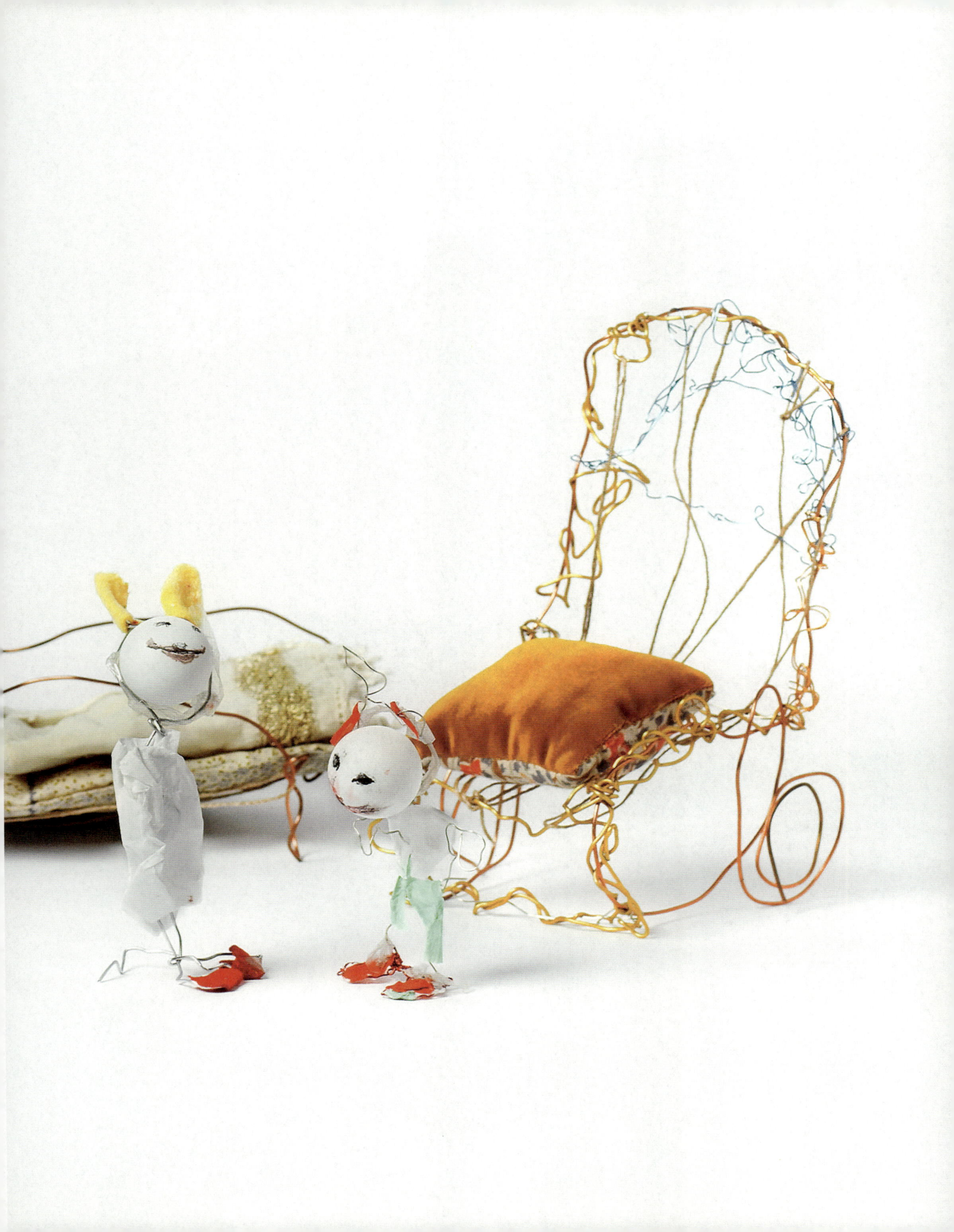

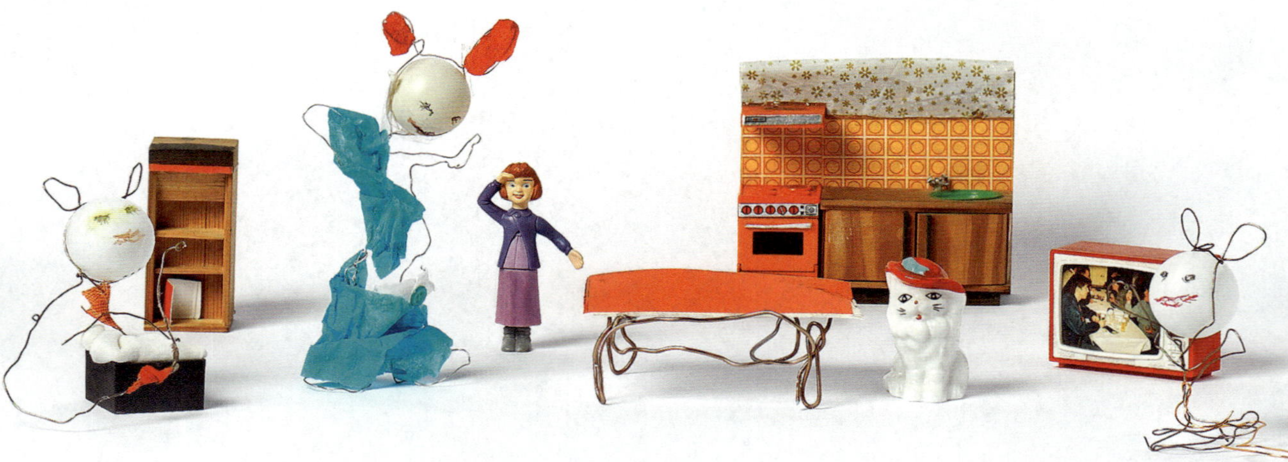

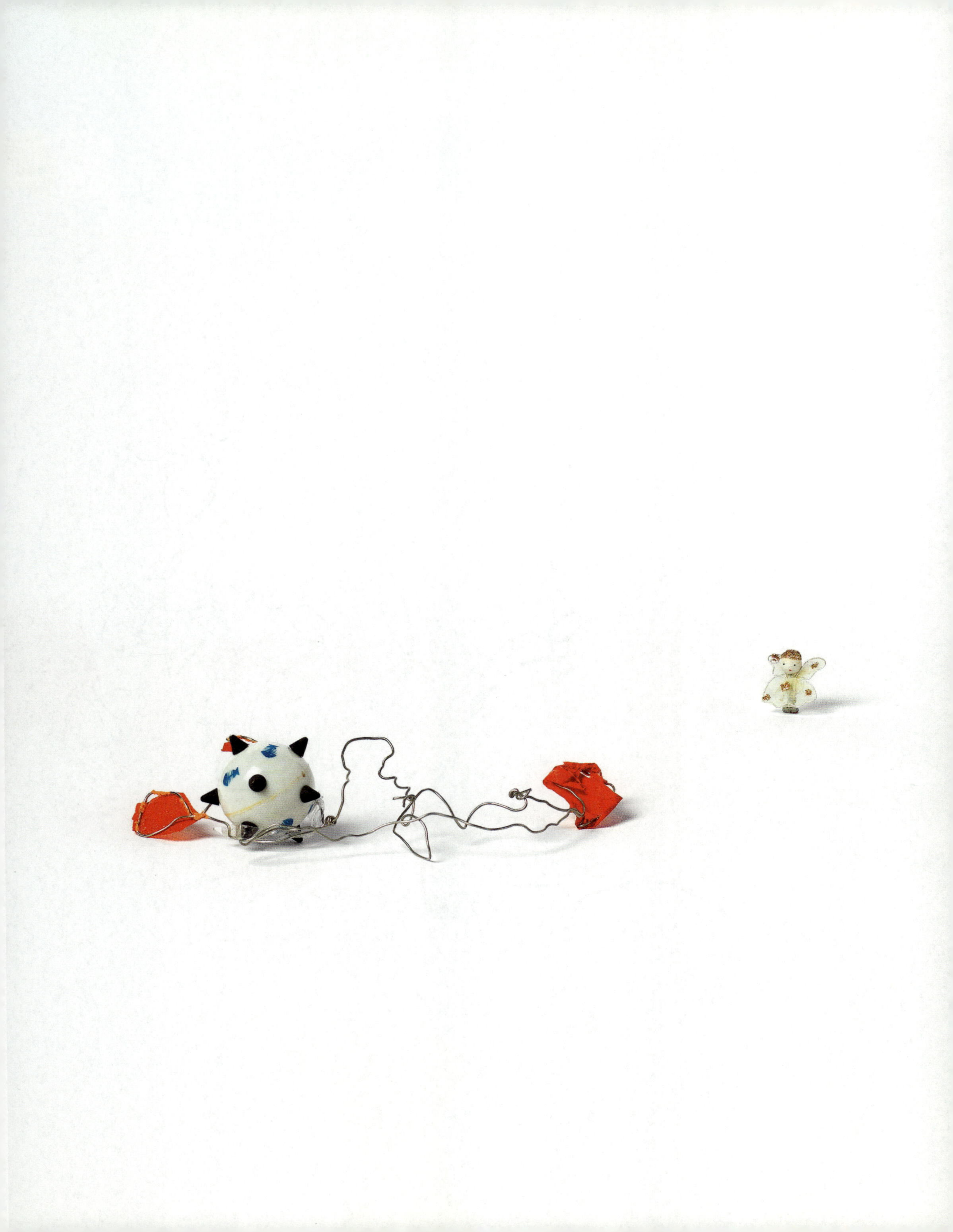

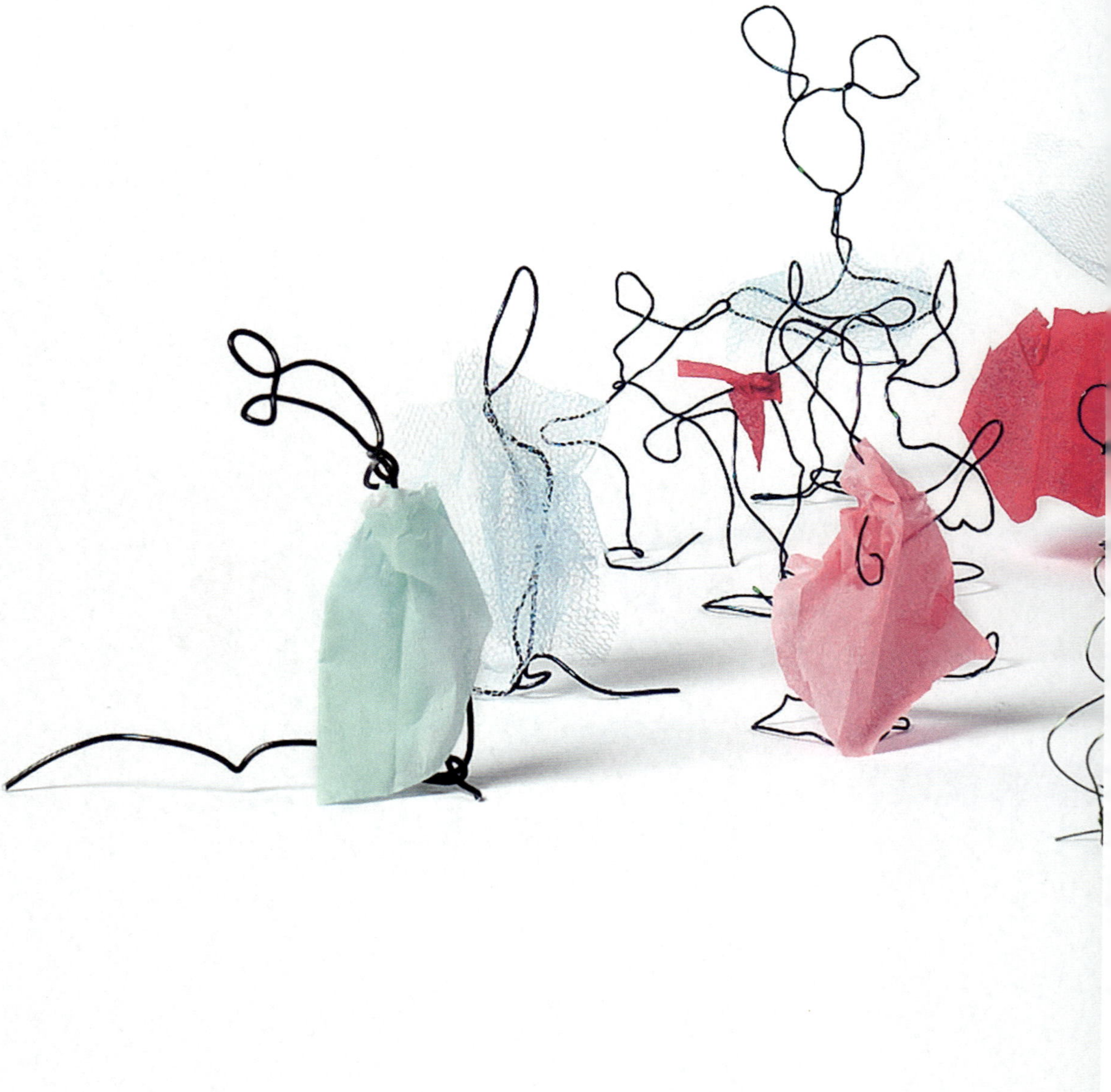

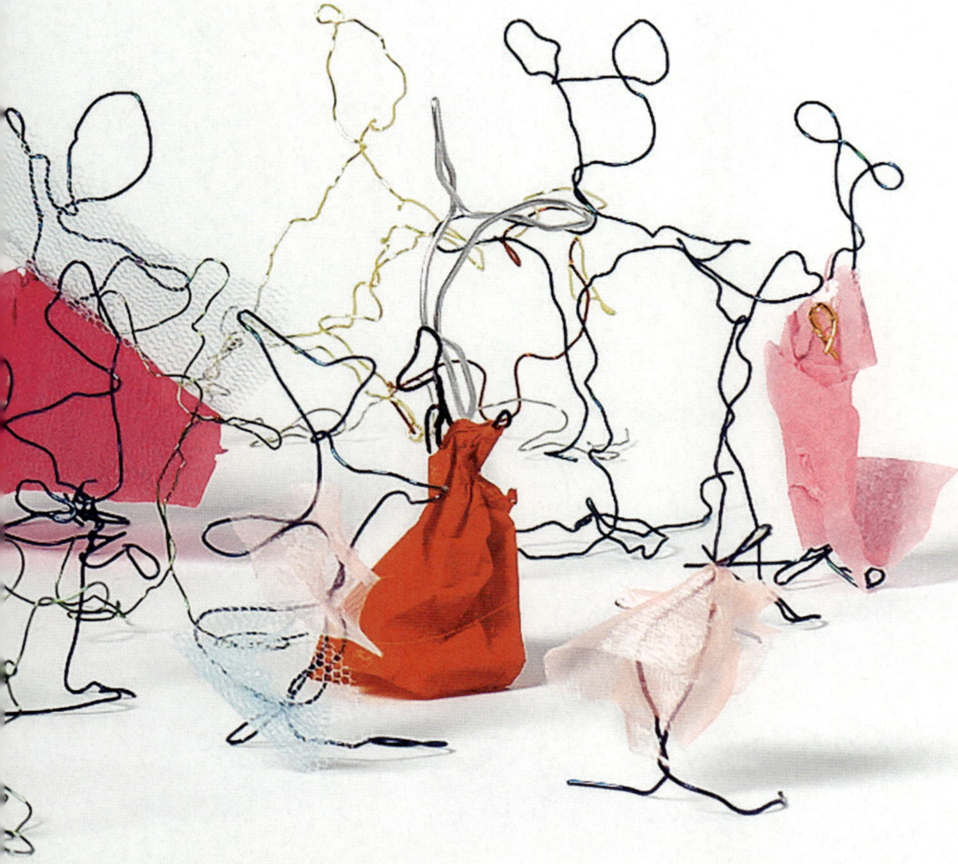

pp. 10–23
Füsun Onur, *Once upon a time…*, 2022
Mixed media installation (metal wire, crepe paper, ping-pong balls, various materials), variable dimensions

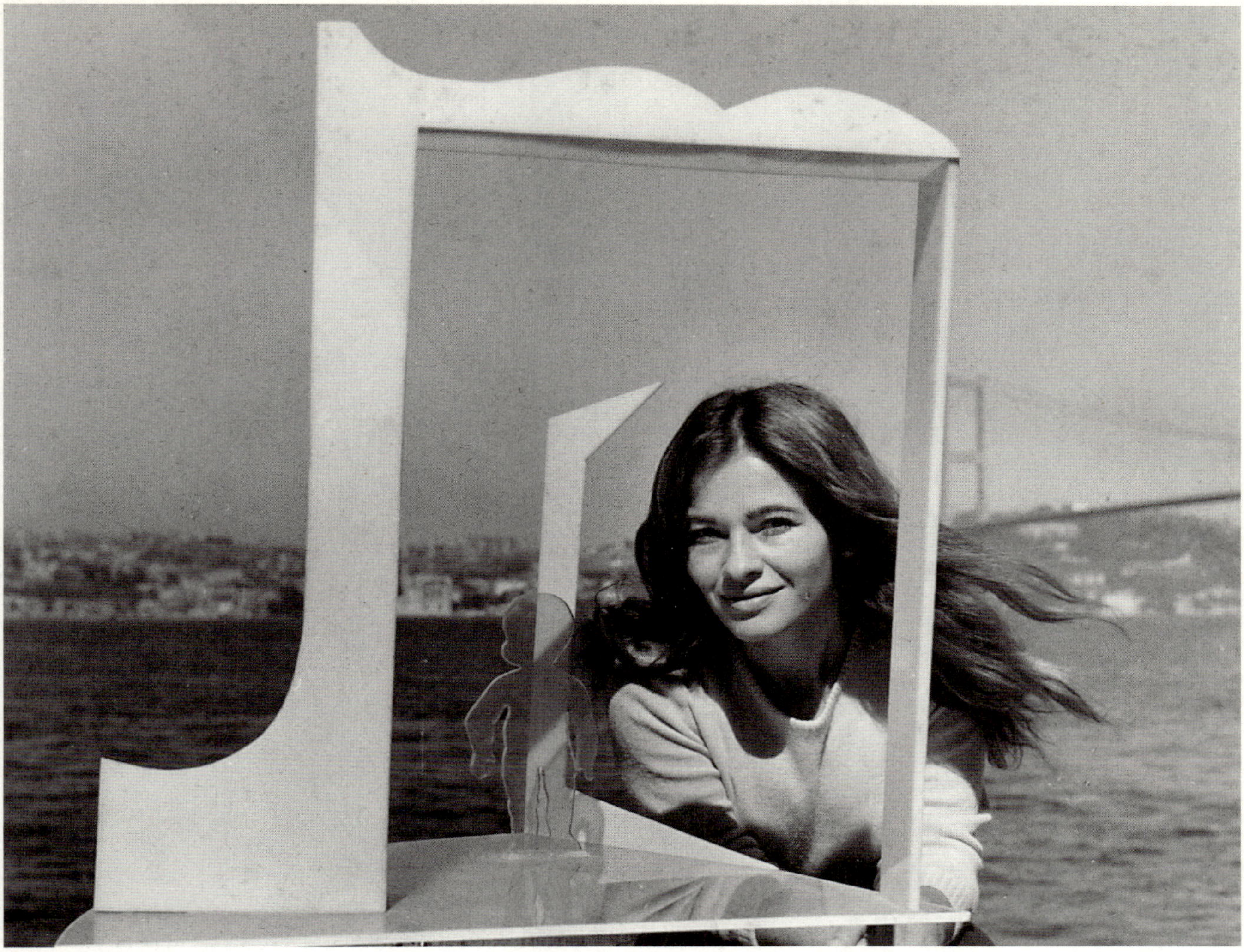

(FIG. 1)

Enchanting Realms[1] by Ahu Antmen

> For him, the quality of oldness was something
> else entirely;
> it was the consecration of time.
> By passing through human hands and entering
> human life,
> an object would assume a warmth independent
> of its own nature;
> become human, as it were.
> —Ahmet Hamdi Tanpınar, *Mahur Beste* (1944)

A photograph taken in 1974: Füsun Onur is posing on the banks of the Bosphorus with one of her sculptures (FIG. 1). The Bosphorus Bridge is in the background, built only a year before. Onur is among the residents of the waterfront houses (*yalı*) on the Bosphorus who must have witnessed the construction of the bridge from their windows day by day; living in the small coastal village of Kuzguncuk on the Bosphorus, she probably observed and heard the bridge's two towers as they rose like gigantic obelisks. Istanbul, a modest city of three million in those years, was rapidly becoming the destination of heavy migration and urbanisation, losing its old image and timbre, becoming impregnated with the mega transformations of the years to come. Against this background, the Onur house was like the pocket watch in the novel *Mahur Beste*, 'simultaneously showing both alla turca and alla franca time.'[2] If you went there today, you'd find both the house and the delicate, childlike woman in that photograph almost unchanged. Onur is eighty-five years old now; in the photograph she was thirty-seven. She'd already held her first solo exhibition (1970) at the prominent Taksim Art Gallery, one of the few exhibition venues of those days; she'd participated in the Paris Biennale of Young Artists (1971), which was then one of the significant art events of Europe; and had a sculpture erected outdoors in Fındıklı as part of the *50 Sculptures for the 50th Anniversary of the Republic* project, which for the first time in Turkey facilitated original artworks other than traditional Atatürk monuments to be installed in public space (1973). In short, she was becoming known on Turkey's small art scene, which was at the time still predominantly centred around the Istanbul State Academy of Fine Arts.

1.
The original Turkish title, *Füsunkâr Alemler*, is a pun on the artist's name, which stems from the word magic in Farsi, and means 'enchantment.' The title is borrowed from a sentence by the writer Safiye Erol which I came upon on Kubbealtı Lexicon: 'Oh the folk song that rings enchanting realms in my mind.' See http://www.lugatim.com/s/EFSUNK%C3%82R. It seemed to express Onur's idiosyncratic mysterious world. However, the pun is lost in translation.

2.
Ahmet Hamdi Tanpınar, *Mahur Beste* [Idyllic Melody] (Istanbul: Dergâh Publications, 2005), 24. The text that initially appeared as a series in the journal *Ülkü* in 1944 was first published as a book in 1975 (Dergâh Publications).

As luck would have it, the sculpture with which she is posing in the photograph is not one of those she threw off the dock of the house to disappear into the waters of the Bosphorus. It is one of her few sculptures included in a collection.[3] She has produced a great many works, so many installations, installed and deinstalled in Turkey and abroad, some remembered some forgotten... Contemporary artworks rarely find a place in private or public collections in Turkey, so it's difficult for artists to bear both the physical and emotional burden of accumulating their works. The question she posed to the reader in an article she wrote in the 1980s seems to have been addressed to herself: 'What remains from my years of work?'[4] However, the fact that Onur is now remaking some of her discarded works so as to exhibit them in Turkey's new art venues and have them included in a new historiography demonstrates that she is no longer rowing against the tide. And one cannot overlook the fact that surrendering work to the currents of the Bosphorus and her inclination towards an ephemeral medium like installation reflect Onur's philosophy on both life and art. Having 'discovered the notion of self-destruction'[5] and existentialist thought through her readings of Nietzsche and Sartre in the 1960s, Onur became convinced that art expanded objecthood into a realm of intuitional and emotional experience, and therefore was quite able to part with her works, saying, 'when they overcrowd me, I take a good photograph of each and throw them in the sea.'[6]

NOSTALGIA AS A GENERATIONAL REFLEX

It is neither easy nor meaningful to discuss Onur's artistic identity as a separate entity from her life. Recognised today as one of the pioneers of contemporary art in Turkey, she shapes her work through direct or indirect reflections on her existence, the city of Istanbul, the Bosphorus, and the habits of *yalı* life. On a fundamental level, her art is based on the perception of time and flux; at a more intimate level, traces of her personal experience within the flow of time are the clues to her work. We should also look beyond an abstract notion of time to the specific time of her life. Onur was born in 1937, a year before Atatürk died.[7] Her childhood coincides with the critical period when Turkey, just after the declaration of the Republic, was in a process of modernist nation-making. She grew up in an environment that was constantly in dynamic flux between the old and the new, amidst the changes in the cosmopolitan fabric of Istanbul due to the economic and social effects of the Second World

3.
This sculpture (50 × 50 × 30 cm) named *Untitled* (1974) is thought to be in the collection of Tomris Atikkan.

4.
Füsun Onur, 'Görsel Sanatlarda Eleştiri Yokluğu' [The Lack of Criticism in Visual Arts], *Hürriyet Gösteri*, no. 82, September 1987, 43.

5.
Defne Ayas, 'Füsun,' *Füsun Onur* (Cologne: W. König, 2012), 12.

6.
Feriha Büyükünal, *Sordum* [I Asked] (Istanbul: Sanat Çevresi Yayınları, 1992), 210.

7.
Füsun Onur's birthdate in all major publications is stated as 1938. During the preparation of this book, she corrected this date to 1937.

War, and the conflicts between different political tendencies during the country's period of transition to a multiparty regime. In this respect, what makes Onur's generation particularly interesting is that they are first-hand witnesses to the evolution of contemporary Turkey. Having spent their childhood and youth during the years when the Republican ideology was experienced most intensely, they carry those modernist ideals like a cultural heritage. The values attributed to the modern as a concept create a conflict between various cultural manifestations of the experiences of modernity unique to Turkey, and that is particularly evident in this generation, leading to a sort of nostalgia.

As Svetlana Boym points out in *The Future of Nostalgia*, 'outbreaks of nostalgia often follow revolutions.'[8] Furthermore, 'nostalgia is not always about the past; it can be retrospective but also prospective.' Onur's recollections of the past as someone whose childhood was spent in the 1940s when the effects of the modernist culture revolution was deeply felt by her generation, resembles those of other middle/upper-middle-class, educated, modern Istanbulites. She emphasises the cosmopolitan and Western modernity of Istanbul, and reveres her late father, whom she lost as a child, as 'a major proponent of modernisation.' She recalls being 'submersed in a passion for the arts, the opera, Shakespeare plays, and ballet' in Istanbul, a place that she describes as intellectually and culturally a 'very modern' city.[9] Despite the fact that she denies a longing for the past, Onur constantly incorporates its traces in her work, bringing feeling to those traces in the present. In this regard, she helps us comprehend the deeper meaning of nostalgia as an elusive state of mind, and opens a door to the personal and cultural manifestations of this emotion.

A FADING FUTURE AND 'OFF-MODERN'

Boym states that unlike melancholy, which is confined to a plane of individual consciousness, nostalgia concerns the relationship between personal and collective memory. She points to a tradition of critical reflection on the modern condition that also comprises nostalgia. She uses the concept 'off-modern' to describe this condition, wherein 'reflection and longing, estrangement and affection go together.' In countries like Turkey, where modernity is experienced in the backwoods, as it were, of the Western world, and among the sociopsychological dynamics of local time, the concept of 'off-modern' evokes a perception of lost potential and faded dreams of the future. Hence nostalgia can appear in the

8. Svetlana Boym, 'Taboo on Nostalgia,' *The Future of Nostalgia* (New York City: Basic Books, 2002).

9. Ayas, 10–11.

form of ideological national/religious revivals, and sometimes it emerges as a more critical interrogation of the forms of modernisation; it offers an opportunity to consider unrealised possibilities and unforeseeable turning points. As such, rather than a longing for the past, it resembles an intense emotional relationship with time in its lived and unlived dimensions. And not only with time but with space, too; according to Boym, nostalgia, which 'charts space on time and time on space and hinders the distinction between subject and object,' predicts an intense relationship with space, and unearthing it requires a 'dual archaeology of memory and of place.'

In this respect, Onur, who has lived for most of her life with her two siblings in the family *yalı*, maintaining traces of the past in the form of various objects like old photographs, fabrics, papers, postcards, dresses, chalices, bric-a-brac, carries nostalgia in both her life and her art. Although she is not an artist who explicitly explores Turkey's makeshift 'off-modern' states from an ideological, political or sociological perspective, her return to Turkey from the States, 'to be useful to her country,'[10] following her Fulbright Scholarship in Sculpture at Maryland Institute College of Art, reflects her personal sensitivity and inclination to a constant 'archaeology of memory and place.' This social sensitivity is an often-overlooked quality of Onur's work. Viewed from the perspective of Boym's concept of 'off-modern' or 'critical nostalgia,' many of her works, and particularly those from the post-1980s, become more 'legible.' Clues can be found by looking at the repertoire in her work of that period of old objects ranging from photographs to robes and textiles, and even their titles: *Dream of Old Furniture* (1985), *Black Roses for Yıldız Palace* (1985), *Atatürk Flower* (1985), *Shadow Play* (1987), *Souvenir de Dolmabahçe* (1992), *Heritage* (1993), *Child's Remembrance of the Word Germany* (1994), *Istanbul Obsession* (1994), *Atatürk's Mother Zübeyde Hanım* (1995), *I Don't Know French* (1995), *Elegy for Tekir* (2009). Various familiar cultural objects, conditions and longings such as imperial tales conveyed from the past to the present; memorabilia of the nation-state; shadow plays – a once-favourite form of entertainment; old furniture carefully draped in cloths; the decorum of speaking French; the idealisation of Europe; the image of the blonde child; and Istanbul's tabby cats (*tekir*) remind us of the sources of our 'off-modernity,' the cultural trauma amidst our visions of the past and of the future. Onur doesn't make lofty statements, but encourages us to feel through the prism of her personal experience, observing forms of cultural modernism that have

10. Büyükünal, 209.

or have not been engraved within us. Artistic modernism, like those modernist ideals, is also part of this framework.

THE LOCAL AND UNIVERSAL ASPECTS OF PICTORIAL SPACE

The Istanbul State Academy of Fine Arts is among the foremost cultural symbols of modernism in Turkey, and holds a very prominent place in Onur's life. A fundamental trait of this idiosyncratic academy of arts, significant in terms of its heritage from late-Ottoman modernity to the Republic, is that although it has followed the Western model of a traditional academy, it has also harboured, in various periods, certain innovative advances. Onur's years as a student there coincide with one of those times. Having entered the Academy during a long period in which the rigidly disciplinary academic era of Rudolf Belling (1886–1972) in the Sculpture Department came to a close, she studied under Ali Hadi Bara (1906–1971), when technical competence was being given less emphasis by instructors who were more curious about contemporary practices within artistic modernism. Onur remembers Bara with profound admiration,[11] asserting that his sculptures would 'make us proud wherever in the world one took them.'[12] His influence on her is evident in her early practice; so much so that some of her sculptures seem to be in conversation with the artist. The rendering of emptiness and fullness, which Bara explores in his open-form geometric iron sculptures or his metal planar reliefs from the 1950s, virtually constitutes a 'grammar' for Onur's early sculpture studies. That said, a comparison between Bara's *Full-Empty* (1952, 1959) (FIG. 2) and Onur's *Composition II* (1971) (FIG. 3), which was invited to the Paris Biennale of Young Artists, reveals that the relationship between teacher and student is not one of imitation but of rethinking and transformation.

The fact that Onur spent her years as a student at the Academy when, alongside Bara, Zühtü Müridoğlu (1906–1992) and the younger İlhan Koman (1921–1986) were breathing new life into a dry environment of formulaic academicism, is among the primary factors that shaped her artistic identity. She had been encouraged by her family and her school environment during her secondary and high-school years, and received a relatively liberal education at the Üsküdar American Academy for Girls, in contrast to the standardised education system in Turkey. We can tell from her own words that she was happy as a student at the Academy. In her interviews, she often reiterates the excitement she felt on her first day there. One can also sense

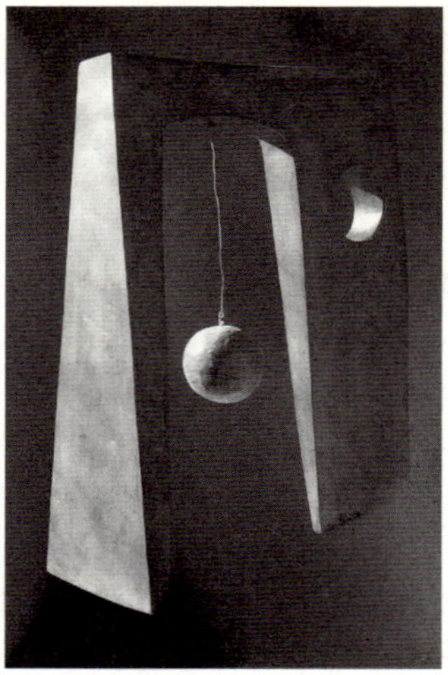

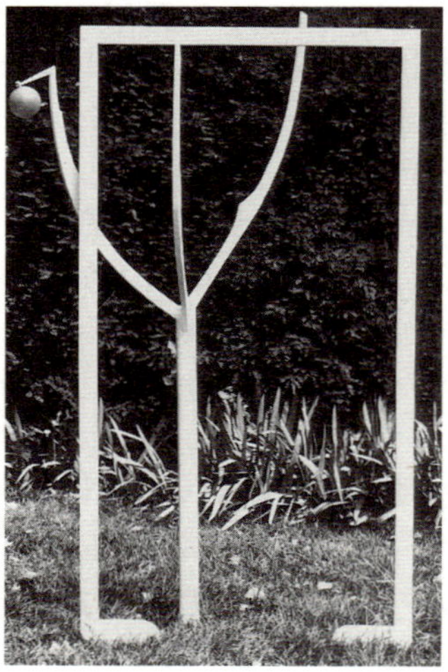

(FIGS. 2–3)

11. Onur says that in later years she understood what a huge opportunity it was to have been a student of Bara in the Sculpture Department of the Academy, and describes the environment of their atelier as follows: 'On the days we had Prof. Hadi, our atelier would be filled with a crowded group of students also from other departments like architecture and painting, and the conversations and discussions would go on until the wee hours. These conversations sometimes involved the atelier and life of an artist, and sometimes they revolved around an architect, a painter, a sculptor, or an art movement. Sometimes it would be about a current issue or our problems as students or it would be a response to our questions. Years later I understood that all his talks honed our skills of reflection, awareness, and perception; these conversations unveiled the action and reaction and awakened all our sensitivity in exploring our environment, ourselves, the world, everything from the simplest to the most complex, and made us love the profession.' See: Füsun Onur, '9 Eylül 1906, Yetmişinci Doğum Yıldönümünde Hadi Bara' [9 September 1906, Hadi Bara on the Seventieth Anniversary of His Birth], *Ankara Sanat*, no. 125, September 1976, 10.

12. Ibid.

her anger in the face of comments that overlook her years as Bara's student at the Academy after her return from the States, where she studied between 1962 and 1967. She feels the need to remind those who associate her with 'the American school'[13] or 'Western crew'[14] that she graduated from the department of sculpture at the Academy as a student of Hadi Bara, defining him as 'a great artist, an esteemed teacher,'[15] pointing to an essential aspect of her artistic roots.

Given his share in the shaping of her artistic identity, a closer look at Bara provides a clue to understanding Onur's artistic evolution. In terms of the development of modernism in Turkey, Bara is certainly an important figure; he is the fundamental bridge between the old and the new, the figurative and the abstract. In the 1930s and 1940s, he was one of the first students of sculpture sent to Paris on a state scholarship during the early Republican period. At this time, he was conservative in his approach to modernity, both as an artist and a teacher, a champion of conventional monument-making based on classical figurative sculpture. However, on his return to Turkey in 1949 after a summer vacation in Paris, where he had seen that he had fallen behind the new tendencies, we find before us an 'abstractionist.'[16] Bara's transformation is woven with psychological and cultural factors far too complex to render in a few sentences, and brings forth important questions about how national/cultural contexts shape the practice of modern art in a country. For Bara's generation, modernism was still about finding the correct formal expression that could represent modern Turkish sculpture in a Western-centric world; the pursuit of subjective identity was experienced as an intricate relationship with cultural identity. Their feelings in striving to attain an original language of art was always somehow bound to what the sculptor Hüseyin Gezer confessed as 'not being able to position oneself in tune with the times.'[17] Sharing the common narrative of many 'other' modernities, Turkey's modern artists had to confront the inevitable burden of such internalised cultural issues beyond individual processes of creation in an effort to reach 'themselves.'

Onur entered the Academy at a time when notions of 'local' and 'universal' were predominant concepts within debates around the idea of originality in 'modern art,' dividing artists into two camps. In the words of Nurullah Berk (1906–1982), an active artist, teacher and writer of the era, those who tended towards a 'local and national' flavour in art and those who embraced abstract art in an 'inclination

13.
Anonym, 'Füsun Onur: Türkiye'de geleneksel heykel sanatı yok' [There is no traditional sculpture art in Turkey], *Milliyet*, 27 February 1985.

14.
Fahir Aksoy, 'Özde toplumcu gerçekçilik ve Taifa-ı-Batıyan' [Social realism in essence and the Western Crew], *Politika*, 16 April 1976, 6.

15.
Füsun Onur, 'Büyük Sanatçı Kıymetli Hoca Hadi Bara' [Great Artist Esteemed Teacher Hadi Bara], *Ankara Sanat*, no. 68, December 1971, 10.

16.
On Bara's transformation, see Nurullah Berk-Hüseyin Gezer, *50 Yılın Türk Resim ve Heykeli* [50 Years of Turkish Painting and Sculpture] (Istanbul: Türkiye İş Bankası Kültür Yayınları, 1973), 24. Also, for a detailed study on Ali Hadi Bara as an artist and an educator, see Ayşe Nahide Yılmaz, *Ali Hâdi Bara ve Atölyesi: Türk Heykelinde Yeni Oluşumlar* [Ali Hâdi Bara and His Atelier: New Developments in Turkish Sculpture] (Ankara: Hacettepe Üniversitesi Sosyal Bilimler Enstitüsü, 2006).

17.
Berk-Gezer, 22.

towards the universal'[18] constituted the two separate poles. Onur's artistic thinking was also based on this dichotomy. Modernist principles, which she attributed to Bara's teaching, such as 'designing and inventing'[19] determined her path like other modern artists of her generation, and even as she was learning how to depict the figure, her work tended towards the abstract. In 1957, when she was in her first year at the Academy as a prospective artist 'preoccupied with forms,'[20] Hadi Bara, Zühtü Müridoğlu and İlhan Koman participated in the São Paulo Biennial with abstract sculptures, and Şadi Çalık – who was to join them as an educator at the Academy – exhibited his *Minimumism*, a black iron rod mounted on a metal pedestal, in a group exhibition at the Istanbul American News Centre. Abstract art was clearly on the rise, providing a basis for interesting experiments and starting to become visible internationally. In the period leading up to the 1960s, the tendency towards abstract art was shared both by teachers such as Bara and Müridoğlu, who wished to free sculpture from the yoke of conventional, traditional busts and monuments, and by artists of a younger generation such as İlhan Koman, Şadi Çalık, Kuzgun Acar and Ali Teoman Germaner. These artists were concerned with creating a new language of sculptural form with elements like space, mass, volume, surface, light and shadow. Onur, who was focused on the relationship between the interior and exterior of form, rather than its outer shape,[21] even when working from the live model, may seem, when compared with others among her generation, to be distanced from sculpture in this sense, but she actually never broke ties with its fundamental aspects. For instance, in her late 'abstract' installations, which seem like musical notations 'rendered three-dimensional,' the desire to shape the spatial void as if it were a mass echoes the concerns of emptiness/fullness of her early period. Constituting a large part of her artistic output since the 1990s, these works are described by the artist as 'sculpture divided into modules through time.'[22] It is as if, in her digressions from sculpture, she left behind a trail of pebbles rather than vanishing crumbs.

Onur internalised the modernist teaching at the Academy, while never becoming a fervent follower blindly committed to it, and this is the staple quality that sets her apart from other sculptors of her generation. Mocking a barren discussion of locality, she questions 'As if pictorial space can actually be deemed American or Turkish!,'[23] also revealing her understanding of the 'universal.' Critics who advised her to work with elements of past Turkish

18. See Ahu Antmen, *Türk Sanatında Yeni Arayışlar* [New Pursuits in Turkish Art] (Istanbul: Mimar Sinan Güzel Sanatlar Üniversitesi Sosyal Bilimler Enstitüsü, 2005), 66.

19. Yılmaz, 88.

20. Büyükünal, 208.

21. 'Füsun Onur, Carolyn Christov-Bakargiev, and Hans Ulrich Obrist, in Conversation,' *Füsun Onur* (Cologne: W. König, 2012), 22.

22. Ibid., Burcu Pelvanoğlu, 'Chronology,' 264.

23. Füsun Onur, 'Bir Cevap…' [A Response], *Sanat Çevresi*, no. 139, May 1990, 71.

culture like 'tombstones' in order to be 'local' appear to her as absurd.[24] It is obvious that for her, locality or universality was never an issue of form, and that she was always aware that the discovery of a 'language of art' urged by artistic creativity was a more personal, more spiritual phenomenon. Her expression, 'Art is my life. I was born with it inside me' captures her idiosyncratic, childlike approach. Interpreting her artistic inclination as a sort of fate, and filtering the language of modernism through her own subjective quest, that language for Onur thus acquired an existentialist, rather than a formalist dimension. Stating that she 'wanted to find herself'[25] before leaving for the States having finished at the Academy, her discovery of a philosophical outlook on art practice constituted a new phase in Onur's process of finding her voice. In this context, predominant features of modernist sculptural practice such as the contrast of full or empty form are tackled and expressed like existential issues of presence and absence. In the early 1960s, while studying for her Master's degree, she strived to find her own voice by questioning, scrutinising and deconstructing the grammar of the modernist language that she had learnt.

SOUNDING AND PRESENCE

Onur's voice as an artist started to become audible in 1966, when she had completed her Master of Fine Arts degree in Maryland before a jury that included well-known American artists such as Norman Carlberg (1928–2018), Grace Hartigan (1922–2008) and Gilbert A. Franklin (1919–2004). And although she was subjected to the unfair criticism of merely copying from abroad, her years in the US were not as formative as her years at the Academy in Istanbul. However, the US was the place where she learnt to listen to her own voice, and realised her longing to expand form into a field of intuition, emotion and presence, and that in itself is no mean feat. The encouragement of a teacher who saw her abstract drawings among her nature studies constituted a milestone for her.[26] The force of existential philosophy, still ripe after its initial impact in the post-war cultural milieu, and especially the influence of Abstract Expressionism as interpreted by existentialist critics such as Harold Rosenberg, constituted the base on which Onur's character, interests and artistic tendencies found ground. She started to explore the ontological foundations of art while questioning its objecthood based on readings in philosophy and literature, and entered a path that would eventually

24. Ibid.

25. 'Füsun Onur, Carolyn Christov-Bakargiev, and Hans Ulrich Obrist, in Conversation,' 20.

26. Büyükünal, 209.

lead her back to herself, to her own past – to Turkey, to Istanbul, and to the house on the Bosphorus.

The excerpt from Walter Kaufmann (1921–1980) quoted in the introduction of her thesis exhibition – 'As a free essence the art object always presents a possible self in a possible world, publicly put forth on its own account as a possibility of being'[27] – formed the basis for her questioning of art's meaning during these years. In this short but extremely rich text, with citations from Kaufmann as well as Hegel and Sartre, she argues that 'art is by nature existential';[28] it occupies the world like any other entity, yet at the same time 'opens our eyes to the world.' The statement accompanying close to twenty black and white drawings and many of the sculptures she left behind in the US, this text proclaimed the voice of a young artist attempting to expand the rigid formalist patterns of modernism in her early artistic renderings. In the drawings submitted for her thesis exhibition, Onur wove intricate compositions by transforming black and white into form; and in her sculptures she rendered these compositions three-dimensionally. The distinct characteristic of these sculptures, comprised of plaster, metal and even found pipes, was a playful quality that evoked the process of their formation. While trying to render space visible through plain and bold forms, she created surface features with light and shadow, evoking the relationship between the interior and exterior aspects of form through recesses and protrusions. Excluding geometric rigidity, and sometimes allowing for organic references to encircle empty space, she betrays neither the influence of Arp's volumetric organic shapes, nor the surface effects that evoke nature in some of Hepworth's work, nor the Constructivists' struggle with industrial materials. It is as if, in her response to Bara's dictum to 'design and invent,' Onur wants to let the viewer peek into her experimenting mind. In this early phase, we perceive a pursuit of artistic meaning beyond visual and formal aesthetics; we realise that this is an artist who questions the meaning of drawing as she draws, or focuses on the meaning of sculpture as she sculpts.

In her first solo exhibition in 1970 at Taksim Art Gallery, Onur continued to investigate the fundamental principles of sculpture, and exhibited a series of larger, more mature sculptures that expanded further into space with a more diverse repertoire of material. Reflecting her interest in the concept of art rather than its aesthetics, and her inclination to exclude the purist attitude of modernism in favour of grappling with the categorical boundaries of

27. Various sources cite this sentence as Onur's thesis title; the artist's text accompanying the Master's thesis exhibition submitted to The Maryland Institute in June 1966 does not have a separate title.

28. Füsun Onur, 'A Statement of Purpose,' Master of Fine Arts Thesis (Baltimore: The Maryland Institute, 1966), 1.

sculpture, the exhibition was an indication that Onur had entered the art scene as a different voice. When we consider an audience familiar with busts, nudes or small-scale abstract sculptures on pedestals shown in isolated exhibitions or at the acclaimed State Painting and Sculpture Exhibition, we can clearly understand that this was an artist setting off on a journey that would not comply with the prevalent understanding of sculpture in her country.

A photograph taken in the gallery space (FIG. 4) can help us visualise the exhibition. The sculptures are not placed on pedestals; they are not made of traditional materials like bronze or wood, nor with conventional techniques like carving/casting; their presence is ephemeral; and although abstract in terms of form, they are not completely autonomous in terms of space or time. With their geometric, organic and sometimes intertwined forms, their soft, frail materials like sponge, canvas, plaster, and with shapes that invoke phenomena like functionality and non-functionality, they evoke the urge to touch, to bend over and look, or walk through them. This attitude continued in Onur's abstract sculptures throughout the 1970s: works with mirrors that preoccupied the viewer with their reflections; works that the viewer would formally transform by stepping on them – for instance, *Composition VI* (1971) (FIG. 5), a pump that required participation; and frames that would enable a perception of here and now – for instance, *Untitled VI* (1977) (FIG. 6) composed of stone, earth, flower and frame – demonstrated that she wanted to include the viewer and reach beyond a passive visual journey.

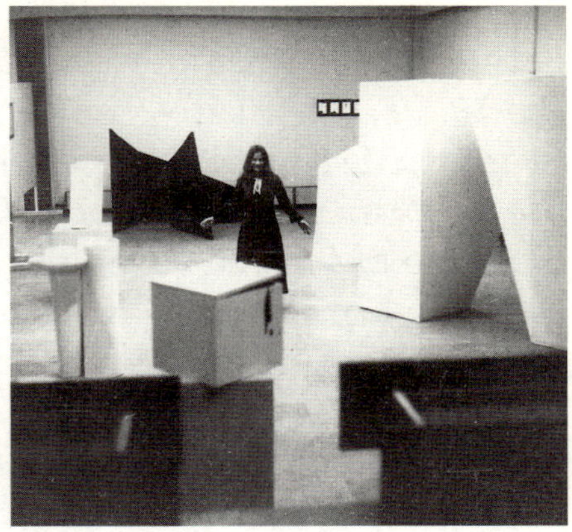

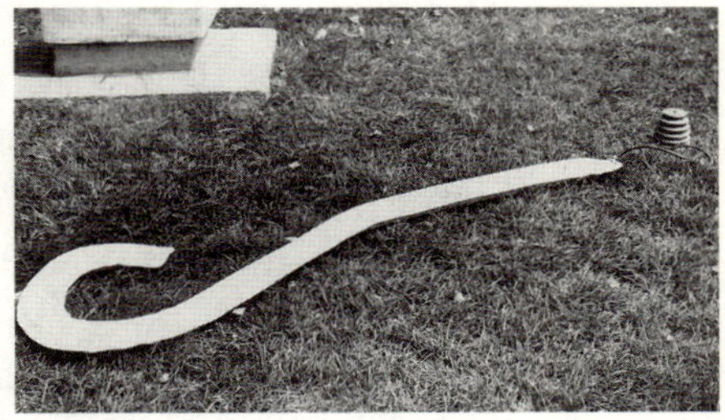

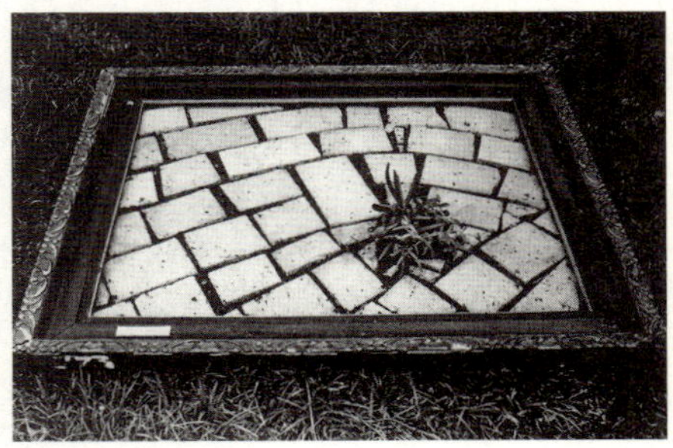

(FIGS. 4–6)

LOCAL ALIEN, ALIEN LOCAL

In the mid-1950s, artists in different parts of the world began to problematise modernism. Artists like Robert Rauschenberg and Allan Kaprow, who contributed to the blooming of movements such as Pop, Minimalism and conceptual art in the States; the Independent Group in the UK; the Situationists in France; Gutai in Japan; Neo-Concretism in Brazil and similar tendencies began to erode traditional categories like painting and sculpture. As feminist art practice came into play, this erosion assumed a character reflective of issues around social injustice in the 1960s and the demonstrations in the streets in demand of change. This was not limited to institutional critique, but shook the foundations of the concept of art. New media such as installation, performance, and video, and the use of the body in an endless array of experimentation well into the 1970s, constituted the general framework for the new avant garde that questioned the boundaries between art and life and the status of the art object. The conventions of art were destroyed through new materials and methods as painting lost its frame and sculpture its pedestal, spreading into what Rosalind Krauss termed 'the expanded field.'[29] A more active art experience, which entailed the constant questioning of the meaning of art, had begun.

In the period from the 1960s to the 1970s, when issues in the Turkish art world were limited to barren discussions around locality and universality as reflections of a figurative vs. abstract art debate, and a tendency towards a kind of Social Realism featuring rural motifs dominated the scene, artists like Onur were marginal figures owing to their new tendencies, and alas, perceived as 'alien locals.' Perhaps they really felt more like local aliens. Altan Gürman (1935–1976), whose efforts to expand the boundaries of painting brought a conceptual dimension to Turkish art in the 1960s, was the pioneer of these marginalised artists. Much like Gürman, Onur consciously opposed turning art into slogans, despite her sensitivity towards social issues, preferring instead to demonstrate her ideological stance through the fight she gave 'in her art.'[30] But the new artistic paradigms in the first solo Istanbul exhibitions of Gürman in 1967 and Onur in 1970 not only failed to receive the attention these artists deserved, but fell into a sort of void in an environment fixated either on the modernist ideology of style, or a political attitude that found its expression in figurative Social Realism.

A number of articles published by Onur in newspapers and journals throughout the 1970s and 80s are particularly worth mentioning; these represent Onur's struggle with yet another type of 'void' and reveal her resilience concerning issues she took to heart. Observing the reflections on Turkish modernism in the art world, Onur touched upon subjects such as the role and function of art in Turkish society as a modern(ising) cultural element; its distorted perceptions; and the outsider status of the artist. While insisting on the hollow understanding of social realist approaches to the 'local,'[31] she also criticised the 'universalist' claims of the Istanbul State Academy of Fine Arts, which she called 'outdated' in a global context.[32] Often pointing to the consequences of the lack of art criticism in the Turkish art world, she did not shy away from polemicising, and openly targeted critics whom she believed to have 'succumbed under the pressure of –isms,' therefore 'harming rather than

29. Rosalind Krauss, 'Sculpture in the Expanded Field,' *The Originality of the Avant-garde and Other Modernist Myths* (Cambridge & London: The MIT Press, 1985), 276–91.

30. Ayas, 11.

31. Füsun Onur, 'Sözde Toplumcu Gerçekçilik' [So-called Social Realism], *Politika*, 14 March 1976.

32. Füsun Onur, 'Modern Heykelin Türkiye'de Korunması' [The Preservation of Modern Sculpture in Turkey], *Hürriyet Gösteri*, no. 66, May 1986, 96.

benefiting the spectator,' and erasing artistic achievement with 'a few stylistic references and narrow, sloppy knowledge.'[33] Onur believed that 'approaching a work of art was not limited to placing it within a movement,'[34] and reacted to being called a 'modernist,' which she denied,[35] as well as being labelled a representative of Minimalism in Turkey, since she had 'nothing to do with Minimalist art,'[36] and even 'being associated with Pop.'[37]

Onur's engagement with the physicality of empty space; her abstract language; her use of materials like light, Plexiglas and mirrors, and her production of 'specific objects' that were neither painting nor sculpture, as well as her focus on the viewer, may seem like grounds for the association with Minimalism. However, it would be more correct to associate her with artists such as Lygia Clark, Lygia Pape, Eva Hesse and Jackie Winsor, who questioned a masculine tradition of sculpture associated with monumental sculpture by removing the art object from the pedestal and levelling it with the viewer, prioritising the artwork's relationship with the soul and the body, and inclining towards soft, tactile, organic materials. There is a common ground between these artists who share a concern with surpassing the formalist idiom of artistic modernism in favour of shaping a more sensory experience that is based on affect. For instance, in a similar way to groundbreaking figures like Clark and Pape in Brazilian contemporary art, Onur in her early work went through a process of thinking and creating with black and white geometric abstractions; and the renderings of interior-exterior appearances/relationships were for her also metaphorical of the relationship between the self and the outside world. Thus, rather than an autonomous, distant sculpture sitting on a pedestal detached from the world, the work was imagined as an entity that reached out to viewers and invited them in. The kinship between Clark's (1920–1988) *Stone and Air* (1966), expanded in space and calling for participation, and Onur's *Composition VI* (1971), a foot-pump filled with air by the viewer, is felt in the simple, everyday materials that both artists use playfully. Pape's (1927–2004) destruction of the rational aspect of geometric abstraction, sometimes by exposing her own manual artisanship and sometimes by transforming it into a game with space, as in the film *O ovo* (*The Egg*) (1967), is an approach we encounter in Onur's artworks as well. It is worth scrutinising how these women from different parts of the world, albeit around the same time, share similar sensitivities and artistic concerns and begin to rethink the idea of the modernist artistic plane in

33. Füsun Onur, 'Son Kırk Yılın İngiliz Heykelciliği' [The Last Forty Years of British Sculpture], *Hürriyet Gösteri*, no. 69, August 1986, 40.

34. Füsun Onur, 'Eleştirmenin Yaklaşımı' [Approach of the Critic], *Cumhuriyet*, 9 September 1976.

35. Anonymous, 'Türkiye'de geleneksel heykel sanatı yok' [There is No Traditional Sculpture Art in Turkey], *Milliyet*, 27 February 1985.

36. Füsun Onur, 'Görsel Sanatlarda Eleştiri Yokluğu' [The Lack of Criticism in Visual Arts], *Hürriyet Gösteri*, no. 82, September 1987, 43.

37. Onur, 'Eleştirmenin Yaklaşımı.'

a way that not only intersects art with life, but encompasses life altogether. In *Third Dimension in Painting – Come In* (1981), Onur constructs a geometric structure with materials like dyed threads, beads, sponge, mirror and cloth. In Pape's *O ovo*, there is the image of a body thrusting out of a designated space, while in Onur's *Third Dimension* a body enters and leaves a designated space; both share an artistic approach that is focused on bodily experience and sensitivity. This approach is based on unlearning the grammar of how to make a painting or sculpture, which instead evolves within a process. The use of alternative materials, methods and forms of exhibition are a natural extension of this process.

Prior to Onur, even when there was a tendency towards unconventional material or methods (Zühtü Müridoğlu's tree branches, Kuzgun Acar's nails and İlhan Koman's radiators come to mind), Turkish sculpture remained based on the autonomous art object with a focus on style. In a historical perspective, Onur is successor to a handful of women sculptors including Iraida Barry (1899–1980), Sabiha Bengütaş (1904–1992), Nermin Faruki (1904–1991), Mari Gerekmezyan (1913–1947), Zerrin Bölükbaşı (1919–2010) and Semahat Acuner (b. 1927), and displays a deconstructive approach that separates her from all sculptors of her generation regardless of gender. We can cite, for instance, Saim Bugay (1934–2008), Servet Büyükbağcı (b. 1934), Tamer Başoğlu (b. 1938), Namık Denizhan (1937–2015), Mehmet Aksoy (b. 1939). Unlike any other of her generation, Onur has questioned, since her first exhibition, the elements that determine how a three-dimensional object becomes a sculpture by using alternative materials and approach. She thus pioneered the new practice of conceptual art through works that stem from questioning not only sculptural space, but pictorial space, especially with her abstract sculptures from the 1970s that evoke frames, vitrines and paintings, like the *Third Dimension in Painting – Come In* (1981) or the three-dimensional construction made of canvas, *Conceptual Visual Images* (1984).

However, the dominant artistic/critical values of the local environment have overlooked the relationship that could have been established between Onur and a transnational artistic context and has caused her artistic approach to be evaluated merely in the context of outer influence. In *Cumhuriyet Dönemi Türk Heykeli*, which still constitutes the only chronological historical account of the history of modern sculpture in Turkey, Hüseyin Gezer's evaluation of Onur as an artist who reflects the 'influences of modern

American sculpture and especially of the minimal art movement'[38] put Onur in a pigeonhole that is more reflective of Gezer's critical approach than Onur's artistic approach. It is obvious that Onur has no affinity with the rigid formalism, geometric sharpness, or the rationalist masculinity of American Minimalists such as Carl Andre, Donald Judd or Dan Flavin. If an affinity is to be sought, it can be established with artists like Eva Hesse (1936–1970) and Jackie Winsor (b. 1941), who embrace a more sensitive, intuitive, fluid form of expression against the Minimalist attitude and thus have been characterised as 'post-Minimalist.' Pursuing an alternative language to the dominant Minimalist attitude, these artists have conveyed, or at least inevitably reflected in their works, the experience of living as women artists. An introspective experimental process realised in modest circumstances, with familiar materials at hand, and without consideration of market conditions can be seen as the outcome of this 'feminine' inclination. As art historian Jenny Sorkin has observed, artists who do not necessarily carry a politically feminist attitude but have served in making possible an alternative sculptural tradition that reflects the various cultural, social, psychological aspects of women's experience have on one hand leaned towards found objects and practical production processes for financial reasons and on the other played an innovative role in shaping a new artistic sensibility and 'transformed the culture of making' sculpture.[39] The same can be said of Onur, who has expanded the limits of sculpture in Turkey. In contrast to the expensive, assertive, and vertical aspects of conventional sculpture, Onur's work is modest, spreading across horizontal ground, having been made in her home/atelier with the life-long support and assistance of her older sister İlhan Onur, and mostly with found/low-cost objects, some from the house itself. Eroding the disciplinary categories of art, this attitude opens a path to a subjective approach that is not shaped by form alone, but the relationship between form and content.

Other pioneering artists, mostly women, representing new tendencies in Turkish art during the 1970s like Onur – Nil Yalter (b. 1938), Nur Koçak (b. 1941), Gülsün Karamustafa (b. 1946) and Ayşe Erkmen (b. 1949) – have not received their due in terms of critical attention, perception and evaluation. The main feature that distinguishes these artists from their contemporaries has been their distance from the dominant conception of art in Turkey and their internalisation of art as a conceptual practice.[40] Onur's small assemblage from the early 1970s, *Nude* (1974), made

38.
I am referring to the book's third edition dated 1984; see Hüseyin Gezer, *Cumhuriyet Dönemi Türk Heykeli* [Republican Period Turkish Sculpture] (Istanbul: Türkiye İş Bankası Kültür Yayınları, 1984), 229.

39.
Jenny Sorkin, 'Five Propositions on Abstract Sculpture,' *Revolution in the Making: Abstract Sculpture by Women, 1947–2016*, eds. Paul Schimmel and Jenny Sorkin (Milan: Skira; New York: Hauser & Wirth, 2016), 155.

40.
Ahu Antmen, '1970'ler Türkiyesi'nde Sanat, Kimlik ve Cinsiyet' [Art, Identity and Gender in the 1970s in Turkey], *Kimlikli Bedenler* [Bodies with IDs] (Istanbul: Sel Yayıncılık, 2013), 94.

as a reaction to the removal of Gürdal Duyar's highly controversial sculpture *Beautiful Istanbul* (1974) from Karaköy Square, can be seen as an important breaking point. Signalling the role women would play from the 1970s, this modest anti-monument was the sign of a new trend in Turkish art pioneered by women who observed the objectified female body from within, through their subjective experiences. We can see that tiny 'sculpture' as a symbol of the expansion of the concept of art in Turkey.

Encapsulating a range of works that break the mould in terms of artistic methods, materials and propositions, Onur's artistic production conveys an extremely introspective and liberated stance, from her first exhibition to the latest: abstract works in the 1970s such as *Composition I, II, III, IV, V, VI* (1970–71) grounded on the deconstruction of the concept of sculpture through basic principles like mass-space, emptiness-fullness, light-shadow; her experiments with new materials like Plexiglas, light, mirrors and foam; the naive assemblages of the mid-1970s in which she began to incorporate figurative elements and narrative, like *Musical Chair* (1976), *Stories for Grown-ups* (1977), *Because You Said Bread and Apple I Remember* (1978), *A Seed Sprouts I, II* (1978–79), *Would You Like to Sit on the Bench* (1983); works such as *Third Dimension in Painting – Come In* (1981) in the late 1980s, where she transformed the abstract idea of space into a real experience with the participation of the spectator; and her installations particularly after the 1990s in which she focused on the idea of 'composition' and undertook the 'orchestration' of empty space using found objects, such as *Cadence* (1995), *Note* (1998), *Opus I* (1999), *What the Earth Sang* (2000), *Prelude* (2000), *Opus II – Fantasia* (2001), *Rondo* (2002), *The Song of the Sea* (2002), *Impromptu* (2003), *Boogie Woogie* (2003), *Whisper* (2010), *Flamenco* (2011), *Silence* (2011) and *Chamber Music* (2019). When we become open to questioning art beyond its conventional grammar, and see how it can become its own limiting structural system of language and knowledge, we can start thinking with Onur.

Her sense of liberation and rebellion can be observed in her solo exhibitions throughout the 1970s and 80s, as well as her active participation in alternative group shows like the *Open Air Exhibitions*, the *New Trends* exhibitions – organised by the Academy of Fine Arts to modernise itself – and later the series of *A Cross Section of Avantgarde Turkish Art* and *A, B, C, D* exhibitions. This in itself is an attitude that goes against the grain of convention, reflecting a genuine avant-garde stance. Her statement, 'Sometimes if

I'm bored of doing something, I rebel against myself. I always want to do something new,'[41] alongside her decision to distance herself from the art market from the very start, can also be seen within this uncompromising and free-spirited attitude. It's worth quoting the text that she wrote in response to criticism she received in the 1990s, because it gives an insider's view to her long struggle in the local art scene:

> After twenty uncompromising years with no financial nor emotional support to make umpteen exhibitions, I simply cannot allow anyone to write me off just like that because they feel like it. I will not, because there are artists lauded in the States today for the kind of work that I did back in the 1970s. Secondly, if there are now sculpture exhibitions in the last couple of years in Turkey, there's my fair share in it because I paved that road, fought for it, made it familiar by exhibiting my work every other year. And finally, I chose the hardest struggle; I fought, then made peace with myself in a foreign country, then chose the hardest path and came back to Turkey. I walked the walk regardless of obstacles. I made no compromise; and let alone change for fear of not being understood. I did not even use cheap slogans; I always spoke the language of art itself.[42]

It's evident from this statement that art for Onur was always an occupation close to her heart. And there is no doubt that the reflections of such an introspective mental journey, internalised like a state of existence that exceeds the concern for survival in the art world, is, at least for 'careful eyes,'[43] laden with interesting clues regarding society, history and art.

HOME AS MOTHERLAND: *NOSTOS* OR HOMECOMING

While relating the urban and cultural transformation of Paris in his *Passages*, Walter Benjamin observes the significance that one's private environment starts to take on in an environment of constant change. He points to how the interior becomes an internal universe of individual fantasies amidst the rush outside. The home thus turns into the voice of its owner. He imagines everyday objects imprinted with traces of living – 'covers, protectors, liners and cases' – recalling the past through the present like a sort of 'phantasmagoria.'[44] Benjamin's image of this phantasmagorical interior universe recalls Ahmet Hamdi Tanpınar, another

41. 'Füsun Onur, Carolyn Christov-Bakargiev, and Hans Ulrich Obrist, in Conversation,' 24.

42. Onur, 'Bir Cevap…,' 71.

43. In a conversation with Margrit Brehm, in reference to her works Onur says, 'Probably it can only be seen by careful eyes.' These words were the source of inspiration for the title of Brehm's Füsun Onur monograph. See Margrit Brehm, *Füsun Onur: Dikkatli Gözler İçin – For Careful Eyes* (Istanbul: Yapı Kredi Publications, 2007), 15.

44. Walter Benjamin, 'Paris, the Capital of the Nineteenth Century,' *Selected Writings 1935–38*, (Cambridge & London: Harvard University Press, 2002), 38–39.

observer of changing times, and evokes Behçet, the protagonist of his novel *Mahur Beste*, who 'sees the tick-tocks of time passing.' There is an unforgettable scene where Behçet, who lives in the sweet serenity of his interior universe comprised of divans, couches, colourful cushions, coffee tables, dolls, crystal bowls, hardbound books, mirrors, gilded postcards and a myriad of other articles of furniture, talks about his dream where clocks with their broken mainsprings pass before his eyes like dancers wrapped in tints of golden yellow. For me, this scene conjures Onur's *Opus I* (1999) installed at the Hagia Irene Museum. Objects like gilded fabrics, glazed porcelain chalices and blue tulle echo the feeling of sanctity in a church like a hymn that we can hear with our eyes, and also give clues pertaining to Onur's relationship with old objects.

Using objects related to the interior space of the home in her installations, Onur has for a long time been making spatial compositions with things that can be found, not in antique shops, but in flea markets, artefacts whose value can be assessed only in an immaterial sense. Founded on an introspective system of signs, these old objects imprinted with personal associations set her apart from other abstract installation artists. While it is generally form, light, and similar abstract elements that dominate such works, Onur's installations open a door by using symbols that we share. Hence their sensory experience is extended to include associations of memory. This can be described as seeing, hearing, experiencing the intangible, precisely like music.

Ever since she was a student, the main impulse in Onur's inclination towards abstract expression has borne an emotional rather than form-oriented dimension, and this is how she draws her spectator into an interior universe similar to the experience of music. This interior universe belongs both to her and to her audience. She knows that an object that enters human life over and over again carries a spiritual dimension. Her solo exhibition *Life-Art-Fiction, Dream of Old Furniture* (1985) at Taksim Art Gallery seems to have paved the way for her mature work; this new form of expression shaped by personal associations of objects inevitably takes the viewer back to childhood. Objects, including a copy of *Alice in Wonderland*, pieces of broken toys, trinkets, tufts, balls, alongside the arrangement that resembles two ballerinas dancing in a separate corner, are notable for their childlike and playful quality. We return to our own childhood; we think about Onur's childhood. Once again, we end up coming home.

The house in Kuzguncuk – Onur's 'motherland' in a sense – where the three Onur siblings and their mother settled following the early loss of their father, is the place to which we return in order to 'hear' Onur. It's no wonder that Margrit Brehm, in her concise monograph on the artist, observed how the heavy atmosphere of the past enchanted visitors to the house, 'conjuring up associations with a cabinet of curiosities.'[45] She describes at length mother Nerime Onur's collection of old photographs, tin boxes, postcards, and implies that her presence can still be felt in the house. And Emre Baykal, in his delightful portrait of Onur also poetically expresses the 'peaceful confluence' of an array of objects including 'Porcelain, crystal, glass, wood, lace, silver, mother-of-pearl, feather, satin and velvet assuming myriad sizes, shapes and colours, filling vitrine cupboards, sideboards, coffee tables and on shelves.'[46] Most of these objects belonged to Onur's mother. As the artist has voiced in an interview, the objects her mother kept, remain kept; they are the things that she values the most and have affected her the most, and she refrains from using them in her work lest she damages them. The house and its stuff – this interior universe – have become a distinctive element surrounding Onur's practice over the years. Is it a mere coincidence that the feel and atmosphere of mother's house is so much in tune with that of Onur's installations?

Just as the wall of objects from André Breton's study taken to the Pompidou constitutes a self-portrait of Breton, the Onur house is a place identified with the artist. Ali Kazma's film *Home* (2014) embodies this identification and contributes to the transformation of the house into an art object of sorts (or perhaps a possible museum?). Onur both emphasises this by agreeing that she was 'very influenced, even as a child, by the objects in the house,'[47] and plays it down: 'We aren't aware [of the house] because we live in it.'[48] But I've visited the house, so I know: despite the dizzying speed of the world outside, time there flows unhurriedly. The extreme changes in Istanbul during the twentieth century can be seen more clearly when looking out of her window. Onur's art makes us witness to an interior universe in Istanbul. And each act of witnessing rings like enchanting bells, carrying us to our own interior realms.

45.
Brehm, 18–19.

46.
Emre Baykal, *Füsun Onur: Aynadan İçeri – Through the Looking Glass* (Istanbul: Arter Publications, 2014), 61.

47.
'Füsun Onur, Carolyn Christov-Bakargiev, and Hans Ulrich Obrist, in Conversation,' 23.

48.
İz Öztat, 'Conversation,' m-est.org, 24 June 2014, https://m-est.org/2014/07/24/conversation-fusun-onur-with-iz-oztat/.

01.06.1966–01.12.2021 by İz Öztat

When *For Careful Eyes*,[1] the first book to bring together Füsun Onur's oeuvre, was first published in 2007, I had just returned to Turkey upon completing my undergraduate studies in the United States. While I was there, I had taken an interest in the processes of Eva Hesse and Claude Cahun's artistic production, and when I returned to Istanbul, I fell for Füsun Onur's artistic practice. As I've worked on my contribution to this publication, which will accompany her exhibition in the Turkey Pavilion at the Venice Biennale, I have revisited my sustained engagement with Füsun Onur's practice over the years, with a particular focus on her own writing.

When Onur defended her Master's thesis at the Maryland Institute College of Art in 1966, she was asked whether or not she wanted to stay in the US. 'I want to go back to my country, be useful there,' she replied.[2] In various publications over the years, she used the same terms, saying that she wanted to return to her country in order to be 'useful,' 'beneficial'[3] or 'helpful';[4] that there was a 'much greater need'[5] for her in her own country. At a time when political suppression and economic difficulties are giving rise to emigration from Turkey, when my friends are leaving and those who left temporarily are choosing not to return, I wonder how and for what Onur's choice to return, to produce her work here, was useful, and which needs she met by doing so.

What's the use of Füsun Onur? What use might I be as I try to answer this question?

In an open letter[6] published in 1990, Onur writes, 'Art is to me so sacred; whenever I see some disrespect committed against it, I know it to be a sacred duty, even if it makes some circles uncomfortable. I will proceed in this duty I've been given without compromising on my art or my beliefs. This is a legacy inherited from my respected teacher Hadi Bara.'[7] In my approach to the artist's work and writing, I am drawn to Onur's relationship with the sense of 'duty.' I try to understand what she means by 'sacred duty,' and what 'use' means in the context of duties given and assumed by her, but not bestowed upon her. I grapple with the burden of what 'duty' and 'use' mean in the context of constructing the nation-state in order to conjure up, as best I can, the ghosts of Turkey's modernisation.

1. Margrit Brehm, *For Careful Eyes* (Istanbul: Yapı Kredi Publications, 2007).
2. 'Füsun Onur, Carolyn Christov-Bakargiev, and Hans Ulrich Obrist, in Conversation,' in *Füsun Onur* (Cologne: W. König, 2012), 22.
3. Feriha Büyükünal, 'Füsun Onur ile Bir Söyleşi' [A Conversation with Füsun Onur], *Sanat Çevresi*, v. 136, February 1990, 18.
4. Brehm, *For Careful Eyes,* 26.
5. Füsun Onur, 'Bir Cevap…' [A Response]…, *Sanat Çevresi*, no. 139, May 1990, 70.
6. This open letter, which Onur published in the 139th volume of the journal *Sanat Çevresi*, was written in response to Yahşi Baraz's essay in the previous volume that admonished artists from Turkey who had gone abroad, either on scholarship or by their own means, for not staging important exhibitions upon their return. See Yahşi Baraz, 'New York'taki Türk Sanatçılarının Yeni Kimliği' [The New Identity of Turkish Artists in New York], *Sanat Çevresi*, no. 139, April 1990, 48; Onur, 'A Response…,' 70.
7. Onur, 'A Response…,' 71.

Attempting to understand what the perspectives on Onur and her work have exposed over the years, I touch upon the myths that spring up around the artist herself, proffering alternative narratives (that might possibly become myths of their own) to meet my own needs. I try to make meaning from my own experiences and observations as an artist producing work from this locality by relating them to the legacy shaped by Onur. Through this effort, I examine what use I am as I attempt to both complicate and reciprocate the meanings of 'duty' and 'use,' though I still find that I am absorbed by the inherent obstacles and impossibilities of such an effort. In this text, grappling with the tensions of rupture and continuity in the intergenerational transmission of artistic practice in Turkey, I arrive, waywardly, at the same points, or else I take a different path, coming to conclusions that contradict one another.

Because the artist has responded with silence to the intense interest devoted to her since she turned seventy years old, dismissing questions by saying that she never looks back to the past, and because she has not referred to her past writings, one is left with the impression that she is an artist who does not like to put her thoughts on art and her work into words.[8] But I want to prevent her past concerns from being overlooked. For this reason, I draw on her works and writings produced between 1966 and 2003 – the Master's thesis[9] titled *Statement of Purpose*[10] that she has characterised as her 'philosophy of art,'[11] the texts she has written about her works, the articles she has published in art journals, her letters – as my primary sources, putting them into conversation with the narratives, contexts and discourses they evoke. In doing so, I choose to quote from both Onur herself, as well as from actors who have been influential in the contexts within which she worked, in an attempt to bring their subjectivity and the spirit of the times into this text. The literature produced during and after her participation in dOCUMENTA (13) in 2012 has emphasised her home on the Bosphorus waterfront, where she has spent her life, and where the traces of her childhood are still apparent.[12] I maintain a distance from the home and from the narratives that try to situate Onur's work in a sphere limited to her individual memory; rather, beginning from the choices she made when she was forming her works and from what she wrote, I grapple with the questions she asks of art, along with the artistic debates that took place in the eras in which she produced.

8.
In the text that Defne Ayas wrote for the publication that accompanied the 2012 exhibition in dOCUMENTA (13), Onur is quoted as asking, 'Why is everyone trying to get hold of me now? Why is everyone interested in my work all of a sudden? Is it because my end arrived?' See Defne Ayas, 'Füsun,' in *Füsun Onur*, 10. In an interview included in the same publication, Onur expresses her indifference toward the past by saying, 'I don't look backward, but I always look forward – what I want, what I can do more of.' See: 'Füsun Onur, Carolyn Christov-Bakargiev, and Hans Ulrich Obrist, in Conversation,' 24.

9.
The text referred to as her 'thesis' in this essay is a document titled *Statement of Purpose* and composed of the text she wrote to receive her Master's degree at the Maryland Institute in 1966 as well as photographs of the works she produced. This document was given signatures of approval from Nicolas Carone, Grace Hartigan, James Hennessey and Norman Carlberg. See Füsun Onur, *Statement of Purpose* (Master's Degree, The Maryland Institute, College of Art, 1966).

10.
In the publication *For Careful Eyes*, the title of her thesis is given as follows: 'The art object as a possible self in a possible world, publicly put forth on its own account as possibility of being.' See Brehm, *For Careful Eyes*, 23. Onur writes, in the original document, 'As a free essence the art object always presents a possible self in a possible world, publicly put forth on its own account as a possibility of being,' footnoting it with 'Walter Kaufmann. *Existentialism from Shakespeare to Sartre* (New York, 1960), p. 24.' One might imagine that she came up with this expression in reference to two separate books by Kaufmann that are titled *Shakespeare to Existentialism* and *Existentialism: From Dostoevsky to Sartre*. Because this quote is placed at the beginning of her thesis and because the cover page of the document says *Statement of Purpose*, I have preferred here to use the expression *Statement of Purpose* as the title of her thesis.

11.
Onur, 'A Response…,' 71.

12.
The artist's home and the childhood she spent there are frequently touched upon in discussions of her work, sometimes at her insistence and sometimes at the insistence of guiding questions. See Ayas, in *Füsun Onur*; Emre Baykal, *Through the Looking Glass* (Istanbul: Arter Publications, 2014).

What is 'sacred' within the project of the secular Republic, and what is the 'duty' ordained for the artist? What legacy did Onur, student of Ali Hadi Bara in the sculpture department at the Academy, inherit from him? Focusing on the figure of the sculptor as we crudely chisel out the official narrative of the artist's duty in Turkey's modernisation, let's take a look at the legacy of Bara.

Because Islam considers three-dimensional likenesses to be idols, the Ottoman Empire had no tradition of sculpture.[13] The earliest manifestations of the tradition are architecturally derived stonework and adornment,[14] as well as gravestones, which might be considered sculptures in the abstract sense.[15] Culture and art have been some of the vehicles in the campaign waged on the way to modernisation. To that end, art education oriented towards the representation of the human figure was institutionalised with the establishment of the Academy.[16] The Academy, a manifestation of the transformation of a 'mentality inherited from centuries of tradition' and an 'educational institution for teaching what had been considered forbidden,'[17] was established in 1882; the Republic of Turkey, in 1923. 'Monuments were erected to persuade the people to embrace the newly established order, to awaken national consciousness, and to build unity,' and these monuments 'contributed to the adoption and spread of sculptural art.'[18] But until sculptors who would build these monuments had 'attained the maturity necessary to fulfil this duty,'[19] the job fell to their European colleagues. Once the first generation of Republican sculptors came of age, they took on this duty. One of the most singular members of this first generation, Hadi Bara, also took on the duty of teaching at the Academy in 1937, in a sculpture department structured around Rudolf Belling's 'principles of sculpture as interpreted through works of antiquity.'[20] Upon his return from his second trip to Paris in 1949, Bara turned to figureless, abstract art. In 1950, the sculpture department was split into two. As the Belling Atelier continued, the Hadi Bara and Zühtü Müridoğlu Atelier was established. A sculptor who made contributions to modernisation and the formation of national consciousness through figurative monuments, Bara ushered in debates over abstract versus figurative art by bringing, through his art and teaching, the artistic developments of the West to his country. In writing the history of art and sculpture, Hüseyin Gezer arrives at the conclusion, 'despite the very brief past of this

13.
Hüseyin Gezer, 'Sculpture,' in Nurullah Berk and Hüseyin Gezer, *Fifty Years of Turkish Painting and Sculpture* (Istanbul: Türkiye İş Bankası Culture Publications, 1973), 3–4.

14.
'Sculpture, as we all know, arrived in Turkey with the establishment of the Republic. Prior to that, there was stonework and the art of adornment. The arts of adornment exhibit the most primitive traces of artistic ways of seeing. Because in their very nature there is the rhythm of life, there is repetition.' Füsun Onur, 'Modern Heykelin Türkiye'de Korunması' [The Preservation of Modern Sculpture in Turkey], *Hürriyet Gösteri*, no. 66, September 1986, 95.

15.
'Our tradition of stonework, connected abstractly to architecture, offers prime examples that follow the trajectory of architecture. In addition, the results achieved in gravestones are each perfect examples of stylisation and synthesis, and can each be considered, in an abstract sense, sculptures.' Gezer, *Fifty Years of Turkish Painting and Sculpture*, 8. 'Representational painting, which aims to give the impression of depth, began in the modernisation movements prior to the Republic. After the Republic, however, subsequent generations returned once again to older traditions (calligraphy, miniatures, mosaics) and selected from among them the foundations for certain modern practises. Sculpture has no such foundation. As Sezer Tansuğ shows, "Over the course of the development of Ottoman art, decorative stonework traced a path ordered by the use of geometric and floral forms separate or together, and the technique of high-relief embossments was not in high demand."' Orhan Koçak, *Modern ve Ötesi: 50 Yılın Sanatına Kenar Notları* [Modern and Beyond: Marginalia on 50 Years of Art] (Istanbul: Istanbul Bilgi University Publications, 2007), 27.

16.
The institution referred to here as the 'Academy' was established in 1882 as the Mekteb-i Sanayi-i Nefîse-i Şâhâne, and began its teaching in 1883. In 1913 it was referred to as The İnâs (Girls') Sanayi-i Nefîse Mektebi, and in 1926 it began offering co-education. Until 1927, it is referred to in both official writings and by the public as the Sanayi-I Nefîse Mekteb-i Alisi. In 1928, the school became the Güzel Sanatlar Akademisi, or Academy of Fine Arts, and in 1969, it was renamed the Istanbul State Academy of Fine Arts. In 1982, it was renamed Mimar Sinan University and in 2004 the Mimar Sinan Fine Arts University. See Mimar Sinan Fine Arts University, 'History,' *Mimar Sinan Fine Arts University*, http://www. msgsu.edu.tr/tr-TR/tarihce/123/Page.aspx (last accessed: 15 November 2021).

17.
Mustafa Cezar, 'Devlet Güzel Sanatlar Akademisi Tarihçesi' [History of the State Academy of Fine Arts] in *Devlet Güzel Sanatlar Akademisi 1883–1968 (Akademi 85. Yıl)* [The State Academy of Fine Arts, 1883–1968 (The Academy's 85th Anniversary)], ed. by Mustafa Cezar (Istanbul: State Academy of Fine Arts Publications, 1968), 5.

18.
Gezer, *Fifty Years of Turkish Painting and Sculpture,* 14.

19.
Ibid.

20.
Ibid., 125.

artistic tradition and the inhospitable environment for its cultivation, Turkish sculpture has, in the 50 years since the foundation of the Republic, shown significant developments,'[21] and he makes reference to Onur as one of Bara's students. In his linear narrative written on the fiftieth anniversary of the Republic, he incorporates notions of sacredness by referring to artists as 'prophets.'[22] As evidenced by this official narrative, the sacred duty that Onur inherited from Bara is part and parcel of the negotiation of duties delegated to artists in the modernisation of Turkey.

Notions of cultural development and progress were instrumentalised in the modernisation of Turkey and, in Onur's thinking on art, they have been transformed by centring the individual's imagination. By maintaining distance from tradition[23] and 'by trusting her own imagination, the artist is able to make progress.'[24] The 'progressive art' that emerges here goes on to improve society.[25] In 1990, in accordance with these beliefs, Onur summarised the effect she has created as follows: [I]f there are now sculpture exhibitions in the last couple of years in Turkey, there's my fair share in it because I paved that road, fought for it, made it familiar by exhibiting my work every other year.[26]

If we look back from the present to summarise the trail blazed by Onur, we see that in the work and writing she produced after her return to Turkey in 1967, for instance, she helped to transform specific debates regarding the national/universal, abstract/figurative, model/copy in the local context by bringing her own analyses to questions implicit to art itself. From the 1990s onwards, the art world began globalising through exhibitions based on national representations,[27] and Onur's works started circulating internationally with greater frequency in this context. In the early 2000s, due in part to the effect of Turkey's negotiations for membership in the European Union,[28] attempts to narrativise the history of contemporary art in Turkey intensified. In these narratives, Onur was situated as a reference point for the beginning of this history,[29] which, it was claimed, dated to the 1970s; she was even described as a 'grandmother'[30] who enabled the generations that followed her. Upon Carolyn Christov-Bakargiev's invitation to Onur to participate in dOCUMENTA (13), her work became visible on the pilgrimage route of the art world, and began to take its place in a global canon. And now, at the Venice Biennale, one of the most traditional spectacles of national representation, she has, at the age of eighty-five, taken on the responsibility of representing Turkey with

21. Ibid., 27.

22. 'In such an environment Rodin, Bourdelle, Maillol, each was truly a Prophet.' Ibid., 20.

23. 'The artist advances with new installations, new articulations. Art is an event of the intellect; it changes as its function changes, as civilisation progresses. Art makes no progress so long as it says, Turkish art was like this a century ago, as long as it insists on traditional art unique to us alone.' Füsun Onur, 'Resimde Üçüncü Boyut – İçeri Gel' [Third Dimension in Painting – Come In], *Sanat Çevresi*, no. 37, November 1981, 15.

24. Füsun Onur, 'İmgelem' [Imagination], *Hürriyet Gösteri*, no. 128, July 1991, 67.

25. 'Though it may be challenged or regarded as odd, progressive art will make society assimilate certain things that will improve it.' Füsun Onur, 'Third Dimension in Painting – Come In,' 15.

26. Onur, 'A Response…,' 71.

27. For a discussion of this subject see Vasıf Kortun, Ayşe Erkmen, Hale Tenger and Gülsün Karamustafa, 'Uluslararası Dolaşım ve Türkiye Sanatçıları' [International Circulation and Artists from Turkey] in *10* (Istanbul: SALT/Garanti Kültür AŞ, 2014), 205–27, first published in *Resmî Görüş*, Vol. 1, 1999.

28. Fulya Erdemci, 'Büyüyü Bozmak, Yeniden-Yön Vermek' [Breaking the Spell, Redirecting], in *Modern ve Ötesi* (Istanbul: Istanbul Bilgi University Publications, 2007), 37.

29. Halil Altındere, 'Giriş: Türkiye'de Güncel Sanat 1986–2006' [Introduction: Contemporary Art in Turkey 1986–2006], in *User's Manual Contemporary Art in Turkey* (Istanbul: artist publications, 2007), 6; Erdemci, ibid., 38.

30. Vasıf Kortun and Erden Kosova, *Ofsayt ama Gol* [Offside But Goal] (Istanbul: SALT/Garanti Kültür AŞ, 2014), 48, first published in *Szene Türkei: Abseits, Aber Tor!* (Cologne: W. König, 2004).

a new work. The relationship between the duty she has undertaken and the needs it meets within a specific context is onerous. The artist's 'usefulness' to the needs of the context in which she produces is reproduced over and over again in its repeated use.

When Onur returned to Turkey, she hoped to be useful as an educator, to be able to teach at the Academy where she studied.[31] At the Academy, there is a master-apprentice system that maintains the institution's traditions by compelling artists to take over their teachers' duties. Within this structure, artists are sent abroad to 'Europe's leading centres'[32] on government scholarships to prepare for the duty of educating, and return indebted to the institution. They have to negotiate the debt and expectations produced by this system in the process of cultivating their pedagogy. Bara, for example, went to Paris, where he worried that turning to abstraction would squander the resources provided by the state.[33] Onur, who went to the US on a Fulbright scholarship, and unlike other artists sent abroad by the state, didn't have to return for mandatory duty, was outside of this cycle. Had she become an educator, she would have been able to develop her own pedagogical approach without feeling indebted to the state. But because the sculpture department only accepted women artists who made monumental sculptures,[34] she was unable, even if she so desired, to take one of those seats handed down as if from father to son. In the 1968–69 academic year, she served as an assistant to visiting Professor Fritz Reuter in the Faculty of Architecture at Istanbul Technical University,[35] during which time she produced a sculpture at the institution in order to prove that she could take on teaching duties. But because she was 'a woman with long hair' and because the sculpture she produced was so disliked that it was recommended to be 'thrown in the trash,'[36] she was unable to enter this institution as an educator either. Onur was never bestowed the duty of educator that she wanted to assume.

LEGACY

In the emerging narrative about 'sacred duties' given and inherited but not bestowed, the ambivalence of Onur's relationship to legacy is palpable. The continuity and rupture that characterise the relationship with the past in Turkey[37] have manifested in art history, too; 'continuity has been frequently interrupted,' and at the heart of these fractures lies the fact that 'the nation and its culture have turned to face the West,'[38] which is also understood as the basis of continuity.

31.
Jane L. Keidel, 'Turkish Student Delays Trip Home: "Lost" Here At First, Now She Relates To America,' *The Baltimore Sun*, 6 December, 1966, A10.

32.
Gezer, *Fifty Years of Turkish Painting and Sculpture*, 12.

33.
Describing how Hadi Bara embraced the abstract art he had once criticised, Hüseyin Gezer quotes from İlhan Koman: 'Hadi Bara came to Paris and saw my pieces in my workshop. He was incredibly disappointed, even angry. "When there's earnest art still to be made, it's meaningless to delve into these fantasies, these games." He denounced me forcefully. He condemned me by saying that "This was a waste of the state's resources." [...] Soon thereafter, Hadi Bara caught onto the work, and he even started working on new experiments himself.' Ibid., 24.

34.
Onur, *Füsun Onur*, 22.

35.
Gezer, *Fifty Years of Turkish Painting and Sculpture*, 205.

36.
'"A woman with long hair?' they asked me. But a Professor who liked my work, his name was Reuter, he said to me, 'You should come to school in February, between semesters, while it's closed and you should make something here to prove yourself.' So I did, and Professor Reuter showed my piece to the department chair. The department chair was a woman architect, she said, 'And what's this? If I saw something like this I'd throw it in the trash immediately.'" See Onur, *Füsun Onur*, 28. Onur specifies, in a conversation on 23 February 2013, that the 'woman architect' was Leman Tomsu, and that the sculpture she so disliked was her work *Composition IV* (1970). See Füsun Onur, 'Saha: Füsun Onur,' *Saha Konuşmaları*, Vimeo video, 1:17:15, 23 February 2013, http://www.saha.org.tr/en/saha-talks/saha-talks-8-fusun-onur-23-february-2013 (last accessed 15 November 2021).

37.
While 'the foundational discourse [...] of Kemalism [...] signifies an absolute rupture with the entire legacy of the Ottoman Empire, and the beginning of immaculate "salvation" and modernisation' (see Tanıl Bora, *Cereyanlar* [Currents] (Istanbul: İletişim Publishing, 2017), 24), the Justice and Development Party (Adalet ve Kalkınma Partisi, or AKP) that has been in power for the last twenty years commits itself to a narrative and world of meaning that rests upon continuity with the magnificent Ottoman past. See Nagehan Tokdoğan, *Yeni Osmanlıcılık: Hınç, Nostalji, Narsisizm* [New Ottomanism: Vengeance, Nostalgia, Narcissism] (Istanbul: İletişim Publishing, 2018), 16.

38.
'Continuity has been frequently interrupted, and at the heart of these breakages is the exact phenomenon that [Kaya] Özsezgin suggests is the foundation of continuity: That the country and the culture "have turned to face the West."' Koçak, *Modern and Beyond*, 2.

What is the legacy of the Ottoman Empire for the Republic of Turkey? Is the inheritance from previous generations a foundation ensuring continuity, or does it become a burden we want to cast off? Is there an uninterrupted lineage connecting the turbans on gravestones, described as the foundation of sculpture here, and the pumpkins that Onur uses in her *Souvenir de Dolmabahçe* (1992)? Is uncompromisingly producing her own work the only legacy of Bara that Onur chose to assume? Might the 'unfillable void'[39] left by the death of her teacher be signified by her sculpture *Untitled (Homage to Hadi Bara, My Teacher)* (1974)? Are legacies simply unfillable voids? 'What use are exhibitions without literature? What traces do they leave for the present or for the generations that follow us?,'[40] Onur asks, helping to forge this literature because she sees it as her duty. Looking closely at this legacy shaped by Onur in her works and her writings, I attempt to find her traces and understand what use they might be.

SACRED

Duty aside, the many plural meanings harboured solely by the 'sacred' can be traced across Onur's work. When she says that the object she shapes has a spirit,[41] she opens the door for the viewer to see into the animistic relationship she has with the world. When she discusses abstract sculpture in her writings, she touches upon the artist's 'inquiry into the spiritual,'[42] the 'hidden force'[43] that drives the artist, the 'spiritual beings'[44] present as she delineates the rhythm she produces, and even the work's 'spiritual truth,'[45] in reference to Sartre. 'Art is by nature existential,' she writes in her thesis, thereby relating existence and art to the sudden invasion of the world.[46] Because it is the worldly, vital response to an existential inquiry that reaches for the spiritual, art is both useful and sacred. Onur both feels and evokes the tension between earth and sky, between sacred and profane, as in the installations where she intervenes in empty space by using the floors and ceilings of her exhibition venues.

The use of gilding in her works might open up connotations of the sacred as well. The reason why she uses gilding, beyond the suggestion that it is because her mother had a collection of postcards gilded in gold leaf,[47] stems from Onur's studies of light and shadow as the basic elements of art. We might say that it is because she wants to achieve the effect of interaction between light and the reflective surface.[48] We might also see her use of gilding as

39. Füsun Onur, 'Büyük Sanatçı Kıymetli Hoca Hadi Bara' [Great Artist and Esteemed Teacher Hadi Bara], *Ankara Sanat*, no. 68, December 1971, 10.

40. Füsun Onur, 'Görsel Sanatlarda Eleştiri Yokluğu' [The Lack of Criticism in the Visual Arts], *Hürriyet Gösteri*, no. 82, September 1987, 43.

41. Onur, 'Saha: Füsun Onur.'

42. Füsun Onur, 'Son Kırk Yılın İngiliz Heykelciliği' [The Last Forty Years of British Sculpture], *Hürriyet Gösteri Sanat-Edebiyat Dergisi*, no. 69, August 1986, 41.

43. Onur, 'The Last Forty Years of English Sculpture,' 41.

44. See the texts written for the artist's works *Doğaçlama* [Improvisation] (2003) and *Boogie Woogie* (2003): Füsun Onur, 'Füsun Onur,' in the exhibition catalogue for *Füsun Onur, Aydan Murtezaoğlu, Hale Tenger* (Lunds: Lunds Konsthall, 2003).

45. Füsun Onur, *Statement of Purpose* (Master's thesis, Maryland Institute College of Art, 1966), 3.

46. In her thesis, she dwells on the relationship between existence and art. She writes, 'Like existence itself art is a sudden invasion of the world. Though it is neutral and particular, it opens our eyes to the world.' She includes a quote from Sartre's novel *Nausea*: 'Existence is not something that may be thought of at a distance; it has to invade you abruptly, fix itself upon you, weigh heavily on your heart like a great unmoving beast.' This quote is followed by a sentence that concludes the text: 'Thus struggle in art is a free struggle embedded in existence in the world.' See Onur, 'Statement of Purpose,' 4.

47. Ayas, 'Füsun,' 12.

48. Discussing her search for the textural qualities of notes in the material, she lists the visible qualities of a surface as follows: 'bright-dark-matte-shining.' We can see the interest she takes in the relationship between light and surface in the title of her 1989 work *Ele Geçirilmiş Işık* [Captured Light], which uses a gold-coloured surface. See the text written by the artist for her work *Dünyanın Söylediği Şarkı* [The Song of the Earth] (2000): Brehm, *For Careful Eyes*, 107–08.

a sarcastic response to criticisms of her use of poor materials, and to recommendations that she apply gold or bronze to her works instead.[49] We might further consider gold as spreading rays of light like the sun, which is a metaphor used by the artist for Atatürk.[50] In the shimmering surfaces of the gold-coloured fabrics she uses, we might feel the movements on the water's surface. And we might go even further, weighing gold's historical relationship with the sacred and how its use in her works is a reminder of its application in ritual objects.[51]

After drifting through these associations of the 'sacred' in Onur's works, we can find the meaning of 'sacred duty' by looking closely at the critical attitude she developed in reaction to the sacred values of the context in which she has produced her work, as well as the beliefs that have conditioned her artistic attitude.

VIEWER AND CRITIC

Onur also touches upon the 'sacred duty' assumed by the artist when she discusses the lack of criticism in the visual arts.[52] She contributes, through her writings, to the formation of the common language and criticism whose lack she has felt.[53] In texts she wrote between 1976 and 1991, she criticises critics, exemplifying the critical writing for which she feels a need and thereby defining the relationship she desires to form between artwork and viewer. She does not believe that the meaning of art can be captured or explained in words.[54] She takes it as her duty to explain not the work, but what methods she uses and what she was thinking.[55] Through writing, she attempts to create a common ground upon which artworks can be discussed.

Onur accompanied her solo exhibitions *From Outside In From Inside Out* (1978) and *Counterpoint with Flower* (1982), as well as *Sign of Sign* (1987) and *Prelude* (2000) with texts written in the first person and addressed to the viewer. In the texts for the first two exhibitions, she expresses her expectations of the viewer.[56] By 1987, she leaves the work entirely to the spectator.[57] In contrast to some of her Turkish contemporaries, who tended to look down on society at this time,[58] Onur believed in the people who made up her viewers, inviting them to participate in the art, and learning from them in turn.[59] She still longs to expand the possibilities of the work, purged of the passive reception, codes, rules, labels, conditionings, prejudices and customs of viewers. She invites them to come to their own interpretations, to approach the work with creativity.

49.
Onur, 'A Response…,' 71.

50.
Explaining her work *Yerdeki Parlak Yuvarlaktan Çağrışımlar* [Associations from a Shiny Circle on the Floor] (1980) in a letter to her friend Cengiz Çekil, who hadn't been able to see it, she discusses the eighth pedestal and the sunny landscape she made, writing 'the sun calls to mind Atatürk.' See Füsun Onur's letter to Cengiz Çekil, 11 June 1980, CEKDIV373, Cengiz Çekil Archive, SALT Research, Istanbul. https://archives.saltresearch.org/handle/123456789/47067 (last accessed 15 November 2021).

51.
Describing her work *Opus I*, exhibited at the Hagia Irene Museum as part of the 6th Istanbul Biennial in 1999, Füsun Onur touches upon how her preference for the shining colour of gold is tied to the sacred: 'I selected materials to give the sense of holiness again, sky-blue, gilded textile, a "rahl" and grails.' See. Brehm, *For Careful Eyes*, 110.

52.
'The artist is entwined with her immediate environment, responding to the stimuli she receives. We've been saying the same thing over and over again for nine years. With such a society, the exhortations of a society with real, progressive critics will be different. Should we artists migrate for this to happen? We're fighting a battle here, we've taken on a sacred duty.' Onur, 'The Lack of Criticism in the Visual Arts,' 44.

53.
'What we are missing is in our common language because what we've made is exhausted before it can reach beyond us. This linguistic dream would open doors for communication, create such interaction, that as-yet unopened doors would open for the viewer, and the artist would come to realise the path she's taken. We do not need the judgement of critics who will see things elsewhere and apply them to us. We fill this void ourselves, we put out our publications ourselves.' Onur, 'The Lack of Criticism in the Visual Arts,' 45.

54.
Voice recording of Füsun Onur's talk as part of her exhibition *İmin İmi* [Sign of Sign], 1987, Maçka Art Gallery Archive, Istanbul.

55.
'I believe that it is my duty to explain how a painter thinks and how she works. I hope it is helpful. This is a job that I want to complete.' Text written for the exhibition *Counterpoint with Flower* (Istanbul: Taksim Art Gallery, 1982). '…for a while now, whichever orientations I find myself taking, what am I thinking, what questions am I asking, what am I exploring, whatever clues I give 'Third Dimension in Painting – Come In' sheds light on them, perhaps I've paved the way for a shift in the field of criticism. Perhaps the possibility of debate has been opened. (I want to be clear that I am writing this text before any text has been published on the new orientations exhibition).' Onur, 'Third Dimension in Painting – Come In,' 14.

56.
'…meanings should multiply and creativity should emerge in the viewer so that they interact with the artist; so that dialogue can be forged between artist and viewer, between viewer and artist […] I want the viewer to look at this work freed of all the traditional stereotypes and habits that have taken form and settled in their mind.' Text written for the exhibition *Dıştan İçe İçten Dışa* [From Outside In From Inside Out] (Istanbul: Taksim Art Gallery, 1982). 'Whoever views this work should only view the works inner flow, they should set aside their own habits of looking so that this flow can continue.

Believing that critics have not fulfilled their duties, Onur chooses to write so that artworks aren't overlooked, so that they don't come and go without leaving a trace, without appraisal, without debate. She admonishes approaches that interpret art according to given conventions, because such approaches 'sterilise, rather than liberate, aesthetic perception in the viewer.'[60] What critics 'lacking in the general concepts of the plastic arts'[61] need to know is the 'alphabet of plastic arts';[62] what they need to do is 'to read the words of the plastic arts.'[63]

THE GAZE UPON HER WORK

Over the course of her life, Onur has reacted against interpretations of art that situate it within movements. Such reactions might be the consequence of debates over imitation that I discuss below, but what bothers her more fundamentally is the risk of foreclosing possibilities through labels and categories.[64] An examination of the categorisations that have haunted Onur's practice makes it possible to reflect on the gaze directed on her work and how this gaze has evolved over time.

In the 1970s, critics associated Onur's work with Minimalism and Pop art. She objected to this reduction of her work to these movements, to which she had no relationship.[65] The attempt to situate Onur in relation to tendencies that belong to twentieth-century modernism is evident in a conversation that she had in 2012 with Carolyn Christov-Bakargiev and Hans Ulrich Obrist. When they try to trace her relationship to Minimalism, Constructivism, Surrealism and feminism, Onur insists that she is indifferent to them all.[66] While the strategic adoption of these kinds of movements might have facilitated her inclusion in canonical narratives, her resistance can be interpreted to support the following critique: 'Although non-Western art has been since then [well into the twentieth century] incorporated into the domain of art history, we are still experiencing the consequences of the initial segregation. The Western art canon continues to function as an implicit measure of all things, by defining the mainstream of the category of "art."'[67]

At certain points, the categories of 'Turkish' and 'Istanbul' have also been used as determinants in contexts where Onur's work has circulated. Though she has never assumed ethnic belonging by using the term 'Turkish' in any text she's written – she even jokes, in explaining how she works with the fundamentals of sculpture, 'As if pictorial space

The void should expand and change so that its emptiness can change with every viewer. This is what I want to happen because this is a visual counterpoint.' Text written for the exhibition *Counterpoint with Flower.*

57.
'I have left the story of the expression of art and its elements (knowing-not knowing, expectations – the unexpected, understanding – misunderstanding), proceeding through time, entirely to the viewer.' Füsun Onur, text written for the exhibition *İmin İmi* [Sign of Sign] (Istanbul: Maçka Art Gallery, 1987). 'Because the finished work is the goal of this experience, it is not so possible to experience the process of its making after the work is complete. At any rate, here I have subjectively worked on the technical side of the production process; the rest is left to the viewer.' Text written for the exhibition *Prelüd* [Prelude] (Istanbul: Maçka Art Gallery, 2000).

58.
'It was impossible for these values, which came to us from a civilisation that developed elsewhere, a civilisation whose intellectual materials we haven't yet accessed, from a culture with a different structure and a different quality, to be brought to us by a few artists, as if they were bringing potted plants, for society here to understand, to embrace and, in particular, to assimilate into themselves.' Gezer, *Fifty Years of Turkish Painting and Sculpture*, 14.

59.
'But the public they said wouldn't understand understood, they followed me. Those who didn't understand were the ones accustomed to mechanical perception through clichés, who claimed that they knew better, because if you make the work truly believing in it, putting yourself into it, the human element enters into it, it becomes social and then the people, even children, can understand it without prejudice.' See Onur, 'A Response...,' 71. 'Whereas meanings should multiply and creativity should emerge in the viewer so that they interact with the artist; so that dialogue can be forged between artist and viewer, between viewer and artist.' See text written for the exhibition *From Outside In From Inside Out*. 'I think the artist can gather information about her own truth even in the course of exhibition. [...] Then I witnessed how a question from a viewer opened me up to something new.' Voice recording, Maçka Art Gallery Archive.

60.
Onur, 'The Last Forty Years of British Sculpture,' 40.

61.
Füsun Onur, 'A Critic's Approach,' *Cumhuriyet* newspaper, 9 September 1976.

62.
Ibid.

63.
Ibid.

64.
'For us, critics are usually people, whether art historians or outsiders, who have not been saved from the pressure of ism's, who have been crushed under their weight. Rather than benefiting the culture, these kinds of writings cause harm to viewers. The artist's journey through art is erased among such narrow, perfunctory wisdom and a few stylistic quotations. The artist, art, and the elements of her art are intertwined with her approach to mental images, designs and physical structures.' Onur, 'The Last Forty Years of British Sculpture,' 40.

65.
Onur, 'Third Dimension in Painting – Come In,' 14; Onur, 'The Lack of Criticism in Visual Arts,' 43.

can actually be deemed American or Turkish!'[68] – many exhibitions in which she has participated have nonetheless featured 'Turkish' in their titles. Until the 2000s, the mindset that defined any artist who produces work in Turkey as 'Turkish' maintained its validity. The Istanbul Biennale was inaugurated in 1987 in the oppressive political environment of the 1980 coup and its aftermath, interceding to improve Turkey's negative image[69] and putting Istanbul on the map for global art. Onur's works have been exhibited in five separate editions of the Istanbul Biennale, including the very first one. In an art world that was being tested by globalisation after the fall of the Berlin Wall, the works of artists from Turkey usually circulated internationally in exhibitions that brought together works from Turkey or from Istanbul.[70] This perspective and infrastructure have led to debates over 'centre' versus 'periphery.'

Another category often used in situating Onur's work is 'woman.' Some of her works have been produced for exhibitions that brought together women artists, or else existing works have been exhibited under this category. It has been said that she tends toward 'materials [...] traditionally ascribed to the realm of women'[71] in choosing her materials; her work has been compared to 'a dowry chest opening and closing.'[72] When asked, 'Does it bother you that the works you've produced are interpreted by way of gender identity?' she has replied, 'I am not bothered by being associated with the identity of womanhood. But I would have been more interested for my work to be read and interpreted within a different context.' To the question 'Does your identity as an artist supersede your other identities?' she has responded, 'No, it doesn't. I don't see things in the context of identity. When I'm producing art, such identities don't matter to me.'[73] The categories of 'Turkish,' 'Istanbul' and 'woman' touched upon here reflect how the gaze directed on the artist's work, and the needs of the context in which she produces, have changed over time.

In fact, Onur's commitments refute the gaze that expects continuity and consistency from her.[74] When Christov-Bakargiev, for instance, observing the variety of works made at different times, asked her whether these contradictions were the result of an ambition always to do the unexpected, Onur replied: 'But I don't think of it that way. Sometimes if I'm bored of doing something, I rebel against myself. I always want to do something new.'[75] In the thesis she wrote in 1966, she foresaw these expectations of continuity and consistency, and expressed an attitude that would thwart them: 'There is not a fixed thing

66.
'Füsun Onur, Carolyn Christov-Bakargiev, and Hans Ulrich Obrist, in Conversation,' 22.

67.
Anna Brzyski, 'Introduction.' *Partisan Canons* (Durham and London: Duke University Press, 2007), 6.

68.
Onur, 'A Response...,' 71.

69.
Banu Karaca, *The National Frame: Art and State Violence in Turkey and Germany* (New York: Fordham University Press, 2021), 205.

70.
In a map of 'Turkey's International Exhibitions' prepared by SALT, which contains 'exhibitions abroad on the theme of Turkey,' Onur's works are included in the exhibitions *İskele. Turkish Art Today* (1994), *Suddenly, Turkish Artists* (1995), *İskorpit: Recent Art from Istanbul* (1998), *From Far Away So Close – Four woman artists from Turkey* (2001), *between the waterfronts. Istanbul – Rotterdam* (2002), *Turkish Art Today: Where? Here?* (2003), *Füsun Onur – Aydan Murtezaoğlu – Hale Tenger* (2003), *Call me ISTANBUL is my name* (2004), *Continuous Variations* (2009), *Tactics of Invisibility: Contemporary Artistic Positions from Turkey* (2010) and *Tanzimat* (2010). SALT, 'Turkey's International Exhibitions' SALT, https://saltonline.org/tr/uluslararasi-turkiye-sergileri (last accessed 15 November 2021).

71.
Brehm, *For Careful Eyes*, 53.

72.
Kortun and Kosova, *Offside but Goal*, 60.

73.
Ahu Antmen, 'The Feminist Paradox: Women and Artistic Identity (Article and survey),' *Kadın/Woman 2000*, Vol. 18, no. 2 (2017), 35–36.

74.
'They are looking for formal consistency and continuity.' Voice recording, Maçka Art Gallery Archive.

75.
'Füsun Onur, Carolyn Christov-Bakargiev, and Hans Ulrich Obrist, in Conversation,' 24.

called self that is known as character or personality, but perceptions, emotions, memories.'[76] We have here an artist who, in place of a continuous and consistent subject, tends toward new questions, toward new sources of the sensory, the emotional, and the remembered with each work, an artist who likes to rebel against and surprise herself. In her work, instead of continuity, the ruptures necessitated by newly asked questions converge with multiplying and diversifying approaches. Though I might resort to specific moments, narratives, or contexts to illuminate some of the artist's choices, I have arrived at these readings with an awareness that Onur has always tended toward the new in her language of expression and her work; she has always used different questions to transform her materials, her works and their contents, and accordingly, no reading of her work can be fixed to one single point. The interpretations I arrive at are the ones I need.

BELATEDNESS

Art in Turkey has, until only recently, been perceived and interpreted in terms of belatedness. While art has developed quickly in the West, so the story goes, Turkey has had to chase after it in order to catch up.[77] The cause of and troubling solution to this feeling of belatedness has depended upon taking the West as a model in order to imitate it.[78] Füsun's anxiety about belatedness, however, was not due to the fact that her works were imitative or failed to capture their times; rather, it was that critics were late in comprehending them.[79] Writing about pieces that she believes have been overlooked, she attempts to create a shared ground for debate without losing any more time.

Saying that she 'chose the hard way'[80] by returning to Turkey, Onur recounts how she had to forcefully grapple with the issue of imitation as she started exhibiting her work. Following the opening of her first exhibition at Taksim Art Gallery, some said that a black book/box containing 'secret information had been brought from the United States,' implying that what she had produced was no more than an imitation of Western art.[81] This experience must be kept in mind in order to understand her ongoing anxieties over influence[82] and her attitude concerning imitation.

Onur has written that she produces 'in a context in which everything foreign or new is regarded as an imitation of Western art,'[83] and the only way to avoid imitation 'as it is regarded by both the national and the universal … is to take up the elements of art one by one.'[84] Artists who

76.
Onur, 'Statement of Purpose,' 3.

77.
Gezer, *Fifty Years of Turkish Painting and Sculpture*, 9–10.

78.
'The Western "model" and Turkish "copy" have been recurring themes […] in social theory for a long time. The distinction historically made between the model and the copy lies at the heart of the hegemonic imaginary concerning the constructs of the East and the West. The Turkish hegemonic imaginary has been structured within an encounter with the West, which imposed a "model" for modernity in its colonialist and imperialist history, and which has always reproduced itself through insufficient "copies."' Meltem Ahiska, 'Occidentalism: The historical fantasy of the modern,' *The South Atlantic Quarterly* 102, no. 2 (2003): 357.

79.
'My suspicion is that critics are lacking in the general concepts of the plastic arts. These concepts are evolving and expanding from day to day without end. We have no time to lose. If it weren't like this, would Cengiz's work in the garden of the archaeology museums be overlooked?' Onur, 'A Critic's Approach.'

80.
Onur, 'A Response…,' 71.

81.
'I returned to Turkey following my graduation. I opened my first exhibition at the Taksim Art Gallery. Back then, you had to present an application and wait. Finally, my turn came and we opened the exhibition. Of course, they were really surprised, saying what kind of work is this, would it be suitable to place them on the grass […] As the exhibitions continued, some people joked, saying 'you've done one, and two, where does the black book end?' I didn't understand what they were saying, what was this black "book"? It turned out they thought I was copying from an American artist they didn't know. Because the overall tendency at the time was to copy.' Füsun Onur and İlhan Onur, 'An Afternoon with Füsun and İlhan Onur,' Interview by Emre Baykal, in *For Careful Eyes*, 7. See also ibid., 31–32; Onur, 'A Response…,' 71.

82.
'When I was in the Academy of Fine Arts, our teacher used to say "Go to the library. If you like a sculptor, you can imitate him, but then you need to do something different and explain to me why you did what you did, and why he did what he did." But I was timid about this because those who always copied stayed there. I was afraid to be influenced.' See: 'Füsun Onur, Carolyn Christov-Bakargiev, and Hans Ulrich Obrist, in Conversation,' 20–21.

83.
Text written by the artist for her exhibition *Counterpoint with Flower*.

84.
Text written by the artist for her work *Sign of Sign* (1987): Füsun Onur, *'Sign of Sign,'* 4. In the *A Section of Avantgarde Turkish Art* exhibition catalogue (Istanbul: Atatürk Cultural Center, 1987).

grapple with these elements will independently yet simultaneously ask themselves, from their geographic locations, similar questions, and will 'come to comparable solutions'[85] because 'the elements of art are universal.'[86]

ART AND ITS ELEMENTS

The following collage of texts, written at different times by Onur, illuminates her thoughts on the relationship between art and life by addressing the process of going from perception to the creative act:

> Art is derived from life. There is a world of perception that unites man to the world and makes him part of it. […] Without presence in feeling and imagination there can be no actuality of a being as presence. […] The aesthetic is presence making element in our experience. The real is what we attend.[87]
>
> She [the artist] perceives the world in this way; through the schema of her rational faculty, through mental images.[88] To perceive is to ascribe a suitable characteristic to the object of attention, to the structure of attention.[89] Art is an event of the intellect; it changes as its function changes, as civilisation progresses. […] The linguistics of the visual image appear incomprehensible to those outside art. But the mindset of the artist, which plucks the visual image from all its undesirable relationships and situates it in brand new, desirable relationships and linkages, gets its strength from psychology, philosophy, the logic of imagination, mathematics, and life itself. Rescuing art from its role as a mere vehicle, incorporating new conjunctions and new uses intrinsic to its lexicon, this mindset begins producing all over again.[90] Signs have to do with how we perceive the world, what we understand of it. What function could art have in the present? A critical reconstruction, a recoding.[91]

In a text titled 'Imagination' that she wrote in 1991, Onur compares a quote from Coleridge that expresses the strength of the imagination[92] to the claim that the imagination has lost its function in the modern sensibility.[93] She criticises how 'the desire for power whatever the cost' takes hold of art, along with the tendency to apply popular clichés to works of art because they are then easily perceived and consumed. She sees these superficial clichés as traps for both the artist and the viewer. Against this, she invites the interrogation of works of art and the use of creativity freed of mental laziness. She explains the consequences of the failure to do so by means of a hypothetical local

85.
Brehm, *For Careful Eyes*, 95.

86.
'To make a concept concrete, to extend toward all areas, from sculpture, painting, architecture, decoration, even music: these are the unending struggles of the artist. This stems from the affluence of her bodily structure, the qualities of her inner structure, the skill with which she chooses and winnows from her perceptions for the conscious mind. Unaware of the flows of history or in her pursuits, an artist can nonetheless work in parallel to another artist in another country. Because the elements of art are universal. […] In summary, the efficacy of these English artists on universal art is clear as day. The path they blazed is the path of art, and it grows out of universal elements. […] They arrive at new conjunctures of meaning and their new worldviews emerge. This is what every artist has dedicated herself to. This is precisely how artists from different countries can understand and coalesce with one another, by following the language of one another's art, without using one another's spoken languages.' Onur, 'The Last Forty Years of British Sculpture,' 42.

87.
Onur, 'Statement of Purpose,' 2–3.

88.
Onur, 'The Last Forty Years of British Sculpture,' 41.

89.
Onur, 'The Preservation of Modern Sculpture in Turkey,' 95.

90.
Onur, 'Third Dimension in Painting – Come In,' 14–15.

91.
Text written by the artist for her work *Sign of Sign* (1987).

92.
'The primary Imagination I hold to be the living power and prime agent of all human perception, and as a repetition in the finite mind of the eternal act of creation in the infinite I am,' Samuel Taylor Coleridge (1815), in Onur, 'Imagination,' 66.

93.
'The modern sensibility no longer believes in the function of the imagination; it has given up its place to the alchemy of the laboratory. Lots and lots of gas, and little imagination: that's the reality of the present.' Wright Morris, 'Territory Ahead,' in Onur, 'Imagination,' 66.

election: 'Our people cannot choose what is useful to themselves because of their trust in clichés and the techniques of propaganda, their laziness in producing thought, the untrustworthiness of their reason, and the inversion of concepts of good and evil.'[94] In order for art to fulfil its function and become a critical recoding, the power of the imagination must be brought alive by the artist, the critic and the viewer, and they must all become part of the creative act.

Reconstructing the perceptible world in the work through the abstraction of imagination, Onur grapples with the elements of art and sculpture – inner and outer space, time, volume, mass, density, weight, verticality, horizontality, texture, colour, light, shadow, rhythm, variation. She does so in order to ask questions that strike at the laws inherent to art and to speak 'in the language of art itself'[95] as she composes answers to those questions.

TIME

Questions about the relationship between sculpture and time have been one of the strongest driving forces shaping Onur's work. Though she may not have outright associated sculpture with time in her thesis, she discusses repetition and rhythm as they spread the work across time and space. Where the repetition of the same elements might be boring and practically impossible, the playfulness brought about by the conjuncture of different materials and the rhythm created by broadening the play of contrasting elements are both characterised as the 'unifying elements of art.'[96] Two works she produced in 1976, *From Outside In From Inside Out* and *Untitled (Variation)*, contain elements that repeat through variation. In the text that accompanied her solo exhibition *From Outside In From Inside Out*, held at Taksim Art Gallery in 1978, she writes that 'in order to save the painting from its fixity, I spread it across time.'[97] In exploring time within the work, she begins to use repetition, rhythm and variation. Discussing *Third Dimension in Painting – Come In* (1981), which viewers had to enter in order to experience it, she suggests that we look at it through these questions: 'What are synchronicity and diachronicity in the plastic arts, and how have they been used before now? Is cubism synchronicity?'[98] Onur followed this work, with *Counterpoint with Flower.* In order to generate an experience of time within the work, she offered a solution in the form of an installation[99] – unprecedented in Turkey – in which the viewer enters the space of the work and experiences it

94. Onur, 'Imagination,' 67.

95. Onur, 'A Response…,' 71.

96. Onur, 'Statement of Purpose,' 4.

97. Text written by the artist for her exhibition *From Outside In From Inside Out.*

98. Onur, 'Third Dimension in Painting – Come In,' 15.

99. Onur says, 'I don't know how it [the installation] came. I myself didn't know about installation. But I was doing it, because I liked to. I didn't know whether I was doing installation or Conceptual art […] I don't care about these names.' This statement supports the idea that she arrived at the solution of installation as she sought answers to questions concerning time in sculpture and the relationship between the mass and space. See: 'Füsun Onur, Carolyn Christov-Bakargiev, and Hans Ulrich Obrist, in Conversation,' 24.

by moving inside it. 'Time is in the work,'[100] she wrote, as well as the viewer.

Counterpoint with Flower is an early portent of Onur's later works that make reference to music. Her departure point is this: 'I am trying to reconcile time and space. I divide sculptures into modules because you cannot adjust time in painting or sculpture, but in music you can. With a painting or sculpture, you wouldn't even spend two minutes in front of it. But with music, you have to make time for it, whether you like it or not.'[101] The solution of 'dividing the sculpture into modules' that she came up with to establish the experience of time in sculpture has parallels with an earlier study she made of Rodin's *Monument to Balzac*. In this work, which treats the figure as a solid mass, 'the sculpture's movement does not manifest as a linear development that coalesces in a single moment.' She writes that the viewer makes sense of this mass 'bit by bit, in motion,' and that 'Rodin had a melodic understanding of space that forces the viewer into motion.'[102] Because Onur splits the mass of the sculpture into pieces and expands it in space, and because the viewer moves with it, time becomes an element of the work. Exploring the experience of time, she arrives at a music that spreads across space through repetition, rhythm and variation.

THE USE OF MATERIAL

In choosing her materials, Onur pays close attention to their visual, sonic and textural features.[103] She creates her own artistic world out of ready-made, everyday materials by purging them of their uses and by 'giv[ing] them a meaning they did not possess before.'[104] Her relationship with ready-made objects in her work coincides with Sara Ahmed's definition of 'queer use': 'how things can be used in ways other than for which they were intended or by those other than for whom they were intended.'[105] Following this line of thought, I prefer to characterise Onur's desire to 'be of use' by returning to her country as a 'use' free of its pragmatic axis, that is, as a queer use.

Onur uses whatever materials she has available.[106] When she has been criticised for choosing poor materials, she has replied, 'I wonder, could bronze or gold have been applied to what I created? The criticism comes without hesitation; gold and silver have their own meaningfulness and if you just apply them they connote certain things. A new material means a new language; who understands that? What I want to say changes with my material.'[107]

100.
Text written by the artist for her exhibition *Counterpoint with Flower*.

101.
Brehm, *For Careful Eyes*, 99.

102.
Onur, 'Modern Heykelin Türkiye'de Korunması' [The Preservation of Modern Sculpture in Turkey], 95.

103.
'The tonal character of music is a perceived process. Its sensory qualities also refer to touch: round-pointed-compressed; in this connection to surfaces' properties: hard-soft, smooth-rough; to sight: bright-dark-dull-brilliant; and subjectively to tone colour: blue, yellow, etc. and to temperature sense: warm-cold. The material character of a tonal body has structural significance in music, such as volume, density, weight.' Text written by the artist for her work *Dünyanın Söylediği Şarkı* [The Song of the Earth] (2000): Brehm, *For Careful Eyes*, 107.

104.
Text written by the artist for her exhibition *Prelude*.

105.
Sara Ahmed, *What's the Use?* (Durham: Duke University Press, 2019), 199.

106.
Füsun Onur, 'Conversation: Füsun Onur with İz Öztat,' interview by İz Öztat, m-est.org, 24 July 2014. https://m-est.org/2014/07/24/conversation-fusun-onur-with-iz-oztat/ (last accessed 15 November 2021), first published as 'Söyleşi: Füsun Onur ve İz Öztat' [Conversation: Füsun Onur and İz Öztat] *Sanat Dünyamız*, no. 141, July–August 2014, 90–99.

107.
Onur, 'A Response…,' 71.

Onur transmits what she wants to say by abstracting it through her material, and in her works she sarcastically embeds the subjects that attracted her attention and her concerns at the time the works were produced but may no longer be accessible to us today.[108] The explanations for her frequent use of tulle, for example, which include her fascination with textiles as a child[109] and her attraction to feminine materials, can be expanded to include sarcasm. In her text titled *Imagination*, she includes in her critique of technologies of development and consumption, artists' production of commercial and decorative works that are quickly consumed in the art context, claiming that 'clichés taken from masterpieces are to be repurposed, repackaged in a brighter, more ostentatious manner.'[110] Perhaps her use of tulle – an easily accessible material used for packaging and decoration – in works like *Any Chair* (1991), where she wraps chairs in the material and elevates them to the status of art, is her own sarcastic form of 'repackaged ostentation' intended to offer a critique of commercial decorative works.

AGAINST MASTERY, ON THE FLOOR

When she works with raw materials, and relies not on technical skill but on intuition,[111] Onur takes a stand against mastery and the sanctification of technique.[112] Intuition is what leads the artist in the first place. Through intuition she becomes sure of the definitude and necessity of what she makes. It is intuition that builds connections within the structure of the work and it is intuition that sustains the process whereby the work changes, takes shape.[113] Onur's confrontation of the value of technical skill and mastery has been criticised by those who speak on behalf of the local understanding of art that she challenges. The work that emerges, based on her conscientious intentions, is thus overlooked. For instance, one of the primary features that defines mastery in sculpture in the context where she produces is durability.[114] In such a context, Onur's non-robust work was considered slack and careless, and was interrogated for its refusal to stand upright.[115] Yet it is clear that Onur has adopted an attitude that refuses hard, durable materials as well as the predictable forms these materials make possible; it is an attitude that proposes a surrender to the horizontality of gravity rather than the solidity of the vertical form. Such an approach, which Robert Morris defined as 'anti-form,'[116] can be seen in Onur's *Conceptual Visual Images* (1983) and *Morning Gymnastics* (1987). Her choice of material and her anti-mastery attitude was interpreted by Canan [Çoker]

108.
When I asked Onur why she wrote 'ÇOCUK YILINDA SAÇLARINIZI SEVİNİZ' [LOVE YOUR HAIR IN THE CHILD YEAR], she replied: 'That was a sarcastic phrase. They come up with slogans like that in advertisements [...] Some children are being raised like race horses. During that time they were supposed to prepare for exams. But most of the children were abandoned to the waves. They were struggling, trying not to disappear.' See Onur, 'Conversation: Füsun Onur and İz Öztat.' In a letter she wrote to Cengiz Çekil immediately after finishing production on the work *Associations from a Shiny Circle on the Floor*, she describes the contents of the sixth pedestal as a 'forceful attack on painters,' and the seventh pedestal as 'a bright-eyed intellectual giving, what's it called, a speech, against a background of spiders.' See Letter, 11 June 1980, SALT Research.

109.
Baykal, ibid., 16.

110.
Onur, 'Imagination,' 66.

111.
'Intuition is the guiding element. If it fails even in one detail the work collapses or the artist can't go on with her process. The materials stand raw with no connection in the work. When the artist is possessed she is not conscious of her ideas through the process. Intuition is a binder I think.' Text written by the artist for her works *Impromptu* (2003) and *Boogie Woogie* (2003): Onur, 'Füsun Onur.' See also Onur, 'A Response...' 71; Onur, 'The Last Forty Years of British Sculpture,' 41.

112.
'I do not believe a perfected mechanical production is a work of art; technique should never dominate the creative intent.' Onur, 'Statement of Purpose,' 4. 'The path to this kind of success passes through clichéd knowledge. In the end, the artist and the viewer are both happy because they have met by the shortest possible route. Abstracted from everything, the individual's intellect and the adventures of their consciousness have been imprisoned. Technical pedantry dominates every section and every area of society. It is so important to know how something was done, to finish the work by the shortest possible route. Clichéd knowledge, divorced from life, might accelerate the arena of practice in our daily lives. But still, for my part, rather than applying the knowledge of 'technically how to do' the task of replacing a screw that has fallen off my car, I will opt for taking an adventurous journey with that single screw.' Onur, 'Imagination,' 66–67.

113.
'Yes I will make it [*Dance of the Crows*] myself. When I work, I will remember things, but if I were to dictate to someone who is doing this professionally, it might not be enough mine. When I am making this, I will perhaps make something different from the idea [...] And the process is very important for me, always.' See: 'Füsun Onur, Carolyn Christov-Bakargiev, and Hans Ulrich Obrist, in Conversation,' 24.

114.
Regarding the non-figurative works by Bara, Hüseyin Gezer writes, 'They strive for order, in search of a balance between emptiness and fullness. Usually in this order there is a durable structure that holds the foundational elements of horizontal and vertical in balance.' Gezer, *Fifty Years of Turkish Painting and Sculpture*, 76.

115.
Sezer Tansuğ, a leading critic of the times, wrote in reference to Onur's piece *Nude* (1974): 'Füsun Onur, whose sculptor fantasy seemed at first to

Beykal, an artist and critic active at the time, as follows: 'By conveying an attitude that stands against the production of art objects, against the commercial, against expensive materials, against skill, and against mastery, this work by Füsun Onur stands against the prevalent understanding of art.'[117] Through the artist's choice and handling of material, the moment she decides the work is complete and the resulting fragility, the works preserve their challenging nature in the present.

Rosalind E. Krauss argues that the attitude that embraces working on the horizontal plane and on the ground refuses the vertical alignments posited by the vertical body of the viewer, the bourgeois salons, and the museum walls.[118] In her studies of the elements of sculpture, one of Onur's abiding questions has to do with the vertical and horizontal reading of art. In producing her work *Third Dimension in Painting – Come In*, she was seeking the answer to the question, 'What is it to read art vertically, or horizontally?'[119] Perhaps this is the question that leads her again and again to works that are on the floor, installations spread across the ground. And, as she represents Turkey at the Venice Biennale, she arrives once again at a work that sometimes necessitates kneeling in close in order to see, and that is humble in terms of scale, mode of production and choice of materials.

DESTRUCTION AND PRESERVATION

Onur's work is animated by the tension between destruction and preservation. One of the narratives that has sprung up around the artist, and one that she herself has sustained, is that she throws old sculptures into the sea from her home/studio on the edge of the Bosphorus in order to make room for new ones. The moment she completes a work, she loses her excitement and embarks on the work to follow. The only reason why a number of her destroyed works are accessible through documents today, and why they all haven't sunk to the bottom of the sea, is because they have been preserved by her sister İlhan, with whom she has a symbiotic relationship.

There is another narrative about the artist destroying her work that comes from her student years. Whenever she was unhappy with what she'd made, she'd destroy it and start all over again. Destroying the work is a practice of putting oneself to the test.[120] Although she does so of her own volition, she has written that artworks are destroyed when they are not understood or when the necessary

be quite robust, has begun exhibiting a perspective that is slack.' Of her works featured at an exhibition held at the American Cultural Center in 1974, he wrote, 'Let's call them works that evoke a sense of both anxiety and indifference, and let's add that this translates to the gaze of the critic as an image of a jocular exhibition visitor describing them as "hideous sculptures, neither standing properly nor falling over."' The 'hideous' sculpture he describes is most likely the sculpture Onur dedicated to Bara. See Sezer Tansuğ, *Sanata Yaklaşım, Eleştiride Duyarlık Çağı* [Approaching Art: The Age of Sensibility in Criticism] (Istanbul: Künmat Publishers, 1976), 269–72, cited in Nilgün Özayten, *Batı'da Obje Sanatı/ Kavramsal Sanat/ Post-Kavramsal Sanat ve Türkiye'de 1965–1992 Yılları Arasındaki Benzer Eğilimler (Doktora Tezi)* [Object Art/ Conceptual Art/ Post-Conceptual Art in the West and Similar Orientations in Turkey, 1965–1992 (Doctoral thesis)] (Istanbul: SALT/Garanti Kültür AŞ, 2013), 98, first published Istanbul University Department of Art History, 1992.

116. Robert Morris, 'Anti-Form,' *Continuous Project,* in *Altered Daily: The Writings of Robert Morris* (Cambridge, MA: MIT Press, 1993).

117. Canan Çoker, 'Füsun Onur ve Çevresel Sanatı' [Füsun Onur and Her Environmental Art], *Sanat Çevresi*, no. 42, April 1982, 24.

118. Rosalind E. Krauss, 'Horizontality,' in *Formless: A User's Guide* (New York: Zone Books, 1997), 93.

119. Onur, 'Third Dimension in Painting – Come In,' 15.

120. Onur, 'A Response…,' 70.

conditions to preserve them do not exist. Her 1986 article titled *The Preservation of Modern Sculpture in Turkey* was written upon the removal of her sculpture in Fındıklı Park that had been created as part of the *Fiftieth Anniversary of the Republic Sculpture Project*.[121] In the article, she suggests that modern sculpture must first be properly understood in order to be preserved. If it isn't, she concludes, it is inevitable that it will be destroyed by the state and/or citizen.[122]

Over the years, in close relationships I've built with women artists of different generations in Turkey, as well as in their publicly accessible statements, I have frequently encountered the notion of 'battling,' a term used by Onur in discussions of her 'sacred duty.' It is disappointing to include this expression here, since it demonstrates that Onur needs to be resolute against the carelessness, indifference and hostility she faces in order to sustain her art practice; she has to demonstrate the willpower necessary to both destroy and preserve the work. For example, in *Plaid 1-2-3-4* (1987), made up of four canvases, we see a girl wearing a plaid dress, some of her body visible and some of it missing, her face indistinct. In the third canvas, where the world surrounding the girl appears in the form of her toys, she takes the canvas by the edges and tears it down, revealing a pink frame and the silhouette of a woman. This work was produced for the *Joint Exhibit* held in Izmir in 1987 through the individual efforts of artists who participated. Cengiz Çekil, Onur's close friend and organiser of the exhibition, wrote the following in the text for the catalogue: 'it was hoped that space would be created for the possibility of once again debating concepts like art, artist, artistic value, etc., but this time with the hope of doing so completely anew.'[123] In this effort, Onur provided a work that destroyed itself by tearing down what was already established in order to render visible the structure residing underneath.

Preservation, however, is also inherent to Onur's work. In the piece *A Seed Sprouts II* (1979), angels protect a sprouting plant.[124] Angels appear from time to time in her later works as well, perhaps in order to protect that which is sacred: art.

PRELUDE

While grappling with the continuities and ruptures, the breakages and fractures in the sum total of the narratives that have emerged in the course of studying what Onur sees as her duty and what she considers sacred in her practice, I approach the question of how to tell the story of the

121. 'As a "celebration of the fiftieth anniversary of the Republic" in 1972, the Governor of Istanbul recommended the placement of works of art in parks and squares and on roads. […] The fate of Füsun Onur's geometric, abstractionist sculpture made of aluminium and installed in Fındıklı Park, was, during construction to rearrange the park under the mayorship of Bedrettin Dalan in 1985, to be removed.' Özlem Diri Bal, 'Türkiye'de Kamusal Alanda Soyut Heykel Sorunsalı' [The Problematic of Abstract Sculpture in Public Space in Turkey] (Master's thesis, Istanbul University, 2019), 132–36.

122. 'We can examine the conceptualisation of modern sculpture in Turkey from a number of perspectives. What is modern sculpture, or even, what is a sculpture, and is there modern sculpture in Turkey? […] It is difficult for modern sculpture to be understood through an exhibition that a handful of people hold once a year. Given such a gaping void, such discontinuity, we simply cannot expect this art to be suddenly understood. […] Not to mention that as parks are rearranged sculptures are torn from the ground, removed, and tossed out. This is another misfortune of sculpture. Many works considered modern sculpture are being destroyed by the municipality today; if not, tomorrow the public will break them; we can do nothing but stay silent.' Onur, 'The Preservation of Modern Sculpture in Turkey,' 96.

123. Cengiz Çekil, 'Toplu Sergi Üzerine' [On the Joint Exhibit], in the *Joint Exhibit* catalogue (Izmir: Izmir Turkish-American Foundation, 1987).

124. In a letter she wrote to Cengiz Çekil, Onur includes a description that accompanies a drawing of her work *A Seed Sprouts* (1979): 'Three angels wave their hands. An angel resting its hand on its head watches over the greenery. One angel shows the path to the sprout. Angels everywhere.' See Letter from Füsun Onur to Cengiz Çekil, 1 November 1978, CEKDIV432, Cengiz Çekil Archive, SALT Research, Istanbul. https://archives.saltresearch.org/handle/123456789/50159 (last accessed 15 November 2021).

relationality between generations through her imagery. Thinking about the works lodged in the memory of Maçka Art Gallery[125] and the generations of artists it has hosted since 1976, I find solace in Onur's 2001 installation *Prelude*. In a space covered in 10 × 10 centimetre ivory tiles – a modernist grid covering the walls and floor, a sealed empty space with associations of cave-womb-bathhouse – nesting tables, hammers and other objects are arranged. The work is accompanied by a text written by Onur:

> If we approach *Prelude* as a soundless musical composition, the opening motif starts with hesitation. The smallest units in this piece are [Legos] and they are unable to form a sentence yet. Then a big form (nesting table) comes in. The little forms follow him, and imitate him. Then the big form doubles, and getting one under each other, the pieces extend. The little forms imitating the big forms do the same thing and expand. Then one big form [*tak*]. Hammers interfere with little strokes; they follow each other. Big forms get together (four of them) get bigger and blur. From left to right, from right to left, from right to low, low to high, they repeat and the great chatterers, the hammers, accompany them. With the little form and three lonely hammers, it comes to an end.[126]

The nesting table becomes a metaphor for an art historical narrative based upon continuity: generations that follow and imitate one another, that emerge from one another. The creation myth embodied by hesitation, by delay from the very start, by an unfulfillable expression. The hammers tied with bows of tulle act as gatekeepers that presume omnipotence over the creation of the official narrative. Another hazy layer of pink and blue tulle covers the surfaces of the nesting tables, both showing and hiding those that follow. The tulle flowing in uninterrupted folds reveals that the continuity created by the nesting tables is an illusion. These are narratives that flow in parallel, that break, that don't intersect, that are all built according to different paradigms…

VOID

Onur grapples in her work with voids: the void in which she installs her work, the 'unfillable void' created when Bara died,[127] the void left by the absence of critique and debate in the visual arts,[128] the void that emerges from the

125.
Maçka Art Gallery was opened in 1976 by Rabia Çapa and her sister Varlık Sadıkoğlu on the ground floor of an apartment building. Architect Mehmet Konuralp, who designed the space, described it as follows: 'All the walls and floors of the gallery, in both its inside and outside spaces, were covered with 26,011 unglazed ceramic tiles, each 10 × 10 cm in dimension, almost too many to count, all manufactured in Bozüyük. The space was purged of all detail, with the intent of removing any reference to planes and to facilitate the continuity of the relationship between inside and outside; composed of basic tectonic-geometric elements to serve as a container, all with the intent of maintaining the plainest form for the created space so it wouldn't compete with its constantly changing contents.' See Mehmet Konuralp, 'Maçka Sanat Galerisi 1976–2016' [Maçka Art Gallery 1976–2016], in *Görünmeyene Bakmak: Maçka Sanat Galerisi'nin 40 Yılı* [Looking at the Invisible: Forty Years of Maçka Art Gallery], edited by Rabia Çapa and Necmi Sönmez (Istanbul: Ofset Yapımevi Publications, 2016), 32. Contrary to Konuralp's intention, the space often defied the works it featured, and many artists across multiple generations reacted to Maçka Art Gallery with site-specific installations, generating a collective memory that reflects the evolution and new orientations in conceptual art in Turkey. It was home to Onur's solo exhibitions *İmin İmi* [Sign of Sign] (1987), *Galeri Işıkları* [Gallery Lights] (1991), *Kadans* [Cadence] (1995), *Prelüd* [Prelude] (2000), *Çeşitlemeler* [Variations] (2012), and *Siz de Bilirsiniz* [As You Know] (2016).

126.
Text written by the artist for the exhibition *Prelude*.

127.
Onur, 'Great Artist and Esteemed Teacher Hadi Bara,' 10.

128.
Onur, 'Third Dimension in Painting – Come In,' 14.

lack of a common language that could make it possible to think about art together,[129] the discontinuity and voids in the emergence of sculptural art in Turkey.[130] Through her writings, she contributes to the formation of that common language, but looking at her writings and her works, I still find myself floundering in the void formed by the absence of this common language. I get lost trying to follow theoretical and philosophical references that emerge across her texts, because paradigms change over time. In fact, I can't even understand the Turkish renditions of a number of the words used, because some time after their invention they lost traction and fell out of use. It seems to me that securing the continuity necessary for the formation of a common language is impossible. Like the fabrics and strings Onur uses to connect one object to another, I am left dangling between her works and her words, and I struggle to follow the traces of what has been passed on from one generation to another, in a history constructed with ruptures and the voids produced by ruptures. While looking at the works that mark certain periods in her art practice,[131] I think of the time that has elapsed between the year when she wrote her thesis to the moment in which I complete this text. Thinking of time as the duration of a thought,[132] I carry these dates to the title of this text and reach for the void to which she directs us.

129.
Onur, 'The Lack of Criticism in the Visual Arts,' 45.

130.
'Our art establishment began gifting our culture its first sculptors in 1928, 1929. The first generation fulfilled their duty, sustained their work as sculptors. Then the art of sculpture made such progress in the world, and we had an enormous void. [...] Given everything I've said, it is clear how modern sculpture is conceptualised in Turkey. Have sculptors been effective in this area? Let's wait and see their efficacy. It is difficult for modern sculpture to be understood through an exhibition that a handful of people hold once a year. Given such a gaping void, such discontinuity, we simply cannot expect this art to be suddenly understood. But I am sure that true works, given over joyfully, will not be made sense of, will not be embraced.' Onur, 'The Preservation of Modern Sculpture in Turkey,' 96.

131.
There are two works by Onur for which she marked the beginning and ending dates of their creation process. In the first instance, she wrote on a plaque, alongside her name, the duration (4.8.1992–16.8.1992) she stayed in Prilep to produce a work that she exhibited at the 9th International Prilep Biennial. In the other, she transformed a dress she wore at her second solo exhibition in 1972 into a work in 1996. She writes about bringing the dress, produced in France, back to France as a work of art: 'I prepared a ceremony for the years between 1972–1996 that it lived with me. I fixed its sleeves and collar, which nobody can wear anymore, with a quilted pillow, placed my glittering gift on its lap, wrapped it in tulle, and packed it with roses.' See Onur, Füsun. Füsun Onur Archive. Istanbul. Later published as 'Sous le Manteau,' in the *Sous le Manteau* catalogue, 59. Paris: Galerie Thaddaeus Ropac, 1997.

132.
'But for the time being I am in the centre of everything that screams and teems. And it's subtle as the most intangible reality. For now time is the duration of a thought.' Clarice Lispector, *Água Viva* (London: Penguin Books, 2012), 16.

POSTSCRIPT: I want to thank Bige Örer and Nilüfer Şaşmazer for inviting me to write on Füsun Onur's practice; Nilüfer Şaşmazer for her support in accessing documents as well as research and editorial support; Sezin Romi for her work on the artist's archives made accessible as part of SALT Research and for facilitating my access to these sources; Katherine Cowan, for support with access and interpretation of documents concerning Füsun Onur's Masters studies, archived at the Maryland Institute; Yasemin Nur, for enquiring into the history of the Academy with me; and Fatma Belkıs and Eda Berkmen for providing comments on the first draft of this text that allowed me to bring it to its final state.

Carolyn Christov-Bakargiev *in conversation with* Bige Örer

BİGE ÖRER

You've worked with Füsun Onur on multiple occasions and you have an ongoing dialogue with her. When did you first encounter her work?

CAROLYN CHRISTOV-BAKARGIEV

Harald Szeemann was the first to tell me about her work, when I was in Australia, working on the Sydney Biennale. The first piece I saw was this sculpture [*Dual Sculpture*, 1970] in the corner of a room in Fulya Erdemci's exhibition, *Modern and Beyond*, at santralistanbul in 2007. And then I saw her work again at the 12th Istanbul Biennial curated by Jens Hoffmann and Adriano Pedrosa. That was a beautiful biennale; it was wonderful. On that occasion, I asked you if I could visit Füsun – I was already working on dOCUMENTA (13). I remember a very long car ride. And the strongest impression I had when she opened the door of her house, was that instead of it opening into an indoor space, it opened into the Bosphorus. So it was almost like a psychological shift of expectation, because suddenly I was overwhelmed by the sound of the Bosphorus, and the light and the shadows of the waves of the Bosphorus on the walls. The entire house gave me the feeling of going through a layer of ghosts or a portal to another world. And that other world was neither an indoor world nor an outdoor world.

I think it was this feeling of going from the street directly into the Bosphorus, and the sense that the habitable living space didn't have the thickness of a house but was just like a thin film, that turned into the piece of art that we ended up making together for the 14th Istanbul Biennial in 2015. She made the work, of course, but when working together with artists, the piece emerges through the conversation.

BÖ

What do you remember about this work, *Deniz* (*Sea*) (2015)?

CCB

It was a little white fisherman's boat with speakers that went back and forth on the Bosphorus. People would barely see it – they had to look for it – but it was a surreal experience because there was sound coming from the speakers.

I remember the photos of some of her earliest works on the Bosphorus. They looked like doors, architectural pieces that you could walk through, or at least she was photographed walking through them, with her long hair and flowery dress. I imagine her as this beautiful young woman in the hippie generation, but when I met her – and her sister, İlhan of course – she was an old lady. And it was kind of scary, because to see two older women in a house full of objects and photographs that are the memories of a past world makes you feel that you could be in a dangerous space – somehow sweet on the outside and dark on the inside. Especially when you see all the little dolls and toys, because they remind that these two women were once children. They've grown into adults, but Füsun still has complete access to her life as a child. It's as if the parents died and the children took over the space. And that's a typical movie trope. So from a psychoanalytical perspective, visiting her in her house and studio is interesting. The studio is downstairs, but more or less everything in the house is a kind of a *gesamtkunstwerk*. So I suppose the most important artwork will ultimately be the house itself in fifty years' time. It should be turned into a foundation and kept exactly as it is, exactly where it is.

BÖ

It's actually been donated to Arter, who will turn it into a museum house and a guesthouse for artists.

CCB

That's wonderful news! It's going to be one of the most special places to go in Istanbul in fifty or a hundred years. It does have this disquieting effect: a combination of joy and possible catastrophe. This reminds me of work she made, *Pink Boat* (2014), the video of these little inflated boats that look like swimming-pool toys. It was a piece made on the occasion of a protest about a bridge that was supposed to be demolished I guess.

BÖ

Yes, it was a proposal for an outdoor work to protest the demolition of the Galata Bridge in 1993. And she wasn't able to realise it at that time. So, many years later, for her exhibition at Arter, the project was produced as a video work in front of the house in Kuzguncuk.

CCB

Right, and I saw that exhibition. I was working on the Istanbul Biennial at that time. So in that video, when you see these boats, you think of childhood and toys at the beach, but there are no children: it's just the water and the boats. It could be the scene after a catastrophe, or it could be a world where there are no children. So there's always something on the edge, something between the lightness and the joy of childhood and a disquieting feeling.

I have the sense that Füsun has this very keen intelligence, which she doesn't always express in words, but you can see it in her eyes, in the way she looks at you, and listens to you. That's a very feminist quality: to have this hidden power that you don't always release. And I don't know if it's true, but I can imagine her being very precise in cutting away things that are just baggage, and not worthwhile.

BÖ

And what was it like working with her on your historical dOCUMENTA (13) exhibition? She participated with an existing work *Untitled*: the chair with a chain and her name on it, which was produced for the first time in 1993, and the new commission *Dance of the Crows* (2012). You also published her artist's book on this occasion. How was working with an artist who doesn't use a computer, or have a mobile phone, and whom you always need to visit in person? And what was it about her work that resonated with you?

CCB

The chair work was very important. That's why I invited her. It had a lot to do with a sense of trauma that was part of the subject matter in the Neue Galerie in Kassel, where her work was shown. For the new work, she was interested in the birds that were flying around the Neue Galerie outside. There are a lot of birds in the Bosphorus as well. She ended up making an embroidered curtain where there were these symbols and images of birds flying and a kind of pictogram alphabet. And the birds are migratory, so you could imagine that the birds at the Neue Galerie would fly to Istanbul in certain seasons of the year. Ultimately, they become little marks, like turning a sketch or something you see through the window outside into a very primitive early human language. What she did was to somehow bring the viewer's attention, not to the space in the Neue Galerie, but to the outside: the whole Neue Galerie becomes a film or a curtain that directs you to look outdoors. Artworks that are portals, doors or windows, towards the outside world are constants in her work.

Like you say, she doesn't look for the latest technology or means of production. Her work is very sophisticated, but she's always used elementary materials and simple gestures, like this embroidery, and it makes me think of a kind of feminist Arte Povera, like what Marisa Merz was doing in the 1960s and 1970s, for example. They didn't know each other, but they were working at the same time: Marisa Merz in Turin and Füsun in Turkey. I would place her in a feminist tradition, but I don't think that her work relates so much to someone like Carol Rama, who was also working in the 1970s in Italy, because she had a very strong idea of the frame of work and of the finished nature of the work, whereas Merz was less traditional and used any means or materials, and did a lot of weaving with copper threads. I think of Füsun's embroideries or spatial works in relation to this. So being an Italian and a so-called expert on Arte Povera [laughs], that gave me a form of situated knowledge which allowed me to understand Füsun's work, even though it has another history to it, which is a refusal of minimalism and the surrealist origin. So that could be something that made me connect with her and invite her to participate in dOCUMENTA (13), which was wonderful. And yes, we did make a book on that occasion which was like a scrapbook of the books that her sister kept of newspaper clippings and personal photographs. Her sister was the archival part of this, let's say, dual personality. There's one part, which is archiving, and then there's the other part, which is playing. And so, the archiving part became a book. I think it was the first monograph, wasn't it?

BÖ
Margrit Brehm has worked on a book in 2001 on the occasion of her exhibition in Kunsthalle Baden-Baden and it was translated and published in 2007 in Istanbul with the title *For Careful Eyes*, but I think yours was the first time that the albums were published in that way.

CCB
Yes, it was the first publication of the albums, which are, if you think about it, like the house. The house contains this compilation of all the objects, and the albums contain a compilation of all the archival materials. So it's a little archive within a larger archive. You could say that the album is a book about her work, so you don't need to make another book; you just need to copy, scan and publish that book. That was the basis of that dOCUMENTA (13) book, which I really like.

BÖ
Apart from Arte Povera, how would you contextualise Füsun's practice in global art histories, starting from the 1960s and coming to our day?

CCB
Well, there is no global art history anymore. Art history is a discipline that's in crisis, and it's only existed since the history of photography in late 1800s, since this allowed people to compare styles of sculptures and paintings and really study the works. Before, there was the story of the lives of the artists and there was the story of the techniques or materials of art, and so on. But this very modern

discipline or field that we call art history has been dramatically re-written with globalisation and the start of multiculturalism and the postcolonial studies in the 1980s, which then developed into anti-colonial studies in the 1990s. What has happened is that there's no global art history, but a lot of regional art histories have been written. There's a multitude of those. So I don't know how one could say where Füsun's work lies in a global art history, even if it did exist.

Her work resonated with me when thinking about women who, around the world, started to work with materials and techniques that recall domestic labour. There are examples all over Europe, and the US, and there have been many exhibitions about feminism and the use of fabric, for example. But it's mainly a tendency from the 1980s. So I guess you could say that Füsun's work enters into that tendency of women, as well as other marginalised communities of artists, doing work that uses the techniques of daily life, which goes back to radical practices in the 1960s. There were also male artists, like Luciano Fabro, who for the work *Pavimento, Tautologia* [Floor, Tautology] (1967) mopped and waxed an area of the floor and put newspaper on top of it to keep it clean. These works, either by men or women, that celebrate daily, domestic labour as a technique for art, was part of a rejection of the parameters of academic and high art. So her work certainly enters into that. And then there's the inflection of locality into abstraction of minimalism, I mean her practice in minimalism in making architectural things is something that happens also in a post-minimalist context.

And again, generally speaking, it's a feminist strategy not to separate the public and the private. Like Mary Kelly's *Post-Partum Document* (1973–79). Most feminist artworks are based on the belief that your work as an artist is also grounded in your daily life and that it's a lie to separate the artwork from that daily life. This breaking of the boundary between public and private was a big theme on a theoretical level in the 1980s, influenced by feminist thinking. So all of this is expressed in Füsun's work, although she was working in a rather isolated way in Turkey and she wasn't part of the public discussion. Her work wasn't published in articles or books about such questions, because the art world is provincial. If you weren't in New York or London at a certain time when these feminist things were happening, if Griselda Pollock didn't know you, if the art critics and art historians like Linda Nochlin didn't know about your work, then how could they put it in the books? It's not out of ill will, so I don't think it's necessary to accuse those feminist art historians of having excluded Füsun; I think it's just normal, because she was in a place that wasn't readily accessible. And even today, when you might think everything is accessible with the internet, it's not true, because we search for things that we know we want to search for. So I don't think it's possible to make some sort of objective art history and include people from all over the world. It's probably better to do regional art histories right now. I think that answers the question.

Rabia Çapa *in conversation with* Nilüfer Şaşmazer

NİLÜFER ŞAŞMAZER

Together with your sister Varlık (Sadıkoğlu), you opened the Maçka Art Gallery in 1976. To start off our conversation, perhaps you could tell us a little about how you invited the artists whom you represented or whose exhibitions you would host. What were your processes of decision-making and working with the artists?

RABİA ÇAPA

Before opening the gallery with Varlık, we made a decision: our gallery, we said, would make a selection from among the artists of the present day. We're not a museum; we'll choose not the old artists but the artists doing contemporary works, and we'll continue working with them by organising solo exhibitions in our gallery every two or three years. And we formed a jury. When people on this jury came by the gallery, we'd give them the artists' dossiers, ask for their opinion, and the jury members would share their views and cast a vote. Varlık and I shared one vote, to avoid giving too much weight to our own individual preferences. We always had that jury. After Varlık's death, I continued working with them. At the Maçka Art Gallery, everything is done collectively. Perhaps that's why it became such a legend. Everything we did was discussed and decided together.

NŞ

And who were the people on this jury?

RÇ

That's something we never revealed, but these ten people were not only from the art world. For instance, one of them was a diplomat whose intellect and art knowledge we trusted. When he came to visit from Ankara, we'd say, 'Here, take a look at this dossier.' Another one was a physicist, who had a sound grasp of painting and had brought me Anselm Kiefer's book from an exhibition held in the States. We'd ask the opinions of these people if they were in Istanbul. If they weren't around, then someone else we trusted would come on board – we'd add them to the list. There was no fixed list of jury members, it varied, but there was always a total of eleven people, including us.

NŞ

How about Füsun Onur? Did someone suggest her to you, or did you previously know her?

RÇ

No, we saw Füsun's work at the exhibition she opened in Taksim Art Gallery, and we liked it a lot.

NŞ

During the 1970s, she opened a total of five exhibitions in that space, in 1970, 1972, 1974, 1975 and 1978. Which was the one you saw?

RÇ

It might have been the last one. We left the gallery saying, 'We must sign this artist to our gallery.'

NŞ

And then, how did your relationship develop after that exhibition?

RÇ

Varlık and I went over to her home. We said, 'We want you to be an artist in our gallery.' She said, 'Okay, alright.' Then we started working on the exhibitions. We got along very well with Füsun; we hit it off from the very first day. She was a kindred spirit. We loved that childlike side of hers, her black humour, her fondness for animals, and of course, her works. Each time we had an exhibition of her work, and I opened the gallery doors at 11:00 in the morning, I'd stop in my tracks as though I was seeing it for the first time, although of course I'd seen it only yesterday, and the day before. Her works make you take a pause: you look again and again, and each time you see something you hadn't seen before, and it makes you happy. There's no end to a Füsun Onur exhibition.

NŞ

Back in that period, how did you appraise Onur's art? What made you invite her to the gallery? Because, in retrospect, her works were actually quite cutting edge. She was already engaged with everyday objects, installations, and back then, even the word 'installation' was known and used by very few people.

RÇ

We'd organised installation exhibitions with Serhat Kiraz in 1984, with Sarkis in 1986, and with Füsun Onur in 1987. At the time, a number of canvas artists criticised us for holding these exhibitions, but that passed.

NŞ

Yes, you embraced new artistic forms in that period. We can see this when we look at, not only Onur but, all the artists you worked with during those years.

RÇ

After all, we'd opened the gallery in order to be different. From the very start, when we chose the basement flat for the gallery, we didn't say, 'Let's paint a random flat white and put some nails on the walls.' Instead, we commissioned Mehmet Konuralp for the architecture of the apartment, Prof. Şazi Sirel for its lighting, and Mengü Ertel for our logo design, and thus transformed the flat into a contemporary art gallery.

NŞ

Plus, at the end of the day, it was a commercial business. Did it pay off back then? Did it meet your expectations?

RÇ

My sister and I both knew that this wouldn't be a commercial venture. It was in 1974 that we decided to establish a gallery. Then we spent the year of 1975 in Rome and Paris; we wanted to see how the galleries there operated. Until that time, we didn't not know that our gallery would be so contemporary. But when we saw the galleries there and the works in the galleries that we liked, we said: 'This is it! This is how a gallerist works.' And when we came back, we set to work on that path. The other alternative is easy: you get the already discovered masters, put their works on the walls, sell them like hot cakes and get your money; that wasn't our intention.

NŞ

Looking back, the path and the position that Onur took seem parallel to yours: working and producing without worrying about who says what, or whether you're going to make money, or expecting any recompense.

RÇ

Birds of a feather flock together, as they say. We loved our gallery, our work, and our artists very much. And we still do love them.

NŞ

What do you recall of Onur's first exhibition at your gallery, *Sign of Sign* (1987)?

RÇ

Füsun came to the gallery having completed all her works, and together with her sister İlhan they arranged the set-up beautifully. At the time, there were a lot of sales and auctions taking place in the art scene; that exhibition was a stance against all this, against the commodification of art. Füsun just writes a little note about her exhibitions on a piece of paper, and then speaks no more. She says: 'Get whatever you understand from what you see,' and leaves it at that.

NŞ

The next exhibition was *References*, organised in 1990, featuring Onur together with Serhat Kiraz, Ayşe Erkmen and Canan Beykal. Was the concept of this group exhibition yours, or that of the artists?

RÇ

We've never interfered with the artists. At the Maçka Art Gallery, the artist is free – they can do whatever they want.

NŞ

What do you remember from the *Gallery Lights* exhibition in 1991?

RÇ

I've always loved Füsun's tulles, beads, little bells. *Variations* was wonderful. It was so beautiful that I still can't understand why no collector bought those works. After every exhibition, I get a blank notebook and write down where and how each piece has been placed. So if one day Füsun wants to reinstall that exhibition, she can easily do it. But then of course, she would never do something she's already done. She does it once and finishes it. Her last exhibition in the gallery, *As You Know* (2016), was also absolutely wonderful. I loved the puzzle she prepared. Then she put a red bucket in front of the work, and turned it upside down, making a stool. That's Füsun's touch.

NŞ

And there are also the exhibitions *Cadence* (1995) and *Prelude* (2000). So you've actually organised a total of six solo exhibitions together.

RÇ

Prelude was beautiful, too, but most people didn't understand that exhibition. And, again, very few people understood *Cadence*. One must know how to read Füsun's exhibitions. It's possible to listen to the music in Füsun's work, just as you can, for instance, in the work of Daniel Buren. And if you listen to the music she creates, then you understand. In the gallery, right above my desk, Daniel had made a work with black and white tape like the keys of a piano. When I sat down, it felt like I could hear its sound. You get caught up in it, because while making it the artist was also completely absorbed by it. All arts are related to one another: architecture, visual arts, music… When you embrace them all together, it becomes much easier to read and to understand the exhibitions.

NŞ

Did you talk to Onur about the musicality of the works in *Cadence* or *Prelude*? Or the concept of silent music?

RÇ

In one of her talks she said: 'I put the music here. I hope you can hear it.' If you know how to read her work, you understand that everything is music. On the way to Kaş, there's a spot filled with crickets. In the afternoon, we'd go there with Varlık to listen to the sound of those crickets. The locals had grown tired of them, but for us it was so beautiful, those crickets... That too is music. If you look for it, there's music everywhere.

NŞ
According to Onur herself, not many people understood her works, and she was often criticised for this. Did you have any difficulties in explaining, or representing the content of these exhibitions?

RÇ
If my artist doesn't explain his/her exhibition, then I have no right to explain it. If there's something the visitor doesn't understand, then they must look more carefully. Of course, Füsun doesn't want her humour to be understood right away. She conceals it. But if you know how to read, then you get it.

NŞ
Beyond the general public, how were her works received in the art world?

RÇ
All of Füsun's collectors were European. There was also an American couple who came and bought works for their own collection. She has plenty of foreign collectors, including René Block. But she had nearly no collectors from Turkey.

NŞ
Over the thirty to forty years during which you've known her, how has the relationship between Onur's works and her materials changed? Or what are the aspects of her practice that have been transformed?

RÇ
The materials that Füsun repeatedly hangs on to are her tulles, beads and bells. Other than those, she's free, and doesn't restrict herself. Her materials change, but in every material that she introduces there's something that makes the work a Füsun Onur.

NŞ
What is it exactly that makes Füsun Onur, Füsun Onur?

RÇ
A good example is the stools in my gallery designed by Mehmet Konuralp for the Kuzgun Acar exhibition. They're forty years old now. She takes those stools, puts her rods on them, covers them with tulles, and stitches on her beads. If she can't stitch the beads, then she ties them on with golden yarns. She plays games. What I love most in Füsun is her childlike approach to everything; I guess she had a very happy childhood, and always carried that happy child inside. And in that childlike approach, there's the candidness of the child. Children can't lie successfully; they can't

pull it off. Füsun can't pull it off either. Whatever she wants to say, she says it. Sometimes she conceals it; sometimes she says it openly; but again, you need to know how to read it.

NŞ

It's possible to describe the works of many artists that you exhibited during the 1980s and 90s as 'pioneering,' but in your opinion, what were the aspects that set Onur apart from her contemporaries?

RÇ

Füsun brings her Füsun-quality to her works. When she takes and installs an old desk, you don't see it only as an old desk or as a nostalgic gesture. She decks it with tulles and beads and brings Füsun to it. She turns it into a sculpture. Moreover, she pays a lot of attention to light, and places emphasis on the relationships between the works themselves. She works with great care. In the *Variations* (2012) exhibition, for example, I offered to help with the paperclips she was using, but she said, 'No way!'

NŞ

She's very much dedicated to her work.

RÇ

She's dedicated to everything she does. That's the beauty of Füsun. She even takes her cat out into the garden with an umbrella, so that it doesn't get sunstroke!

NŞ

She has a profound relationship with material. As you say, in the exhibitions she held at Maçka Art Gallery, she presented works where she used both the materials inside the gallery and everyday objects, as well as canvases and embroidery threads. Taking into consideration your own fondness for sewing, clothes and your collections of different objects, would you say that you share a special sort of bond with her?

RÇ

Yes, I collect, and yes, I like sewing, but I like Füsun's works because Füsun made them. Of course, the old baby dresses, fabrics, etc. that I collect are outstanding, very meticulous works, but I don't attribute my appreciation of Füsun's work to this association. I like the art that Füsun does. I like her freedom, her uncompromising attitude.

NŞ

Of course, but on the other hand, perhaps this creates an intellectual and emotional connection for you or adds another dimension to your relationship.

RÇ

Of course, after each exhibition I understood her better, liked her more.

the generosity of small things[1] by Fatih Özgüven

CAROLYN CHRISTOV-BAKARGIEV
But you love the past.

FÜSUN ONUR
No.

CCB
But you live with many things from the past.

FO
They are here and now.[2]

I

Like Füsun Onur, whom I've known for thirty years, I'm a collector of small things. Occasionally, I'll arrive at her home with a bag filled with small things that I've gathered over time from here and there. 'This will be of use to Füsun,' I must have thought as I stored each one away. After the requisite tea and cookies ceremony – this is the ritual in the doll's house where she lives – Füsun and her sister İlhan take the objects one by one from the bag and look them over. None of these objects – the candlestick that consists of a spike in the middle of a yellow sphere where the candle sits, the small red plastic boat made for kids to play with in the bath, tarnished silver spoons, a box of pins with coloured heads – ever surprises Füsun Onur. When she takes them out of the bag, I imagine that she not only identifies what they *are* – their hidden, true meanings – but also what they might *become*. That's why she seems so calm when she looks at them. I'm both pleased and enchanted by this ceremony. Later, at the opening of some exhibition, she'll say to me, 'Look, do you recognise those brass globes you brought me?' Of course I do, but now they've become fragments of an altogether different topography, pieces in the landscape of the work itself. It's marvelous.

'At times [Füsun Onur] keeps intact the objects that become her materials,' writes Defne Ayas, 'at other times she completely transforms them, as in the case of her ensemble *Dream of Old Furniture* (1985) in which the found objects became almost unrecognizable.'[3] This was in fact the very first installation by Füsun Onur that I ever saw, at Taksim Art Gallery, which is now nothing more than a grassy slope on the end of Gezi Park near Elmadağ.

1.
Feyyaz Kayacan, *Çocuktaki Bahçe* [The Garden Inside the Child] (Istanbul: self-published, 1982), 51. The original sentence in the book is 'I learn about the generosity of small things.'

2.
'Füsun Onur, Carolyn Christov-Bakargiev, and Hans Ulrich Obrist, in Conversation,' *Füsun Onur* (Cologne: W. König, 2012), 23.

3.
Defne Ayas, 'Füsun,' *Füsun Onur* (Cologne: W. König, 2012), 12.

The small and (seemingly) unrelated figures that sat atop a table wrapped in canvas that looked like a kind of saddle – perhaps because of the horse on it? – were so captivating that the other things in the exhibition *spread* across the entire floor of the exhibition space, as if they were caught in their centrifugal force. Füsun Onur says of this installation: 'I want the viewer to look upon this work freed of all the traditional, conventional habits ingrained in their mind. I spread the image across time to save it from its stillness, because much of our attention is based upon change and time.'[4] We might also consider this to mean spreading the story across time and space, because most of Füsun Onur's works hold in tandem both gesture and story.

To me, the spread of the furniture parts in *Dream of Old Furniture* was rather like the old dresses in Ahmet Hamdi Tanpınar's *Dresses of Times Past*:[5] they stopped being the mere displaced dream things, and became parts of a story we don't know, or else, a waking dream. 'El mâ'nâ fi batnı'ş-şair,' reads an Arabic proverb: 'the meaning dwells in the gut of the poet.' But that wasn't the whole story here. Although at first glance the pieces of furniture seemed closed – *dreamlike* – on second glance, I was overcome with a feeling that they carried fragments of inspiration from familiar stories. The great poet and short-story writer Sait Faik, who always gave the unknown its due in his own incomparable fashion ('Well then. Guess what it is, then'),[6] was there, along with that strange yet so familiar secret from Orhan Veli's poem *Grand Bazaar*, which was also hinted at in the tulle-swathed chairs of Füsun Onur's *Any Chair*: 'You don't know my sister. / [...] These threads are her threads / And this bridal veil, her bridal veil.'[7]

I may not have recognised some of the pieces used in Onur's works, but I *knew* all of them. As she says, they were 'here and now,' their evocative strength always intricately layered, always working, always open. The tulle she used to wrap the furniture didn't cloak it in nostalgia, because for her, the mystique of the object – let's call it that – always corresponds to some concrete point in social history. From tulle to embroidery, from canvas to plastic, from the chairs she uses in her works, to the dolls and children's clothes from Germany, the diverse materials each occupy a place in both the history of manufactured goods and in the history of manufactured goods in Turkey, where these objects arrived late or not at all – in other words, they occupy a place in the memory of the object.

Margrit Brehm, who wrote a comprehensive monograph on Onur, elaborates on this notion in depth:

4. Füsun Onur, text written for the exhibition *From Outside In From Inside Out*, in Margrit Brehm, *For Careful Eyes*, 76.

5. Ahmet Hamdi Tanpınar, in *Hikâyeler* [Stories] (Istanbul: Dergâh Publications, 2011).

6. Sait Faik Abasıyanık, 'Yılan Uykusu' [Sleep of the Snake] in *Alemdağ'da Var Bir Yılan* [There is a Snake in Alemdağ] (Istanbul: Türkiye İş Bankası Kültür Yayınları, 2005), 116.

7. Orhan Veli, 'Kapalı Çarşı' [Grand Bazaar] in *Bütün Şiirleri* [Complete Poems] (Istanbul: Yapı Kredi Publications, 2003), 111.

> Onur's use of objects in her art not only testifies to the respect she has for them (and has little to do with any relic-like stylisation or nostalgic emotionality), [but] it also directs our gaze to that mass product, the commonplace object that has seemingly nothing to show for itself apart from its functionality and no longer points to 'homo faber,' the tool maker. The artist, as a 'homo ludens,' sees in the banal thing, the block of Lego not used to build a house or the knitting-needle not used to knit, a quality which she sees as the point of departure for the role she allots to that object in her work.[8]

II

I knew all of these objects, yes, 'knew without knowing,' and in fact, there have been objects among Onur's works that have seemed so familiar to me, that they have left me feeling bewildered. When I was a schoolboy, cab drivers were in the habit of hanging clusters of things from their rear-view mirrors; among the objects they hung were not just baby booties or tiny chicken-scratch prayer books, but also erotic things, Pirelli-style calendars, perhaps given out by companies as gifts. One of the most paradigmatic examples of this was the busty girls made of soft plastic, sitting up, legs joined, their bodies tilting slightly forward as they teased their hair up with their hands. In their miniscule dimensions, each of these dolls had an individual 'design' that bore the innocence of a child's toy, as well as the seductiveness of a sex toy. One of these appeared in a work of Onur's (*Nude*, 1974), placed inside a box, its body split into two or three sections by thin sheets of celluloid, its reflections proliferating in the mirrors on the box's walls. It was when looking at this work that I realised how these dolls were dedicated to watching/being watched; I saw the whole story of how they exist as individual objects as well as how they evoke the fragmentary nature of narcissism. It is not possible to watch and be watched without being split, being fragmented, and the game of eroticism is just the arena of such fragmentation. This whole story was being told through an object that was once conspicuously 'here and now,' but eventually disappeared. Perhaps you can still find them at the flea market, but they're no longer 'here and now.' And yet in Füsun's work, they come back from beneath the rear-view mirror, frozen in time, and continue to be present ('here and now').

8. Margrit Brehm, *Füsun Onur: For Careful Eyes* (Istanbul: Yapı Kredi Publications, 2007), 131–32. Brehm continues: 'Rather (and this takes us back to the beginning of art's dialogue with the object) Onur's use of objects starts where their disappearance as an expression of human work and their status as commodities begins. Georg Simmel described this situation in his *Philosophy of Money* in 1900, asserting that when so many things are replaced by money and lose their direction-giving meaning for us, the change in our relationship to them elicits a practical reaction, namely, the desire for them to have a new even deeper meaning – be it that each in itself gains a more valuable, spiritual emphasis, or that it receives this through a new context, through being saved from its atomisation.'

'Frozen' may not be the correct word when it comes to the majority of Füsun Onur's works. As Brehm claims: 'in the work of art, time gels into a static object. Onur works against this stasis by continually reducing the materiality of the individual element and by never arranging just one but many of them in one space.'[9] And as Carolyn Christov-Bakargiev argues, Onur's task 'is to work against the obsolete idea of the stasis of things.'[10] The object, both on its own and together with other objects, wriggles. They wriggle together. Or they writhe. What author Sevim Burak did with words, Füsun Onur does by working with the demonstrative power of objects – a power that sometimes totemises them. 'The spark of life is suddenly kindled in the dead object [...] the artist again continues a tradition of her own, the dialogue between things, and finds a new language with which to pursue the conversation.'[11]

'Lapidary installations of impeccably arranged elements have been her stock-in-trade for more than three decades, well before "unmonumental" became the dominant sculptural style.'[12] This apt observation by Defne Ayas summarises not just Füsun Onur's consistency in producing her work, but also the relationship between the sculptural and the monumental that is at play in it. The relationship that Onur forges between rhythm, music, and musical structures in her work is a subject upon which both she and others have dwelled. It is pertinent to touch upon these relationships that she makes not just with musical compositions, but also sometimes with semiology. In fact, though, as Brehm says, 'Onur does not work with *music* but rather *parallel to the idea of music*.'[13]

III

Almost all of Onur's 'musical compositions' operate on the plane of, and together with, small objects that form a whole. The viewer cannot help but see this. It is the key not only to her storytelling and her poetry, but also to her particular sense of humour. In her piece *Opus II – Fantasia* (2001), for instance, an installation comprised of knitting needles, balls of gold braid, porcelain figurines and plinths, insofar as your attention is drawn to the tricks these objects play on you, insofar as you can see the broken 'being-there' of these small things in all their atypicality (never randomness, though – everything has been intricately planned and devised), you, too, are 'there.' The knitting needles trick you; while they sometimes compose rectangles that you might regard as formal elements, they surprise you when

9. Ibid., 99.

10. Carolyn Christov-Bakargiev, 'Füsun Onur: What the Crows Know,' *Füsun Onur* (Cologne: W. König, 2012), 7.

11. Brehm, *Füsun Onur: For Careful Eyes*, 125, 127.

12. Defne Ayas, 'Füsun,' *Füsun Onur*, 12.

13. Brehm, *Füsun Onur: For Careful Eyes*, 98.

they suddenly cross one another like swords. In an instant you reflect on the knitting needles not just as blatant fragments of traditional domesticity, but as potential weapons of defence, in every sense (the 'purple needle' of feminists). You reflect on 'Knitting Lady,' a Turkish brand of yarn, and from afar you hear the ceaseless clicking of the knitting needles in the hands of countless grandmothers. Or else you may contemplate the relationship between mass-produced trinkets and the glittering braid that stretches to them from the balls, proceeding tensely in every sense of the word, until suddenly the yarn slackens in rings as the little statues turn their backs. Or else, you may wonder what we should call the balls of yarn that sit like talons in front of white pedestals that hold no statues, lifting them gently off the ground, making them weightless.

Though a majority of her works avail themselves of ephemeral (transitory, intangible, temporary) materials, these materials exceed their temporality with a resoluteness unique to Füsun Onur's art: they confront time; they are still 'here.' While the material is truly ephemeral, the relationship built between space and material is anything but. It is perhaps because the materials exceed the temporality of the works that they can throw down the gantlet to time. They can change *with time* and *according to the time* in which they are situated, so that 'those chairs' do not have to remain 'those chairs.' (Füsun once told me jokingly that it would be very easy to restage *Any Chair*, a work true to its name, in any venue – or, in fact, every work of hers – summing up her relationship with galleries by saying 'Their chairs, my tulle.') But in the relationship between things and space, what is perhaps most fundamentally musical (let's call it a murmur, a babble, a barely audible noise), stems from the perception of time unique to this relationship that it calls forth and expands.

One of the other truly astonishing things about Onur's work is how she manages to achieve the same effect, perhaps even a greater effect, with very little material or reduced material – often by means of a spontaneous, momentary decision. When we see her economy of materials, we realise, with admiration, that all the works are an attempt at 'reduction,' that Füsun Onur's art has, since the beginning, been oriented toward speaking with fewer words. *Elegy for Tekir*, for example, remains perhaps the most minimal and the most romantic of her works. The crocheted forms evoke the shadows that cats cast on the floor and walls. In Search of Lost Cats, you say? A theme suited perfectly, if not to Proust, then to Onur! And yet, precisely because it is produced with light and shadows cast on the wall, it might be one of her most enduring works. As Onur might say, it is the work that is the most 'here and now.'

In her exhibition *Variations* (2012) at Maçka Art Gallery, a space that she had inhabited a few times already, each of the square tiles covering the floor and walls were treated as the foundation of writing; in fact, she used the tiles like the paper on which she writes her work, correlating them with colourful plastic paper clips and transparent celluloid rectangles that echoed – and reinterpreted – the tiles, thereby sweeping that demanding space off its feet. It wouldn't be inaccurate to call this playing a trick on the space. Onur's hidden playfulness, the casual 'femina ludens' in her work, is all the more effective precisely because it is not part of some plan or intention. Its story becomes poetry, and vice versa; its humour pays no heed to whether anyone notices it or not. In the back room at the same exhibition, featureless white canvases bore forms that looked almost like sentences in some strange language, forms akin to the notations of silent music. John Cage and Morton Feldman came to mind.

In a later exhibition, the 2019 *Chamber Music* at Galeri Nev Istanbul – the exhibition's name emphasises, as always, the chamber as much as the music – crumpled letters seem thrown to the ground, while coloured pencils are scattered like Mikado sticks to evoke childhood and serve as a transition to the subsequent musical phrase within the logic of an arrangement of colour-lined envelopes, and a number of small or scaled-down things. These are the miniature totems we are used to seeing in Füsun Onur's work, totems that she continues to use – covering the space with a system, a syntax that only she understands, while on the walls, we see – or rather, we *intuit* – the traces of an A4-size paper. When Füsun Onur goes 'in search of lost time,' if we suppose that time is a kind of space and that space spreads like time, then she is also in search of lost space.

Let's leave the last word to her. She has this to say about time/space, or about 'emptiness':

> Visual art seems to explain itself at first glance. What is needed is to enter into its inner structure, which is *successive and expanded in space, as the function of time*. I want the viewer to go through the work, leaving his expectations and memories behind. [...] time is most important. Those forms are being seen together for the first time. [...] Time is in the work. Whoever looks at it one after the other, enters

inside. So *I wanted time to be spread out around the space* of this work and I wanted people to see all these elements without having what they expected. Just watch the elements. Whoever watches this work, should only follow the inner stream of the work and not their habits, so the flow can continue. *Emptiness must change with extension, so that emptiness is changed with each visitor.*[14]

14.
Füsun Onur, text written for the exhibition *From Outside In From Inside Out*, in Margrit Brehm, *For Careful Eyes*, 101–02.

The Sound of Water by Paolo Colombo

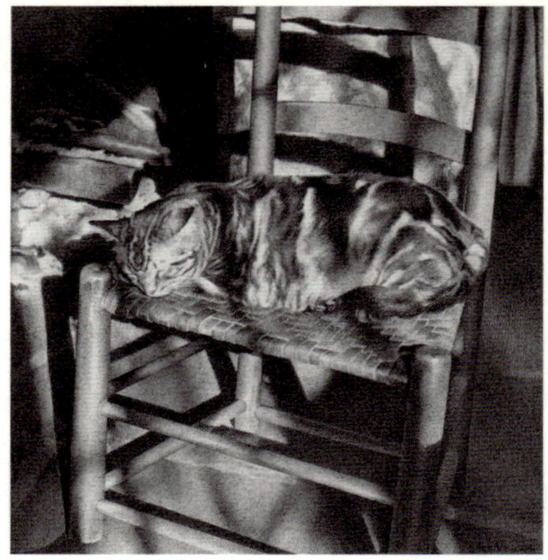

(FIG. 1) *Feline Felicity*, Harvard Art Museums / Fogg Museum, Louise E. Bettens Fund, Photo © President and Fellows of Harvard College, 1934.182.

Lore has it that some of Füsun Onur's works lie in the waters of the Bosphorus. They have been returned to their source of inspiration, which fills her red house on the Asian shore of Istanbul with its light, reflections and sounds.

I imagine the drowned works, like living organisms, grasping the seabed and swaying with the flow, covered in algae and corals. The image recalls Ariel's song in Shakespeare's *The Tempest*, when the boat that carries King Alonso and his son Ferdinand from Tunis to Italy is shipwrecked during a storm conjured by the sorcerer Prospero. Ferdinand is tricked into believing that his father is dead, and his body now lies underneath the water transformed by the sea. The spirit sings:

> Full fathom five thy father lies.
> Of his bones are coral made.
> Those are pearls that were his eyes.
> Nothing of him that doth fade,
> But doth suffer a sea-change
> Into something rich and strange.
> Sea-nymphs hourly ring his knell.[1]

I cannot think of Onur's oeuvre other than as part of a flow. Among them are schools of *palamut*,[2] leaping dolphins and *iskorpit*.[3] They are at times delicate and refreshing, and at times imperious and willful. I remember a set-up of a chair and a chain;[4] an installation of a brass vessel and organdie;[5] and wooden cream-coloured doors on a series of paintings – doors that open and close to reveal painted black cats in a blue evening light.[6]

During my last visit to her house and studio, a gentle cat, a dark tabby, was curled up on a chair, bathed in sunlight: the live *Doppelgänger* of the cat in *Feline Felicity* (1934) by Charles Sheeler (FIG. 1). As we visited, he slowly got up and followed us on his cushiony paws from room to room, periodically closing his eyes, a feline sign of love.

To the sound of the water, we now add a new noise: a cat purring.

Think of a red house. Think of the Bosphorus. Hear the sound of flowing water and the light drone of a purring cat. Now add the musicality of Onur's lilting voice.

1. William Shakespeare, *The Tempest*, Act I, Scene II, 399-405.
2. Bonito fish.
3. Scorpionfish.
4. *Untitled* (1993).
5. *Opus I* (1999).
6. *From Outside In From Inside Out* (1976).

It is a house of whispers. Its murmur will be interrupted by her gentle laughter, and by her guest's exclamations of pleasure when seeing her art, so organic to each wall, nook and cranny. There is a canvas on which is attached a shawl;[7] old family photographs are gracefully displayed among objects scattered on the furniture. I believe that the figure of a man playing the violin is the house's guiding spirit, guarding the premises from the top of a tall bureau.

These are the songs and murmurs we hear from Onur's house.

There is more to be said about her art: visually engaging and absolutely personal, poetic and metaphoric, far from the art manifestos of the past.

We have mentioned songs. Let us imagine that there is more than one visual language, just as there are two written languages: the language of prose and the language of poetry.

'The nature of prose,' Paul Valéry said, 'is to perish.'[8]

Kenneth Koch added: 'Poetry lasts because it gives the ambiguous and ever-changing pleasure of being both a statement and a song.'[9]

Onur's work calls on a shifting coherence and valency, like the language of poetry, mixing 'oil and water,' creating a visual rhythm that gives emphasis to the elements that compose it. Often her assemblages are made up of incongruous elements; incongruous, yet musically consistent. They are meant to be enjoyed emotionally, with no expectation of precise information nor the description of facts.

In conceptual art, the elements that compose a work are there for the benefit of practical goals: the orientation of a line in a wall painting or on a sheet of paper; the positioning of a word in a wall text; the slant of a neon light… Unimpeded by a poetic voice, they stand up starkly to the viewer's understanding and appreciation. Onur's work, however, brings us the song of poetry and the trace of a soul. Her works are not statements, nor the production of facts. Hers is the work of an artist who grew and grows with her art, who understands the passing of time, and the different feelings that time, with time, will disclose. We are captivated by the layering of past and present embedded in her work, that 'ambiguous and ever-changing pleasure' that resonates with our emotions.

In an article on Istanbul in *The New Yorker*, titled 'Flight from Byzantium,' Joseph Brodsky writes:

> […] an awareness of time is a profoundly individualistic experience. [I]n the course of his life every

7. *Flamboyant* (2007).

8. Kenneth Koch, 'The Language of Poetry,' *The New York Review*, May 14, 1998 issue, https://www.nybooks.com/articles/1998/05/14/the-language-of-poetry/

9. Ibid.

> person sooner or later finds himself in the position of Robinson Crusoe, carving notches and, having counted, say, seven of them, or ten, crossing them out. Such is the origin of the ornament, regardless of preceding civilizations, or of that to which this given person belongs. And these notches are a profoundly solitary activity, isolating the individual and forcing him toward an understanding, if not of his uniqueness, then at least of the autonomy of his existence in the world.[10]

It is Onur's systematic tracing of these notches – the silent recording of emotional passage – that enraptures me. A feeling for time conveyed through her voice offers us a journey through poetry that is both one of language and of sight.

10.
Joseph Brodsky, 'Flight From Byzantium,' *The New Yorker*, October 20, 1985.

Untitled (MAGICAL DAY) 'colours' by Seza Paker

Beginning the day on the Bosphorus strait, passing to the
Asian side from Beşiktaş
Starts the magic always ...
Suadiye, Selamiçeşme get mixed up in our minds ...
This time we're going to Kuzguncuk,
Searching for the Red Yalı[1]

Red,
A colour to be defined;
Red,
A rosy red with a dash of framboise
    Matte and glossy
    At the same time,
With no saturation in it.

Just as
Füsun (Onur)
Who opens the door

THE Yalı
Freshly painted (auguri)![2]

New coats, draw
New horizons, always;;;

The two sisters welcome us in ...
Füsun with her striped pullover and her incredibly
    hearty smile
And her sharp gaze and her comfortable
Petit carré red and black patterned trousers
Settles down on her (most probably) familiar armchair
In the defined elegance of the old Mansion ...

1.
A *yalı* is a house or mansion built on the waterside, particularly on the Bosphorus strait in Istanbul.

2.
(It.) Congratulations.

We settle in the dark red satin sofas,
Sipping our 5 o'clock tea,
And watch the dreamy orangered sunset across
the Bosphorus

Ms. İlhan on my left side with her check capri pants
Comfortable and sporty

(Füsun's sister, her admirer and protector,
both / a continuing story of sisterhood)
Not having any brothers or sisters
I've just been an observer to these kinds of
Relations)

Füsun is telling stories and she completes them …
There is sisterhood, there is trust,
There is shouldering.
Unison of two beings.

Both of them are ageless

Füsun is more TODAY // for sure …
İLHAN, with her eyeliner/makeup, white complexion,
and her sporty check trousers
Her posture
Carrying a coat of the age-old family elegance
With smart, meaningful and lovely looks …
She fiddles with the bandaid on her finger
Which got caught in the doorway;

Füsun shows her photo of her cat
'Tekir'

I'm rather looking at Füsun
'Sensuelle';[3] 'Câline,'[4]
'Truly' (I think I understand …)

We lend an ear to the afternoon rush
Of the motorboats and the crashing waves

3. (Fr.) Sensual.
4. (Fr.) Cuddly.

While İlhan is boiling some more water under
the TEA POT,
Füsun continues chatting with us

DOWNSTAIRS /// LOWER GROUND FLOOR

MEMORIES // FÜSUN'S ARTWORKS //

Other artists' works,
All entangled ...

All of them; as always
And most probably as they are in her memory
One beside the other
Just like her creations.

The swashing waves
Outside
Seem to have blended into her inner strength

She opens a cabinet
Like a DOLL HOUSE
But 'HUMAN SIZE'

Her mother arranged her childhood belongings,
Just as they were ...
The INSTANT she opened the cabinet
(I remembered what I have kept)
I felt like saying
'There's a young girl inside every woman'
Just like Lewis Carroll.

The Mother, woman, daughter, grandmother
Collide
In the chains of time,
As in Almodovar pictures

This also reminds me in a way, Gülsün KARAMUSTAFA's
video …
Checking on precious pieces of glass as in
(THE GLASS MENAGERIE) Tennessee Williams …

Moving ahead …
A sculptural form appears in the mirror
Through an open door

Gently, Füsun
Steers us toward the bathroom
And starts telling us about the
Story of the broken sculpture
Belonging to Hadi Bara …

And then, the conversation continues upstairs about
The broken, those who want to break
The desire of,
ACADEMIA, STILL IN THE DAWN OF TIME

The sculpture that we see from the mirror
Looks like the photograph of KRAMER[5]
Placed by Sarkis in an exclusive room, in the exhibition …

(Apparently Selçuk also knew KRAMER quite well,
And he had a lot to say after the exhibition)

We leave a LIFETIME behind

And head upstairs,
To our day-to-day life,
Continuing our conversation,
On success, ambitions, vulnerability,
Talent,
joyfully and peacefully …

As we're sipping our teas
İLHAN hands us

5.
American film director, screenwriter and actor Robert Kramer (1939–1999) was a beloved friend of contemporary artist Sarkis (1938), who used his image in some of his works.

Some of Füsun's
Small-scale, rare, elegant,
Chinese porcelain-like
ceramics
Made in her childhood

And we carefully pass them around

I feel like I am living inside
(The text of) THE GLASS MENAGERIE … THIS TIME,

THE DIFFERENCE:

IS LIVING THIS EXPERIENCE;
ON THE SEA, NATURE,
The red, AND wine red reflections …

Time goes by; we ask permission to bid farewell
(Let the magic continue
Forever) ………

Taking three steps up,
I see on the little door,
A rattle,
Just like the one in Füsun's *SHRIEK* installation;
Her childhood doll placed on a
Small golden cube
Under
The flaggy pink beige purple pastel-coloured tulle,
From which hangs a rattle
And during her exhibition in RUSSIA
The doll disappears, she says in a fading voice!
(probably stolen)

While we are slowly heading towards the door

Füsun waves us
goodbye

(Reminding me of the last photo of my
The day after the wedding
PHOTO SEQUENCE INSTALLATION...
(Delphine bidding AU REVOIR[6]
1986
As a happy bride
In her Normandy village
LES PETITES DALLES)

Ending this magical day,
On the last rays of the sunset
Shutting rapidly, and OPENING my eyes
I have a vision

Of OLAF NICOLAI
Of his two gold rings;
With the inscription inside
'MUNDUS TOTUS EXILIUM EST'[7]...

Suggesting
The perfect being would be
ONE who
Looks at the whole world
As a foreign realm ...

from history
to
TODAY,

The displacement of mankind
IS THE CURRENT EVIDENCE ...

Kuzguncuk, Istanbul 2009

6. (Fr.) Goodbye.

7. Latin phrase meaning 'All the world is a place of exile.' In Edward Said's book *Orientalism* (1978), it is translated as 'The whole world is a foreign land,' quoting Hugh of Saint Victor, scholastic theologian from the twelfth century.

Dividing Space on a White Piece of Paper, 1965–66
Through the Looking Glass, 2014
Dark Deep Darkness and Splendor, 2017
Border of Time, 2018
7th Valley, 2021
The Dollhouse, 1970s
Through the Looking Glass, 2014
Heartbreak, 2019
Untitled, 1970
Taksim Art Gallery, 1970
Untitled, 1970
Taksim Art Gallery, 1970
Untitled, 1970
Taksim Art Gallery, 1970
Dual Sculpture, 1970
Taksim Art Gallery, 1970
Modern and Beyond, 2007
Untitled, 1970
Taksim Art Gallery, 1970
Composition IV, 1970
7th Paris Young Artists Biennial, 1971
Untitled, 12th Istanbul Biennial, 2011
Composition III, 1970
Taksim Art Gallery, 1970
7th Paris Young Artists Biennial, 1971
Composition V, 1970
7th Paris Young Artists Biennial, 1971
Through the Looking Glass, 2014
ThisPlay, 2022
Composition I, 1971
7th Paris Young Artists Biennial, 1971
50 Sculptures for Istanbul in the 50th Anniversary of the Republic, 1973
Through the Looking Glass, 2014
Border of Time, 2018
Composition VI or *Untitled (Shapeless Form)*, 1971
7th Paris Young Artists Biennial, 1971
Through the Looking Glass, 2014
Composition II, 1971
7th Paris Young Artists Biennial, 1971
Untitled, 1971
Through the Looking Glass, 2014
Border of Time, 2018
Untitled, 1972
Through the Looking Glass, 2014
Untitled (Mirrored Labyrinth), 1972 (2014)
Through the Looking Glass, 2014
Nude, 1974
Nude, 1974
A Section of Contemporary Women Artists, 1985
Modern Turk: Turkish Art in the Second Half of the 20th Century, 2001
FOOTNOTES on Geopolitics, Market and Amnesia, 2007
Through the Looking Glass, 2014
Untitled, 1974
Istanbul Archaeology Museums Open Air Exhibitions, 1974
Recalls, Reminders, 2007
Untitled, 1974
American Cultural Center, 1974
Untitled, 1974
35th State Painting and Sculpture Exhibition, 1974
Dual Composition, 1974
Taksim Art Gallery, 1970
Modern and Beyond, 2007
Free composition, 1975
13th Middelheim Biennial, 1975
Untitled, 1975
Heartbreak, 2019
Tree with Seed, 1975
Istanbul Archaeology Museums Open Air Exhibitions, 1975
Untitled, 1975
Life Behind Walls, 1975
Through the Looking Glass, 2014
Untitled, 1975
Life Behind Walls, 1975
Untitled (Variation), 1976
Istanbul Archaeology Museums Open Air Exhibitions, 1976
Through the Looking Glass, 2014
From Outside In From Inside Out, 1976
Tarabya Art Gallery, 1976
The Passion and The Wave, 1999
The Song of the Earth, 2000
Who Killed the Painting?, 2008
Who Killed the Painting?, 2009
Border of Time, 2018
Musical Chair, 1976
Through the Looking Glass, 2014
Heartbreak, 2019
Untitled, 1977
Istanbul Archaeology Museums Open Air Exhibitions, 1977
Stories for Grown-Ups, 1977
1st New Trends, 1977
From Outside In From Inside Out II, 1978
From Outside In From Inside Out, 1978
Because You Said Bread and Apple I Remember, 1978
Group show, 1978
Through the Looking Glass, 2014
A Seed Sprouts I, 1978
Exhibition of the Turkish Preserving Nature Foundation, 1978
A Seed Sprouts II, 1979
Exhibition of the Turkish Preserving Nature Foundation, 1979
Untitled, 1979
International Year of the Child Exhibition, 1979
Through the Looking Glass, 2014
Untitled, 1980
Exhibition of the Turkish Preserving Nature Foundation, 1980
A Seed Sprouts, 1980
Exhibition of the Turkish Preserving Nature Foundation, 1980
Untitled, 1980
Group show, 1980
Fool's Paradise, 2020
Associations from a Shiny Circle on the Floor, 1980
Associations from a Shiny Circle on the Floor, 1980
Water by the Sidewalk, 1981
Realisation, 1981
Through the Looking Glass, 2014
Border of Time, 2018
ThisPlay, 2022
The Nightmare, 1981
Realisation, 1981
A Section of Pioneering Turkish Art, 1984
Dream, 1981
Realisation, 1981
Untitled, 2011
Through the Looking Glass, 2014
Border of Time, 2018
Third Dimension in Painting – Come In, 1981
3rd New Trends, 1981
Through The Looking Glass, 2014
Border of Time, 2018
Untitled, 1982
BBC 50th Anniversary Exhibition, 1982
Counterpoint with Flower, 1982
Counterpoint with Flower, 1982
Through the Looking Glass, 2014
Untitled, 1983
Six Women Six Actions, 1983
Galleries '83, 1983
The Passion and The Wave, 1999
The Song of the Earth, 2000
Through the Looking Glass, 2014
Untitled (July), 1983
Six Women Six Actions, 1983
Galleries '83, 1983
A Section of Pioneering Turkish Art, 1984
The Passion and The Wave, 1999
The Song of the Earth, 2000
Who Killed the Painting?, 2008
Who Killed the Painting?, 2009
Through the Looking Glass, 2014
Border of Time, 2018
Conceptual Visual Images, 1983
4th New Trends, 1983
A Section of Pioneering Turkish Art, 1984
Would You Like to Rest on the Bench?, 1983
5th New Trends, 1985
Contemporary Turkish Plastic Arts Exhibition, 1986
Girl with a Turquoise Bracelet, 1984
Through the Looking Glass, 2014
Bird, 1984
Through the Looking Glass, 2014
A-Z, Z-A, 1984
A Section From Pioneering Turkish Art, 1984
Dream of Old Furniture, 1985
Life-Art-Fiction, Dream of Old Furniture, 1985
1st International Asia-Europe Art Biennial, 1986
Modern and Beyond, 2007
Invisibility Tactics, 2010
Invisibility Tactics, 2010
Invisibility Tactics, 2011
Through the Looking Glass, 2014
Black Roses For Yıldız Palace, 1985
A Section From Pioneering Turkish Art II, 1985
Atatürk Flower, 1985
Inspirations from Creative Turkish Women, 1987
In Memory of Joseph Beuys, 1986
Another Art Collective Exhibition in Memory of Joseph Beuys, 1986
Afternoon Window Front, 1986
A Section From Pioneering Turkish Art III, 1986
Morning Gymnastics, 1987
6th New Trends, 1987
Untitled, 1989
Shadow Play, 1987
1st International Istanbul Contemprary Art Exhibition, 1987
Sign of Sign, 1987
Sign of Sign, 1987
A Section From Pioneering Turkish Art IV, 1987
Plaid 1-2-3-4, 1987
Joint Exhibit, 1987
Through the Looking Glass, 2014
Aesthetic Applications, 1988
Joint Exhibit, 1988
Group Exhibition, 1988
Modern and Beyond, 2007
Continuous Variations, 2009
Continuous Variations, 2011
Untitled, 12th Istanbul Biennial, 2011
Through the Looking Glass, 2014
The Table, 1988
A Section of Pioneering Turkish Art V, 1988
Captured Light, 1989
Untitled, 1989
From an Exhibition, 1989
10 Artists 10 Works: A, 1989
Modern and Beyond, 2007
Untitled, 12th Istanbul Biennial, 2011
Heartbreak, 2019
From the Exhibition, 1989
Great Exhibition II, 1990
Through the Looking Glass, 2014

From the Exhibition or Through the Looking Glass, 1989
Great Exhibition II, 1990
Modern and Beyond, 2007
Through the Looking Glass, 2014
Icons of Time, 1990
Icons of Time, 1990
Through the Looking Glass, 2014
Border of Time, 2018
Seeing Unseen – Recognizable Unrecognizables, 1990
8 Artists 8 Works: B, 1990
Gallery Lights, 1990
Gallery Lights, 1991
References, 1990
References, 1990
Any Chair, 1991
10 Artists 10 Works: C, 1992
Women in Anatolia Throughout History, 1993
Suddenly, The Turks, 1995
Kunst Stoff, 2004
Tanzimat, 2010
Through the Looking Glass, 2014
Souvenir de Dolmabahçe, 1992
Art-Texnh – Fourteen Turkish and Greek Artists, Dolmabahçe Palace, 1992
FÜSUN ONUR (4.8.1992–16.8.1992), 1992
9th International Prilep Biennial, 1992
This Place, 1993
10 Artists 10 Works: D, 1993
Through the Looking Glass, 2014
This Place, 2021
Heritage, 1993
Istanbul, 1993
Suddenly, The Turks, 1995
Call me ISTANBUL Is My Name, 2004
FOOTNOTES on Geopolitics, Market and Amnesia, 2007
Through the Looking Glass, 2014
Untitled, 1993
Kır4b1r: 41 years 41 artists 41 works, 1998
Dream and Reality, 2011
dOCUMENTA (13), 2012
The I is Always in the Field of the Other, 2019
Constellation, 2020
Pink Boat, 1993 (2004)
Through the Looking Glass, 2014
Border of Time, 2018
ThisPlay, 2022
Child's Remembrance of the Word Germany or War through the Eyes of a Child, 1994
İskele (Turkish Art Today), 1994
Suddenly, The Turks, 1995
Modern and Beyond, 2007
Through the Looking Glass, 2014
Istanbul Obsession, 1994
İskele (Turkish Art Today), 1994
Suddenly, The Turks, 1995
FOOTNOTES on Geopolitics, Market and Amnesia, 2007
Through the Looking Glass, 2014
Art of Islam, A Past for A Present, 2021
Untitled, 1994
7th New Trends, 1994
Those Who Have Washed Here, 1994
Artists from Turkey: Tomur Atagök & Füsun Onur, 1994
Kunst Stoff, 2004
Through the Looking Glass, 2014
Hear Me Whistle, 1994
Maryland Institute Alumni Exhibition, 1997
Tolerance, 1995
Intolerance, 1995
Atatürk's Mother Zübeyde Hanım, 1995
Traces, 1995
ARHAT, 1995
Train Station, 1995
Let's Meet at the Orient, 1995
Orient/ation – The Vision of Art in a Paradoxical World, 1995
Cartographers: geo-gnostic projection for the 21st century, 1998
EindhovenIstanbul, 2005
Through the Looking Glass, 2014
I Don't Know French, 1995
Suddenly, The Turks, 1995
Cadence, 1995
Cadence, 1995
Untitled, 1995
Uludağ University 1st Sculpture Symposium, 1995
Time to Love and to Return Home, 2008
1972–1996, 1996
Under My Coat, 1997
Through the Looking Glass, 2014
Note, 1998
İskorpit: Contemporary Art from Istanbul, 1998
Turkish Art Today: Where? Here?, 2003
Caprice, 1998
Mediterranea – Contemporary Art from Mediterranean Countries, 1998
Opus I, 1999
The Passion and The Wave, 1999
What the Earth Sang, 2000
The Song of the Earth, 2000
Fantasy for the Bells, 2000
strange home, 2000
Untitled, 2000
Feature Presentation/Coming Attractions, 2000
Prelude, 2000
Prelude, 2000
Modern and Beyond, 2007
Plurivocality, 2014
Opus II – Fantasia, 2001
From Far Away So Close, 2001
Invisibility Tactics, 2011
Border of Time, 2018
Opus II – Fantasia, 2021
Nocturne, 2001
Regrets, Reveries, Changing Skies, 2001
Through the Looking Glass, 2014
Rondo, 2002
From Far Away So Close, 2002
The Song of the Sea, 2002
Between the Waterfronts, 2002
Impromptu, 2003
Füsun Onur, Hale Tenger, Aydan Murtezaoğlu, 2003
Boogie Woogie, 2003
Füsun Onur, Hale Tenger, Aydan Murtezaoğlu, 2003
Opus II – Variation, 2003
Organized Conflict, 2003
Odd Time Beat, 2010
Prelude II, 2003
X times I, 2007
Call me ISTANBUL, 2004
Call me ISTANBUL Is My Name, 2004
FOOTNOTES on Geopolitics, Market and Amnesia, 2007
Magic, 2004
Shaman's Diary, 2004
Shriek, 2006
FOOTNOTES on Geopolitics, Market and Amnesia, 2007
Continuous Variations, 2009
Continuous Variations, 2011
Man in the Moon, 2002–2006
Nested in Kuzguncuk, 2006
Evolve, 2017
Bells, 2007
Erratum Musicale, 2007
Through the Looking Glass, 2014
Flamboyant, 2007
Nested in Kuzguncuk, 2007
Through the Looking Glass, 2014
Heartbreak, 2019
She Has Been Here, 2008
Women of Light, 2008
Ladder, 2008
Women of Light, 2008
Through the Looking Glass, 2014
Elegy for Tekir, 2009–2012
Elegy for Tekir, 2012
Through the Looking Glass, 2014
Light Like a Bird Not Like a Feather, 2019
Whisper, 2010
Silence / Storm, 2010
Untitled, 12th Istanbul Biennial, 2011
Through the Looking Glass, 2014
Border of Time, 2018
For Eyes That Listen, 2020
Flamenco, 2011
Continuous Variations, 2009
Continuous Variations, 2011
Silence, 2011
Continuous Variations, 2009
Continuous Variations, 2011
Through the Looking Glass, 2014
Dance of the Crows, 2012
dOCUMENTA (13), 2012
Untitled, 2012
all that shines ain't no gold, 2012
Variations, 2012
Variations, 2012
Miracle (symphonic poem), 2013
Signs Taken in Wonder, 2013
Intervention for the MAK Collection Textiles and Carpets, 2014
Signs Taken in Wonder, 2013
Pegged, 2014
Through the Looking Glass, 2014
Border of Time, 2018
Sea, 2015
SALT WATER: A Theory of Thought Forms, 2015
As You Know, 2016
As You Know, 2016
Chamber Music, 2019
Chamber Music, 2019
Imagine, 2019
Chamber Music, 2019
This Story Will Continue, 2021
This Story Will Continue, 2021

1937 Born in Istanbul
1949–1956 Üsküdar American Academy for Girls
1956–1960 Istanbul State Academy of Fine Arts, Sculpture Department
1962 Fulbright Scholarship, American University, Washington D.C., USA
1964–1966 Maryland Institute College of Arts, USA
1972 Milliyet Art Magazine, Sculpture Artist of the Year Award
1974 35th State Painting and Sculpture Exhibition, Achievement Award
1974 Hadi Bara Competition, Second Prize
1975 Archaeology Museums Open Air Exhibition, Silver Medal
1976 Archaeology Museums Open Air Exhibition, Silver Medal
1981 *New Trends* Exhibition, Istanbul Art Festival, Silver Medal
2004 International Association of Art Critics (AICA) Turkey 50th Anniversary, Artist of Honour Award

SOLO SHOWS

1970 Taksim Art Gallery, Istanbul
1972 *Drawing in Space*, Taksim Art Gallery, Istanbul
1974 American Cultural Centre, Istanbul
1975 Taksim Art Gallery, Istanbul
1978 *From Outside In From Inside Out*, Taksim Art Gallery, Istanbul
1980 *Associations from a Shiny Circle on the Floor*, Taksim Art Gallery, Istanbul
1982 *Counterpoint with Flower*, Taksim Art Gallery, Istanbul
1985 *Dream of Old Furniture*, Taksim Art Gallery, Istanbul
1987 *Sign of Sign*, Maçka Art Gallery, Istanbul
1990 *Icons of Time*, Garanti Art Gallery, Istanbul
1991 *Gallery Lights*, Maçka Art Gallery, Istanbul
1995 *Cadence*, Maçka Art Gallery, Istanbul
2000 *Prelude*, Maçka Art Gallery, Istanbul
2007 *Erratum Musicale*, Yapı Kredi Kazım Taşkent Gallery, Istanbul
2012 *Variations*, Maçka Art Gallery, Istanbul
2012 *Elegy for Tekir*, Pilevneli Project, Istanbul
2014 *Through the Looking Glass*, Arter, Istanbul
2016 *As You Know*, Maçka Art Gallery, Istanbul
2019 *Chamber Music*, Galeri Nev Istanbul, Istanbul
2021 *Opus II – Fantasia*, Arter, Istanbul
2021 *This Story Will Continue*, ChertLüdde Gallery, Berlin

GROUP SHOWS

1971 7th Biennial of Young Artists, Paris, FR
1973 *50 Sculptures for Istanbul in the 50th Anniversary of the Republic,* Fındıklı Park, Istanbul
1974 *Nude*, Taksim Art Gallery, Istanbul
1974 Istanbul Archaeology Museums Open Air Exhibitions
1974 35th State Painting and Sculpture Exhibition, Ankara
1975 13th Middelheim Biennial, Antwerpen, BE
1975 Istanbul Archaeology Museums Open Air Exhibitions
1976 Istanbul Archaeology Museums Open Air Exhibitions
1976? Tarabya Art Gallery, Istanbul
1977 Istanbul Archaeology Museums Open Air Exhibitions
1977 *1st New Trends*, Istanbul Art Festival
1978 Özar Art Gallery, Istanbul
1978 AKM (Atatürk Cultural Centre), Istanbul
1978 Turkish Association for the Conservation of Nature Exhibition, Istanbul
1979 Turkish Association for the Conservation of Nature Exhibition, Istanbul
1979 International Year of the Child Exhibition, Istanbul
1980 Turkish Association for the Conservation of Nature Exhibition, Istanbul
1980 Özar Art Gallery, Istanbul
1981 *Realisation*, Seramar Gallery, Istanbul
1981 *3rd New Trends*, Istanbul Art Festival, Istanbul State Academy of Fine Arts
1981 Pangaltı Fine Arts Gallery, Istanbul
1982 BBC 50th Year Exhibition, Bush House, London, UK
1983 *Anatolian Civilizations*, Council of Europe 18th European Art Exhibition, Istanbul Archaeology Museums
1983 *Six Women Six Behaviours*, Seramar Gallery, Istanbul
1983 *4th New Trends*, Istanbul Art Festival State Academy of Fine Arts
1983 *Turkish Painting and Sculpture Art in the 100th Anniversary*, Istanbul Painting and Sculpture Museum
1983 *Galleries '83* – Contemporary Turkish Art Exhibition, 4th Istanbul Art Festival, AKM
1984 *A Section of Avantgarde Turkish Art*, AKM, Istanbul
1985 *A Section of Avantgarde Turkish Art II*, Yıldız Technical University, Istanbul
1985 *A Section of Contemporary Women Artists*, Istasyon Art House, Istanbul
1985 *6th Contemporary Artists Istanbul Exhibition*, Istanbul Painting and Sculpture Museum
1985 *5th New Trends, Istanbul Art Festival*
1986 *Contemporary Turkish Plastic Arts Exhibition*, Hacettepe Fine Arts Faculty, Ankara
1986 *Contemporary Dimensions Painting and Sculpture Exhibition*, Artnet Gallery, Istanbul
1986 1st International Asian-European Art Biennial, Ankara Türkocağı Painting and Sculpture Museum
1986 *Another Art Collective Exhibition in Memory of Joseph Beuys*, Izmir German Cultural Centre
1986 *A Section of Avantgarde Turkish Art III*, AKM, Istanbul
1987 *6th New Trends*, Mimar Sinan Fine Arts University, Istanbul
1987 Military Museum, 1st International Istanbul Contemporary Art Exhibition
1987 *Joint Exhibit,* Izmir Turkish American Association
1987 *A Section of Avantgarde Turkish Art IV*, AKM, Istanbul
1987 *Inspirations from Creative Turkish Women*, AKM, Istanbul
1988 Üsküdar American Academy for Girls alumni show, Soyak Art Gallery, Istanbul
1988 *Joint Exhibit*, Izmir Turkish American Association
1988 *A Section of Avantgarde Turkish Art V*, Hareket Köşkü, Istanbul
1989 *10 Artists 10 Works: A*, AKM, Istanbul
1989 *Untitled*, Derimod Art Centre, Istanbul
1990 *References*, Maçka Art Gallery, Istanbul
1990 *Great Exhibition II*, Istanbul Painting and Sculpture Museum and Ministry of Culture, AKM, Ankara
1990 *8 Artists 8 Works: B*, AKM, Istanbul
1991 *Eurodialogue 13 Female Artists from Istanbul*, Yıldız Palace
1992 *Art-Texnh – Fourteen Turkish and Greek Artists,* Istanbul Painting and Sculpture Museum and Dolmabahçe Palace
1992 9th International Prilep Biennial, MK
1992 *10 Artists 10 Works: C,* AKM, Istanbul
1993 *10 Artists 10 Works: D*, Koleksiyon Mobilya and Maçka Art Gallery, Istanbul
1993 *Exhibition Dresses*, Maçka Art Gallery, Istanbul
1993 *Women in Anatolia Through the Ages: Women Artists from the Republic to the Present,* Istanbul Archaeology Museums
1993 *Istanbul*, AKM, Istanbul
1994 *7th New Trends*, Mimar Sinan Fine Arts University, Istanbul
1994 *İskele (Turkish Art Today)*, ifa-Galerie Berlin and ifa Galerie Stuttgart, DE
1994 Alumni exhibition, Maryland Institute College of Art, USA
1994 *Artists from Turkey: Tomur Atagök & Füsun Onur*, Art Gallery Skopje, Davut Pasha Hammam, Skopje, MK
1995 *Traces*, Yıldız Technical University, Yüksel Sabancı Art Centre, Istanbul
1995 *Intolerance*, Yıldız Palace Armoury Building, Istanbul
1995 *Train Station*, TCDD Art Gallery and train station venues, Ankara
1995 *Orient/ation – The Vision of Art in a Paradoxical World*, Hagia Irene, 4th Istanbul Biennial
1995 *Suddenly, The Turks*, Parvi Paris, FR
1995 *Meeting*, Derimod Art Centre, Istanbul
1995 1st Uludağ University International Sculptors Symposium, Bursa
1997 *Under My Coat*, Galerie Thaddaeus Ropac, Paris, FR
1998 *Cartographers: geo-gnostic projection for the 21st century*, Zagreb, HR; Warsaw, PL; Budapest, HU; Maribor, SI
1998 *İskorpit: Contemporary Art from Istanbul*, Haus der Kulturen der Welt, Berlin, DE
1998 *Mediterranea – Contemporary Art of Mediterranean Countries*, Le Botanique, Brussels, BE
1998 *Kır4b1r: 41 Years 41 Artists 41 Works*, Marmara University Fine Arts Faculty, Istanbul
1999 *The Passion and The Wave*, Hagia Irene, 6th Istanbul Biennial
2000 *The Song of the Earth*, Museum Fridericianum, Kassel, DE
2000 *strange home,* Historische Museum, Kestner Museum, DE
2000 *Feature Presentation/Coming Attractions*, Yapı Kredi Culture and Arts, Hacopulo Passage, Istanbul
2001 *From Far Away So Close – Four Female Artists from Turkey*, Kunsthalle Baden-Baden, DE
2001 *Regrets, Reveries, Changing Skies*, Karşı Sanat, Istanbul
2001 *Modern Turk: Turkish Art in the Second Half of the 20th Century,* Topkapi Museum Stables, Istanbul
2002 *From Far Away So Close*, Govett-Brewster Art Gallery, New Plymouth, NZ
2002 *Between the Waterfronts (Contemporary Art from Istanbul and Rotterdam)*, Las Palmas, Rotterdam, NL
2003 *Füsun Onur, Hale Tenger, Aydan Murtezaoğlu*, Lunds Konsthall, SE
2003 *Turkish Art Today: Where? Here?*, Museum of Modern Art Saitama, JP
2003 *Organized Conflict*, Proje 4L, Istanbul
2004 *Kunst Stoff*, Galerie nächst St. Stephan, Vienna, AT

2004 *Call me ISTANBUL Is My Name*, ZKM, Karlsruhe, DE
2004 *Shaman's Diary*, Proje 4L, Istanbul
2004 *From Bosphorus to Moine: Aspects of contemporary art from Turkey in France*, Art and History Museum of Cholet, FR
2005 *EindhovenIstanbul – Contemporary Art Selection from Turkey*, Van Abbemuseum, Eindhoven, NL
2006 *Paper Works*, Galerist, Istanbul
2006 *Nested in Kuzguncuk – 45 Artist Portraits*, Kuzguncuk, Istanbul
2007 *Nested in Kuzguncuk*, Kuzguncuk, Istanbul
2007 *X times I*, Städtische Galerie Fruchthalle Rastatt, Rastatt, DE
2007 *FOOTNOTES on Geopolitics, Market and Amnesia*, State Schusev Museum of Architecture, 2nd Moscow Biennial, RU
2007 *Modern and Beyond*, santralistanbul, Istanbul
2007 *Recalls-Reminders*, Galerist, Istanbul
2008 *Time to Love and Return Home,* Şefik Bursalı Art Gallery, Bursa
2008 *Women of Light*, Galerie Davide Gallo, Berlin, DE
2008 *Who Killed the Painting?*, Neues Museum Nürnberg, DE
2009 *Who Killed the Painting?*, Neues Museum Weserburg, DE
2009 *Continued Variations*, Centre d'art contemporain d'Ivry, FR
2010 *Silence / Storm*, Port Izmir 2nd Contemporary Art Triennial
2010 *Tanzimat*, Augarten Contemporary, Vienna, AT
2010 *Odd Time Beat*, Rodeo Gallery, Istanbul
2010 *Tactics of Invisibility*, TBA Contemporary, Vienna, AT
2010 *Tactics of Invisibility*, Tanas, Berlin, DE
2011 *Tactics of Invisibility*, Arter, Istanbul
2011 *Dream and Reality*, Istanbul Modern, Istanbul
2011 *Continued Variations*, Akbank Sanat, Istanbul
2011 *Untitled (Abstraction)*, 12th Istanbul Biennial, Warehouse no. 3 and 5
2012 dOCUMENTA (13), Neue Galerie, Kassel, DE
2012 *all that shines ain't no gold*, Rodeo Gallery Istanbul
2013 *Signs Taken in Wonder*, MAK, Vienna, AT
2014 *Plurivocality*, Istanbul Modern, Istanbul
2014 *Do it Moscow*, Garage Centre for Contemporary Art, Moscow, RU
2015 *SALT WATER: A Theory of Thought Forms*, Istanbul Modern, 14th Istanbul Biennial
2017 *Dark Deep Darkness and Splendor*, Galerist, Istanbul
2017 *Evolve,* Gallery A, Port Izmir 4th Contemporary Art Triennial
2018 *Border of Time*, Neues Museum, Nürnberg, DE
2019 *The I is Always In the Field of the Other: A Selection From the Agah Ugur Collection*, Evliyagil Museum, Ankara
2019 *Heartbreak*, Ruya Maps, Venice, IT
2019 *Light Like a Bird, Not Like a Feather*, SIGNS, Istanbul
2020 *For Eyes That Listen*, Arter, Istanbul
2020 *Fool's Paradise*, Galeri Nev Istanbul, Istanbul
2020 *Constellation*, Troya Museum, 7. Çanakkale Biennial
2021 *Seventh Valley*, Galeri Nev Istanbul, Istanbul
2021 *THIS PLACE*, Yapı Kredi Culture and Arts, Istanbul
2021 *Arts of Islam. A Past for A Present*, Roger-Quilliot Art Museum, Clermont-Ferrand, FR
2022 *ThisPlay*, Arter, Istanbul

PUBLISHED ARTICLES

'Büyük Sanatçı Kıymetli Hoca Hadi Bara' [Great Artist and Esteemed Teacher Hadi Bara], *Ankara Sanat*, no 68, December 1971: 10–11.

'İlerici Sanat Üzerine' [On Progressive Art], *Politika*, 30 January 1976.

'Sözde Toplumcu Gerçekçilik' [So-called Social Realism], *Politika*, 14 March 1976.

'Resim Heykel Sorunları' [Problems in Painting and Sculpture], *Politika*, 29 May 1976.

'Eleştirmenin Yaklaşımı' [Approach of the Critic], *Cumhuriyet*, 9 September 1976.

'9 Eylül 1906, Yetmişinci Doğum Yıldönümünde Hadi Bara' [9 September 1906, Hadi Bara on the Seventieth Anniversary of His Birth], *Ankara Sanat*, no. 125, September 1976, 10.

'Gün doğuyor' [The Day Breaks], *Aydınlık*, 28 September 1978.

'Sorumlu Kim' [Who is Responsable], *Sanat Çevresi*, no. 79, May 1985: 75.

'Modern Heykelin Türkiye'de Korunması' [The Preservation of Modern Sculpture in Turkey], *Hürriyet Gösteri*, no. 66, May 1986: 95–96.

'Son Kırk Yılın İngiliz Heykelciliği' [The Last Forty Years of British Sculpture], *Hürriyet Gösteri*, no. 69, August 1986: 40–42.

'Görsel Sanatlarda Eleştiri Yokluğu' [The Lack of Criticism in the Visual Arts], *Hürriyet Gösteri*, no. 82, September 1987:43–45.

'Bir Cevap' [A Response…], *Sanat Çevresi*, no. 139, May 1990: 70–71.

'İmgelem' [Imagination], *Hürriyet Gösteri*, no. 128, July 1991: 66–67.

BİGE ÖRER is the Director of Istanbul Biennial and İKSV Contemporary Art Projects. Örer's breadth of activity embraces both the artistic and the academic fields. Her curatorial projects include the exhibitions *Flaneuses*, Istanbul (2017), *Linear Transcendency*, Amman (2016), and *Agoraphobia*, Berlin (2013, co-curated with Fulya Erdemci). She has participated in curatorial residency programmes at Whitechapel Gallery (2016) and Palais de Tokyo (2018). Her contributions to various publications include the research she co-conducted on the financing of international contemporary art biennials. She co-wrote the children's book *A Colourful Journey in a Time Machine: Istanbul Biennials for Children* with Süreyyya Evren, *Haz / Cızzz*, with İz Öztat. Örer has written extensively about biennials and taught courses on the subject. She is one of the founding members of the Curatorial Studies programme at Kadir Has University. She has been a consultant and jury member for numerous arts institutions and has been the vice-president of the International Biennial Association since its foundation in March 2013. She is also on the editorial board of the association that conceptualised and edited the inaugural issue of its journal, *Pass*.

Chronology

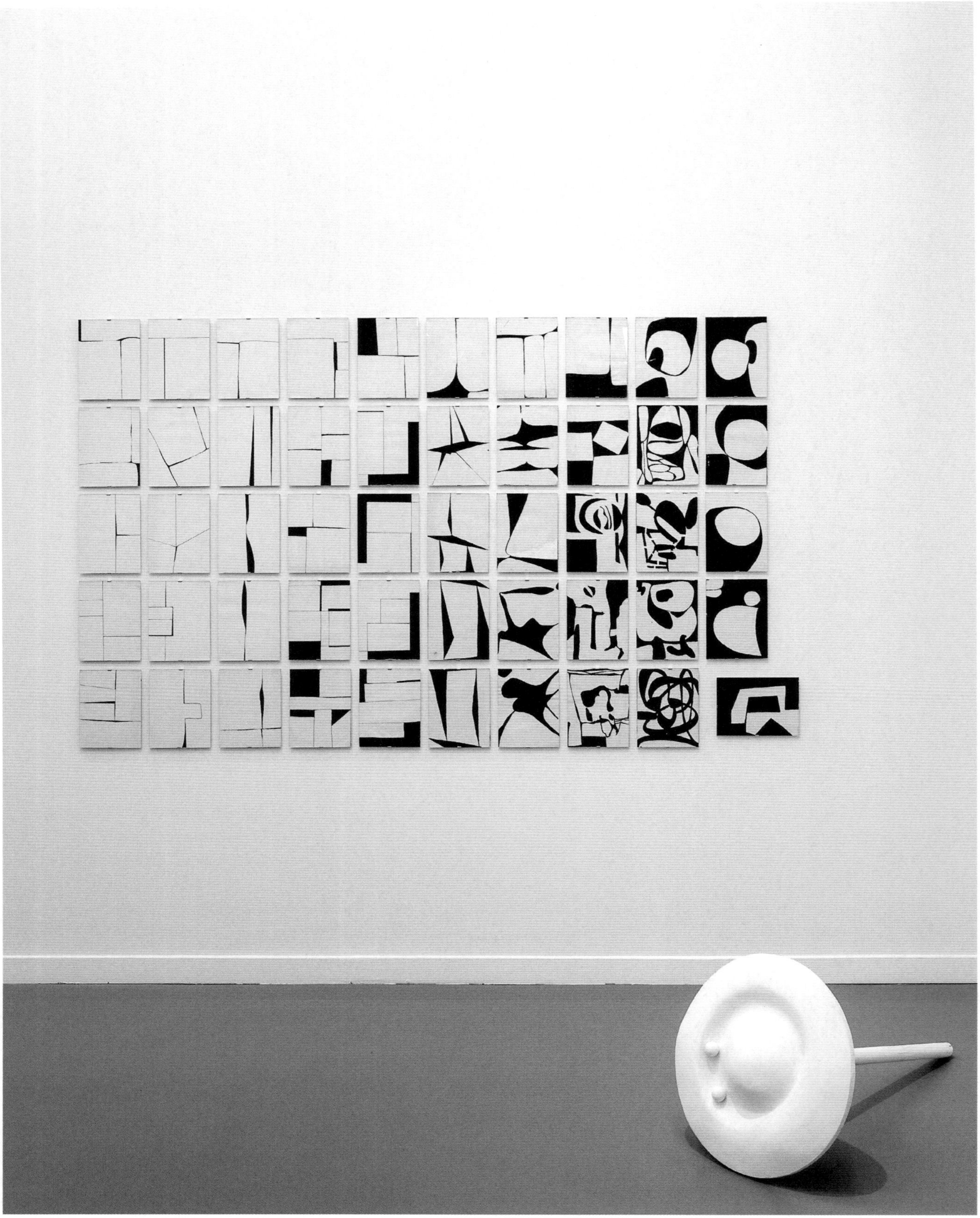

Ink on paper, 50 pieces, 30 × 22.5 cm each

[*Dividing Space on a White Piece of Paper*] interpret the surface of the paper as a space. Often, a swelling and narrowing of the black lines is enough to suggest a three-dimensional structure that could also be realized as a sculpture. The drawings anticipate Onur's work in several ways, highlighting her aim to shape the space as a whole.

Thomas Heyden, excerpt from the *Saum der Zeit (Border of Time)* exhibition booklet, Neues Museum Nürnberg, 2018.

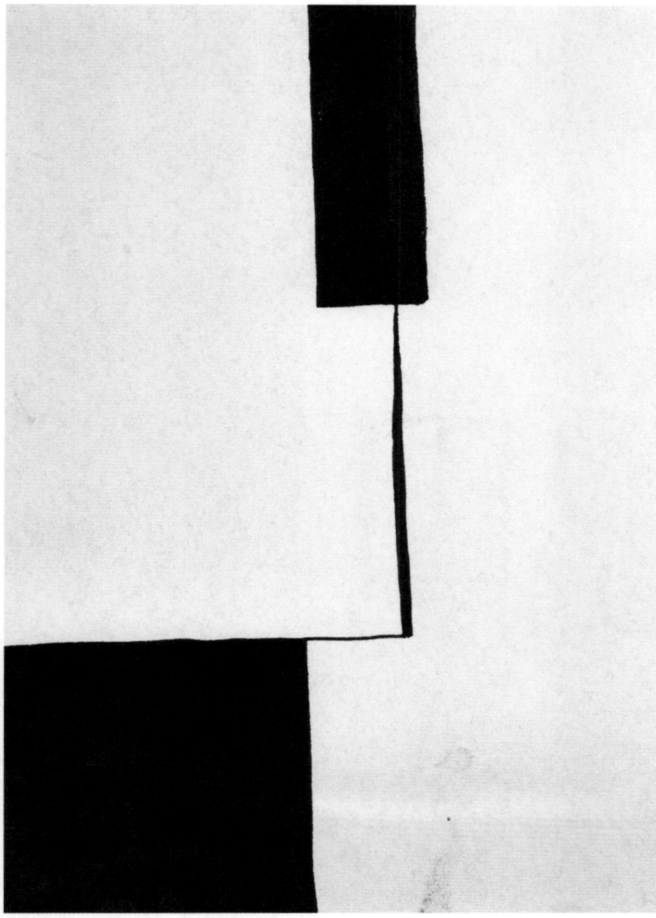

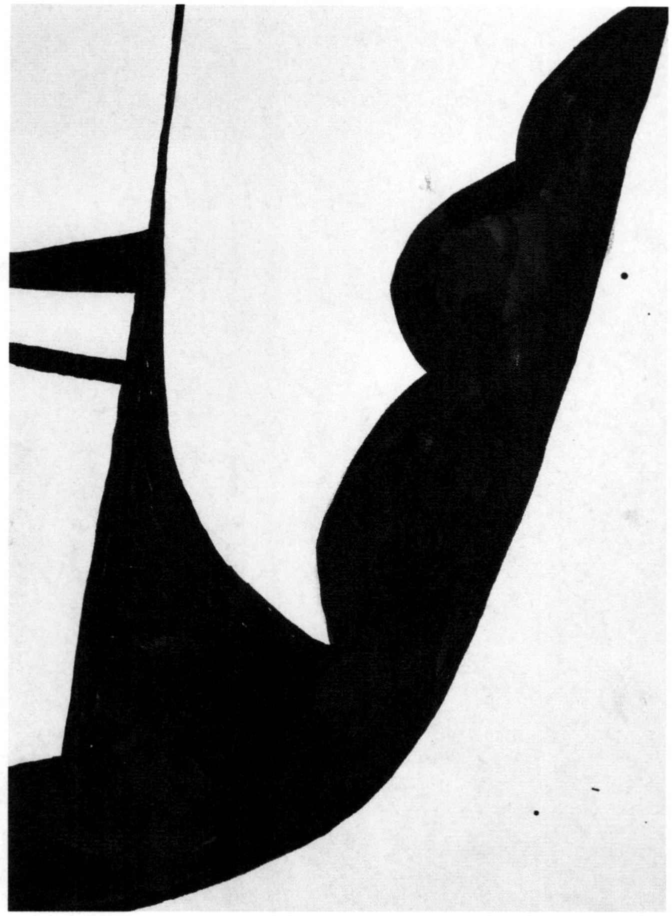

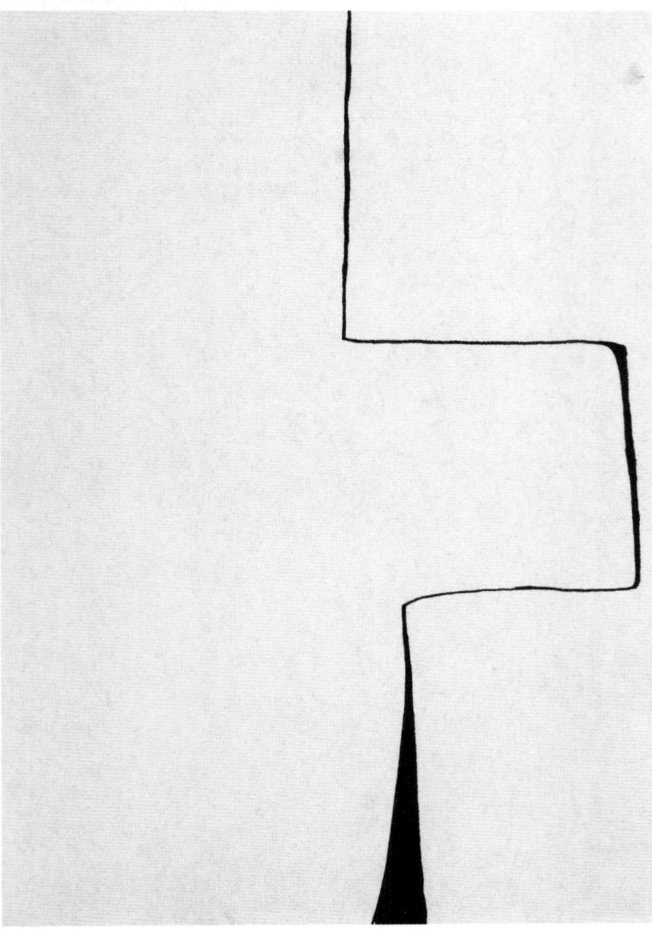

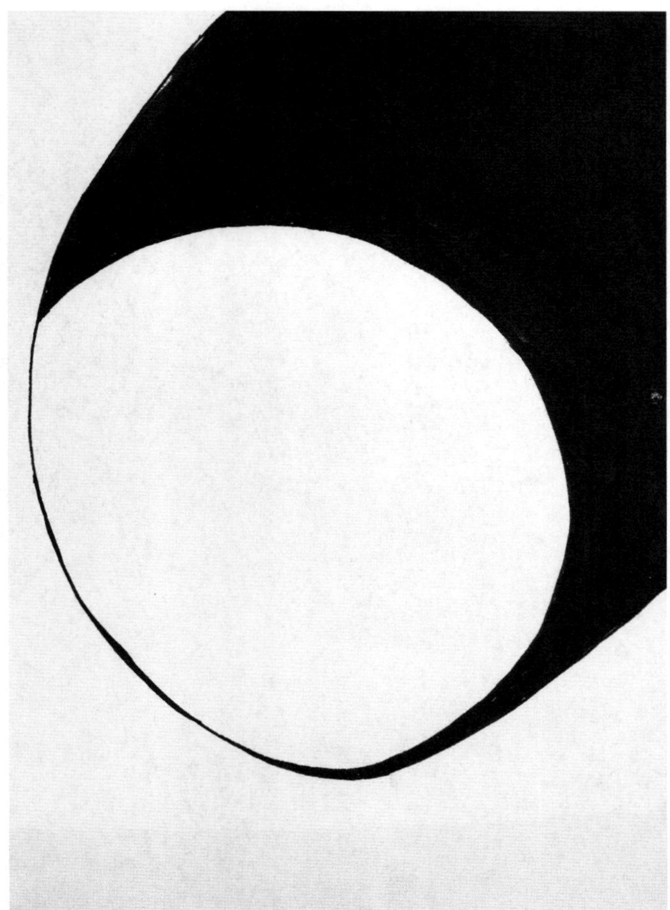

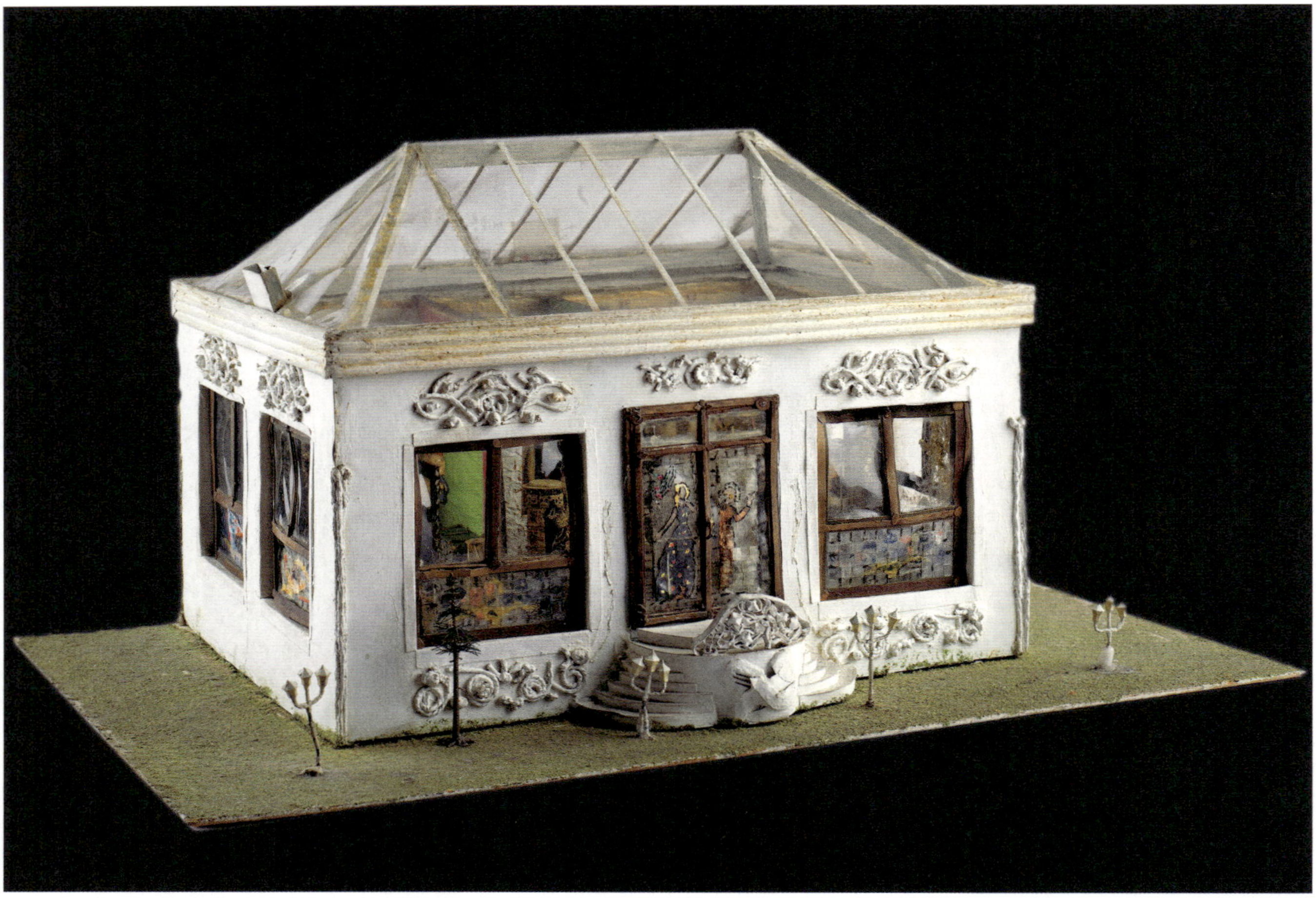

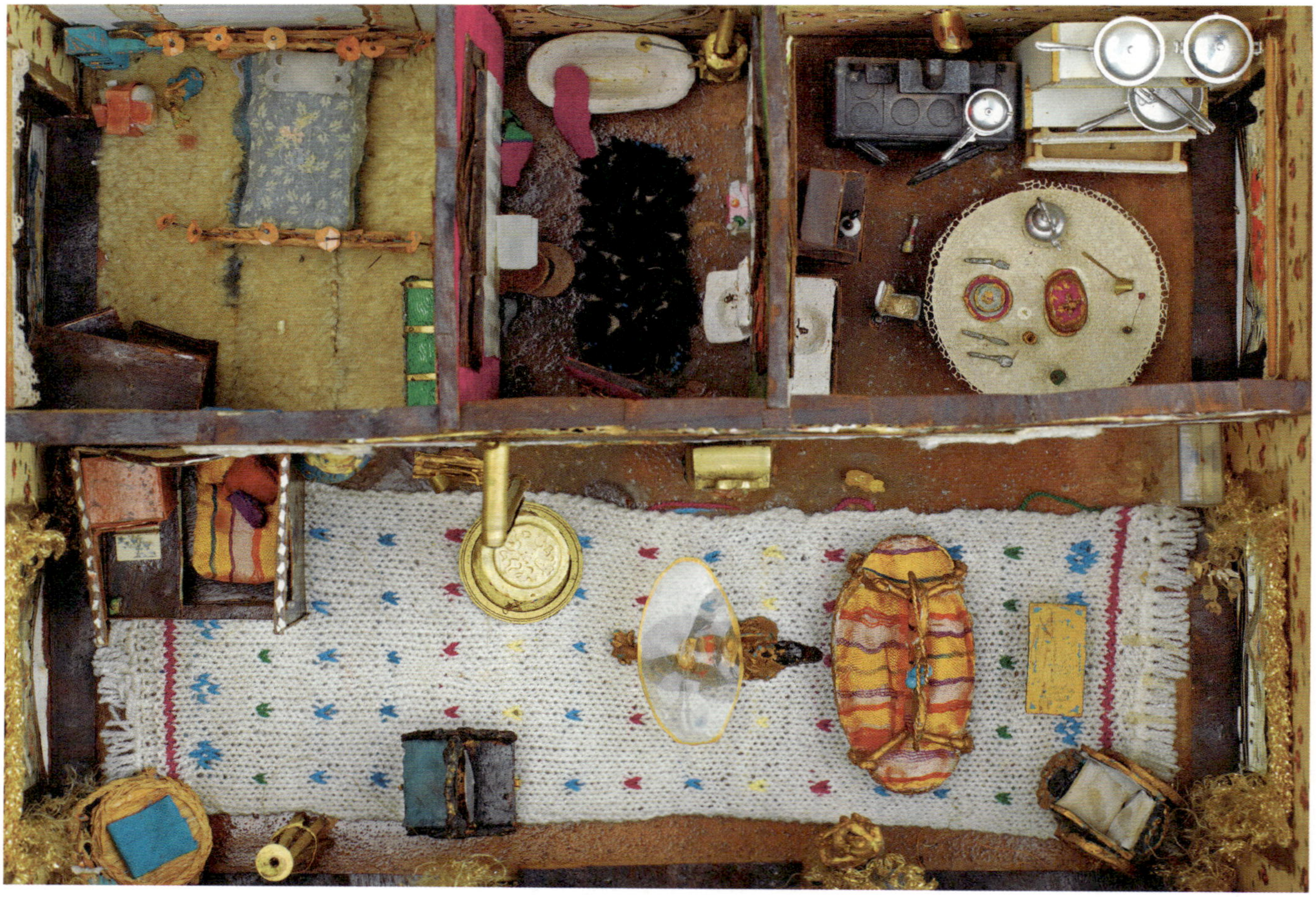

Wood, paint, metal, fabric, ceramic, 72 × 50 × 38 cm

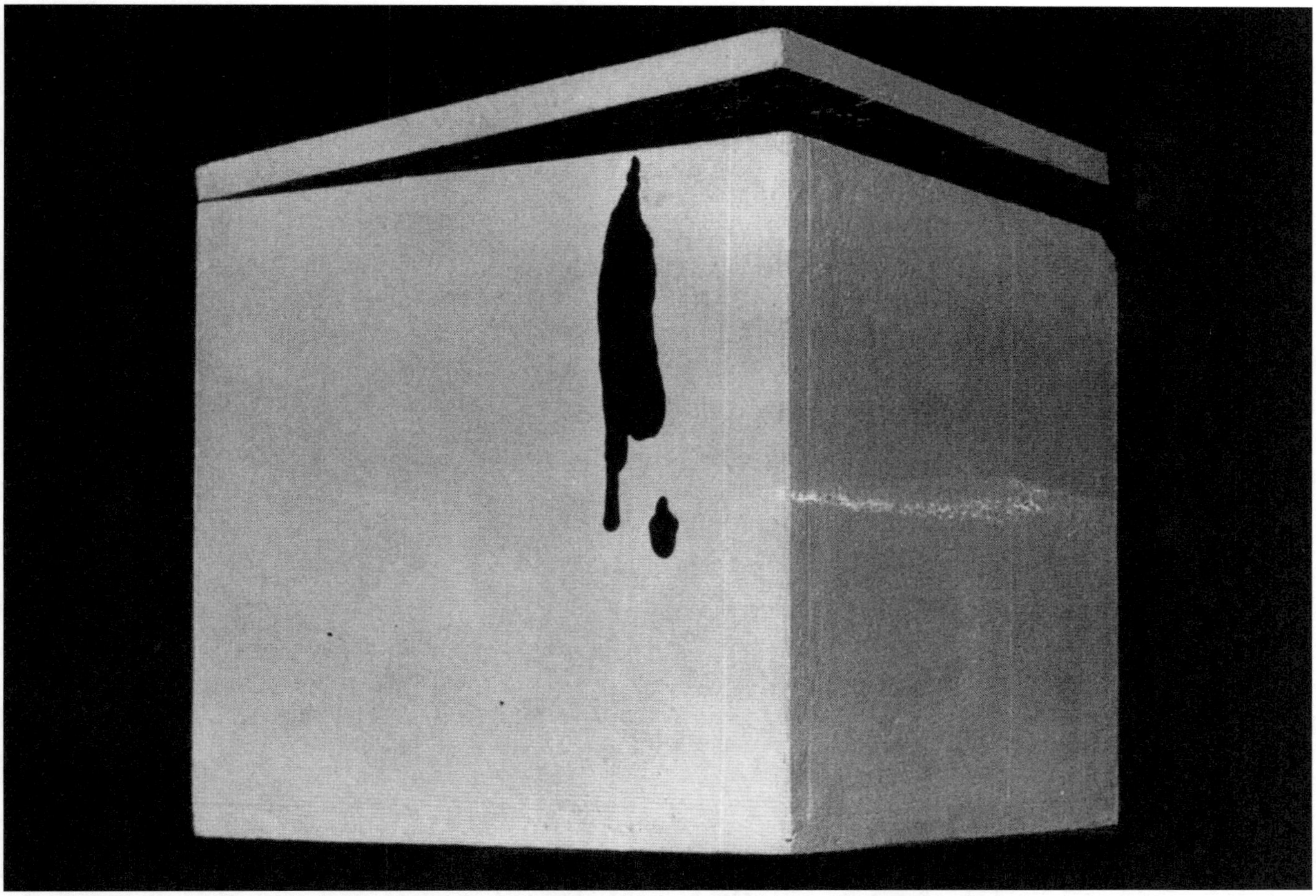

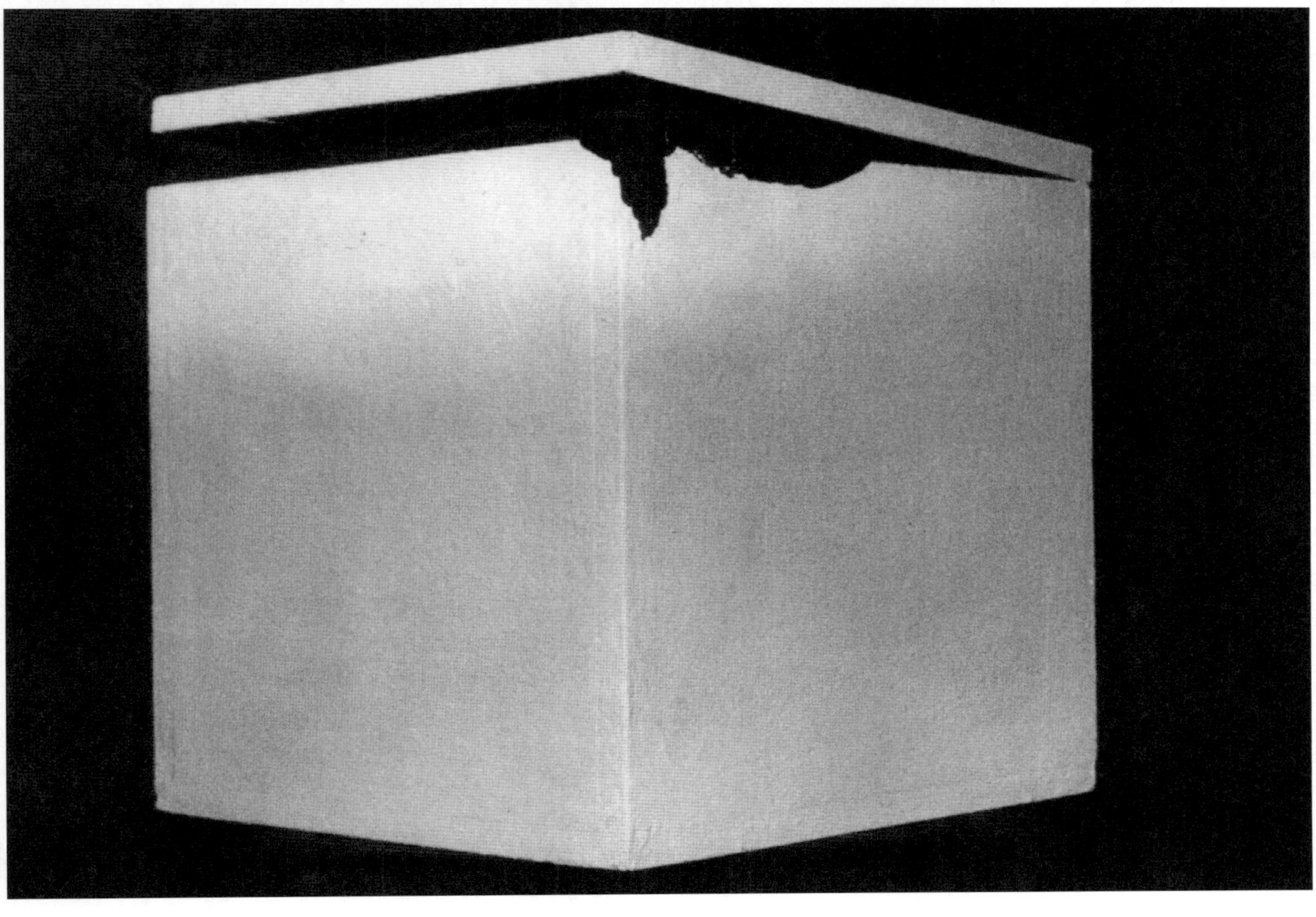

Wood, paint, plaster, 50 × 50 × 50 cm

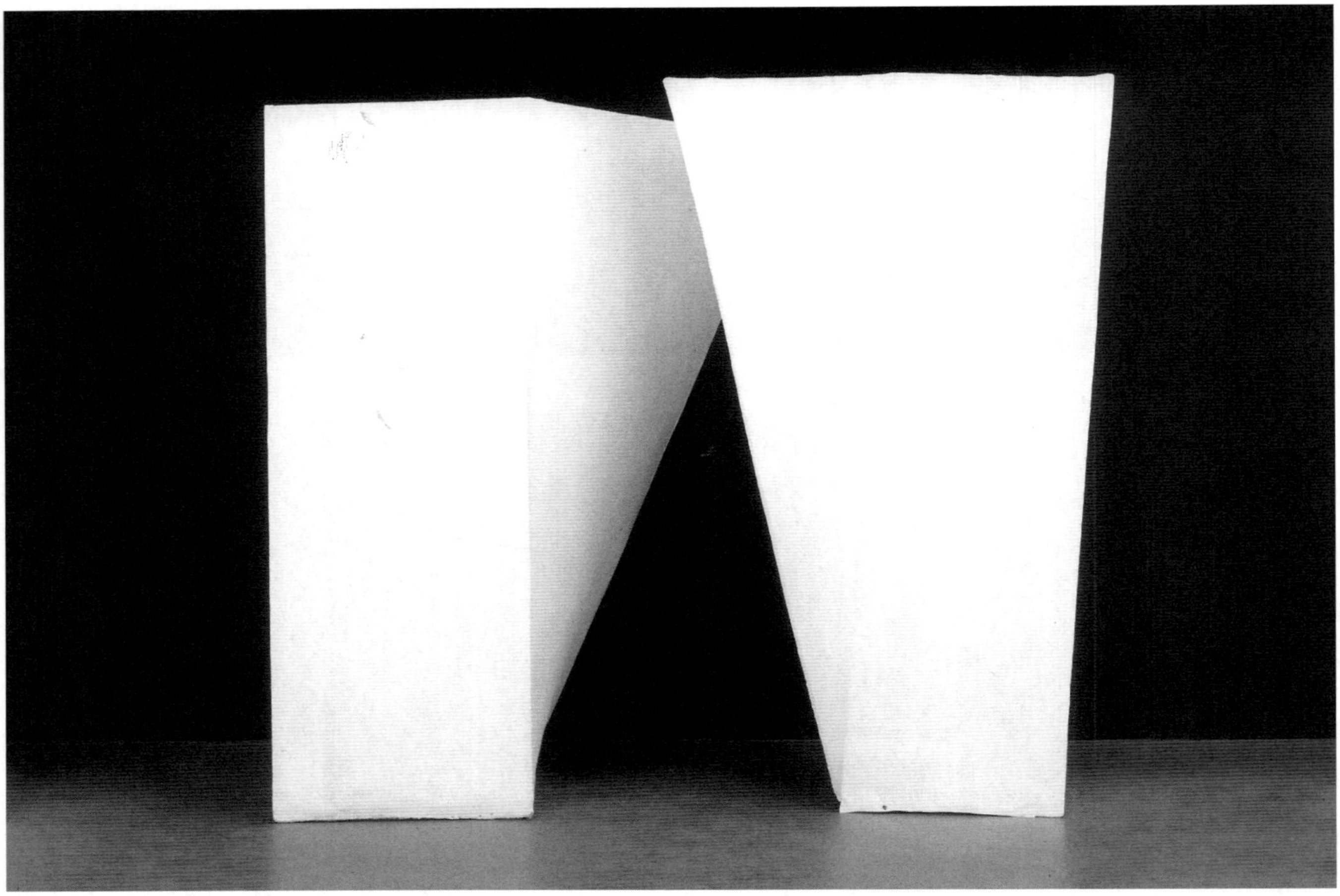

Canvas, wood, 200 × 320 × 80 cm

1970 UNTITLED

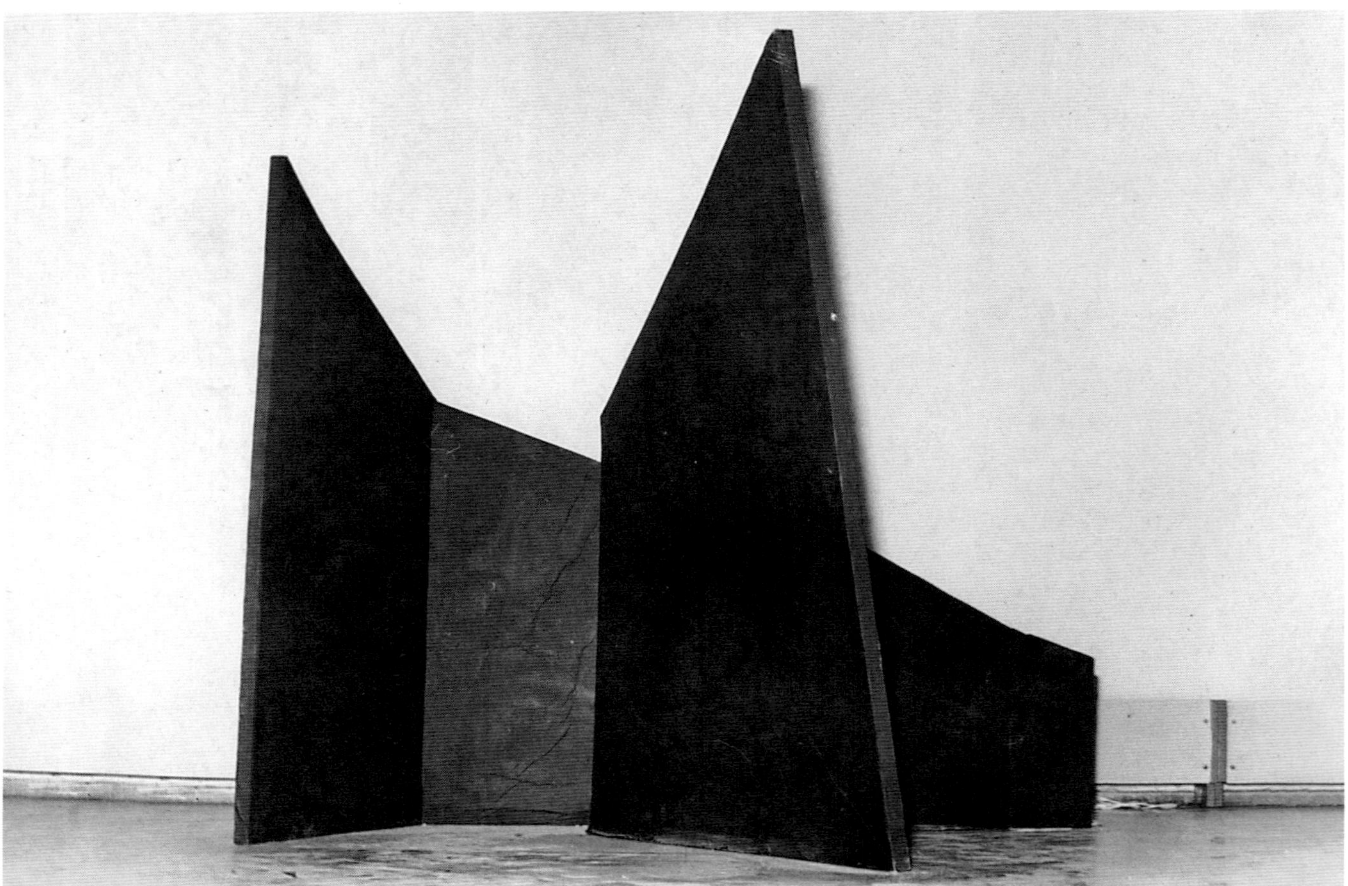

Sponge, 145 × 225 cm

1970 UNTITLED

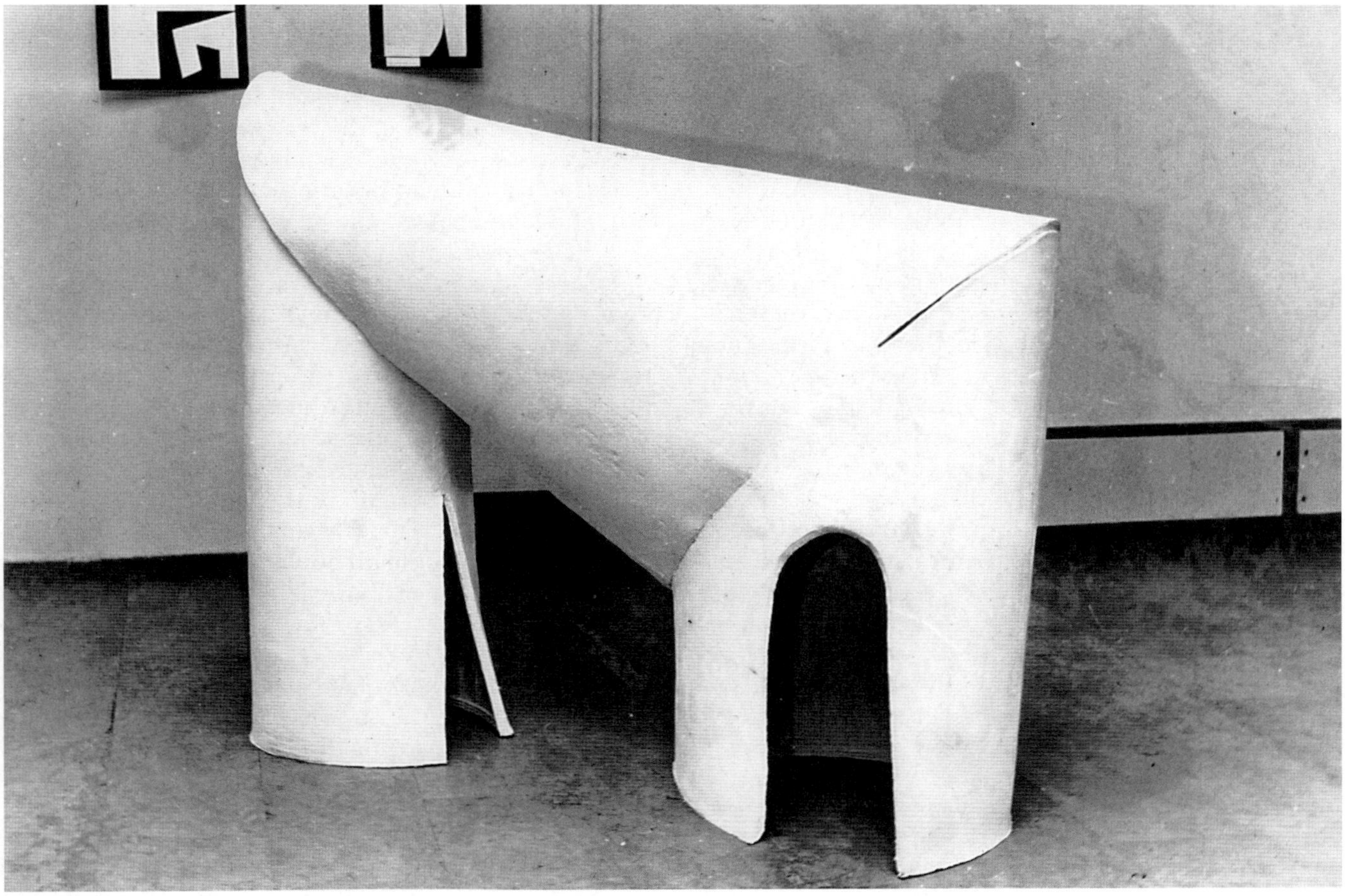

Sponge, 175 × 50 × 75 cm

1970 UNTITLED

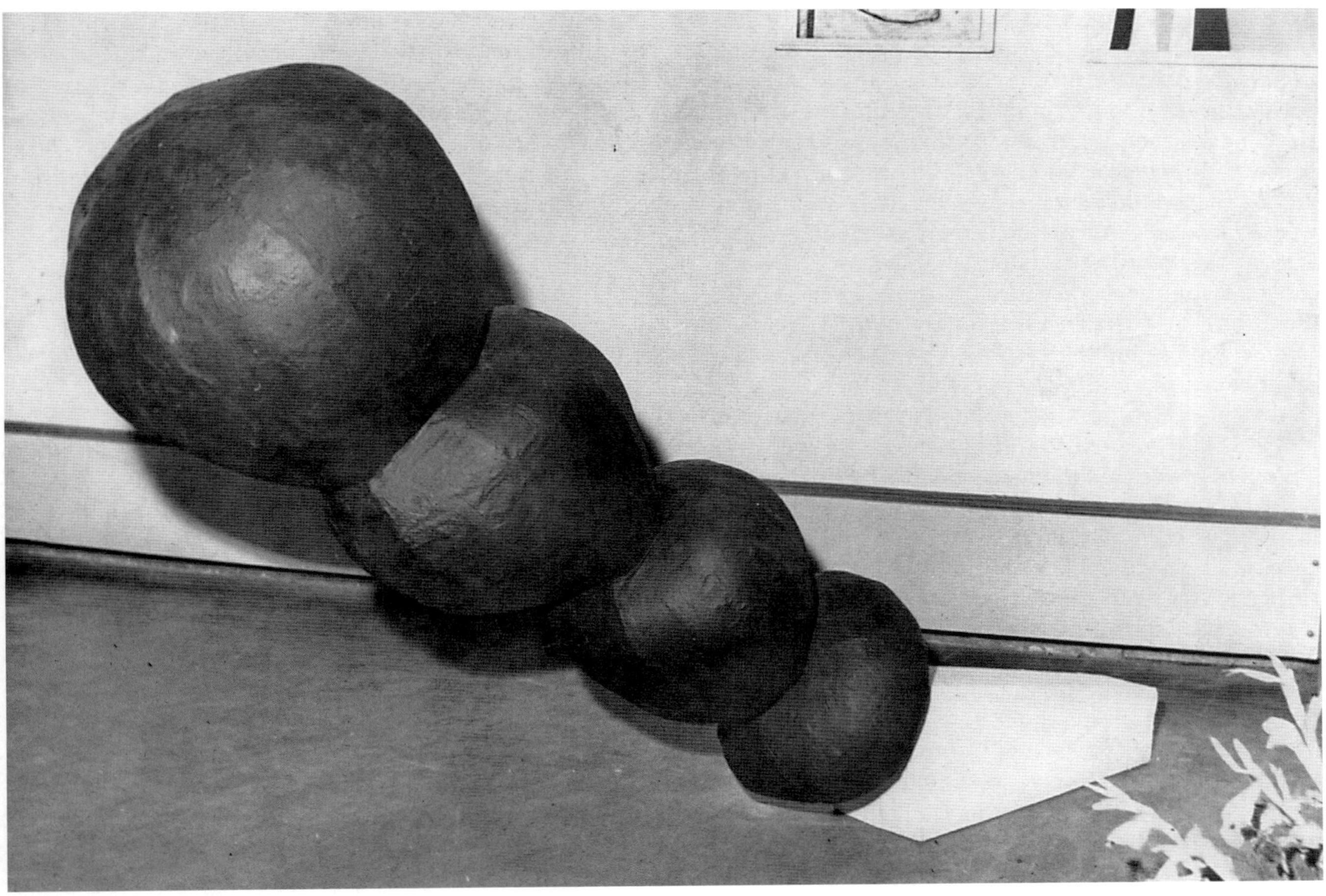

Wood, paint, sponge, 210 × 65 × 40 cm

Produced between 1968 and 1971, selected and presented as part of Turkey's participation at the 7th Paris Young Artists Biennial, a series of six sculptures bridges Füsun Onur's formative years in the US and her first exhibitions in Turkey and abroad. Although two of the six sculptures having been damaged during transportation, and only four were exhibited at the biennial,[1] when considered together as a series of six, remaining true to the original selection, these sculptures shed light on Onur's early esthetics and on this esthetic's resistance to politics of exhibition and display her works circulated through. Taken as an ensemble, as they were in the framework of the 7th Paris Biennial, they encapsulate her lifelong interest in themes and variations, and announce a double shift in her early practice: from abstract modernist sculpture towards assemblages and installations deployed in space and time, activated by the viewer's body and movements; and from plaster to lighter materials like painted wood, found objects and textiles. As such, and especially when contemplated side by side, they foreground her core concerns over the following decades.

I imagine the juxtaposition of these sculptures and the conversation between them from a distance of fifty years, by scanning black and white photographic archives. Seriality and movement are at work in *Composition I*, where sculpture becomes architecture on a human scale, with a clear tension between object, drawing and space. Both *Composition I* and *II* (1971) carry a reflection on the relationship between frame, image and architecture, variations of which are activated as the viewer moves in space and shifts perspective. Both works seek a human form and scale, and in this sense, they are precursors to Onur's Plexiglas installations that would follow a few years later. While in these works, it is the external movement of the viewer and the shifting perspective that complement the work, by contrast, in *Composition III* (1970), an internal movement unfolds, a concentration on the object's inner space. *Composition II* and *Composition V* (1970) are linked by an engagement with play and games: the two disk-like shapes placed within the circular cavity of the round plane in *Composition V* and the red plastic ball – one of Onur's first uses of found objects – both have associations with games, playgrounds and toys.

The formal structure of *Composition IV* (1970) reveals a constancy over the years and across materials such as cloth, glass, paper: the tear instantiates fragmentation as a potential inner space cracks the plane, volume merges with its negative space, setting the form in tension with both its process and its material and metaphysical conditions of possibility. Moving from the incised surface of *Composition IV* back to *Composition V*, the red plastic ball operates almost like an incision on the formal reduction of the ensemble, bringing not only colour but also the everyday into the realm of these white surfaces and abstract forms. Similarly, the geometric abstraction of the frame and the organic branches of the tree interrupt each other and create a unique assemblage ripe with tension between abstraction, imitation and life itself in the form of a found object.

Composition VI (1971), titled elsewhere *Untitled (Shapeless Form)*,[2] is Onur's first work requiring audience participation to be physically activated: an air pump connected to the horizontally laid, meandering shape made out of sailcloth – like a serpent or a question mark – invites the spectator to inflate and move it. Once pumped, the sculpture deflates gradually over a period of time, a movement closely associated with the rhythm of breath or the wind. The horizontal layout, the potential for movement and audience interaction, which would all be central threads in Onur's rhythmic spatial installations in the years to come, appear here in gestation.

The privilege of hindsight allows me to reflect on the position these works held at the time of their first public presentations as 'outsiders' within various frames of presentation. Since it is the 7th Paris Biennial, organised in 1971, that provides the context for the first ever grouping of these compositions as a series, it is worth revisiting various frames that this exhibition put into play, and how Onur's works resisted categorisation within each of them.

The experimental nature and the constantly evolving formats and selection procedures of the Paris Biennial are well documented.[3] The seventh edition of the event insisted upon the 'youth' aspect of its participants and encouraged audacious experimentation. It boasted of offering 'for the first time in France, the most rigorous and theoretical ensemble of conceptual art presented in Europe.'[4] The national curators were

1.
This information is taken from Füsun Onur's statement quoted in the article 'Artist in Paris' which appeared in *Alma Mater*, Spring Summer issue, 1972, published by Üsküdar American Academy for Girls.

2.
See *Füsun Onur: Through The Looking Glass* (Istanbul: Arter Publications, 2014), 56.

3.
A research project on the archives of the Paris Biennial, supported by the Institut National d'Histoire de l'Art in partnership with Les Archives de la Critique d'Art in Rennes and the Kandinsky Library, results of which have recently been exhibited at Musée national d'art moderne – Centre Georges Pompidou, underlined the controversial, experimental and ever-evolving formats of the event through a double display focusing on the diversity of materials on one hand, and moments of crisis on the other. See 'A Space for Something Else: the Paris Biennale 1959–1985,' Centre Pompidou, 4 June – 31 December 2021.

4.
See the introduction to the biennial catalogue by George Boudaille, 'Préface,' *Septième biennale de Paris: Manifestation Biennale et Internationale*

1971 COMPOSITION I

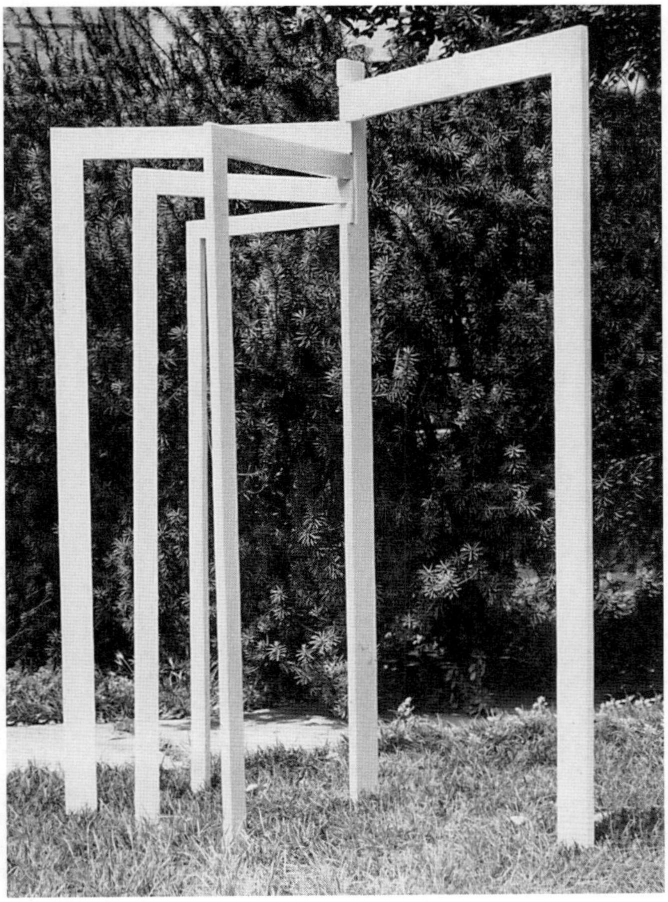

1971 COMPOSITION II

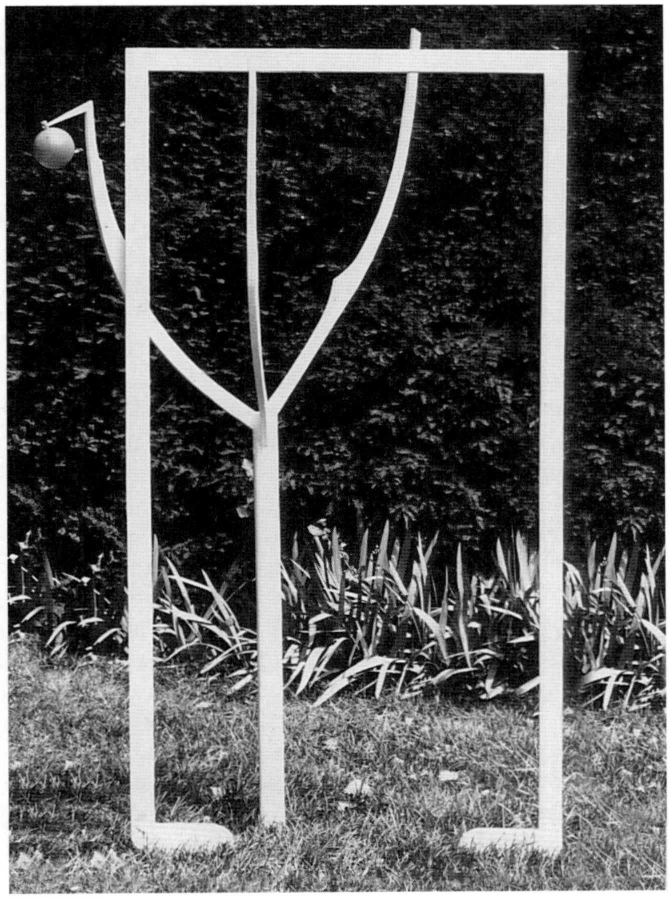

(Left) Wood, 195 × 160 cm
(Right) Wood, paint, 200 × 100 cm

1970 COMPOSITION III

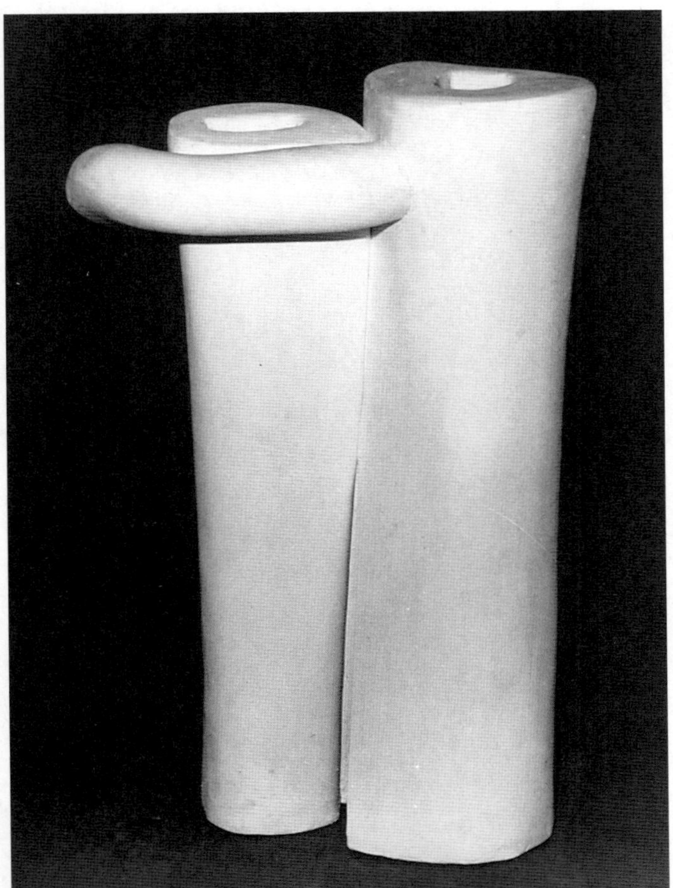

1970 COMPOSITION IV

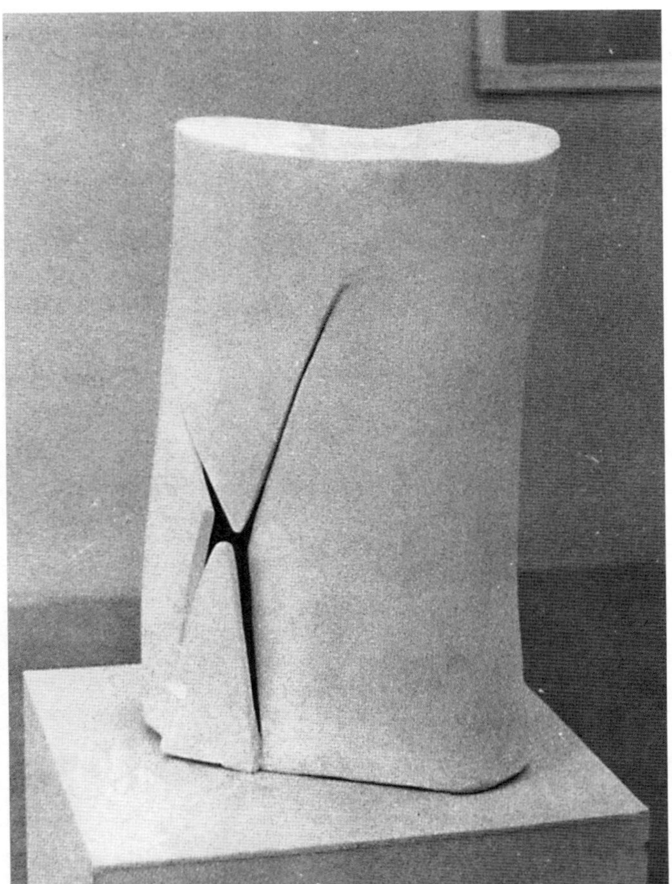

(Left) Plaster, 100 × 62 cm
(Right) Plaster, 62 × 37 cm

asked to align their selections with one of three artistic tendencies identified as emergent at the time: conceptual art, hyperrealism and performance-oriented practises such as Land art, body art or happenings. In line with the insistence on the generational aspect of the event, the national curators were also expected to be under the age of thirty-five, in order to be closely associated with this young generation of artists.[5] Despite this detailed framework, the biennial organisers remained open to proposals that fell outside of this frame, particularly from countries of the 'Global South,' whose artistic production remained attached to traditional modernist forms, distant from the aforementioned avant-garde movements.[6]

In response to this framework, the Turkish national selection was put together by the artist Bedri Rahmi Eyüboglu, then professor at the Istanbul State Academy of Fine Arts and approaching the age of sixty. The curatorial presentation privileged works of figurative painting and engraving.[7] It remained attached to the formal debate opposing abstraction and figuration, coupled with the duality between Eastern-Islamic traditions and Western rationalism. It expressed regret regarding the importance recently gained by 'cerebral work.' As such, despite having selected the young Onur's works as a valuable contribution to national representation, the curator seems to have failed to recognise and articulate the multiple experiments and potential towards both conceptualism and performativity in her works.[8]

Just as Onur's sculptures and installations fall outside the national presentation, the national selection itself falls outside of the curatorial frame developed by the biennial curators. The series of sculptures in fact resists both these frames, and stands out as an ensemble of avant-garde propositions creating their own interiority, coiling in and folding out around a unique, multi-centred gravity, constituting a source of energy filled with resistance, reaching and embracing us across decades.

des Jeunes Artistes: du 24 septembre au 1er novembre 1971: Parc Floral de Paris, Bois de Vincennes, Biennale de Paris, 7, 1971, 13.

5.
On close inspection, this framework proves to be the result of an unstable compromise between a desire to emancipate the Biennial from its previous attachments to diplomacy and national representation towards a more democratic and participatory structure, and the organisers' need to rely on existing structures to meet curatorial, logistical and budgetary challenges.

6.
We should note that the designation 'Global South' is a contemporary one. A term more appropriate for the time, following the decolonisation movements of the 1950s and 1960s and the emergence of the non-aligned movement, would be 'Third World' countries.

7.
Besides Füsun Onur, Gündüz Gölönü and Oya Katoğlu were among artists selected for the national presentation; the curatorial text however mentioned only the works of those two artists: Bedri Rahmi Eyüboğlu, 'Turquie,' *Septième biennale de Paris: Manifestation Biennale Internationale des Jeunes Artistes: du 24 septembre au 1er novembre 1971: Parc Floral de Paris, Bois de Vincennes,* Biennale de Paris, 7, 1971, 255–56.

8.
'But just as Turkish art kept pace with the West, abstract painting made its appearance, and decorative values, which have nothing in common with nature, took on capital importance. The Turkish painters, who since the beginning of the century, studied and observed nature, suddenly found themselves without support. Cerebral work replaced everything. A peasant rug designed without a sketch, without a design, without a pencil stroke took on a new value. [...] As for our sculptors, the environment is not so welcoming. The word "icon" has meant for thirteen centuries the greatest enemy of Muslims. Any sculpture was an "icon" to break and many were broken...The chosen sculptors express themselves with a language that is rather universal.' Bedri Rahmi Eyüboglu, 'Turquie,' *Septième biennale de Paris: Manifestation Biennale Internationale des Jeunes Artistes: du 24 septembre au 1er novembre 1971: Parc Floral de Paris, Bois de Vincennes,* Biennale de Paris, 7, 1971, 255–56. (translated from French by the author).

1970 COMPOSITION V

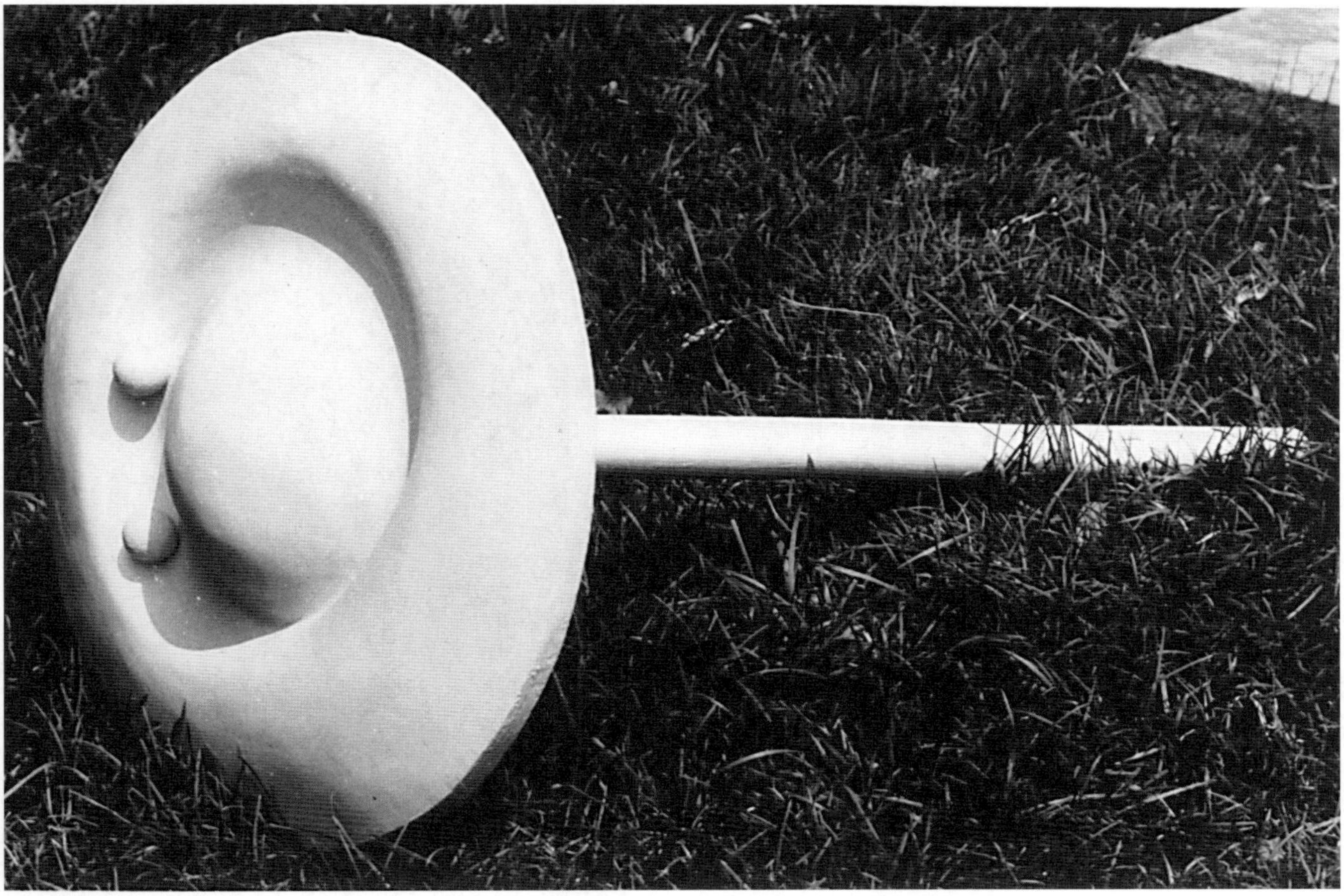

Plaster, wood, 59 × 100 cm

1971 COMPOSITION VI or UNTITLED (SHAPELESS FORM)

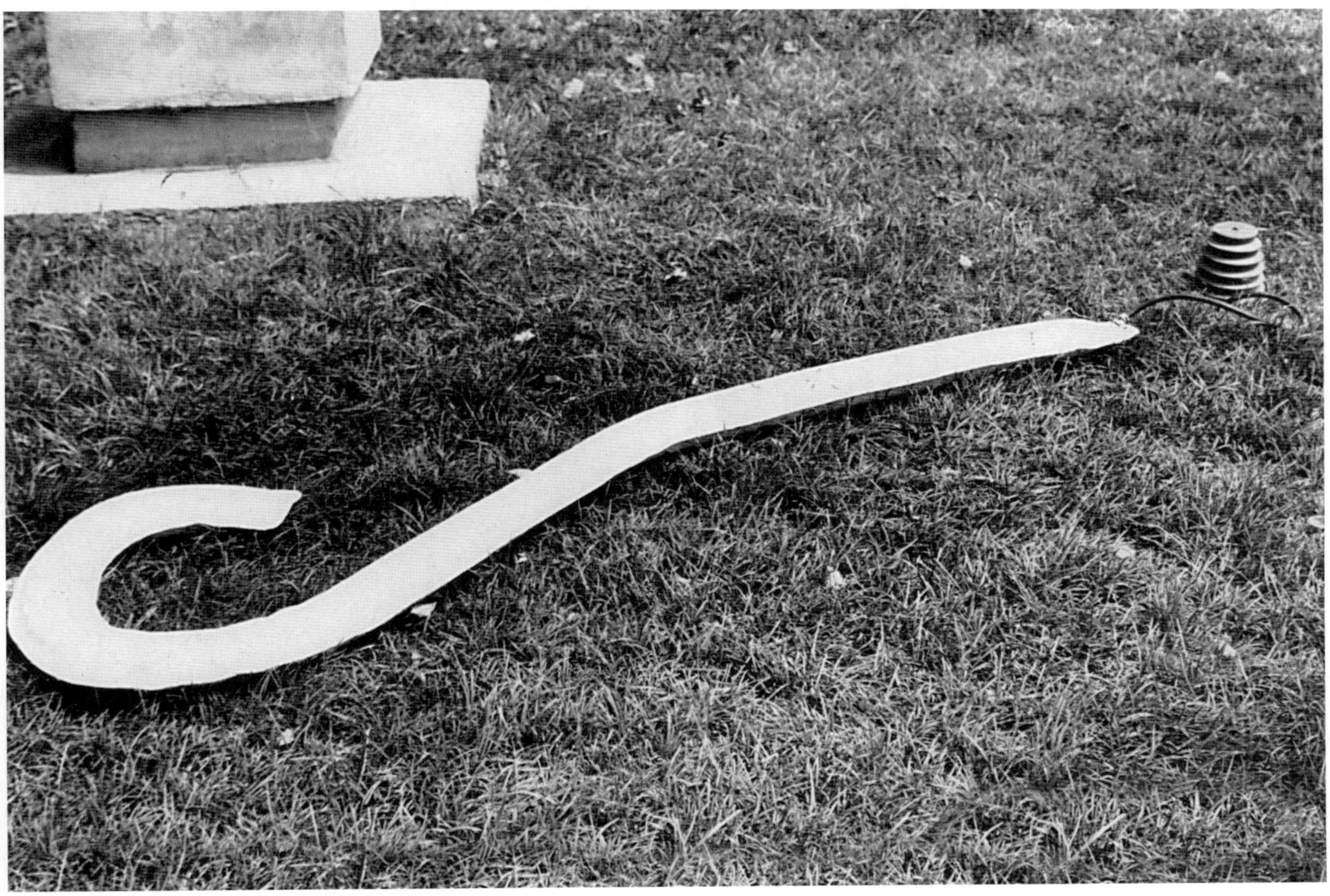

Sailcloth, pump, 250 × 20 cm

1971 UNTITLED

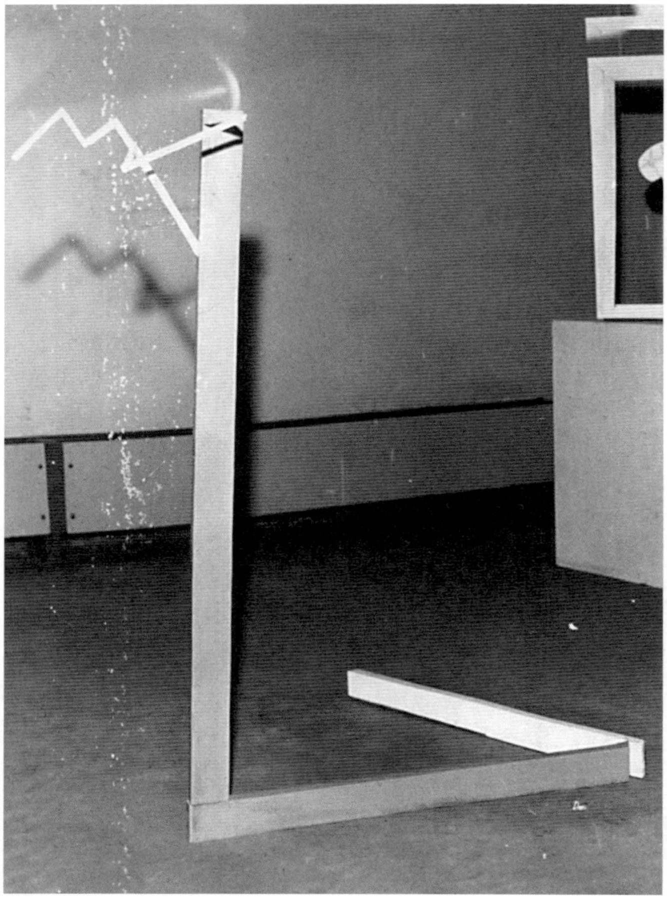

1971 UNTITLED

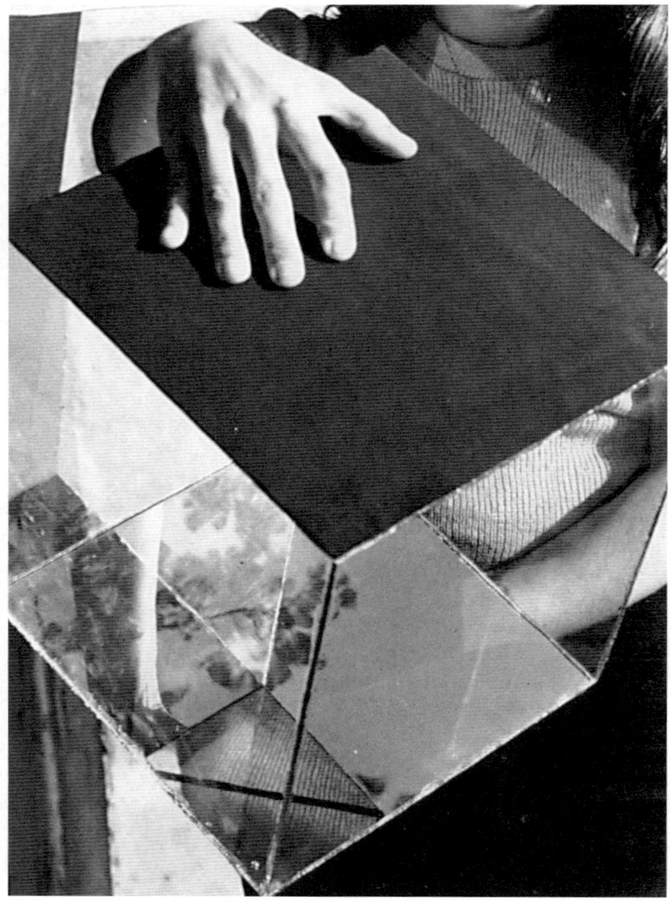

(Left) Wood, paint, unknown dimensions
(Right) Glass, mirror, 35 × 30 × 30 cm

1971 UNTITLED

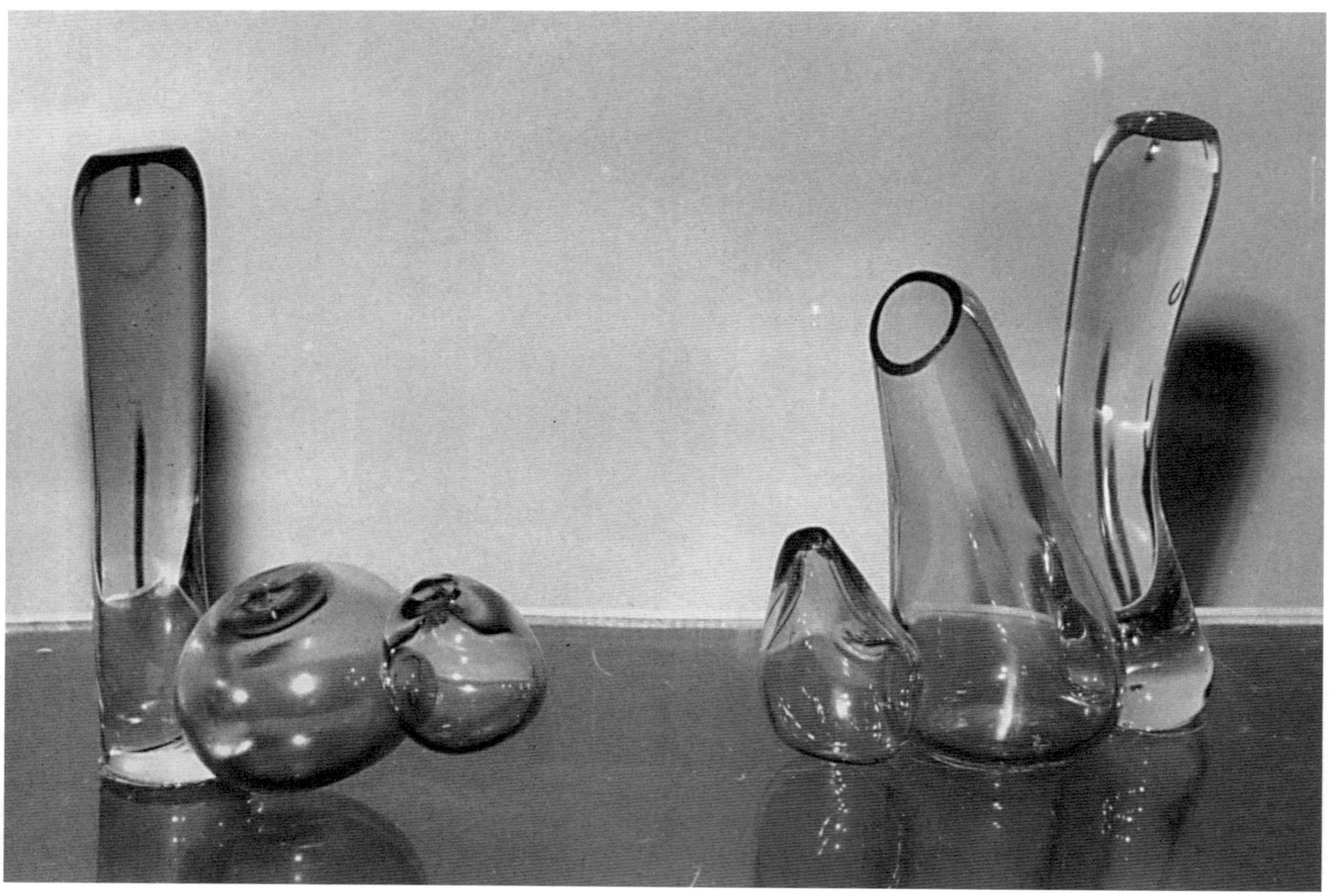

Glass, variable dimensions

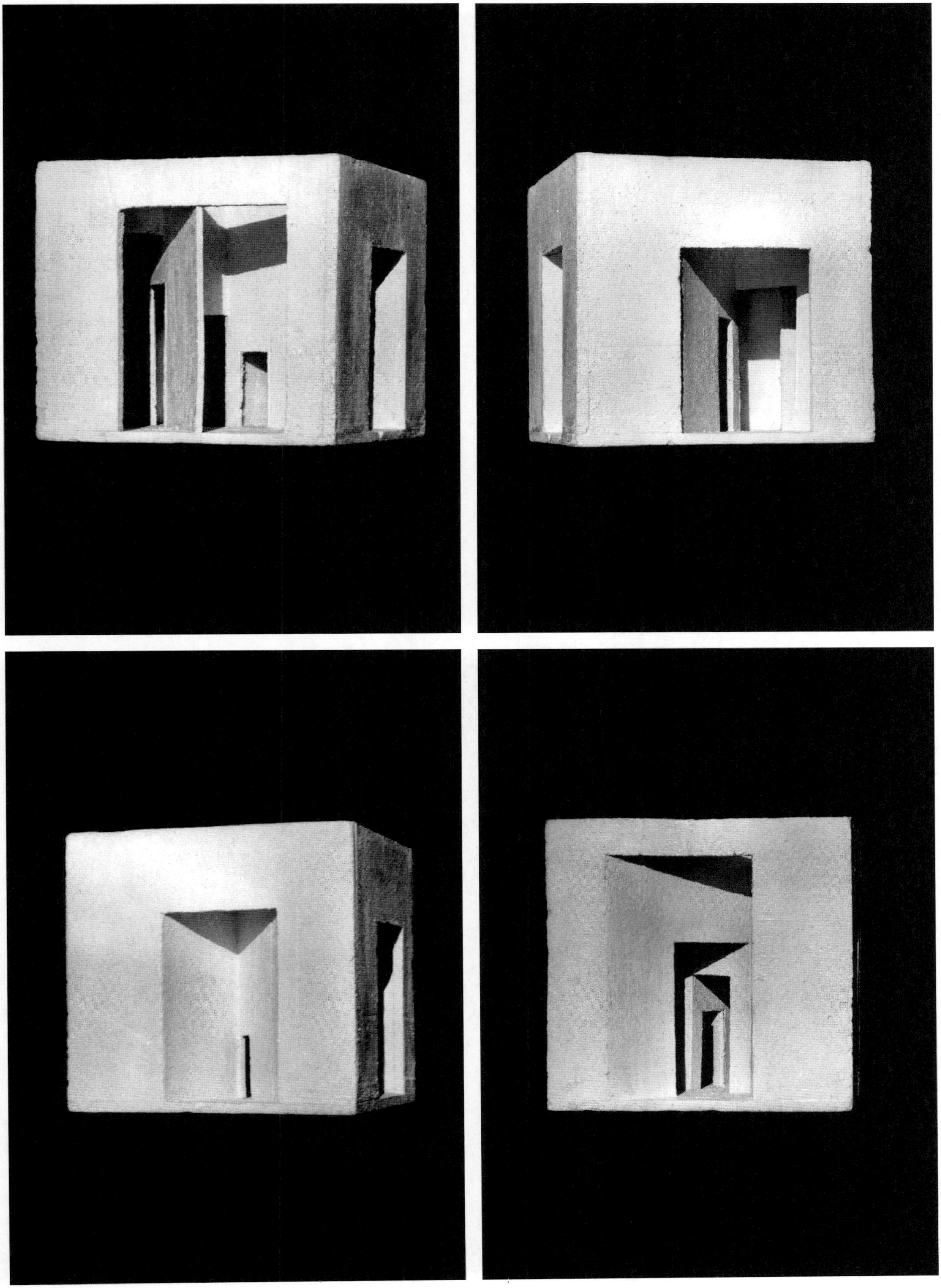

Foam, 100 × 100 × 100 cm (see *Mirrored Labyrinth*, p. 237)

1972 UNTITLED

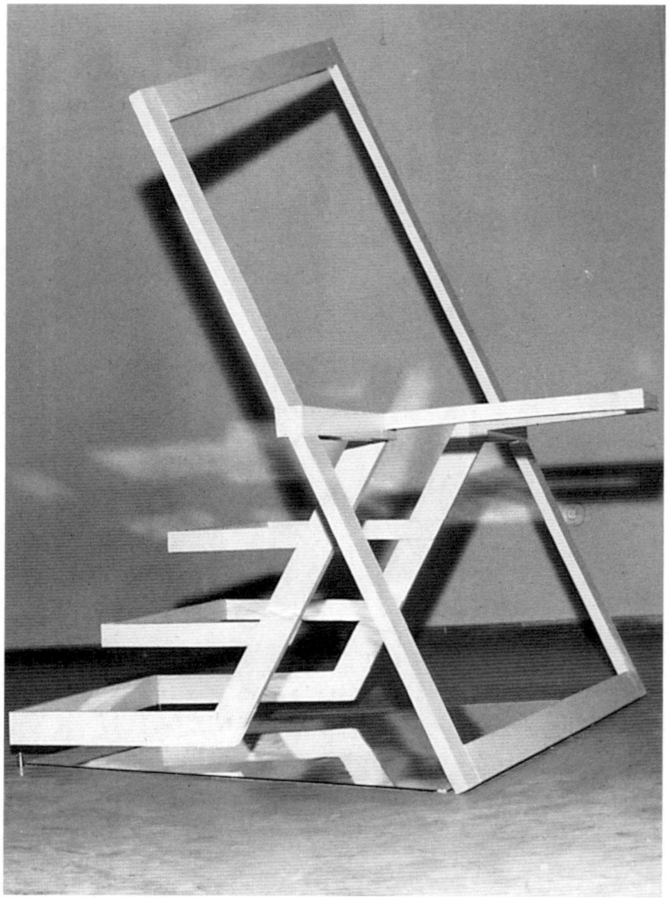

1972 UNTITLED

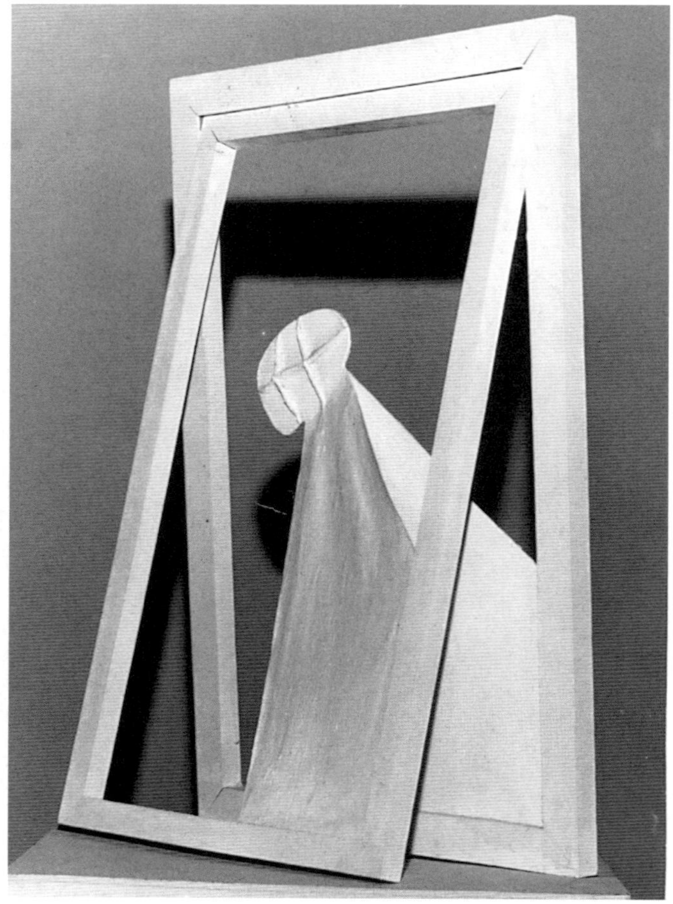

(Left) Wood, mirror, paint, 155 × 125 cm
(Right) Wood, paint, canvas, 75 × 50 cm

1972 UNTITLED

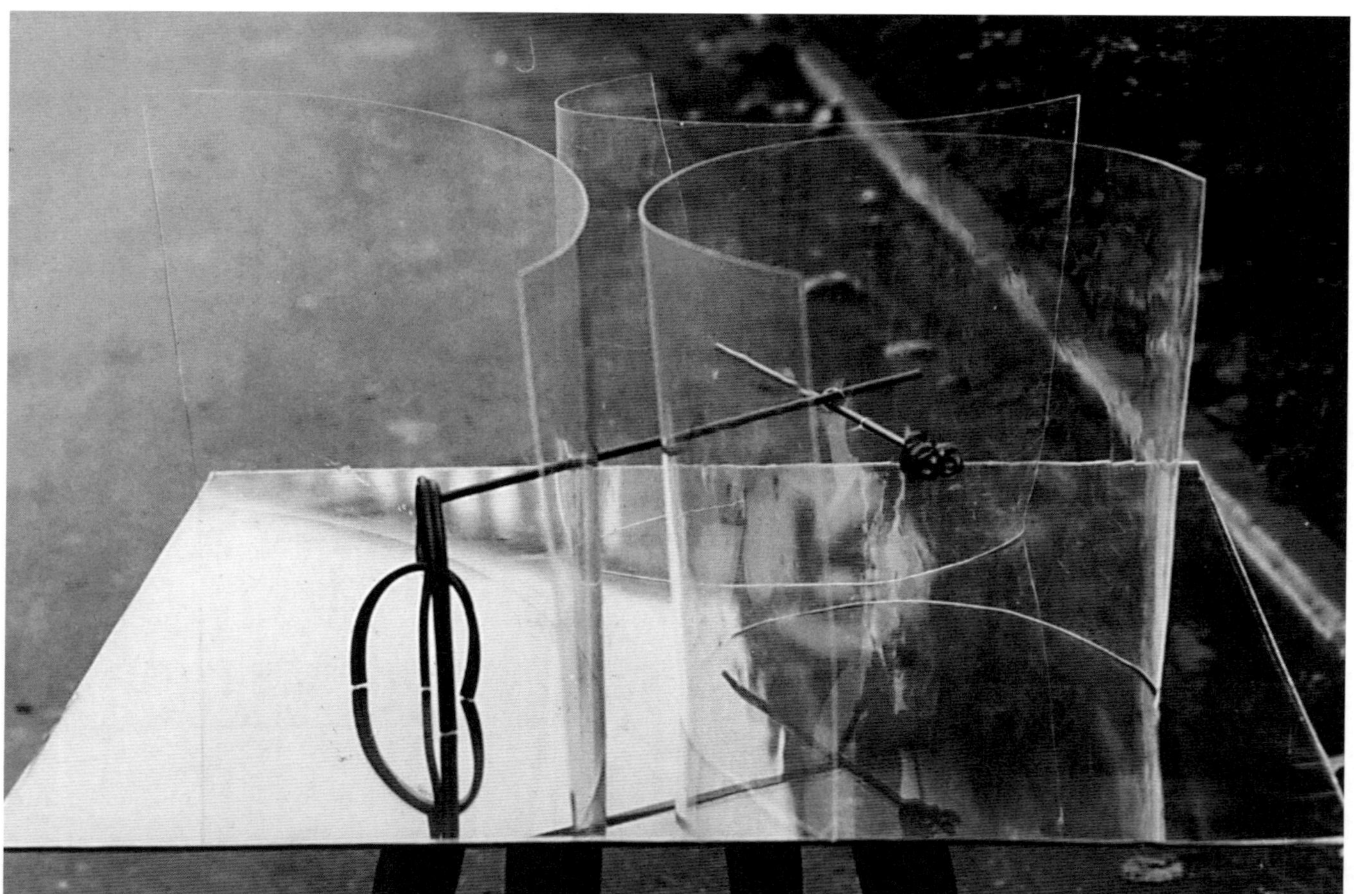

Plexiglas, 100 × 80 cm

Nude
by Chus Martínez

Nude: a woman's body trapped in a box. Is it a cage, or rather a safe, where no one can touch her? Two mirrors project out strangely, reflecting the female nude. She is holding up her beautiful hair with her hands in a suggestive pose. She seems to be by herself, unaware of what is happening outside. Wait! Her body is sectioned into three parts. Her legs, her torso, her head appear like fragments of a body. Who cut her up? Is it painful? Is she aware? It is maybe our gaze that is the issue. We might not be ready to see her body as she does, at ease, absorbed in her morning rituals, coming to terms with the day ahead… Yes, we are outside of her world. She is innocent. We are not. Our mental habits so deeply affect our social behaviour, our perception of gender, that we hurt the body with our thoughts. Luckily she doesn't seem to know. She is a doll. Or is she? She seems to be real, a real woman, a youthful being, coming to life. Her calmness says: no context is inescapable, it only seems so in a moment of history, from the outside of innocence, but this box speaks about a secret, the secret hope it holds.

1974 NUDE

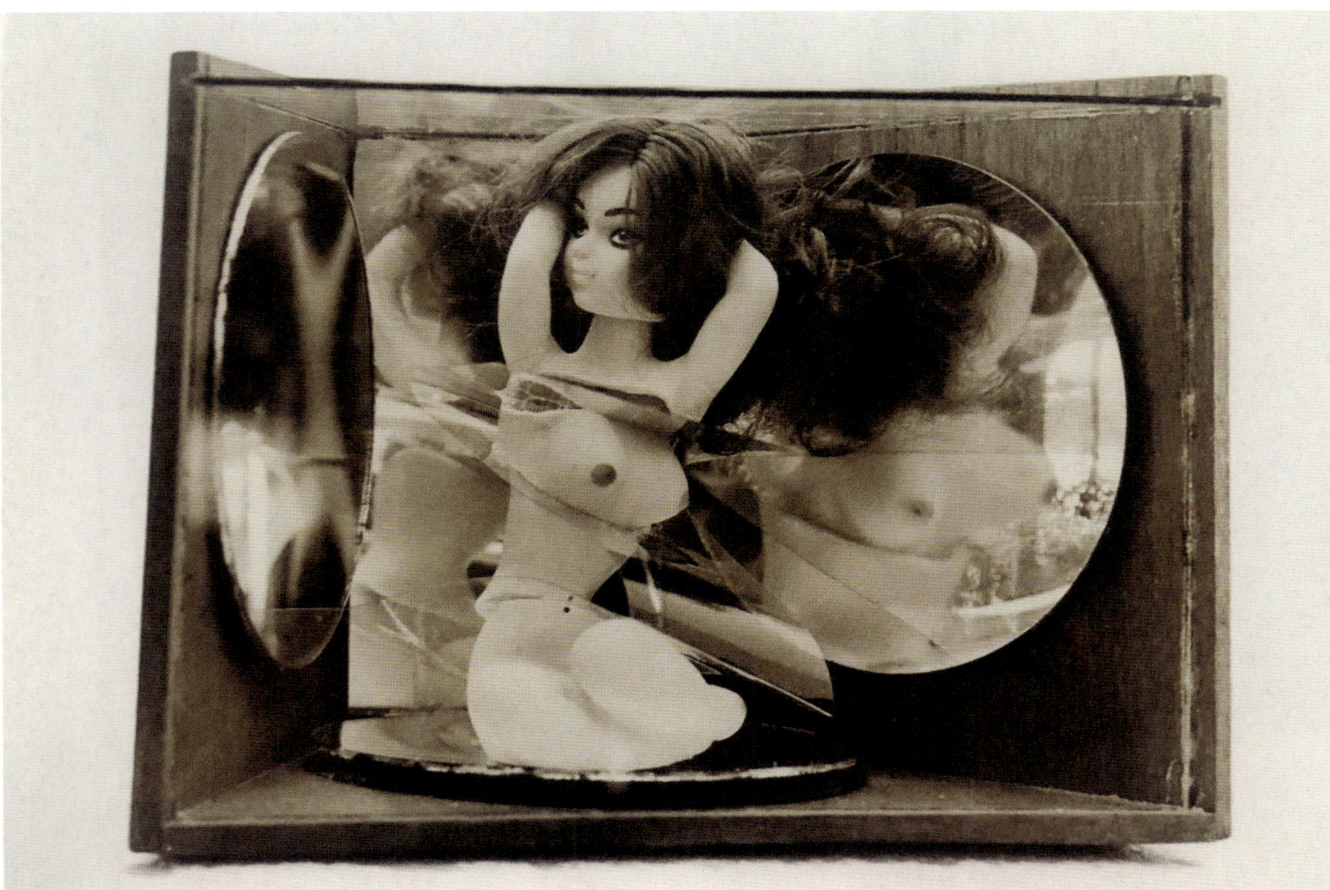

Wood, glass, mirror, doll, 20 × 30 × 15 cm

1974 UNTITLED

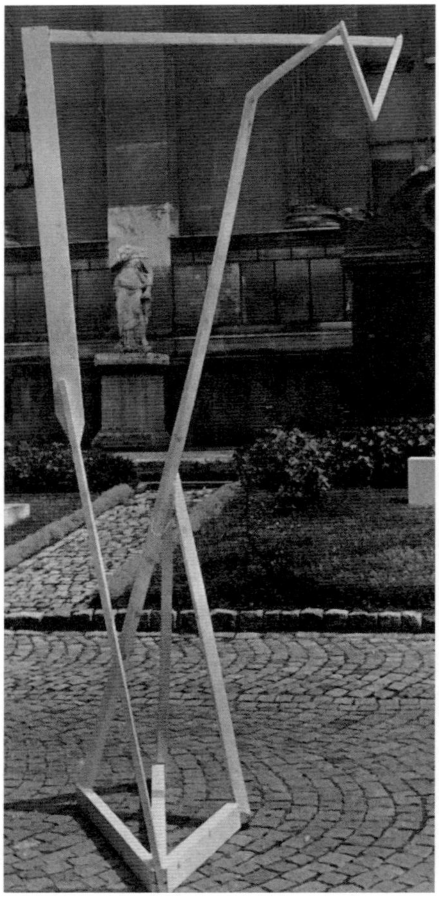

1974 UNTITLED

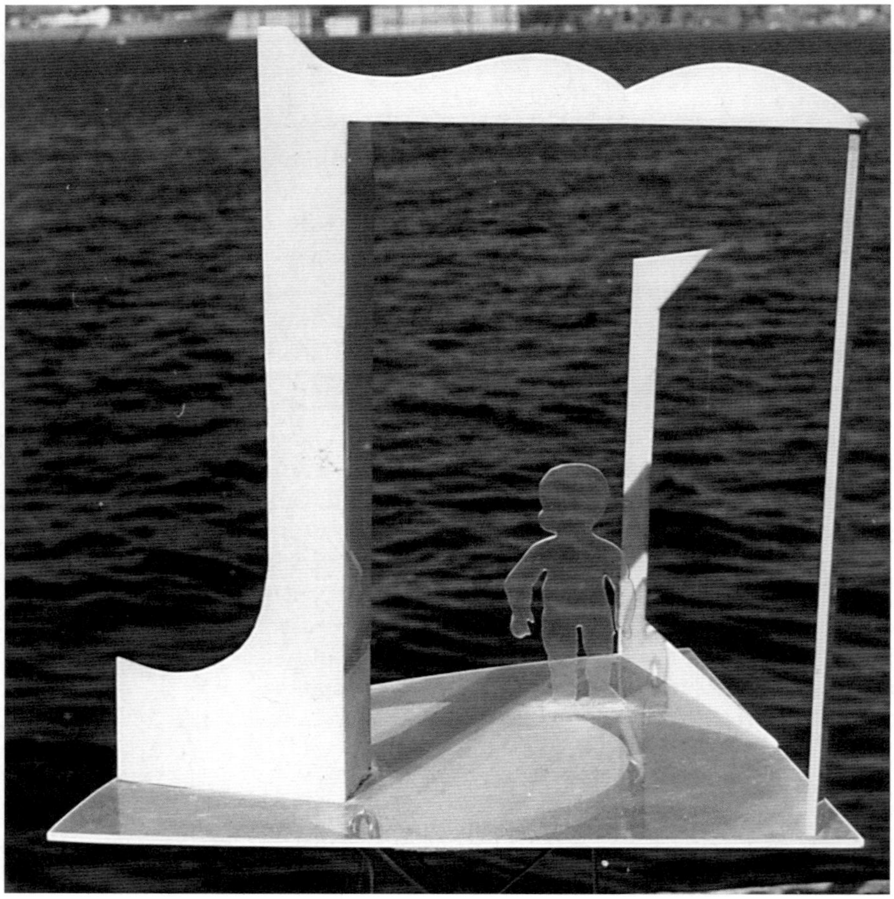

(Left) Wood, 300 × 110 cm
(Right) Plexiglas, 50 × 50 × 30 cm

1974 UNTITLED

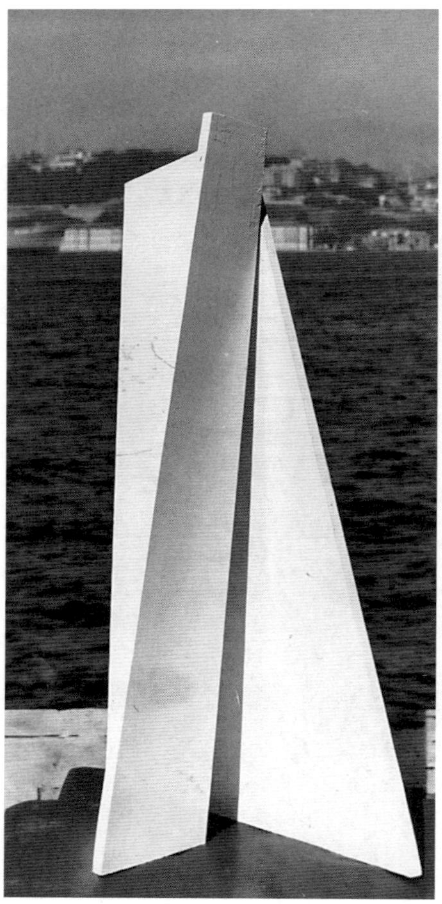

1974 UNTITLED

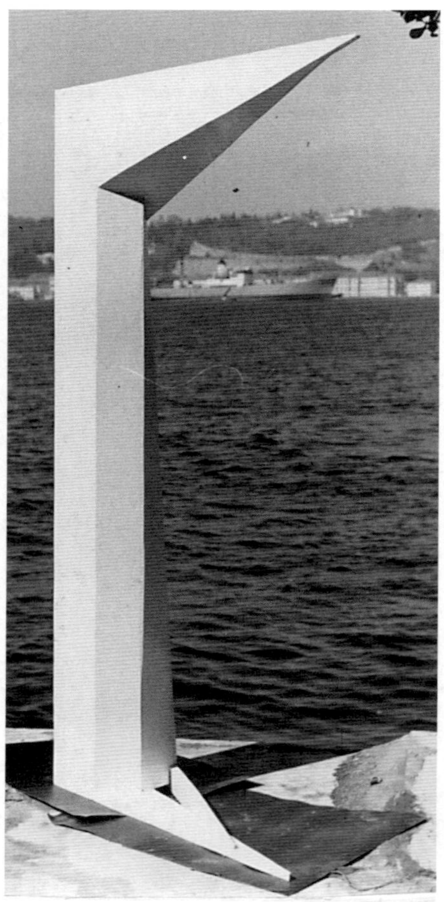

1974 UNTITLED

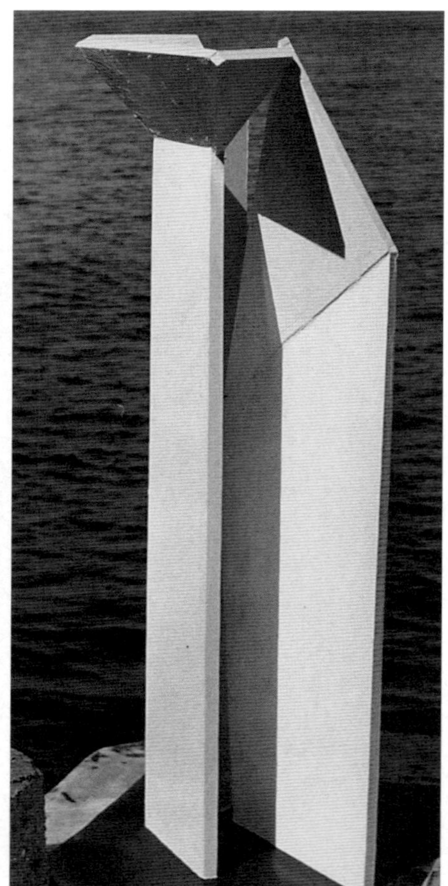

(Left) Wood, paint, 96 × 52 × 40 cm
(Center) Wood, paint, 160 × 70 × 20 cm
(Right) Wood, 108 × 45 cm

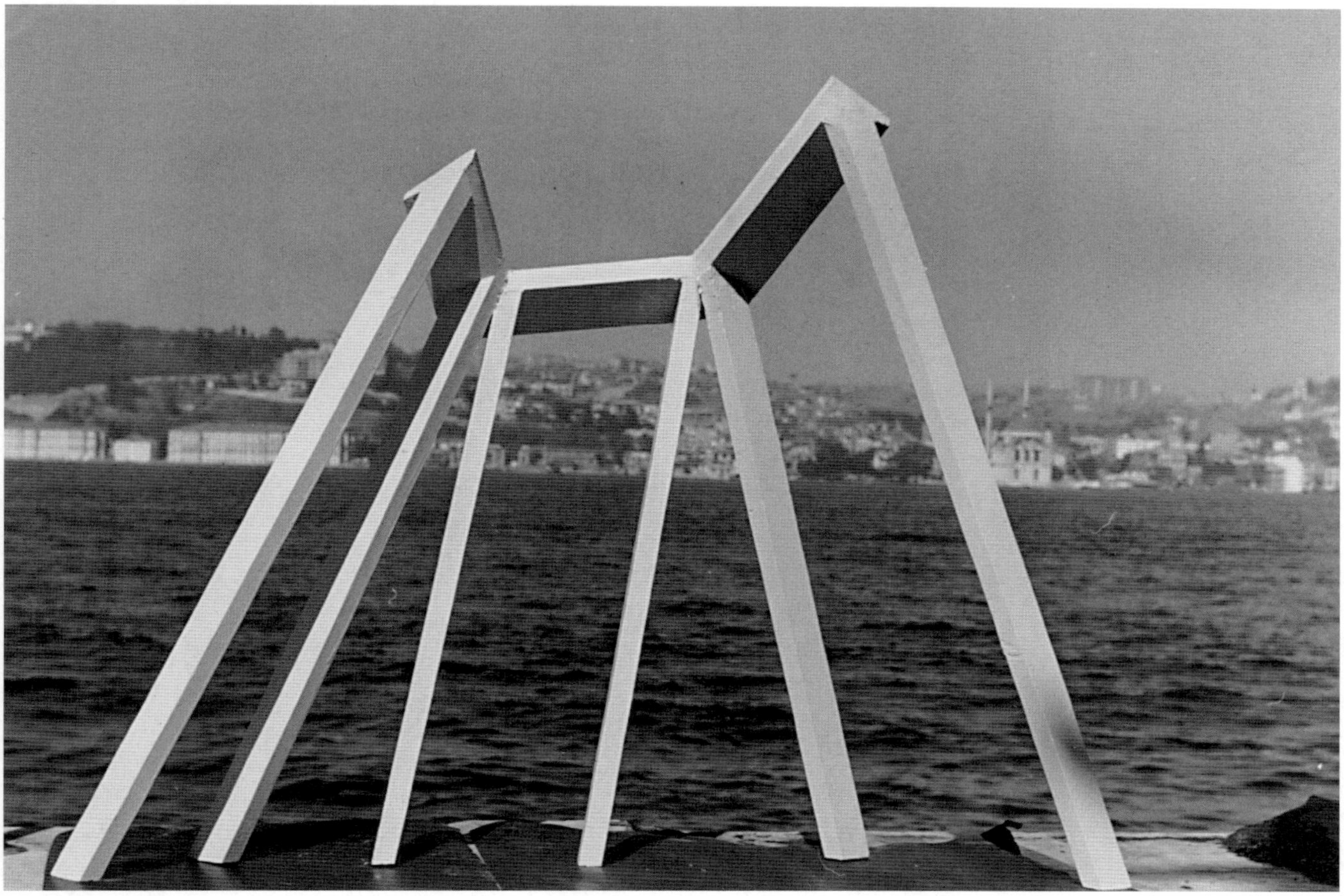

Wood, 87 × 112 × 27 cm

1974 UNTITLED

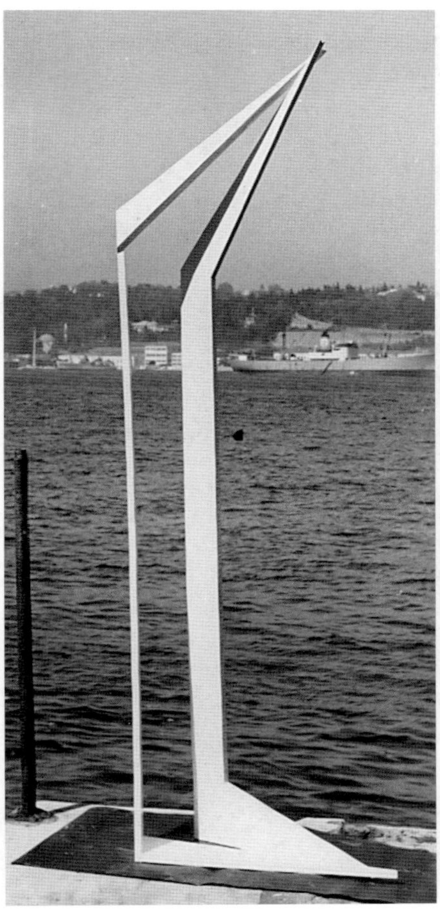

1974 UNTITLED

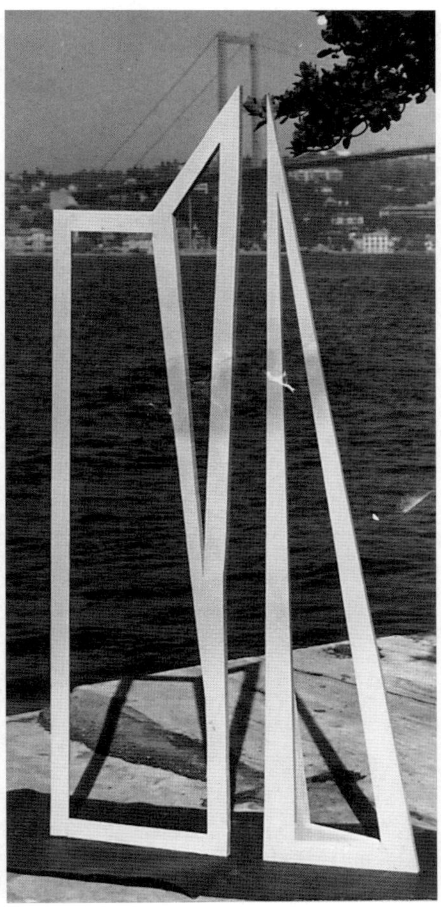

1974 UNTITLED

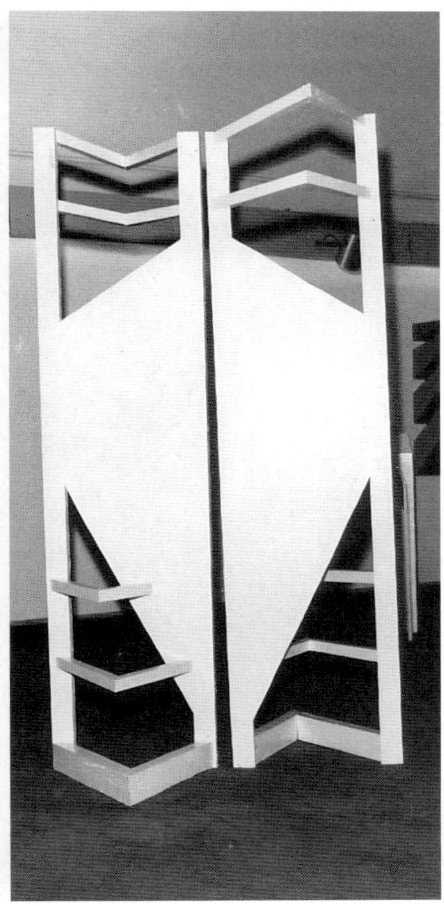

(Left) Wood, 190 × 65 cm
(Center) Wood, 160 × 80 cm
(Right) Wood, 204 × 97 × 53 cm

1974 UNTITLED

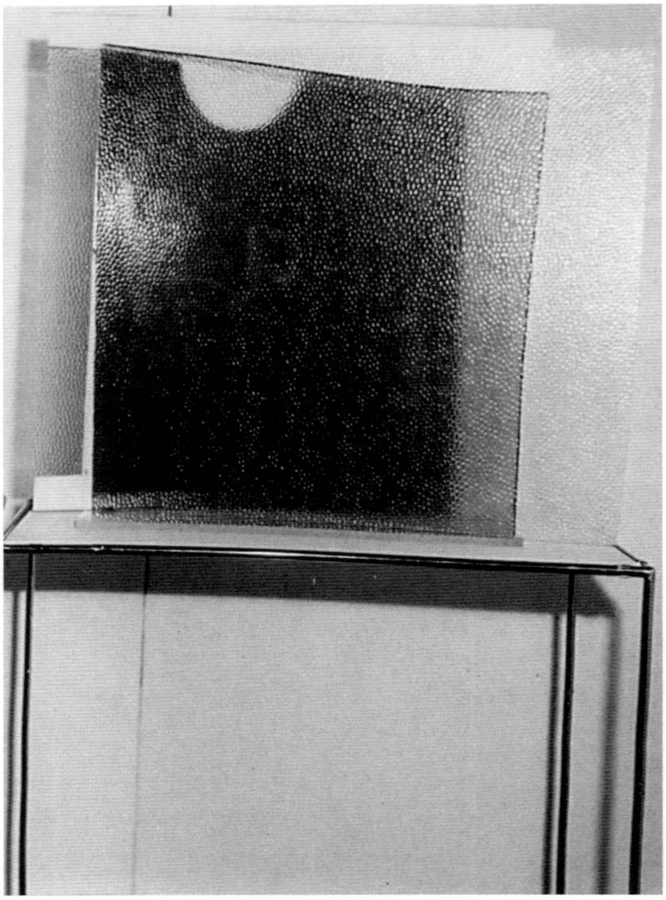

1974 UNTITLED

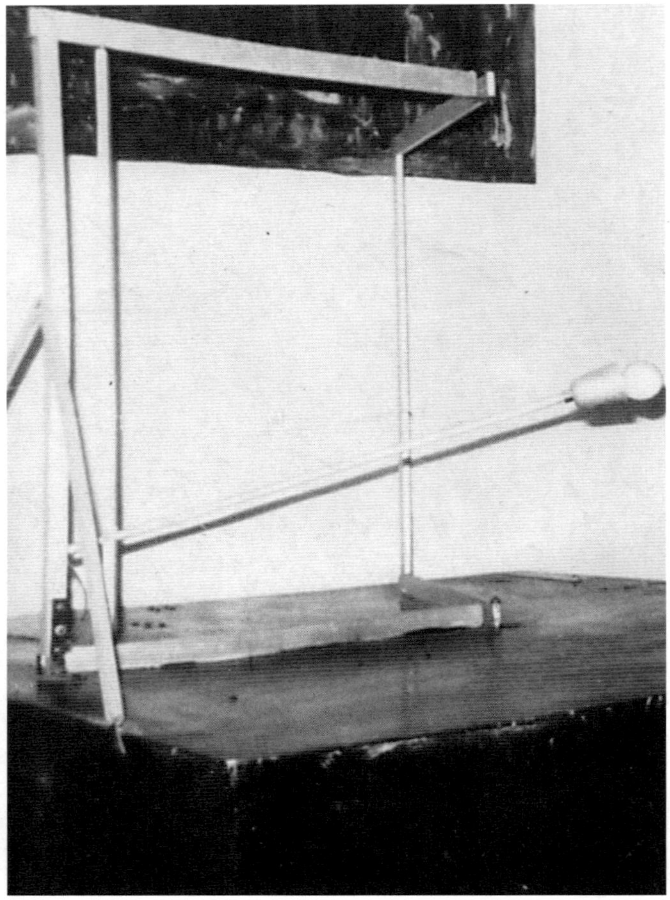

(Left) Plexiglas, 50 × 50 × 40 cm
(Right) Mobile and lighted sculpture, aluminum, 50 × 100 cm

1974 UNTITLED

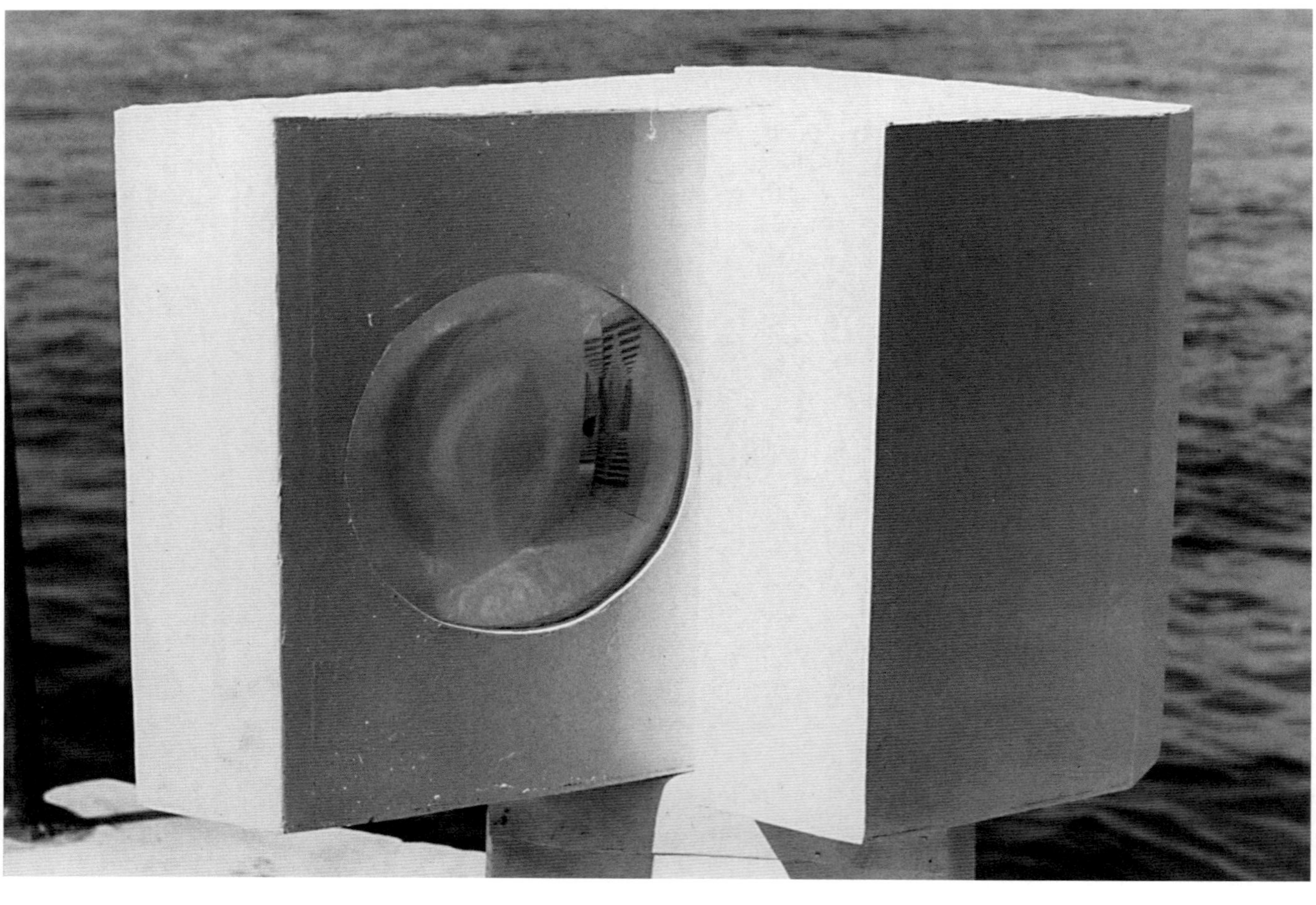

Wood, Plexiglas, 70 × 52 cm

1975 TREE WITH SEED

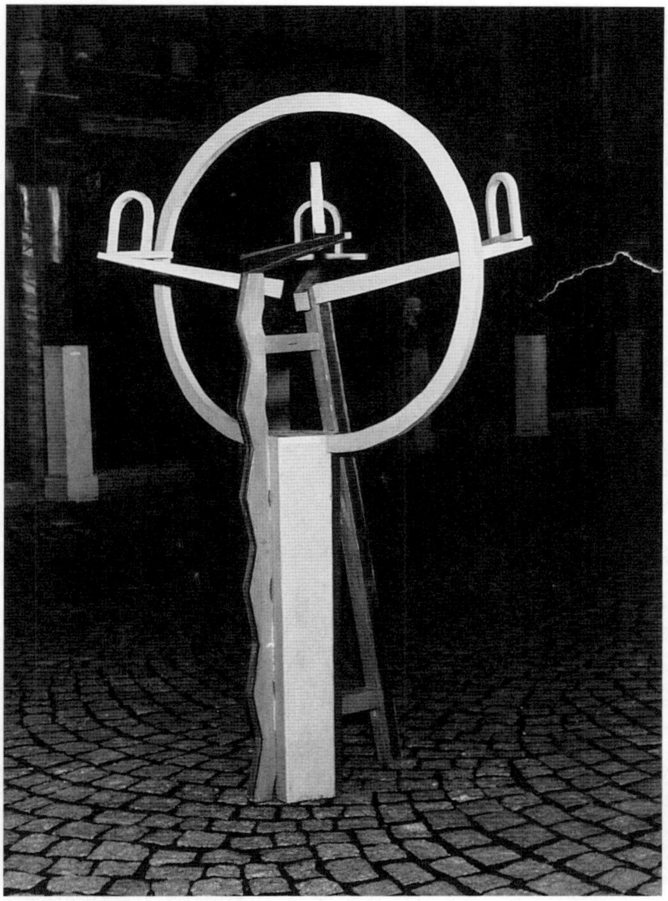

1975 UNTITLED

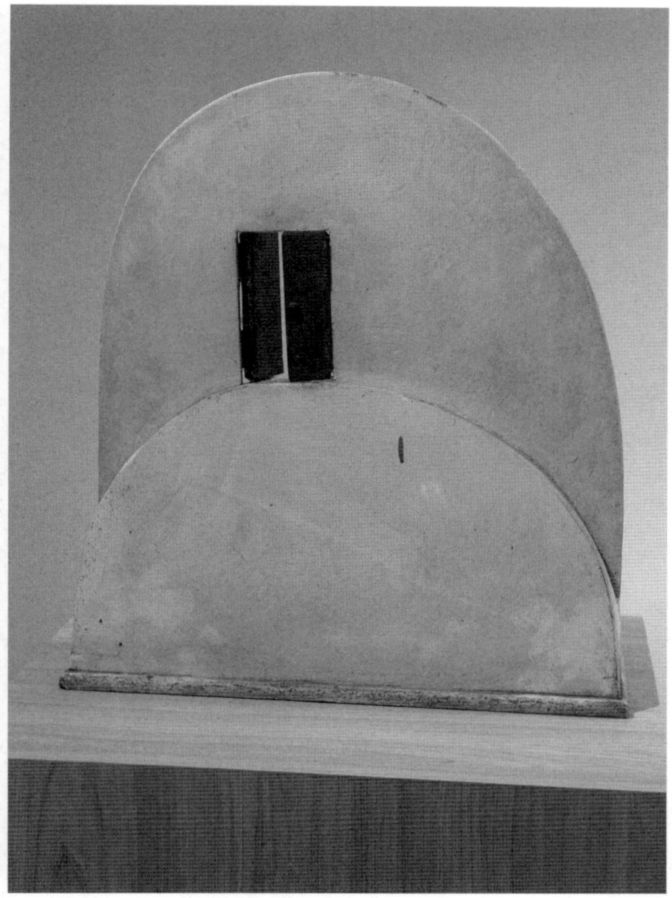

(Left) Wood, brass, 165 × 108 cm
(Right) Plaster, paint, 70 × 60 cm

1975 FREE COMPOSITION

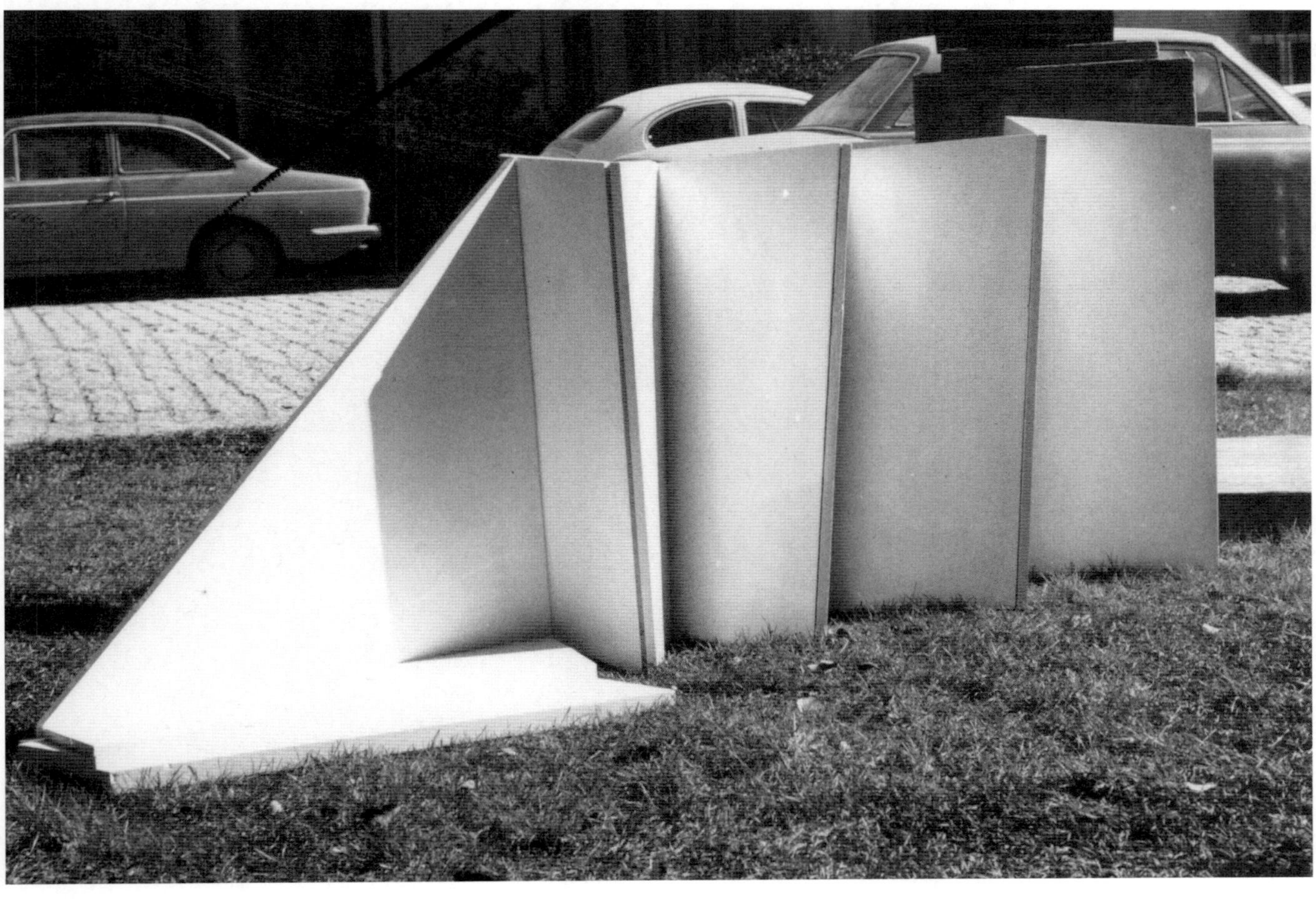

Wood, paint, 97 × 238 cm

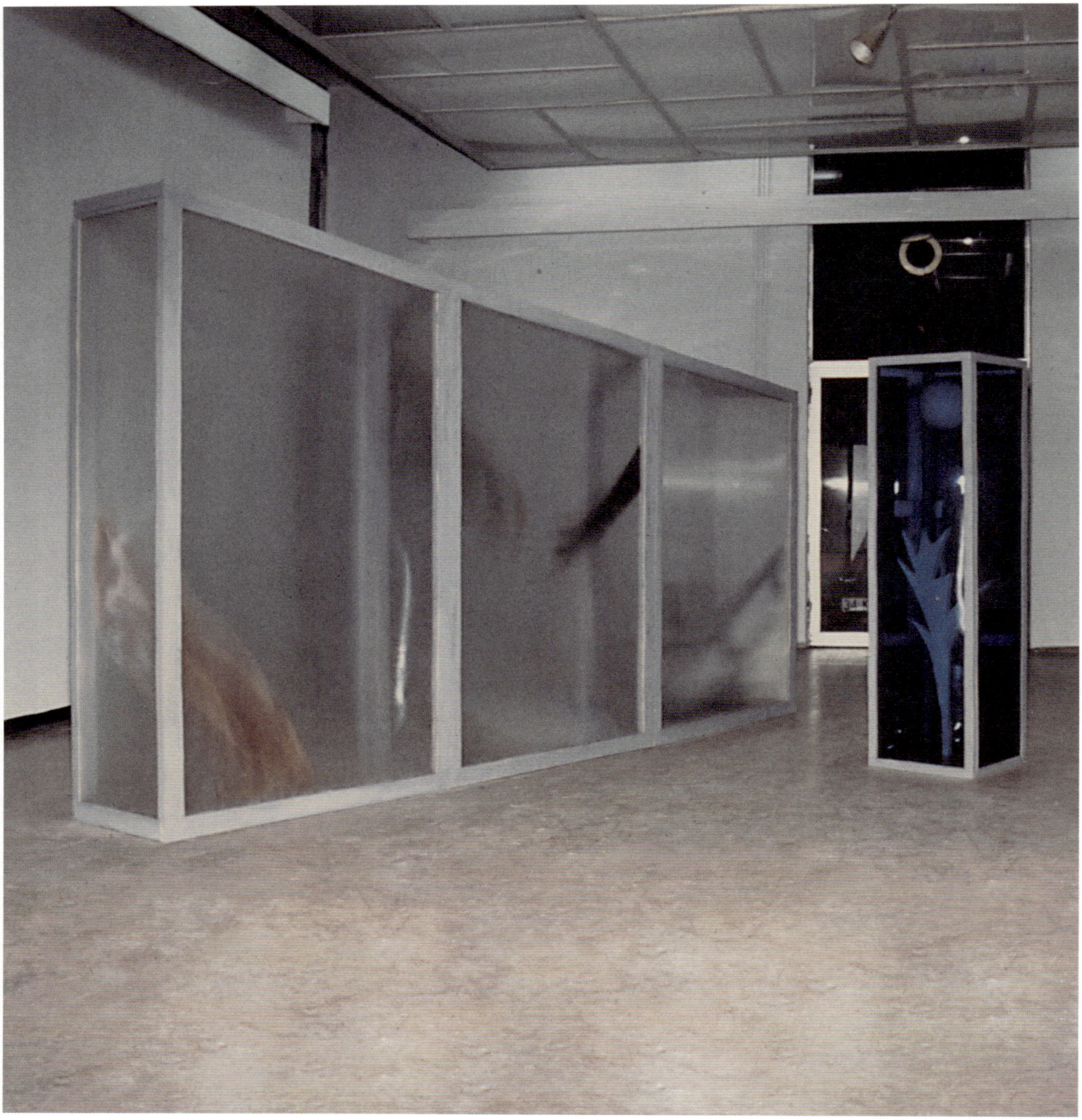

(Left) Plexiglas, wood, 385 × 200 × 50 cm
(Right) Wood, Plexiglas, styrofoam, 165 × 45 × 45 cm

Our valuable young sculptor exhibited two large sculptures at Taksim Art Gallery last month. This is the fourth exhibition she has held since her return from the States. Having brought us new views in the field of sculpture art, Onur conveys new and different forms in this exhibition. This time she displayed a more dashing, marvellous artistic persona. She has also incorporated transparency into her studies of space, which she accomplishes by doing justice to three dimensions and with a simplicity that is very difficult to capture in art. In the present day and age, when our sculpture art is only just beginning to emerge and is difficult to make head or tail of, especially such new views, Onur's honest exhibition of these objects rests on the power and courage of a true artist. This is also the sound foundation on which I ascribe the marvellous persona to her.

Güzin Fuat Okbay, 'Istanbul Exhibitions,' *Ankara Sanat*, January 1976, Issue 117, p.14.

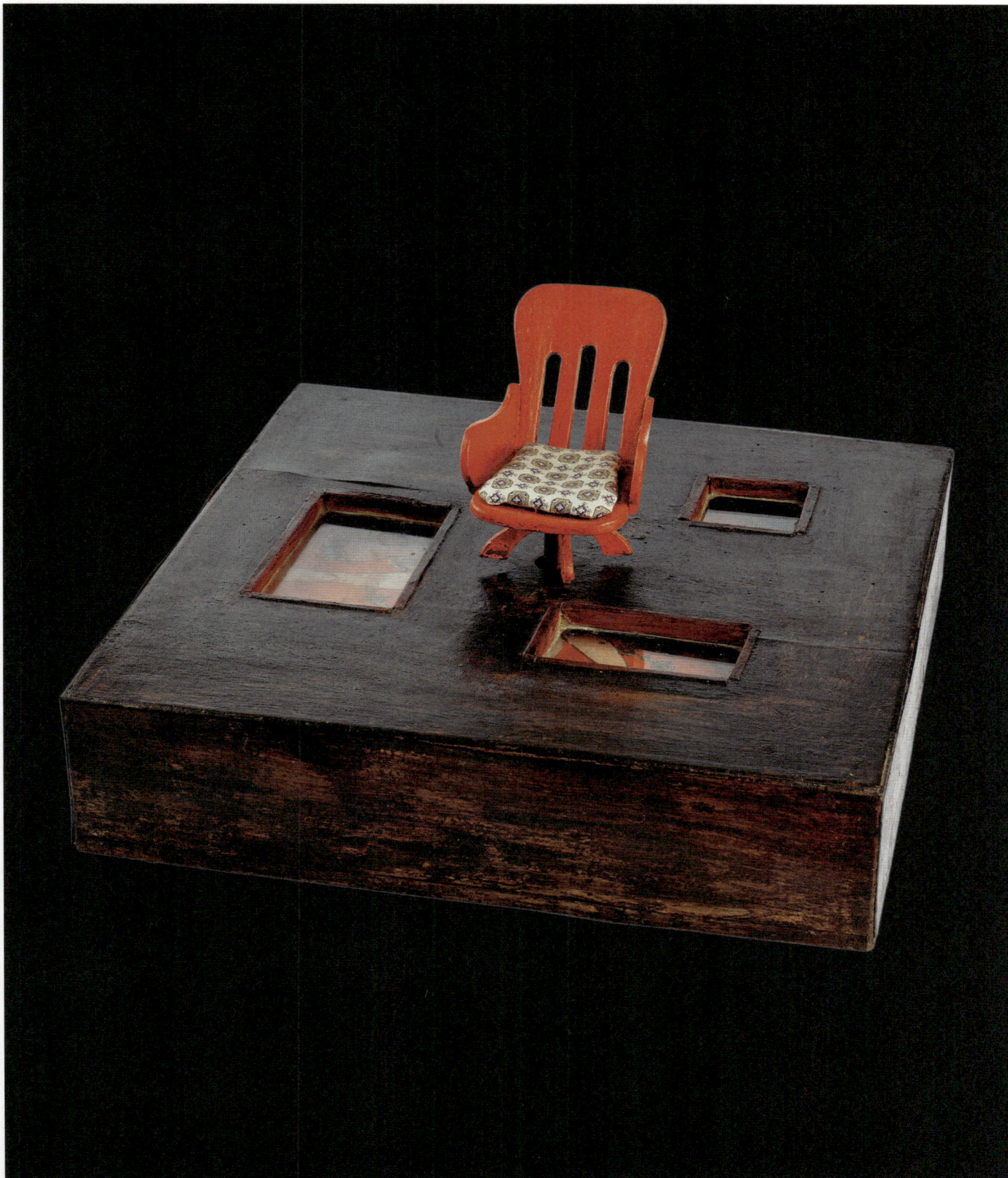

Mixed media, 40 × 40 × 20 cm

The focus of this piece is a bright red chair, set at a slightly off-kilter angle as though it has been tipped back and held just before the moment of falling. A music box mechanism can be used to turn the chair slowly. This reveals a painted plate underneath with a figure made out with watercolours, only parts of which can be viewed through small, square windows. The figure's limbs spin round in an unsupported free fall; suggesting a ghostly quality to the empty seat of the chair above.

Excerpt from the *Heartbreak* exhibition catalogue by RUYA MAPS, Venice, 2019.

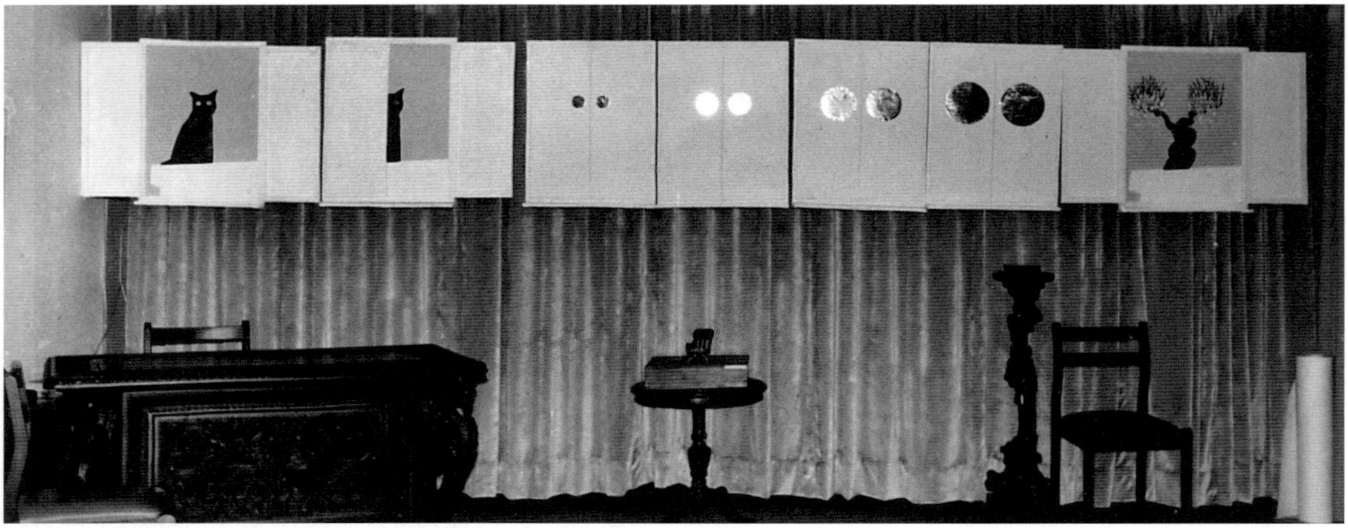

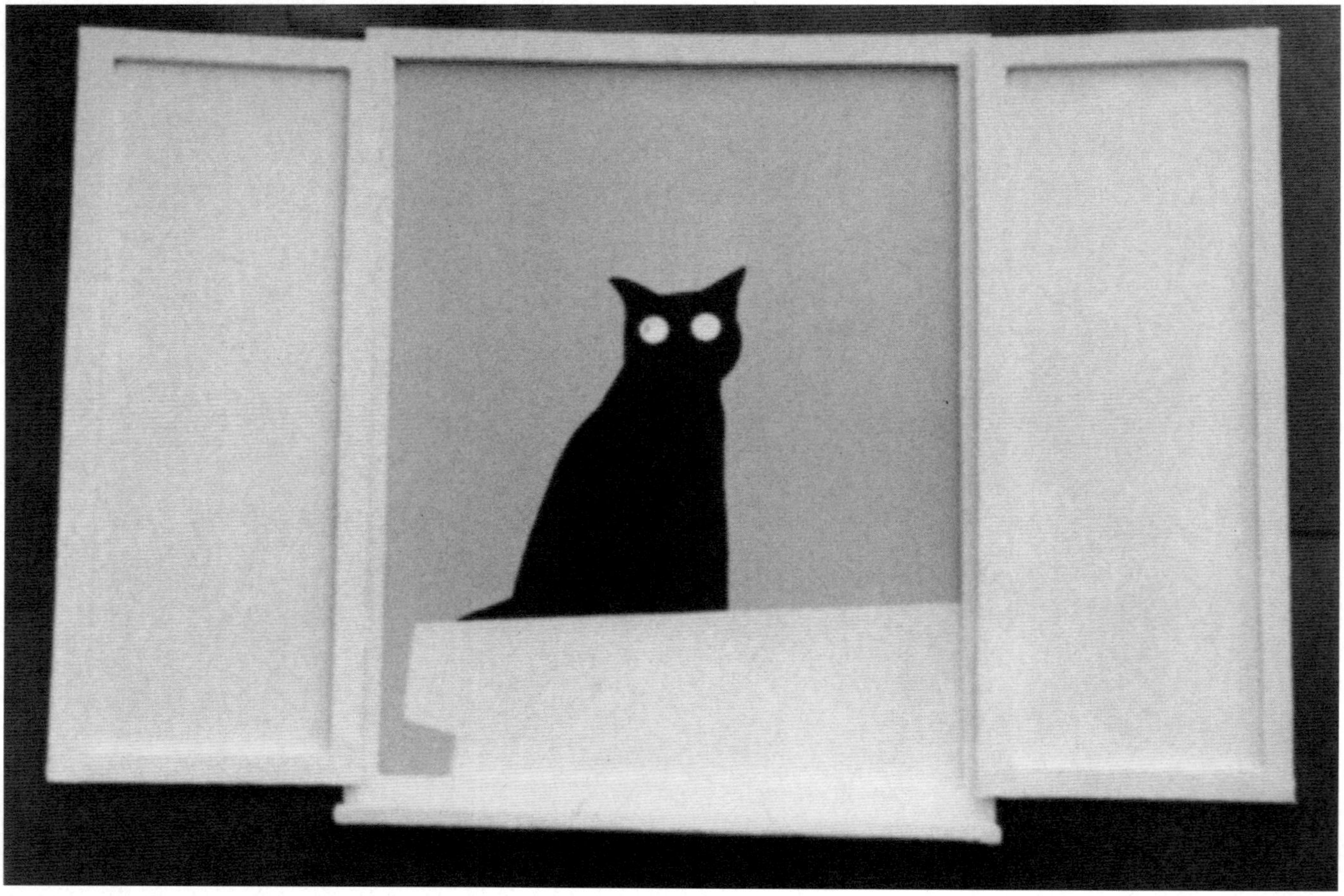

Wood, canvas, aluminum, 7 pieces, each 75 × 70 cm

I think 'electrifying' the audience as if struck by lightning in the face of the exhibited works is Onur's primary concern [...] The common essence of the declarations presented at the 'Symposium of Arts Toward the Year 2000' also underlined the fact that the art of our age is an explosion of 'Events' and 'Spiritualities' that do not fit into any traditional aesthetics or classification [...] Onur decries the attitude of our era's classical art and artists, and all the superficial, 'snobbish' behaviours that approach art without a conscious understanding. The figures, like 20,000, 25,000, on the greengrocer's price tags placed in gilded frames that she hung on empty wooden vegetable crates covered with cellophane are examples of this satire [...] No doubt, Onur is a young intellectual concerned with contemporary/realist thought [...] And therefore, instead of searching for very profound 'mysteries' in her exhibition, or dredging up 'judgements' at length, she appears before us with these simple, in a way tragi-comic satires. In a sort of manifesto/declaration that she added to her statement and also put in her exhibition, Onur talks about 'SIGNS.' She touches upon this problem of 'SIGNS' in her works, which comprise seven pieces, and in a cat story that she calls *From Outside In From Inside Out*. In her aforementioned declaration she says, 'animals abide by signs by force of their nature...' and adds, 'humans too run after signs all day long and abide by them.' I guess the artist is conflicted on this point [...] But Onur is interesting. I believe that she will present us with increasingly more interesting and consistent exploits.

O. Zeki Çakaloz, excerpt from 'Three Exhibitions at Taksim Art Gallery,' *Cumhuriyet*, 14 February 1978.

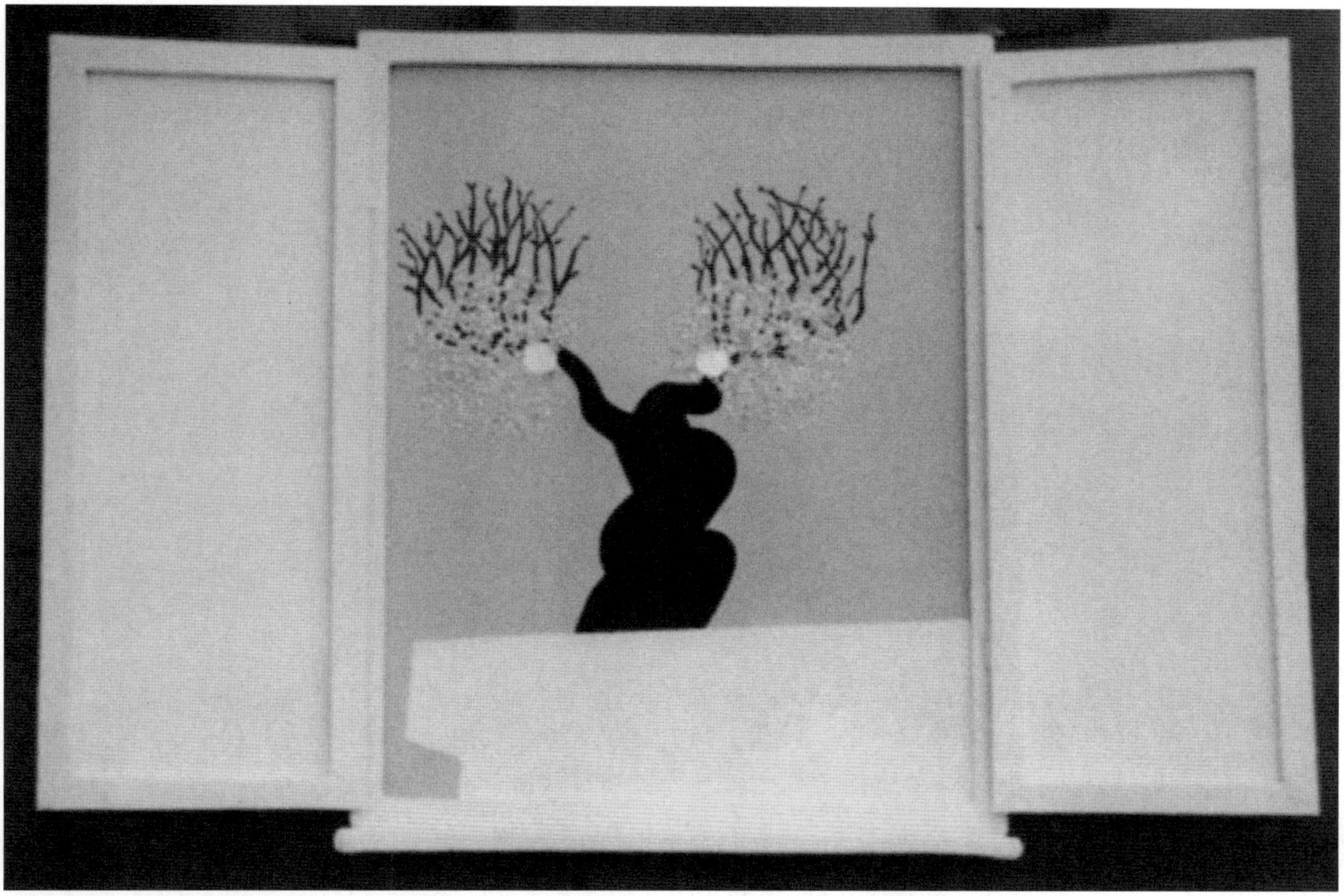

1978 FROM OUTSIDE IN FROM INSIDE OUT II

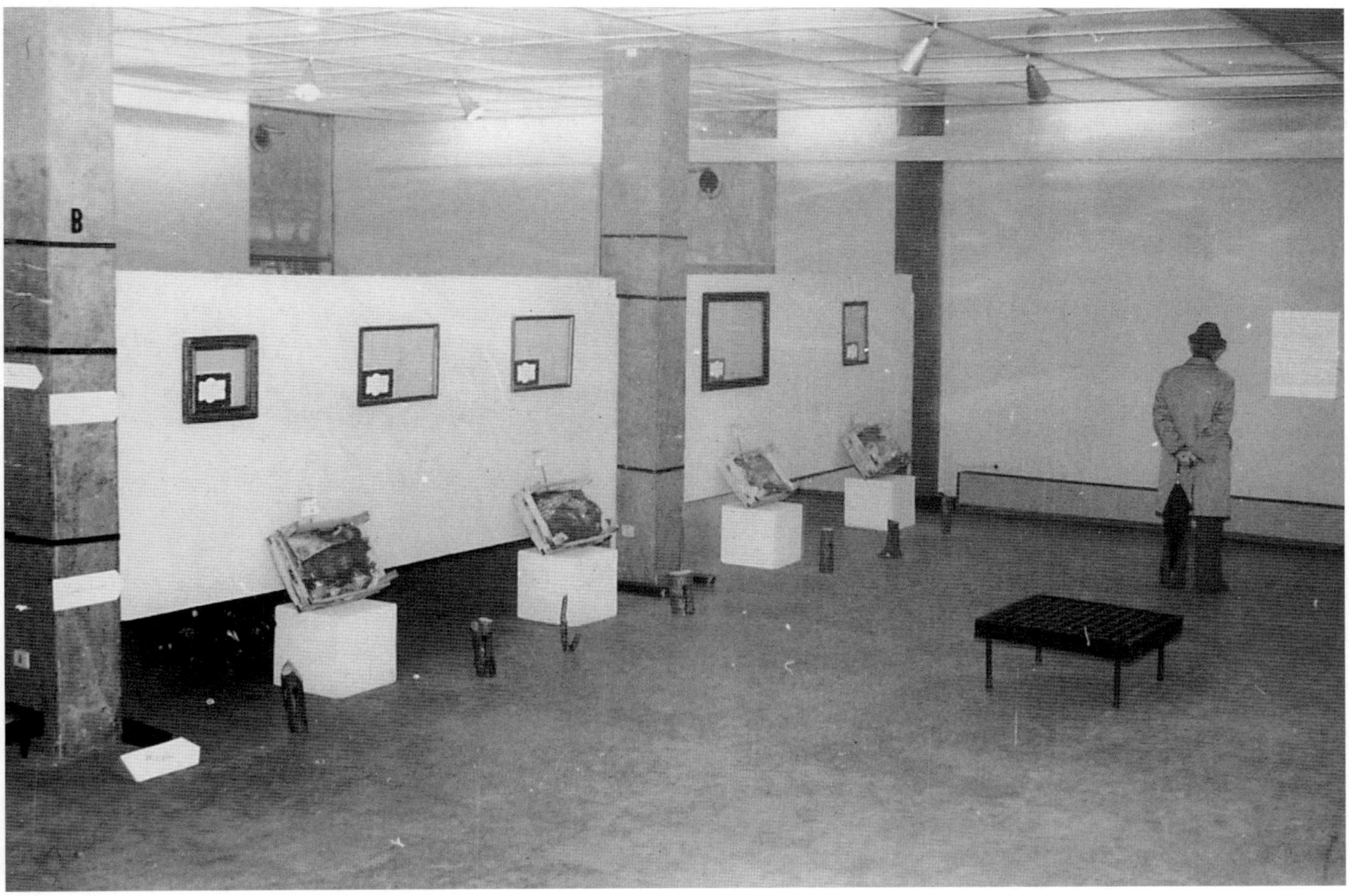

Mixed media installation, variable dimensions

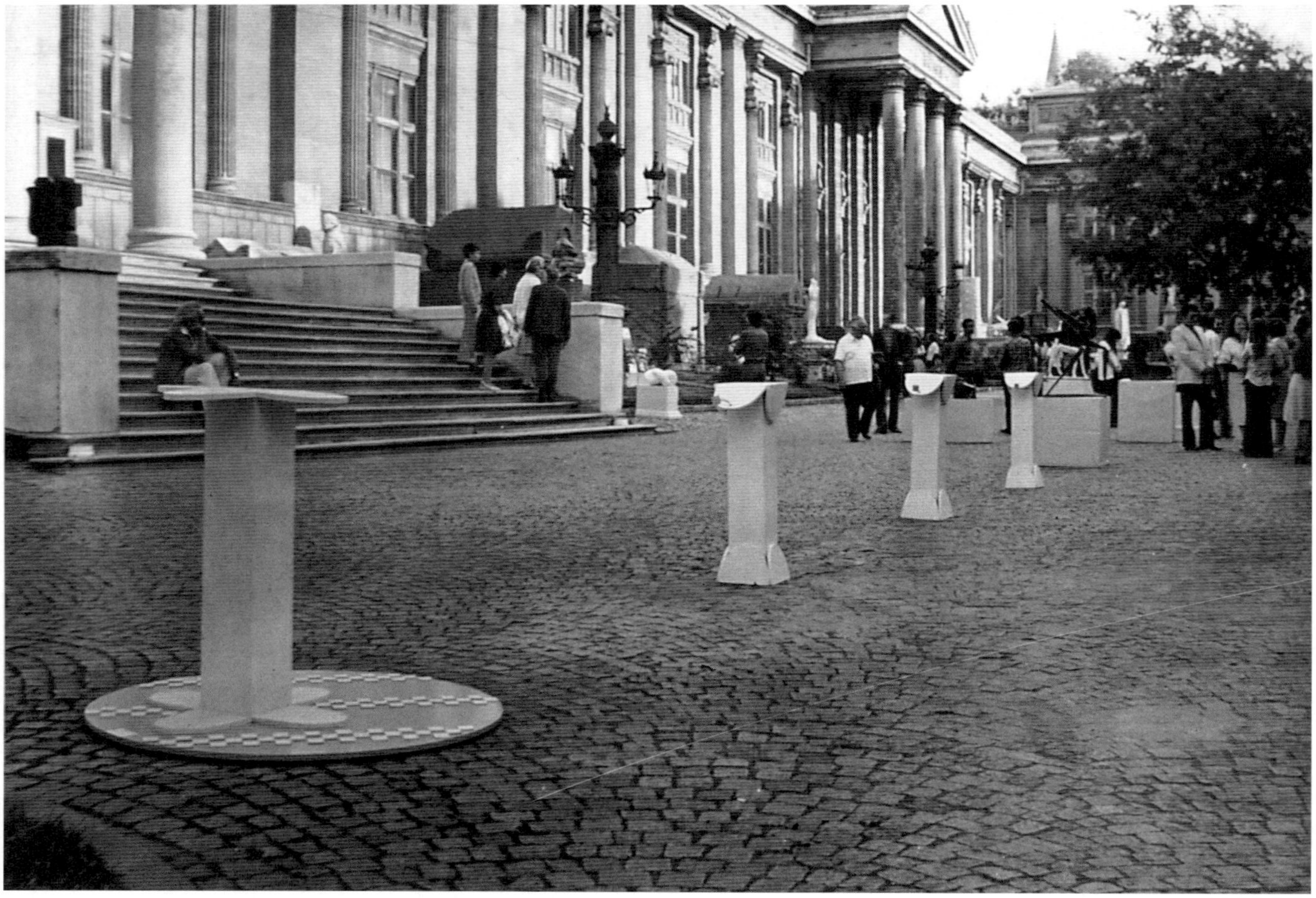

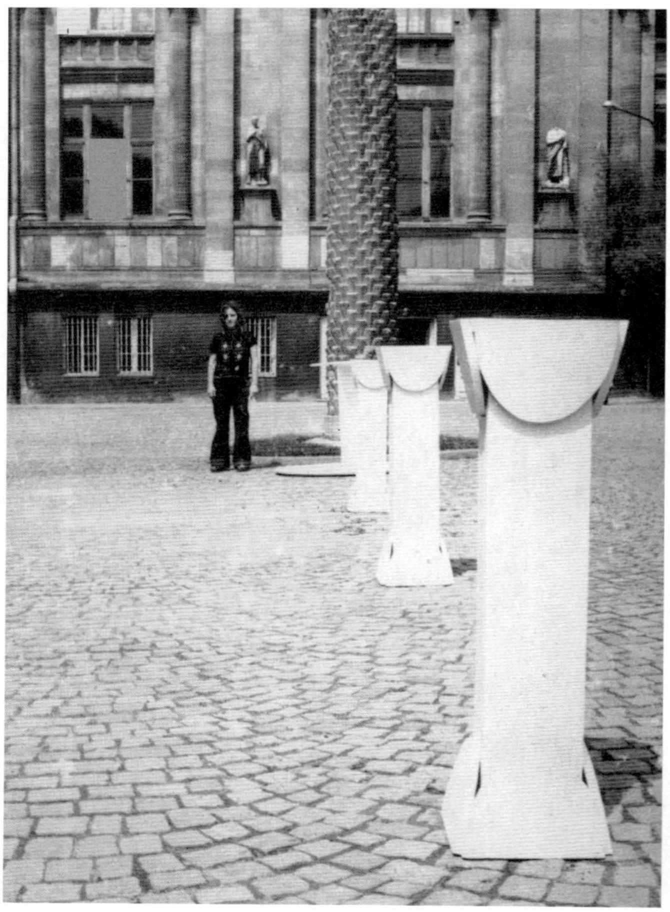

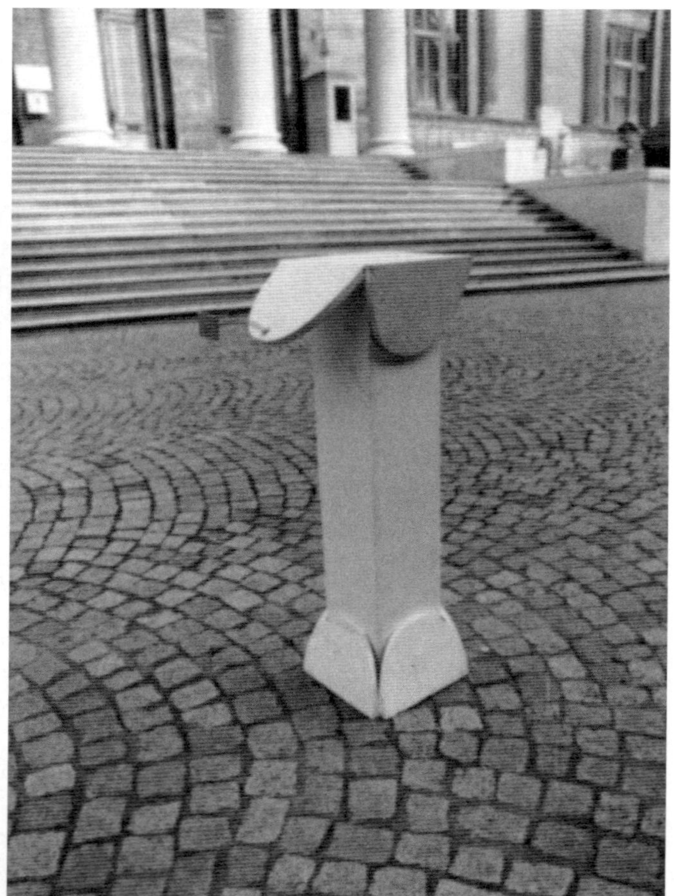

Wood, paint, wire, variable dimensions

Füsun Onur's *Untitled* was created for the 1977 Open Air Exhibition at Istanbul Archaeology Museums. Acting as a kind of intervention in the grounds of the museum, the work responded not to historic contexts or narratives but rather to the physical nature of the site itself. Using pieces of sandstone and earth, Onur emulated the patterns of the pathway, creating a 'surface on a surface' – in essence, another version of that reality. An embedded plant disrupted the layer of stones, its shape from certain perspectives resembling a small figure: an unlikely protagonist in balletic pose. As an ephemeral element of organic life whose form would inevitably change and deteriorate, its presence also introduced the dimension of time. An antique gilt frame defined the border of this composition, communicating that it *was* an artwork. Yet in being viewed from above, it created an experience of looking that was far from the typical gaze at artworks on a museum or gallery wall. This was a construction that was clearly artificial: art, life and nature co-existed in this poetic, playful gesture.

Untitled (1977) reflected Onur's increasing experimentation with forms in sculpture through her conceptual installations that began in the early to mid-1970s, as evidenced in the use of found or ready-made objects, and a shift away from more conventional sculptural materials. It also encapsulated elements of what would become key preoccupations for Onur in subsequent years, from her interest in the position of the viewer to her preoccupation with the relationship between image and frame, art and daily life, and the constructed and the real. As such, *Untitled* was a poignant precursor of what was to follow.

1977 UNTITLED

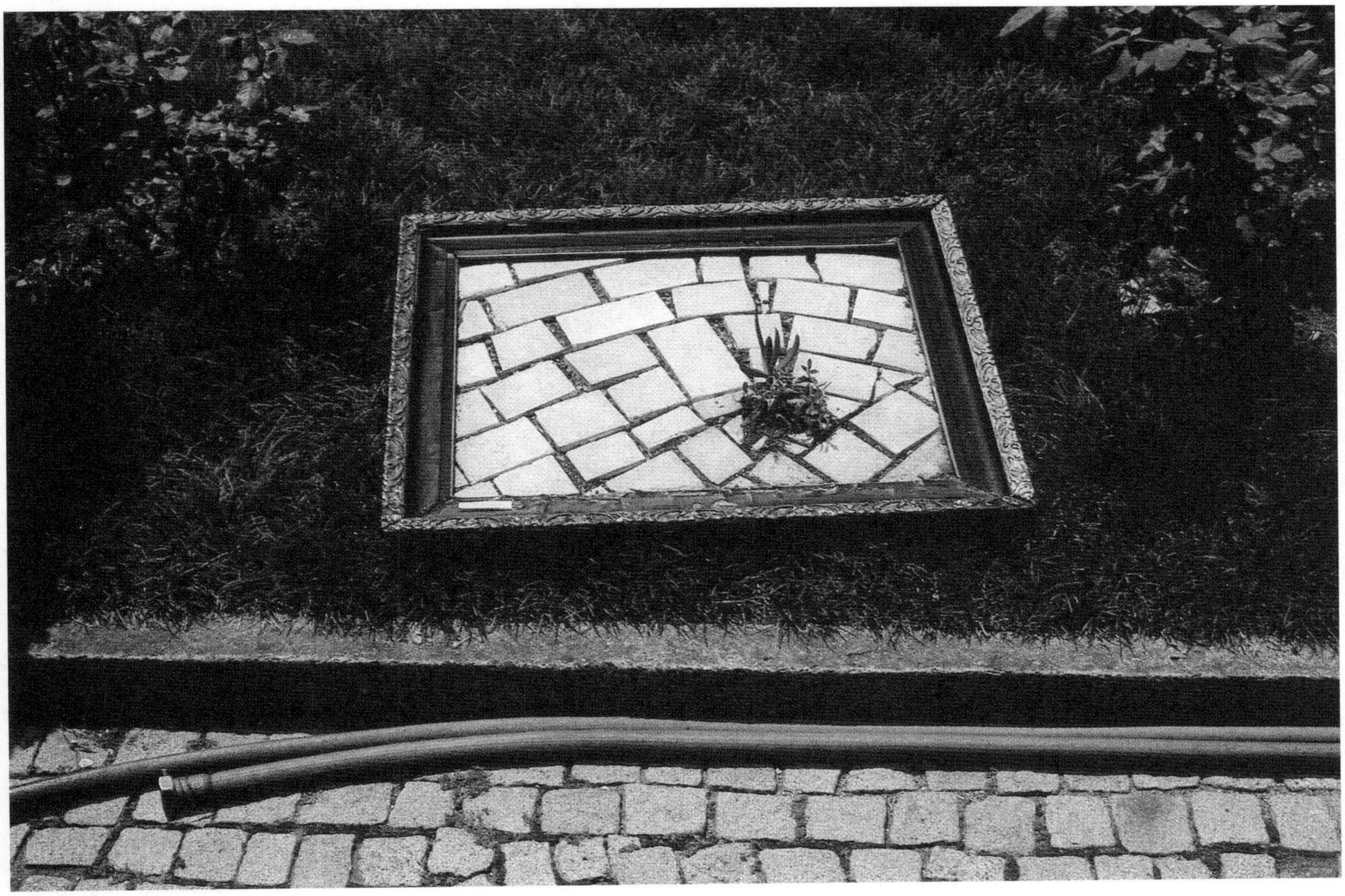

Stone, soil, flower, frame, 100 × 85 cm

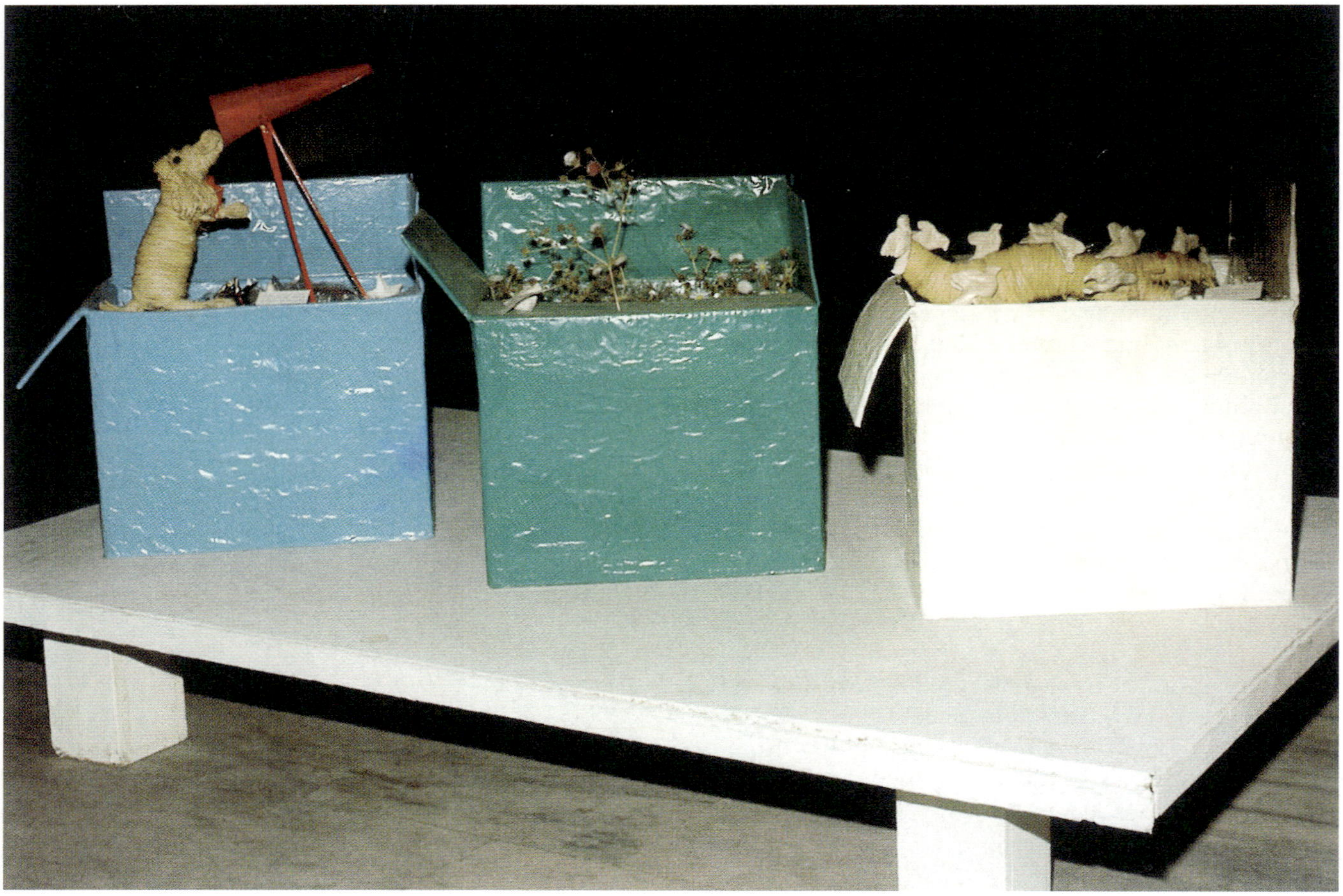

Cardboard, raffia, gilding, gelatin, each 60 × 60 cm

1978 BECAUSE YOU SAID BREAD AND APPLE I REMEMBER

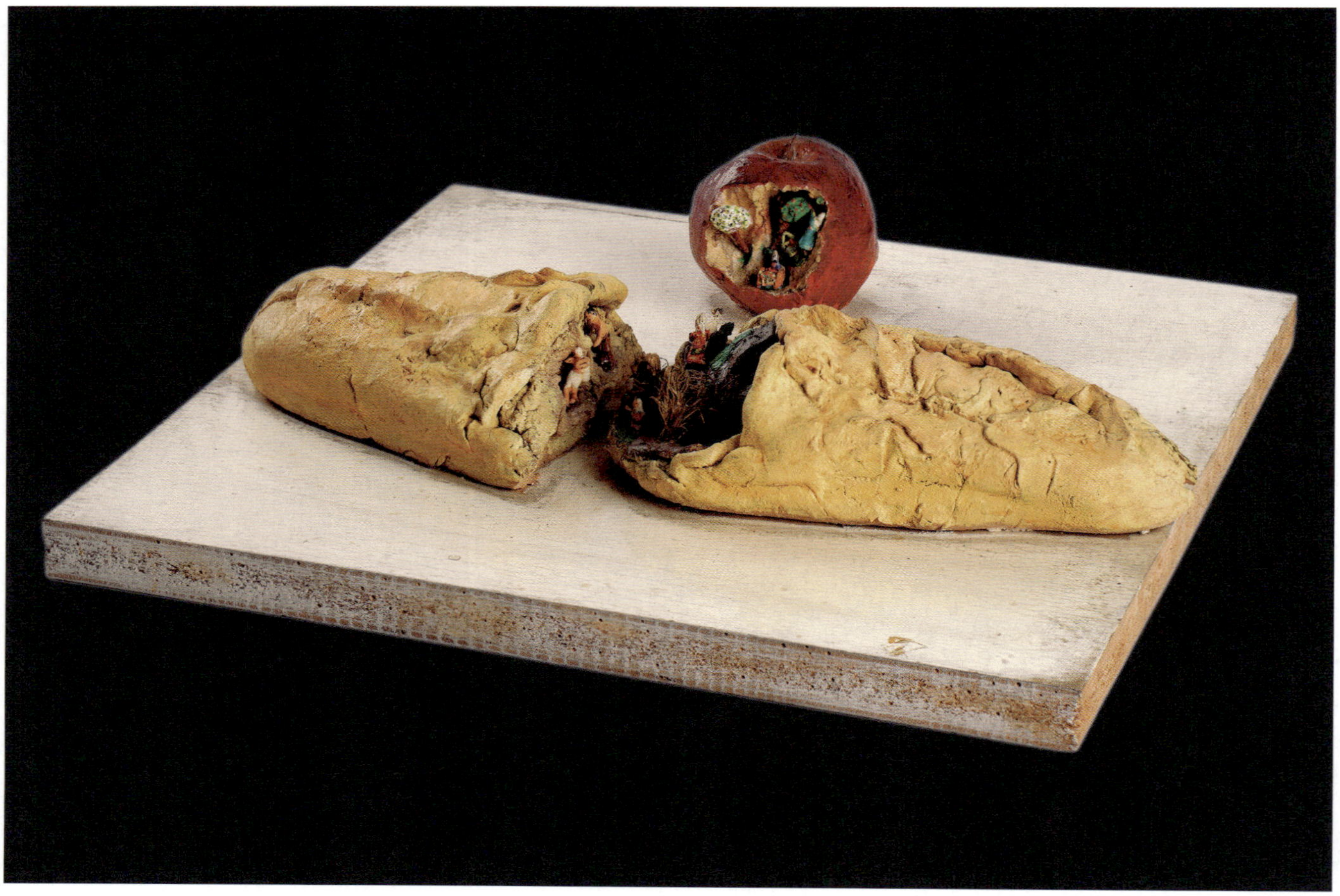

Wood, ceramic, 45 × 45 × 11,5 cm

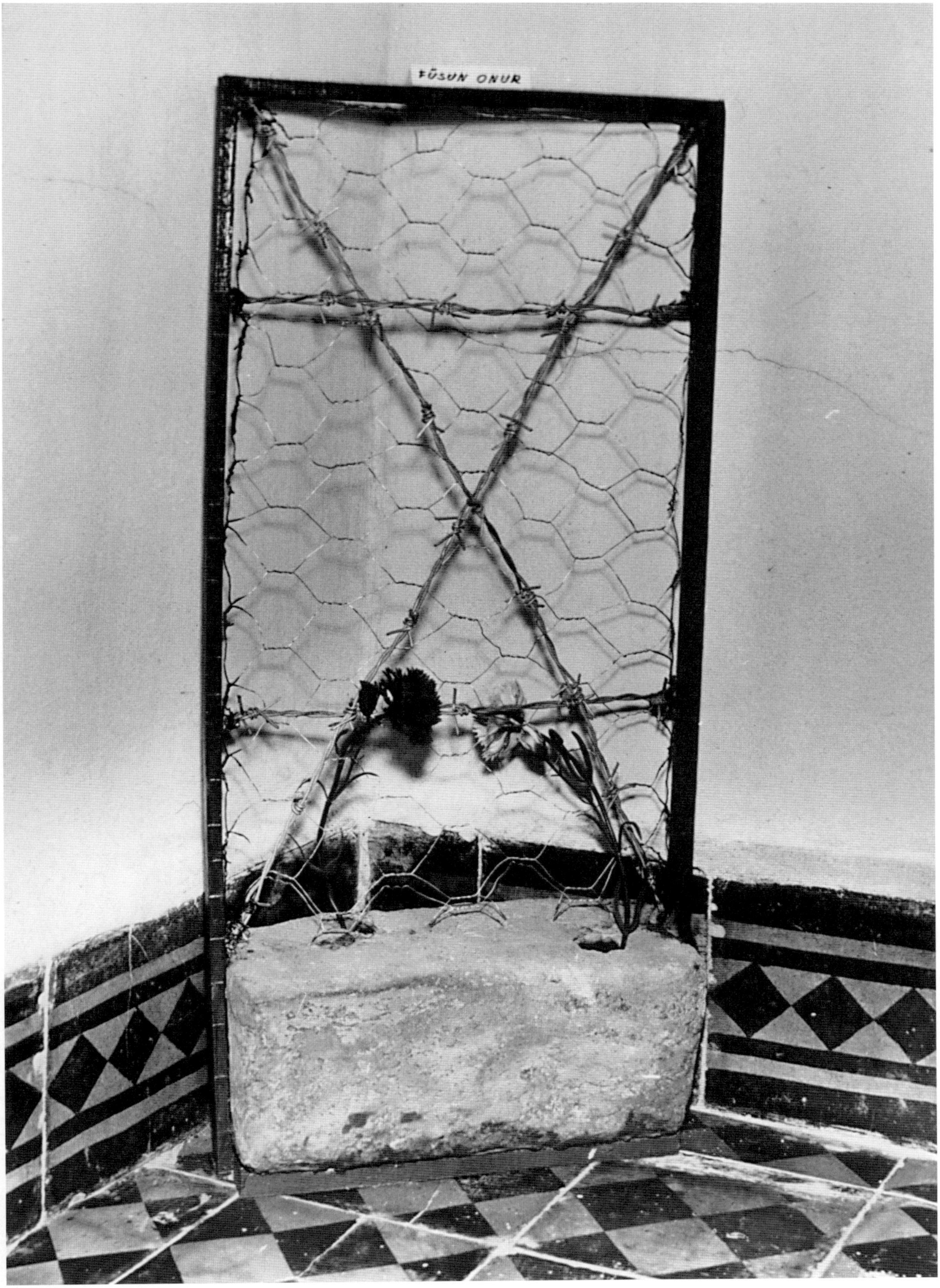

Concrete, wood, wire

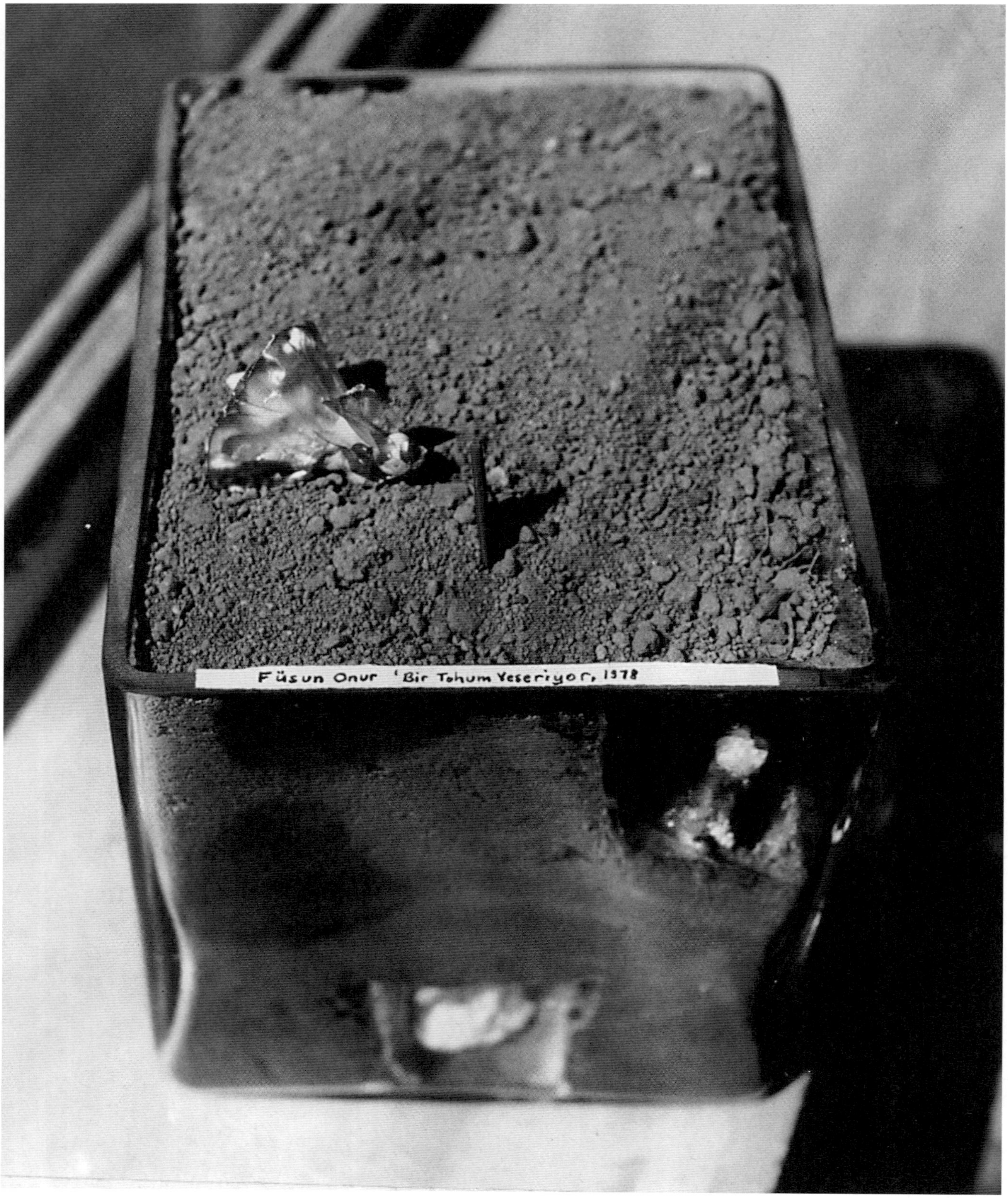

Glass, clay, soil

I'd given a sculpture to the Association for the Conservation of Nature. The association president liked it a lot. He gave it as a gift to Ecevit [the Prime Minister of the time]. I was there too – we presented it to Ecevit together. Its name is *A Seed Sprouts I*. It's a glass cube filled with soil. Inside there's again glass, and inside the glass there are angels separated from soil.

three angels clap hands
ready to be unearthed
resting its head on its hand
angel is watching the greenery
angel is showing the way to the right
angel on all four sides

I am out of paper
much much much love
write me

Excerpt from Füsun Onur's letter to Cengiz Çekil, 1 November 1978, SALT Research, Cengiz Çekil Archive, Istanbul.

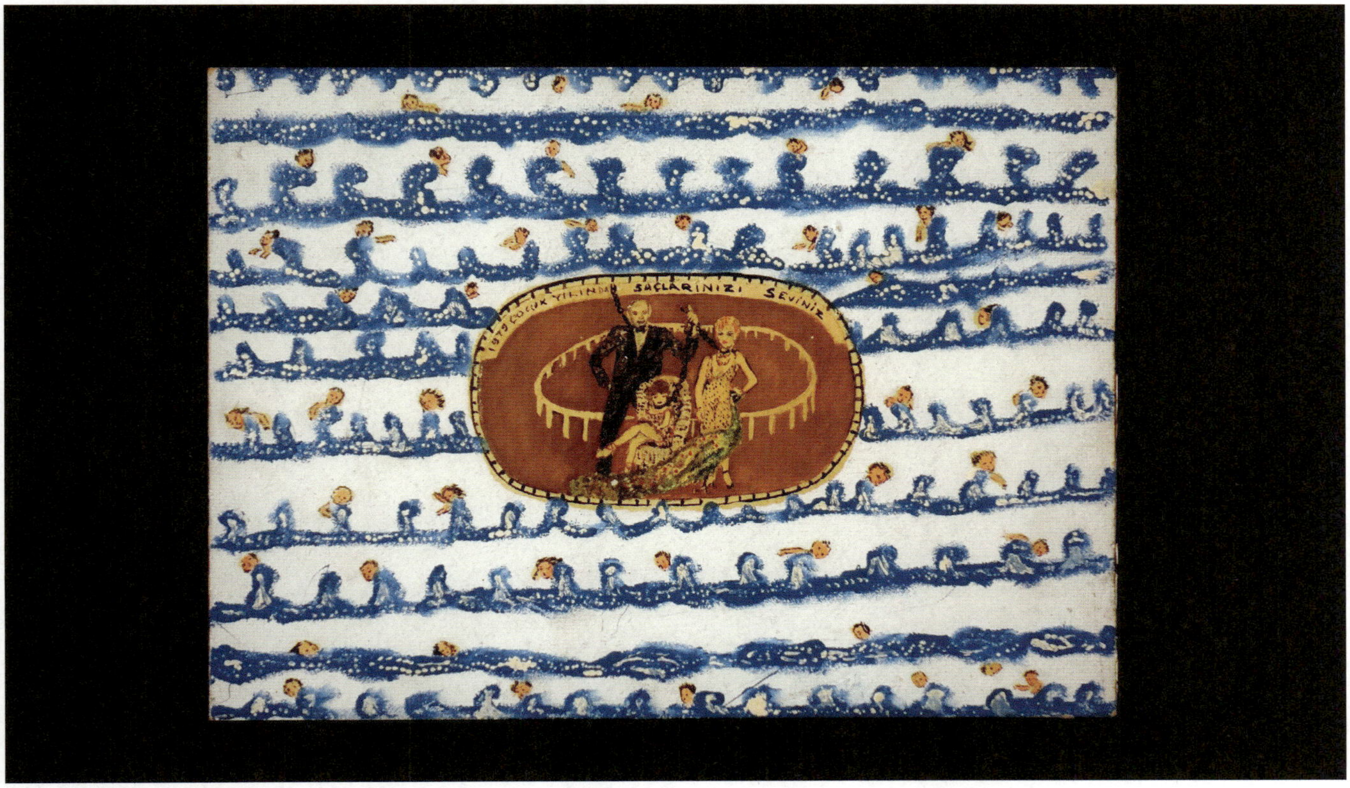

Oil on chipboard, 34 × 45.5 cm

1980 A SEED SPROUTS II

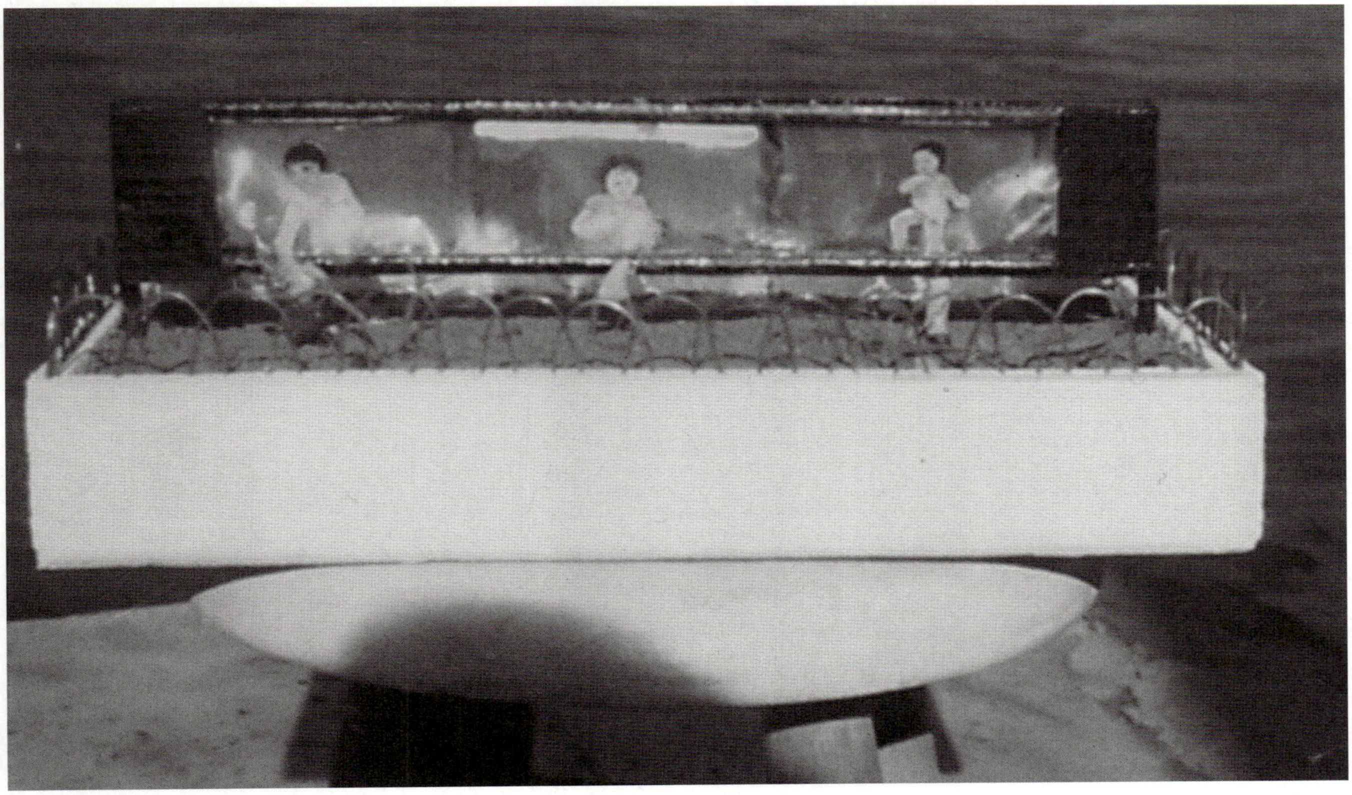

Wood, soil, clay, mica, 18 × 35 cm

Before that, in Ankara, the Association again opened a group exhibition. For that I made something called *A Seed Sprouts*. On top is painting like a film; its side is mica, and on it the colourful important parts are done in clay: a child with a bucket is watering a plant, a bee has alighted on his hand; 2. here he flings the bucket and pulls up the plant and 3. he crushes the plant under his feet.

Excerpt from Füsun Onur's letter to Cengiz Çekil, 11 June 1980, SALT Research, Cengiz Çekil Archive, Istanbul.

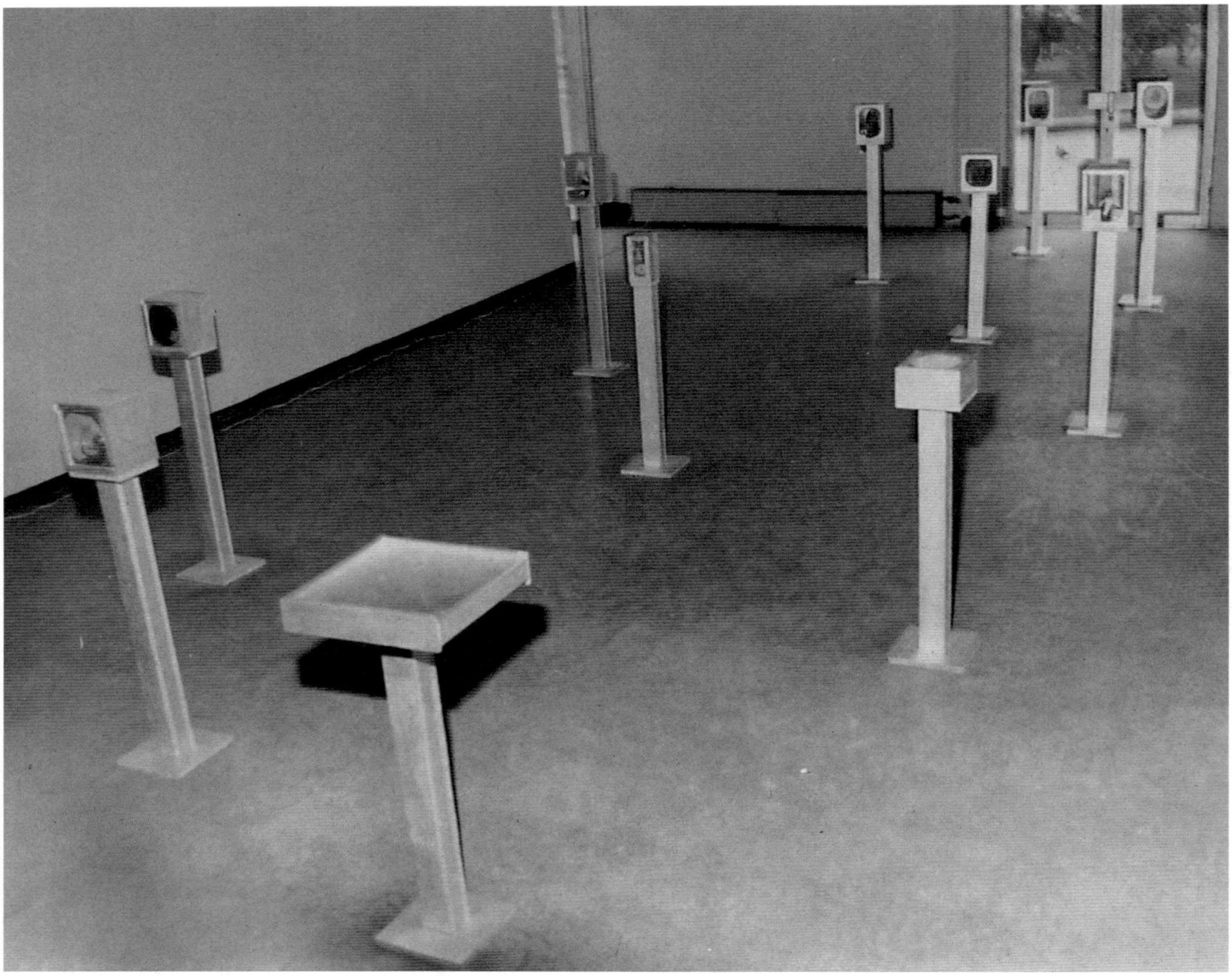

Wood, glass, Plexiglas, clay, 116 × 25 × 25 cm, 97 × 39 × 39 cm, 110 × 25 × 25 cm, 115 × 25 × 25 cm, 125 × 25 × 25 cm, 116 × 25 × 25 cm, 140 × 25 × 25 cm, 125 × 25 × 25 cm

Yet another reason why I'm writing you is to explain the work I made for the exhibition. As time goes by, one loses one's excitement; it becomes difficult to talk about something done and gone, but I will explain it for your sweet sake. I know you'll nevertheless say that you don't understand without seeing it, but you'll at least get an idea. In this exhibition, the work consisted of eleven pieces. Its name is Associations from a Shiny Circle on the Floor. I put a five-lira coin on the floor, isolated it with a hoop circling it, and put a spot on it. That's where we start from. Let's come to the first piece (view from above. It's not exactly like this, but anyway, the downstairs hall on the left in Taksim [Art Gallery] with the glass door).

First of all, they're all on special thin pedestals reaching 90 to 115 centimetres in height. The bearers vary according to the boxes on top, so they come right to the top; there's no overflow on top. Above, bottom and sides. Two sides are glass boxes of 40 × 40 and 20 × 25 cm in dimension. They're all aluminium, bronze painted. Inside the first piece there is again this five-lira coin, seeming to be sunk in the bottom of the water the coin flung off the wheel; a fish gnaws on the scaly but transparent wheel of Plexiglas. 2. Sea inside there are shiny rounds, squares, forgetting the quantity of the money, but its qualities, the associations evoked by its shiny roundness. You know how you see a red car and it takes you back to many places, like a t-shirt you owned when you were five years old? (The materials of these are mica, Plexiglas with various transparencies; others are painted clay) 3. A sofa. From under the sofa, the glittering eyes of a cat who's just woken up 4. A mask coming (?) to your mind like any light 5. A clock on it the solar system (concept of time) 6. Painters' red round sold stickers pasted on the glass. When viewed from the back, it's emptied out; from the front, you see a little painter, hitting on the buttons of a machine and producing art, in front of it a price list (loaded numbers) The paintings coming out from the back are in the style of M. Pesen, Ramiz Seyit Bozdoğan [...] 7. Again an intellectual (say whatever you want) and his empty eyeglasses are shining, he is preachifying. His back is spidery and on its rear front a snake is strangling a rabbit (couldn't change the laws of nature) 8. A forest roots, trees, pines, leaves. I painted dried flower petals, a sunny landscape with light trickling in 9. When someone says 'sun,' Atatürk comes to mind. You know the transparent Atatürk I made? I pasted those on the glass outside on both sides, back and front. A yellow light, shiny sun 10. Atatürk with binoculars, on a hill in the back. Women and men, soldiers mounting the hill, the castle is taken, the flag on the hill. In the front, this tiny (?) binocular is turned to the audience, detail, soldiers, one or two are seen clearly 11. Sun on its front, glass, and inside a mass moving towards it. It is made with painted clay of course all of them 3-dimensional tiny miniature statuettes.

Excerpt from Füsun Onur's letter to Cengiz Çekil, 11 June 1980, SALT Research, Cengiz Çekil Archive, Istanbul.

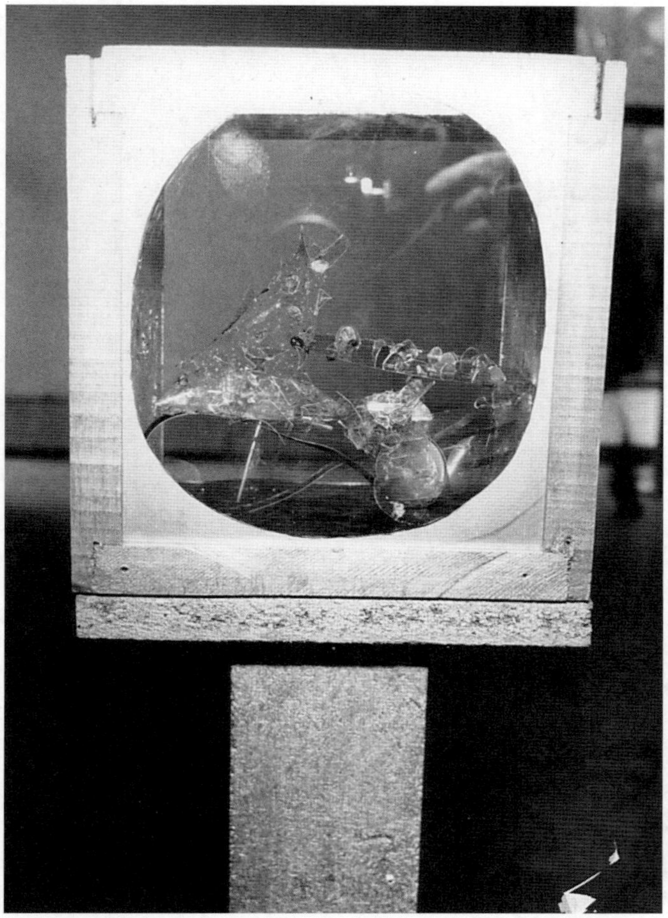

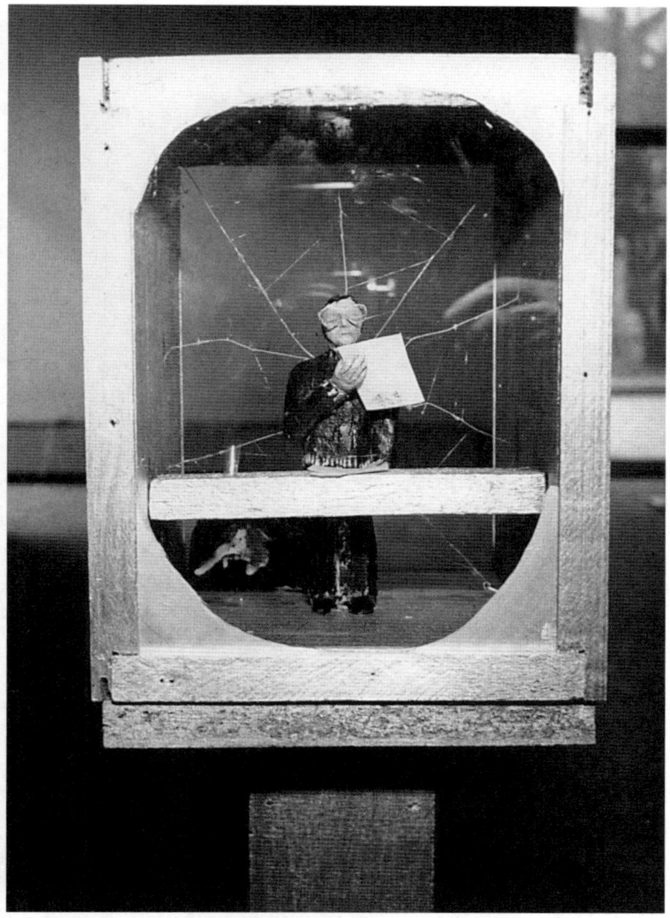

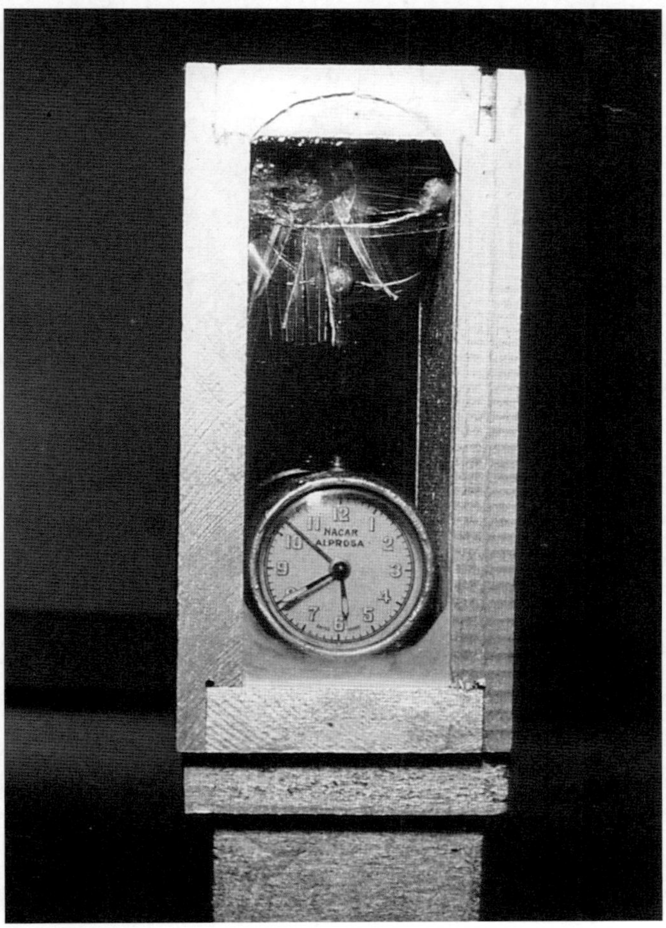
NACAR
ALPROSA

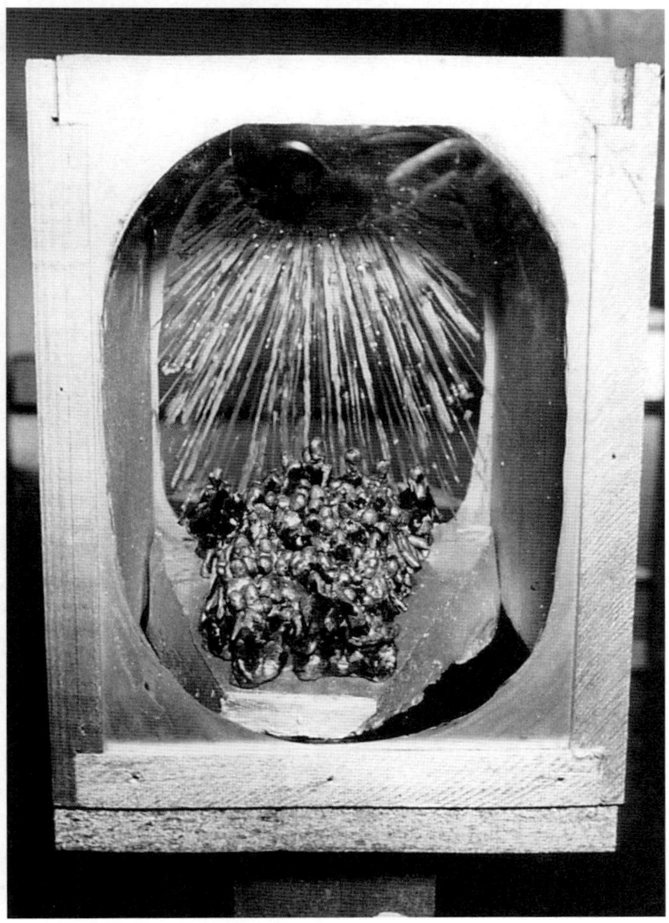

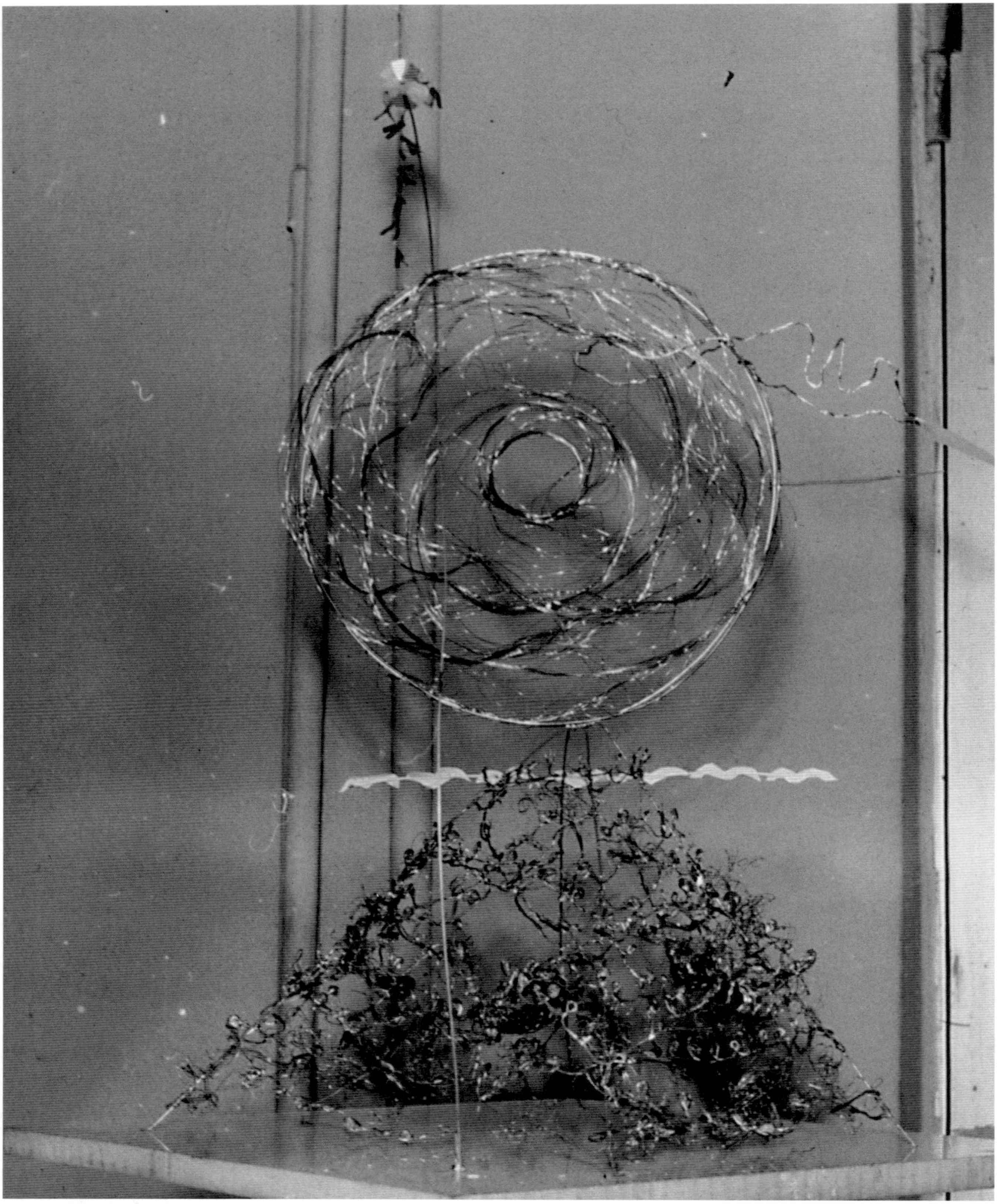

Wire, clay, Plexiglas, 55 × 40 × 40 cm

Then there was a group exhibition organised by the Association for the Conservation of Nature. For that exhibition I made something […] by twisting copper wires. The bottom hill is green, but made of wire. On it are tiny red clay flowers; between them are tiny bushes of wire. The top is like the sun – copper left in its natural state. At the very top a colourful kite. These are the latest things I've made.

Excerpt from Füsun Onur's letter to Cengiz Çekil, 11 June 1980, SALT Research, Cengiz Çekil Archive, Istanbul.

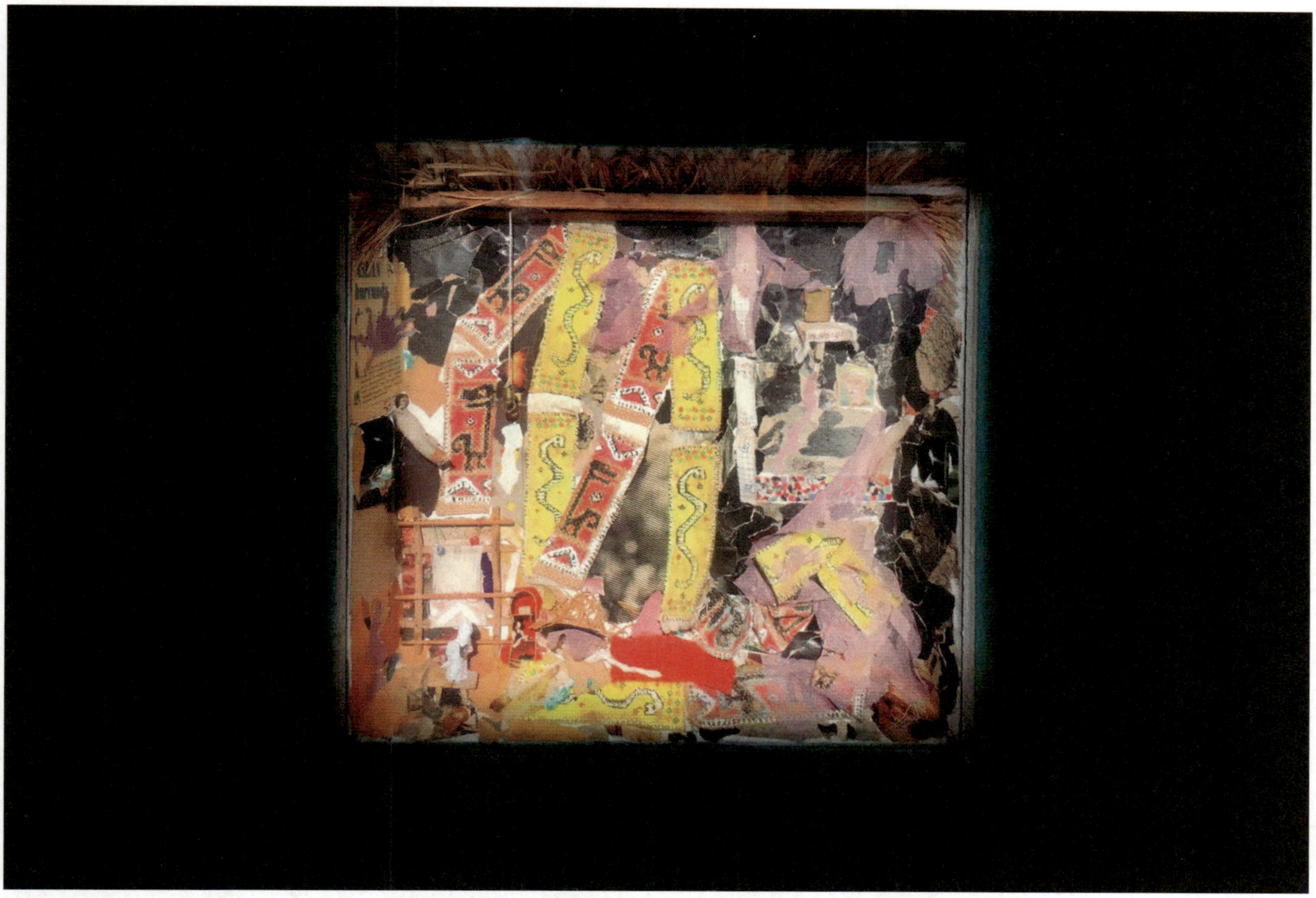

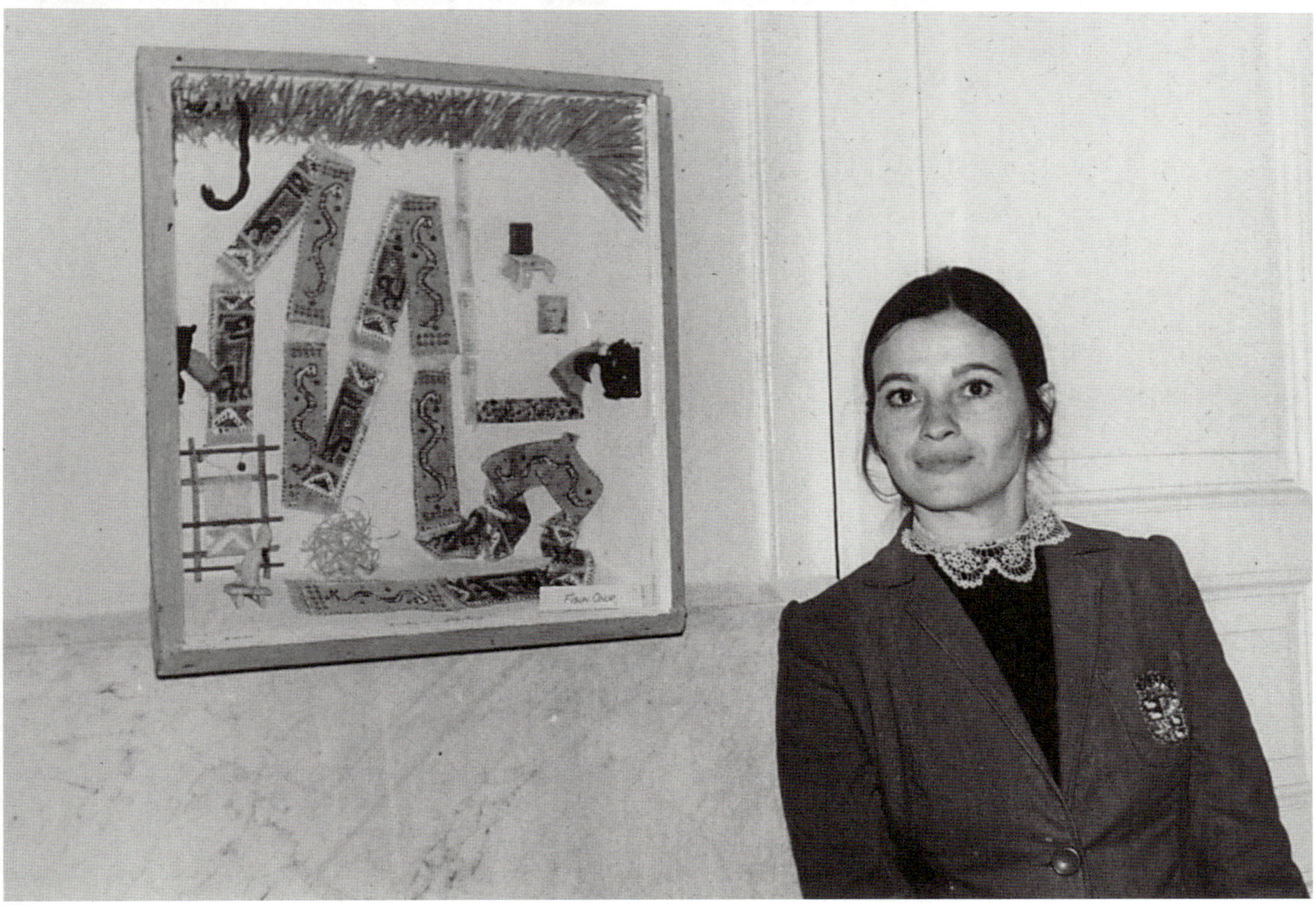

Wood, raffia, clay, fabric, 50 × 50 cm

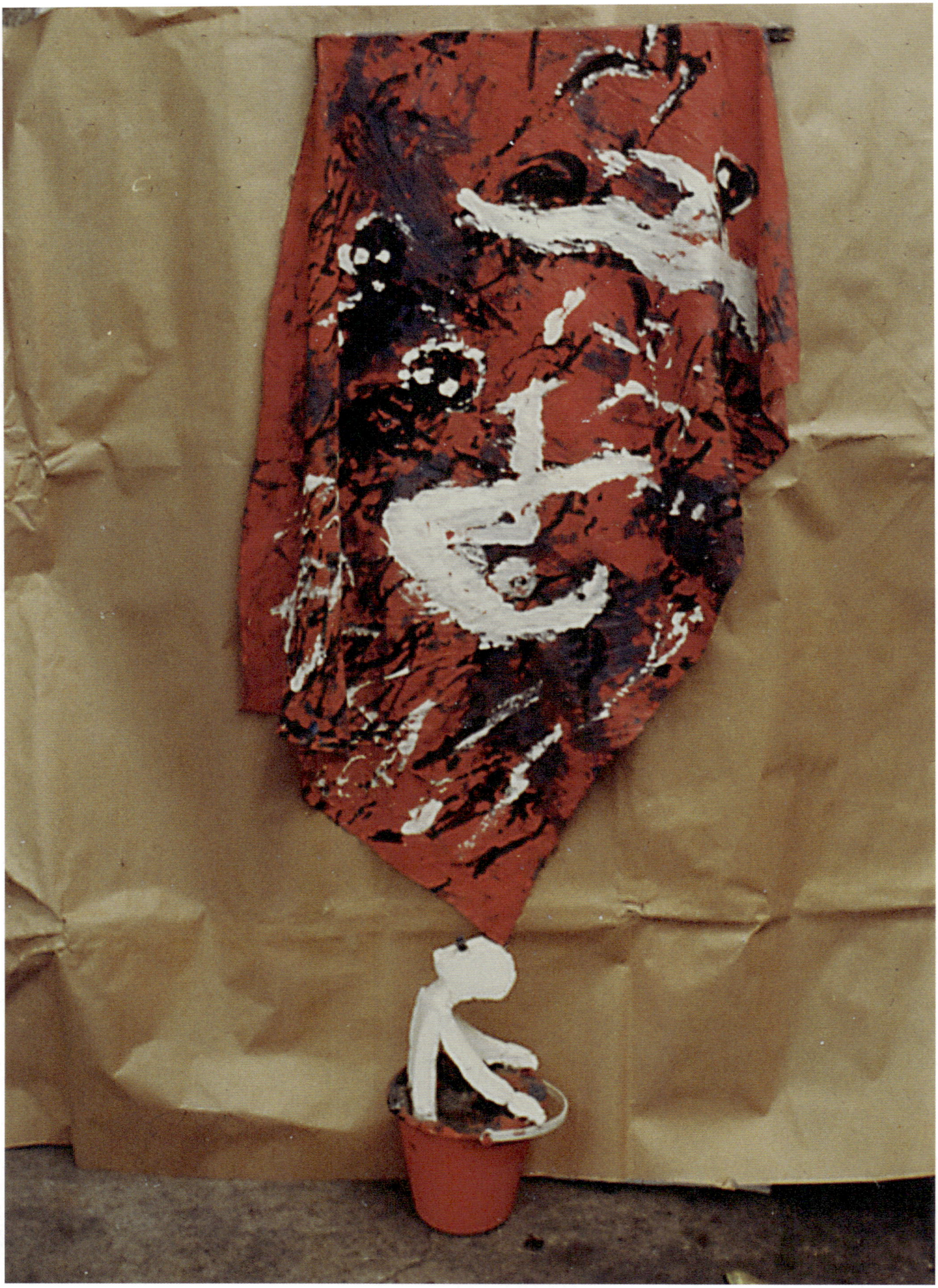

Canvas, acrylic and mixed media, dimensions unknown

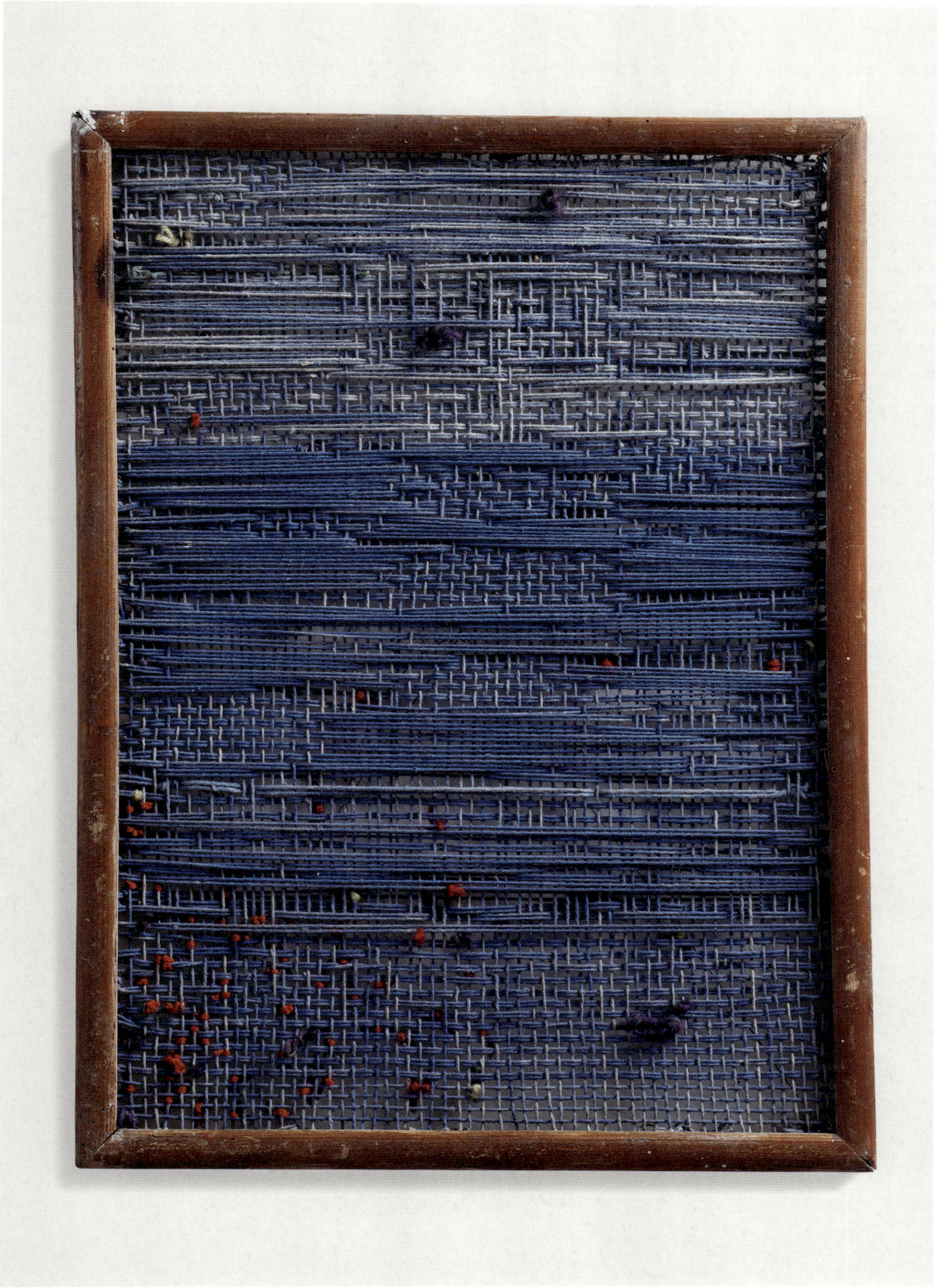

Painted thread, wooden frame, 48 × 35 cm

If we try to imagine how freeform jazz might look as a work of art, the early geometric abstractions of Füsun Onur come to mind. Her hard-edged compositions are rhythmic improvisations in line and shape. Blocks of pure black jive with white voids. Like a saxophonist improvising on a single note, Onur elongates, repeats and doubles back on her rectangles and circles to release their vibrancy in forms that dance before our eyes. There is also something of nature invading the space of culture: solid monochromes split and fissure as if on geological lines; the Euclidean perfection of geometry is bent and fractured as if by some elemental force. The kinaesthetic movement of these black and white images gives equal valence to presence and absence, the seen and the invisible, silence and sound.

Over the years, the graphic lines that once contained solids and voids escaped from the surfaces of Onur's modestly scaled, minimalist compositions to embark on a series of adventures. They metamorphosed into the fibres of a textile or into a thread connecting found objects in poetic lines of association. The two-dimensional diagram walked out of the image and into real space and time to become an architectonic form. Intimations of rhythm and movement became fully fledged sound installations. These early works are, in a way, prototypes, the foundations of an epic journey that came to absorb a life and its histories into its gyrating geometries.

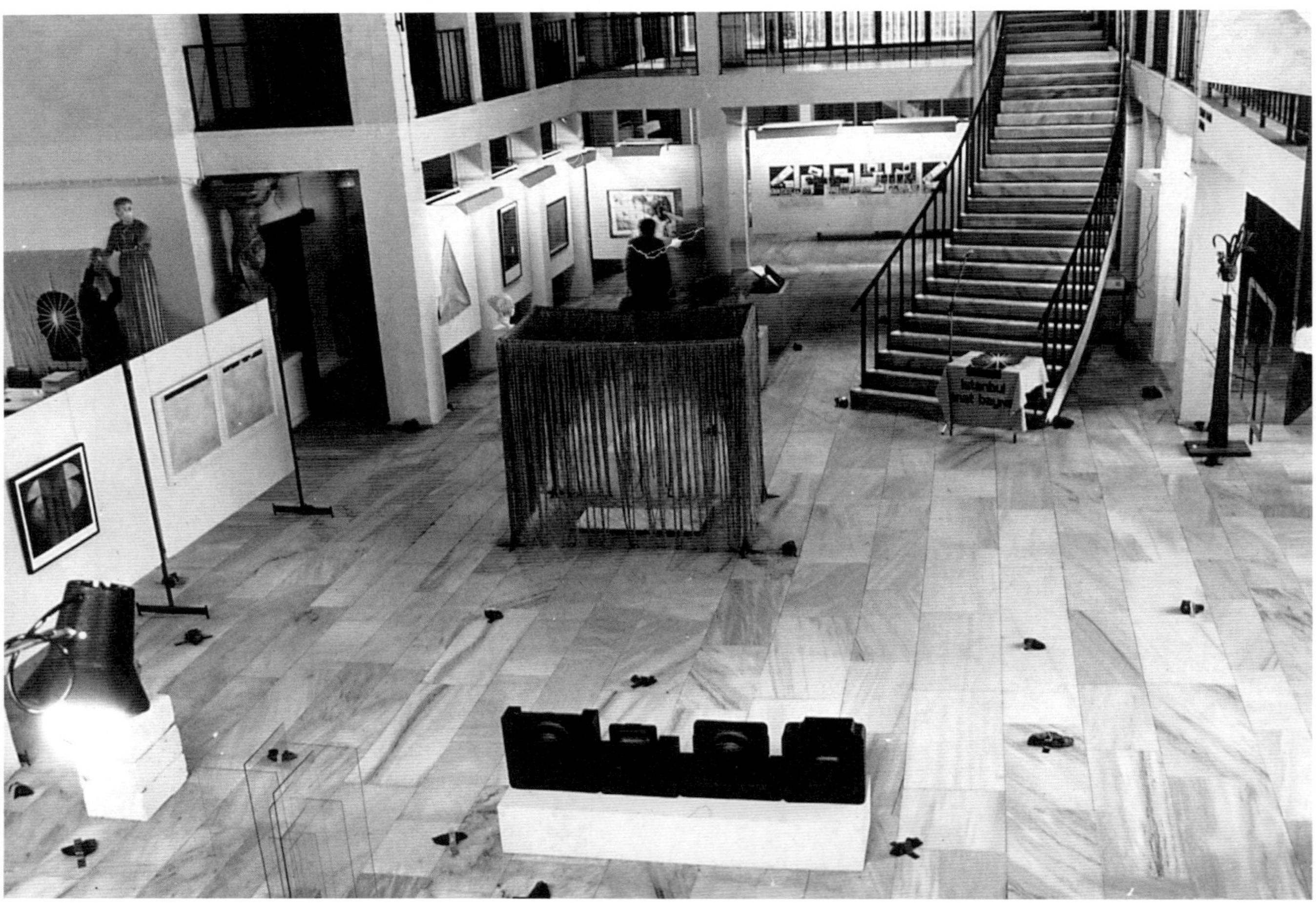

Installation with wood, painted thread, rubber, fabric and spangle, 183 × 200 × 140 cm
View from the exhibition *3rd New Trends*, in 3rd Istanbul Art Festival, Istanbul Academy of Fine Arts, 1981

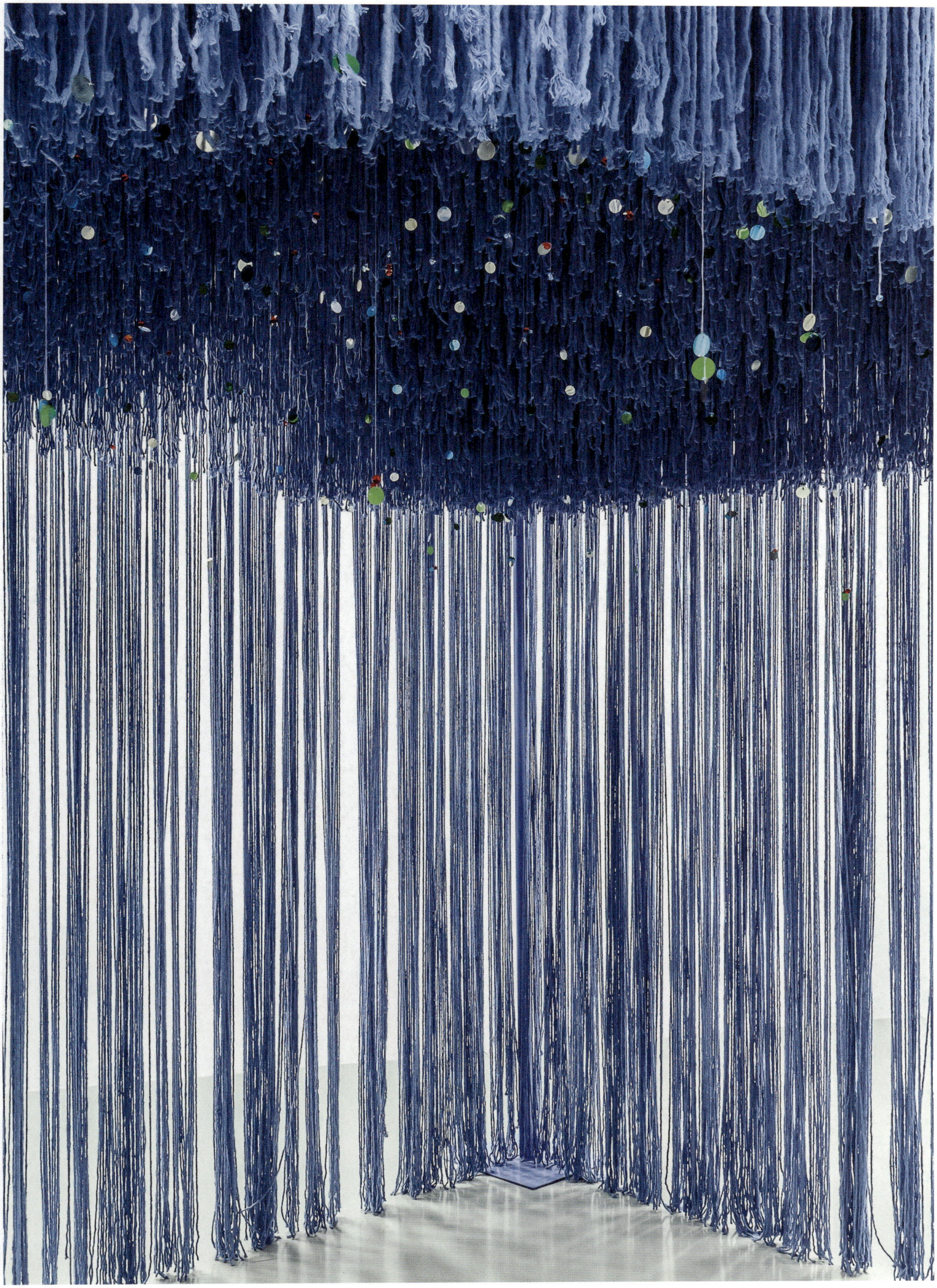

Installation with wood, painted thread, rubber, fabric and spangle, 275 × 300 × 210 cm
View from the restrospective exhibition *Through the Looking Glass* in Arter, 2014

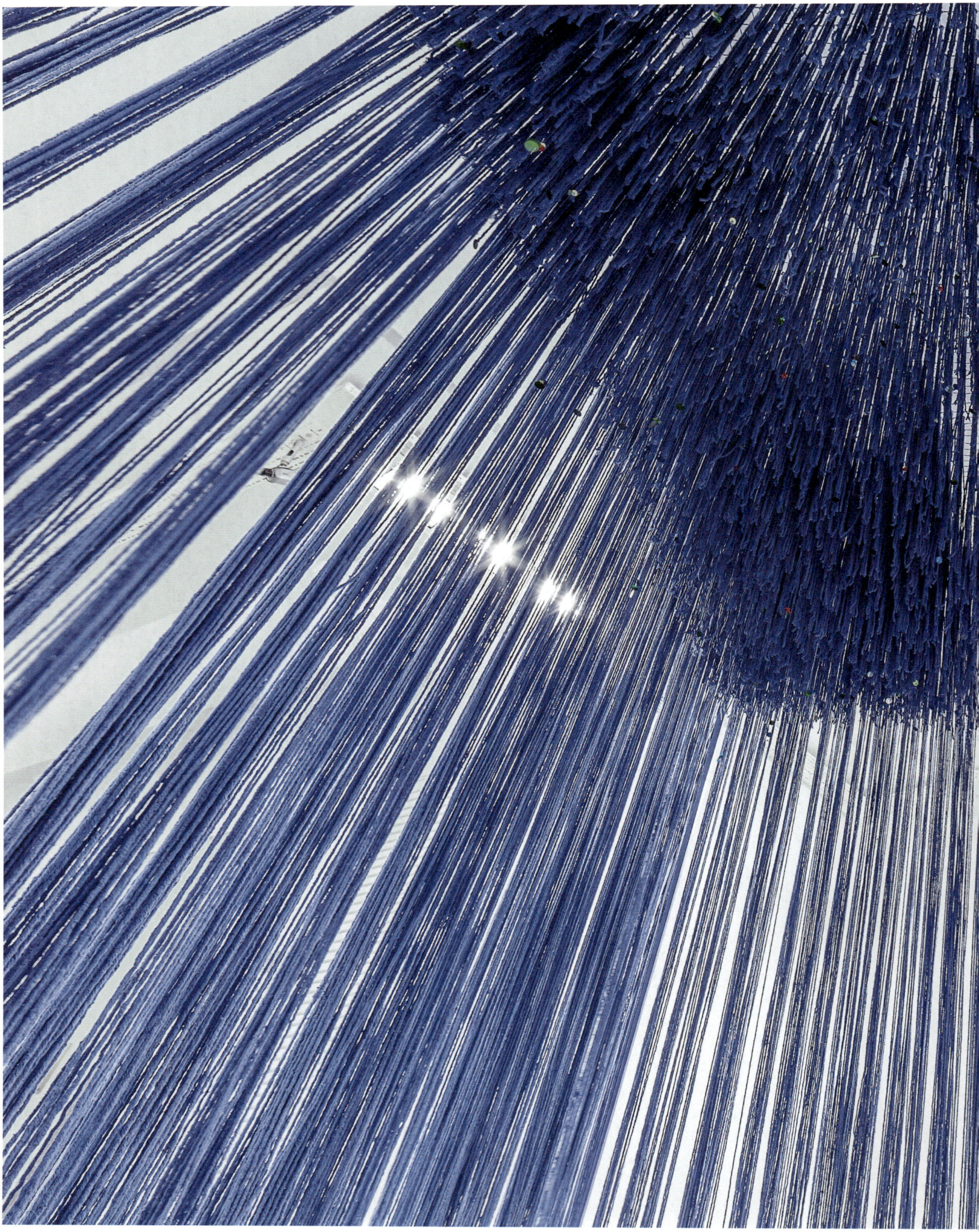

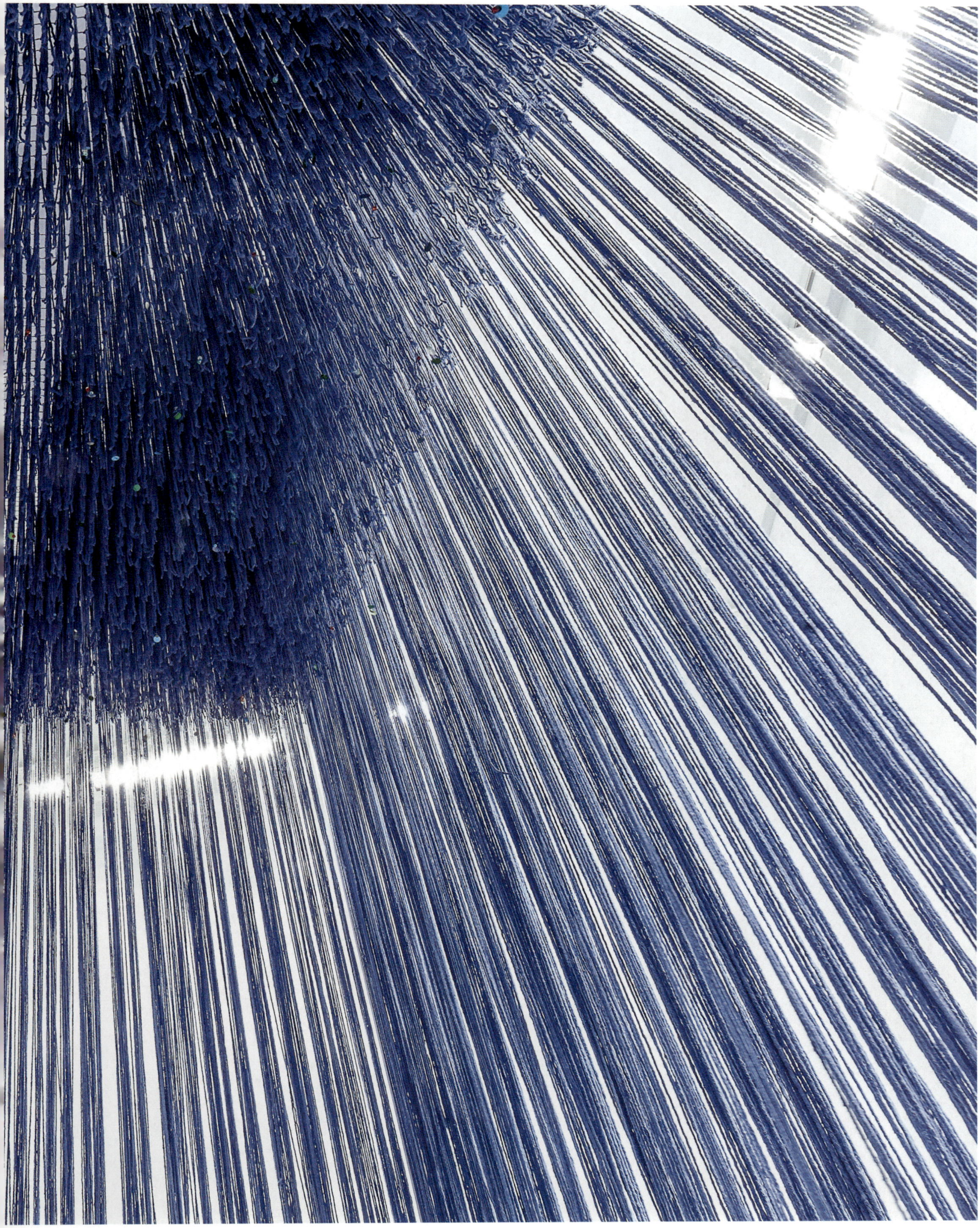

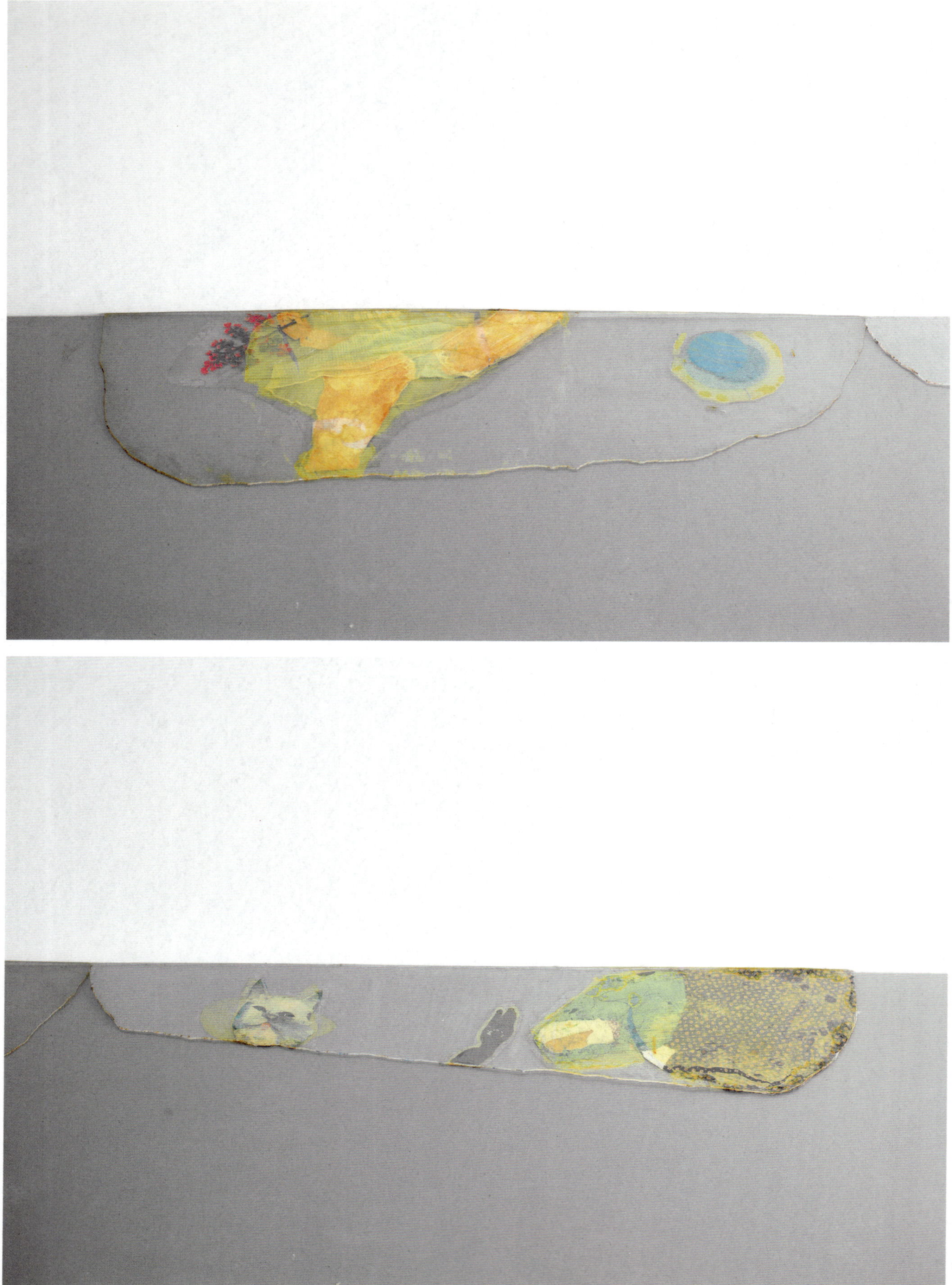

Installation, collage on Plexiglas, two pieces: 100 × 30 cm, 100 × 40 cm

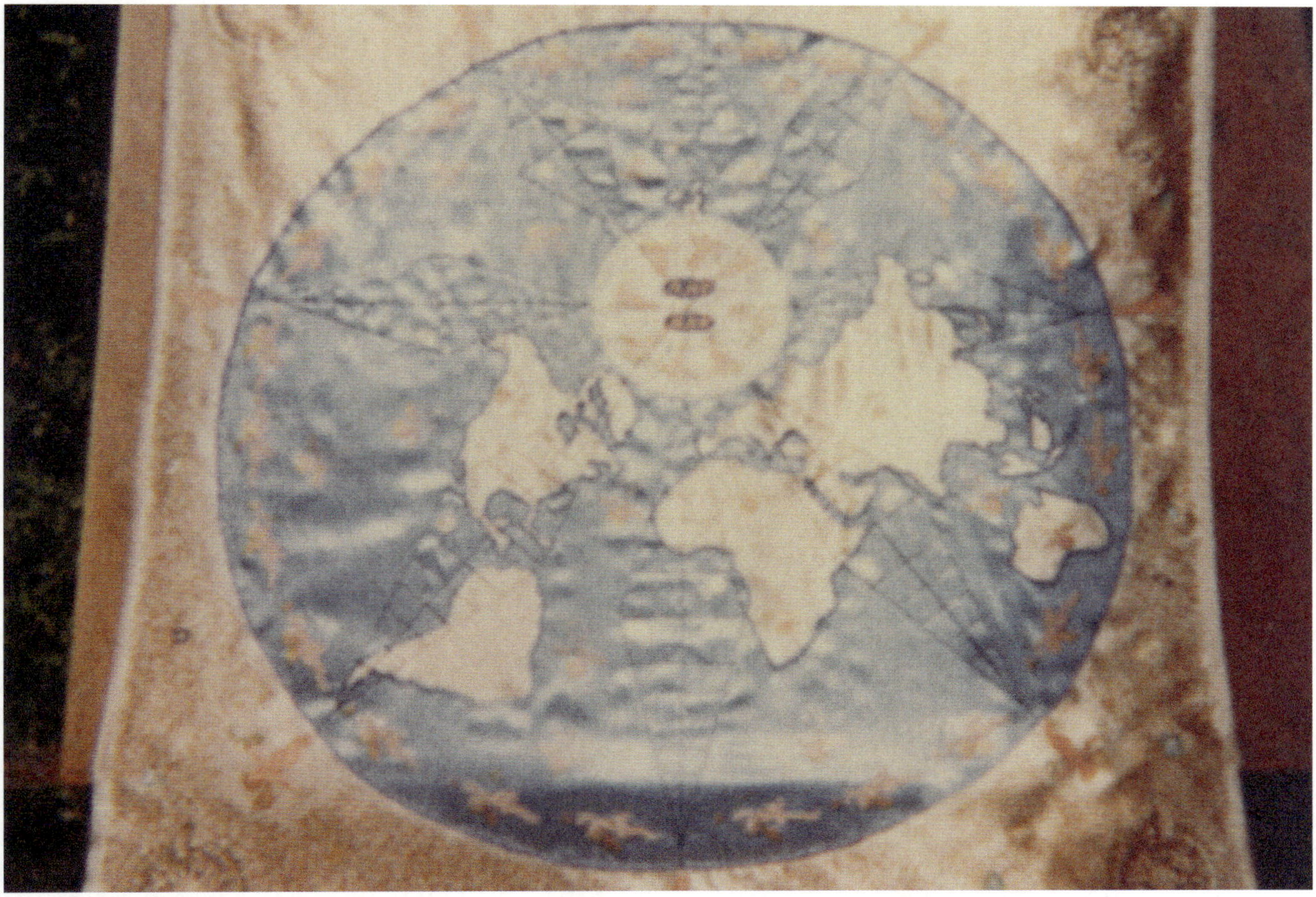

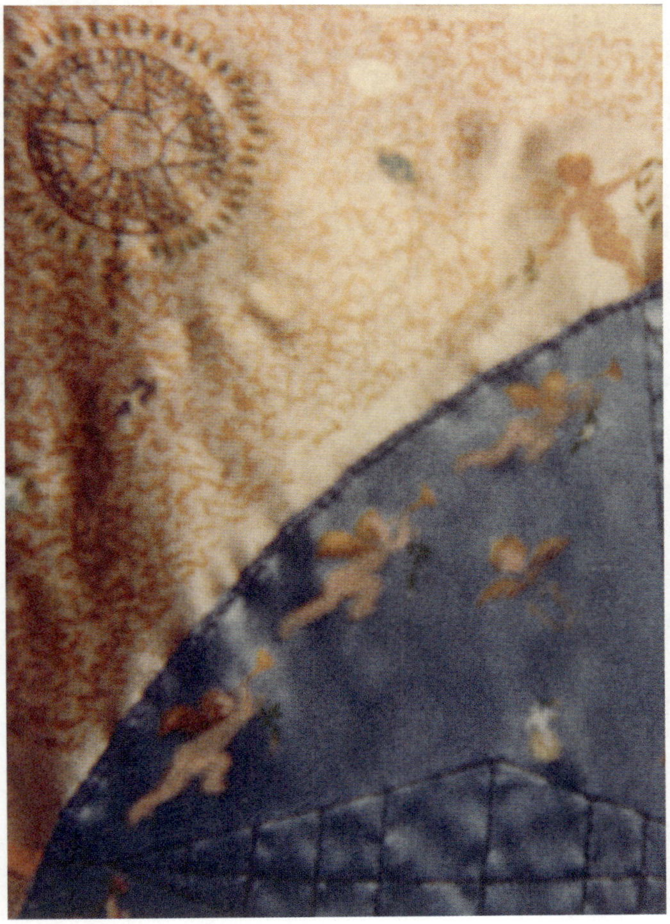

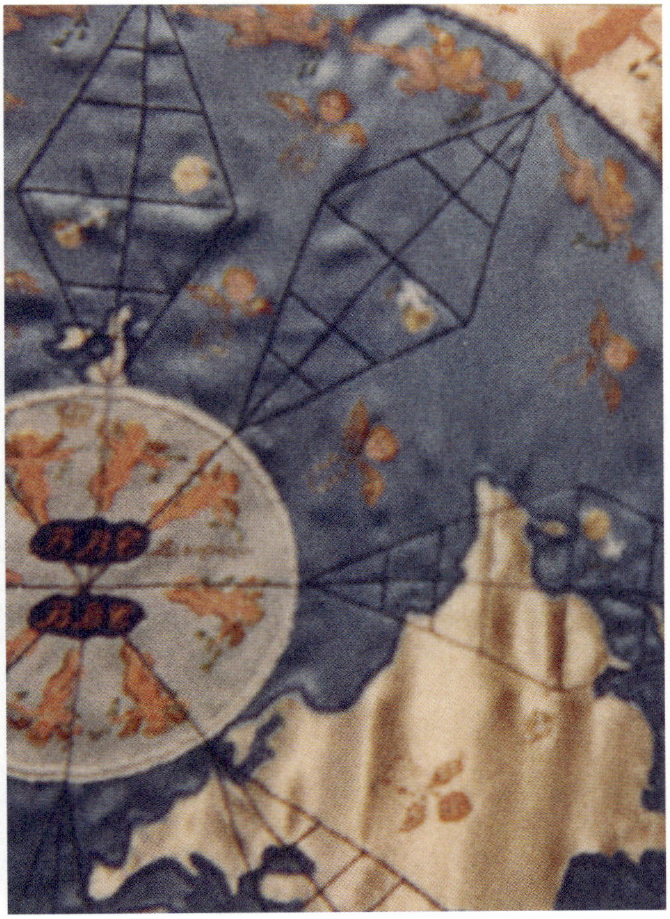

Paint, embroidery, gilding on silk satin, 100 × 100 cm

> No water, no life. No blue, no green
> —Quoted from a speech given by American marine biologist Dr Silvia Earle.

We are emerging from over a year of isolation and loss, due to the global pandemic. Processing and coming to terms with what we've experienced, we struggle to find a language to speak about the intolerable uncertainty and grief that we're collectively facing, and it is art and artists that provide us with a way through.

So to enter a world drenched in blue light, a place filled with poetry, is a relief from the chaotic and confusing world we navigate. This magical, dreamlike place exists inside the silent and joyful world of Füsun Onur's *Counterpoint with Flower* (1982).

This installation punctures the everyday and offers shelter. We find ourselves immersed in a spatial and temporal experience. Imagine sitting in a volume of water or at the bottom of a pool holding your breath and taking a profoundly silent moment to listen and to experience a visual counterpoint. This calm environment creates a space for us to rest and make sense of the world. It transforms everyday materials into magic and poetry, tree branches and rocks into bright red flowers and leaves. The dreamlike scene seems to unfold in a hopeful, silent musical pause.

This work requires time. It rewards those who are open to the possibility of making and experiencing a new world – it is a gift to those who can allow themselves to experience it.

Written in New York overlooking the East River, while thinking about Füsun Onur overlooking the Bosphorus, and about Venice, a city engulfed by rising waters.

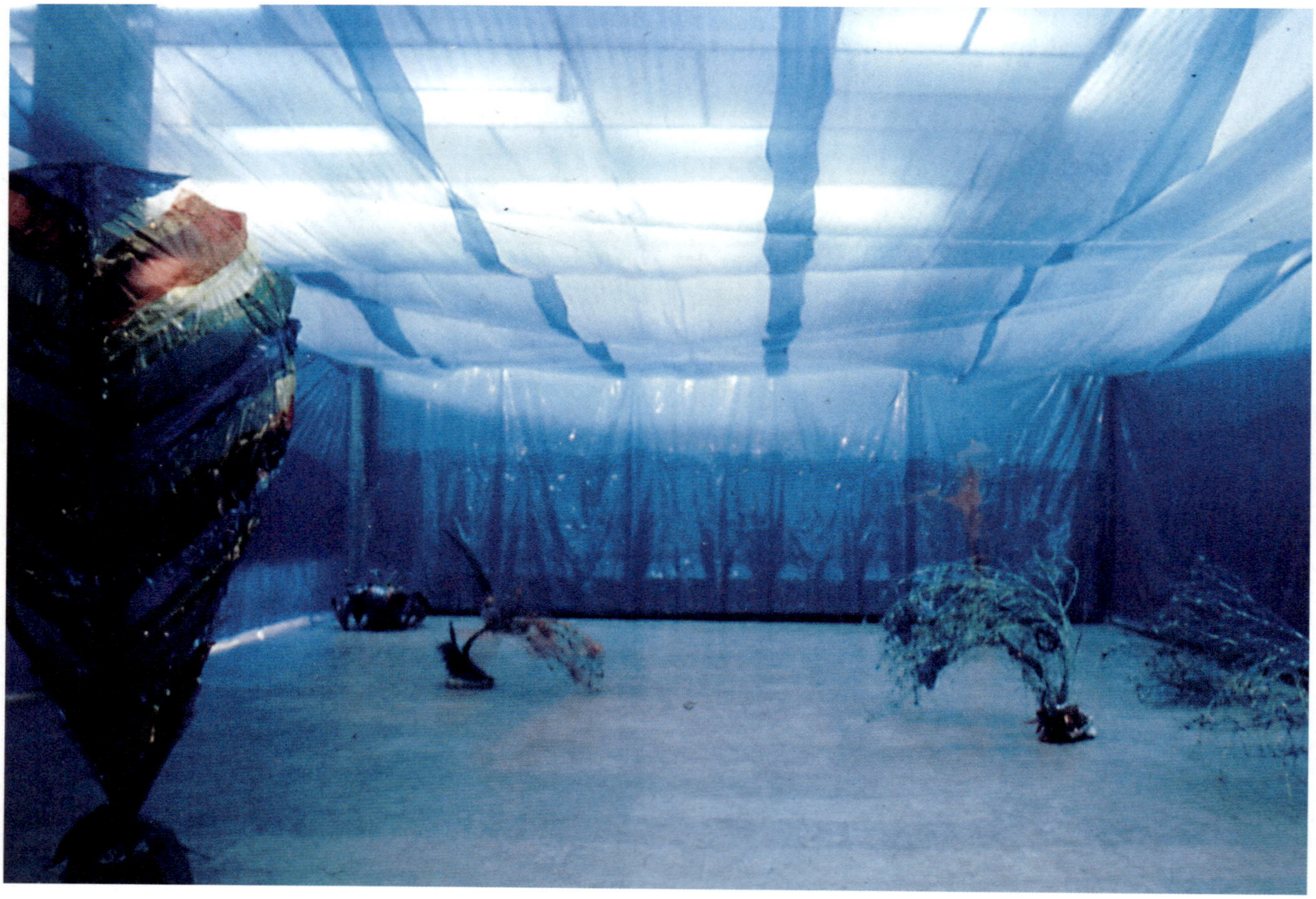

Installation, 215 × 650 × 850 cm
View from the exhibition *Counterpoint with Flower*, Taksim Art Gallery, 1982

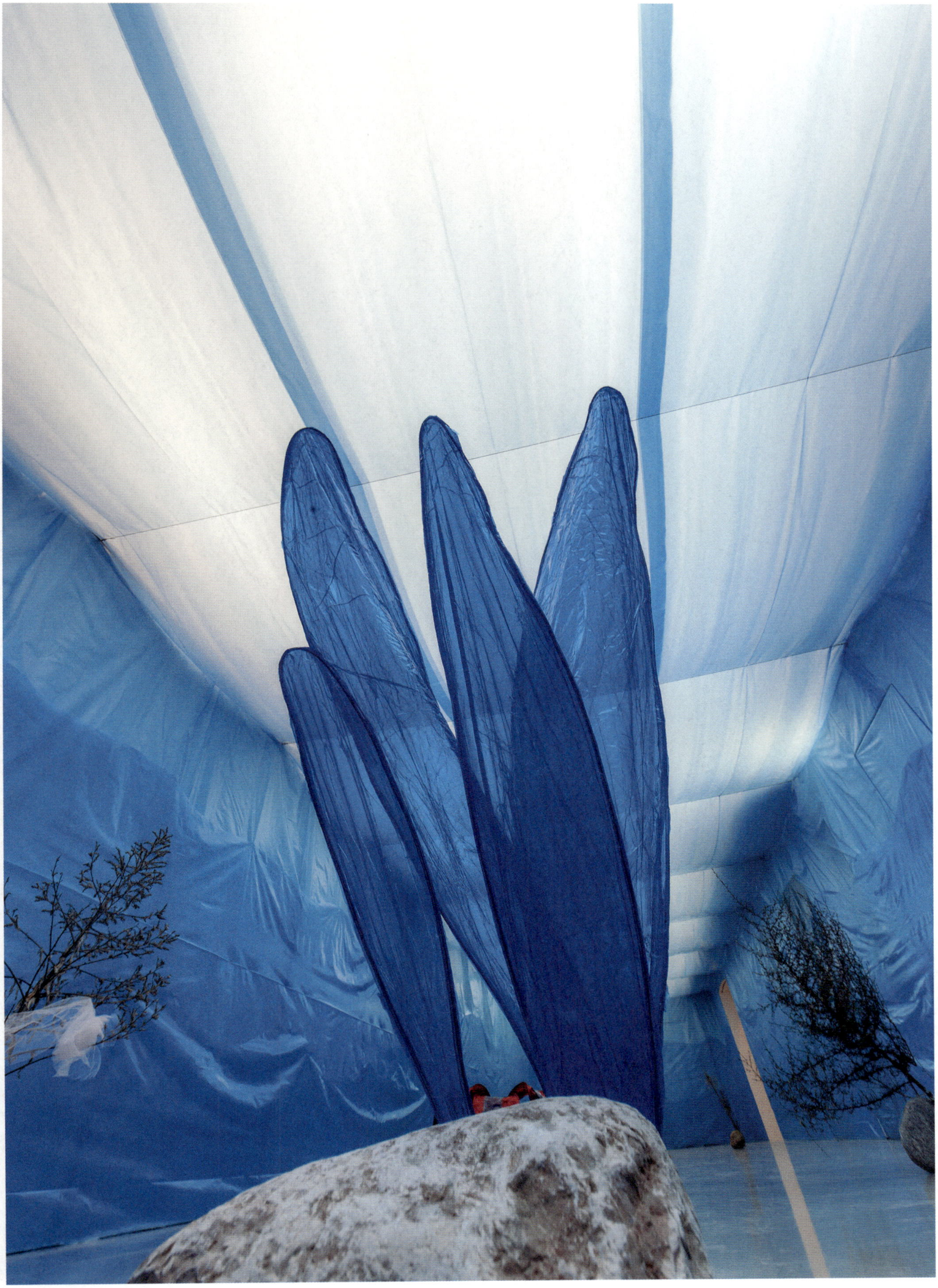

Installation, 215 × 650 × 850 cm
View from the exhibition *Through the Looking Glass*, Arter, 2014

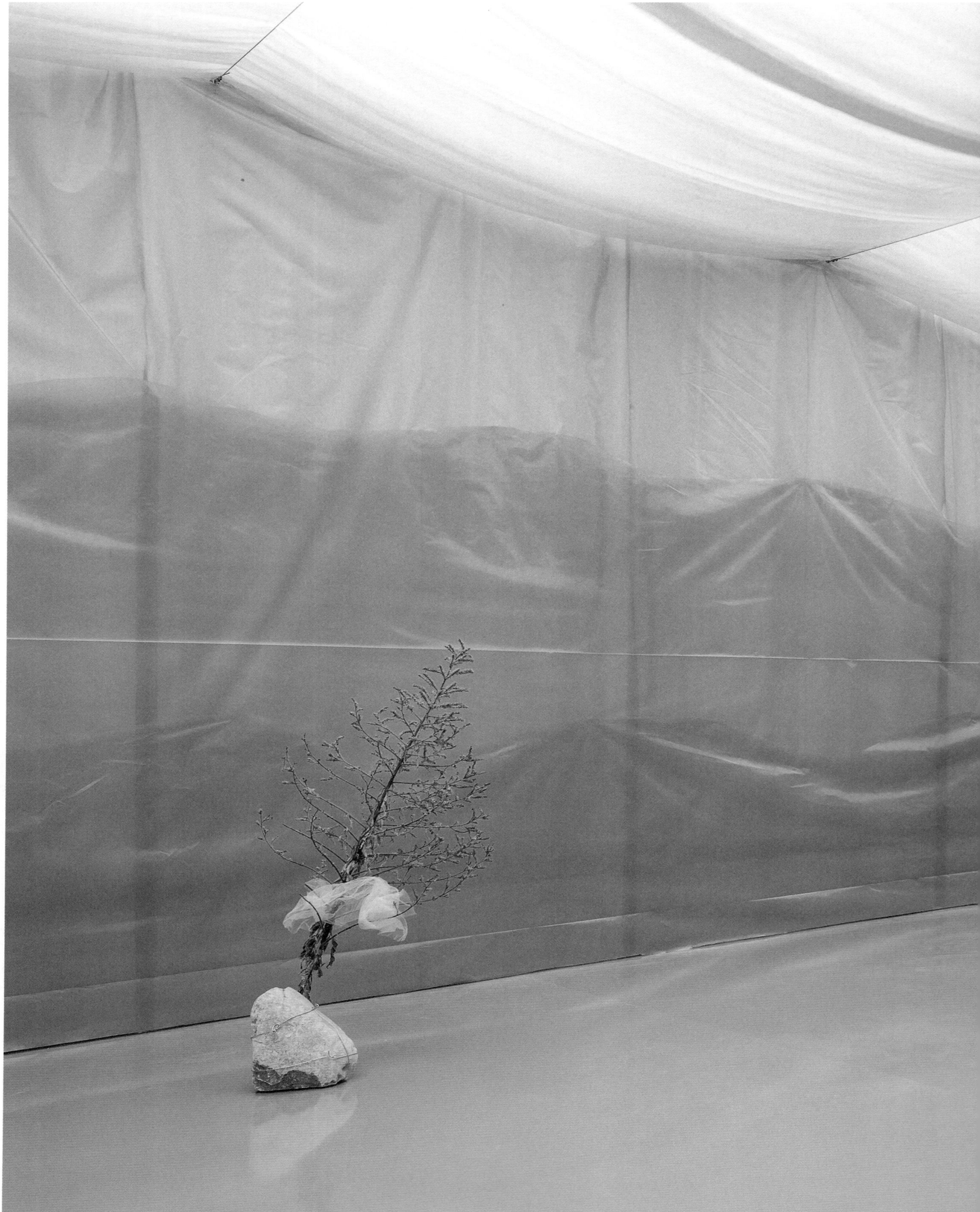

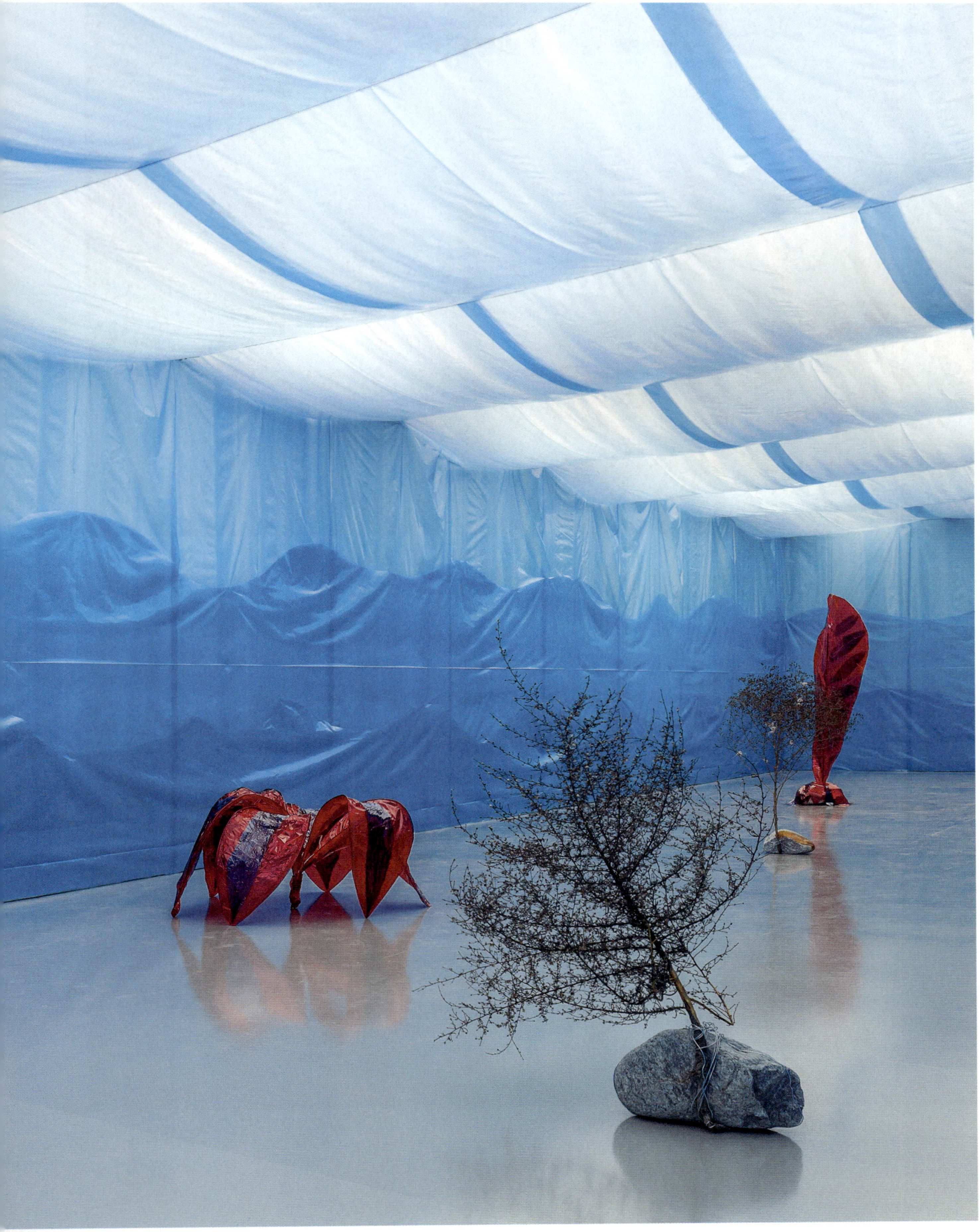

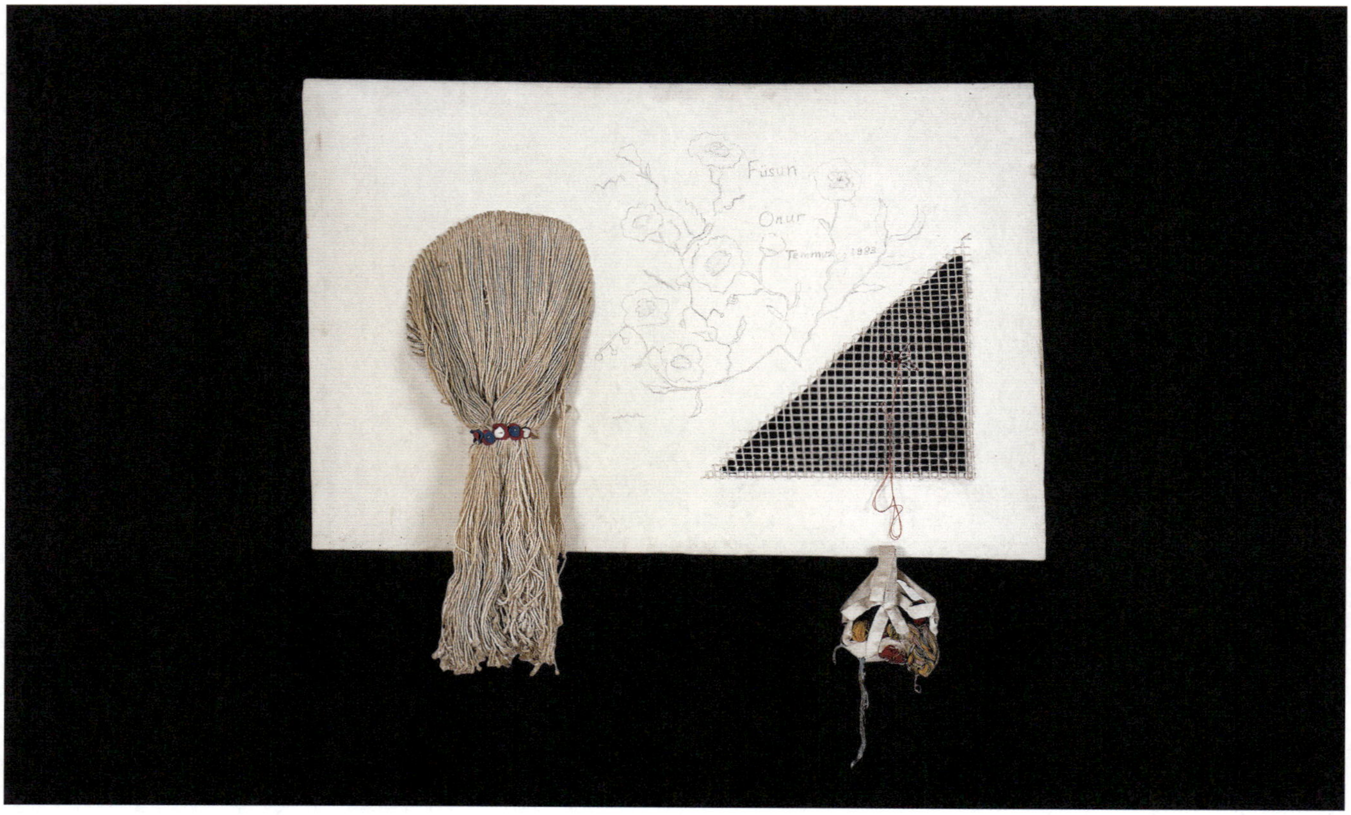

Oil, pencil, fabric, needle and threads on canvas, 87 × 90 × 8 cm

1983 UNTITLED

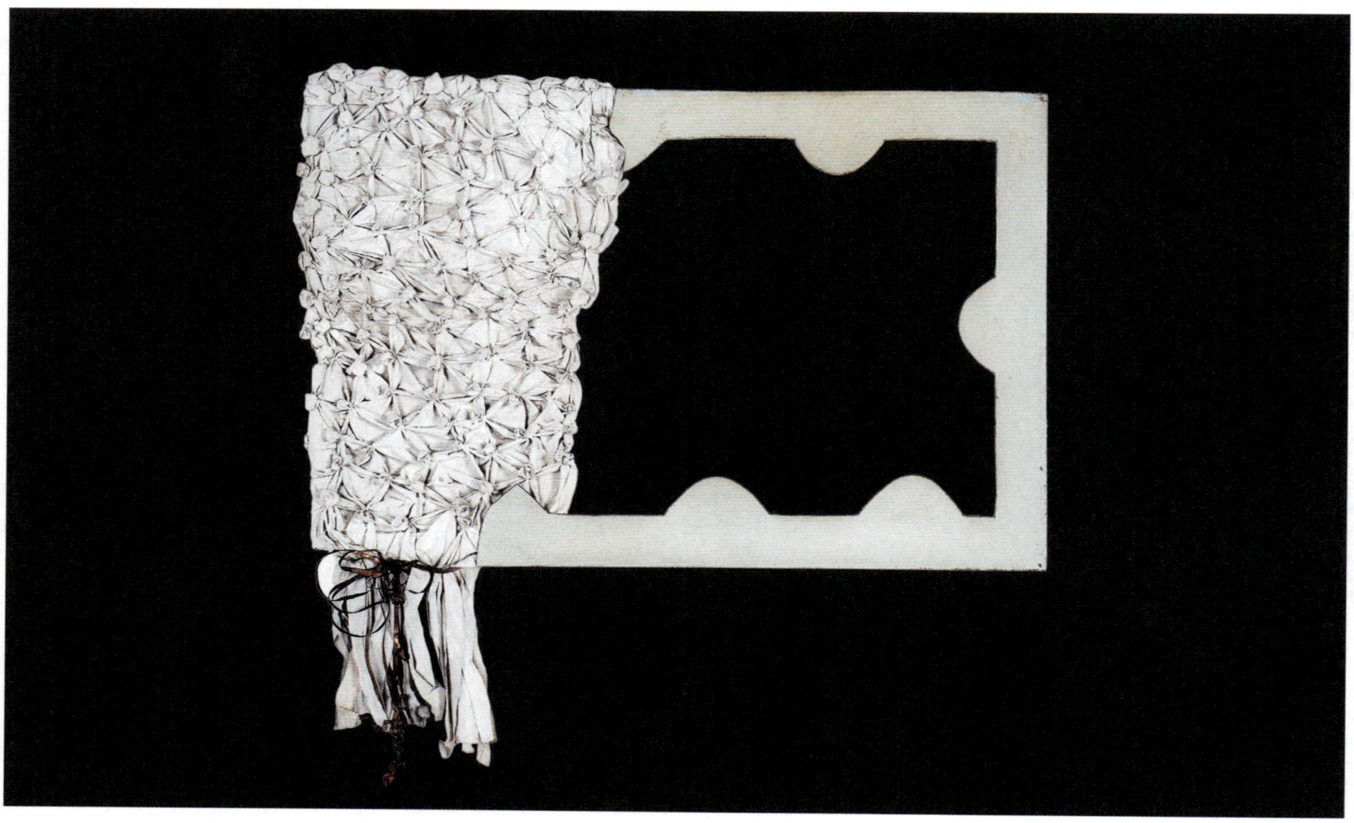

Oil, wood, fabric and copper band on canvas, 93 × 90 × 3 cm

In *July*, the artist seems to have been interrupted while embroidering. The needle is still stuck in the triangular net structure and below it hangs a small bag with thread. The woolen shock of hair in the same work signals a reflection on the expectations associated with female roles that are inseparable from textiles.

Thomas Heyden, excerpt from the *Saum der Zeit (Border of Time)* exhibition booklet, Neues Museum Nürnberg, 2018.

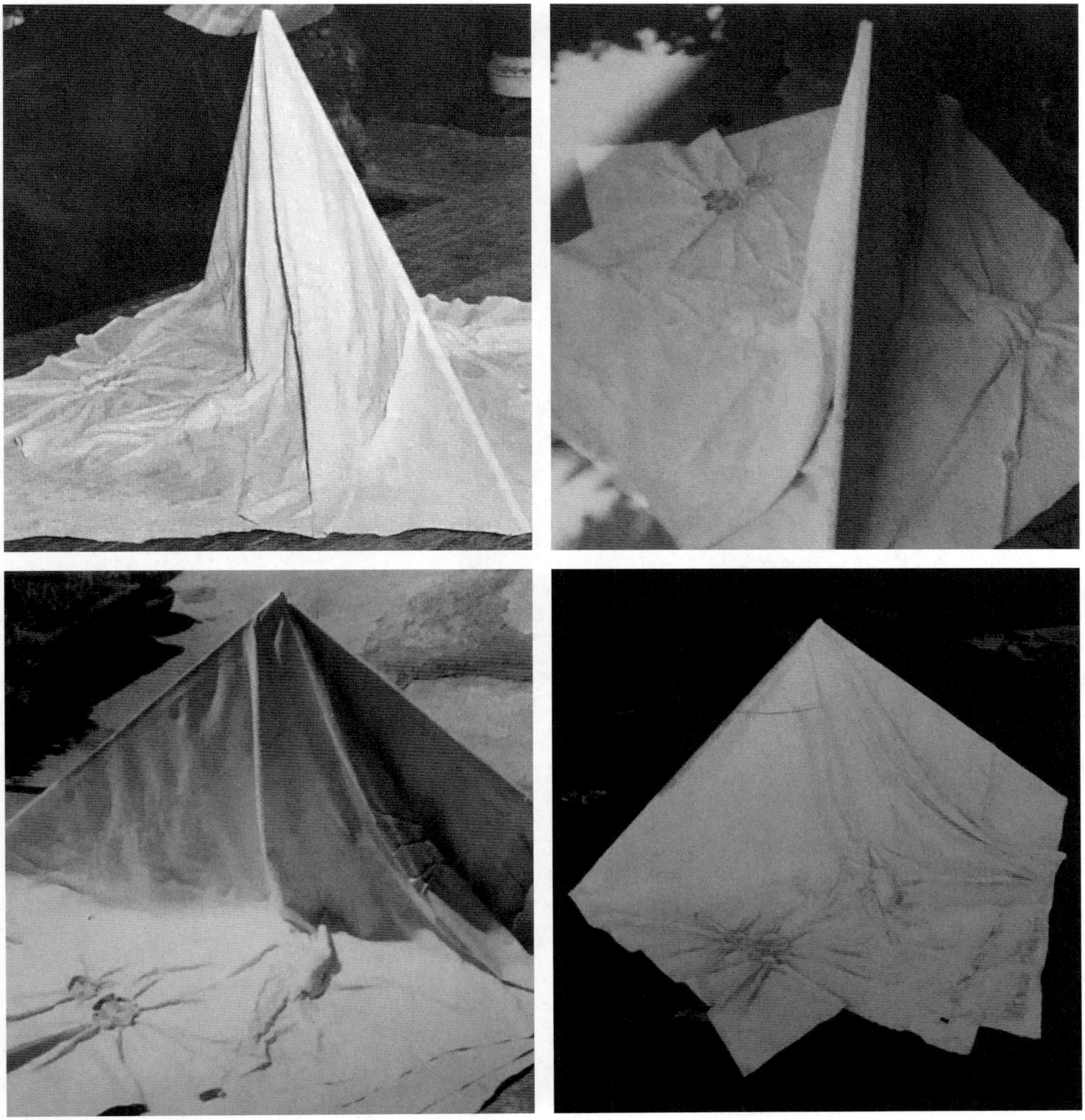

Canvas, 145 × 140 × 75 cm

Conceptual Visual Images (sic.) (1983) is solid in shape. Here, the visual discrepancy lies in the fixing of a movement. The apparently spontaneous form that emerges when the cloth is lifted is made permanent; the fabric is stiffened with glue. Onur also tests the three-dimensional potential and the different appearances of textiles in wall objects, such as *July* (1983) or *Untitled* (1983), two works shown in the context of the 6th Istanbul Biennial at the Dolmabahçe Palace in 1999. In the first one she weaves a mesh that spans an empty space in the woven fabric and arranges the same strands of wool into a pony tail growing out of the image; in the second she makes the different perception of the same material visible by partially covering a piece of canvas stretched behind a wooden frame with a kind of smocked curtain, the same fabric in a three-dimensional form.

Margrit Brehm, excerpt from *For Careful Eyes*, Yapı Kredi Publications, Istanbul, 2007.

1983 WOULD YOU LIKE TO REST ON THE BENCH?

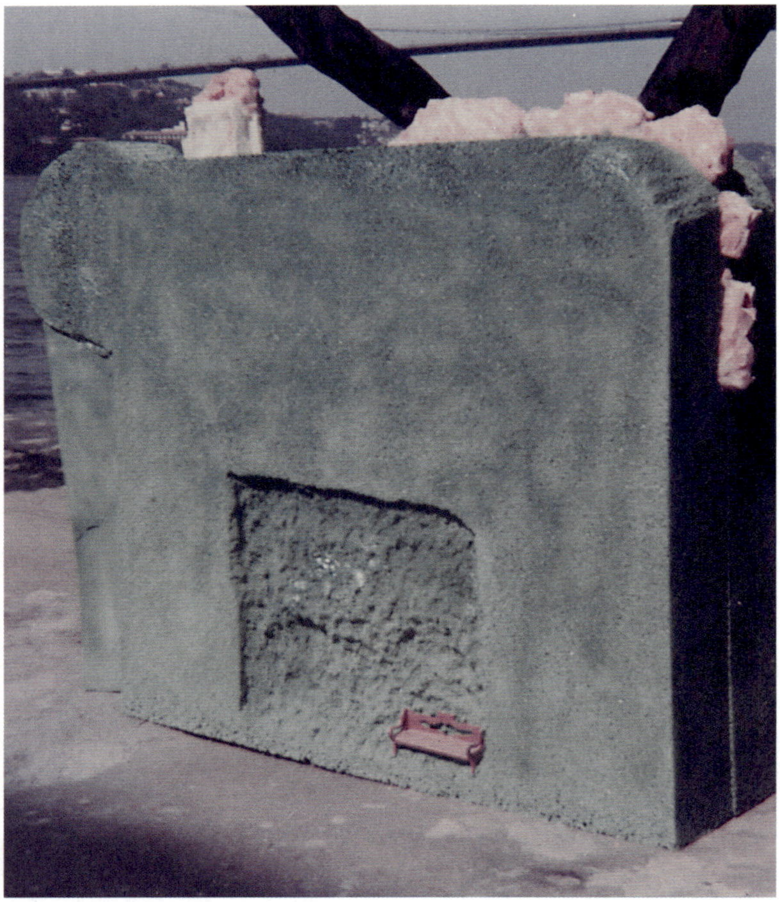

1984 GIRL WITH A TURQUOISE BRACELET

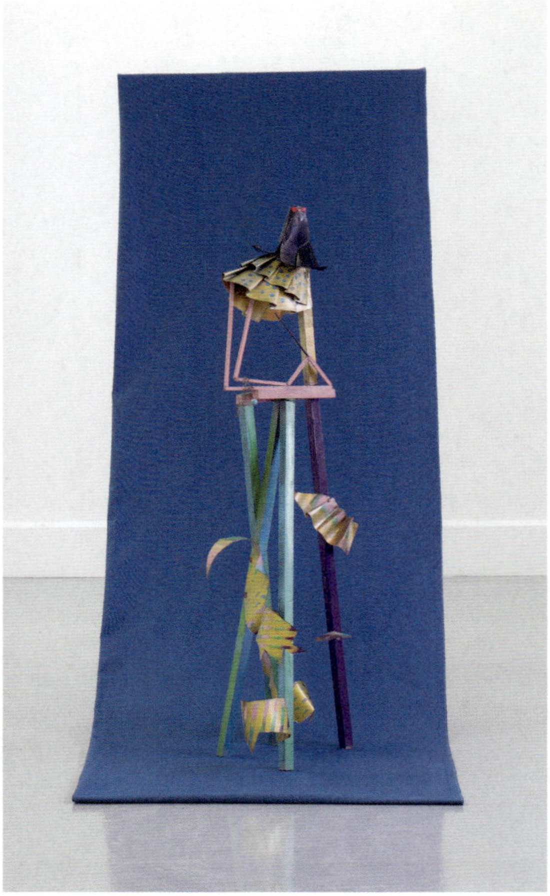

(Left) Foam, 150 × 150 × 30 cm
(Right) Wood, brass, bead, metal, paint, 115 × 35 × 45 cm

1984 A-Z, Z-A

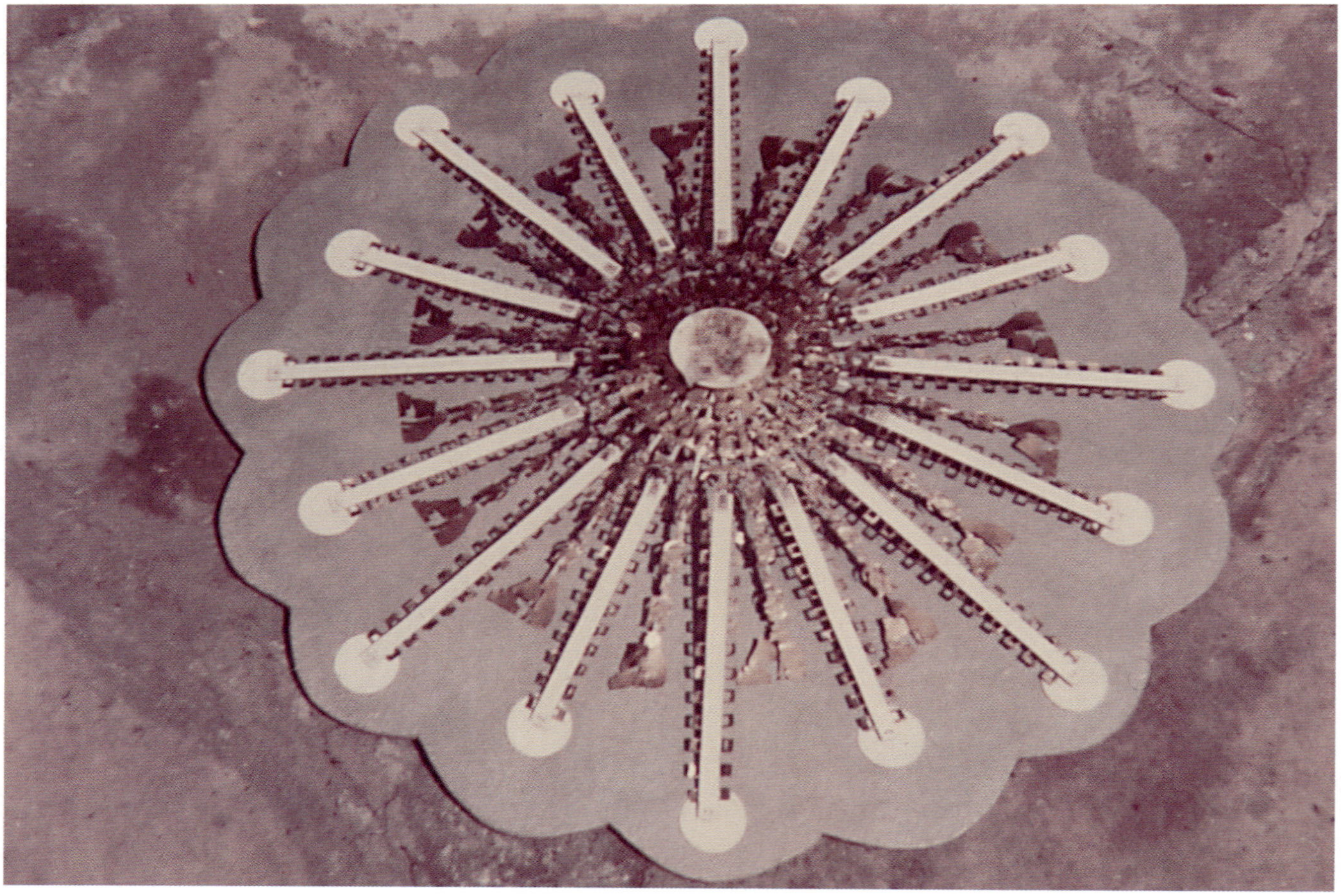

Wood, brass, bead, metal, paint, ∅ 100 cm

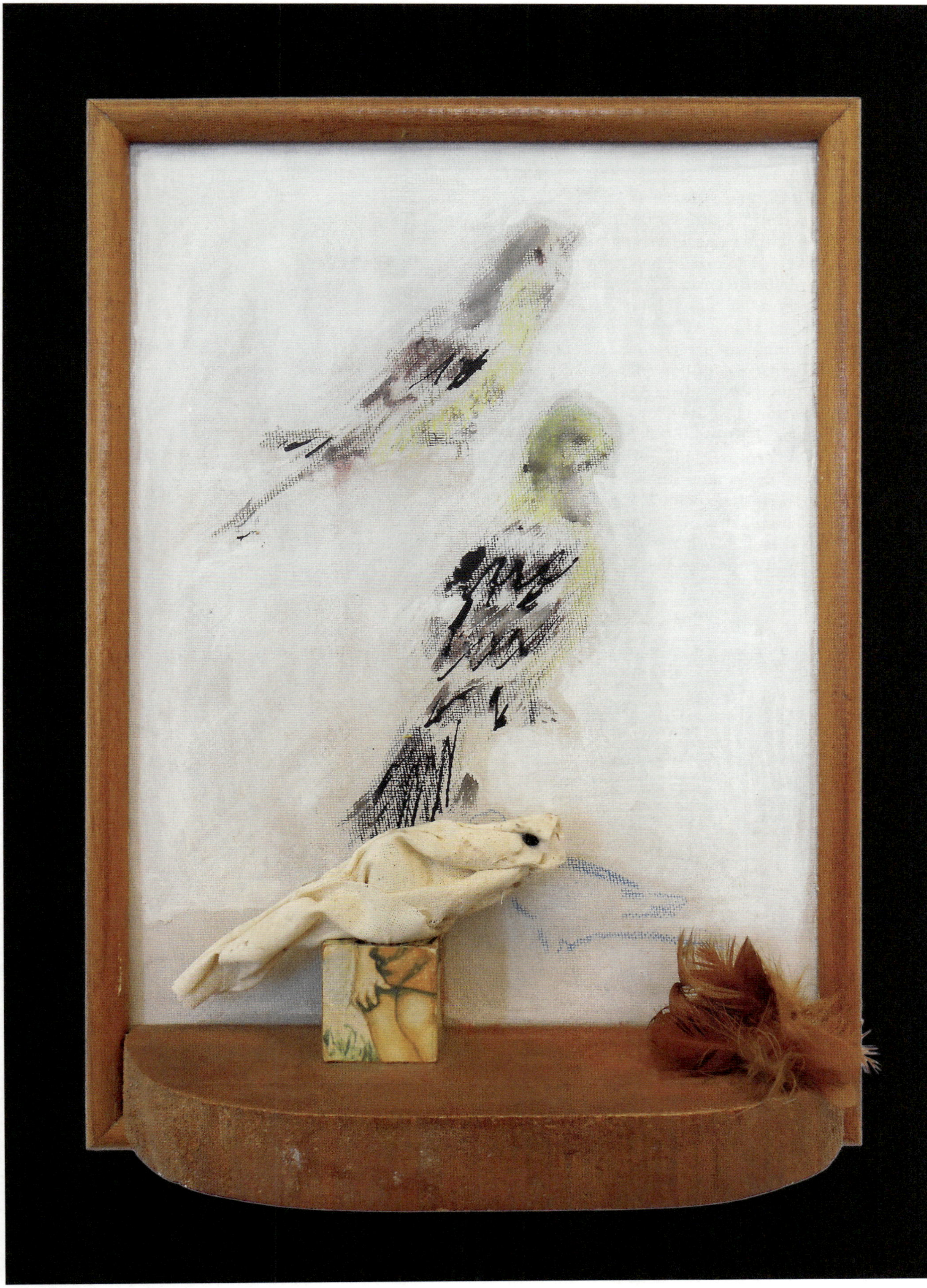

Oil, wooden cube and feather on hardboard, 37 × 26 × 8 cm

Füsun Onur's artistic practice and conceptual art are like distant relatives – we might not discern any resemblance at first. Her creations draw from things of daily life and their haptic evocations within us. An assembly of domestic objects, *Dream of Old Furniture* (1985) brings with it the materials – their appearance, their threads, their dust, their scent – of a home, and creates an uncanny space within the purported neutrality of the white cube. The dynamic is deliriously awkward – the objects are intensely familiar, but appear disturbed and dislocated. The pair of doll's legs, draped with a strand of common lace, stands on a wooden pedestal, but the rest of the figure has vanished. The cover of an ungainly armchair is stitched and bunched like a figure in confinement. A family portrait appears embroidered on a tabletop, along with two larger busts and their five little loved ones, but the table is disassembled, lying on its side with a wooden leg next to it. On the other side of the room, a lectern has wrapped itself in blankets and a tasseled woven net, as if it is trying to disappear. These are odd objects, each seeming to be playing and simultaneously refusing a role in this domestic arrangement. There's a surfeit of personality and absence of functionality. What Onur's installation reminds us of, in the objects' displacement into this carpet-less, evenly lit, temperature-controlled art venue, is that we inhabit our possessions to such an extent that we become inseparable from them. And they also remind us that the white cube is life's mausoleum, shattering any illusions we might carry into the museum, just as any good member of the conceptual art family would.

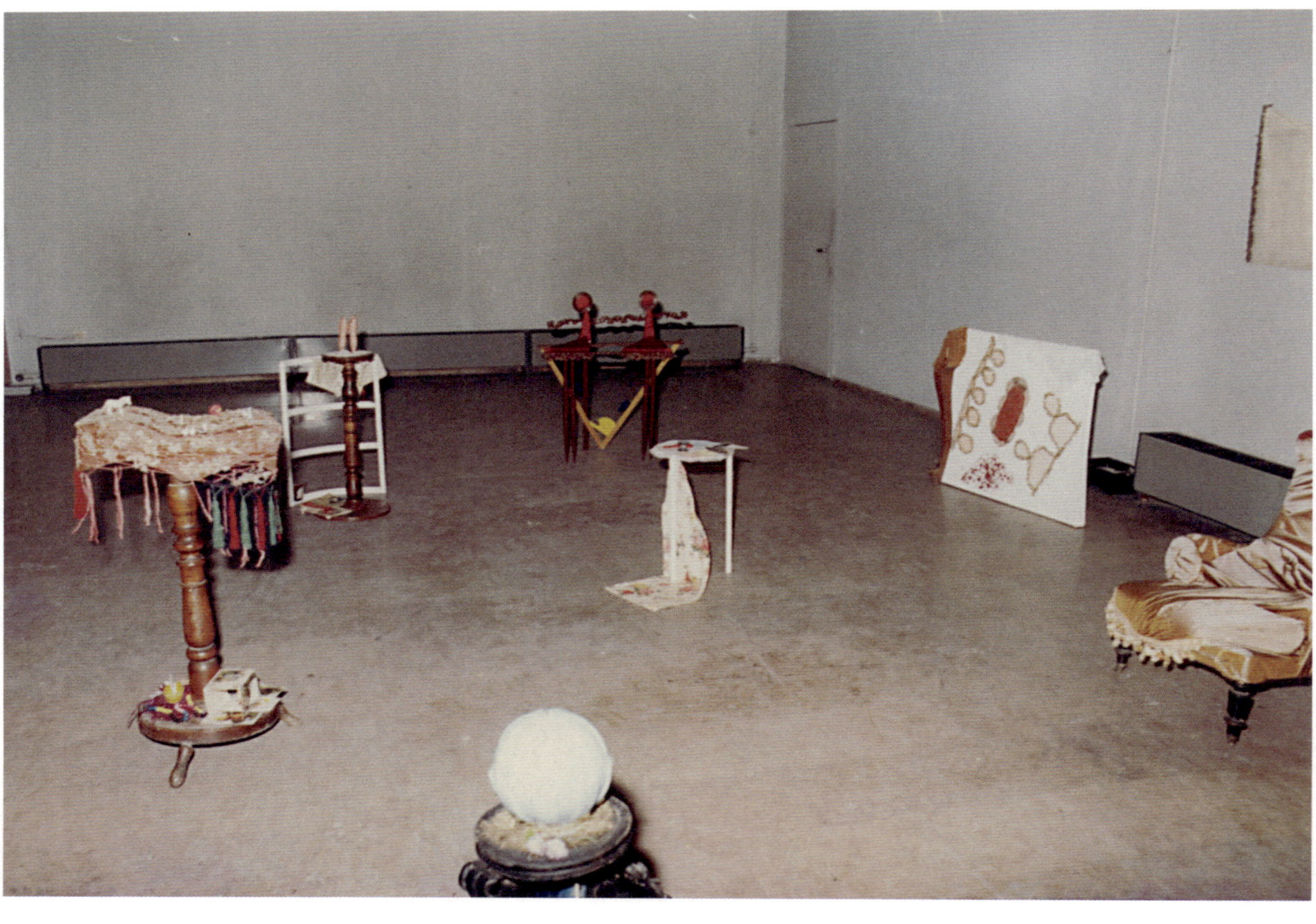

Installation with old furniture, textile and various objects
View from the exhibition, Taksim Art Gallery, 1985
(pp. 148–149) View from the exhibition *Through the Looking Glass*, Arter, 2014

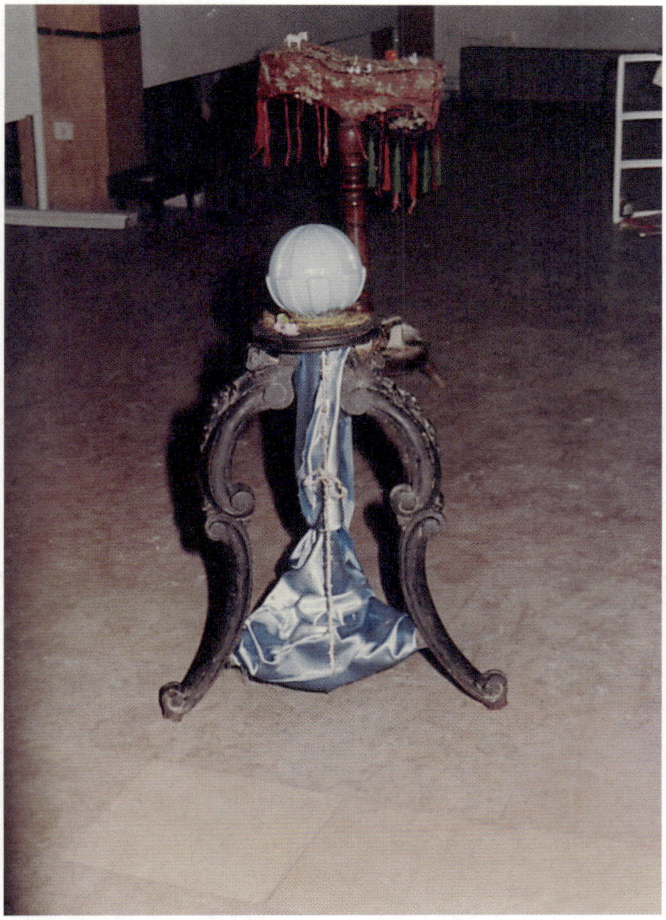

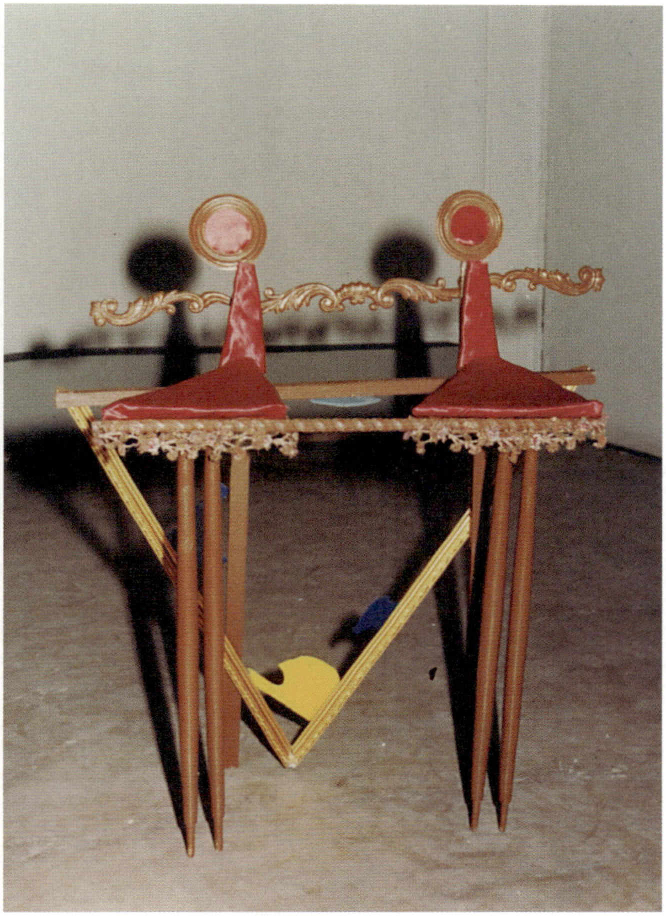

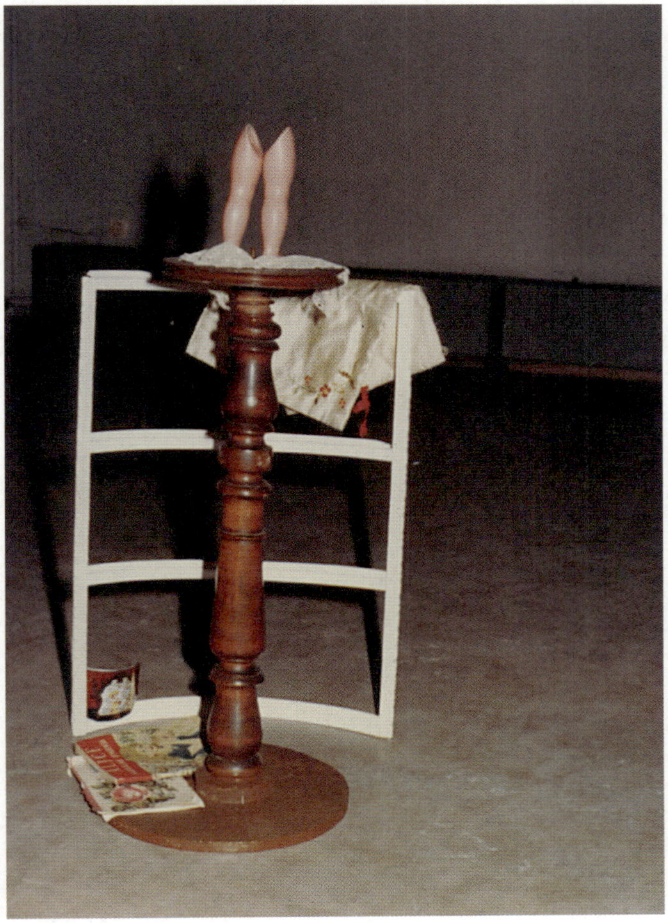

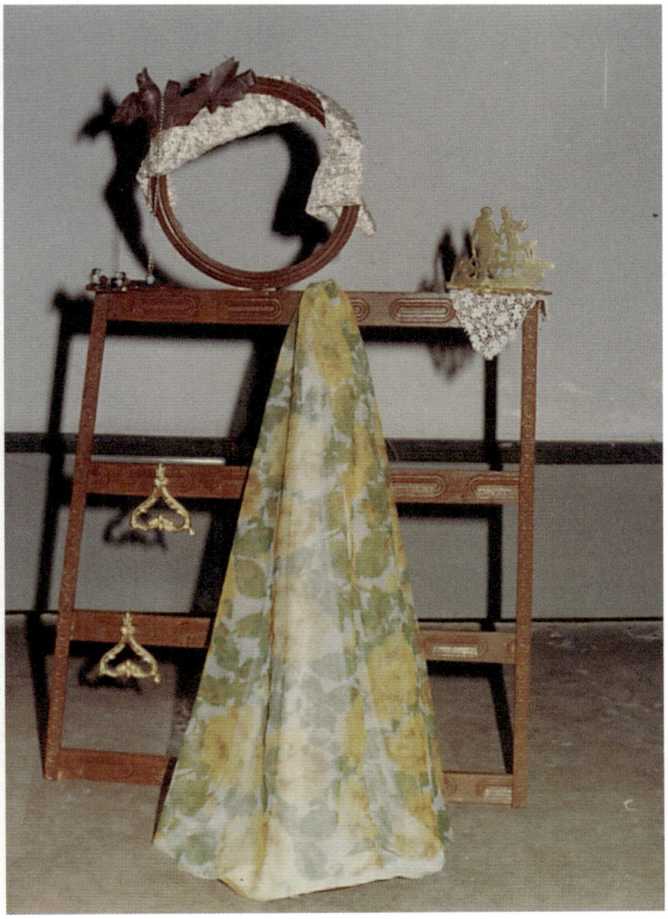

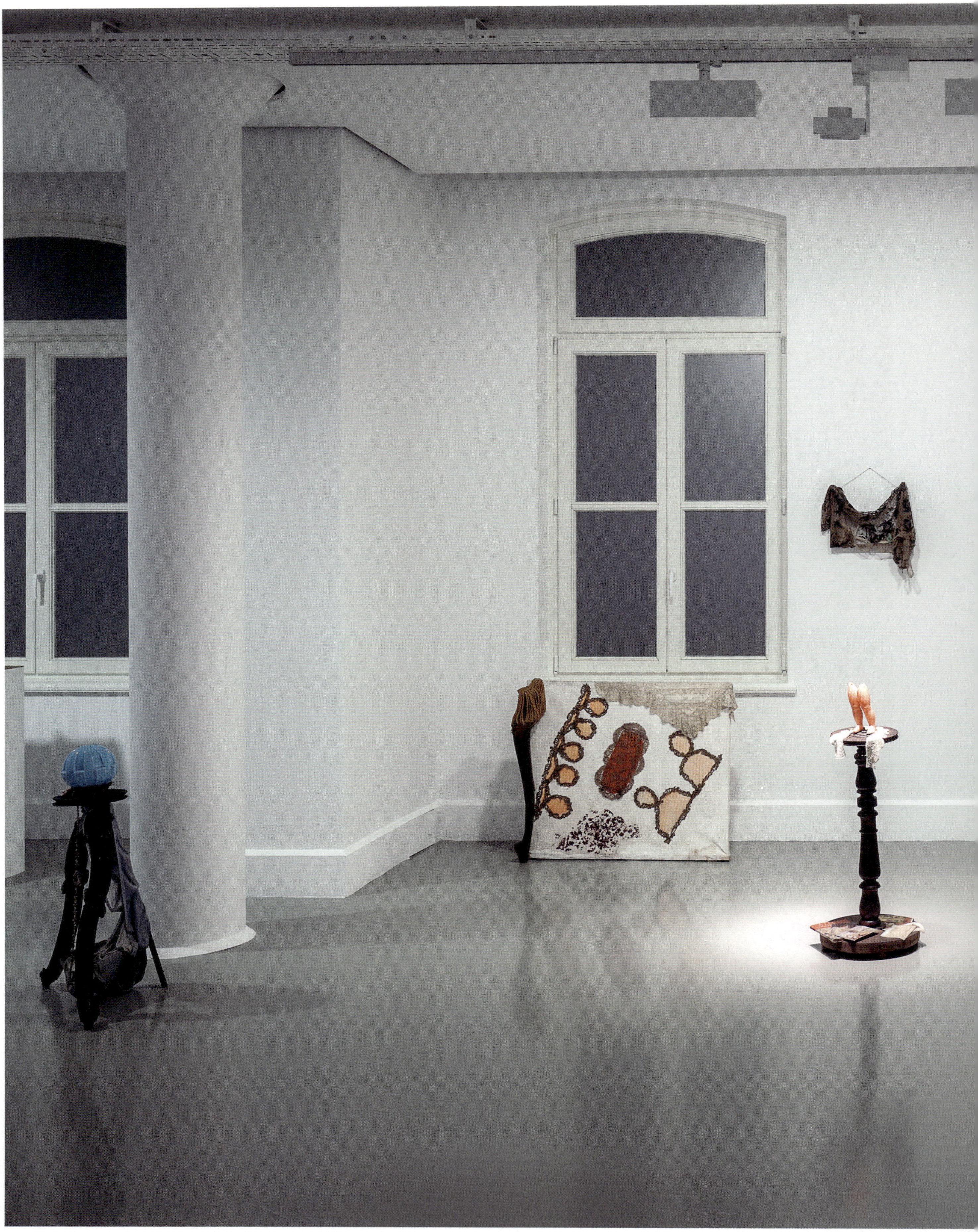

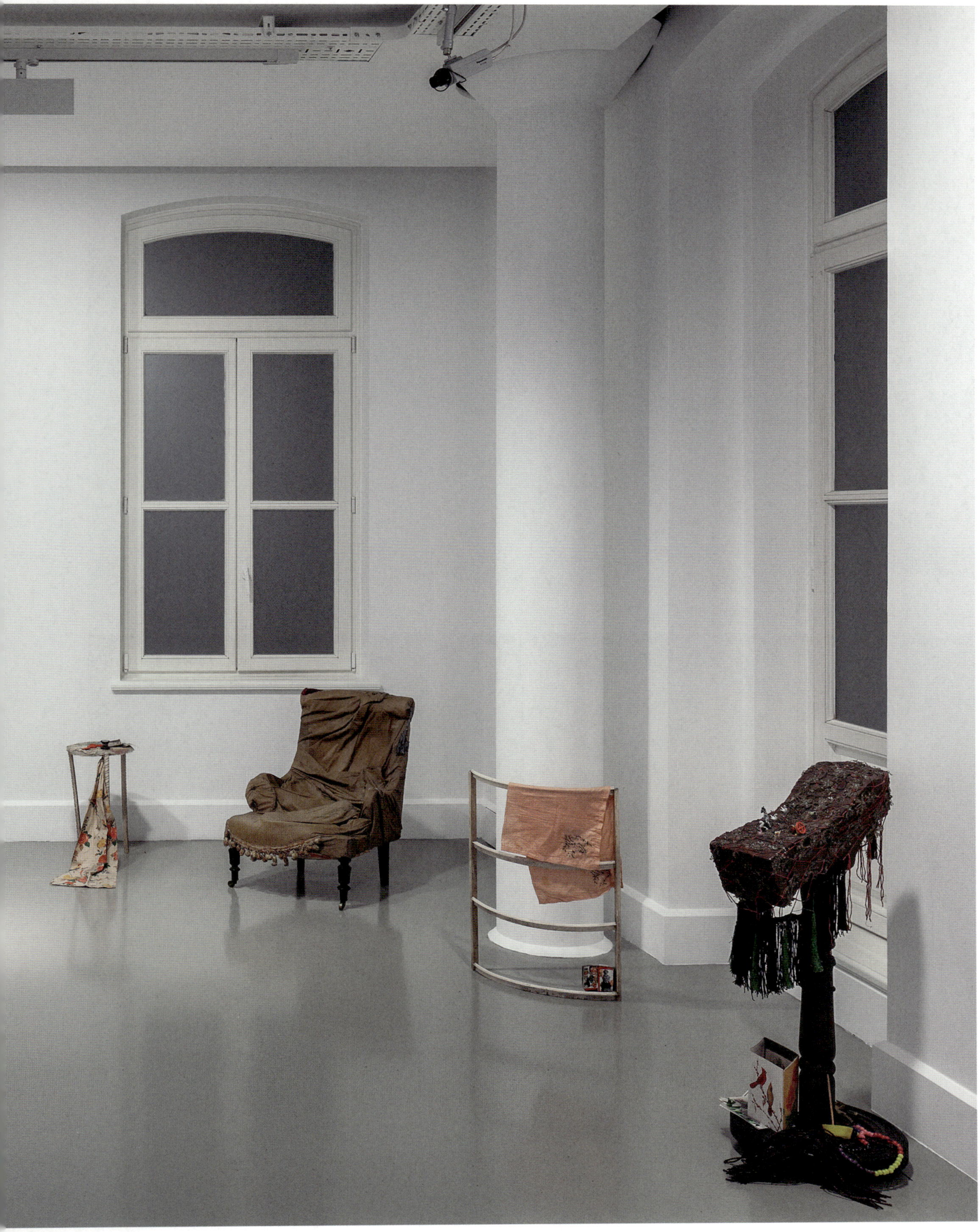

1985 ATATÜRK FLOWER

1985 BLACK ROSES FOR YILDIZ PALACE

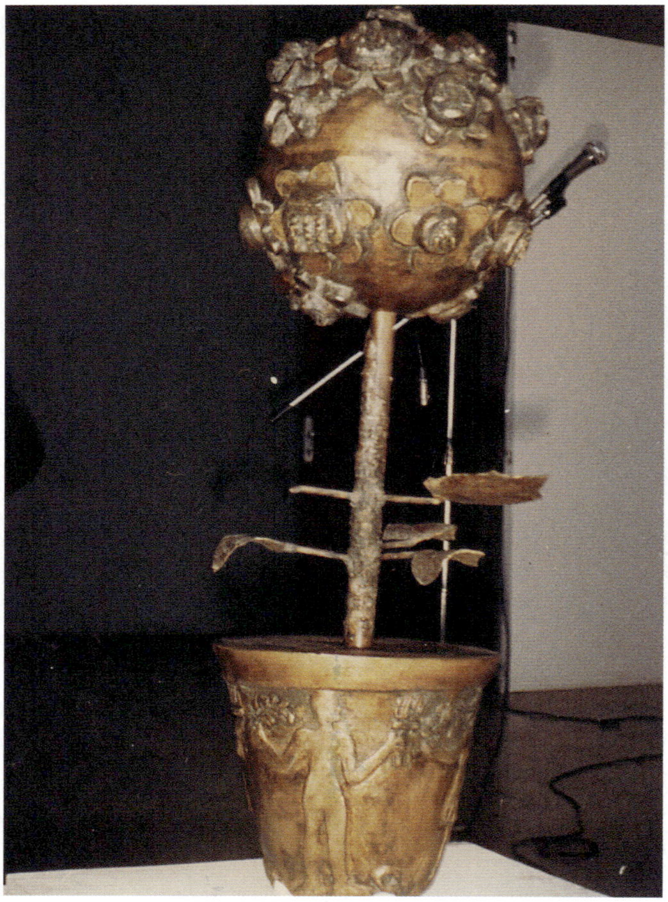

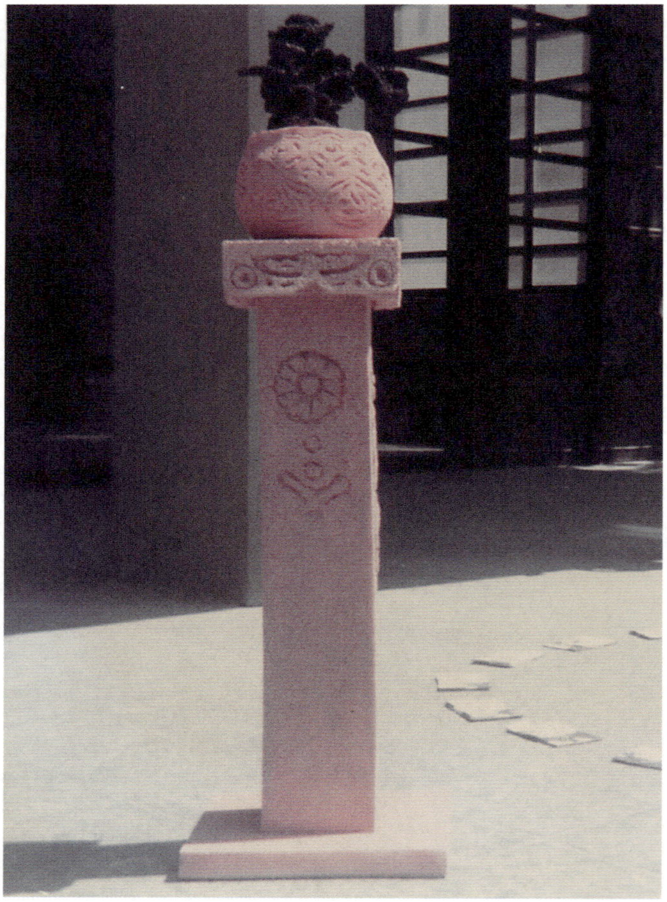

(Left) Bronze sculpture, 82 × 32 cm
(Right) Mixed media, 150 × 100 cm

1986 AFTERNOON WINDOW FRONT

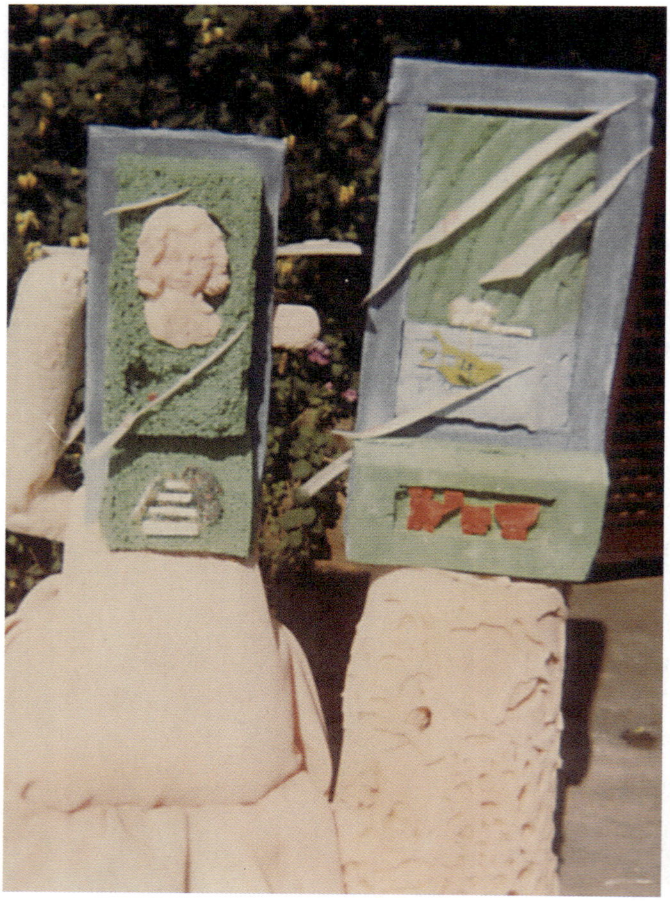

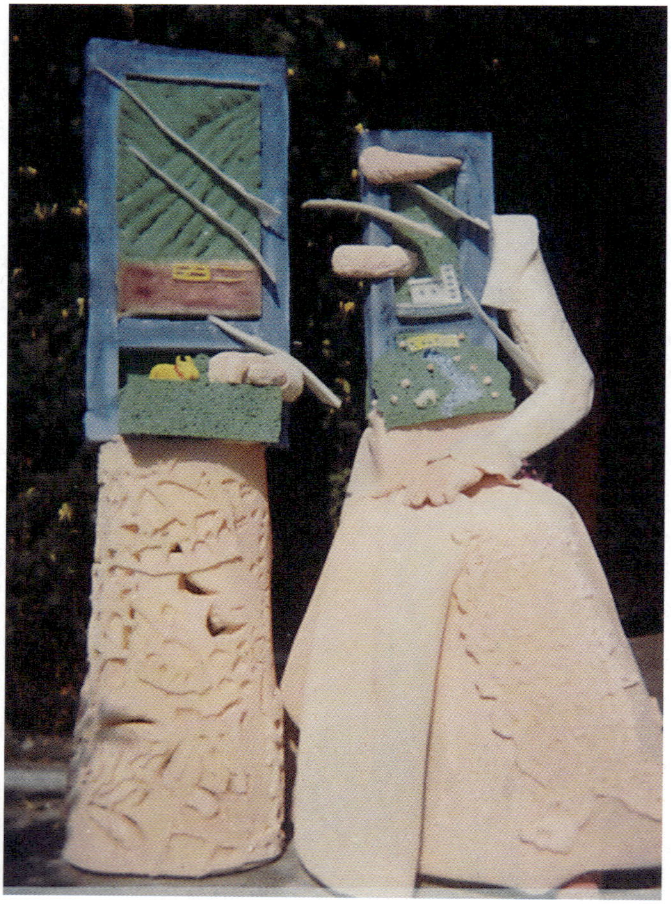

Mixed media, 120 × 80 × 85 cm

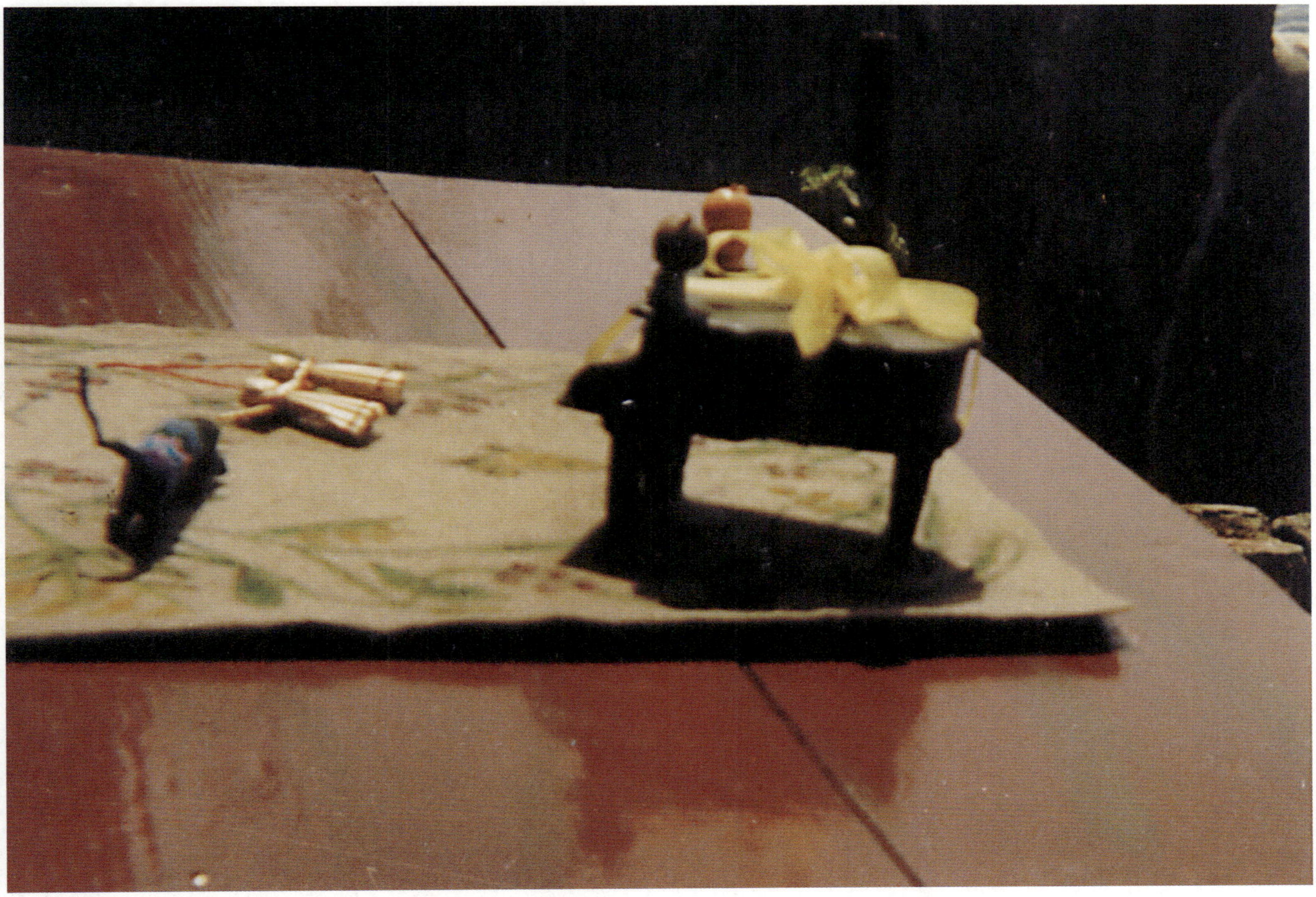

Mixed media, dimensions unknown

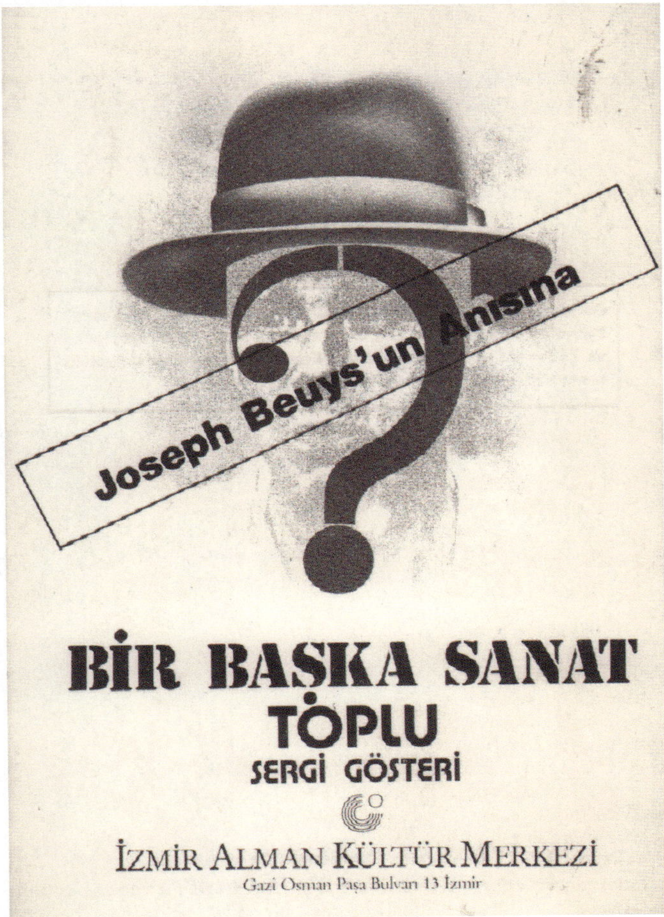

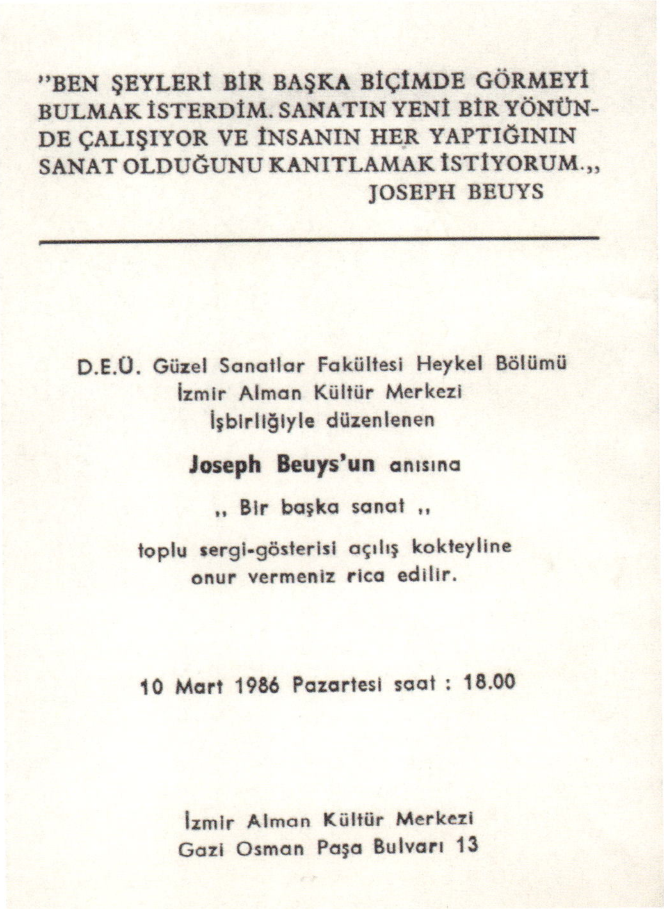

"BEN ŞEYLERİ BİR BAŞKA BİÇİMDE GÖRMEYİ BULMAK İSTERDİM. SANATIN YENİ BİR YÖNÜNDE ÇALIŞIYOR VE İNSANIN HER YAPTIĞININ SANAT OLDUĞUNU KANITLAMAK İSTİYORUM.,,
JOSEPH BEUYS

D.E.Ü. Güzel Sanatlar Fakültesi Heykel Bölümü
İzmir Alman Kültür Merkezi
İşbirliğiyle düzenlenen
Joseph Beuys'un anısına
,, Bir başka sanat ,,
toplu sergi-gösterisi açılış kokteyline
onur vermeniz rica edilir.

10 Mart 1986 Pazartesi saat : 18.00

İzmir Alman Kültür Merkezi
Gazi Osman Paşa Bulvarı 13

Invitation of the exhibition *In Memory of Joseph Beuys*, 1986

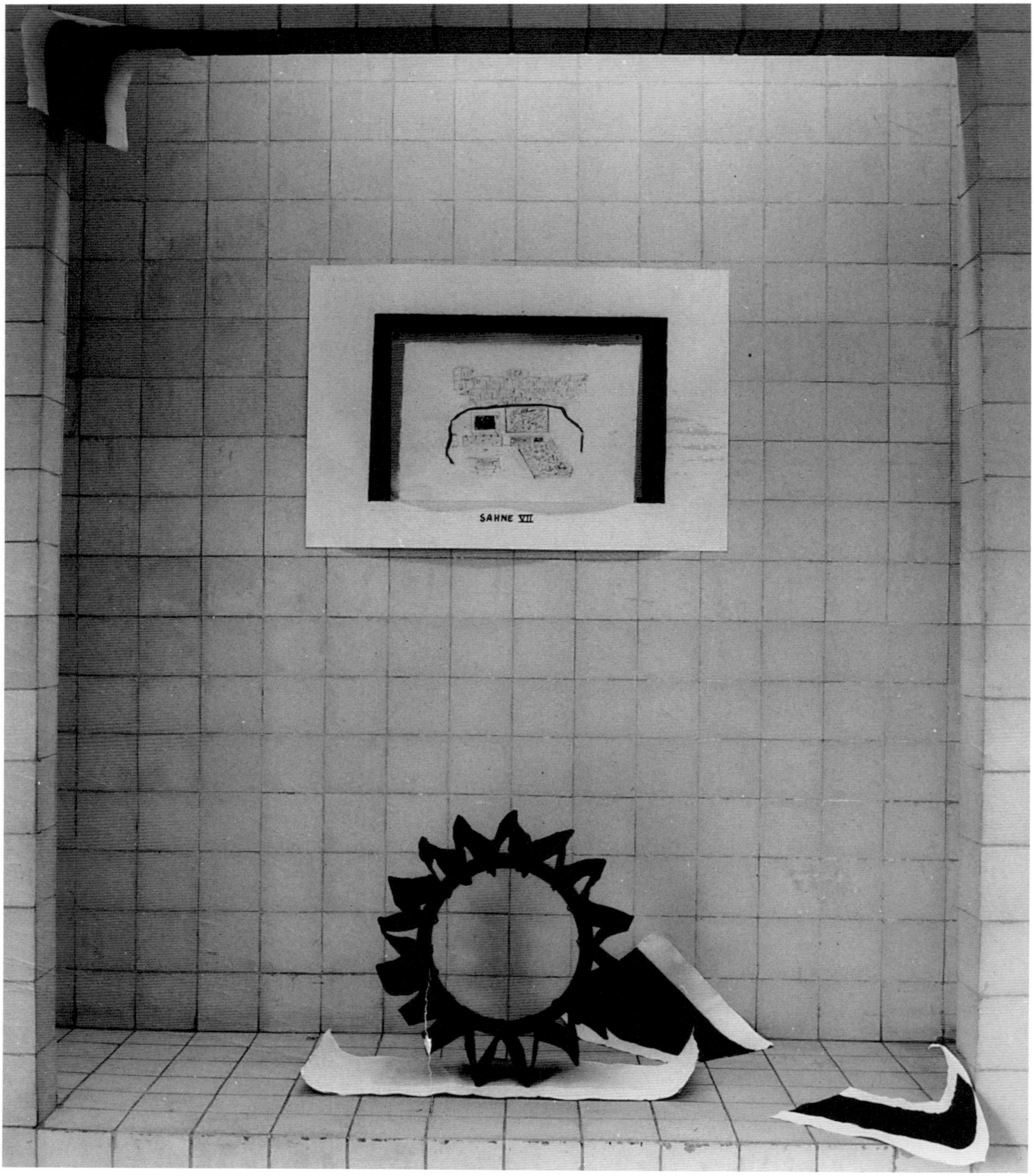

Installation (canvas, wood)

In all fields of life, there is multiplicity but deterioration, degeneration and lack of quality. The bombardment of TV commercials, video-films and gimmicks. A passive outlook! People are playing certain parts; they have each grabbed a part in the play: they have got carried away with the codes and the rules of the game. It is the same in art. If we want to practice real art without looking back, without eclecticism, and without imitation (of which I have never approved, whether national or international), we have to take up the elements of art one by one. 'What is art?' I keep asking myself. What was it in the early ages? What is it today? Painting and sculpture help us perceive the existence of what does not exist. Attention is mostly focused on the image, not on the meaning. Signs are related to how we perceive the world and what we understand from it. What can the function of art be today? A critical re-structuring and re-coding. I want art to render the 'innocent' element, the intact element with such expectations of sharing the experience of art as knowing/not knowing, reading/not reading, participating/not participating and understanding/not understanding.

Text written by the artist for the exhibition, from the artist's archive.

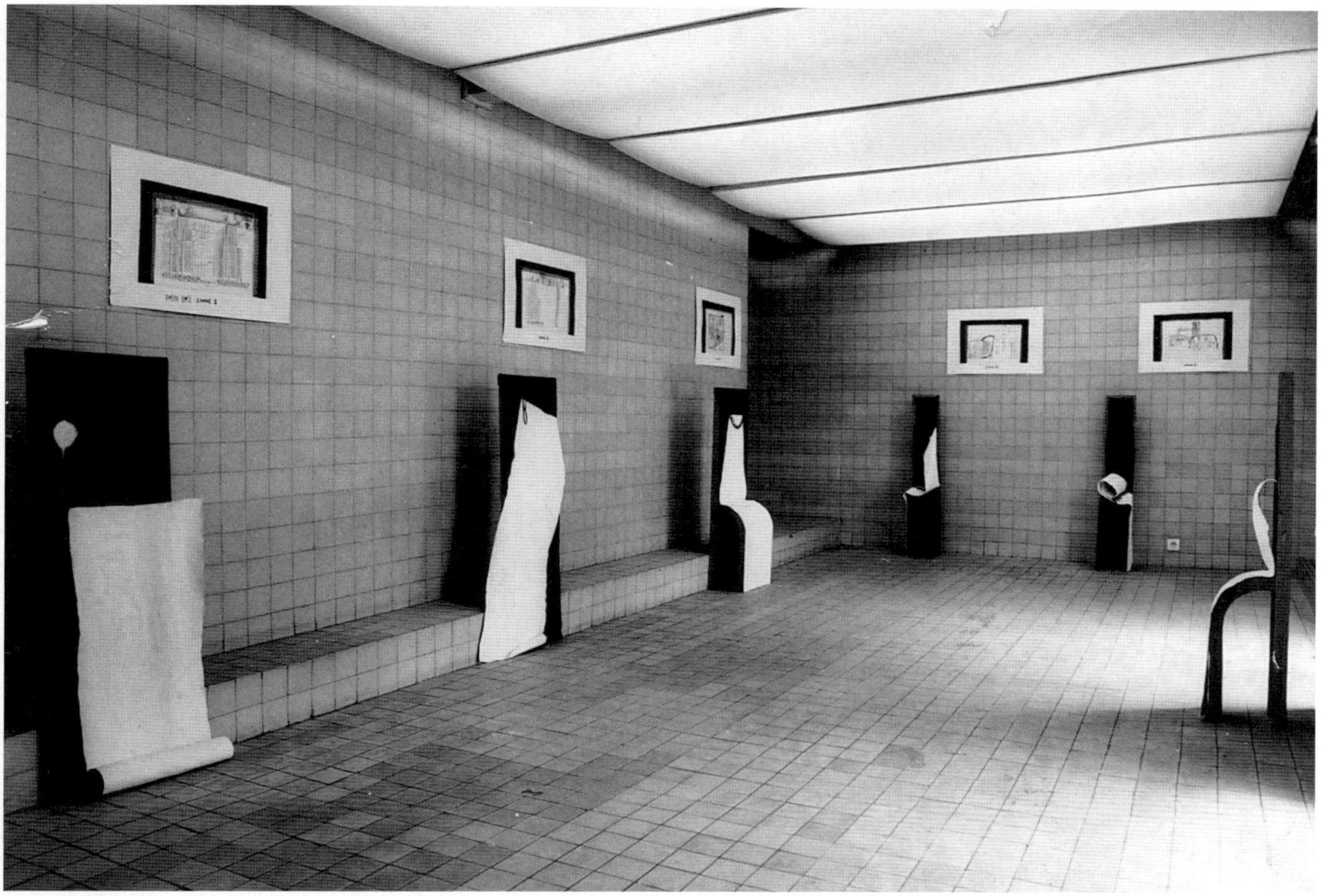

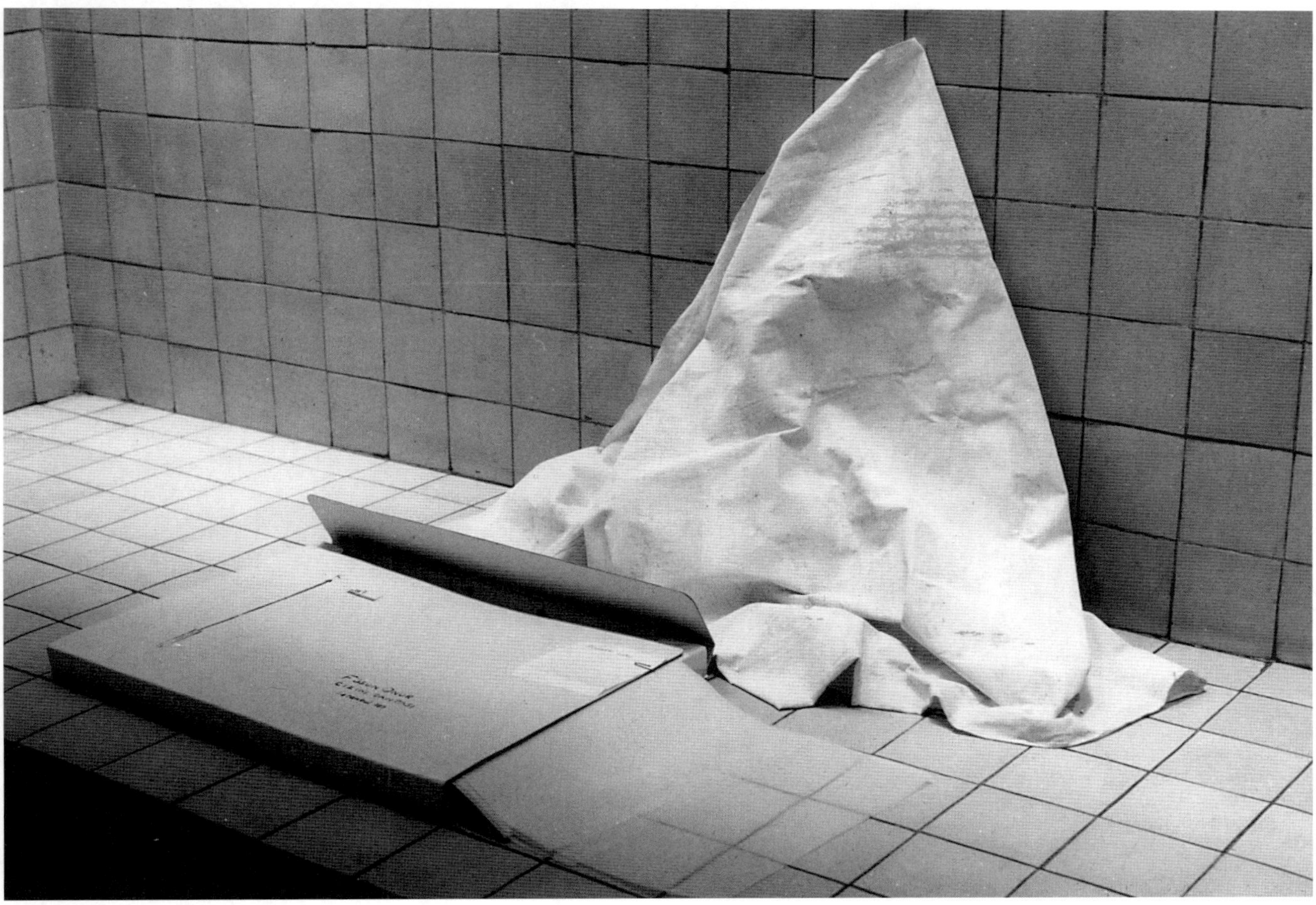

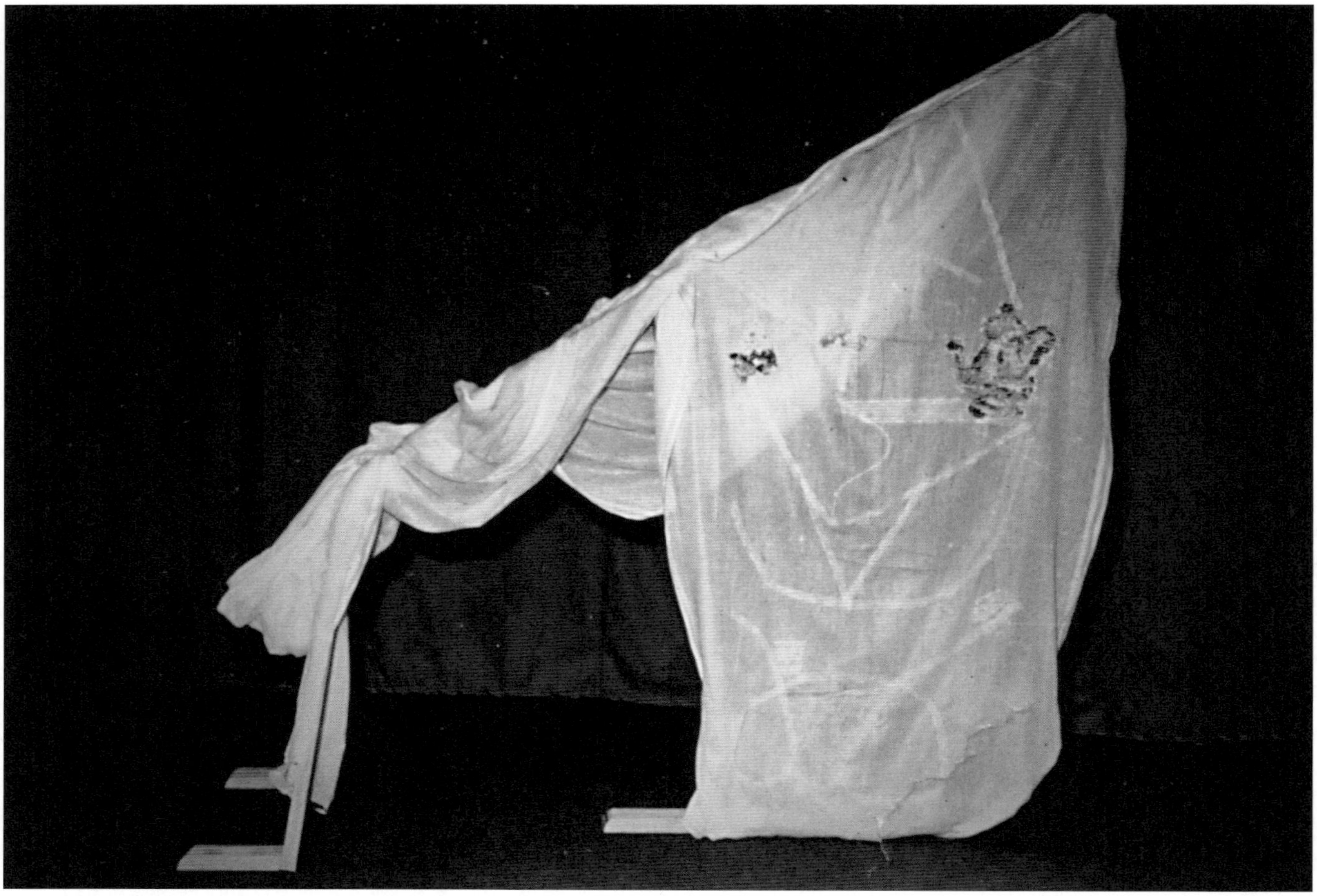

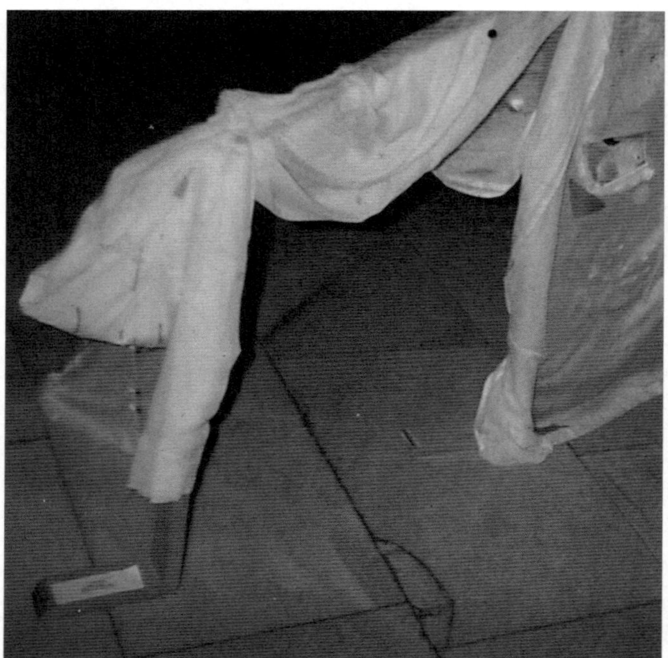

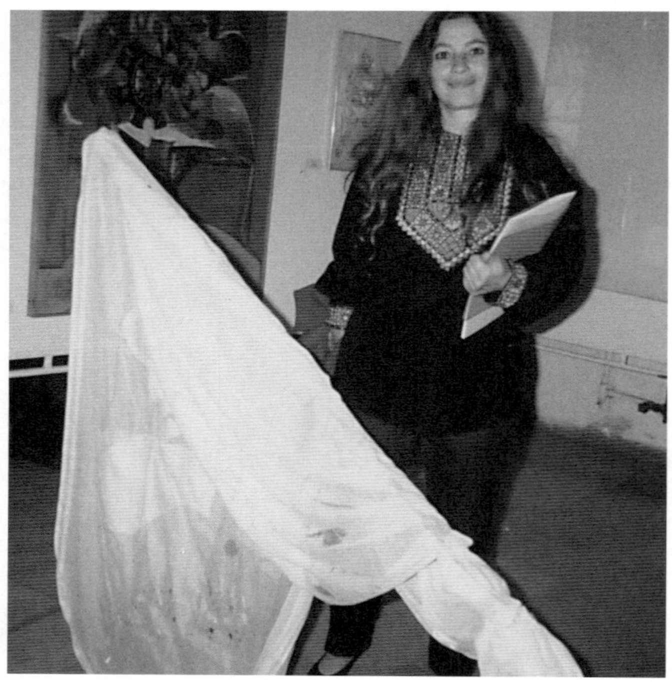

Mixed media, 140 × 20 × 45 cm

It would not be wrong to say that underlying Füsun Onur's interest in spatial arrangement or volume and space is her strong sense of sculpture. In some, this comes across in the form of her memories through nostalgic ready-found objects, and in some, it comes across us with morning gymnastics. The materials she uses may not be elegant or meticulous like Aysan's, but an ordinary construction, one element, suffices to express what she thinks.

Yusuf Taktak, excerpt from the text 'For A Nameless Exhibition' written for *Untitled* organised at Derimod, 1989, SALT Research, Istanbul.

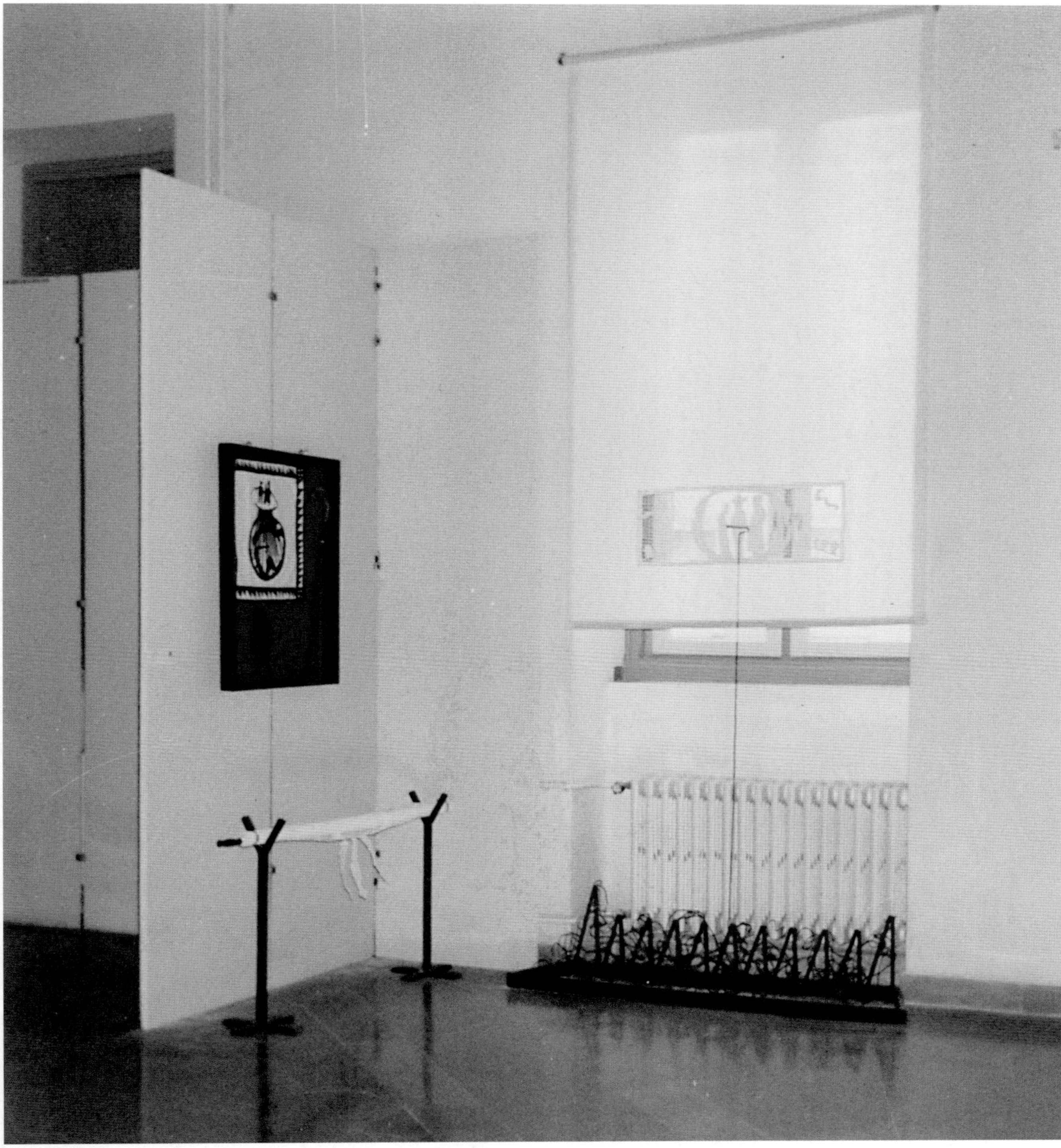

Mixed media, variable dimensions

I too was allocated a place in the Military Museum at Harbiye, in the space where mostly the sculptors would be exhibiting their works. Am I going to make a sculpture or an installation? I thought about what sort of a place I was in. I opted to make an installation in front of one of the windows there. There was also a radiator under the window I'd chosen. I thought about what I could do to this window in that space. I'd be making a work that hadn't been exhibited before. First, I developed the idea of making a curtain for the window; other details followed that idea. I liked the light of this window. At the time, I was perhaps making more narrative works, works with more content, but however much content it comprised, its content could only be perceived by more careful eyes. When I exhibited the work, those who saw it made comments such as, 'Oh what beautiful light … The light comes in differently in the morning, and it's also different in the evening,' but no one understood the content! In terms of material, I used a lacelike – well actually not exactly lace – but a curtain woven with thread; wood in front of the radiator; and human figures made of cables rolling inside the shadow cast by that wooden material. The materials were wood, metal, fabric and cable. On the curtain were the three major powers: USA, Russia, China. I made ropes descending to the cable-people that seemed to be rolling inside the wooden material in front of the radiator. The ropes were in their hands … I tried to make all of them look like museum pieces. The fact that the exhibition space was a museum also evoked this idea.

From the interview made by Özge Araslı Yardım with Füsun Onur on 19 February 2001. See Özge Araslı Yardım, 'Turkish Artists Who Participated in the International Istanbul Biennials Organised Between 1987–2001,' unpublished Master's thesis, Mimar Sinan University Institute of Social Sciences, Istanbul, 2001, p. 231.

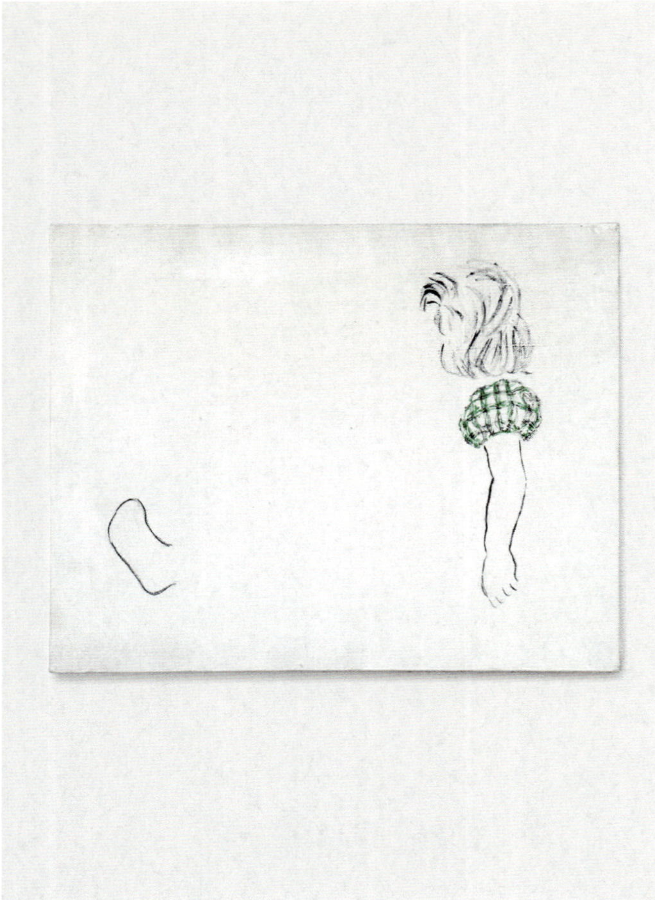

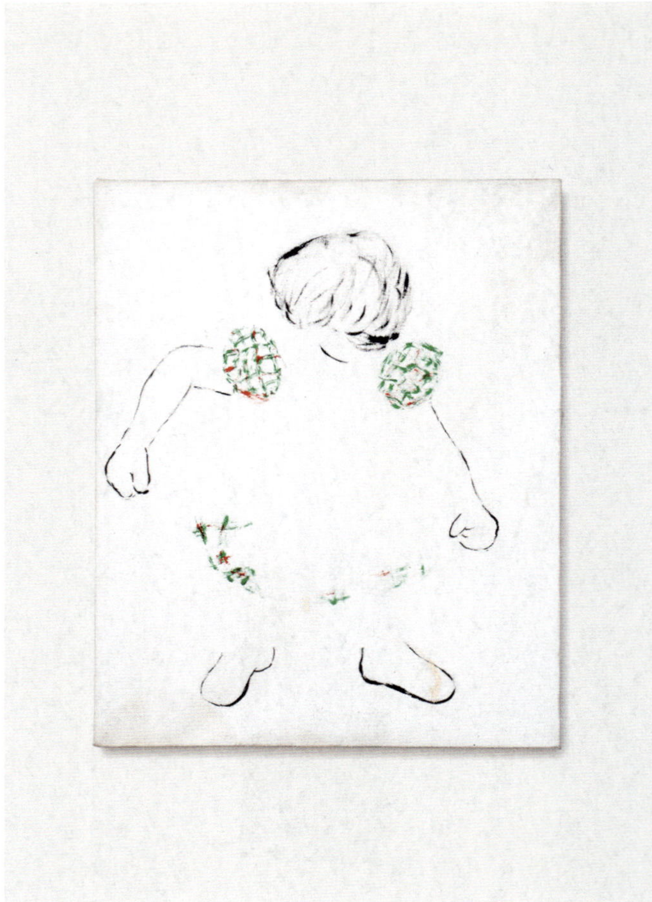

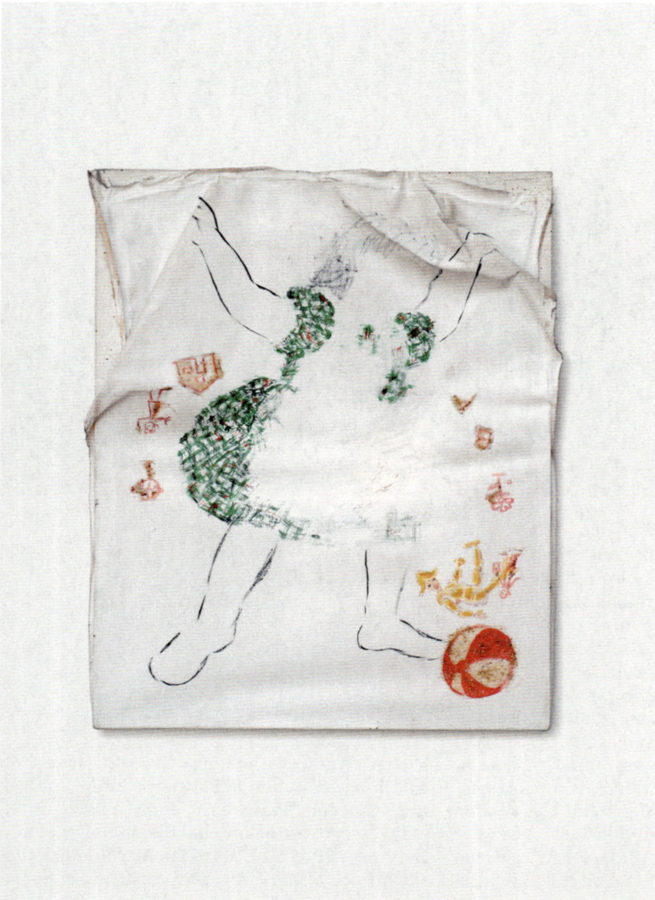

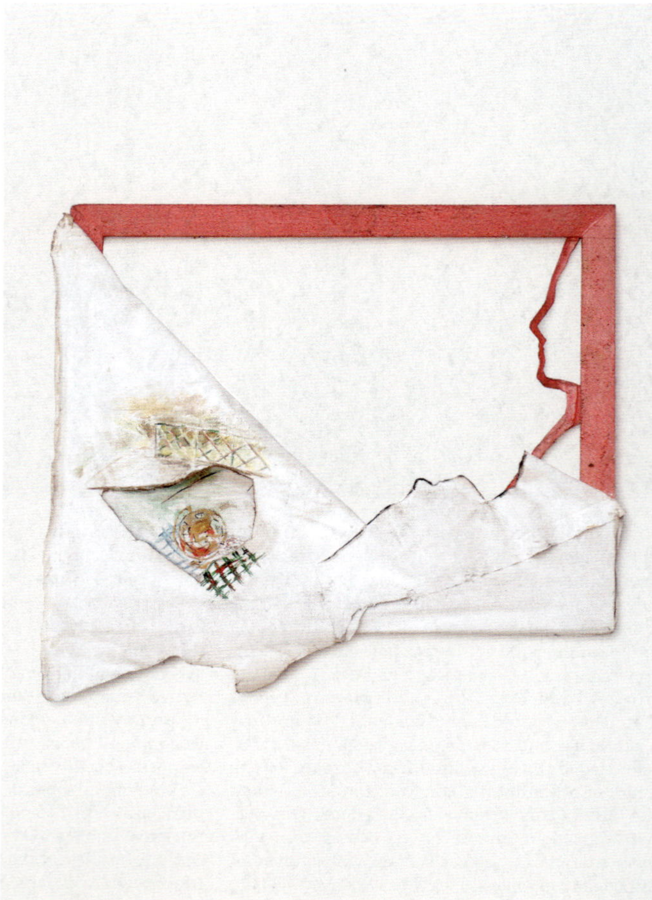

Mixed media on canvas, 4 pieces, each 40 × 50 cm

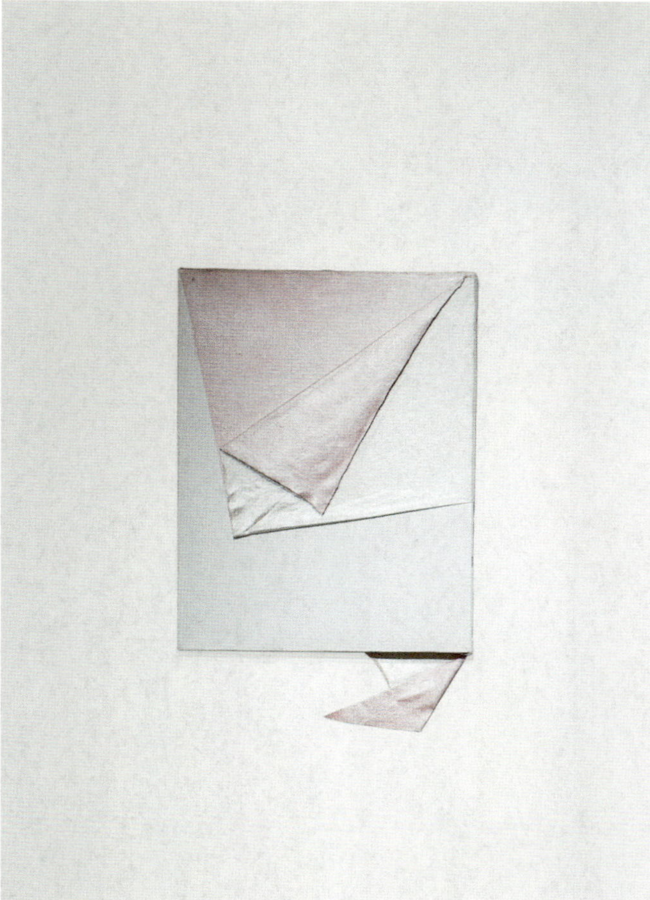

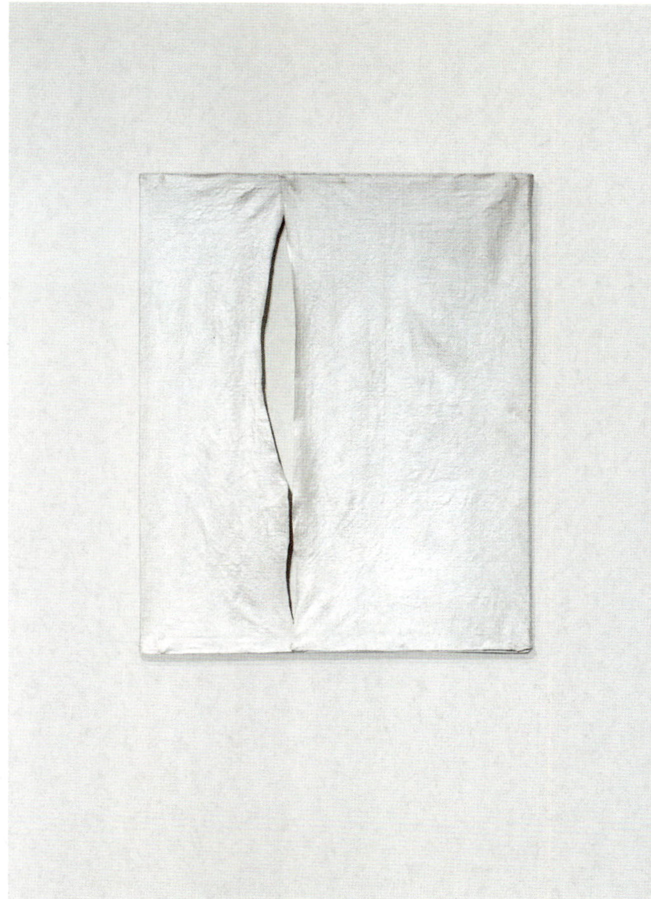

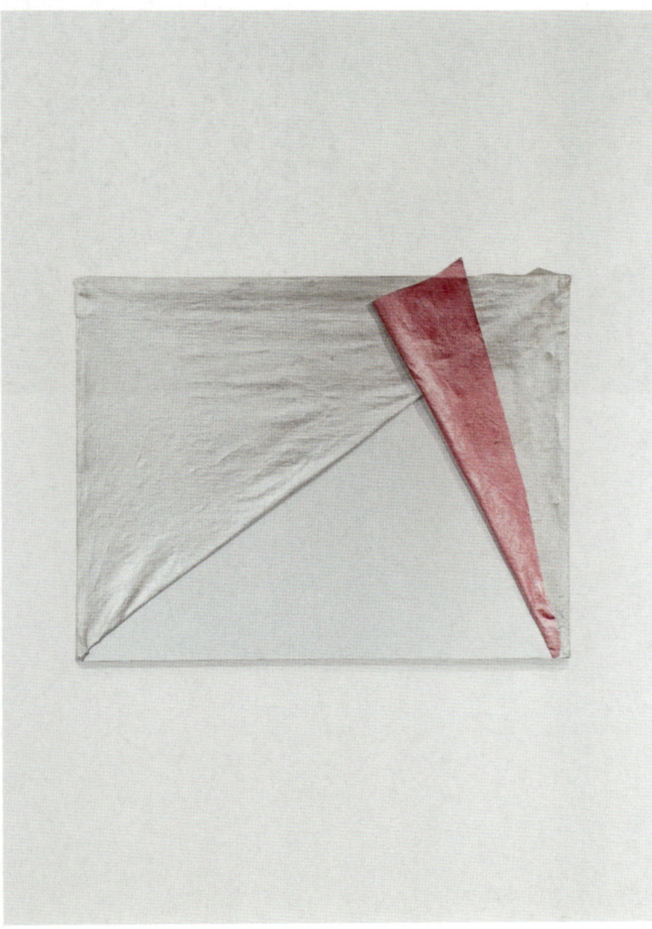

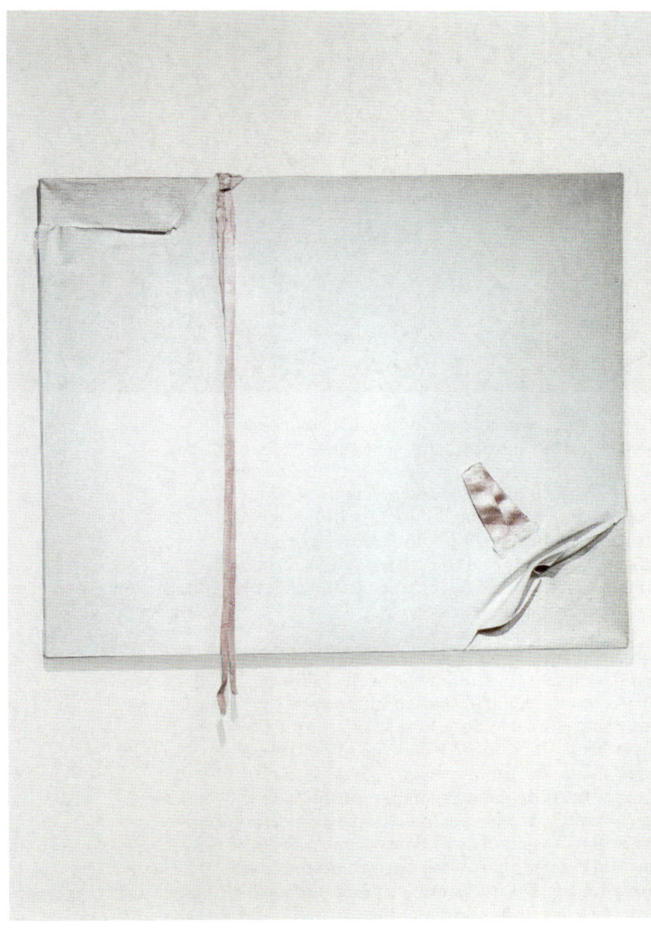

(From left to right) Mixed media on canvas, 49.5 × 59.5 cm, 50 × 39.5 cm, 39.5 × 50 cm, 48 × 30 cm

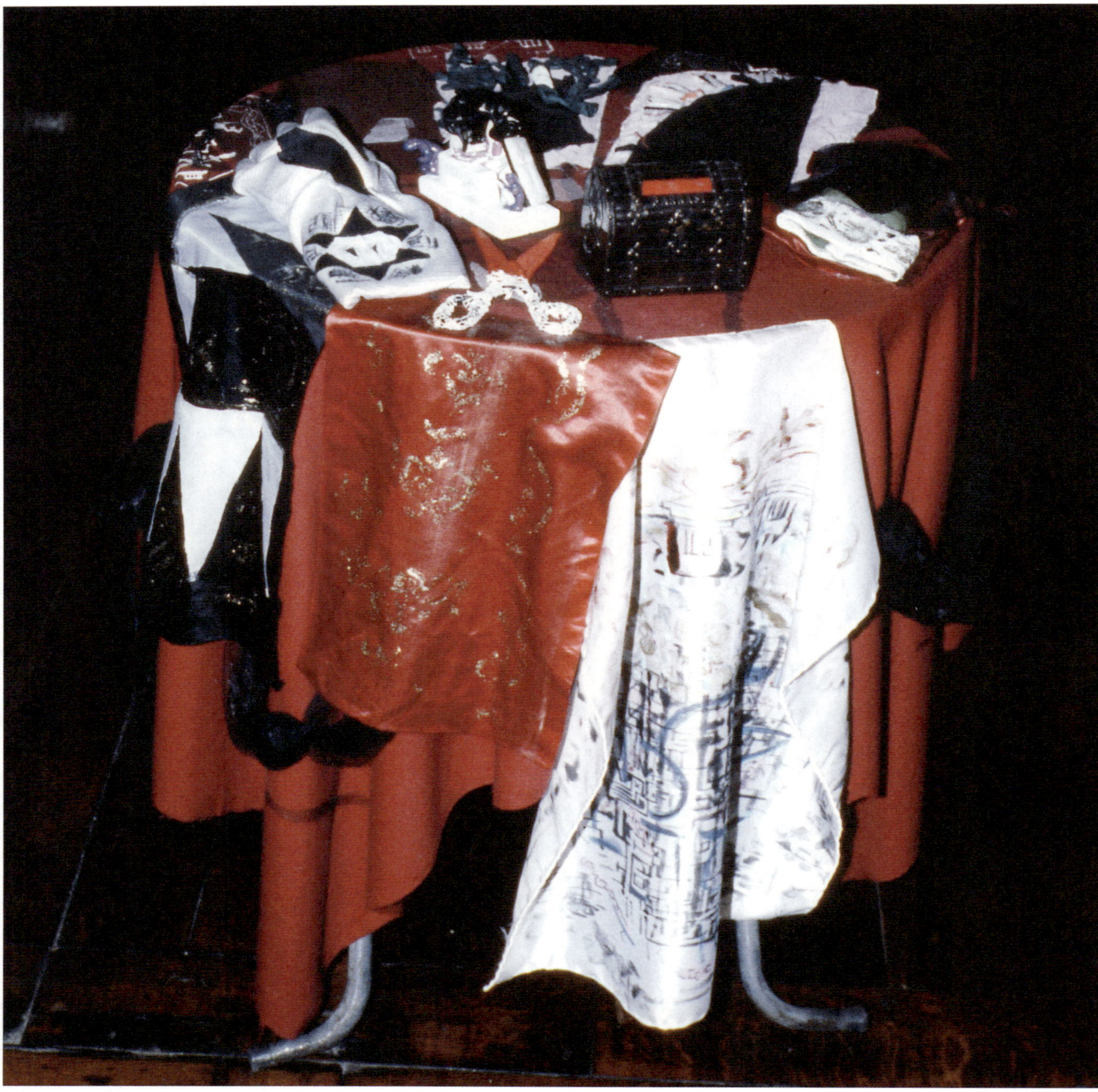

Mixed media

The age we live in compels many of us to look at everything mechanically in every sense [...] art, as well. A few phrases penned in fancy words may subdue the audience and procure a mechanical look. [...] but I insist on it, I will not write such phrases because I want creativity to elevate the audience and the critics and lead them to compound. A 'table,' look and see how, why it has been assembled.

Füsun Onur, excerpt from '12 Years Before the New Age,' *Cumhuriyet*, 31 May 1988.

As we continue to walk around in the kiosk, we come across a table under the stairs. This is Füsun Onur's table. In the exhibition catalogue, Onur says, 'A table, look and see how and why it has been assembled.' What the artist brings together on the table are tiny statuettes, fabrics, contrasting colours, transfigured tools ... On this table, Onur also includes the tiny statuettes that she made in middle school and, with the intervention of her older sister, desisted from throwing out. Onur's work [...] has to be seen by drawing near and even touching.

Lale Filoğlu, excerpt from 'Avantgarde Art in Hareket Kiosk,' *Cumhuriyet*, 7 June 1988.

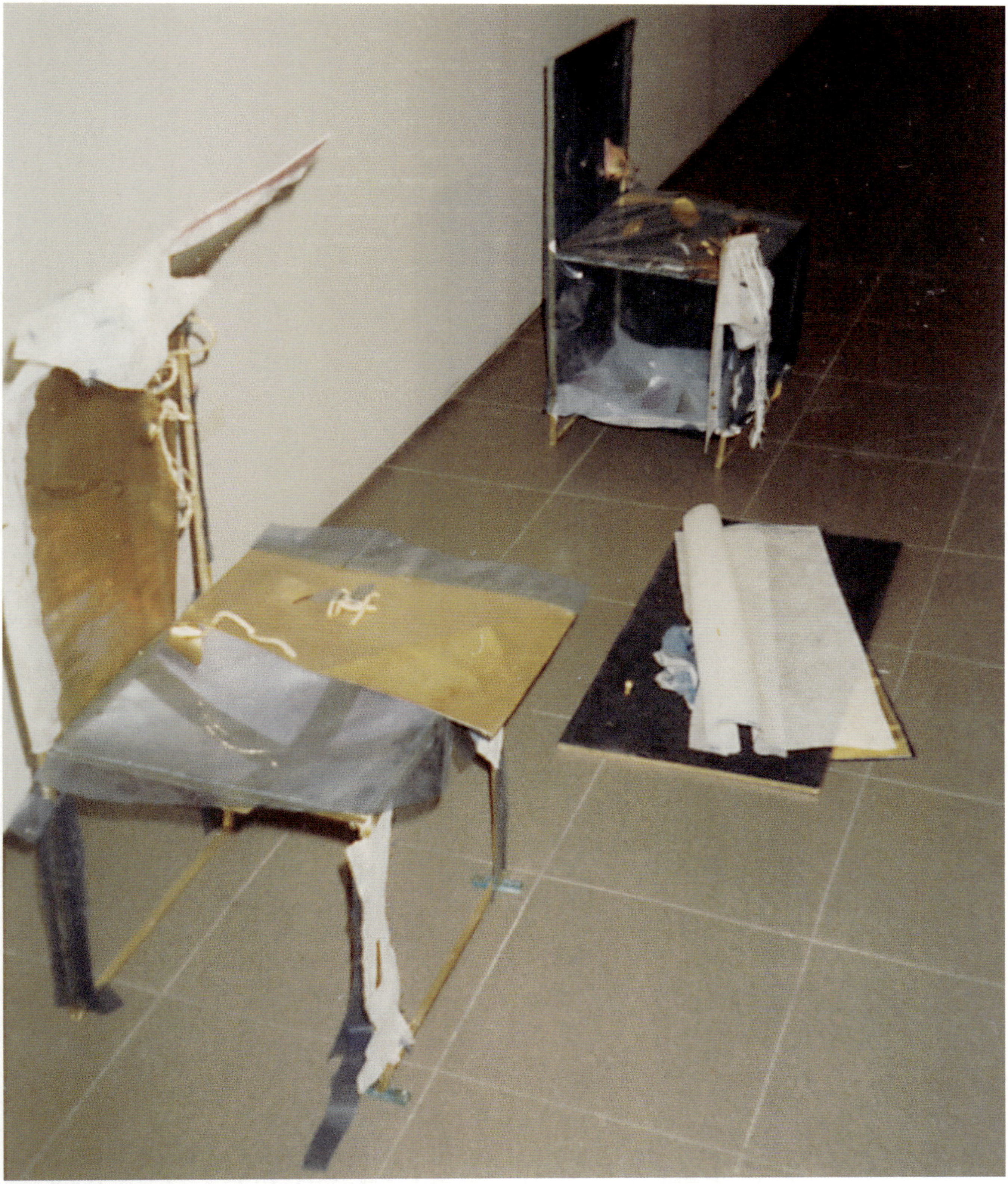

Mixed media

Füsun Onur has produced yet another of her toy-like artworks, which she has been producing for some time, that probes the concept of 'space-time' and draws on the sensory quality and associative power of various tools. In this new artwork titled *Captured Light*, which she constructed with gilded paper, cardboard, buckram, coloured threads, nylon and laths, Onur has transformed the room through the special light that enters it into an associative and symbolic 'installation.'

Author unknown, excerpt from 'Exhibitions,' *Milliyet Sanat*, 1 September 1989, issue 223.

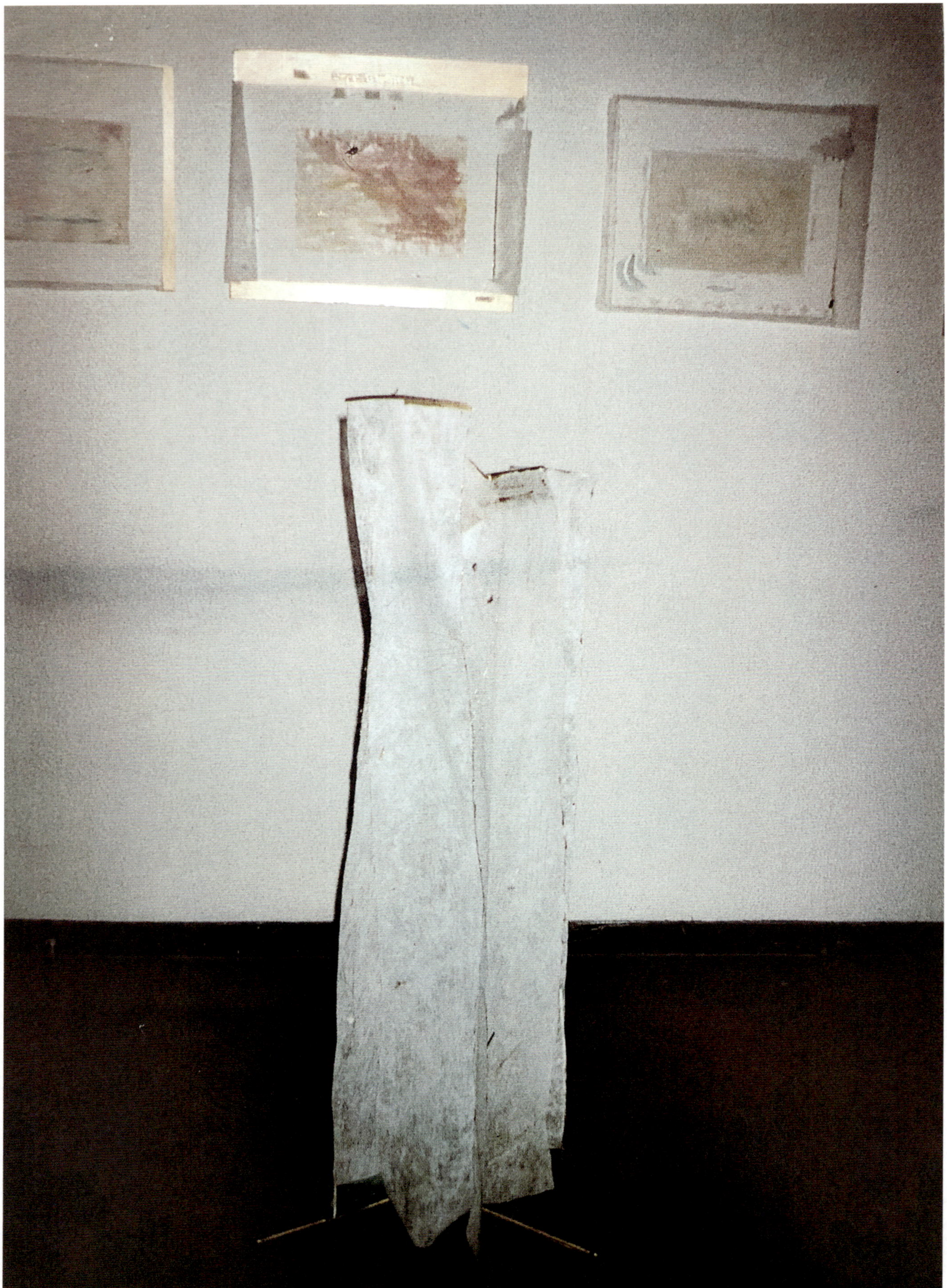

Canvas, wood, gauze, gilding, paint

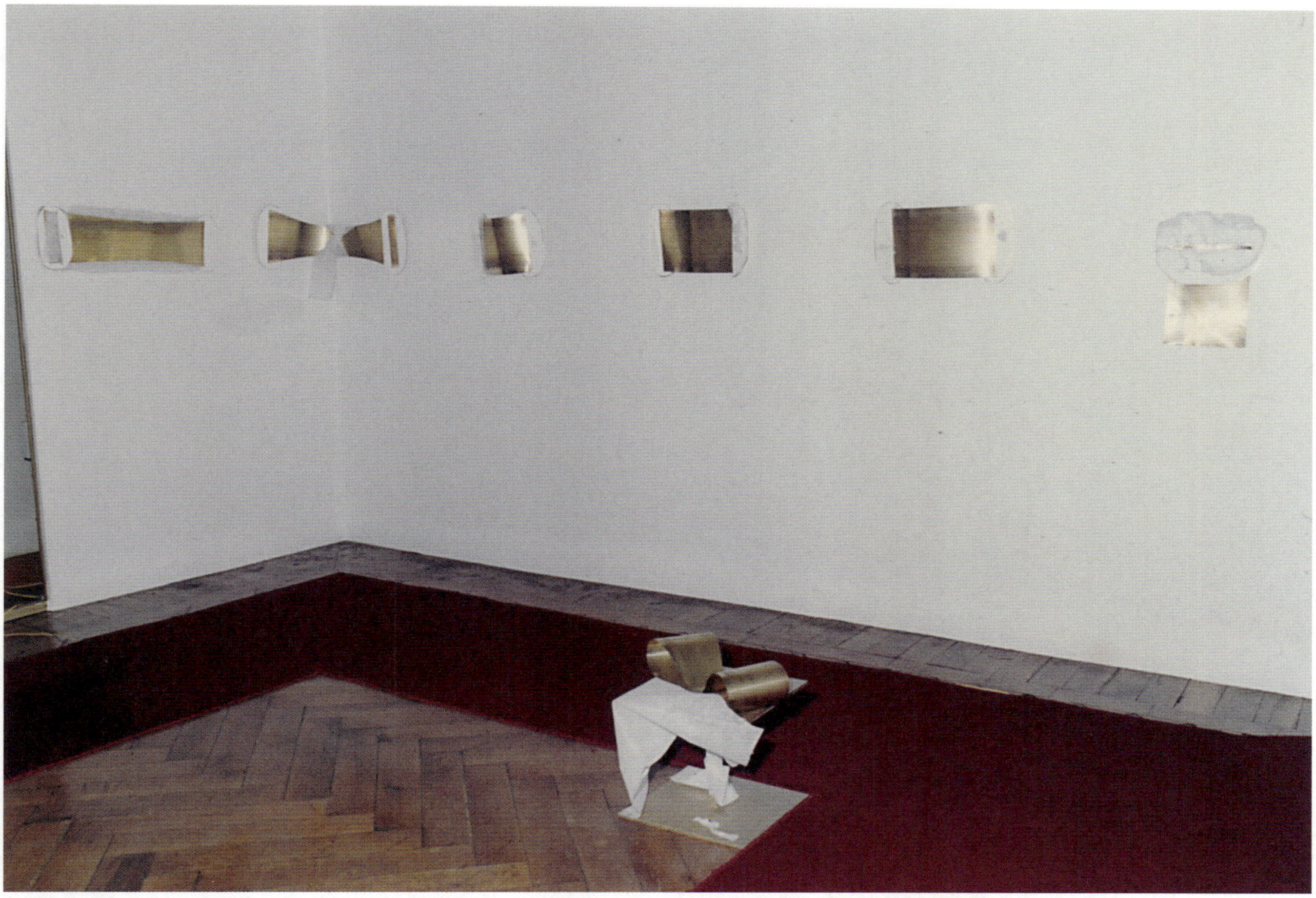

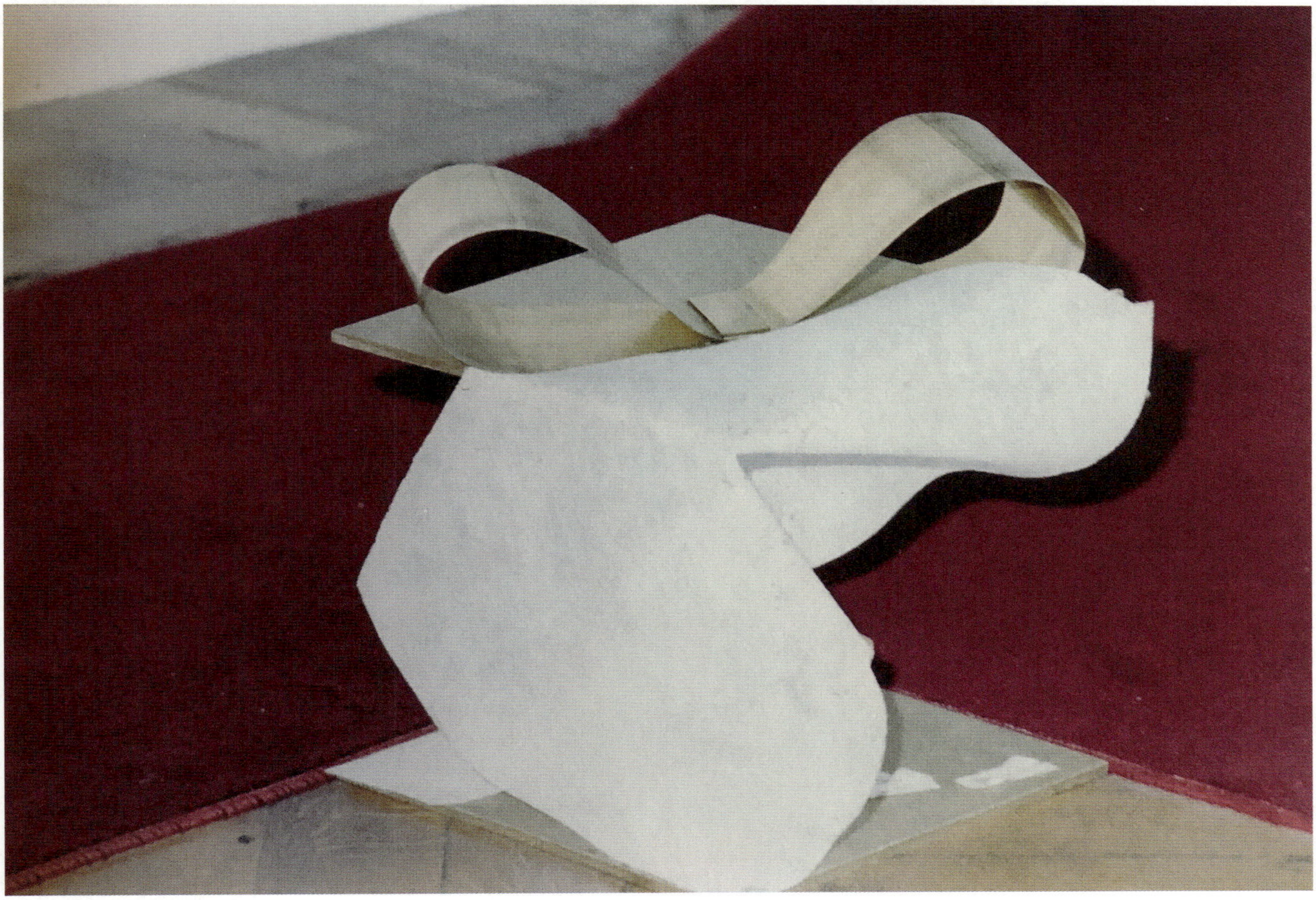

Canvas, wood, gauze, gilding, paint

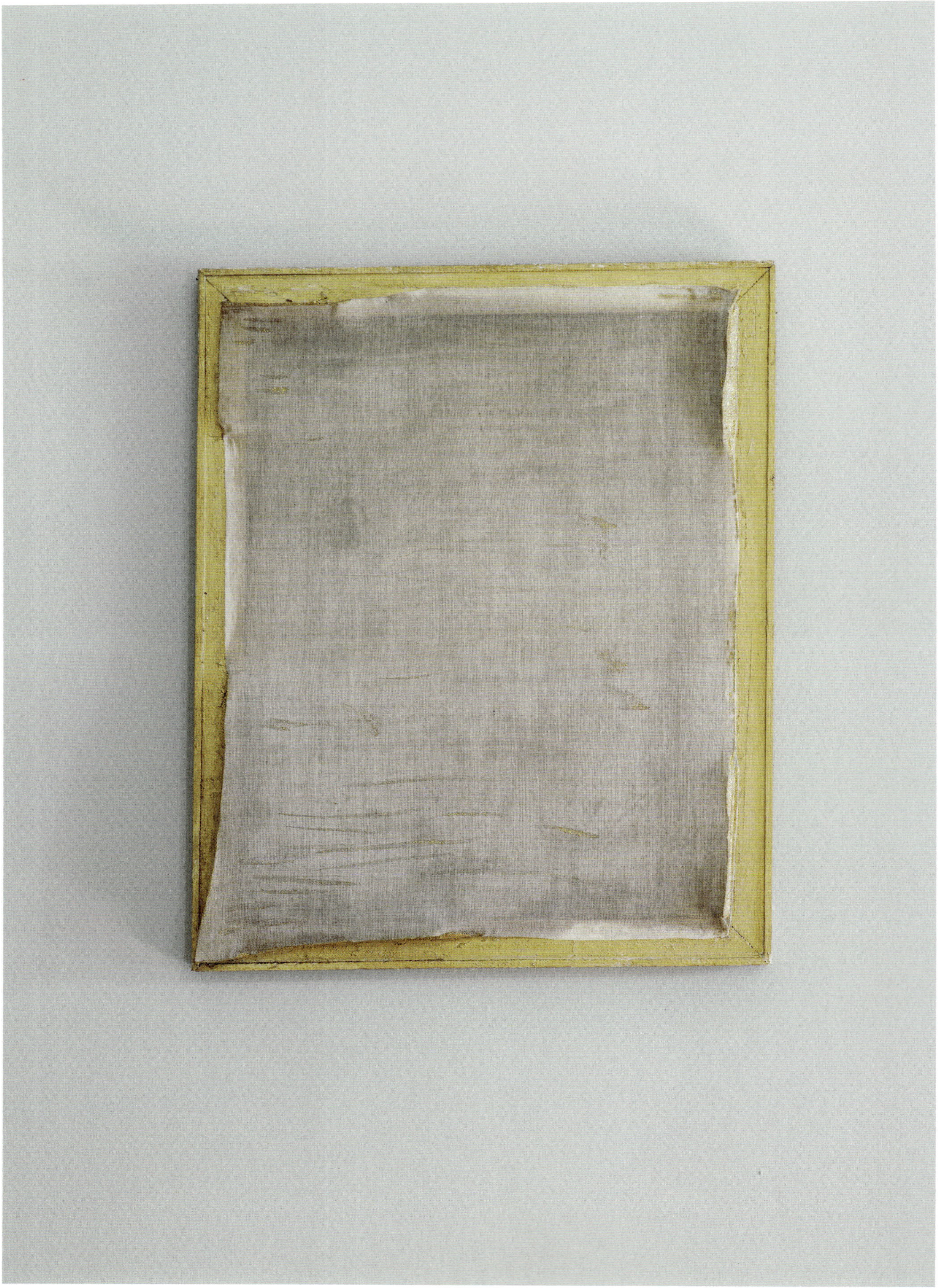

Canvas, wood, gauze, gilding, paint, thread, 50 × 40 cm

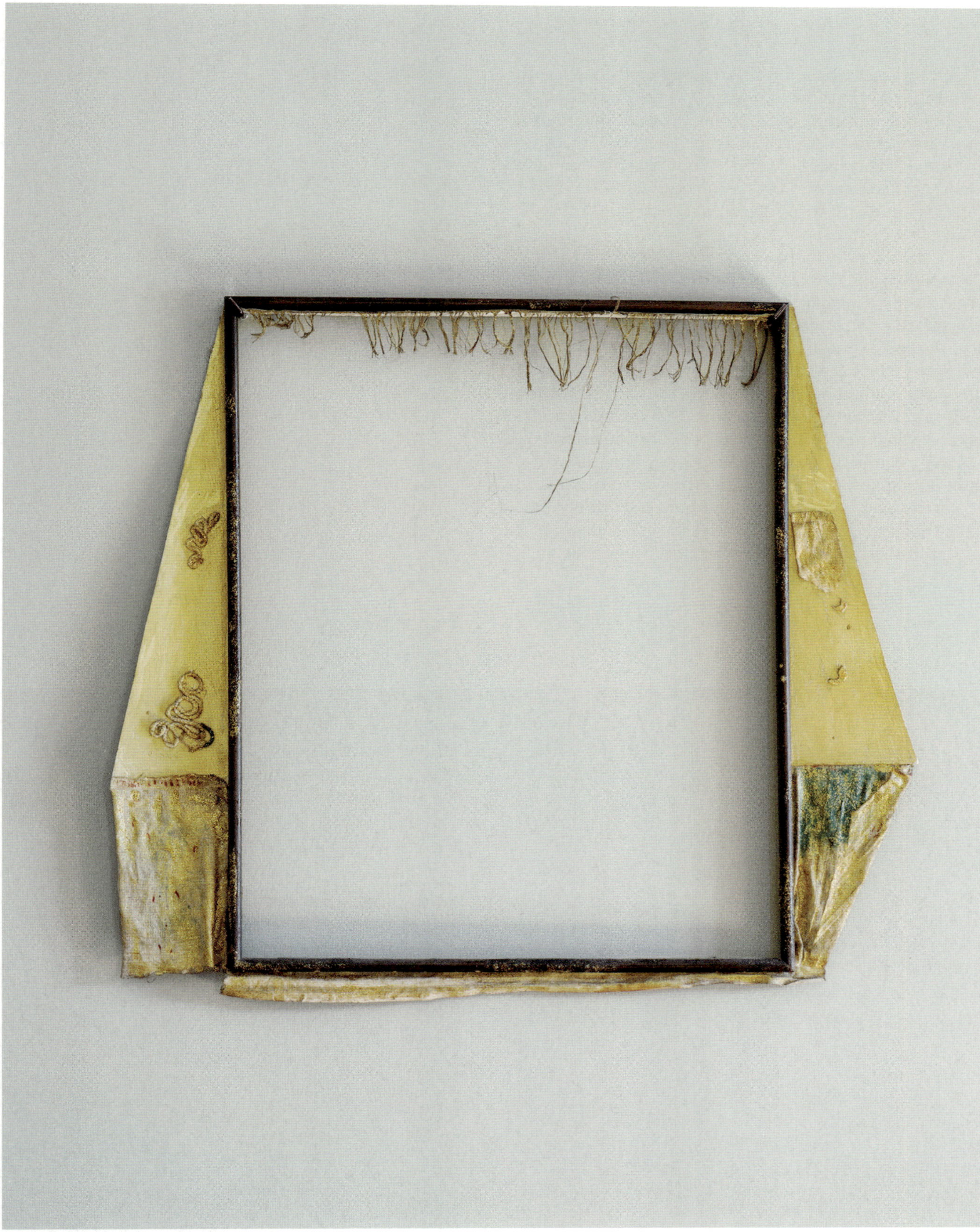

Mixed media, 48 × 41 cm

[…] in *Through the Looking Glass* (1989) it is the empty frame that is the artwork -its embroidered and gilded sides striving to offset the missing subject. In this way, Onur uses the shape of the canvases to suggest a longing for that which cannot be retrieved. The work is deeply intimate work, even though it is abstract.

Excerpt from the *Heartbreak* exhibition catalogue by RUYA MAPS, Venice, 2019.

Which structures should be stripped bare to allow the possibility for broader meaning? What reductions can possibly capture the shadows of relations, hierarchies and values, as well as represent the cracks and gaps of this fragile world? What psychic and social constructs correspond to the unequal conditions of visibility and suffering? What artifacts constitute the lens of love?

In this work, one can sense how Onur probes these questions. Hers is a proposal for the experience of art as the experience of the human condition. And to express this overarching quest, she embarks on the bold pursuit of questioning what constitutes physicality, lovingly replacing cold formalism with tender poetry. She pushes the constraints of form, masterfully assembling organic materials in an ecology of intimacy and care. As such, in *Icons of Time* (1990), she creates an achingly beautiful work in a timeless dialogue with light and space. In a curative to the weariness of it all, exploring and exposing the strained nature of our dance around the question of life, she reminds us of the outdated abstractions that we humans have become.

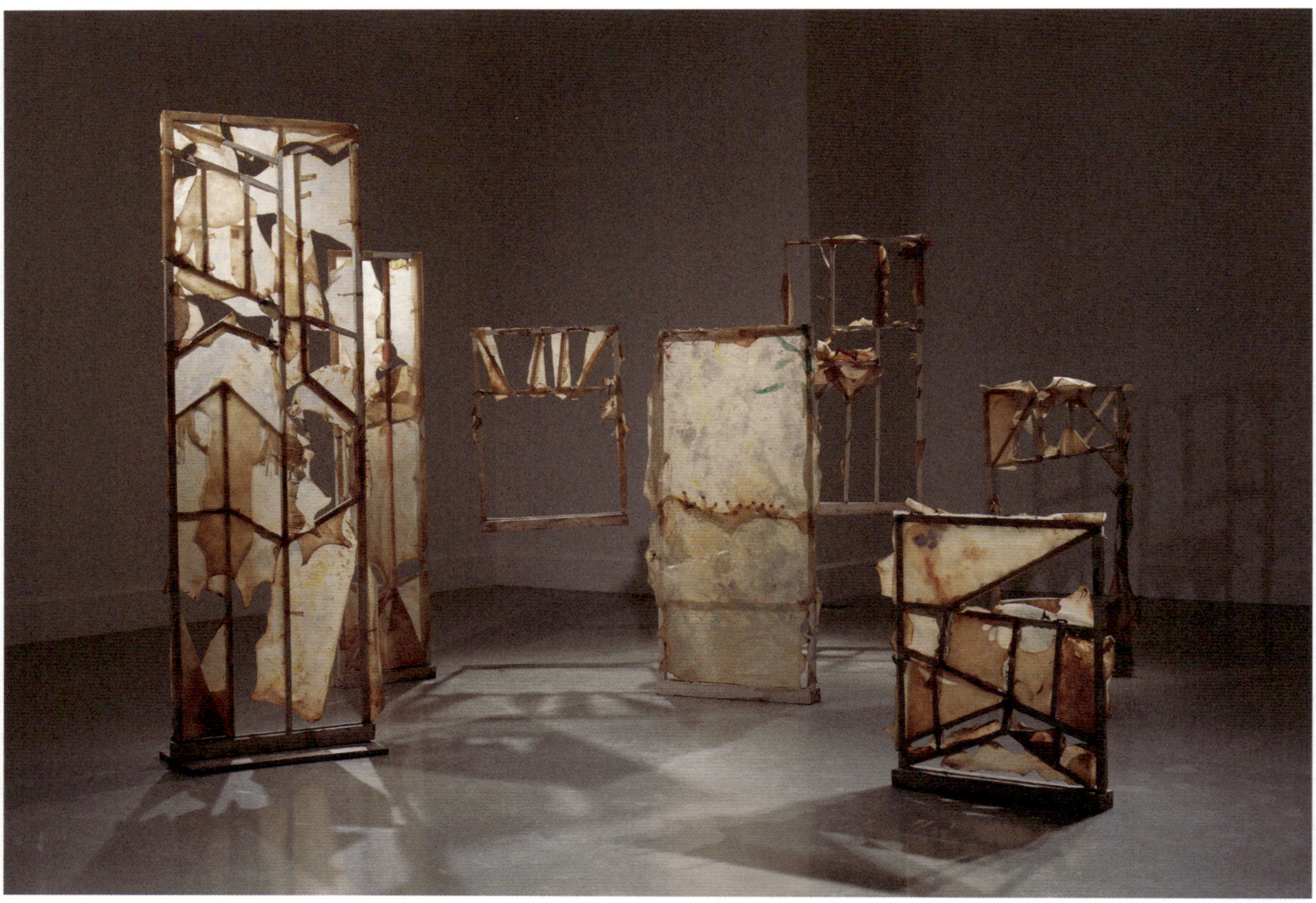

Installation (wood, leather, metal, paint), 7 pieces

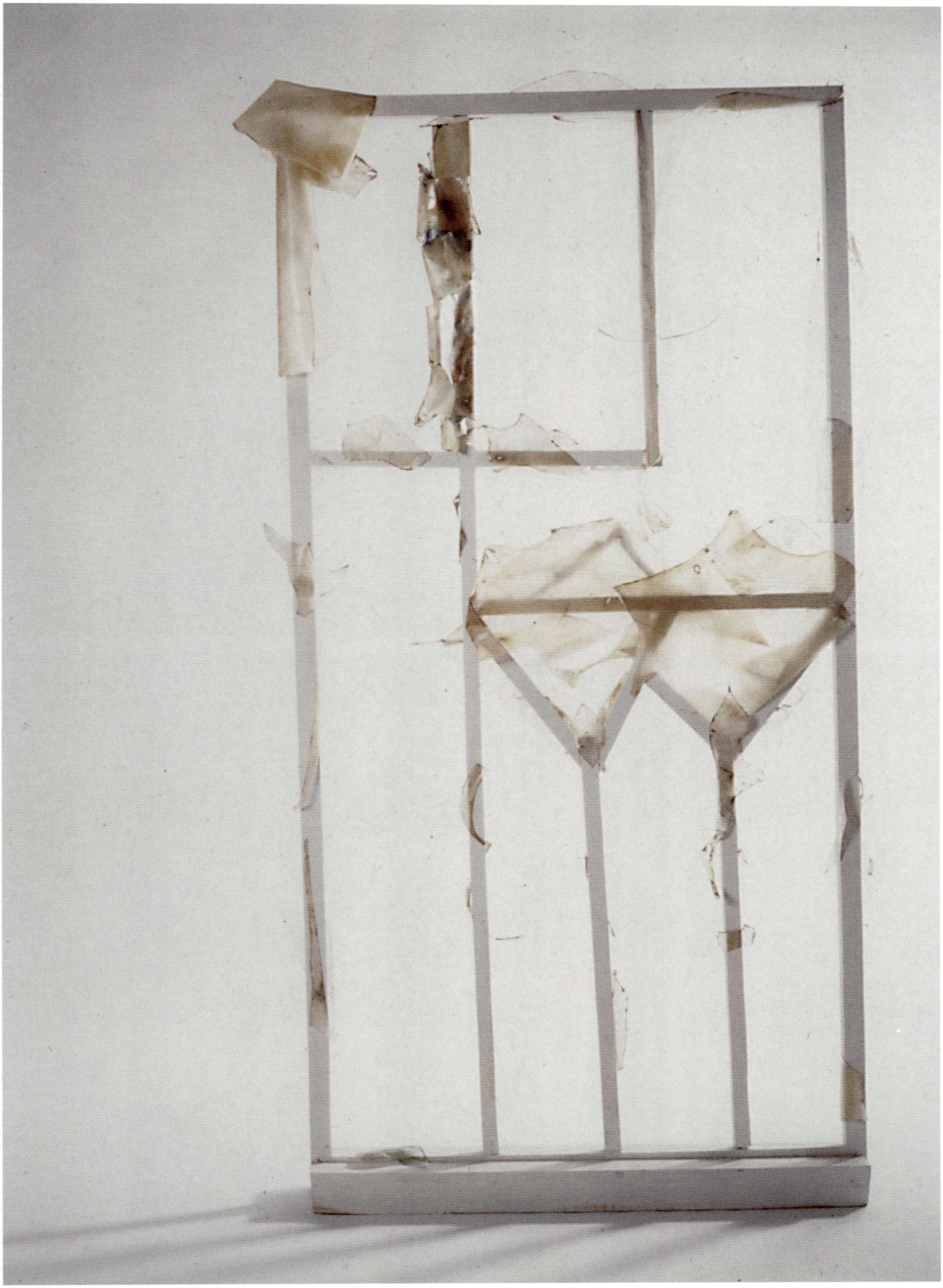

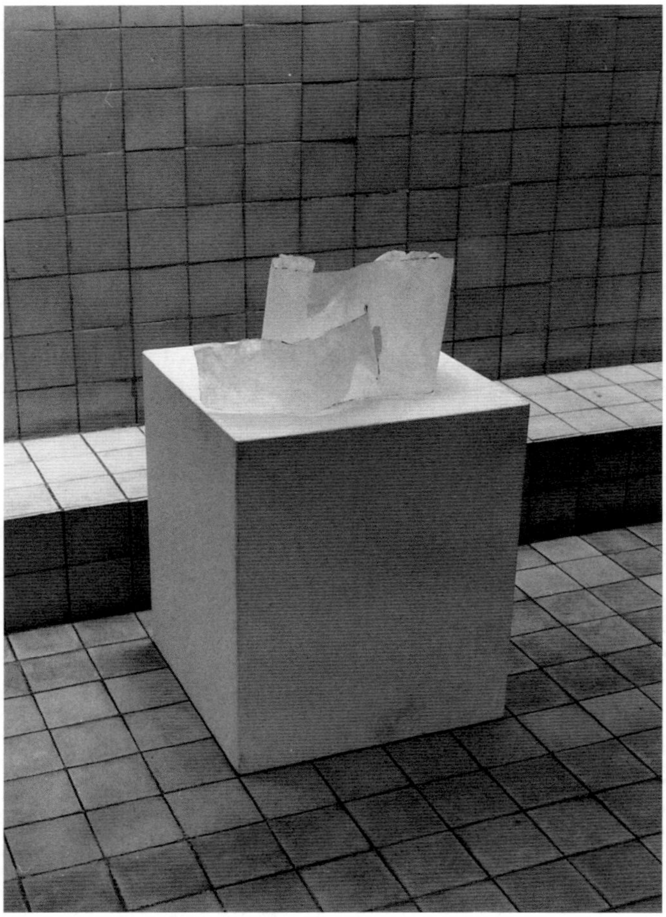

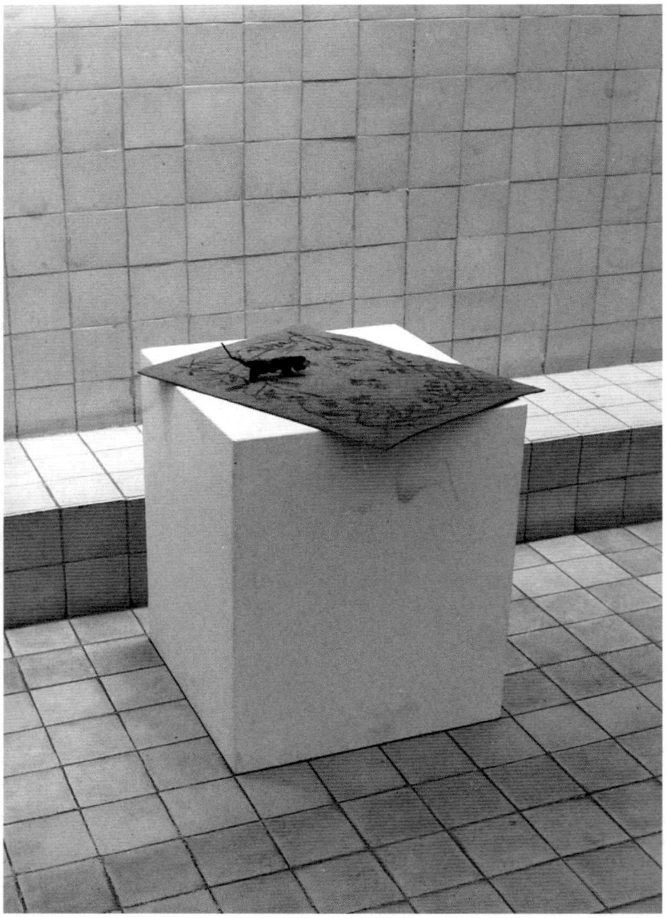

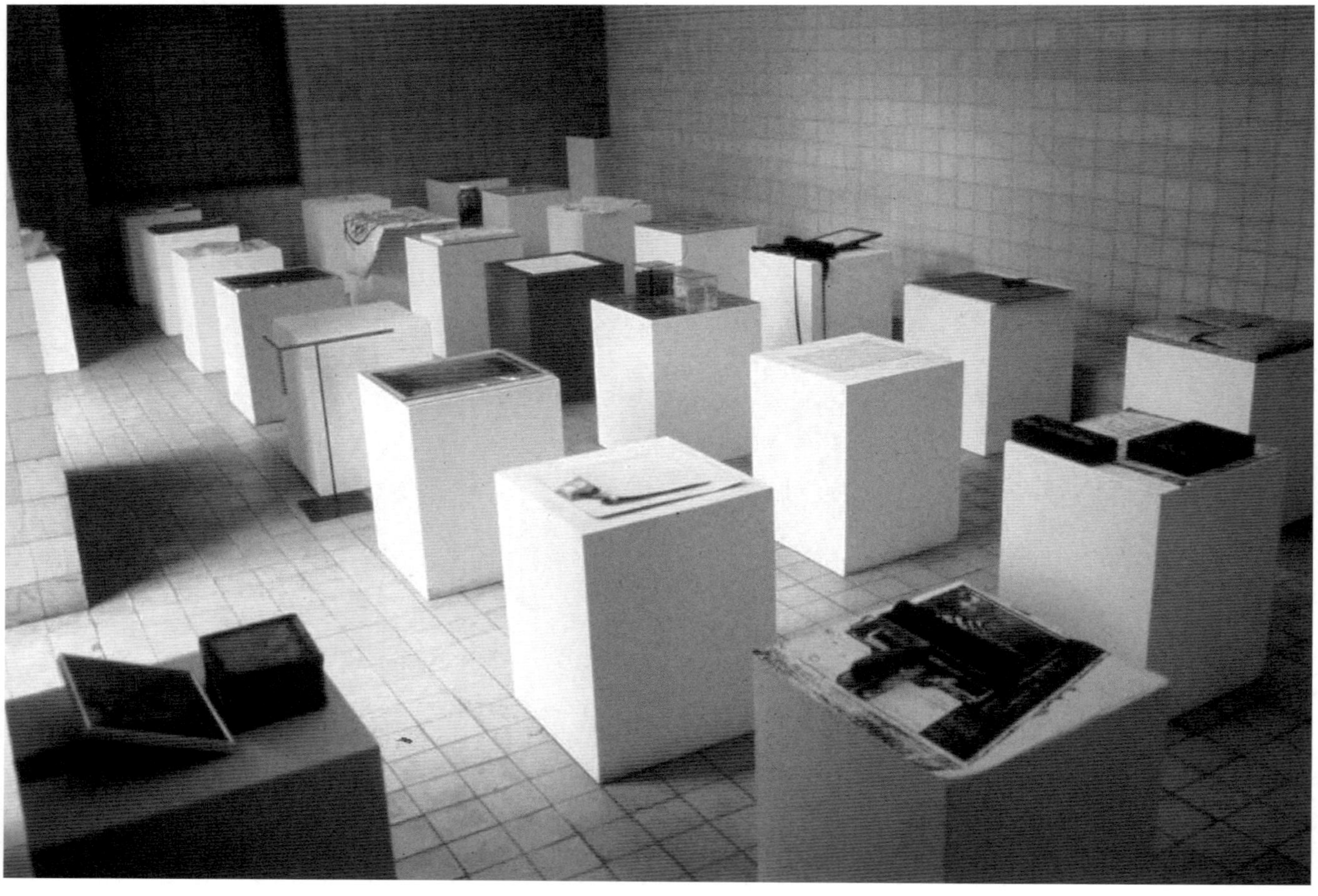

Installation view from group show *References*, Maçka Art Gallery

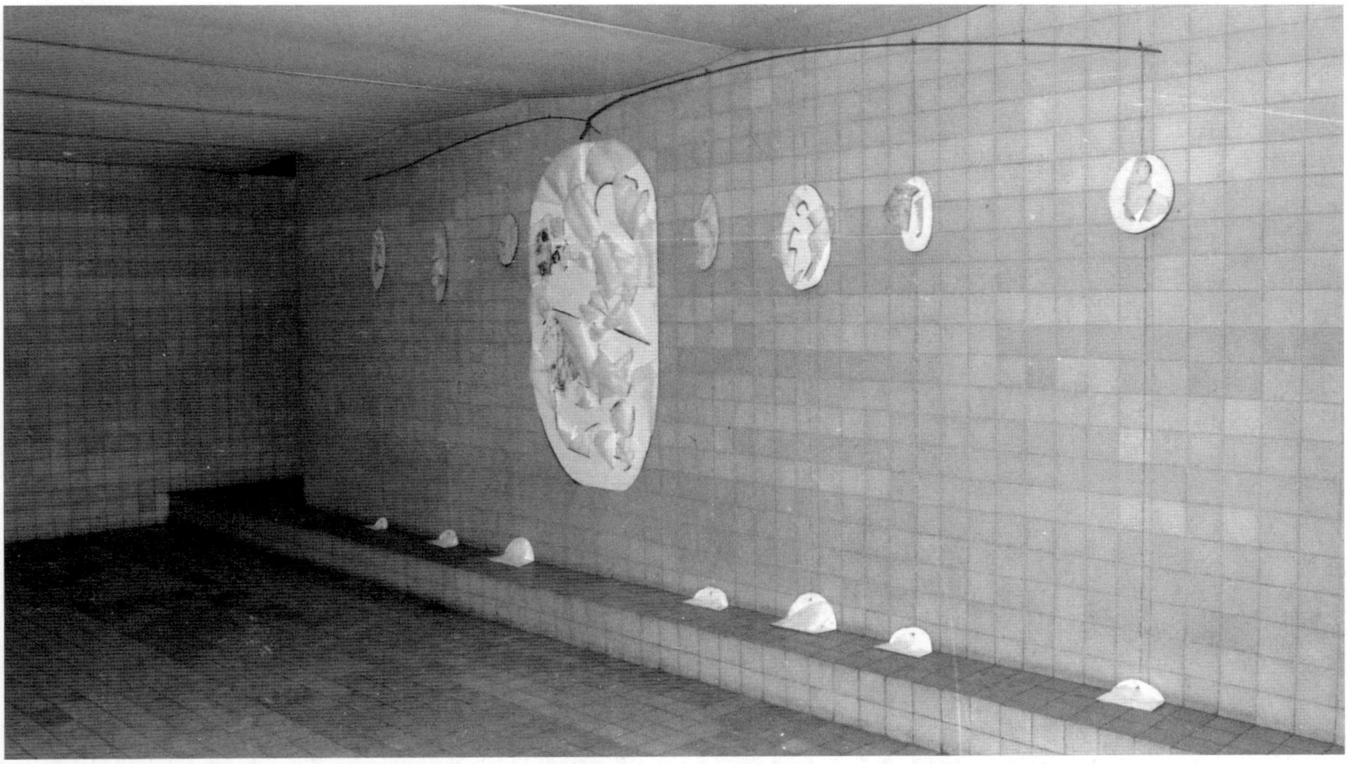

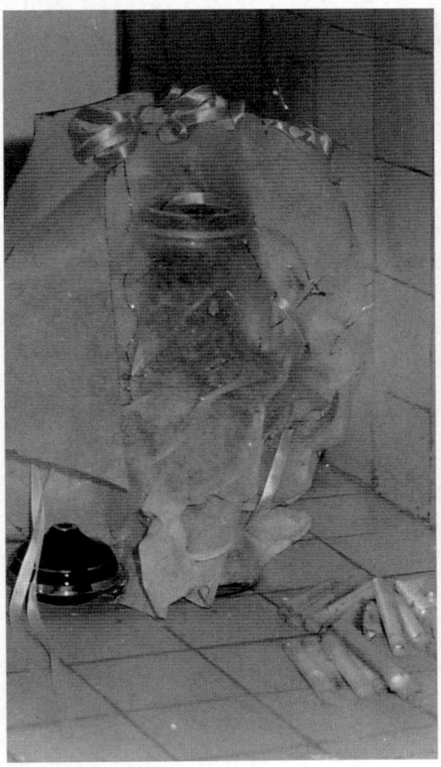

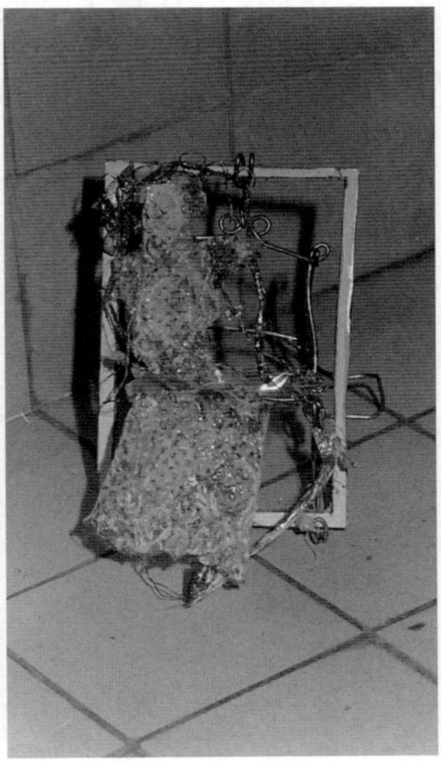

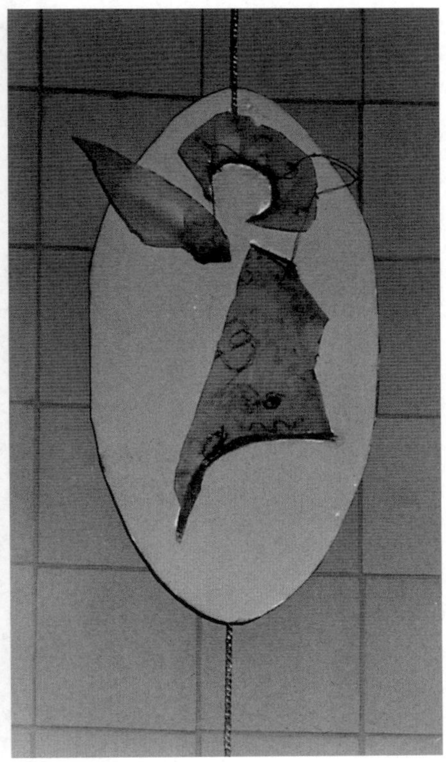

Mixed media installation, variable dimensions

Exhibiting two arrangements in the gallery space that are extensions of one another, Onur, with her unique use of material, employs objects that have distinct characteristics at once. These are objects that engage in a warm communication with the chequered walls of the Maçka Art Gallery: a kitsch vase, cartoon angels, an old frame converted into a baby chaise longue. Onur does not use nostalgic elements or those that allude to the splendour of the past. While interpreting these objects within a composition, she wants to render them as native to herself as they come. [...] When viewed in the dark, the composition with the angel and the *Arrangement with Lights* may perhaps convey to the audience more profound meanings. Other than the lighting of the gallery space, the light that the artist uses (which is a simple bulb) falls on the colourful chalks wrapped in crepe paper. The vase on the corner lit by the bulb and its lid wrapped in tulles is a continuation of the angel composition on the wall: can the tulles, bronze paint, small, blue, red spots be perceived as the signs of a symbolic expression? Symbols in Onur's work are conspicuous for their descriptiveness rather than for their associative qualities.

Necmi Sönmez, excerpt from the article 'Interrogation under Gallery Lights,' *Cumhuriyet*, 3 January 1991.

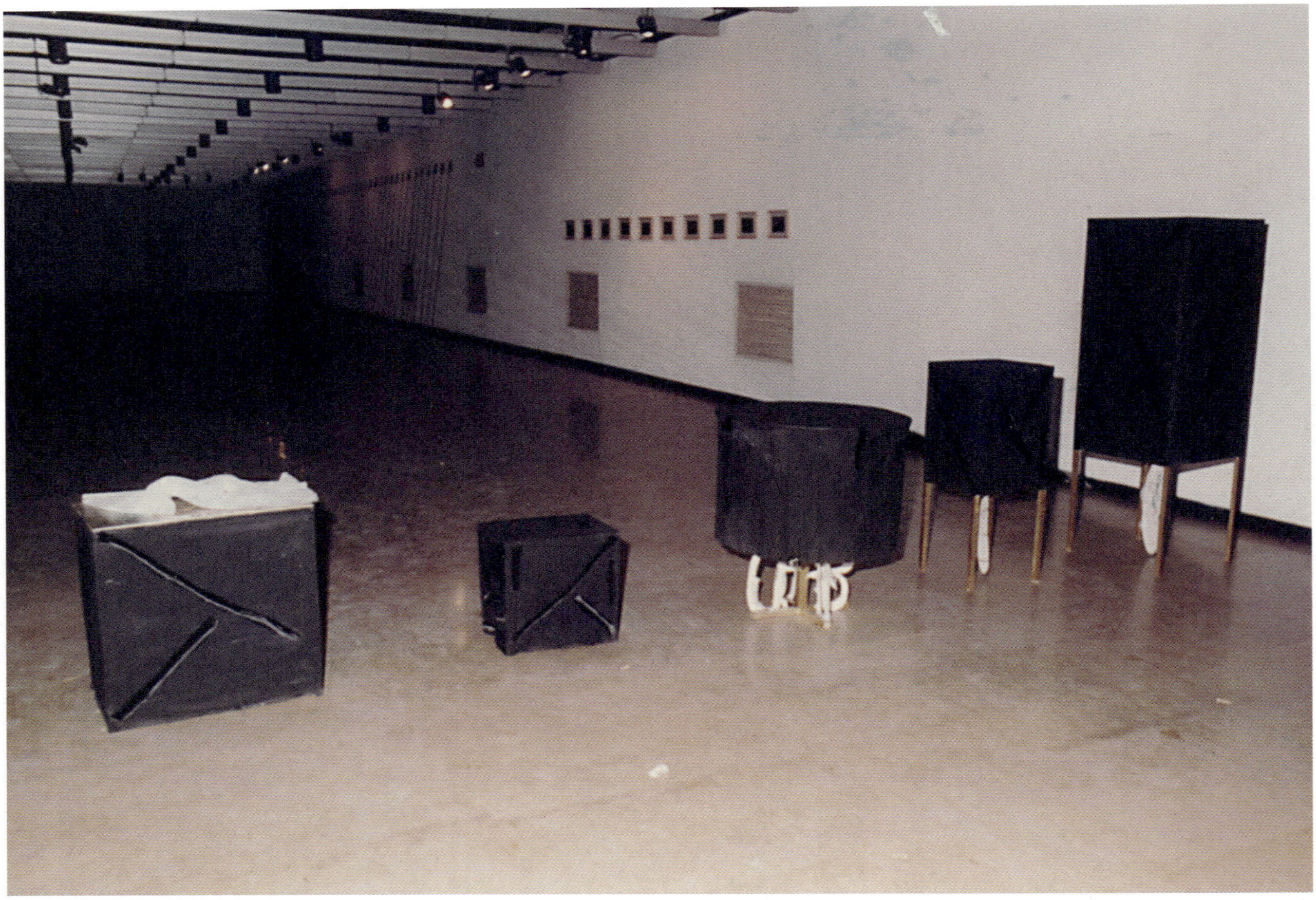

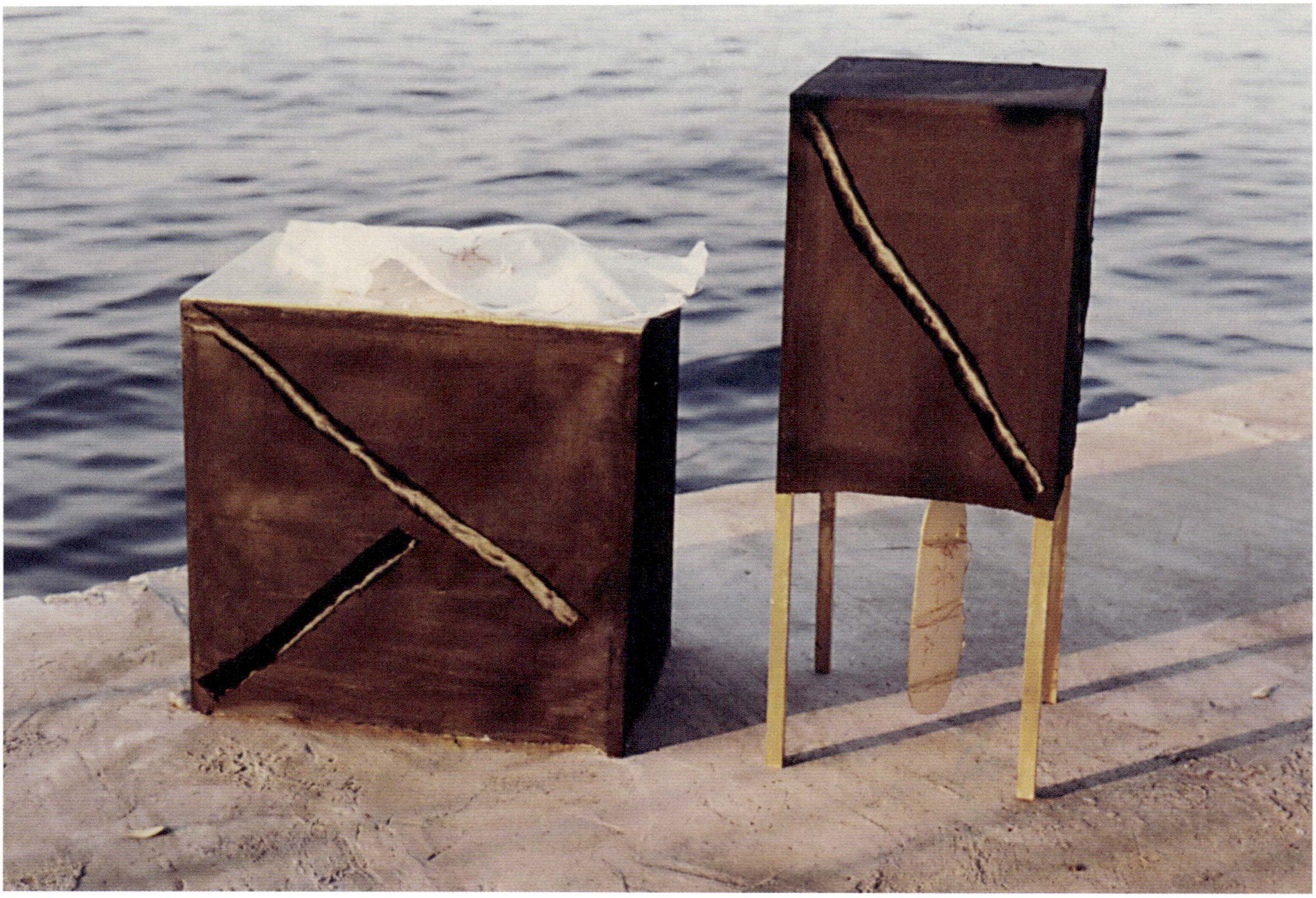

Wood, canvas, paint and mixed media

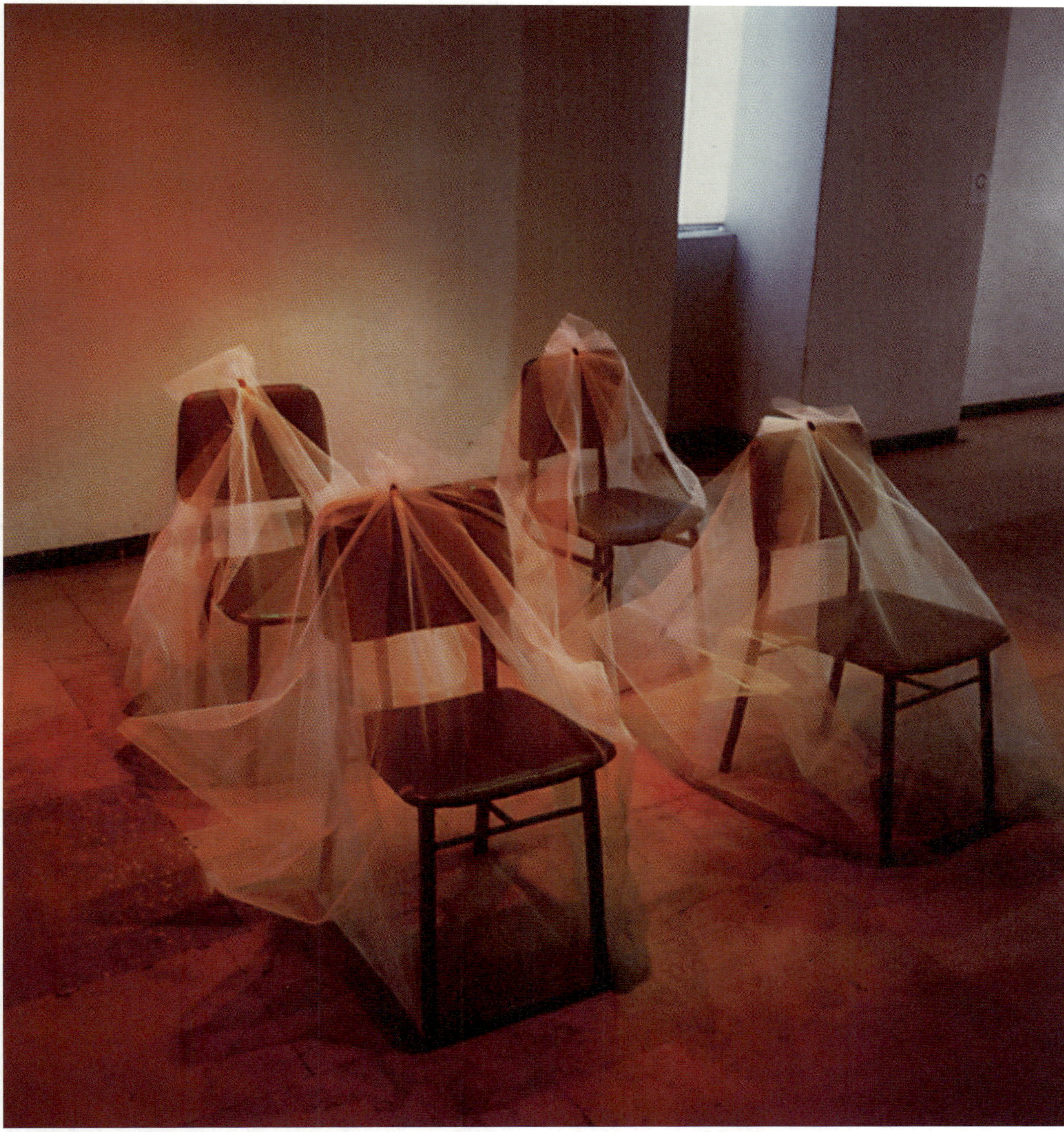

Tulle, chair, variable dimensions

In this exhibition, Füsun Onur uses a readymade object. This is a chair available in Atatürk Cultural Centre (AKM) or easily brought from outside. She bundles the chair with an ordinary and inexpensive material, with tulle. The artwork turns into a fetish that one almost does not have the heart to touch. A bundle is an element of traditional culture; it evokes nomadism and humble property. Meanwhile, the chair demonstrates the state of being settled, as well as power (domination). Here, we come face to face with Füsun Onur's twist. Political, social, economic, cultural dualities are exhibited through the synthesis of two simple materials. The masterful use of theoretical and conceptual values hidden behind these simple materials constitutes the 'permanence' of Füsun Onur's 'temporary' artworks.

Beral Madra, excerpt from the *10 Artists 10 Works: C* exhibition catalogue, 1992.

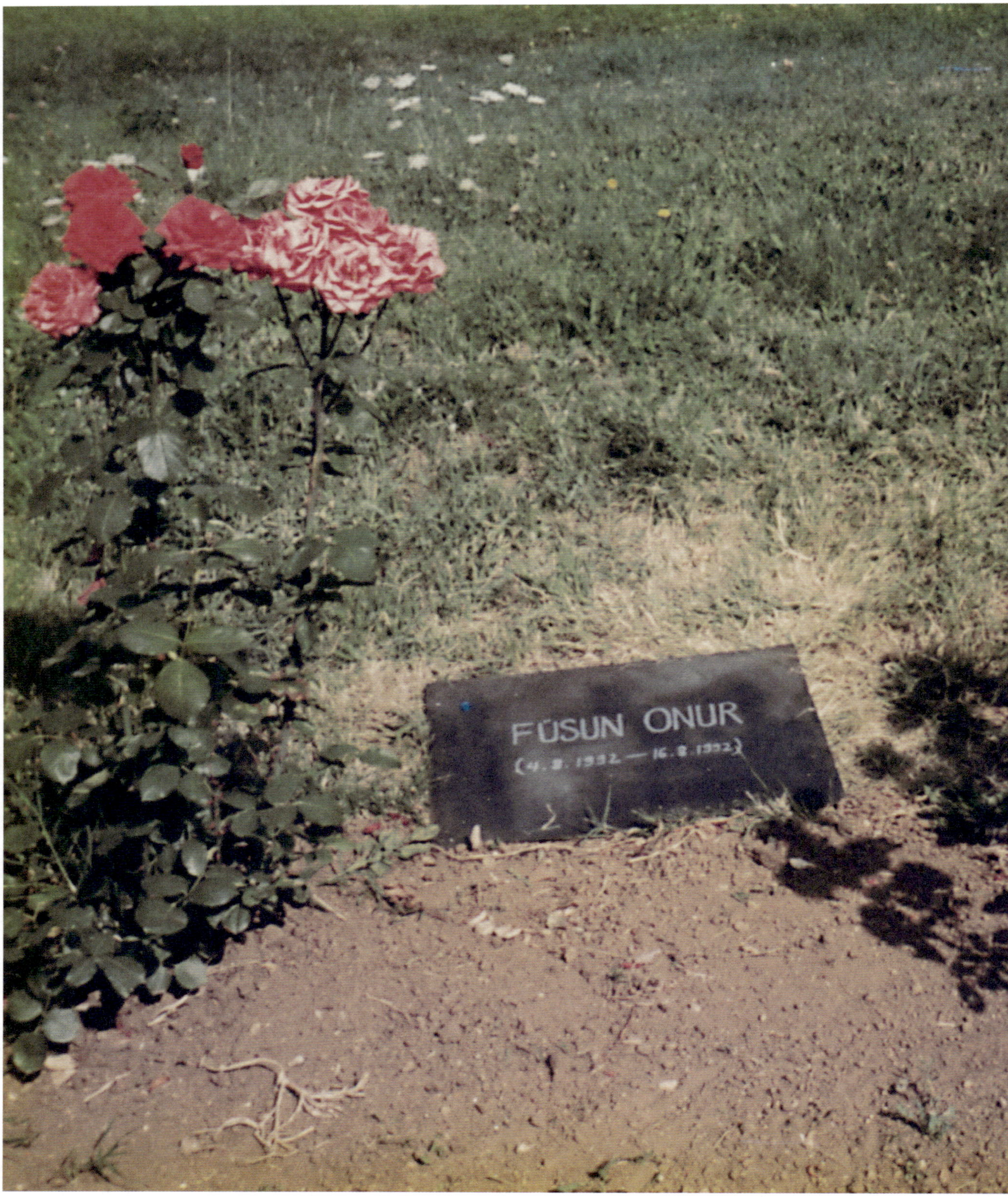

Metal plate, paint, 60 × 40 cm

[...] Exactly these naive conceptions about our understanding of time and our existence in it are questioned by Füsun Onur's work. The tin plate, with written the name of the artist and the dates of her arrival and leaving Prilep on it, alludes to a common memorial tablet with its form. But, while the memorial tablet's function is to help remind us of the former existence of the defunct person, here we have a case of 'immortalization' of one short period of life, a period that once was present but now is past.

Excerpt from the text *Is the time 'Flowing By'?* by Suzana Milevska.

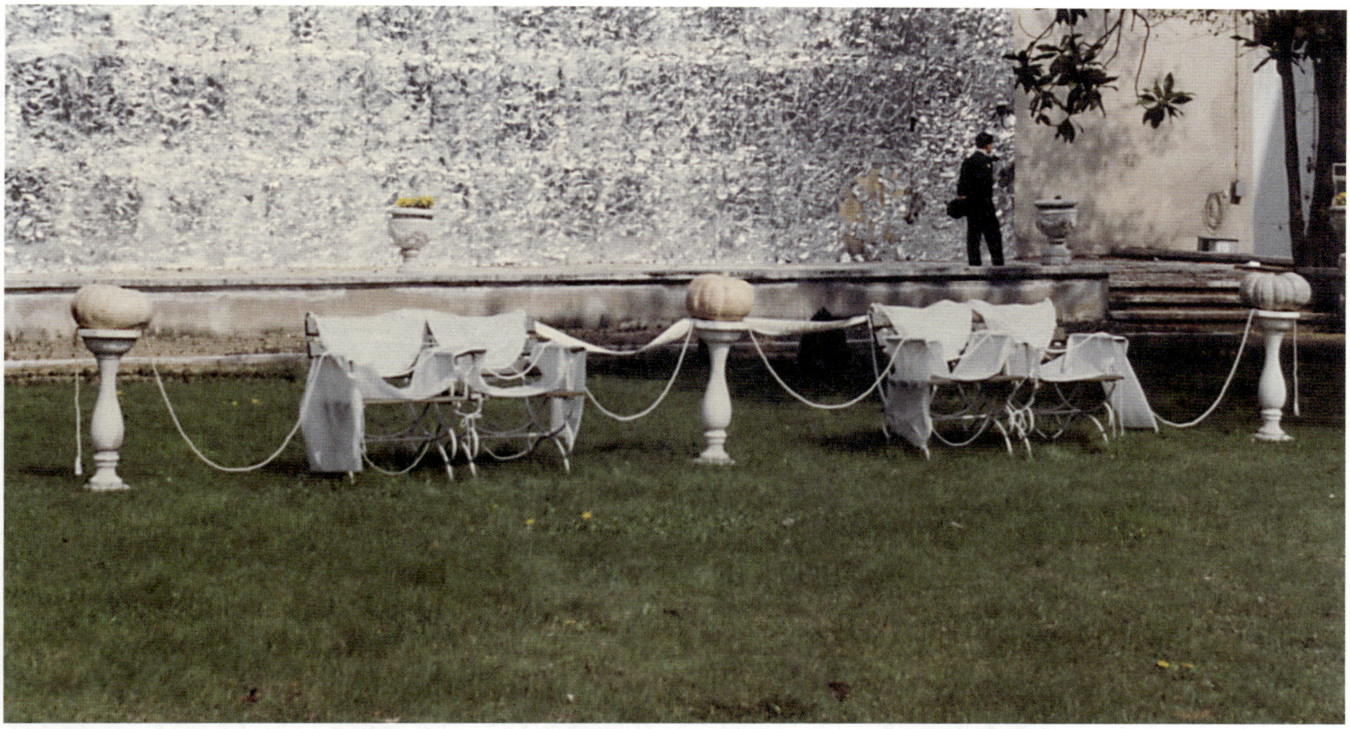

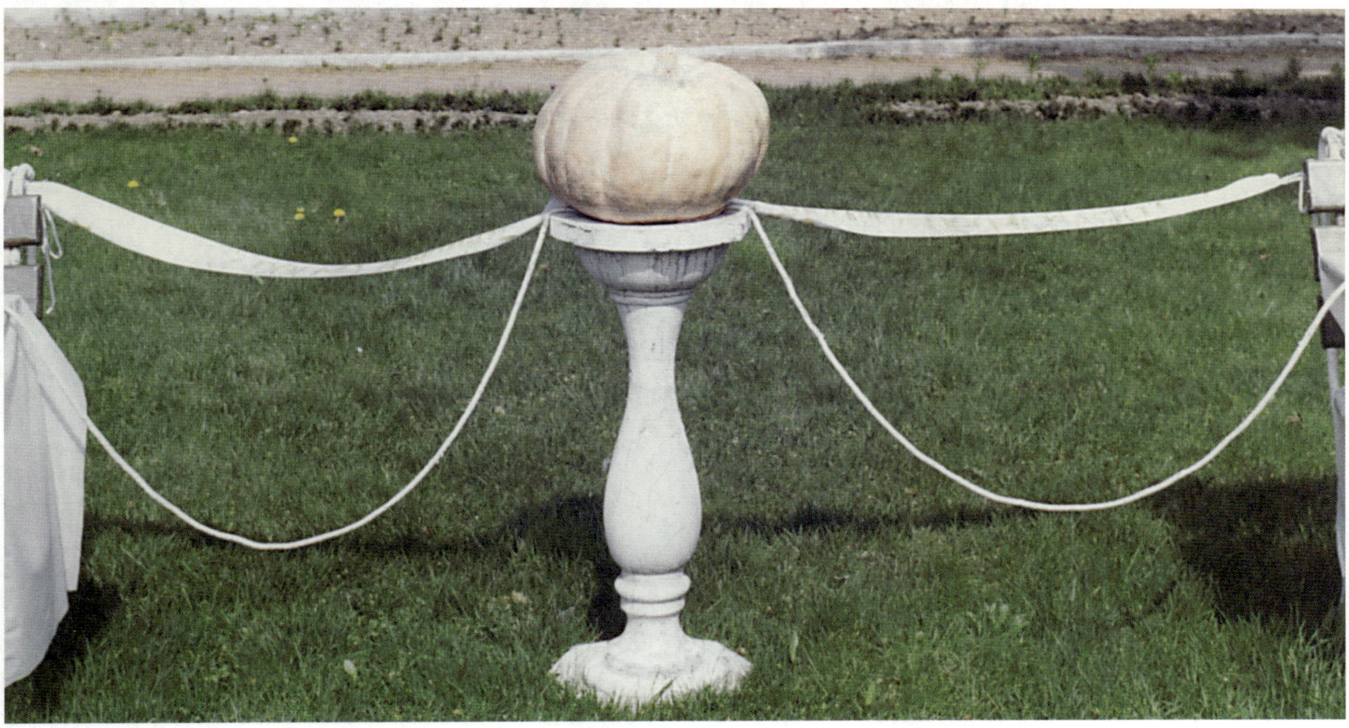

Installation, variable dimensions

In *Souvenir de Dolmabahçe* (1992) the artist made a reference to the ornamental rhythm of the famous 19th-century palace, linking the local with the non-local through her linear arrangement. The garden chairs covered in white tulle were linked to plaster plinths, belonging to the park, by cords and white bands with gold writing. This gold-white playful yet majestic composition was accentuated and made ironic by large pumpkins resting like sculptures on the plinths, their very shape reminiscent of the opulent turbans of the palace's former inhabitants. The rhythmic arrangement of this installation, the serial repetition of the elements and their variations make *Souvenir de Dolmabahçe* a direct precursor of Onur's musical compositions.

Margrit Brehm, excerpt from *For Careful Eyes*, Yapi Kredi Publications, Istanbul, 2007.

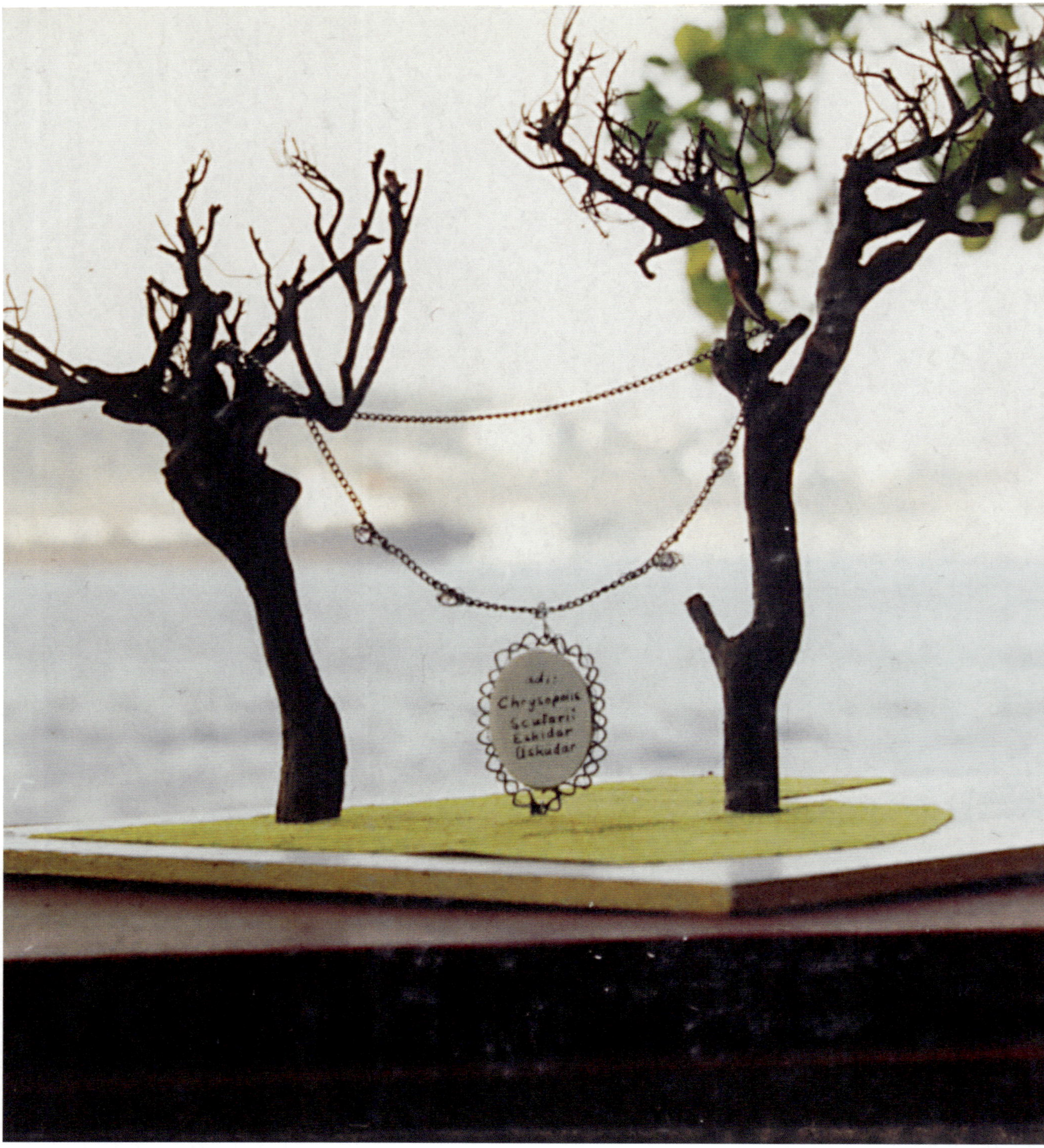

There was a contest. I'm not sure who organised it … [We were asked to make works] for different localities in Istanbul. I chose Üsküdar, the park past the pier. I wanted to [hang] a chain on a tree there, but so that the chain wouldn't harm the tree or the branch. The chain would reach down, and it would have a pendant on its end […] round, with an inscription … and [the area] around it would be decked in iron, embedded into the ground. On the chain, there were pieces of glass. The … sunset in Üsküdar is very picturesque. In that light, the glass would shine on the chain and on it would be written all the names that Üsküdar has been given throughout the ages. […] It remained a project: it wasn't selected; they didn't like it.

Füsun Onur, excerpt from the artist's talk at SAHA Association, 23.02.2013, https://vimeo.com/61336653, 54:24.

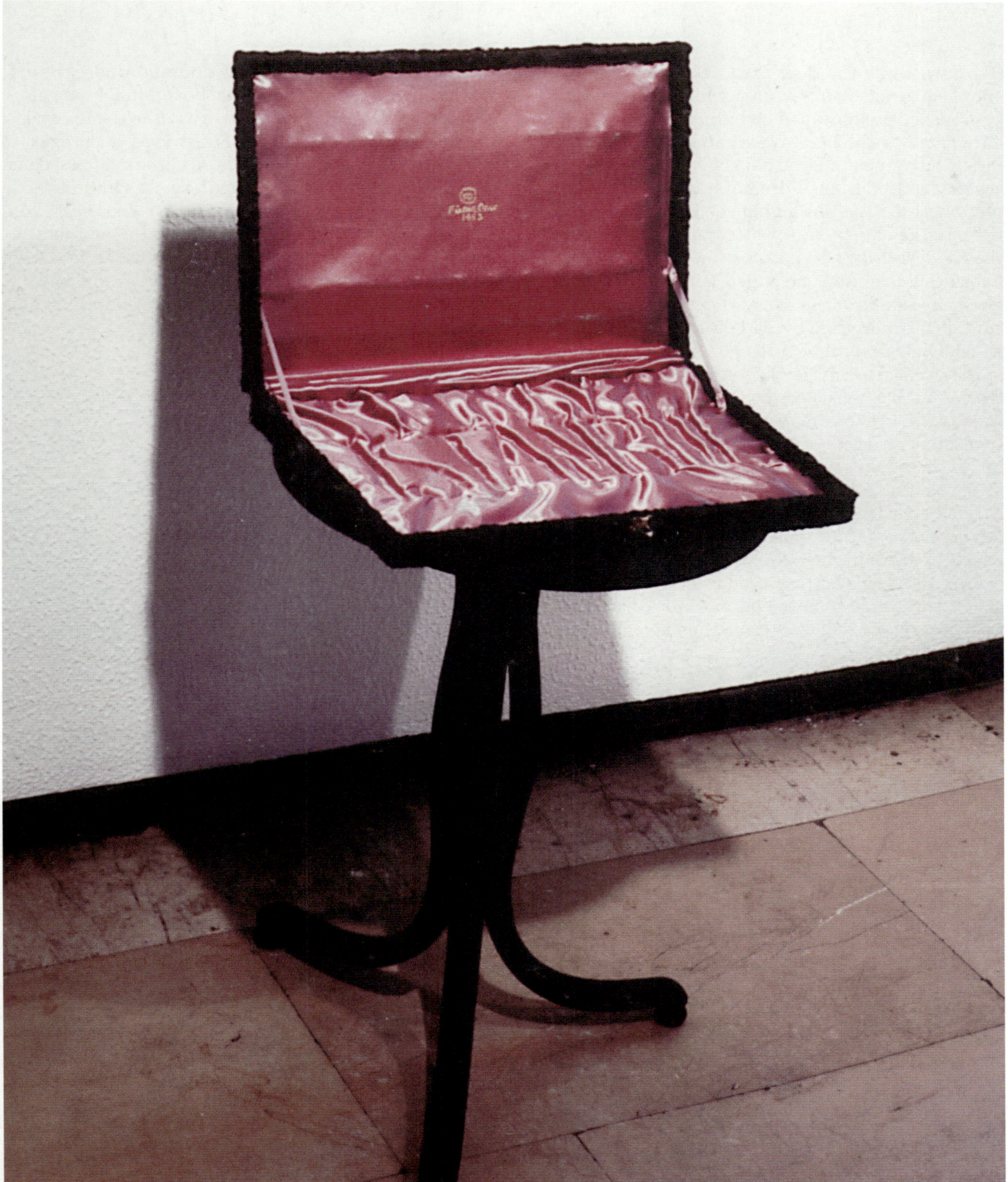

Wooden box, satin, 50 × 40 cm

This time, in her work titled *Heritage*, Füsun Onur presents the audience with a box covered in rumpled black satin that from the outside looks like astrakhan. Inside, the box is again satin and designed like a jewellery case. On the concave surface that holds jewellery, or another valuable object, is simply one word to be read: 'Istanbul.' Just like the void left behind when a necklace is removed from its box, Istanbul too has disappeared.

Nilgün Özayten, excerpt from the *Istanbul* exhibition catalogue, AKM, 1993.

(I am watching the *Pink Boat*.) The other day, during one of our usual swims at daybreak, the coast guard approached our group of swimmers and told us, 'It is forbidden to swim here. We are in international waters.' I have spent a large part of my life looking at this sea, hearing of its past, dreaming about the geography where the Cyrillic alphabet – which I learned from the passing ships – was written, about Odessa and the Eastern Black Sea, about the Mediterranean and Gibraltar. It neither belonged here nor anywhere else: this sea belonged everywhere. As my father once said, it is an organic living being. The Pink Boat, which Onur dreamt of putting to sea in 1992, the year of the great fire on the Galata Bridge, revives the traces of that time when the Galata Bridge, along with its stories, broke away from Istanbul's daily life. It recalls the traces of the decisions required in its aftermath, which somehow could not be taken, and of the waves and dilemmas. I am thinking about how this old structure by the sea has been ravaged and abandoned by a new ongoing urban renewal project, which I read of in the news this morning; about the century-old glass bottles, produced in long-gone workshops, that came from the bottom of the sea, which I heard of on the radio yesterday; and about the whisper forever oozing from above ground and underground. I am turning back to the Pink Boat. Unable to get away from the sea, it surrenders itself to the unexpected rhythms and oscillations of the waves; it changes colour with the light, becomes dark, glitters, falters, dances. Does it create a dark image? No. As Onur says, it is not nostalgic either. She does not like nostalgia. To me the Pink Boat evokes coolness and lightness, much like what Onur says about the sea she sees from her home in Kuzguncuk: a momentary sense of ease about the future. Life goes on with the unpredictable rhythms of the sea.

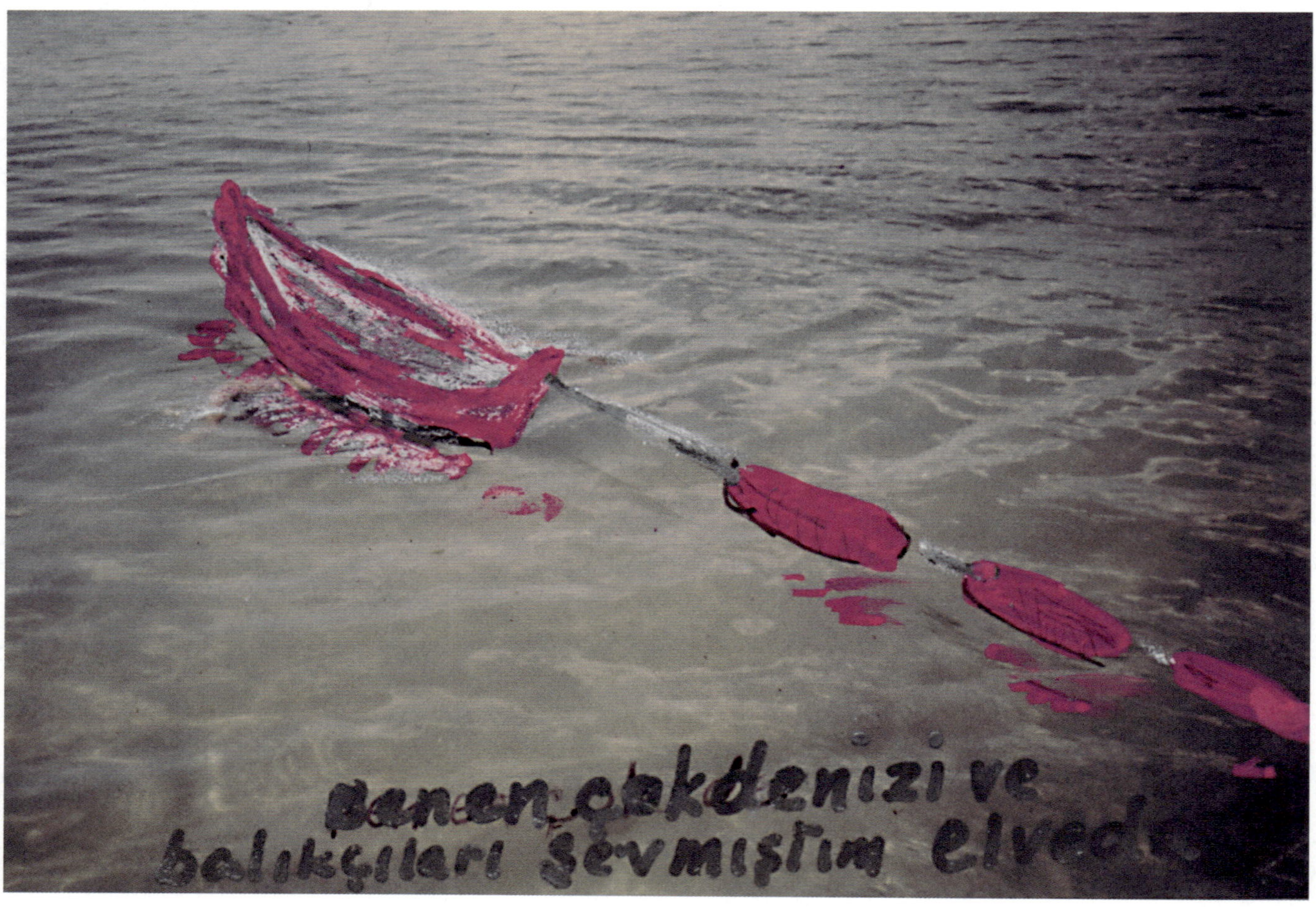

Initial sketch for *Pink Boat*, 1993

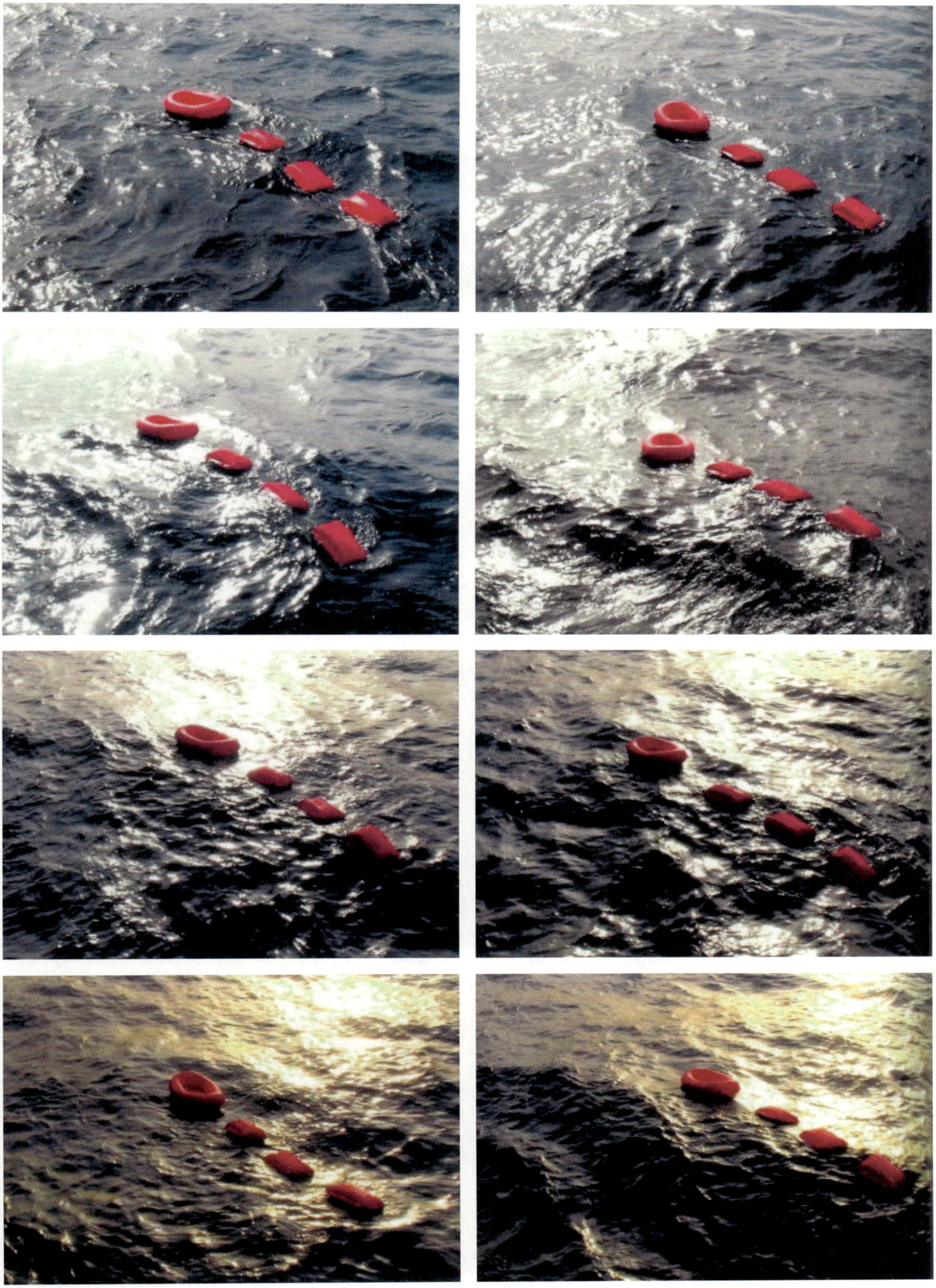

Video (colour, silent), 8 hours

Füsun Onur produced *This Place* in 1993 for the fourth and last of the group exhibitions *A, B, C, D* held from 1989–93. The exhibition, whose full title was *10 Artists 10 Works: D* (1993) was realised in three different locations on Mim Kemal Öke Street in Maçka: No. 9 and No. 23, the site of the furniture shop Koleksiyon Mobilya, and No. 31, which hosts the Maçka Art Gallery.

By distancing themselves from the use of traditional techniques and materials, the artists in the *D* edition of the exhibition series aimed to open a space for the then contemporary modes of production and expression such as installation, conceptual art and object art. In *This Place*, Onur explores the relationship of installation art with space. According to her, an installation is site-specific and proposes a spatial and temporal encounter that is possible only in the here and now. The work, which consists of a rusty metal plate with the word *BURASI* (THIS PLACE) written on it in red paint, questions the politics of sculpture's traditional vertical relationship with space, highlighting its dialogue with the horizontal and existential conditions of space. Onur exhibited *This Place*, like a doormat, outside the store at No. 23. Here, it simultaneously points at Maçka, at Istanbul and at Turkey in the early 1990s, one of the dark periods of its history, and announces: 'This is the place you have been searching for!' The red paint also recalls the political grafitti of this period, marked by a violent crackdown on public space. By placing her writing on the floor rather than the wall, however, Onur transforms the image of propaganda into an image of bearing witness, of claiming responsibility and of action. The place where the subject, the action, the space and time can be reorganised, she suggests, is exactly where we are standing now; it is precisely 'this place.'

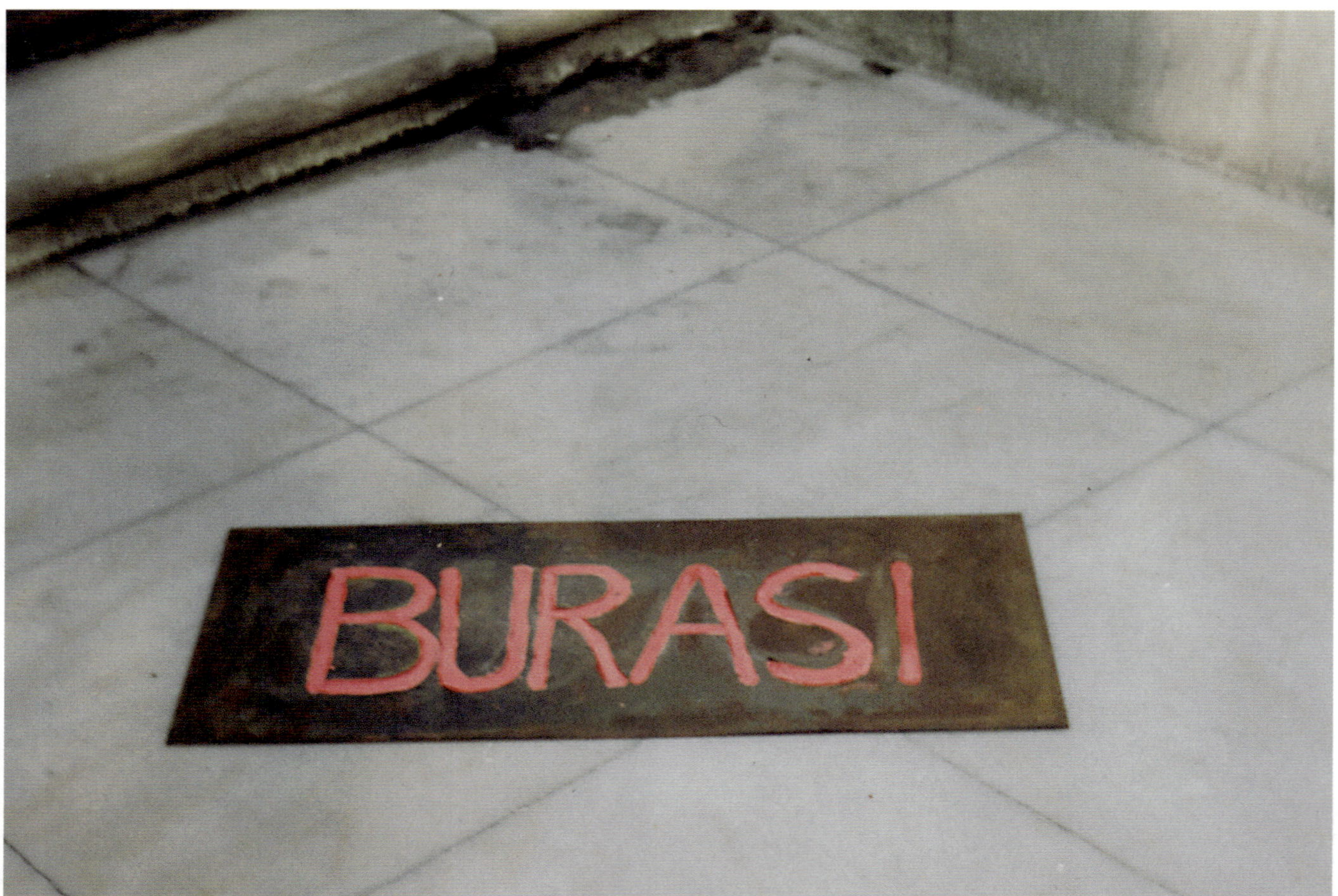

Metal sheet, paint, 34 × 74 cm
View from the exhibition *10 Artists 10 Works: D*, Koleksiyon Mobilya, 1993

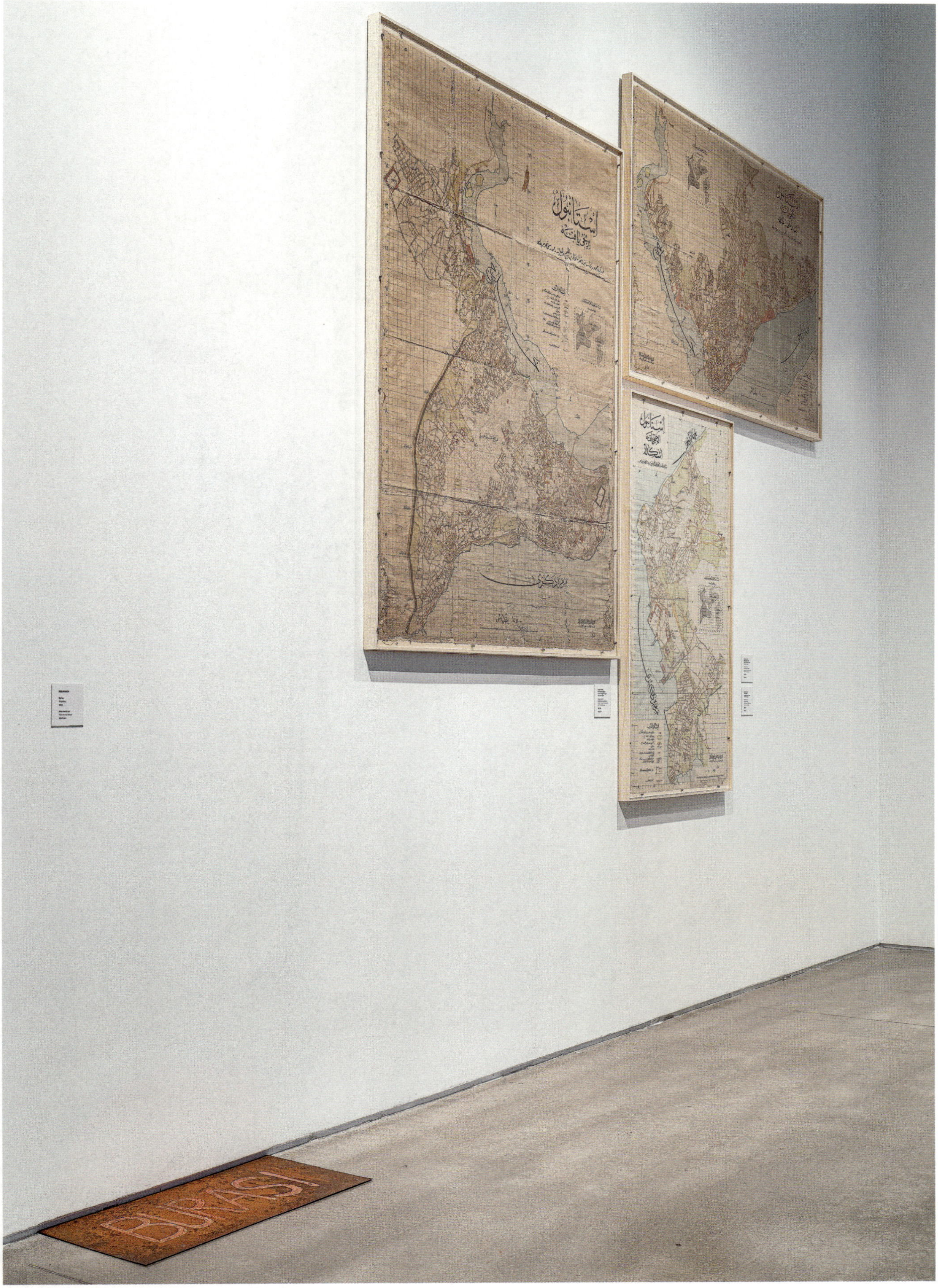

View from the group exhibition *This Place*, Yapı Kredi Culture and Arts, 2021

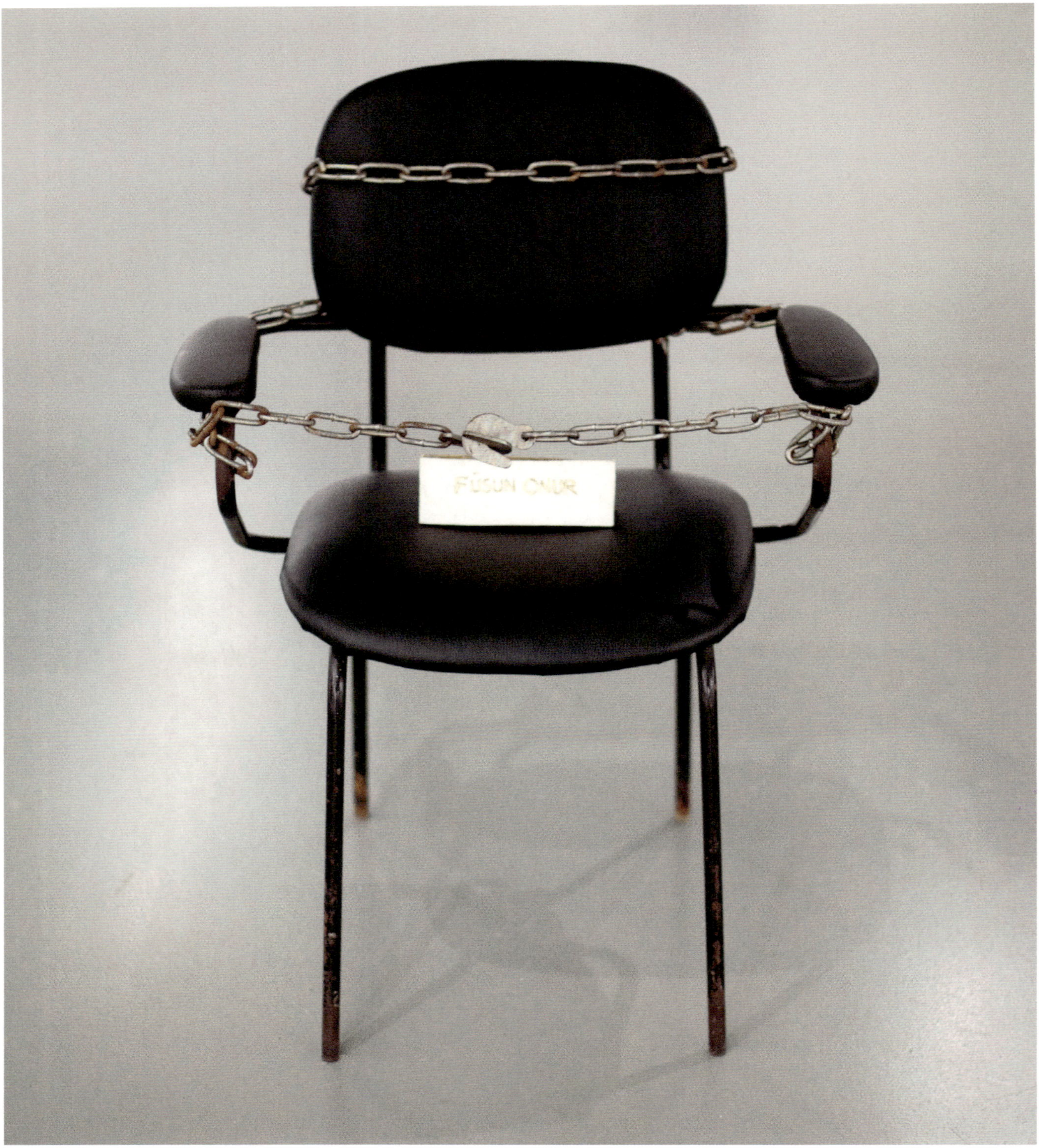

Chair, chain, nametag

Chairs often appear in Füsun Onur's work as symbols of power, property and social status. The fabric, gauze, and various accessories used with the chairs deprive them of function and reference the public space where they belong. In this work, instead of the insubstantial and decorative materials used by the artist in similar works, there is a chain stretched over the chain. Giving the impression that it belongs to a government office, and redolent of bureaucracy, this chair has masculine elements. The artist's name tag is on the chair. The fact that a place set aside for the artist is 'chained' may be read as an expression of the idea that she has not found the place she deserves in the society.

Excerpt from the *Dream and Reality* exhibition catalogue, Istanbul Modern, 2011.

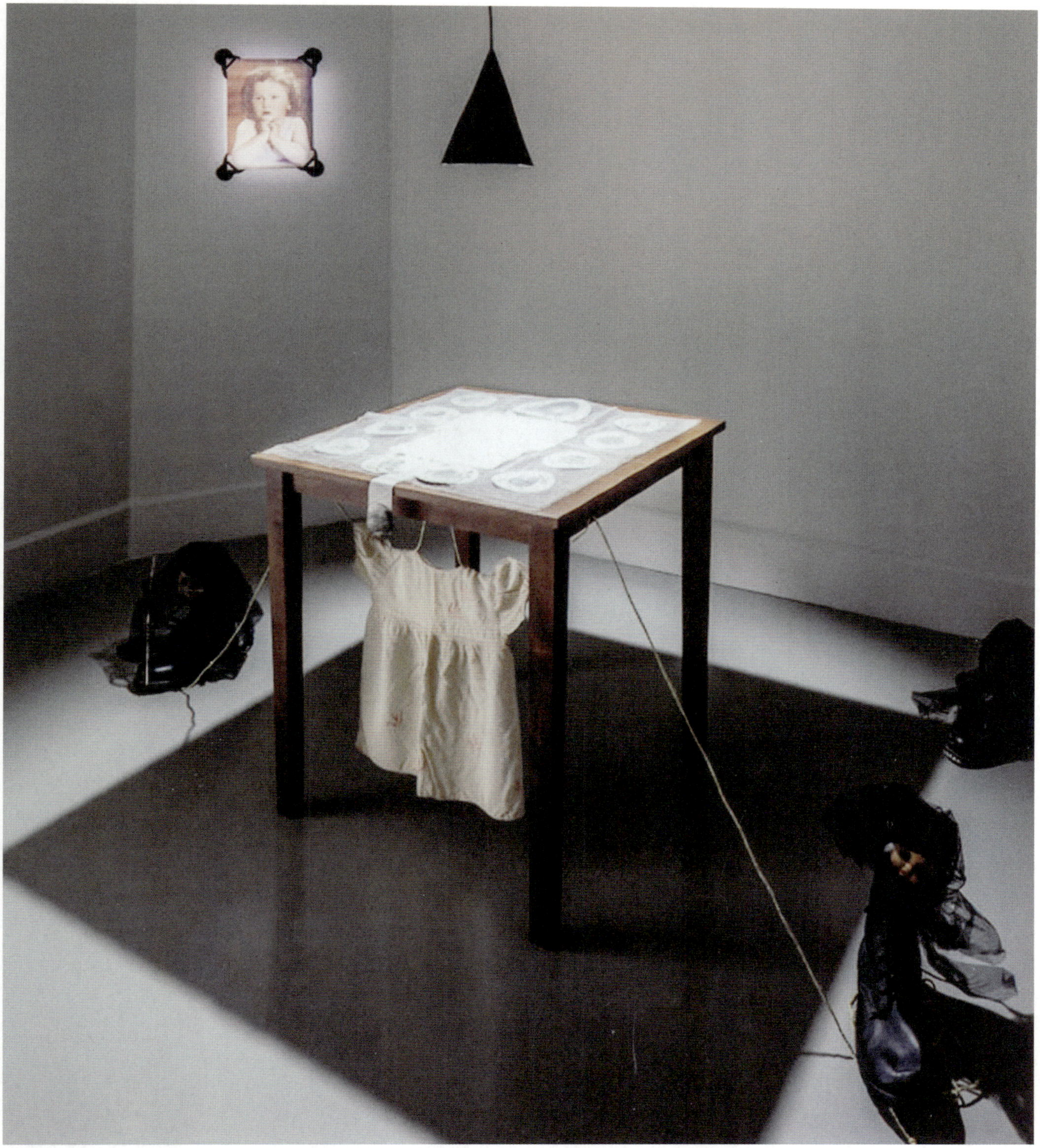

Installation (table, photographs, boat, doll, baby dress)

In her environments she condenses and rectifies individual experiences into a spatial reference system, her plastic structures embody enigmatic symbols. The assemblages do not function as a vehicle for something outside of art. Füsun Onur invents new objects from their own imagination, according to their own laws. In this way, the things she creates achieve a hermetic self-image, as if, in all modesty, they had always existed. Memories crystallize into strange situations that oscillate between abstraction and concretion. For this exhibition, Füsun Onur researched the terrain of tangible and text-light memory and staged a tableau of her ideas about Germany: *My first memory of the word Germany* as a child.

Excerpt from the *Iskele (Turkish Art Today)* exhibition catalogue, ifa-Galerie, 1994.

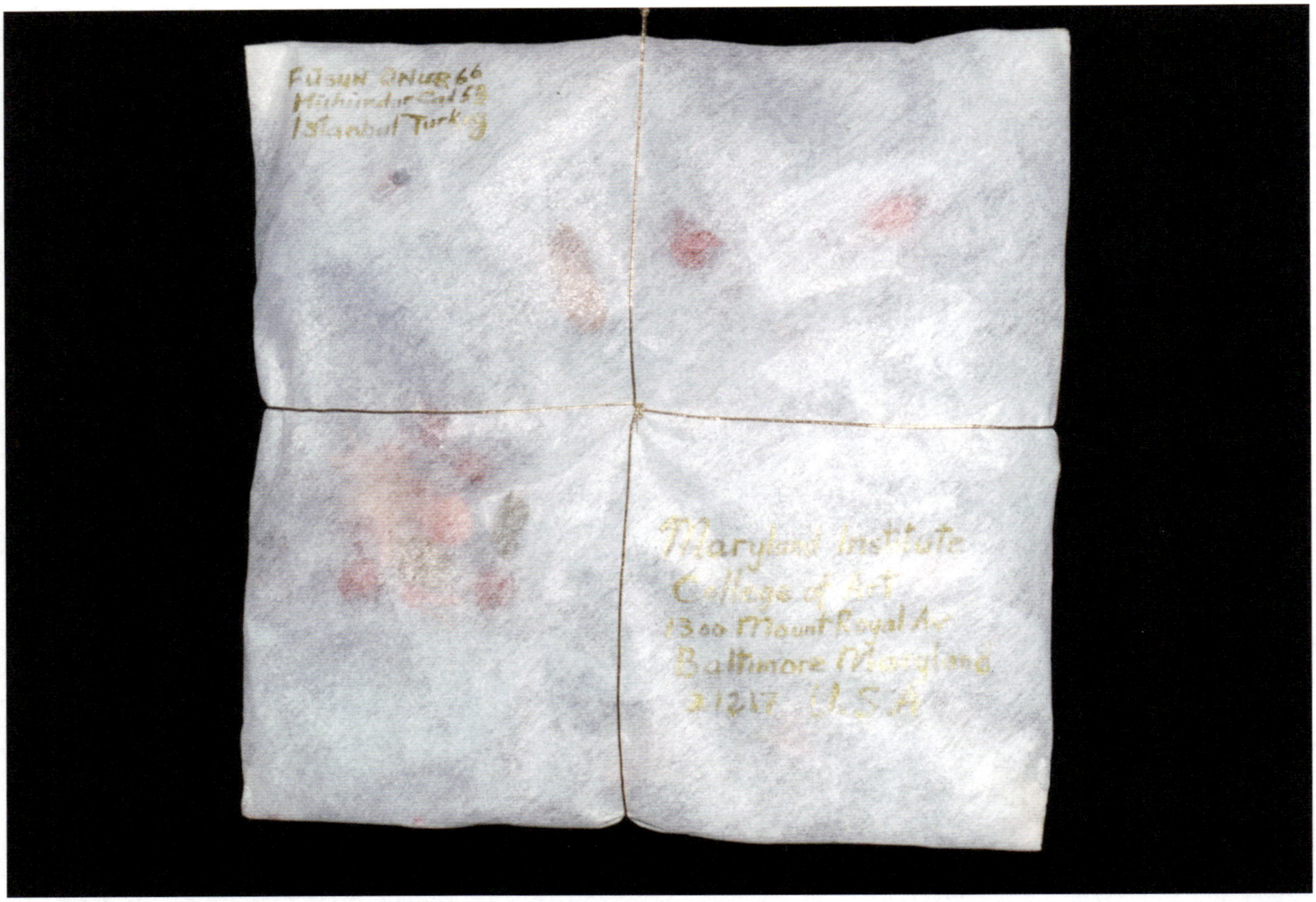

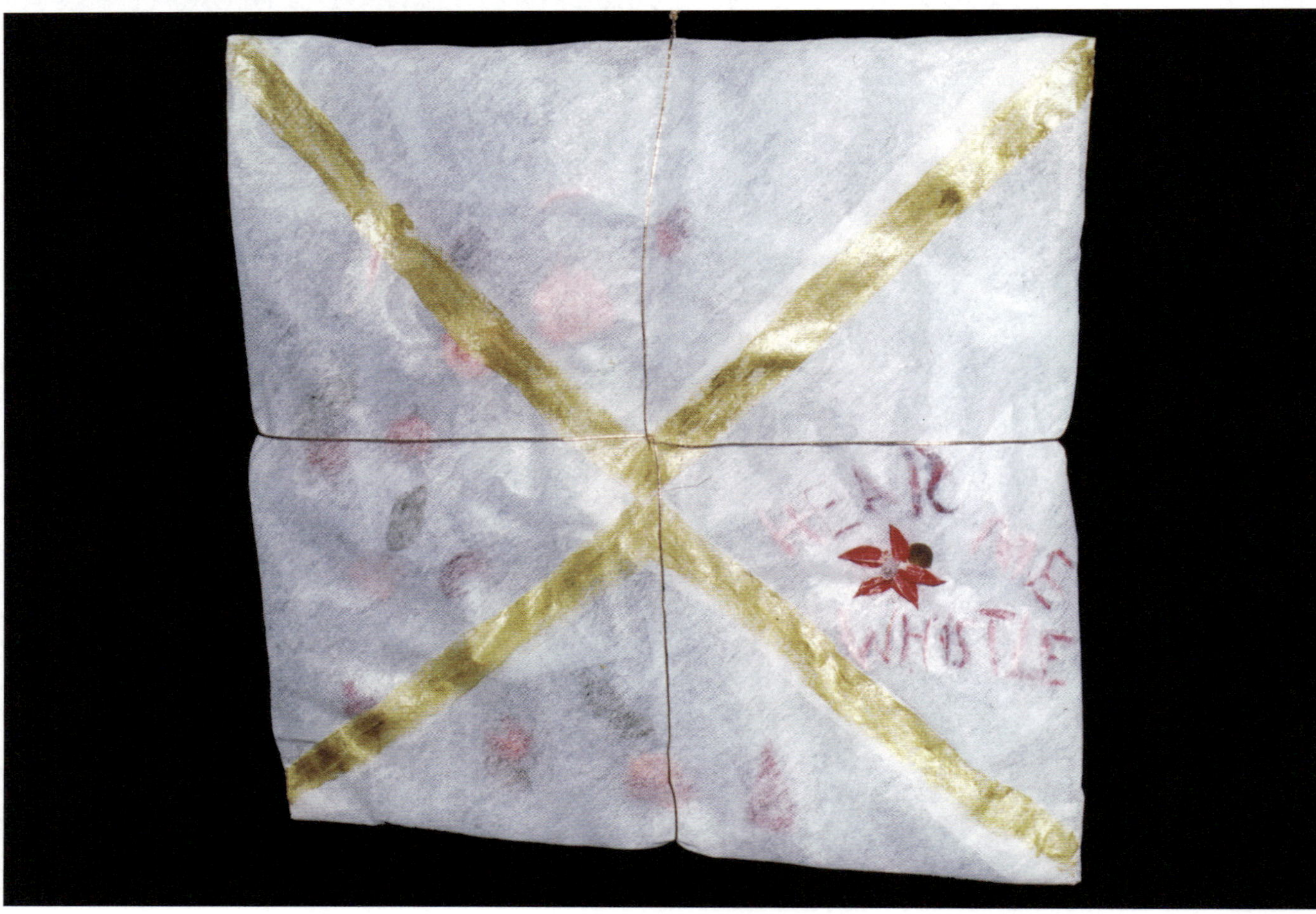

Fabric, paint, 15 × 15 cm

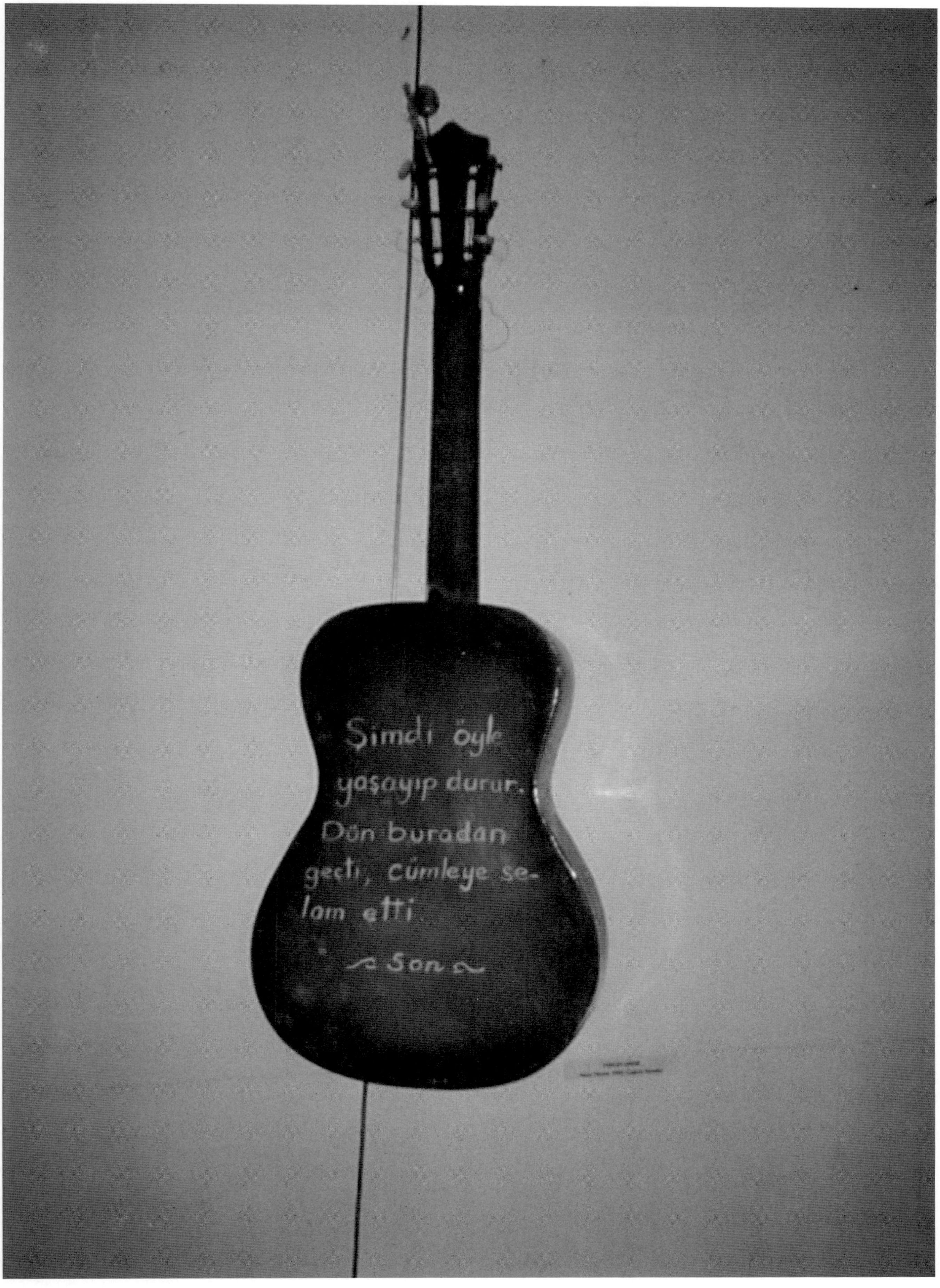

Classic guitar, paint

A flighty line advancing according to its own undulating rhythm reconstructs a current that has passed, drawing fragile yet imposingly flexible curves, suspended in purgatory between earth and sky.

This line that unites the visible and the invisible eternalises the moment between the water's contact with the body and its evaporation, and categorically transforms the tangible and intangible borders of the venue, once a hammam, through the abstract language it builds.

The formal components of *Those Who Have Washed Here* (1994) have a temporary physicality, yet with its linear structure it is also a mediator that traces the invisible. Like washing and purifying, the perpetual act of erasing and redrawing creates an intertemporal space, opening up the form and the venue with a movement from the inside out.

By transforming semi-visible, ephemeral objects, Füsun Onur brings into being once again the spirit of the water fused into the heavens of the venue in the moment of purification. Thus, with the projection of this current that defies gravity, she determines the linear and intuitive kinetic effects of water on no longer existent bodies. By activating an unfinished dream with the notation of the crystals and the refined curves of this blue tulle that preserves the time within, she virtually recalls the stagnant history of the venue.

The confluence of the blue tulle and crystals fastened on the wall with golden chains induces their serene silences to speak. Like the symphonic echo of an audible silence touching constantly flowing time, it starts at an unexpected place, glides through the venue and fades away, blending into space.

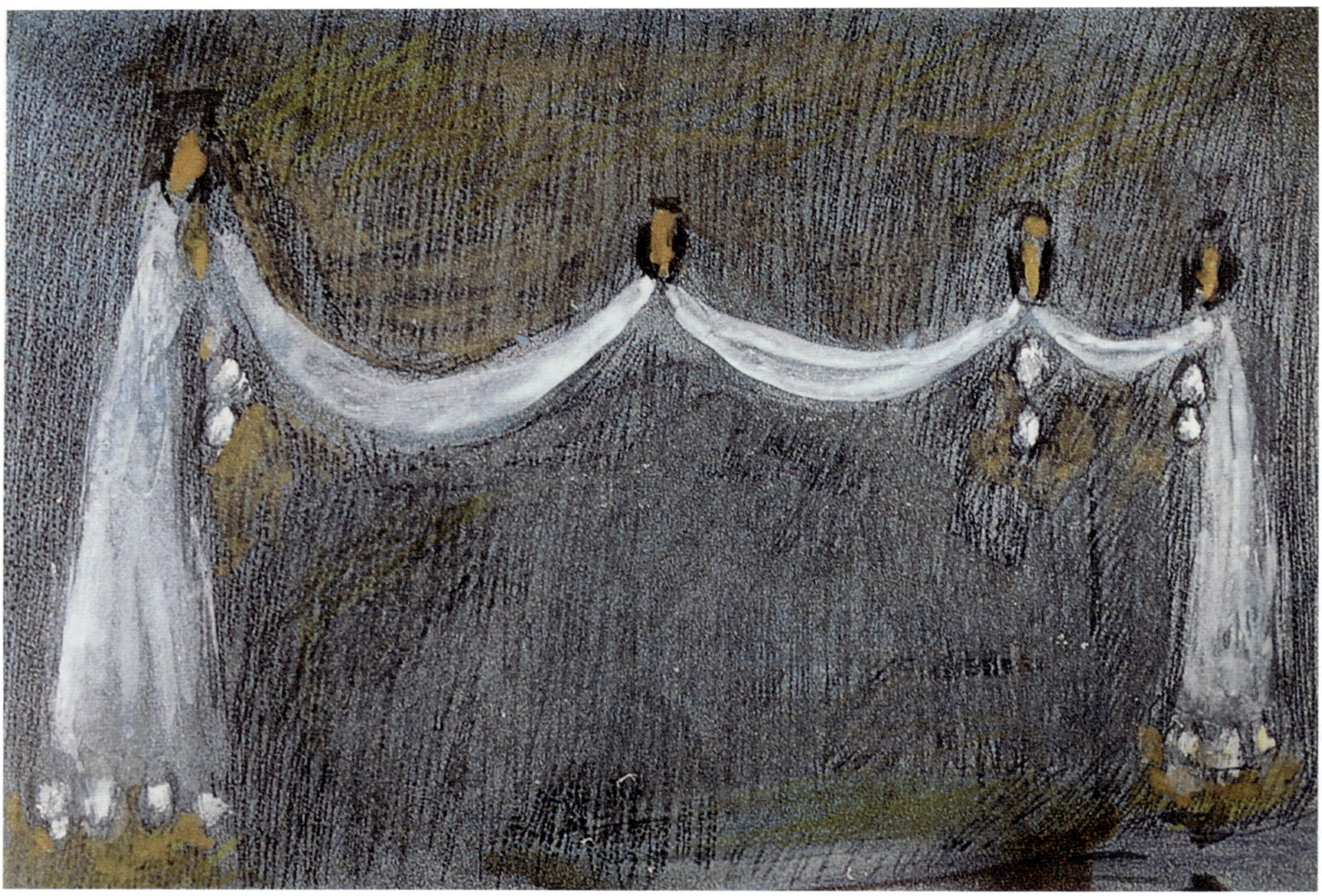

Sketch for *Those Who Have Washed Here*, 1994

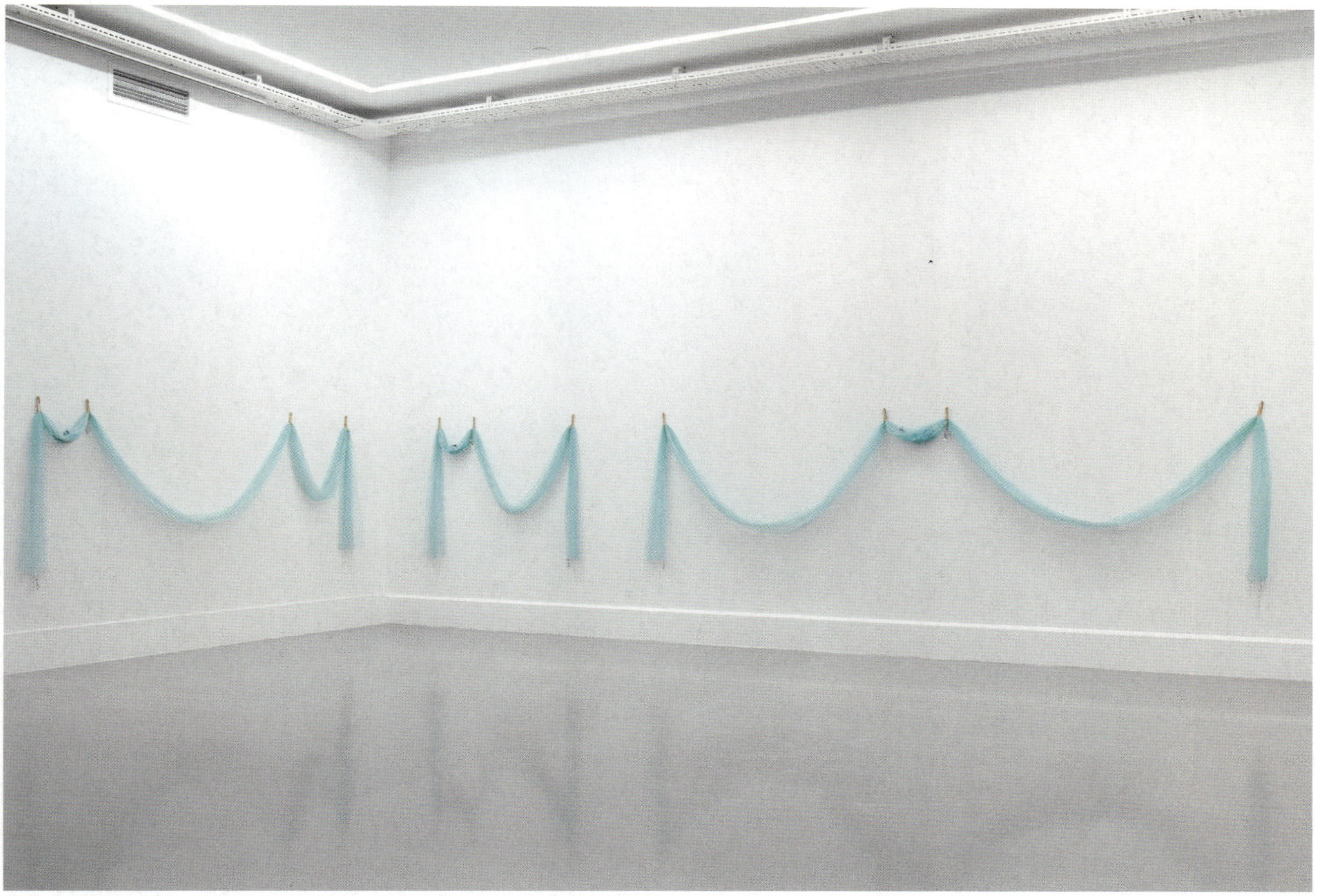

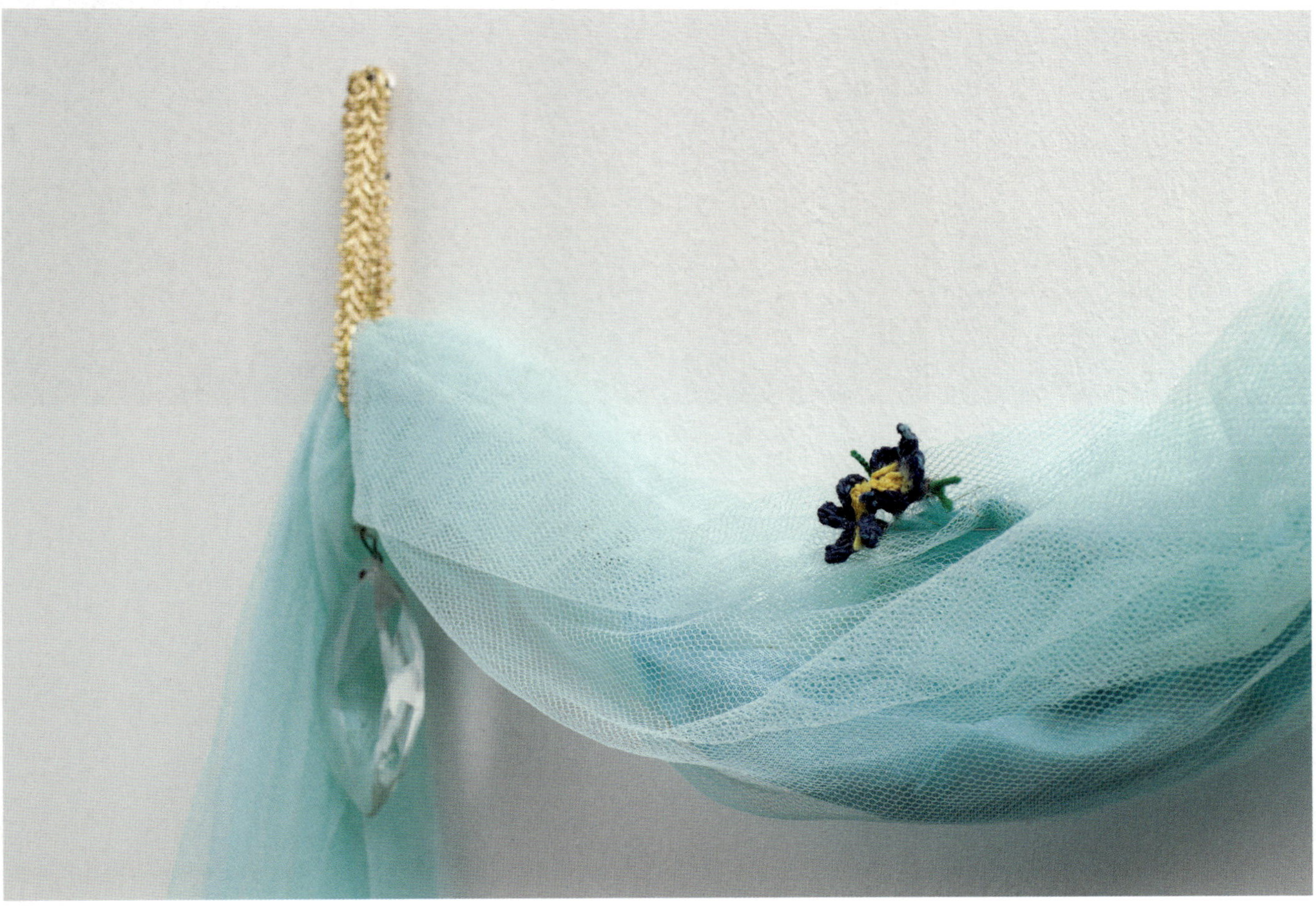

Tulle, fabric, thread, pieces of crystal, 1994, variable dimensions
Installation view from the exhibition *Through the Looking Glass*, Arter, 2014

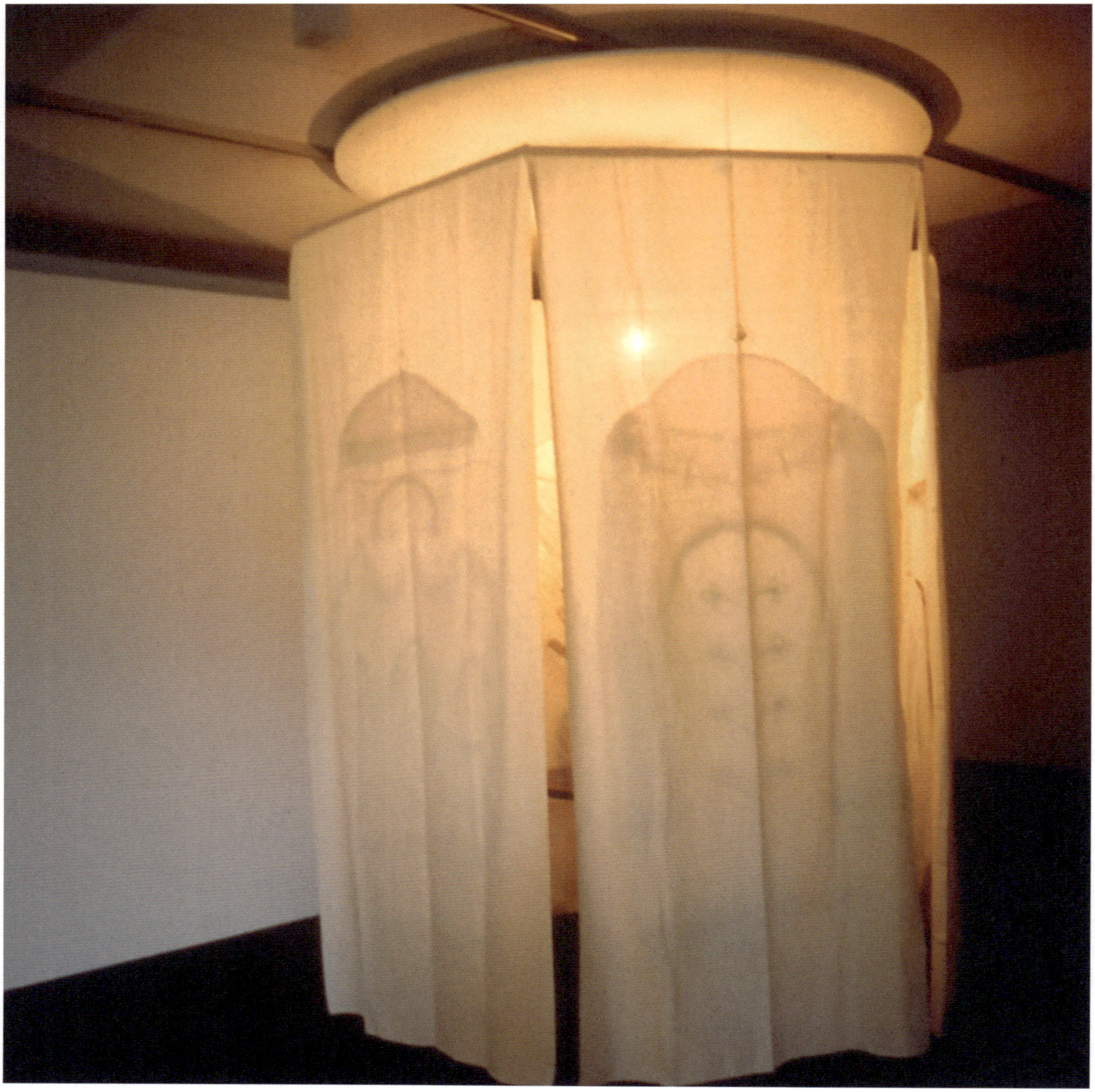

Installation (fabric, tulle, thread, beads, metal)

Above all else, a scenery definitely worth seeing, still breathtaking.

Recently, I've been looking out the windows and observing how the other shore of the Bosphorus seems spiky as the back of a hedgehog, the ways it's riddled with tall residential blocks, skyscrapers, and commercial towers. The more we look outside, the bigger the annoyance, at times evoking an outcry in the house. 'Oh look, yet another one,' says İlhan with exasperation in her voice. 'But this is too much,' Füsun mutters angrily. As the cranes keep turning their heads this way and that, the city's silhouette continues to change rapidly, becoming ever more surly and irritable.

Istanbul Obsession... What an obsession indeed!

Reclining in my resting place by the window, I think of yet another old work she made long before we met. When I enter this tiny room which she made by arranging fabric panels in a hexagonal format so that it resembled a honeycomb, I feel like I am embraced tightly inside a haute-couture outfit. These fabric walls on which she hung garments of transparent organza decorated with bright stones and glitter feel as if they might ruffle and wave, and take to the wing at the gentlest breath of air.

Füsun has bent the hangers – from which she has suspended the clothes – so that they conform to a dome-like shape; and on the transparent clothes she has added embroidery that evokes traditional motifs. The first time I imagined the room from outside, I was completely swept away by the shadow-shapes playing out on its cloth curtains, and the silhouettes of touching beauty they produced, which reminded me of Istanbul. As I open the photo album lying on the coffee table, looking through photos of old Istanbul, I once again find myself daydreaming.

Whoever enters this room shall become part of this silhouette.

Emre Baykal, excerpt from the catalogue *Through the Looking Glass*, Arter, 2014.

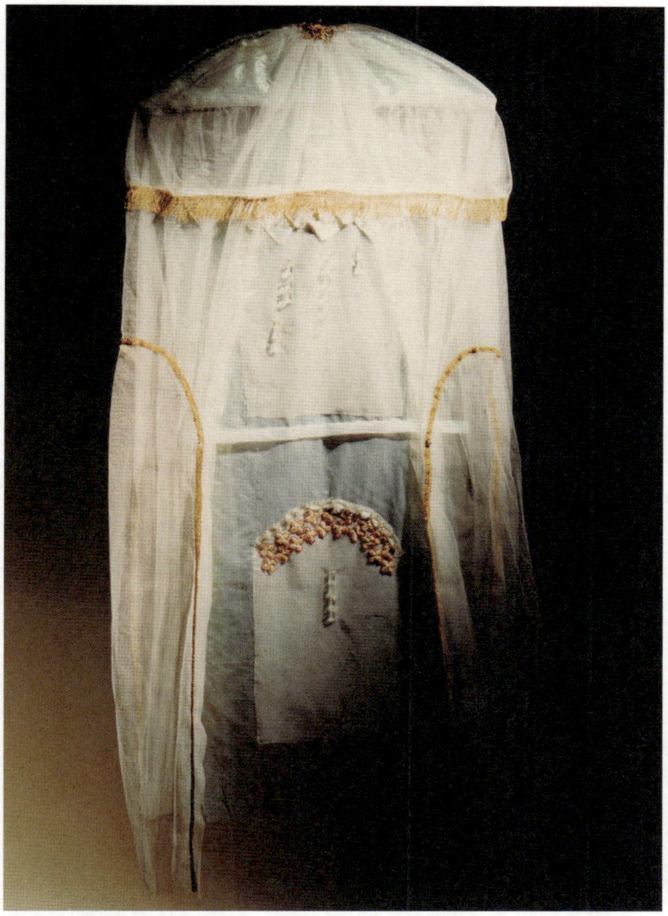
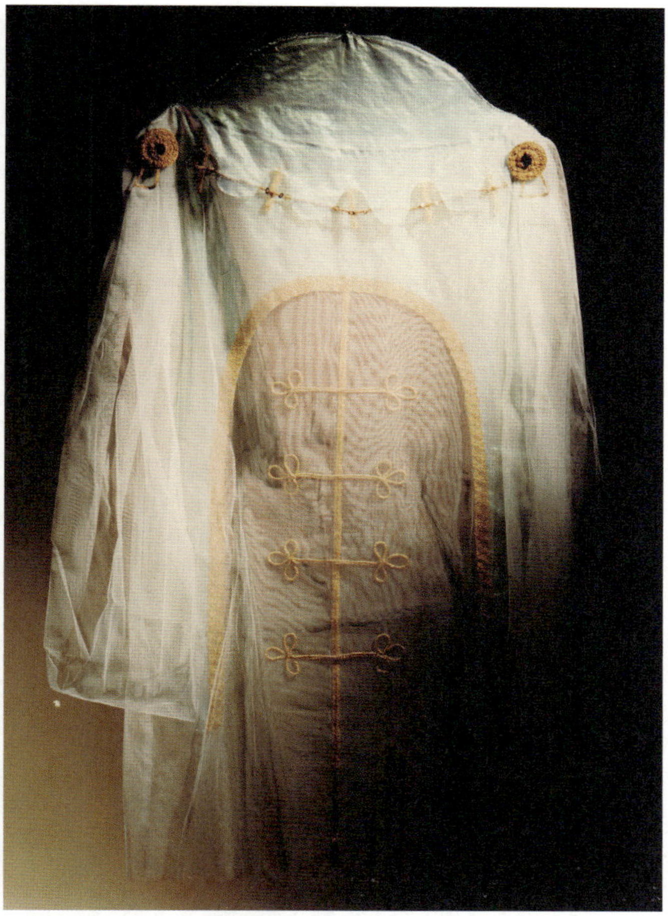
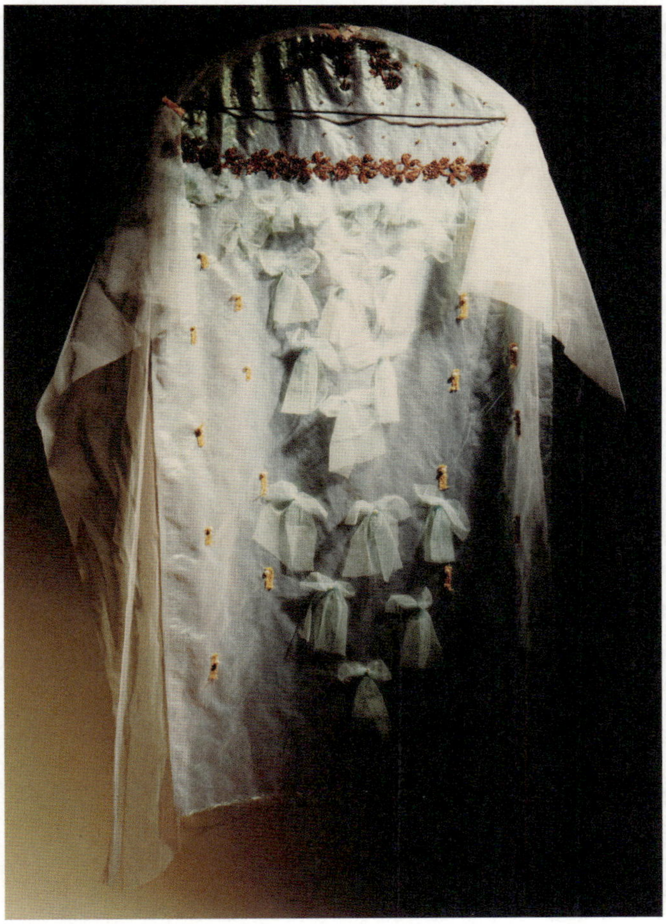
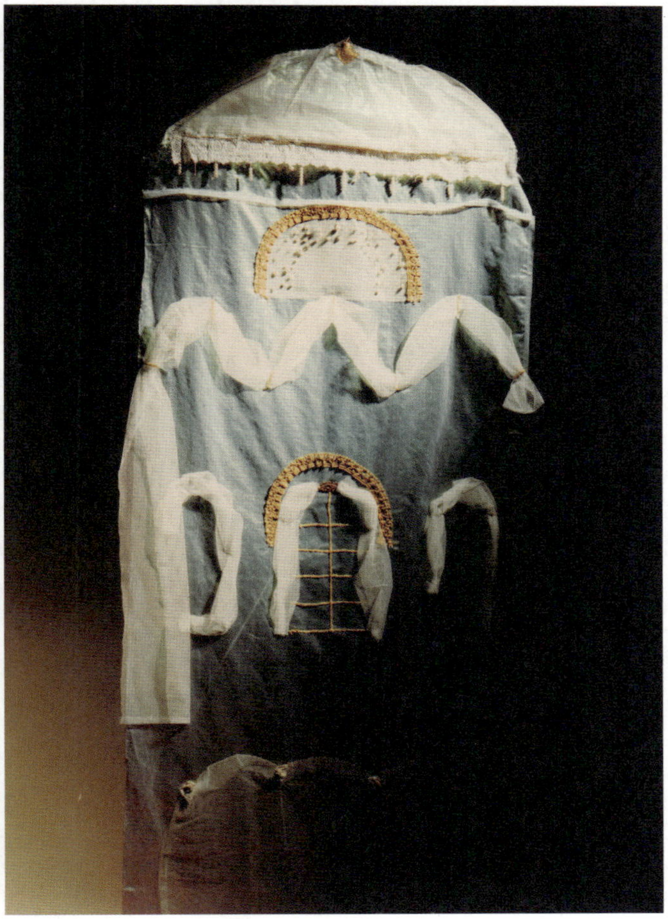

When I was asked to write about the work Füsun Onur made for the Train Station [GAR] exhibition held in May 1995, I took a trip twenty-seven years down memory lane. I had participated in several joint exhibitions with Onur, installed some of her works with her and photographed many of them. It was the same with this show. Unfortunately, the two sole photographs I took that day can't tell us much about her work. It's always very difficult to capture a site-specific installation, especially this one, which was of such subtlety.

For the exhibition, Onur folded a rowboat out of glittery purple wrapping paper. On the bow was an inscription written in crayon that read 'ARHAT'. There were also five, palm-sized gift packages wrapped in shiny black paper and bound with fishing line. On each one of these, a sticker bearing one letter of the word ARHAT was randomly placed. One of the boxes had its lower surface cut out in the shape of a heart.

Room Number 4 was a high-ceilinged space, overlooking the railroad. It was lit with a fluorescent tube suspended from the ceiling on a chain. Onur installed her paper rowboat behind the roller blind that was covering the window. The light from outside cast the shadow of the boat onto the blind. We installed four of the five gift boxes on the floor in the corners and the last one on the fluorescent light hanging from the ceiling. The task of installation didn't take long, but Onur spent almost the entire day in the room, occasionally leaving only to go back in a little later. It was as if each time she re-entered the room she was trying to forget the work and discover it anew like an ordinary visitor. The next day at the opening, Onur would once again meet her own work as if for the first time.

When visitors entered Room Number 4, it seemed at first glance to be empty. Only after spending some time in this space would they begin to discern the objects around them. They were inside a space true to the meaning of the word arhat, purified and ready to attain nirvana. This was the station of leaving and arriving. Onur was inviting us on a spiritual journey, and we even had the chance to bring along our gifts.

Istanbul 03/2022

*In Buddhism an *arhat* (Sanskrit) is one who has gained insight into the true nature of existence and has achieved *nirvana*; a person free from all defilements, existing without greed, hatred, delusion, ignorance or craving. The term is also used for people far advanced along the path of Enlightenment, but who may not have reached full Buddhahood. en.wikipedia.org/wiki/Arhat

1995 ARHAT

Installation (paper boxes, paper boat)

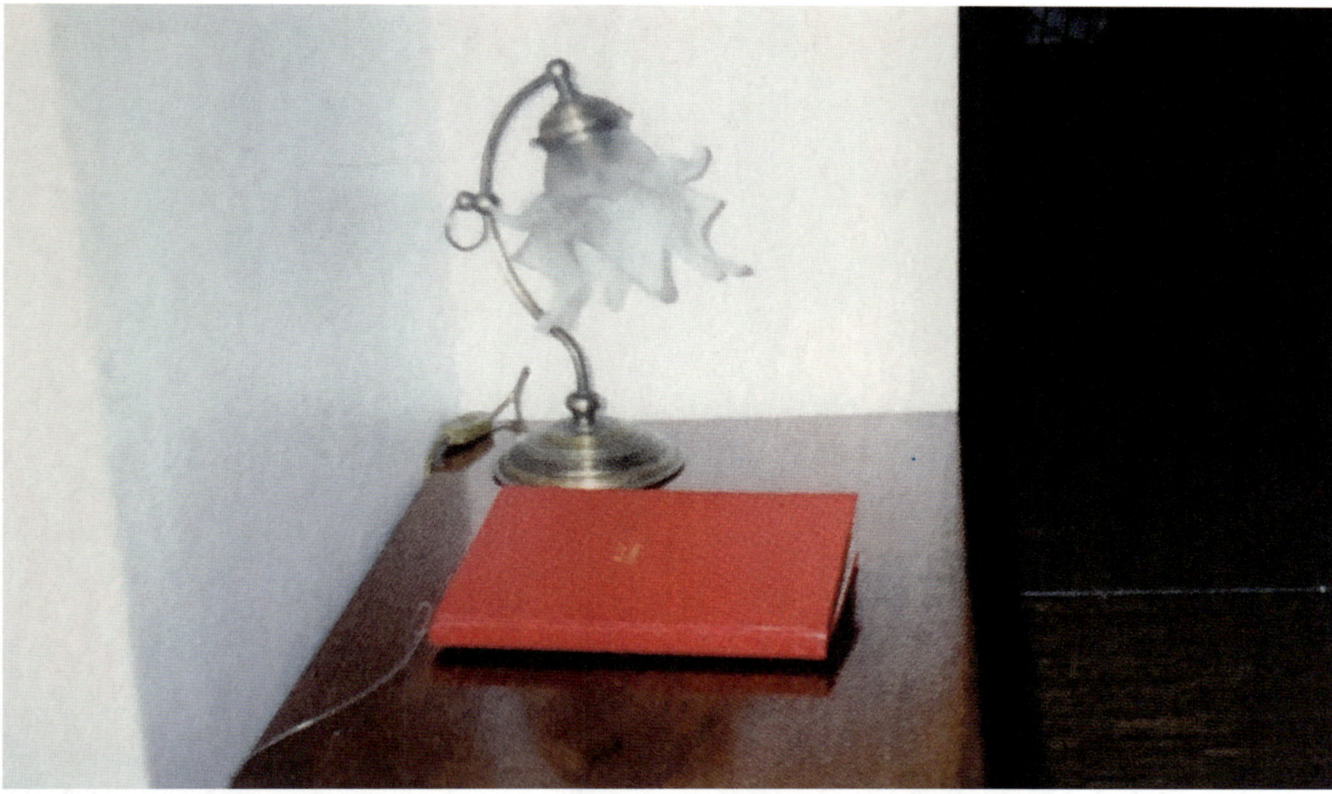

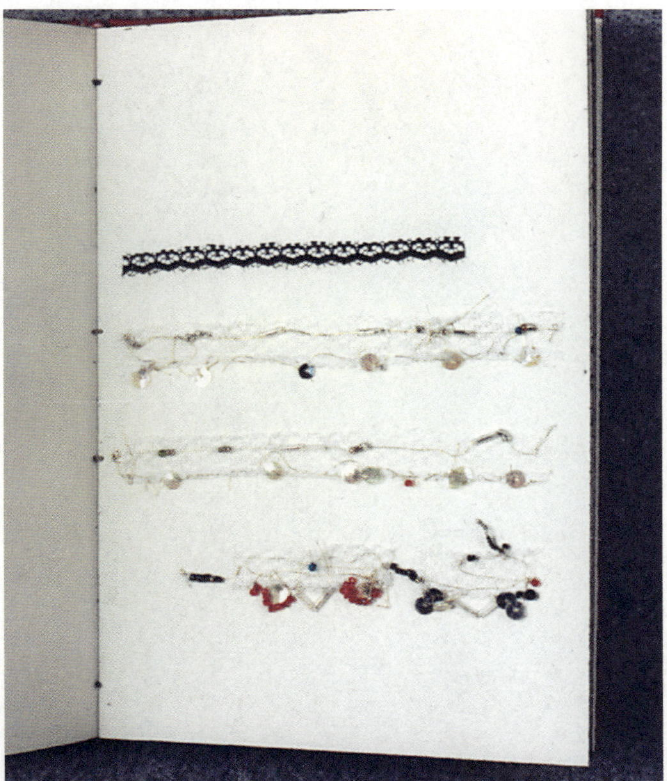

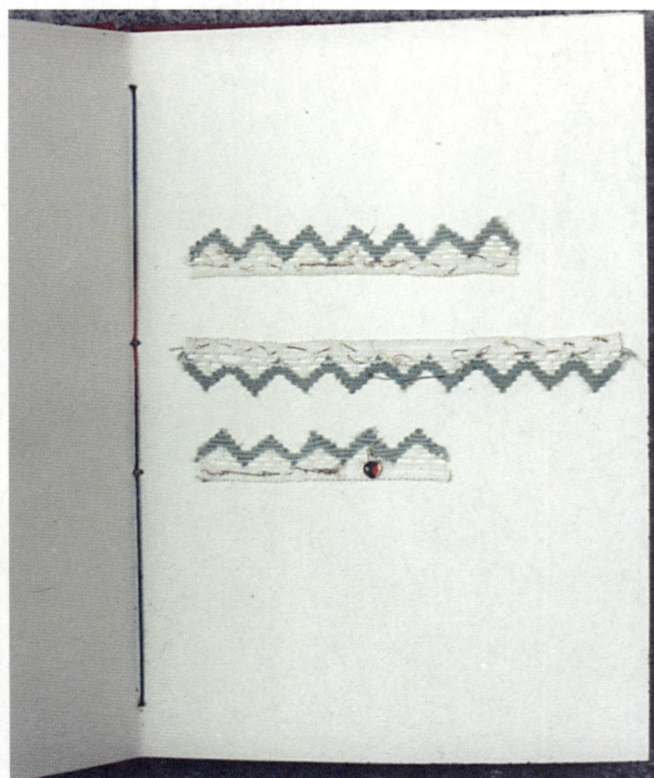

Artist book

In a Paris gallery she combined transparent gauze dresses she had sewn herself with the presentation of a book *I don't know French*. On the pages of the book were fragments of lace, ribbons and beads, once collected by her own mother or other women and added to by the artist herself. In this way, Onur gently confirms her own language, one of universal brilliance which is characterized by handiwork, touching and female tradition.

Angelika Stepken, excerpt from the *The Song of the Earth* exhibition catalogue, Kassel, 2000.

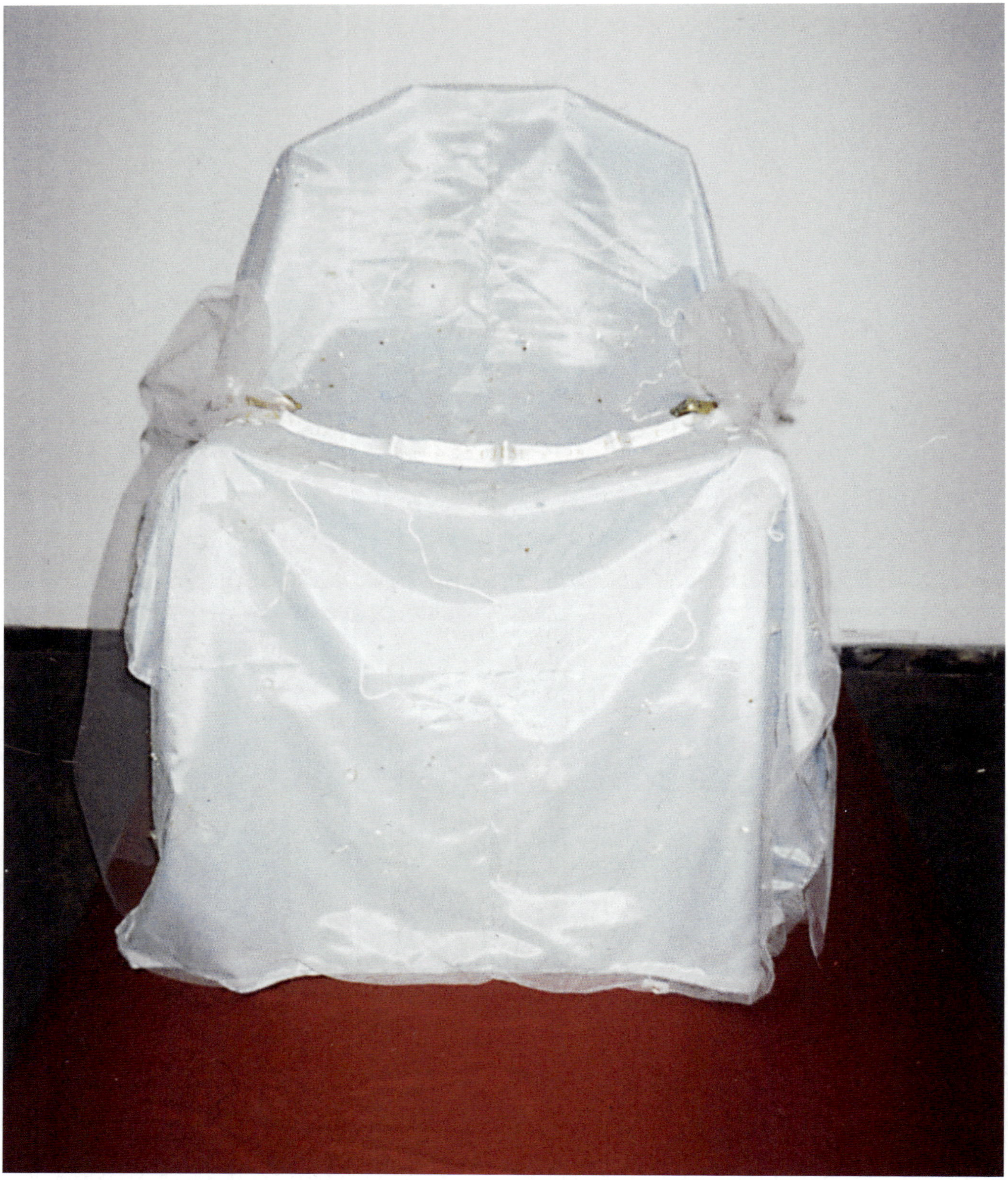

Installation (fabric, armchair)

[…] the chair which the artist decorated with satin, tulle and beads for Zübeyde Hanım, the mother of Atatürk, looks like a throne. Here too, we see the name of the woman, this time written in gold on a band and held by two small brass hands. While this work surely includes admiration which the artist has for Atatürk, whose reform policies on equality and the separation of state and church she repeatedly emphasises, it makes no reference to the woman's son. The focus of attention is women, understood as representatives of their gender, irrespective of the names mentioned. As in other works in which Onur has used chairs to signify the place assigned by society, this work tells of the social disadvantages of women. As an artist, Onur attacks this state of affairs not only in a personal statement but also through the place of honour ascribed to Zübeyde Hanım (who is usually seen merely in the role of mother) she points out that it is up to women to write their own history, as this will otherwise remain unwritten.

Margrit Brehm, excerpt from *For Careful Eyes*, Yapı Kredi Publications, Istanbul, 2007.

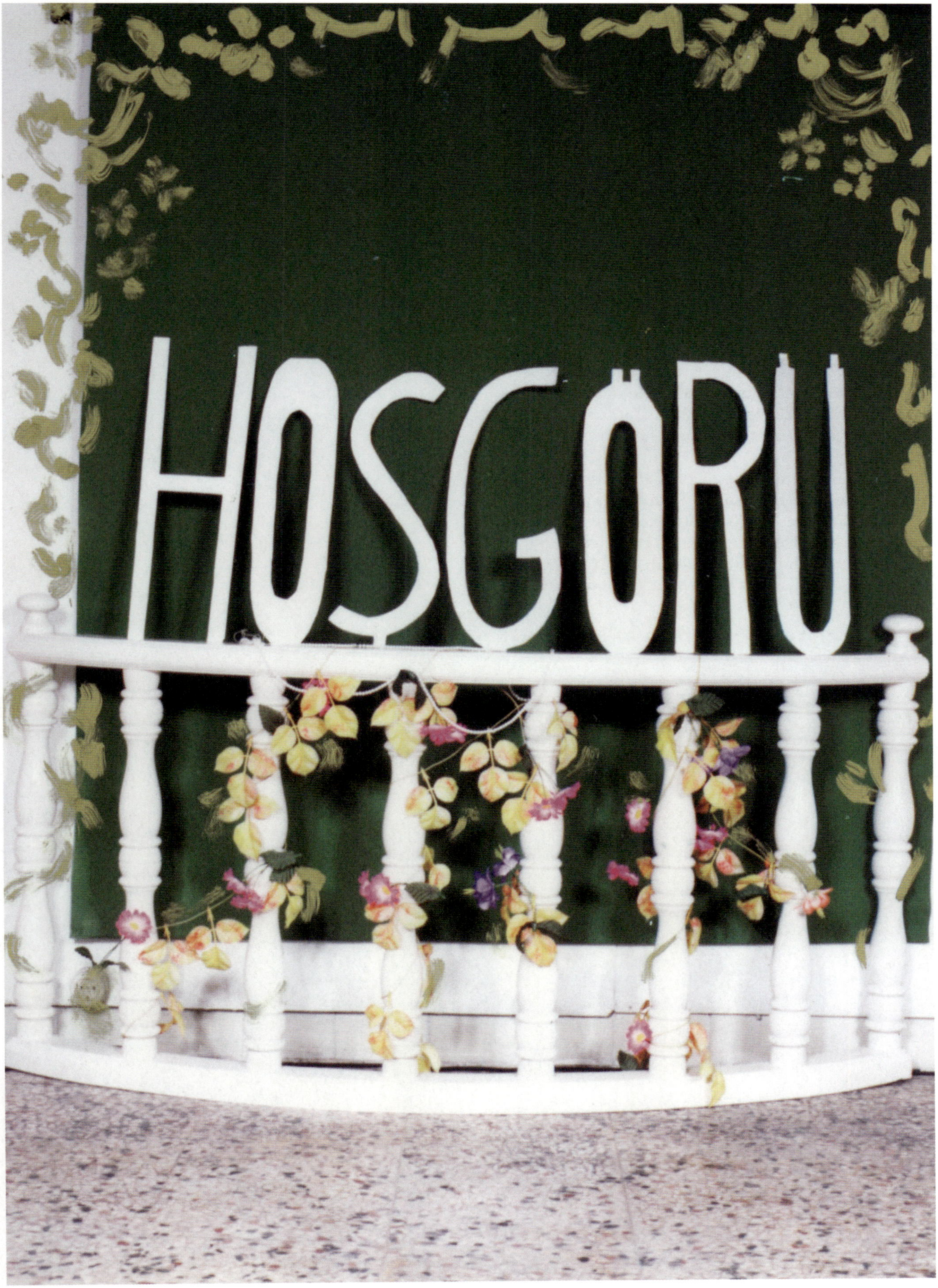

Mixed media installation

Cadence (1995) has left reflections in my mind like the shards of a shattered mirror. When it caught my eye in the 1990s, my twenty-year old self could see that it was no cute or playful work, but nor was it a stern critique of the institution. The artist had pinned a note to the work, saying that she wished us to 'hear' it.

I remember trying to solve the work's relationship with its title. Perhaps the romantic connotations of the word were equivalent to the pieces of tulle, illuminated with a theatrical colour, gently covering the freestanding ashtray. There was a tension between the wooden stools of the art gallery, and the metal rods reclining on them – the mechanisms used for hanging paintings. One could hardly say that Onur took pleasure from the plain gallery stools. They simply served as a sort of pedestal, just as the tiled gallery space resembling a checkered page constituted a background. The focal point was the picture hanging rods and their hooks.

Cadence deconstructed and alienated these mechanisms for the display of paintings to such an extent that they no longer contributed anything. So was the word 'cadence,' which means the close of a musical phrase, alluding to the death of painting? I think not. Onur's issue is not with painting, but with the elements that discipline it. It is difficult for the painting to breathe in such formal conditions. The fact that this critique came from a sculptor and not a painter indicates that profound lessons for painters are hidden in fields like sculpture, dance, music, theatre and film.

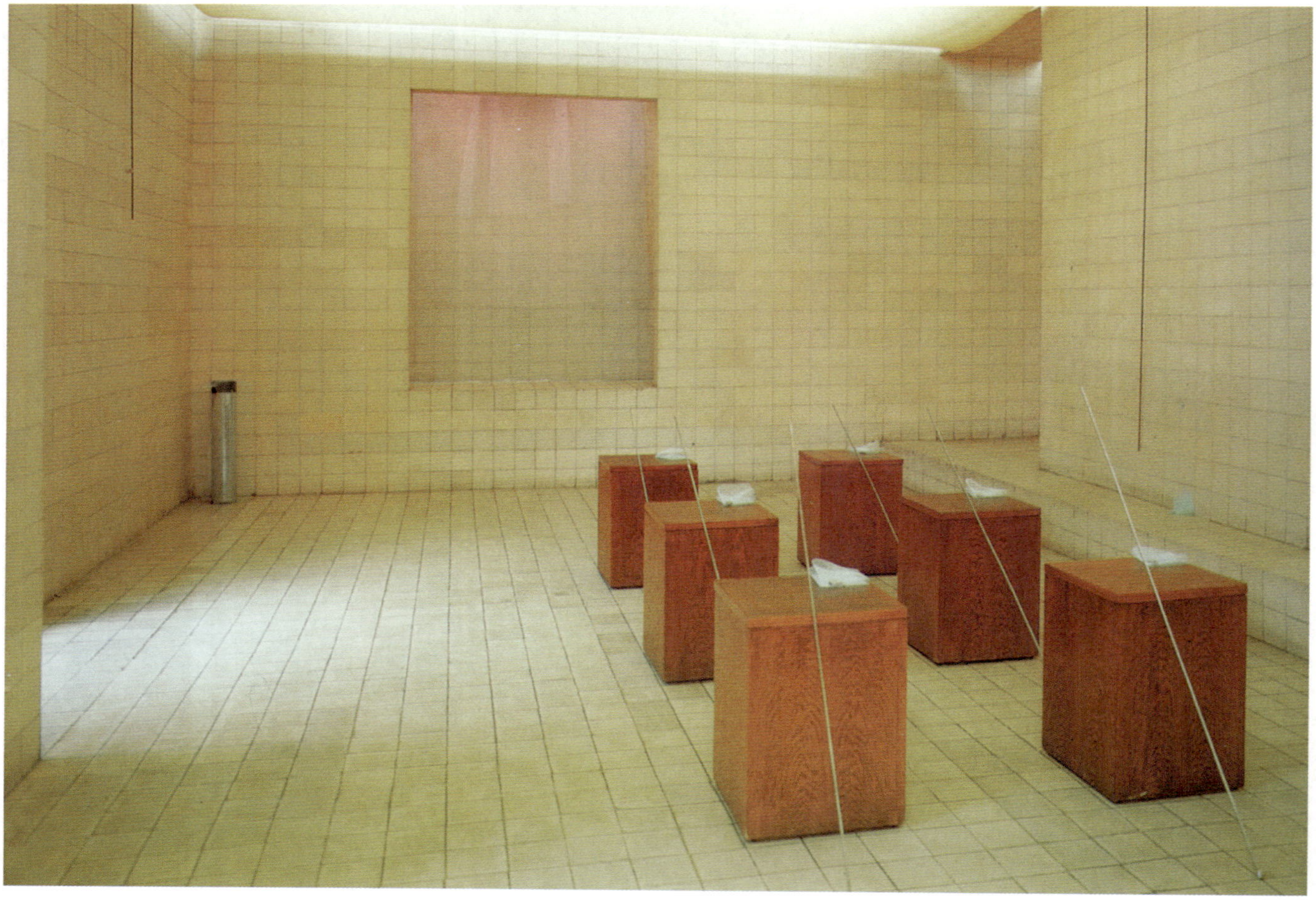

Installation (tulle, pedestal, apparatus to hang painting)

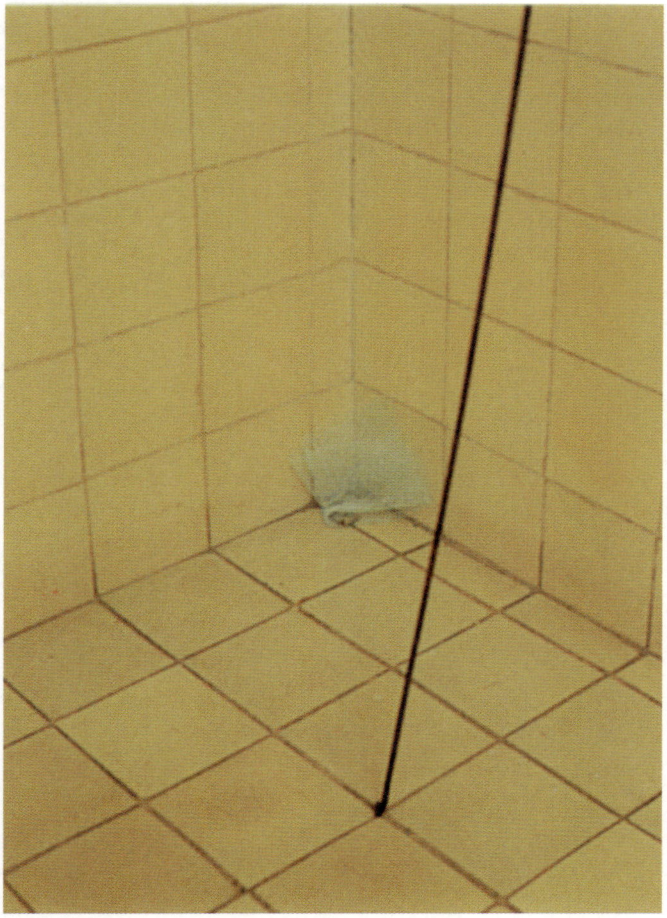

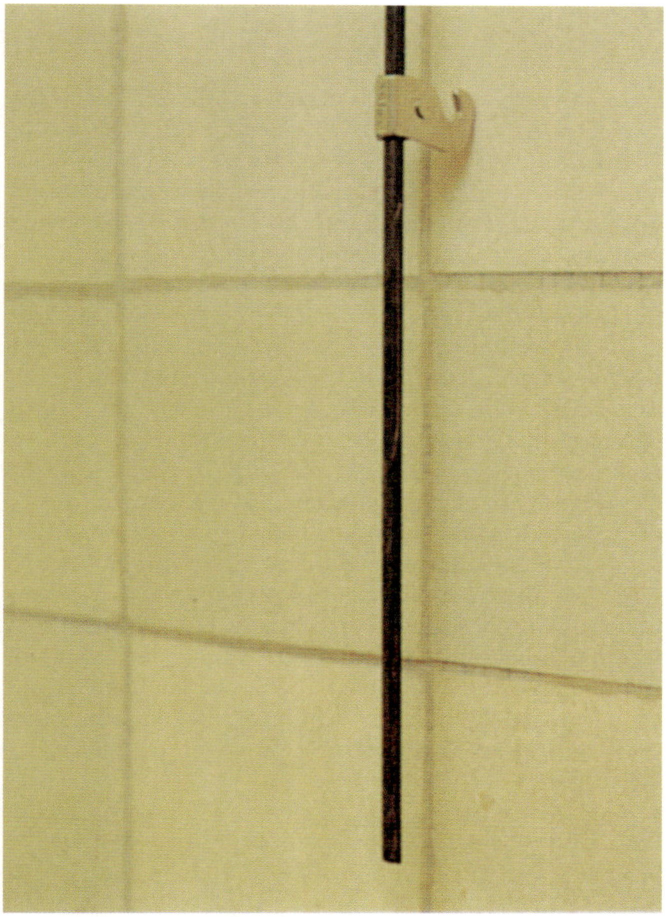

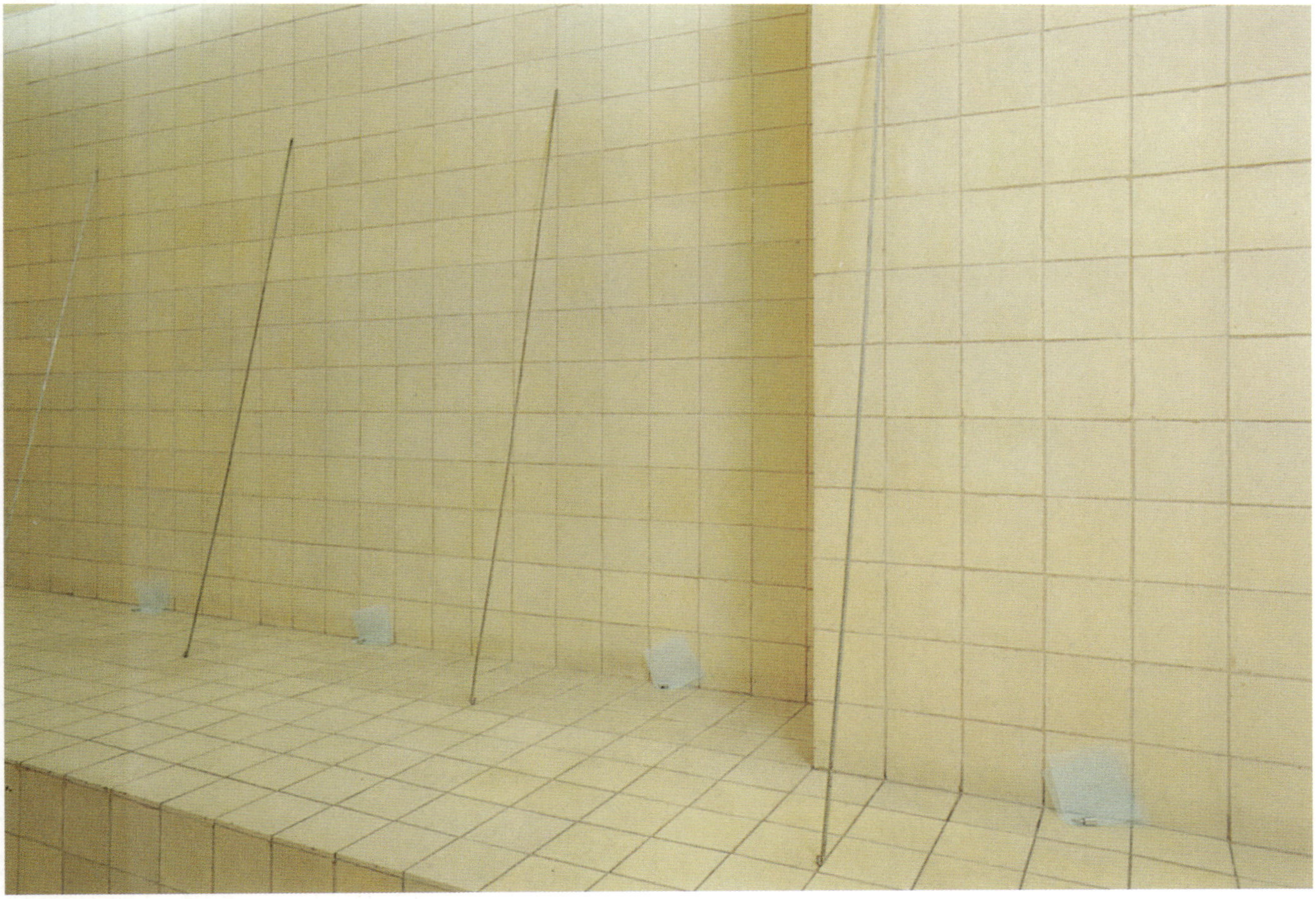

Füsun Onur made her renowned installation *Let's Meet at the Orient* (1995) for the visionary 4th Istanbul Biennial, *ORIENT/ATION*, curated by René Block, where it was exhibited in the impressive Hagia Irene, an Eastern Orthodox church that dates to the fourth century. This 'elemental and utopian' (Onur's term) work is as meaningful now as it was back then – perhaps even more so.

A sizable blue rubber balloon hanging overhead in a beaded net suggests a solitary party decoration, but also Earth seen from space – our gorgeous blue planet floating in the universe. Onur excels at imbuing commonplace objects and materials with driving ideas, and at giving them surprising connotations. An embroidery hoop dangles below; draped over it is a somewhat ragged silk swath, shaped like all the continents but without countries and borders – perhaps Earth as it was 200 million years ago before humans. It is the artist's vision of a holistic world that has transcended virulent nationalism and endless conflicts. On the floor is a copper washtub filled with water. In raised brass letters on its bottom are the names of countries, as if they've fallen here to be cleansed.

Deftly combining diverse objects into an enthralling whole, Onur's installation hints at huge world-shaping forces, including the formation of continents; domestic activities like washing and embroidery; the divisions and borders that we, as humans, have imposed on the world, and what it might be like to be freed from them. Her installation of twenty-seven years ago is still uncannily relevant now, with a pandemic requiring global cooperation, not antagonism and strife.

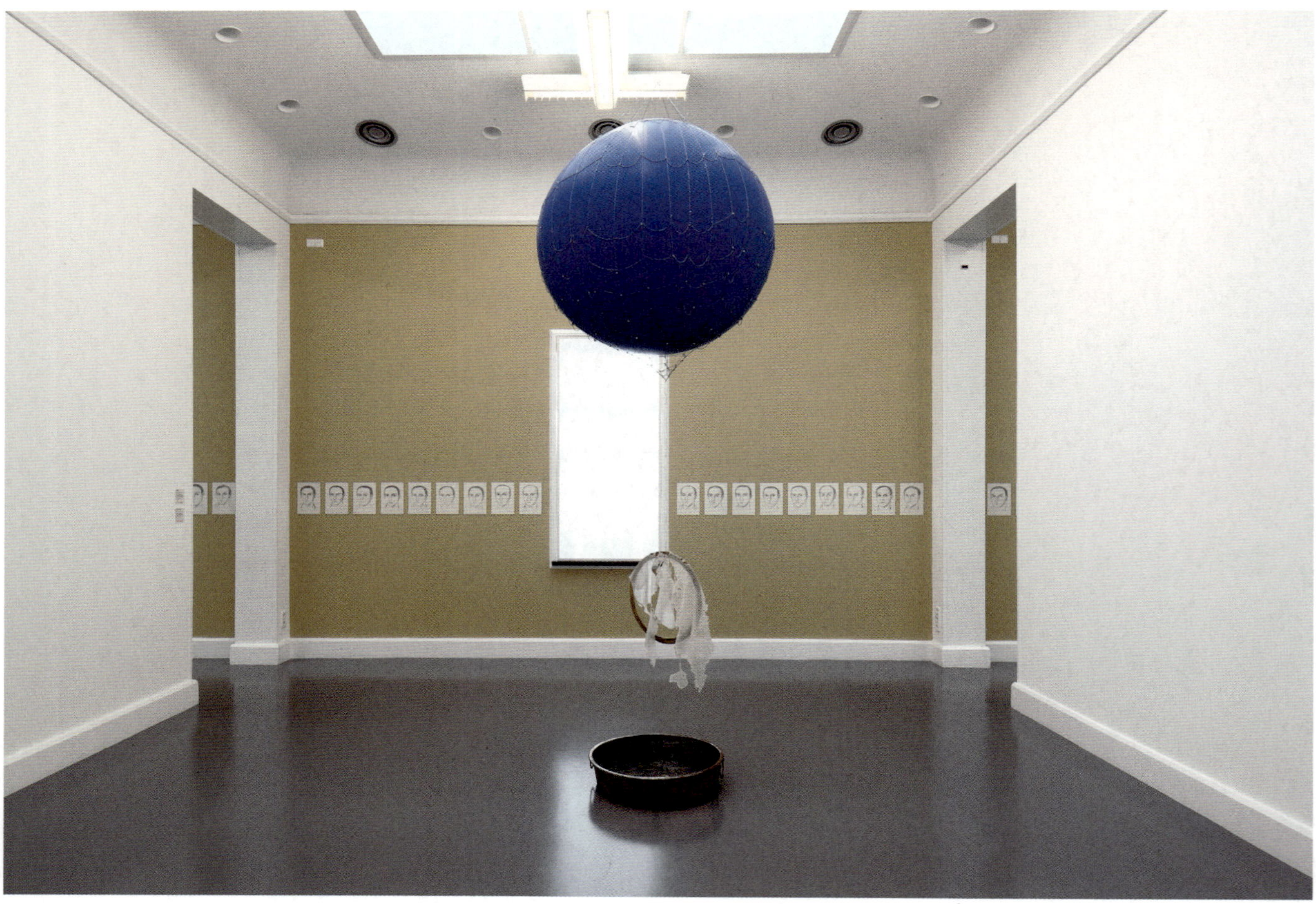

Installation view from *EindhovenIstanbul*, Van Abbemuseum, 2005

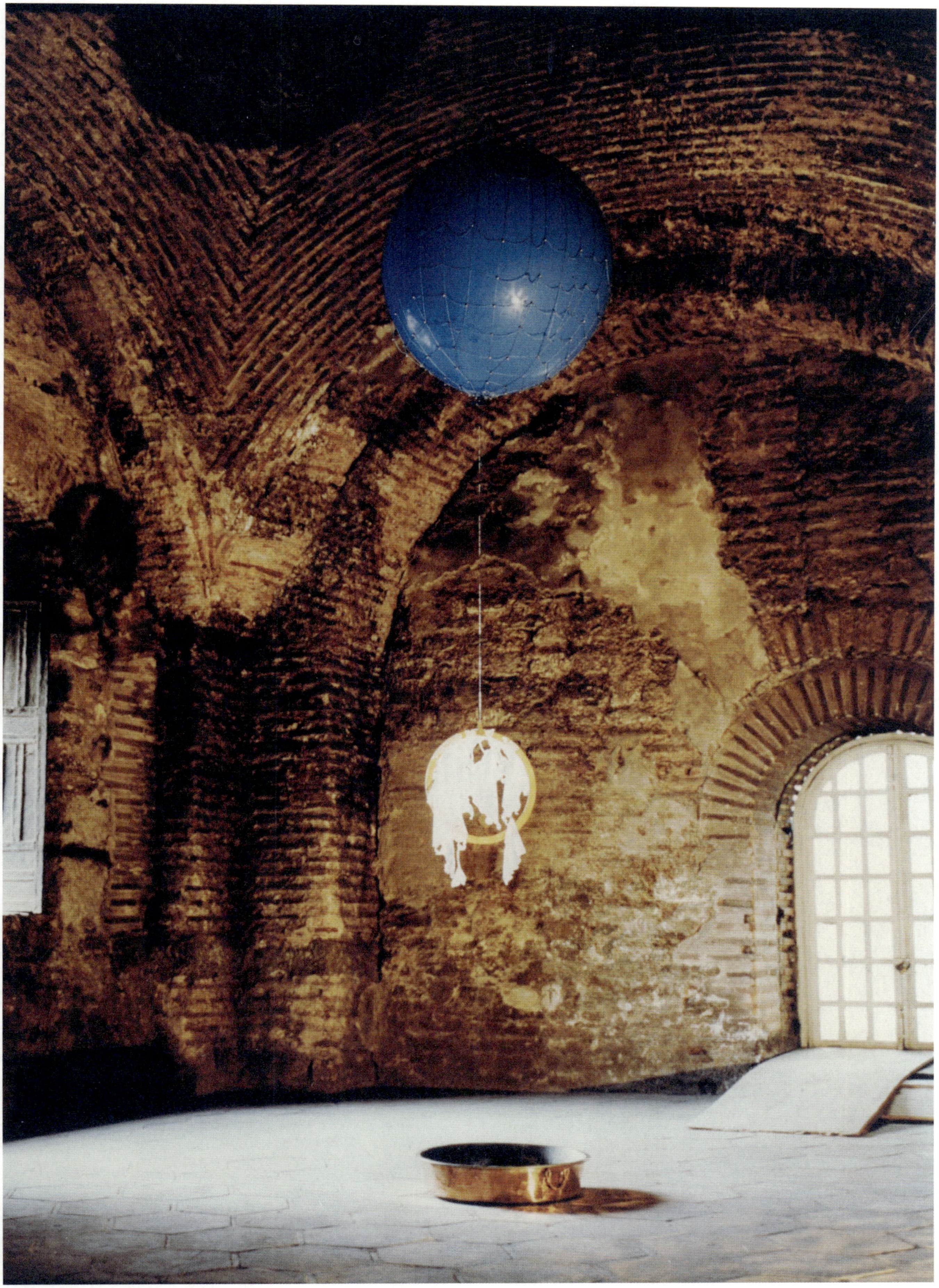

Rubber balloon, silk, rope, wood, copper washtub. Collection Van Abbemuseum, Eindhoven, The Netherlands
Installation view from the 4th Istanbul Biennial, *Orient/ation*, Hagia Irene, 1995

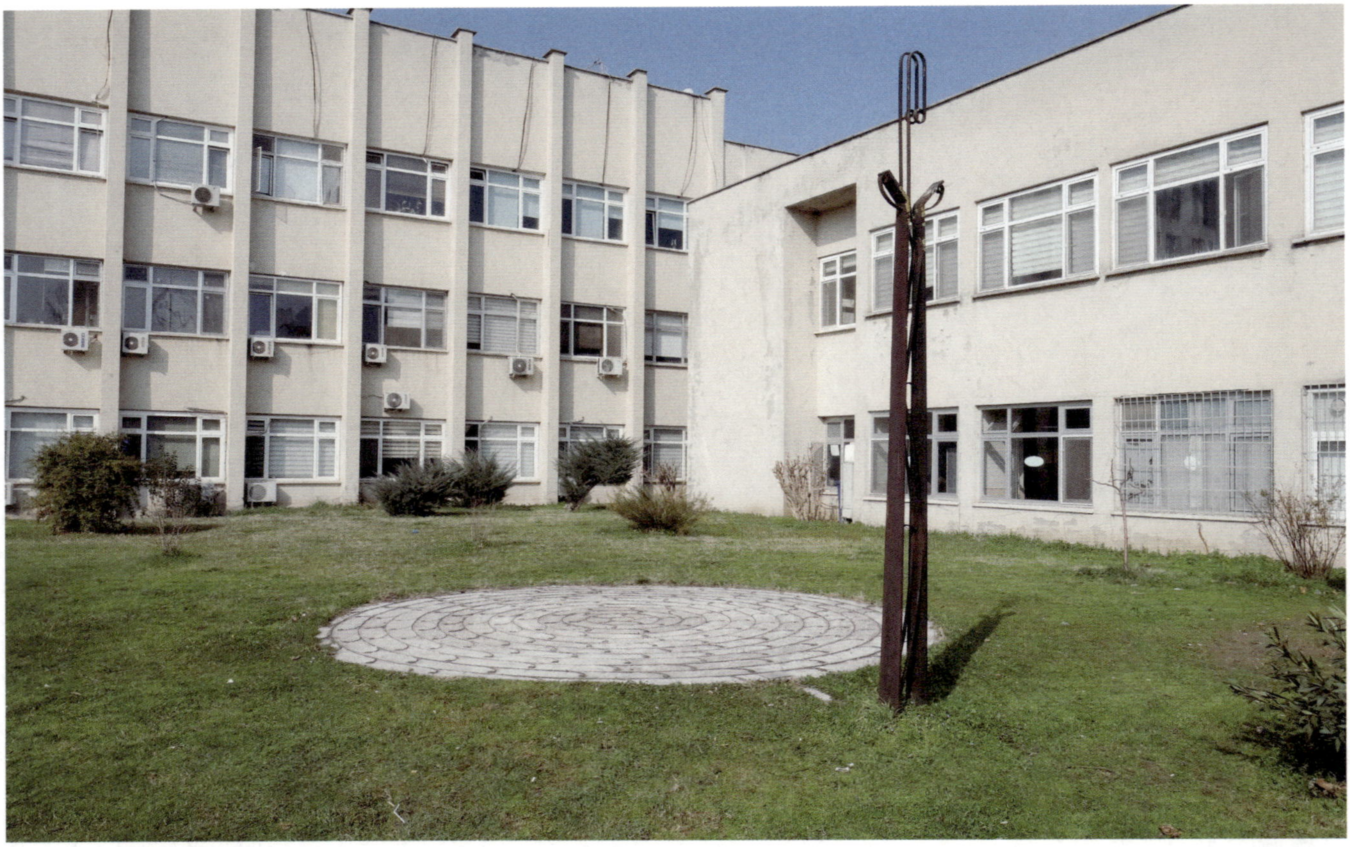

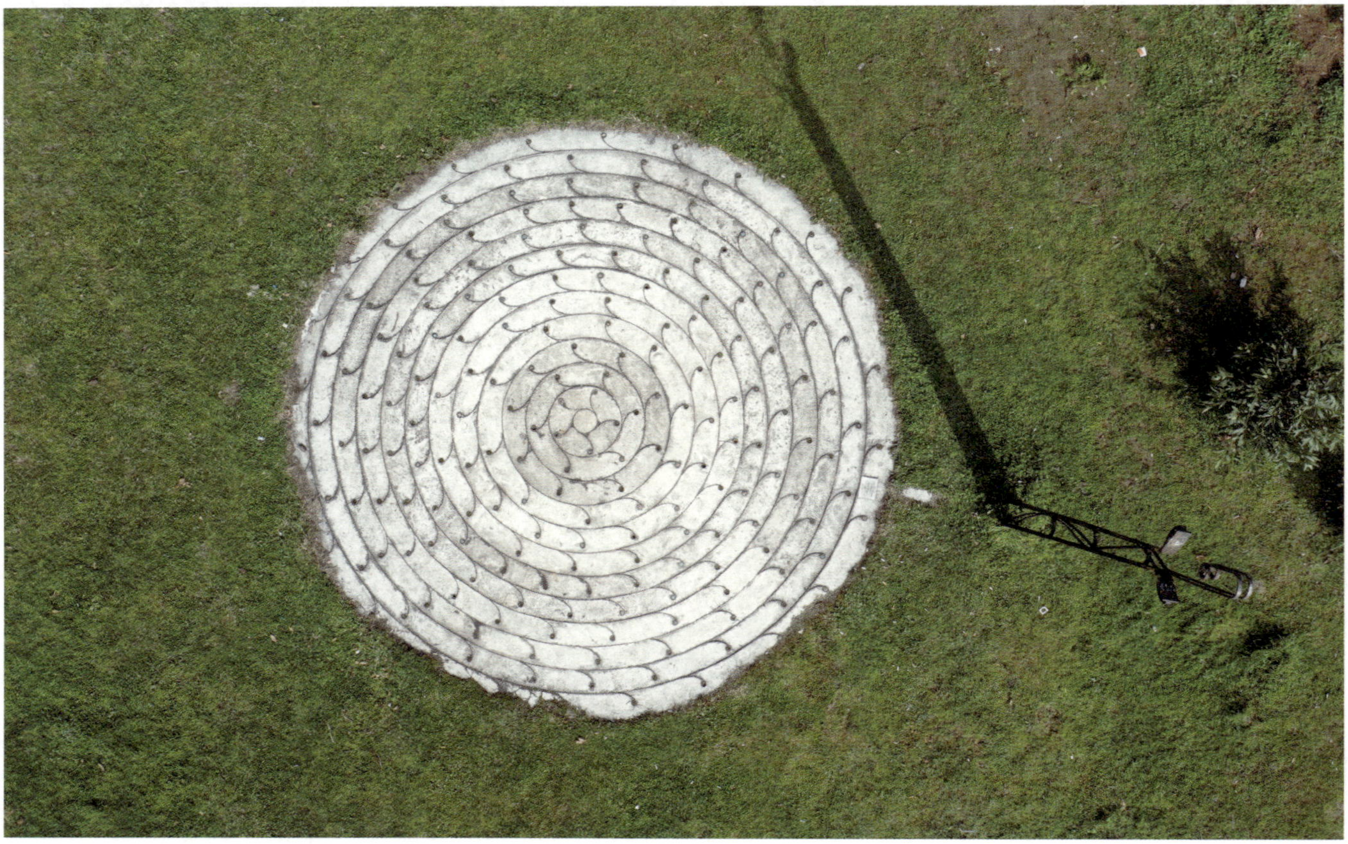

Concrete, metal, ceramic

At the Sculpture Symposium of Uludağ University, I made a work for the floor using metal and blue ceramics. First, concrete was poured on the ground, then with metals I repeated a motif from İznik pottery, and blue ceramics were to be placed on the commas at the connection points.

Füsun Onur, excerpt from the *Prelude* exhibition catalogue, Maçka Art Gallery, 2000.

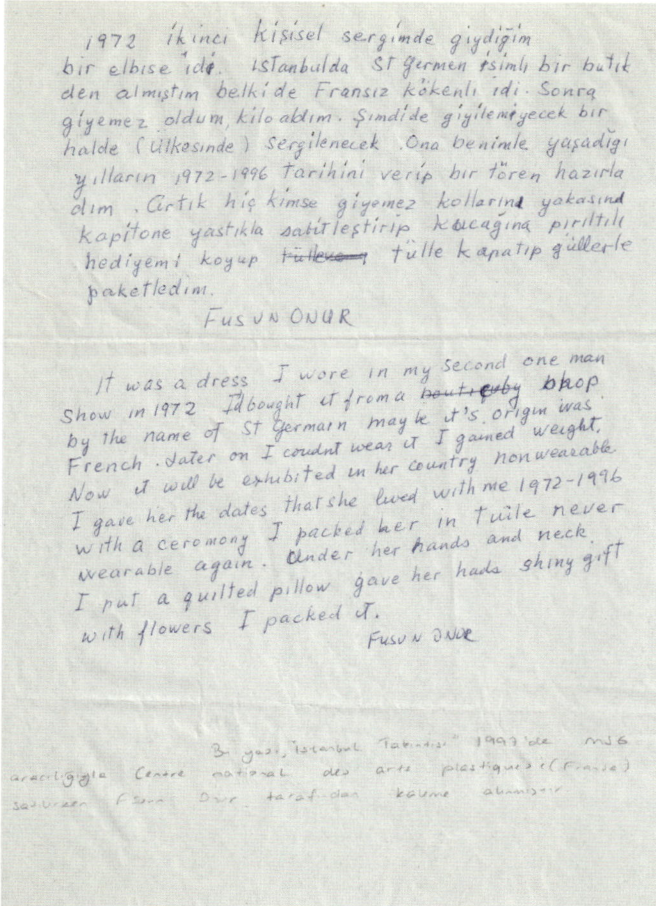
1972 ikinci kişisel sergimde giydiğim
bir elbise idi. İstanbulda St Germen isimli bir butik
den almıştım belki de Fransız kökenli idi. Sonra
giyemez oldum, kilo aldım. Şimdide giyilemeyecek bir
halde (Ülkesinde) sergilenecek. Ona benimle yaşadığı
yılların 1972-1996 tarihini verip bir tören hazırla
dım. Artık hiç kimse giyemez kollarına yakasına
kapitone yastıkla sabitleştirip kucağına pırıltılı
hediyemi koyup ~~tülle~~ tülle kapatıp güllerle
paketledim.
FUSUN ONUR

It was a dress I wore in my second one man
show in 1972 I bought it from a ~~boutique~~ shop
by the name of St Germain may be it's origin was
French. later on I coudnt wear it I gained weight.
Now it will be exhibited in her country nonwearable.
I gave her the dates that she lived with me 1972-1996
with a ceromony I packed her in tulle never
wearable again. Under her hands and neck
I put a quilted pillow gave her hads shiny gift
with flowers I packed it.
FUSUN ONUR

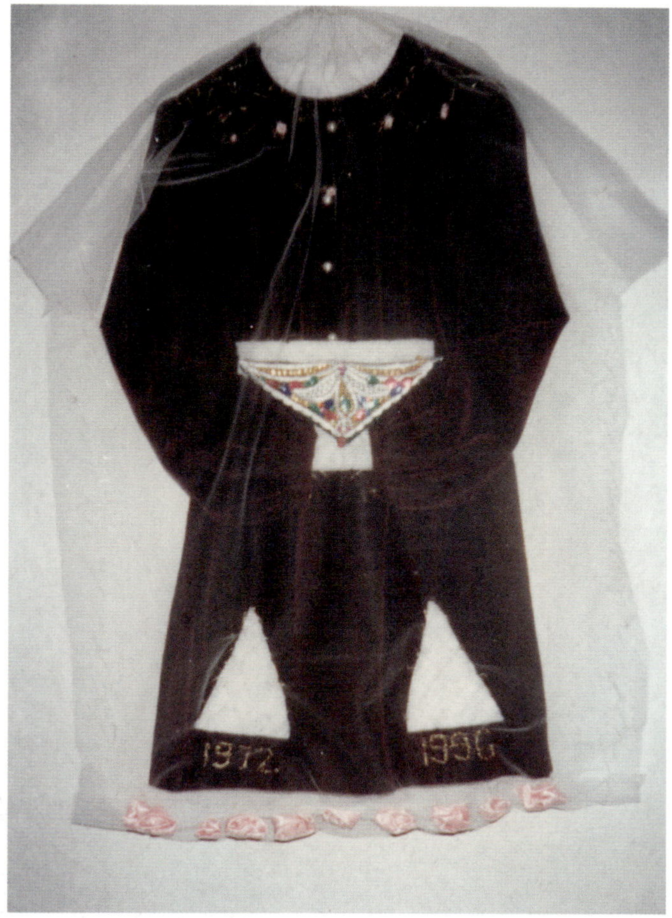

(Left) Füsun Onur's note on the work
(Right) Dress, tulle, embroidery

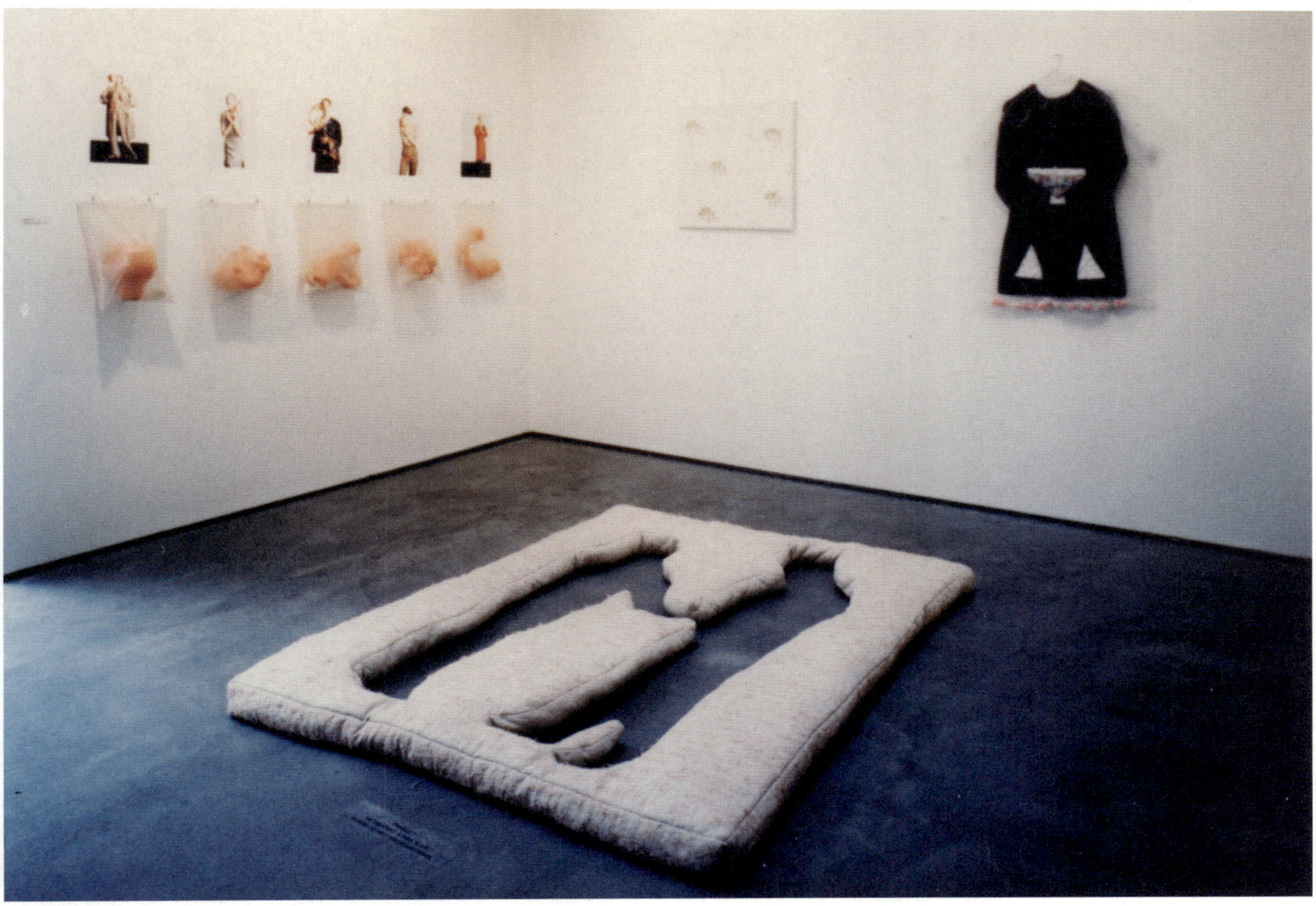

Installation view from *Sous Le Manteau*, Thaddeus Ropac, Paris, 1997

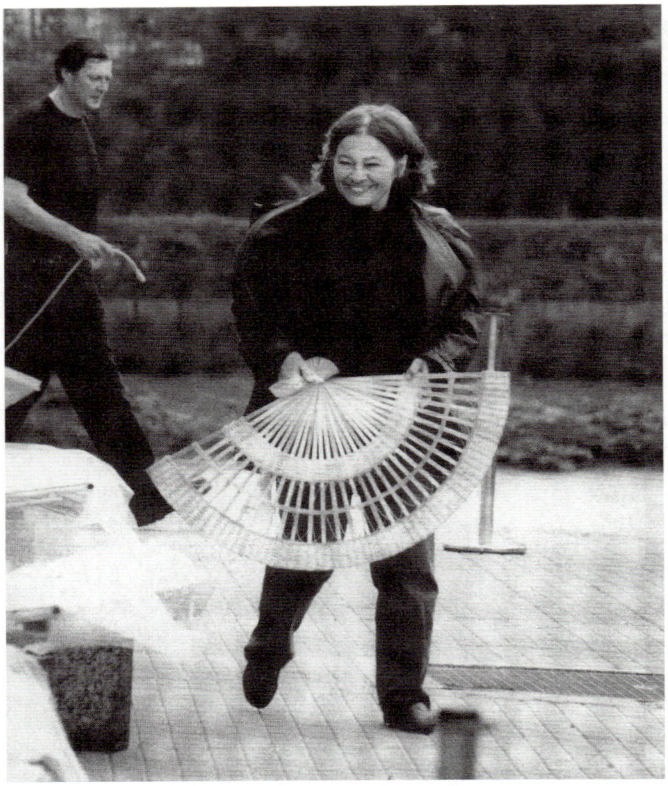

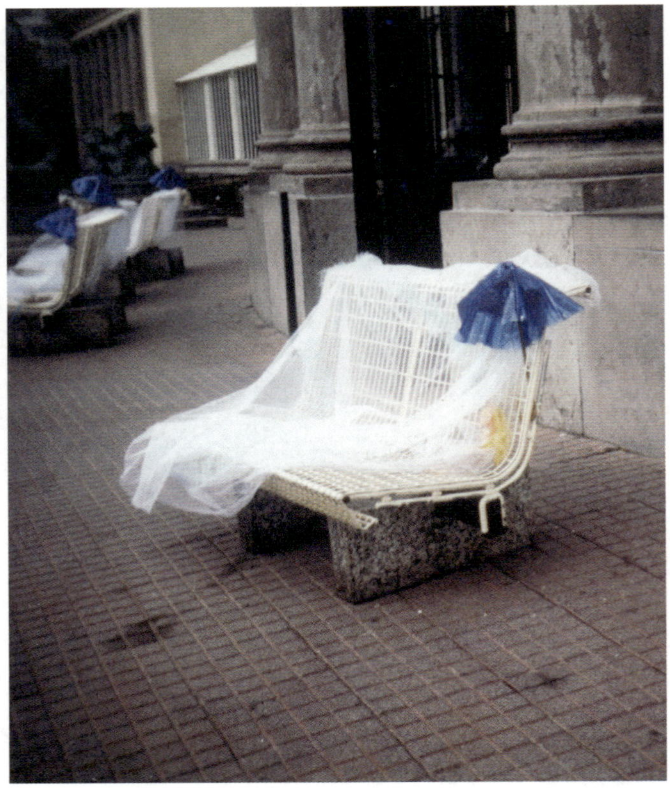

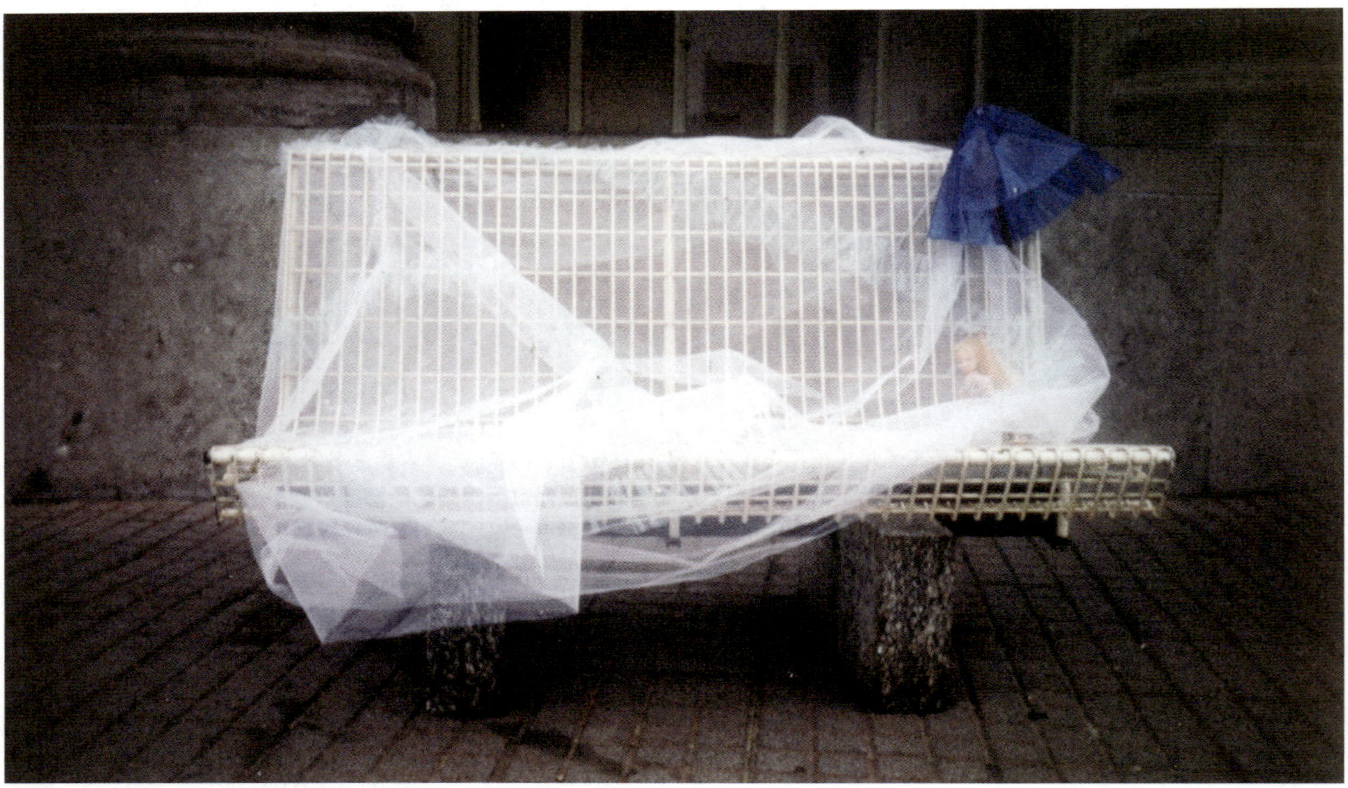

Mixed media installation for garden benches, variable dimensions

As soon as I received the photos of the place, I decided what I was going to do for this exhibition. I was preparing something else but all of a sudden I saw the pictures of the Botanique Gardens, with a row of benches. As soon as I saw these benches I fell in love with them and soon *Caprice* was born. These benches were running up and down in a rhythm following the curve and the shape of the park path. Somehow my little Barbie dolls wanted to occupy those fantastic benches. The small size of each doll was no excuse: they capriciously wanted to sit on them. On one side she sits at the top of the bench, on the other at the seat. In the middle, on the right, on the left, or laying at the top of it, rhythmically exchanging places. Somehow, they own the benches by their own means. Their main instrument is their veil, sometimes extending from their hand, sometimes from their waist, spreading all over the bench. When she fails then she has a fan twice her size. In case it rains, she has her own blue umbrella.

Excerpt from the *Mediterranea – art contemporain des pays méditerranéens* exhibition catalogue, Le Botanique, Brussels, 1998.

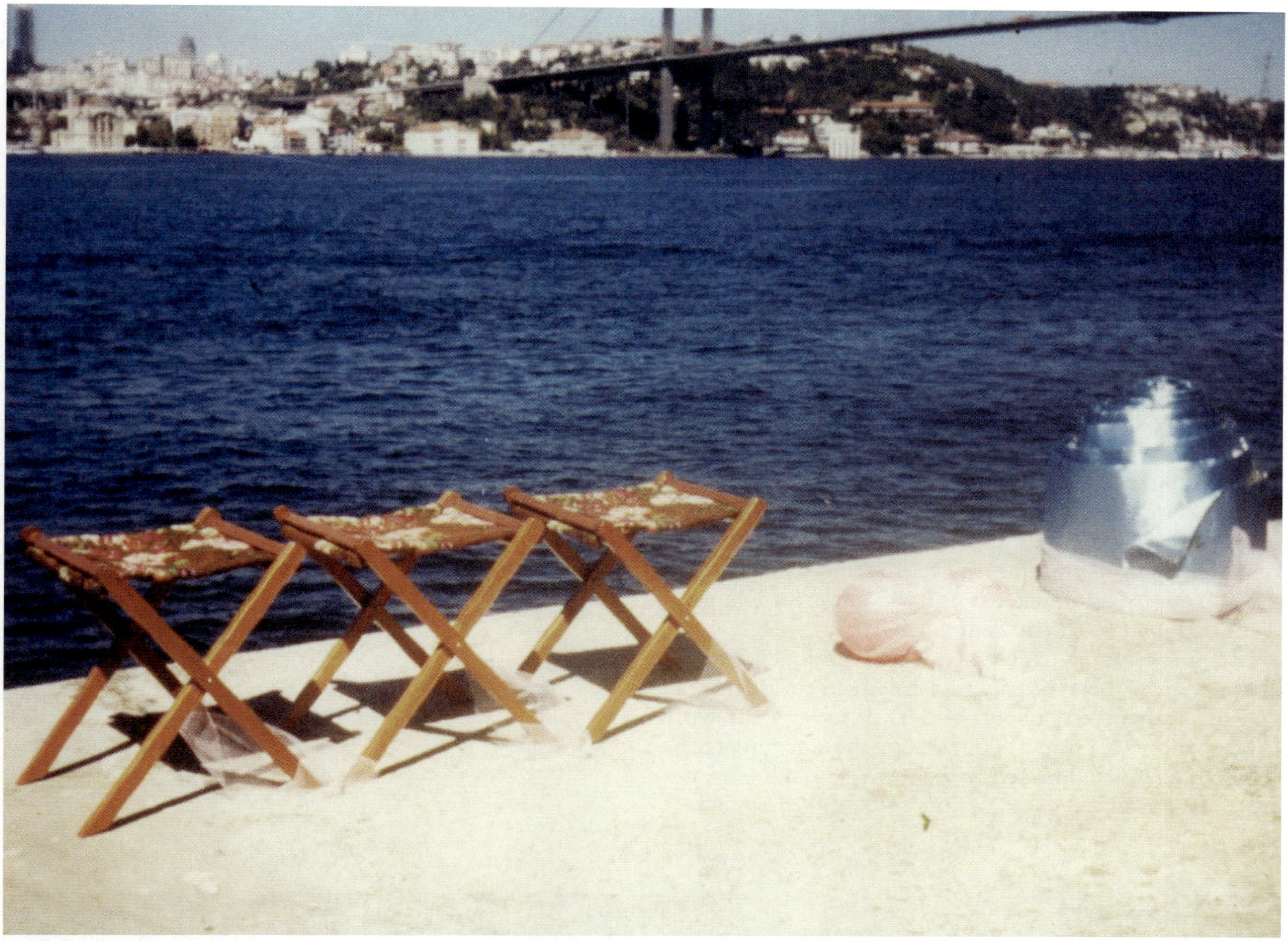

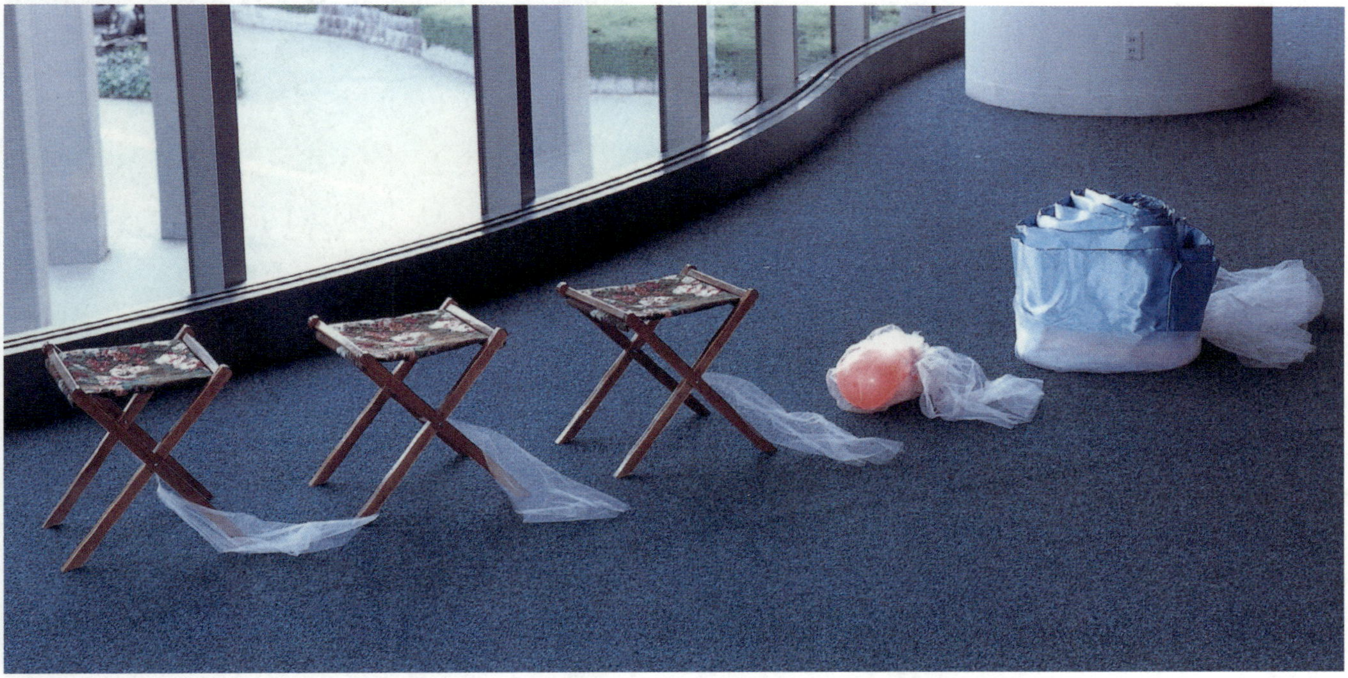

Installation (wooden footstools, cloth, plastic balls, plastic rose)

In Füsun Onur's *Note* (1998), a playful installation with rolls of gauze and wooden stools topped with pieces of embroidered tapestry, music appears visually almost as a thought, in the poetical rhythm of the sequence of her objects. All memories, fantasies and childhood games are encompassed in the simplest of compositions.

Fulya Erdemci, excerpt from the exhibition catalogue *Iskorpit*, Haus der Kulturen der Welt, Berlin, 1996.

An artist who builds tightly knit formal relationships between her life and her art, which have each taken root in the other, Füsun Onur has a privileged position in contemporary Turkish art. One of the sharpest curves of her long and solitary art adventure was her site-specific installation titled *Opus I* (1999), which was shown at the 6th Istanbul Biennial, curated by Paolo Colombo. The abstract images we encounter in this work, displayed on the second floor of Hagia Irene Church, were shaped using materials that refer to Onur's own world of mythology. Although they have a tantalising simplicity and essentiality, it is not possible to comprehend their qualities immediately, since they are based on subtle references. In Onur's own words: 'The artist builds a multilayered structure by processing it with his/her own inner dynamics, by responding to it and passing it through a complex filter. Yet, to its audience it might seem as simple as if it happened at the drop of a hat.'[1]

This site-specific installation made with ribbon shaped forms, bric-a-brac, gold-coloured cloth bows, glasses and tulle, whispers into the viewer's ear while taking the risk of disappearing in the enormity of the venue. This approach, which can be likened to musical abstraction, heralds Onur's post-2000 period, when she began to explore the relationship between sound and vision by concentrating on the constitutive elements of classical music.

1.
This note was taken from a one-page document written by Füsun Onur between 1985 and 1990. It was signed by the artist for me on 9 January 2018 to be included in the book about her on which I was working at the time. As in all of her papers, on the back are two little drawings.

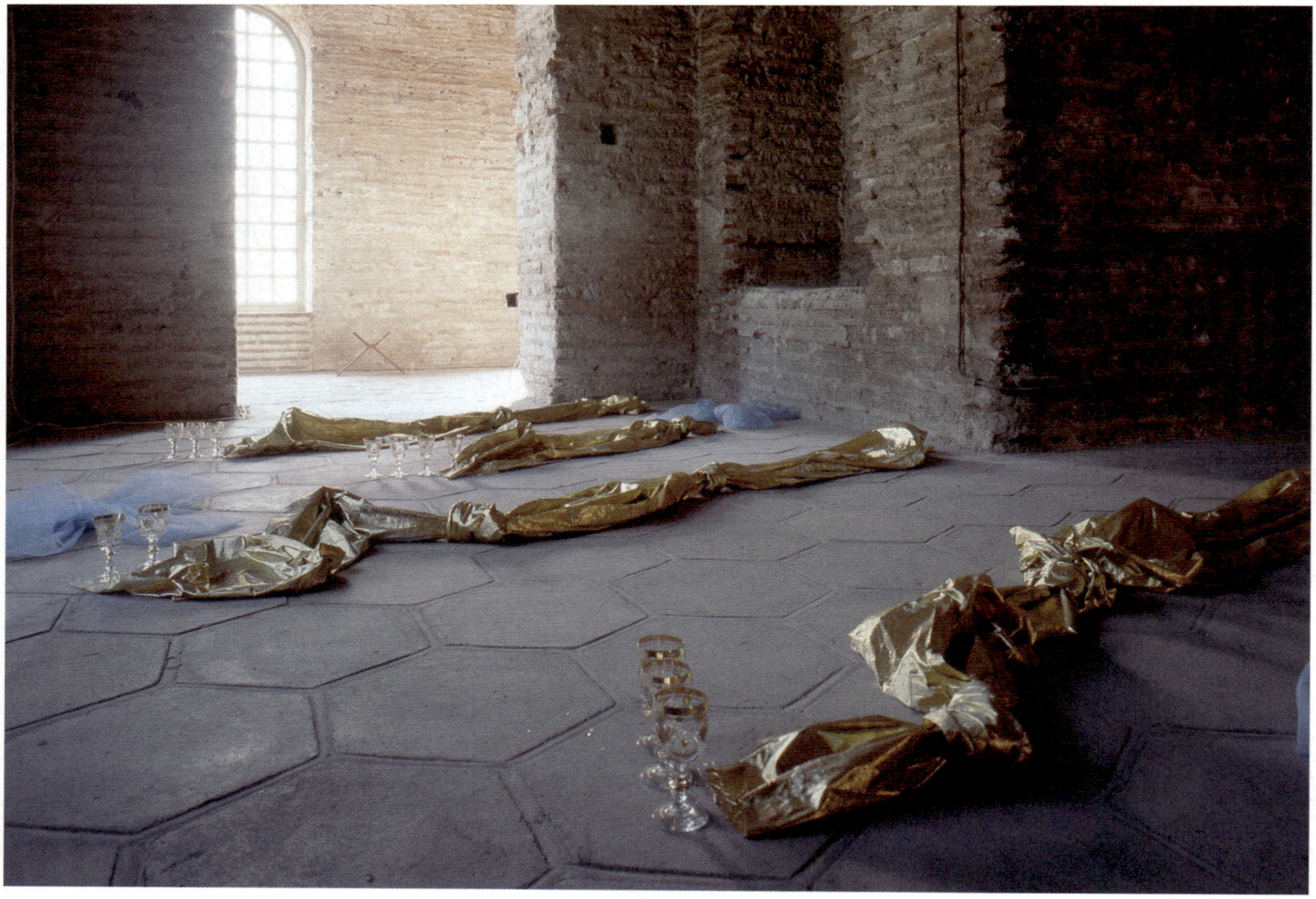

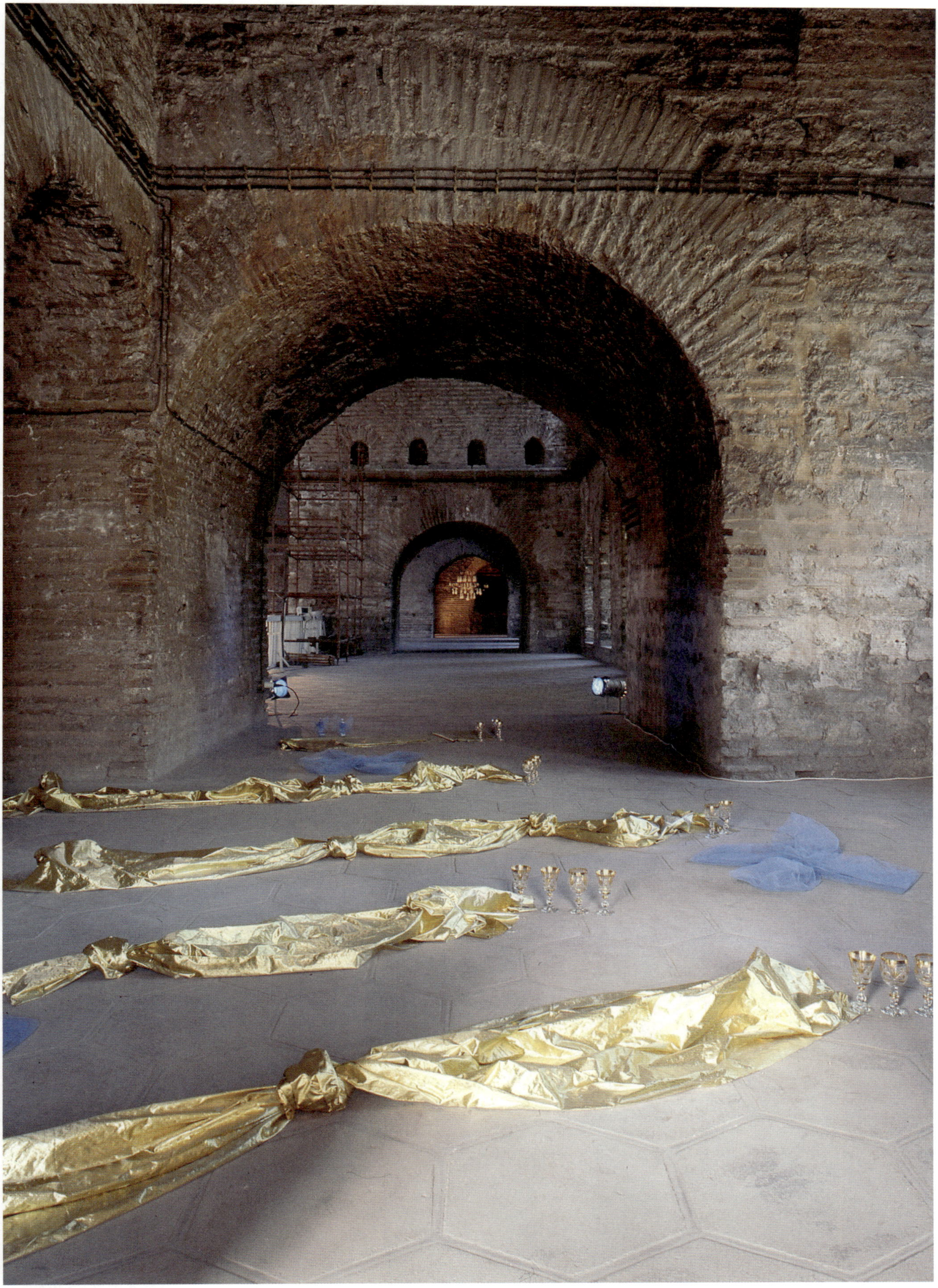

Installation (mixed media, wood, fabric, glass), variable dimensions

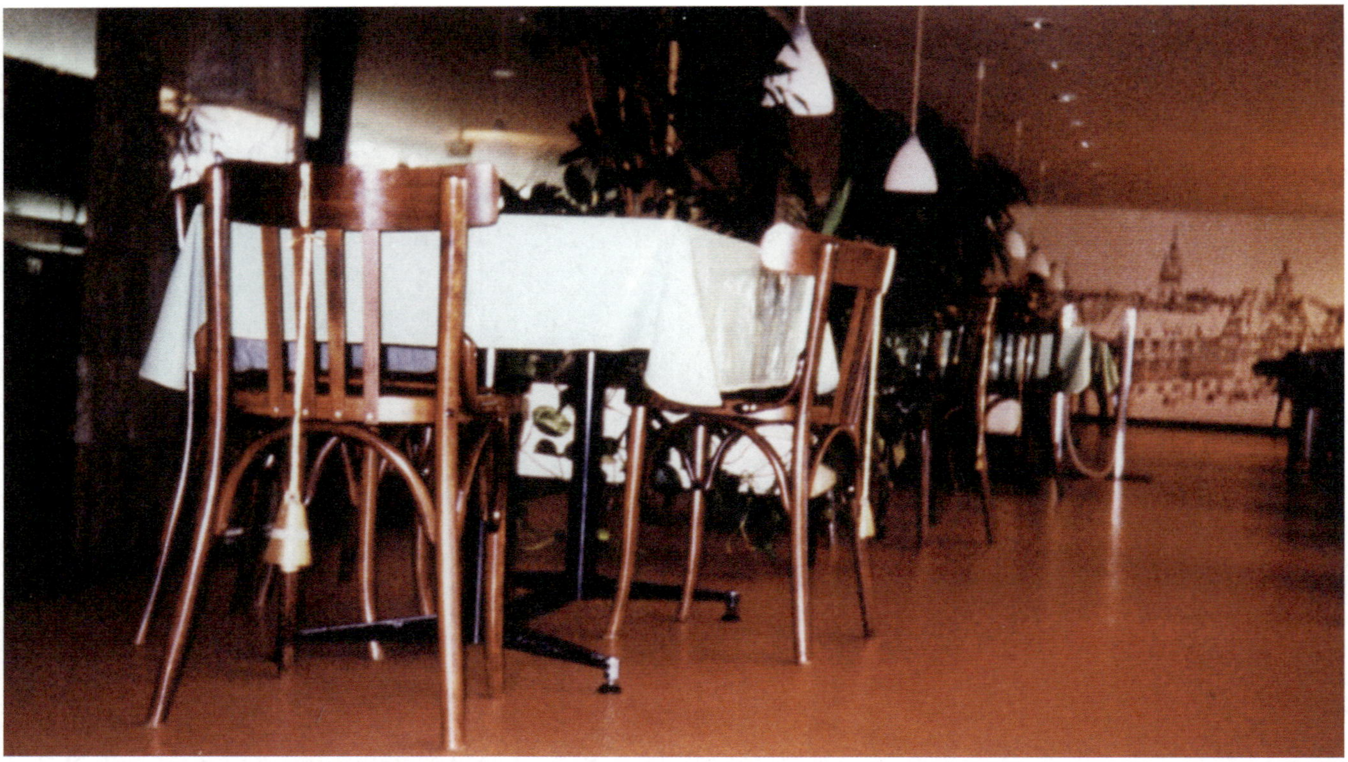

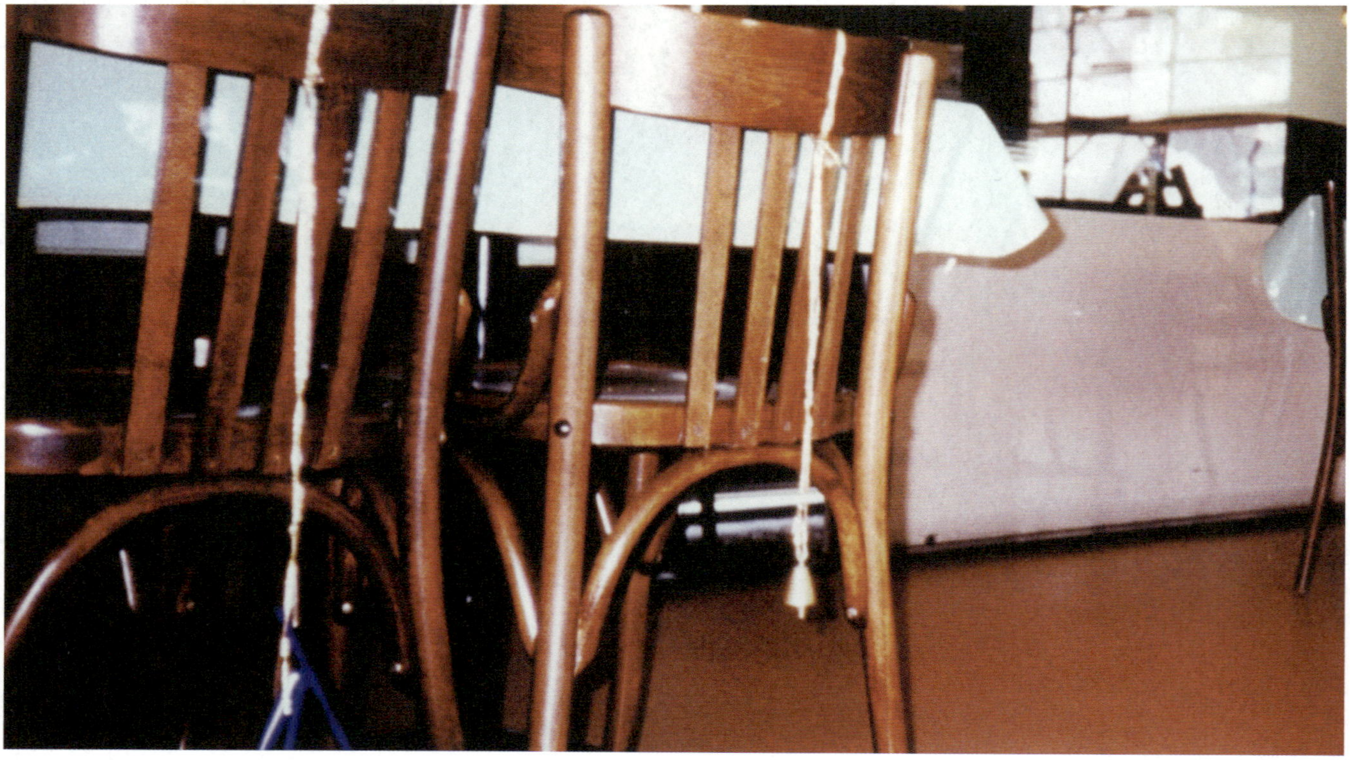

37 bells on different sizes

Musical Spaces / Communities – The late artistic production of Füsun Onur, who has been living and creating in Istanbul since the 1970s, is marked by a wish to make 'musical artworks.' For the Hanover exhibition, rather than an 'objective' collection space, she opts for a subjective gathering spot: the cafeteria of the Historical Museum, which is set up on a kind of glass balcony. From each of the cafe's 37 chairs hangs a gilt ribbon with a bell attached to the end. When visitors move the chairs, they emit a sound, make music, even randomly perform together. Onur has a repertoire of materials and things that she repeatedly incorporates into her work, notably fabrics, chairs, ribbons and balls. These combine allusions to childhood, playfulness and references to the body and its time, stance, disguise. The artist plays with hiding and showing bodies, seeing and not seeing the content. In the cafeteria, only the moving bodies of the visitors –and the chairs– make the work sound. Onur's work always maintain a close relation to a personal existence, her own existence, her life as an artist in Istanbul; a theatrical being-at-home/one-with-oneself in a foreign country, which can also be one's own homeland; a poetic self-portrayal of biographical fragments.

Angelika Stepken, excerpt from the exhibition catalogue *strange home*, Historisches Museum & Kestner Museum, Hannover, 2000. Translated from German by Niyazi Zorlu.

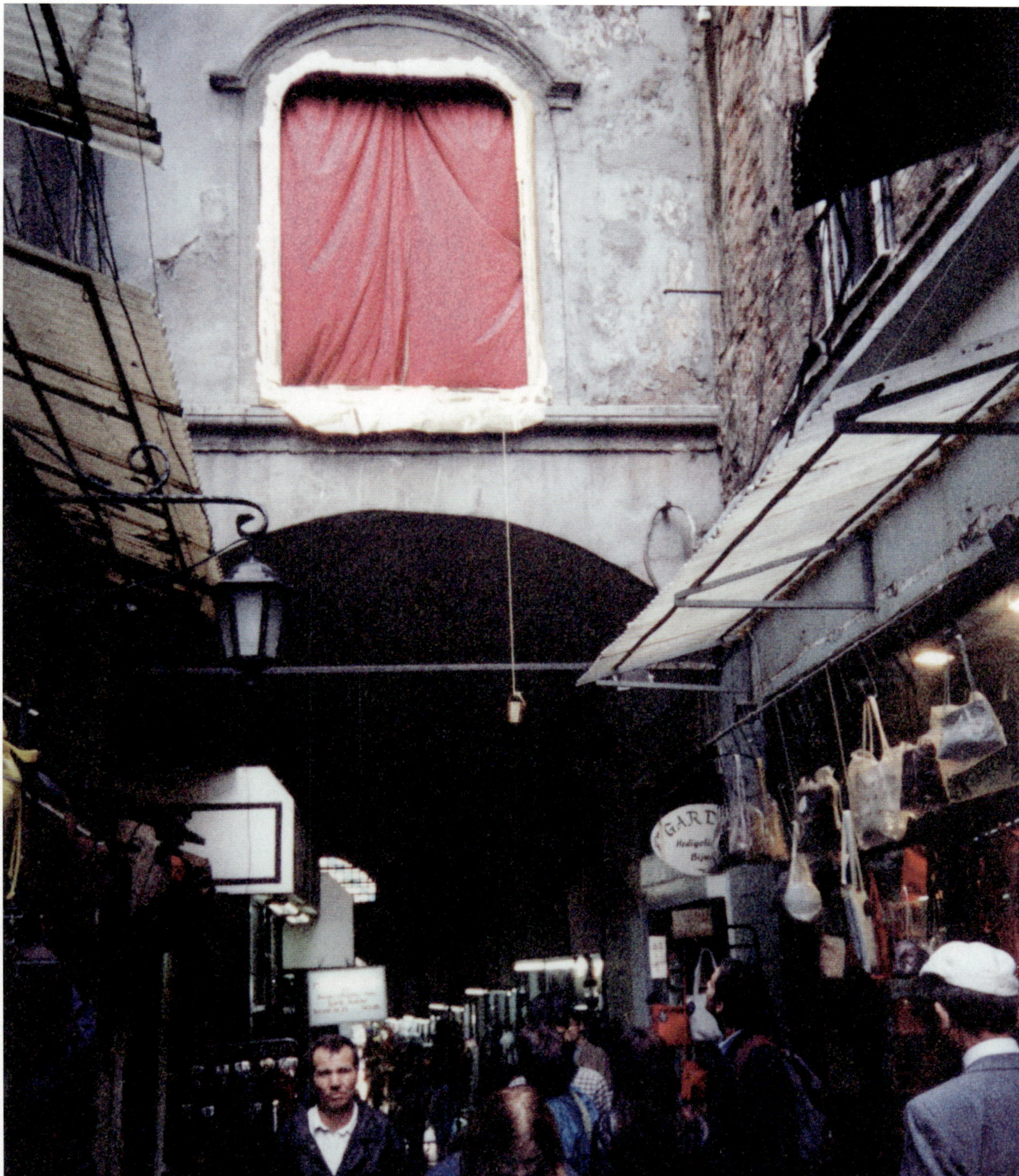

Installation (bell, rope), variable dimensions

Füsun Onur set a '1871 Stage' in the Hacopulo Arcade; under the neon lights, all the grace and ugliness of Beyoglu, all its splendor and violence, craftsmanship and depravity; all this theater of memories. Füsun Onur's very personal, timid, shy voice, momentary touches, the lyrical placement, space woven with sounds, textures and light becomes a temporary map. An equipment for exchange, a shopping list. Füsun Onur claims everything that may vanish under the weight of time, all that may evaporate into thin air; collects ready-made objects, gold colored baskets, lace curtains, decorates spaces like home, makes them live. The Hacopulo Arcade is 'an original ready-made.' It is impossible to find the authentic owner, author, no one can estimate at first glance the boundaries of Onur's involvement, originality has been overthrown and thus the work of art is at once present and absent. The city is overflowing with an infinite number of 'Füsun Onur Artworks,' an infinite number of 'lost scenes' that Füsun Onur has once made real, has completed only in her head; with what she has not seen once, has not encountered or ever brushed by.

Cem İleri, excerpt from the *Feature Presentation-Coming Attractions* exhibition catalogue, Yapı Kredi Culture and Arts, 2000.

Füsun Onur is 'thinking music.' She perceives music not as some 'thing' that one listens to or thinks about, but as a state of thinking, a state of being; she talks about 'silent music.' When you remove the sound, that is, the fundamental object of music, from the equation, you are left with structure, space and form. These are what Füsun Onur is working with in *Prelude* (2000), as well as with intensities, textures, abundances, distances. When it comes to art, such concepts, which are essentially the determining aspects of every human endeavor, facilitate transitivity from one branch to another, allowing for breaches of the perimeter.

Historically, 'prelude' is the name given to a short introductory musical piece that precedes the main work, with which it is sometimes closely, sometimes remotely linked. That is, a prelude is a precursor; it points at that which will follow. Nineteenth-century Romantism, especially Chopin, broke this historical unity, deactivating the prelude's role of introduction. Henceforth, this musical form stood on its own legs without being the prelude to that which will follow.

Füsun Onur's *Prelude* conveys this historicity and takes it even further. The technical terms she uses in the work's description – motif, passage, small forms, expanded forms, themes, variations, duplications, counterpoints, repercussions etc. – are terms that we use in explaining the form known as fugue in music. *Prelude* can also be read as a modular spatial fugue in terms of the objects' rhythmic relationships in space.

Can *Prelude* be its own precursor? Such a self-contained prelude/fugue underlines the fact that Onur is thinking 'music' and not 'about music.'

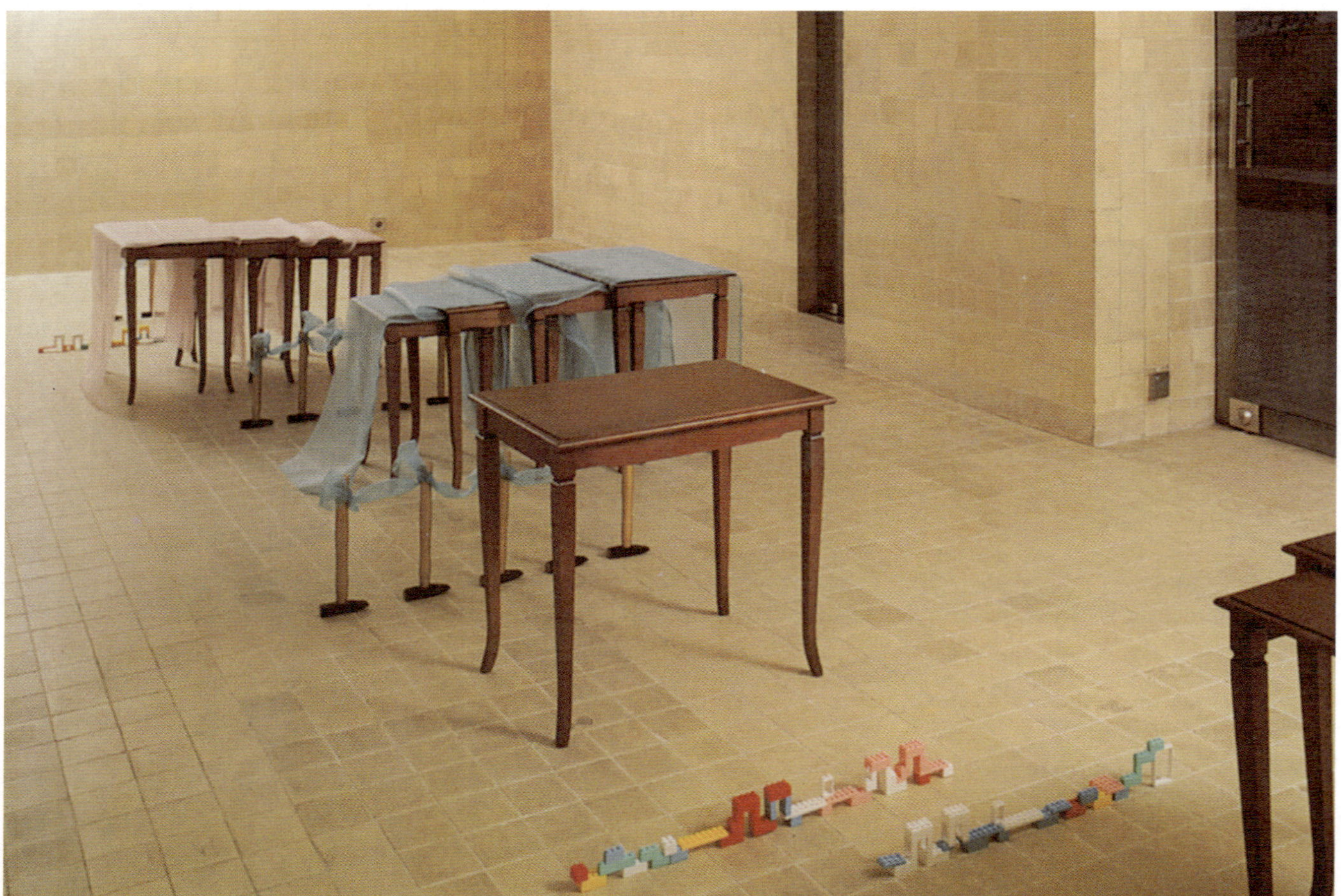

Installation, variable dimensions

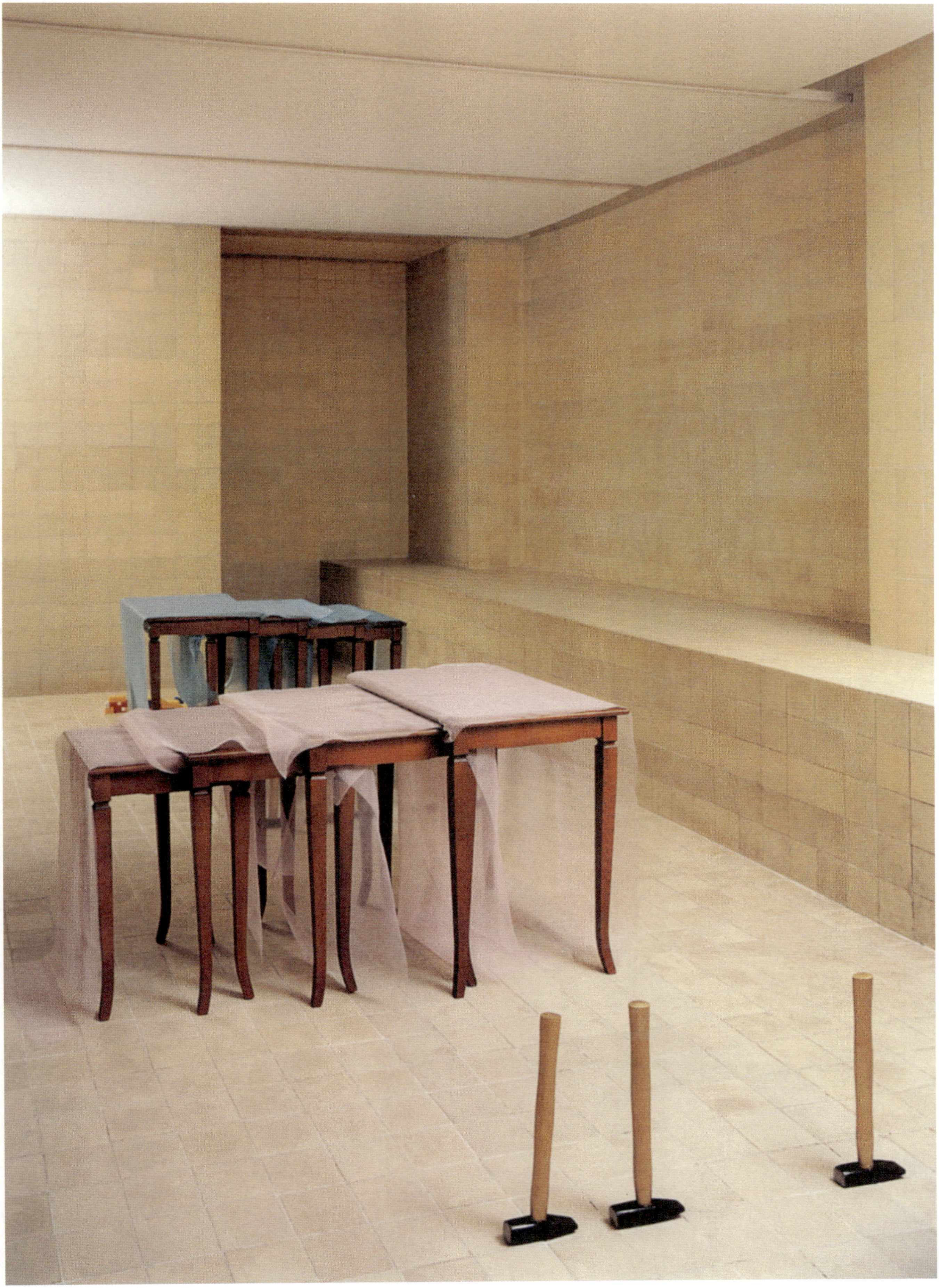

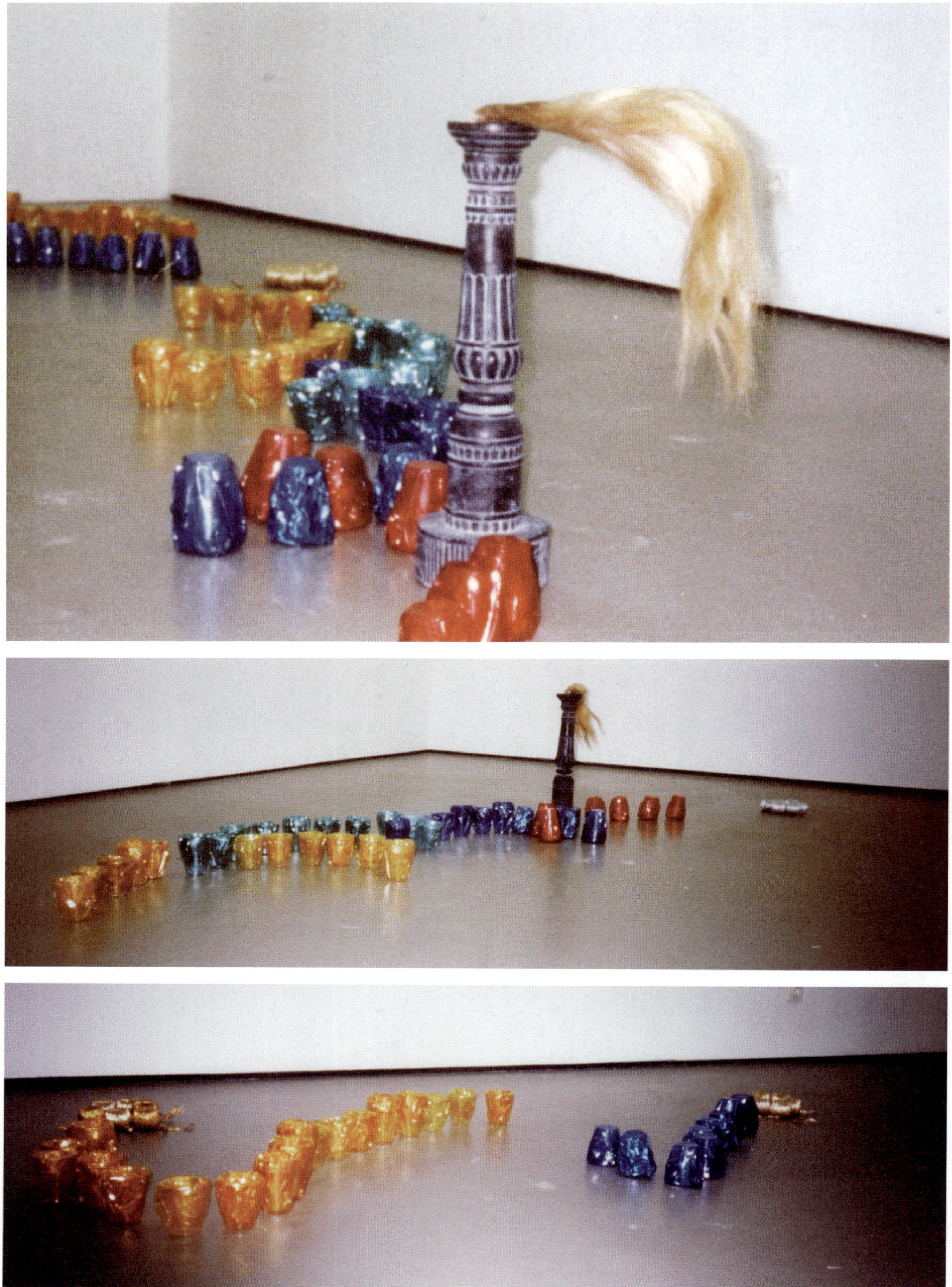

Installation (plastic cups, gelatin paper, gold and silver thread, wood, animal hair), variable dimensions

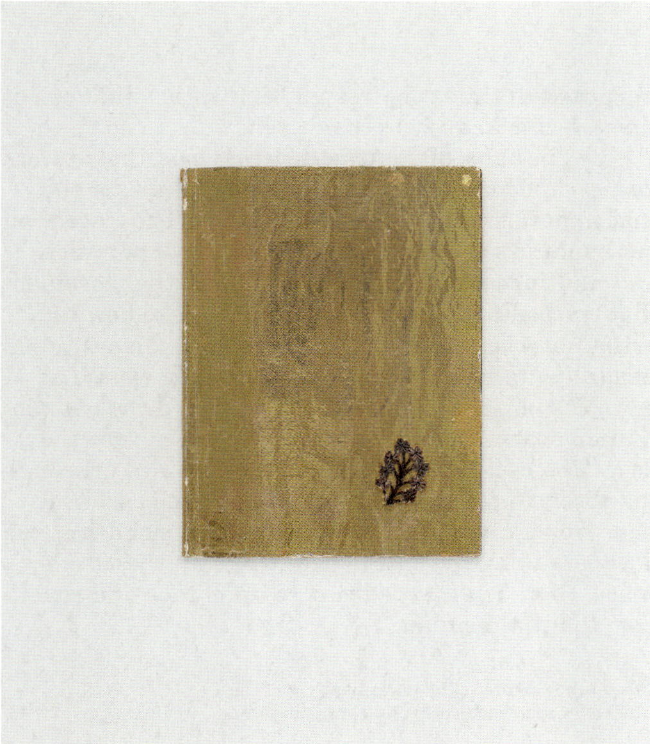

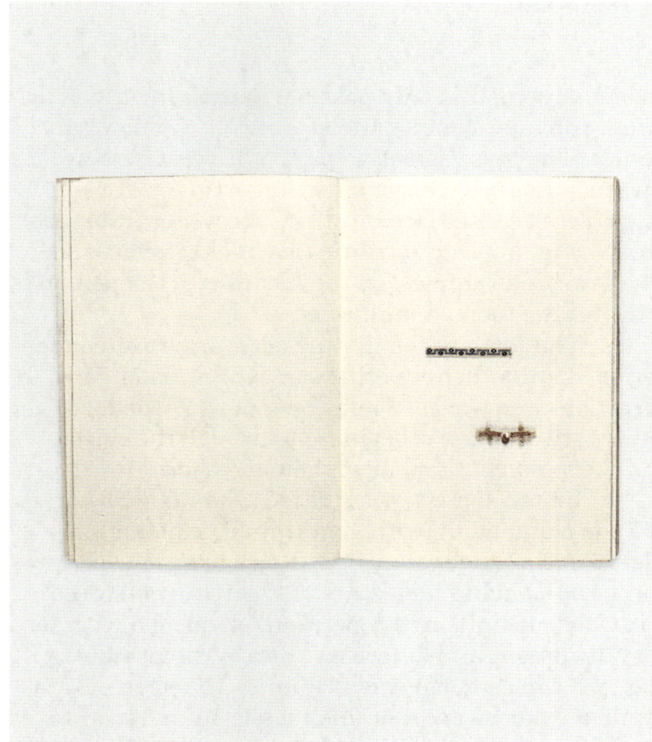

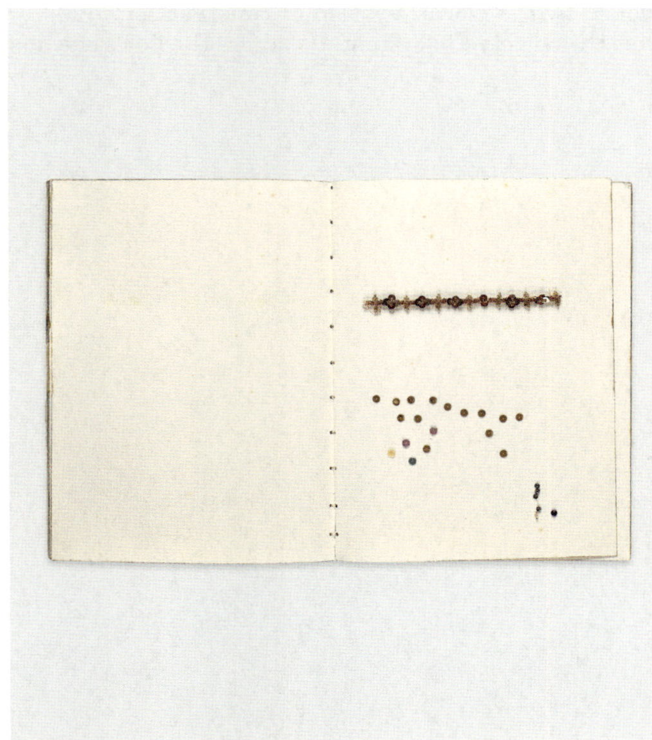

Ornamental beads on notebook, 31.5 × 21.5 × 1.5 cm

With materials like old fabrics and furniture, insignificant objects like plastic glasses, braids, tulle, whatever is available in her house and neighborhood, she composes silent songs, opuses and preludes like *Note* (1998), *Opus I* (1999), *What the Earth Sang* (2000), *Prelude* (2000) and *Opus II – Fantasia* (2001). In her musical pieces, the shapes of the objects, the distance and relation between them are delicately arranged to accentuate the rhythm of her inner music. […] She is also preparing a musical piece, a dreamy *Nocturne* for the *Regrets, Reveries Changing Skies*, in which she reduces installation into a drawing.

Fulya Erdemci, excerpt from the *Regrets, Reveries, Changing Skies* exhibition catalogue, Karşı Sanat, Istanbul, 2000.

Inside a room, it is only possible to imagine the whirlwind, the hurricane or the storm, yet the flow can be felt. The most sensitive part of a person's skin, for instance, her neck, lower back, fingertips contact an invisible yet sensed stream of air. The work (the breeze)* on the window-door axis hits manifold surfaces, is swallowed by volumes. In the meantime, the person is a nod in the room, a multiplier.

The force is too disturbed to warrant condensation. Let us then imagine the escalation of gaps, directions and waves. Some queer flow! We deduce that we are still inside a room merely through the objects that keep us here and now, then and there.

Füsun Onur's work titled *Opus II – Fantasia*: strings clumped up with gold thread, knitting needles, porcelain figures girded up for baroque or perhaps rococo, venturing pedestals... A setting clustered with various units and repetitions, stratified with sensory deviations and differences hardly discernible to the eye, wherein the waves fluidise the space. An assemblage whose creation inclines from material to incorporeality and will not be encapsulated in forms evoked by the words, system or construction, likewise the objects Füsun installs across the flows she has unpacked in time conjures multiple moves that are at times vectorial and at others cyclic.

The name of this experience is *Opus*, that is, work (*breeze*): the manifestation without beginning or end that comprises the making of the artist. The traced can be sought in the assortment of the acts of partition and multiplication. On the other hand, the movement that traces Füsun Onur's work pertains to how the artist observes the gaps. Through their dispositional in situ (not alluding to any circumstance even if at rest), the objects – needles, pedestals – draw out ventilation spaces within the room. We are nearby the floor. The oscillations conceived in the mind through the absence of situs, which might be traced as deviations from gravity, can be read as waves mobilising the flow pervading the room. Meanwhile, in the visible space, there is an expedition to difference and repetition, to infinitesimals.

*The author points to the homonym root of the Turkish words 'eser' (work) and 'esinti' (breeze).

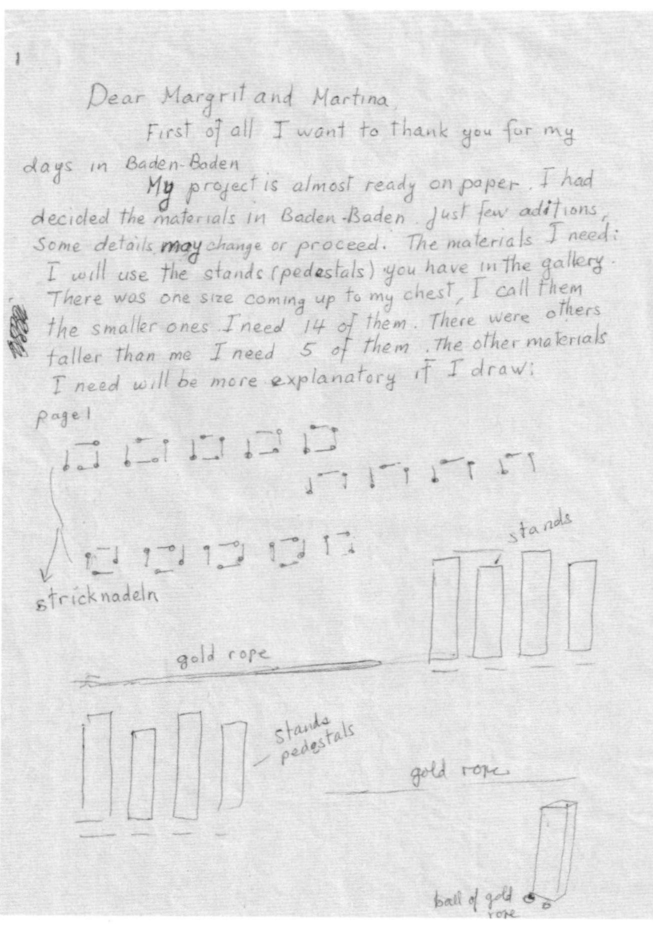

1

Dear Margrit and Martina,
First of all I want to thank you for my days in Baden-Baden
My project is almost ready on paper. I had decided the materials in Baden-Baden. Just few additions, Some details may change or proceed. The materials I need:
I will use the stands (pedestals) you have in the gallery. There was one size coming up to my chest, I call them the smaller ones. I need 14 of them. There were others taller than me I need 5 of them. The other materials I need will be more explanatory if I draw:

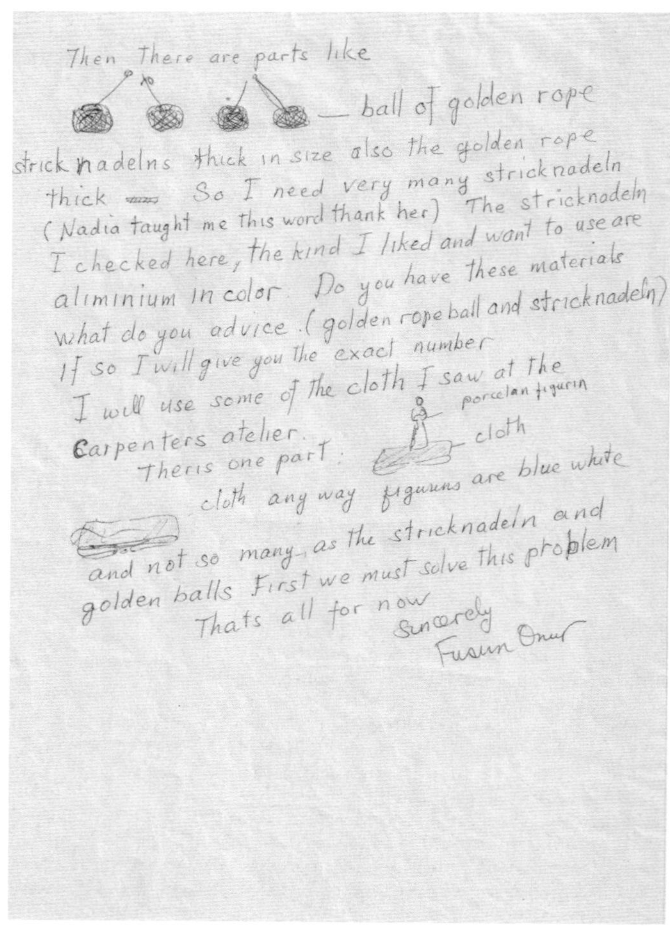

Then there are parts like

stricknadelns thick in size also the golden rope
thick So I need very many stricknadeln (Nadia taught me this word thank her) The stricknadeln I checked here, the kind I liked and want to use are aliminium in color. Do you have these materials what do you advice. (golden rope ball and stricknadeln)
If so I will give you the exact number
I will use some of the cloth I saw at the Carpenters atelier.

Theris one part:
cloth any way figurins are blue white
and not so many, as the stricknadeln and golden balls. First we must solve this problem
Thats all for now
Sincerely
Füsun Onur

Füsun Onur's note to Margrit Brehm, curator of *From Far Away So Close*, Kunsthalle Baden-Baden, 2001

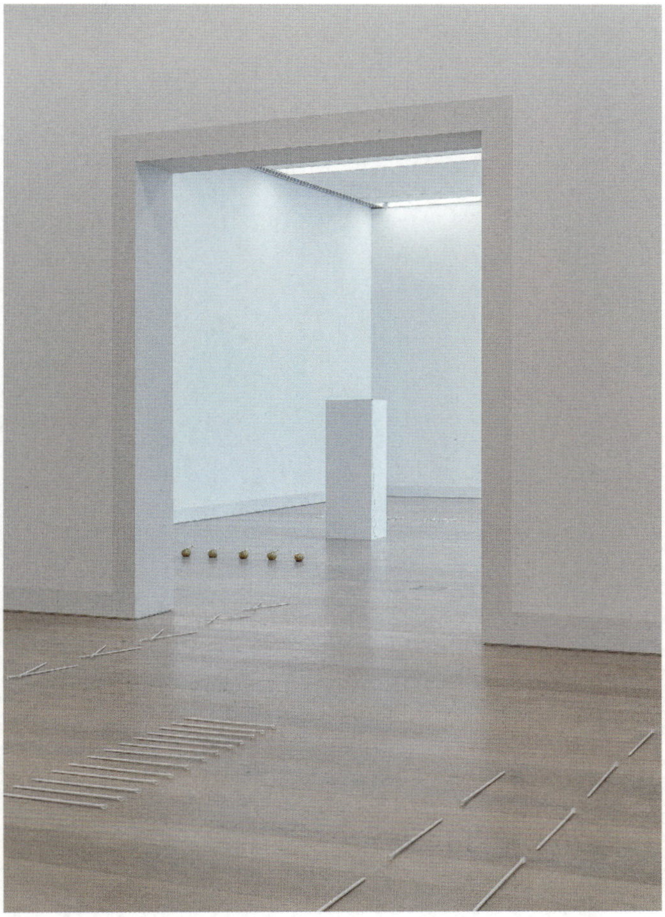

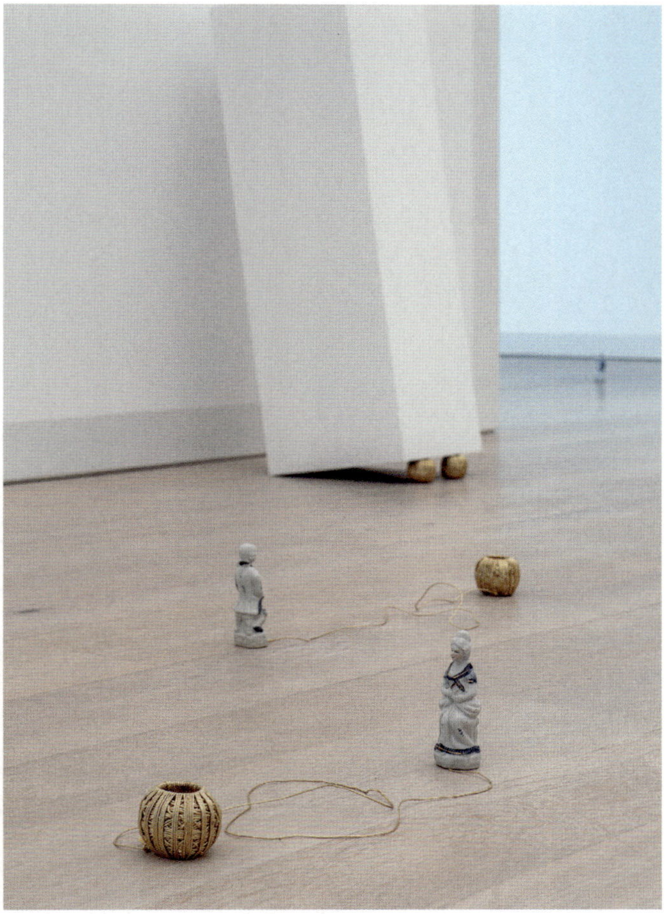

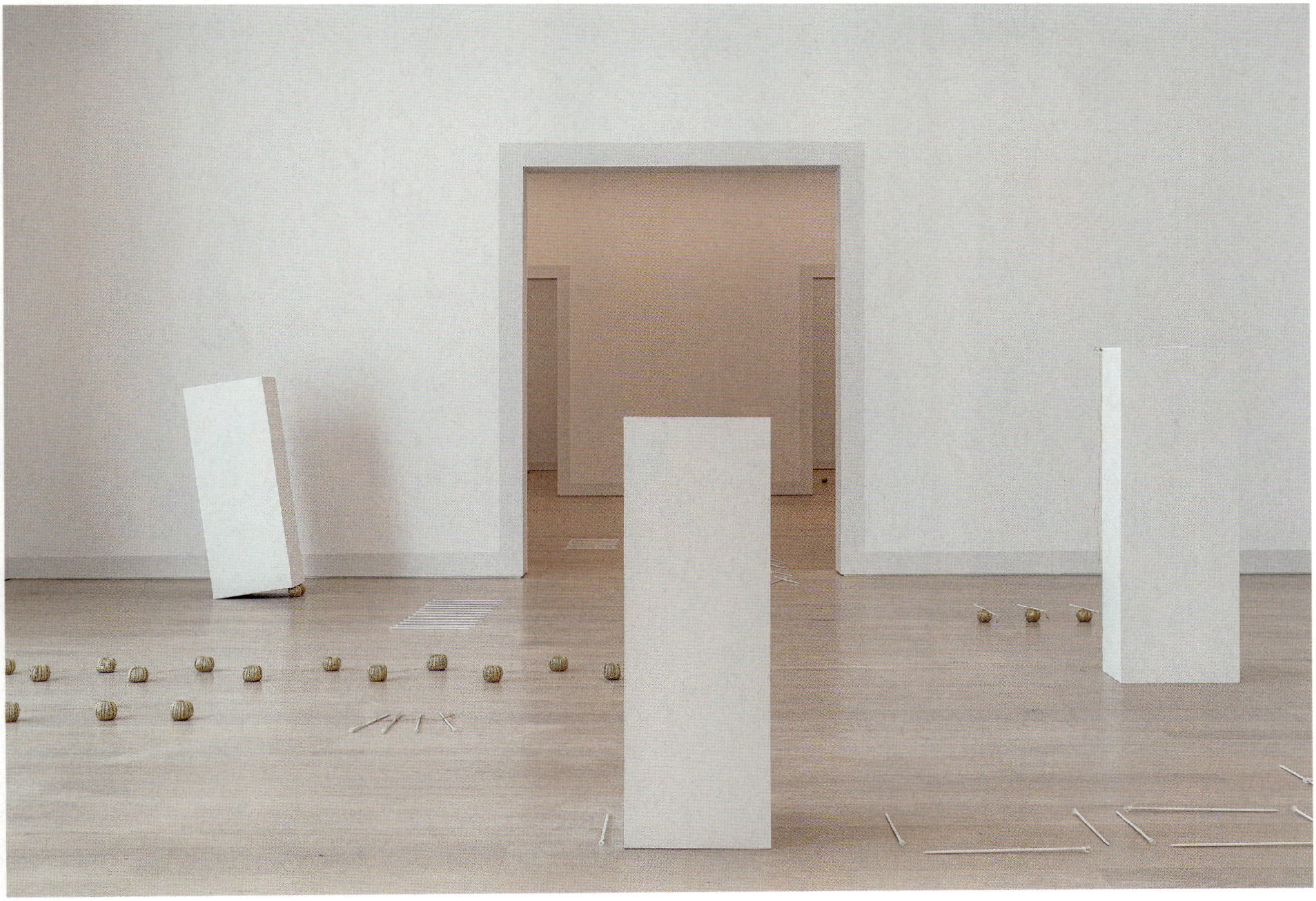

Knitting needles, balls of gold braid, porcelain figurines, plinths

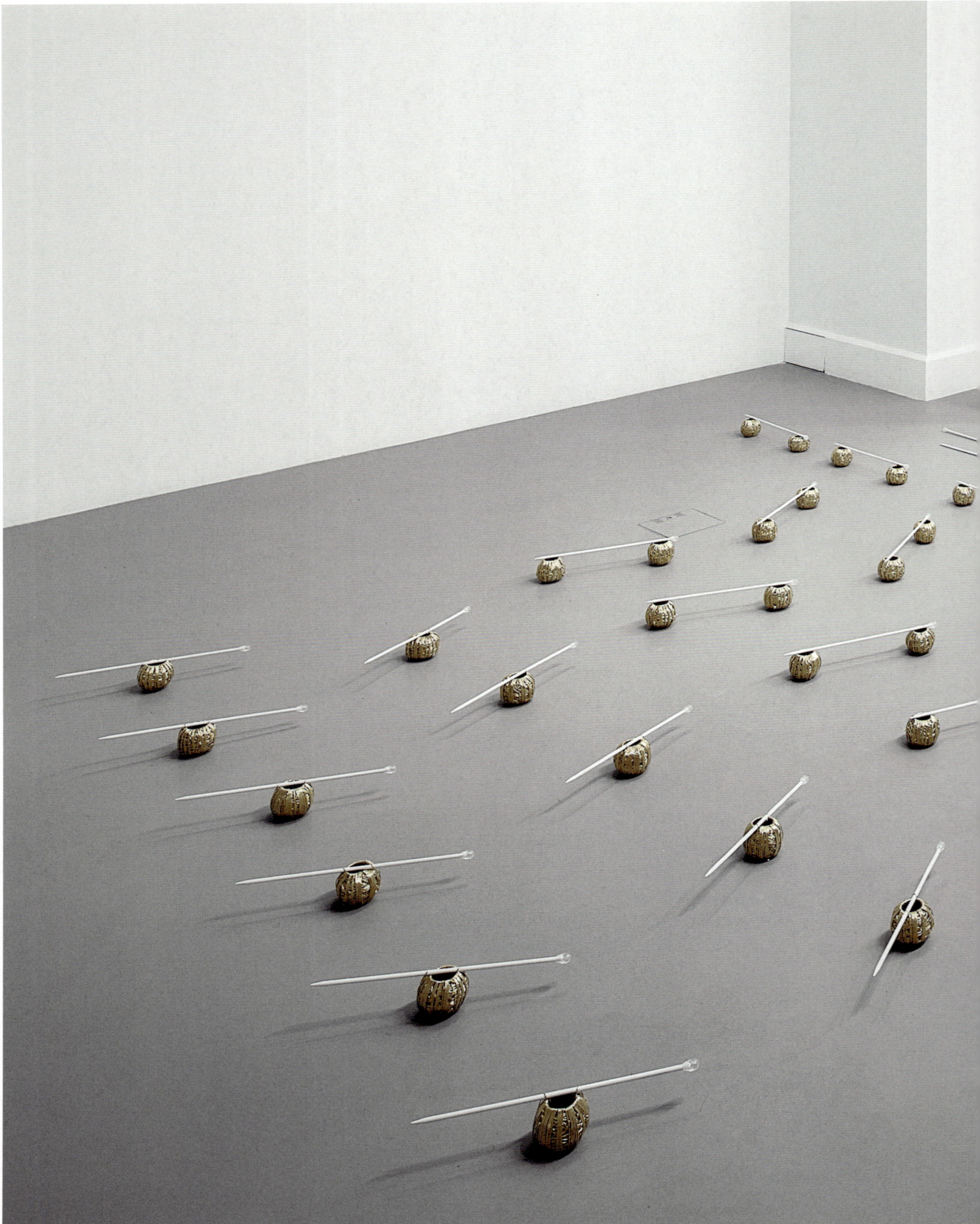

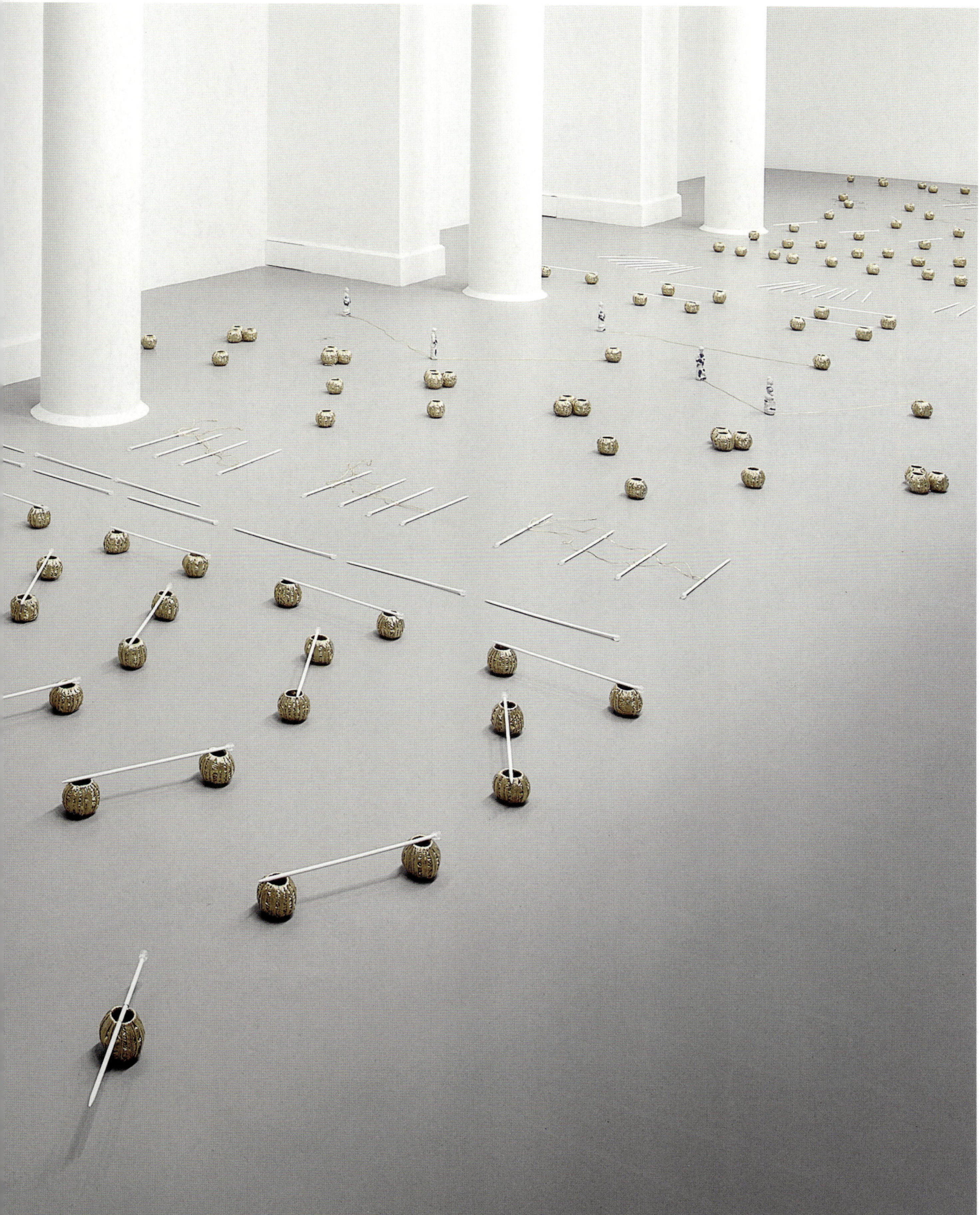

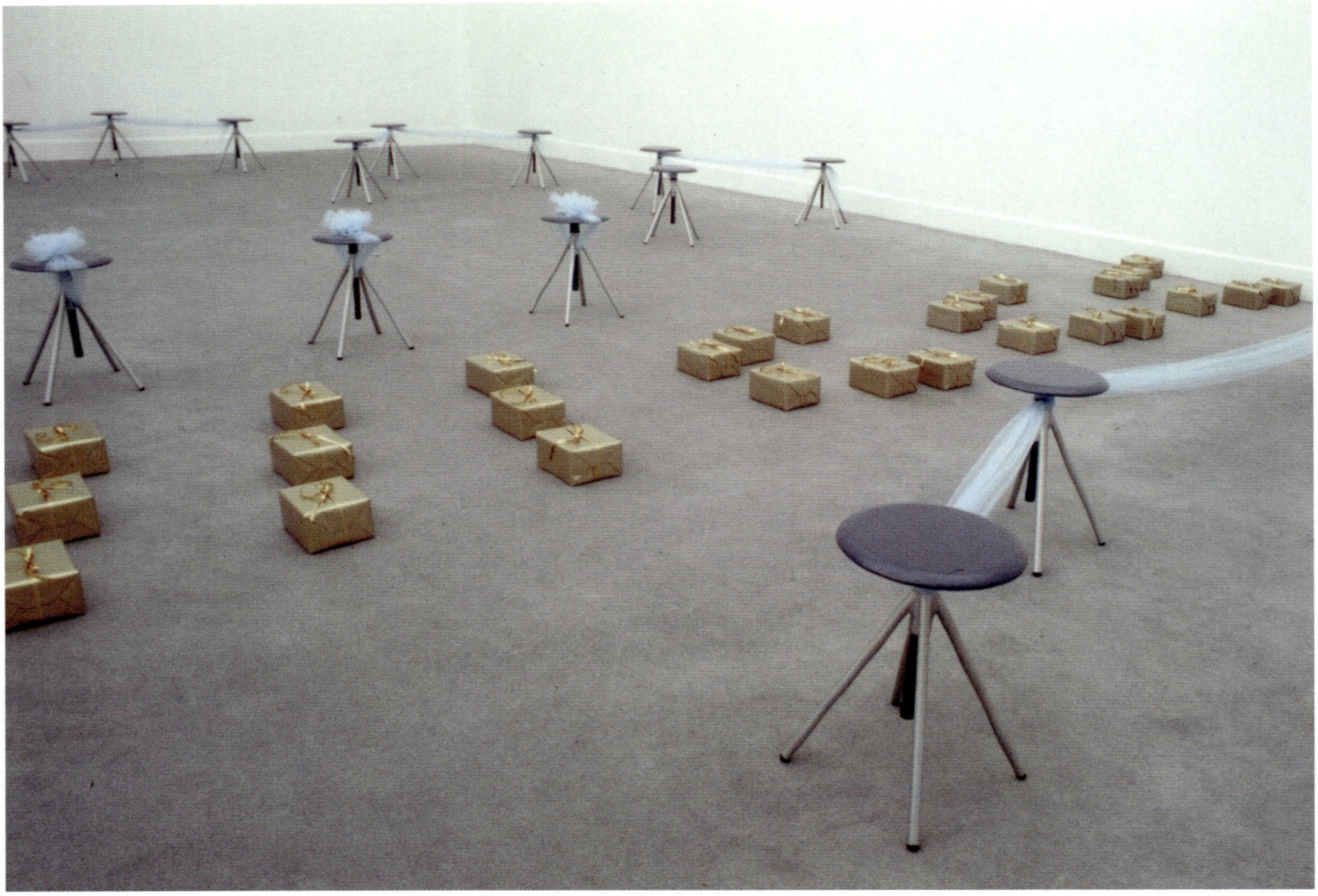

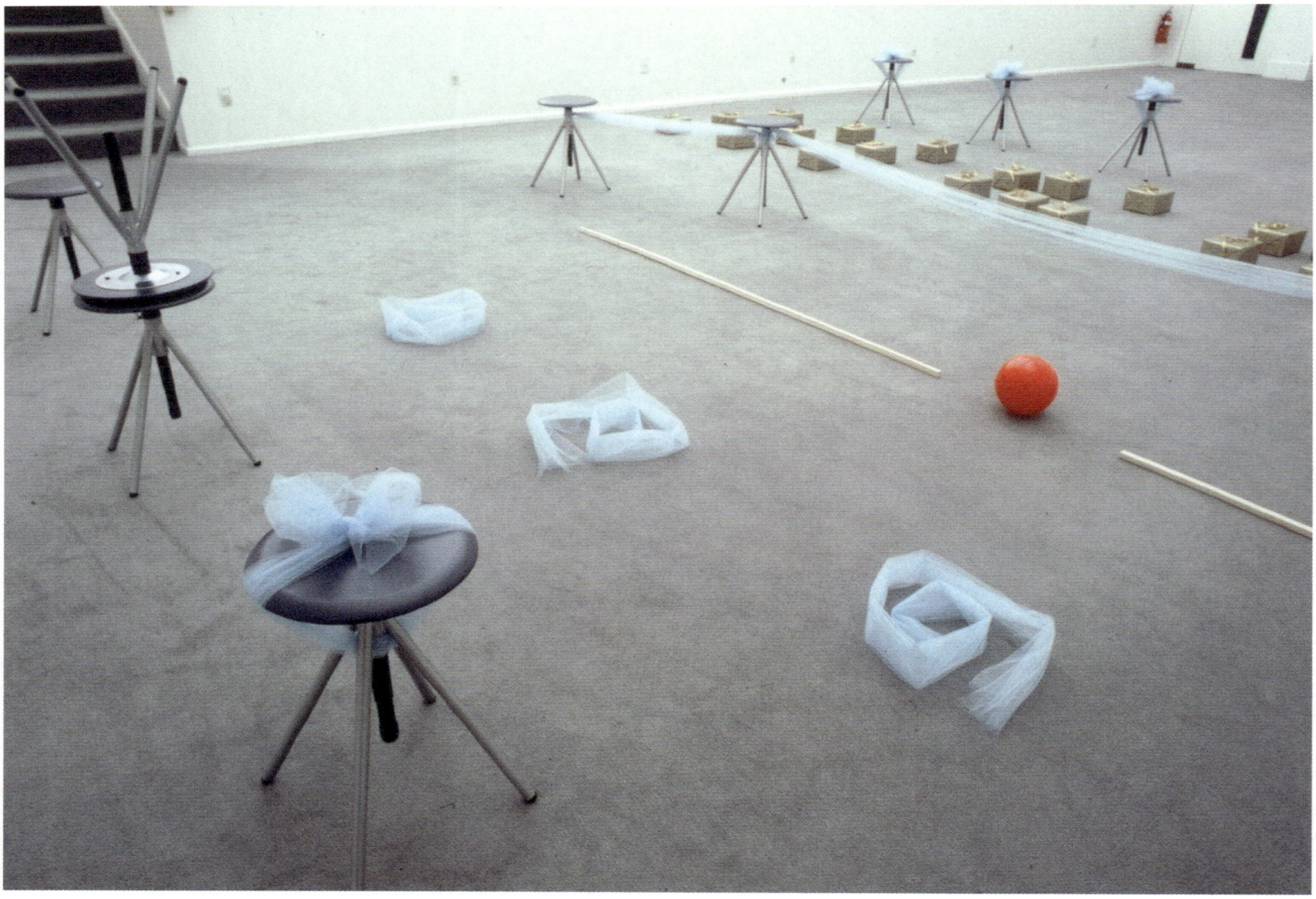

Installation, variable dimensions

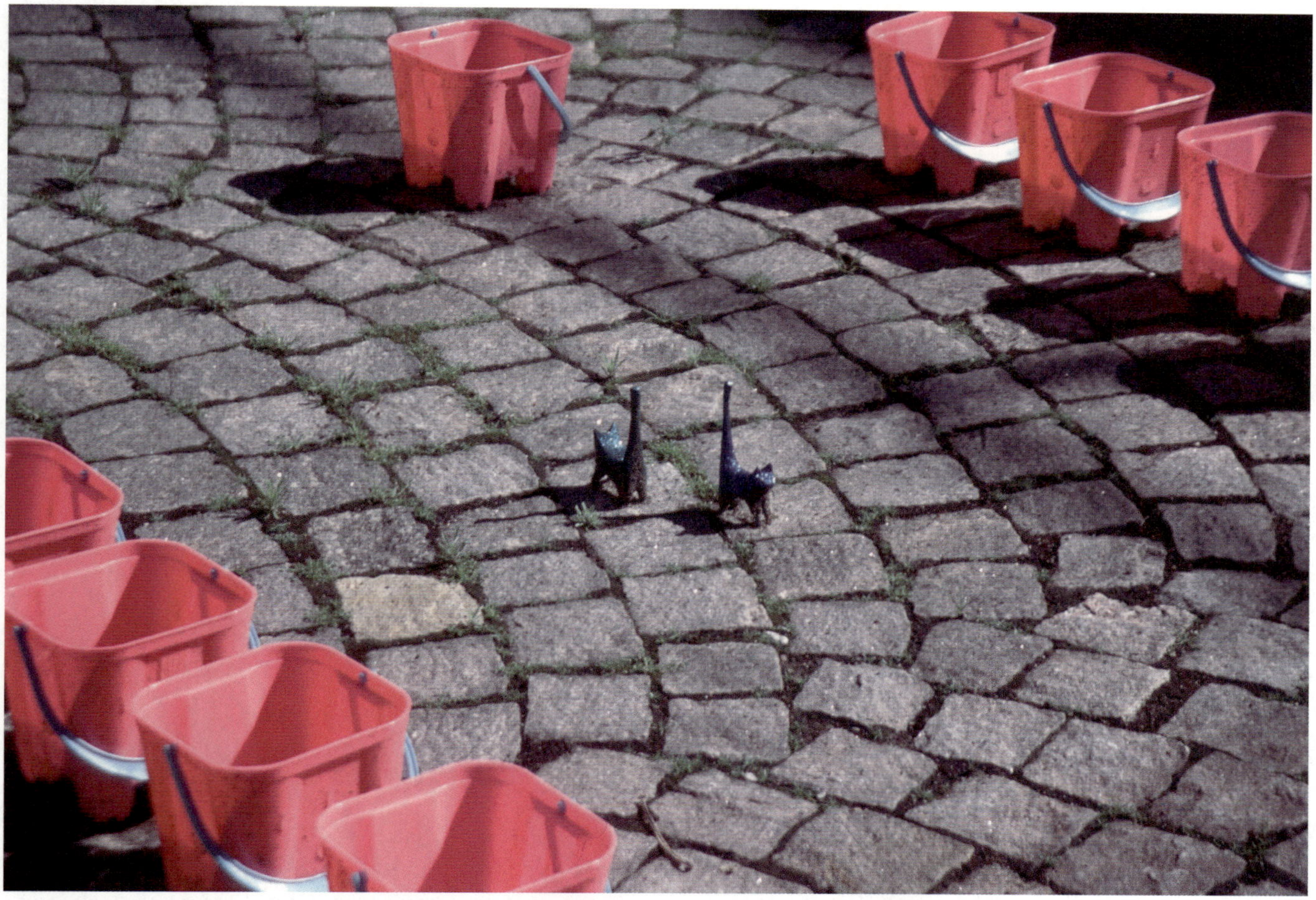

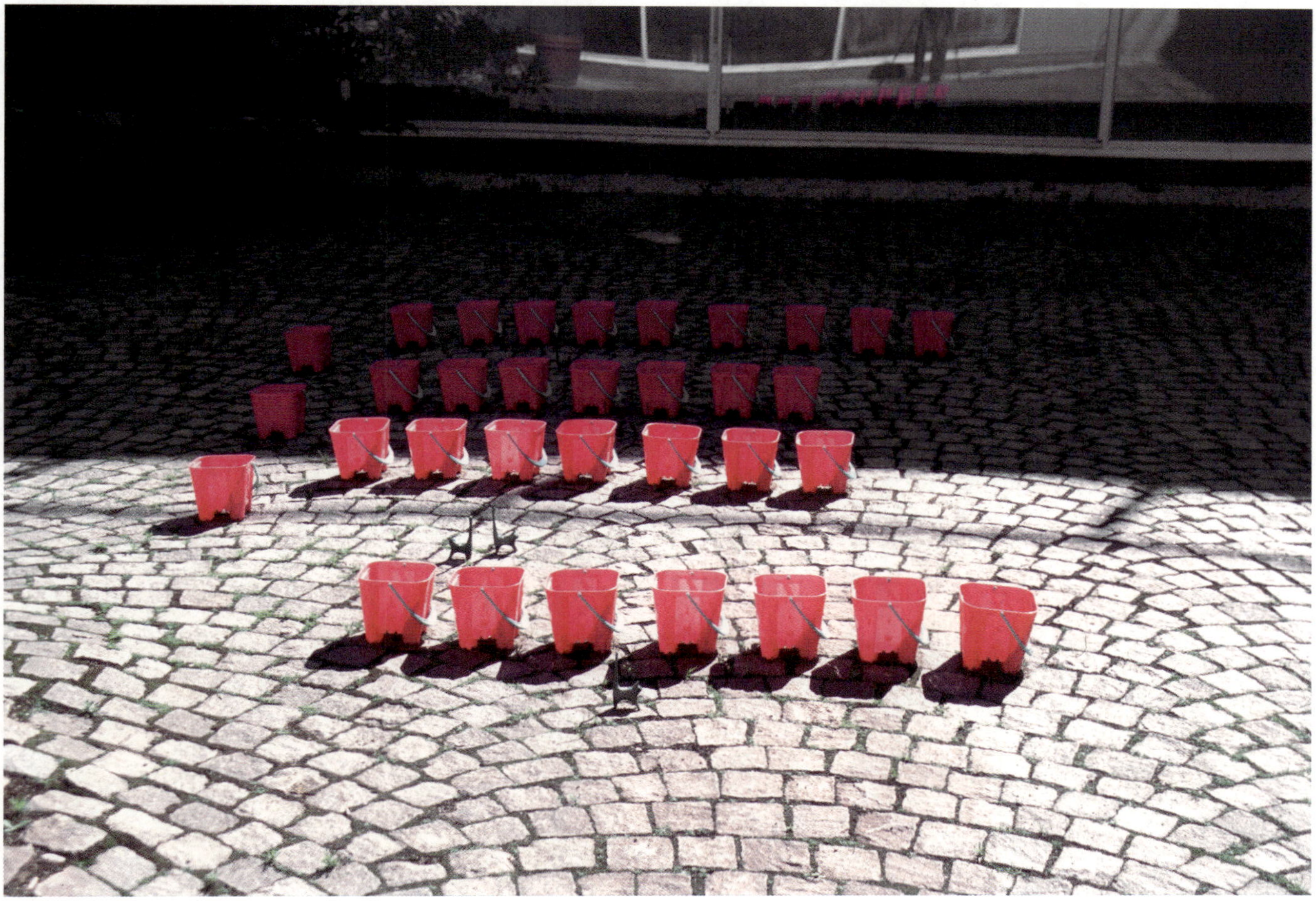

Installation, variable dimensions

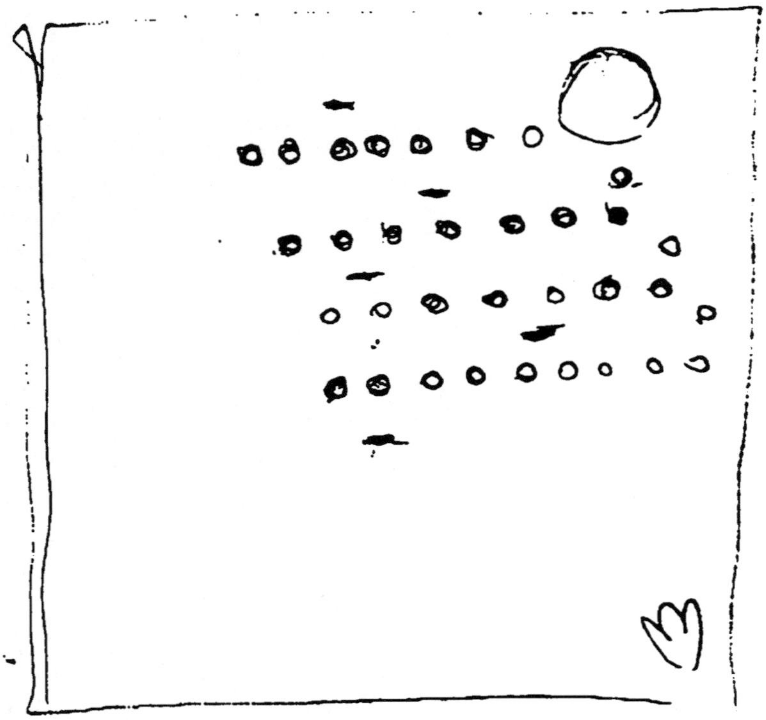

Dear Veronica,
For the garden I thought
something can you find 33 buckets
the one children play in the park, little ones
bright pink in between I have something
to bring.
For the big saloon if you can
find 9 bottles between 10-15 -8-5
approximately, and some of them with
color like blue I will arrange them
like so 3 of them the same
size 3 of them the same size and so
~~I will~~ that is the only addition I can make
I will look fo them here too. Love
Fusun

Onur's sketch for *Boogie Woogie*

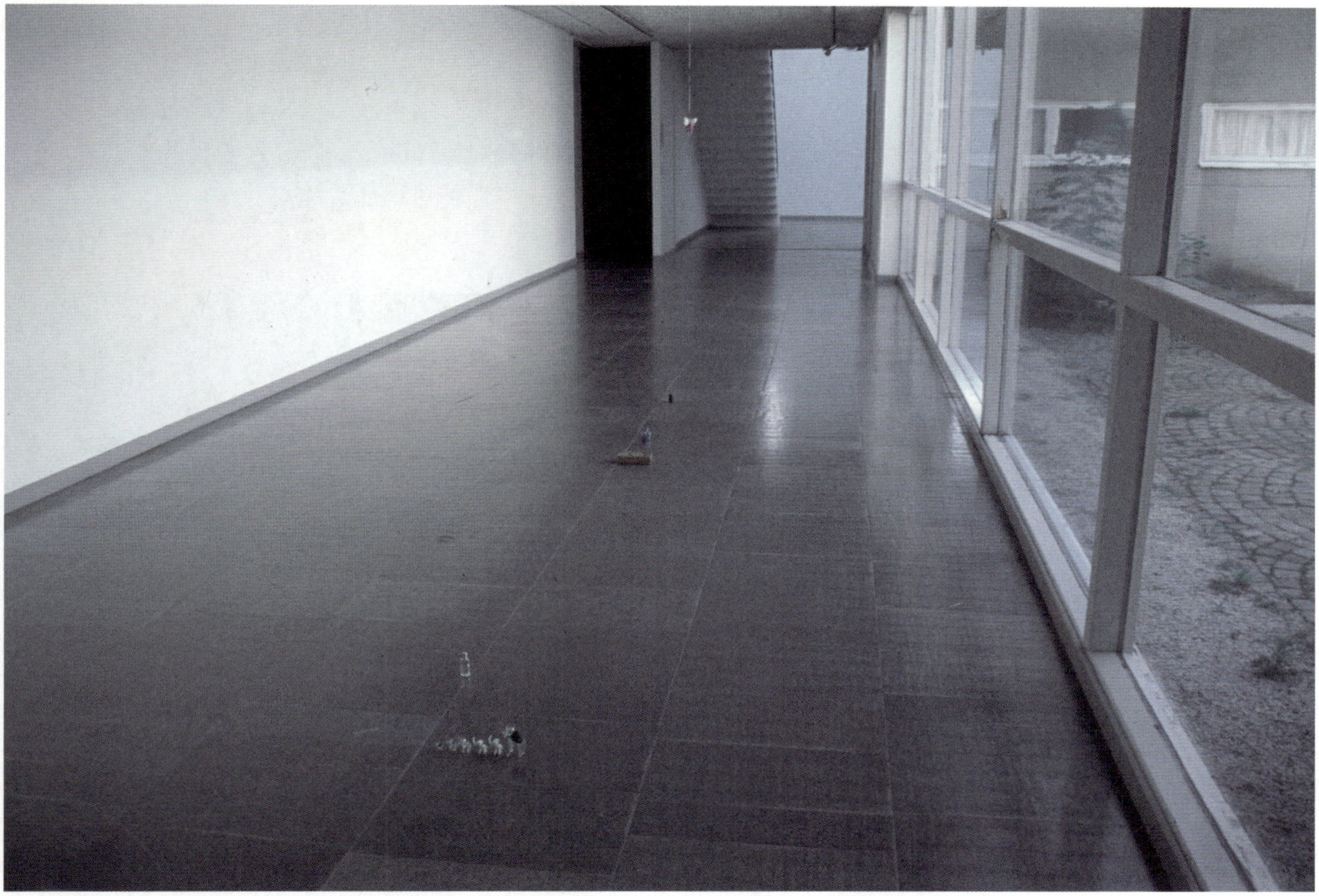

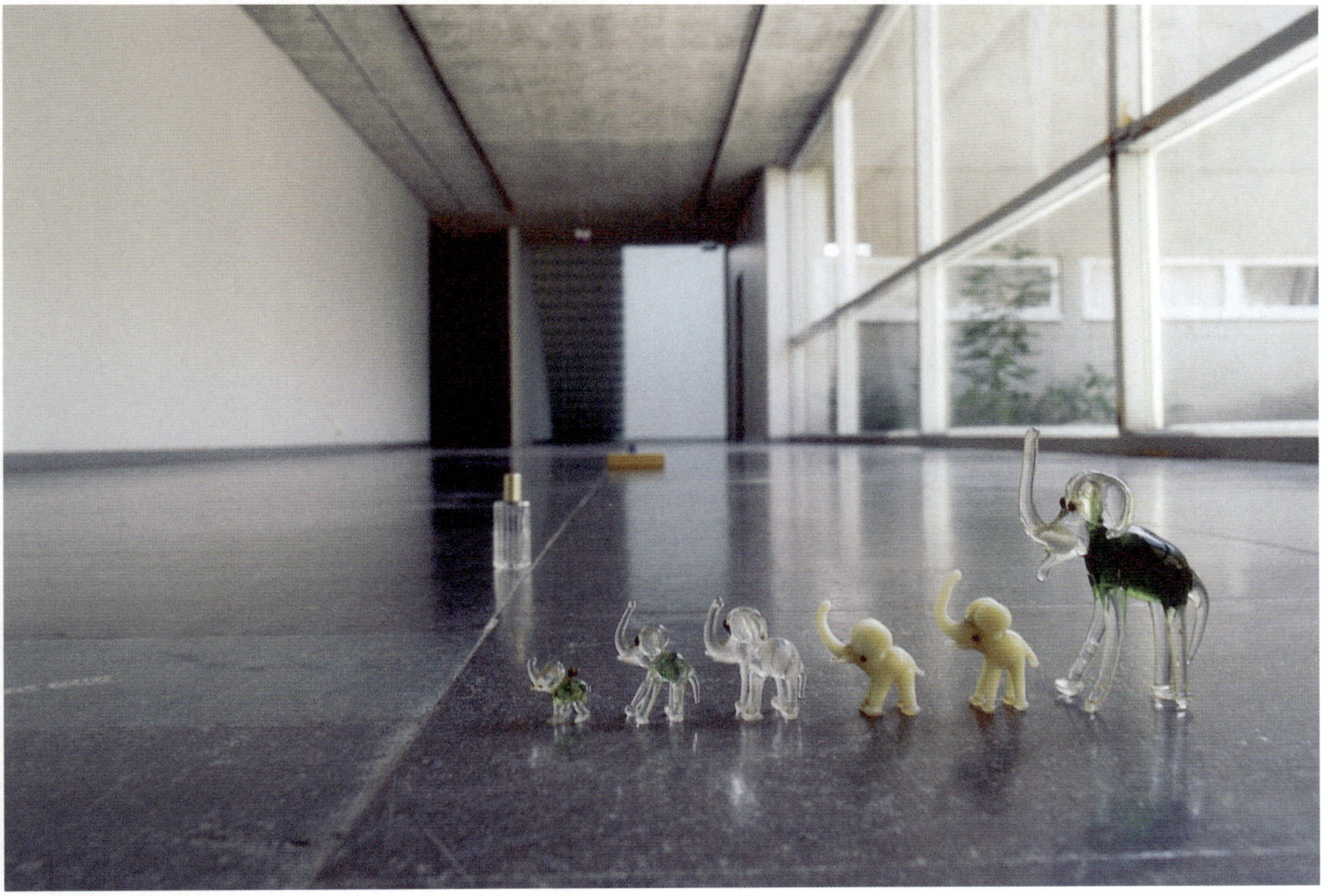

Installation, variable dimensions

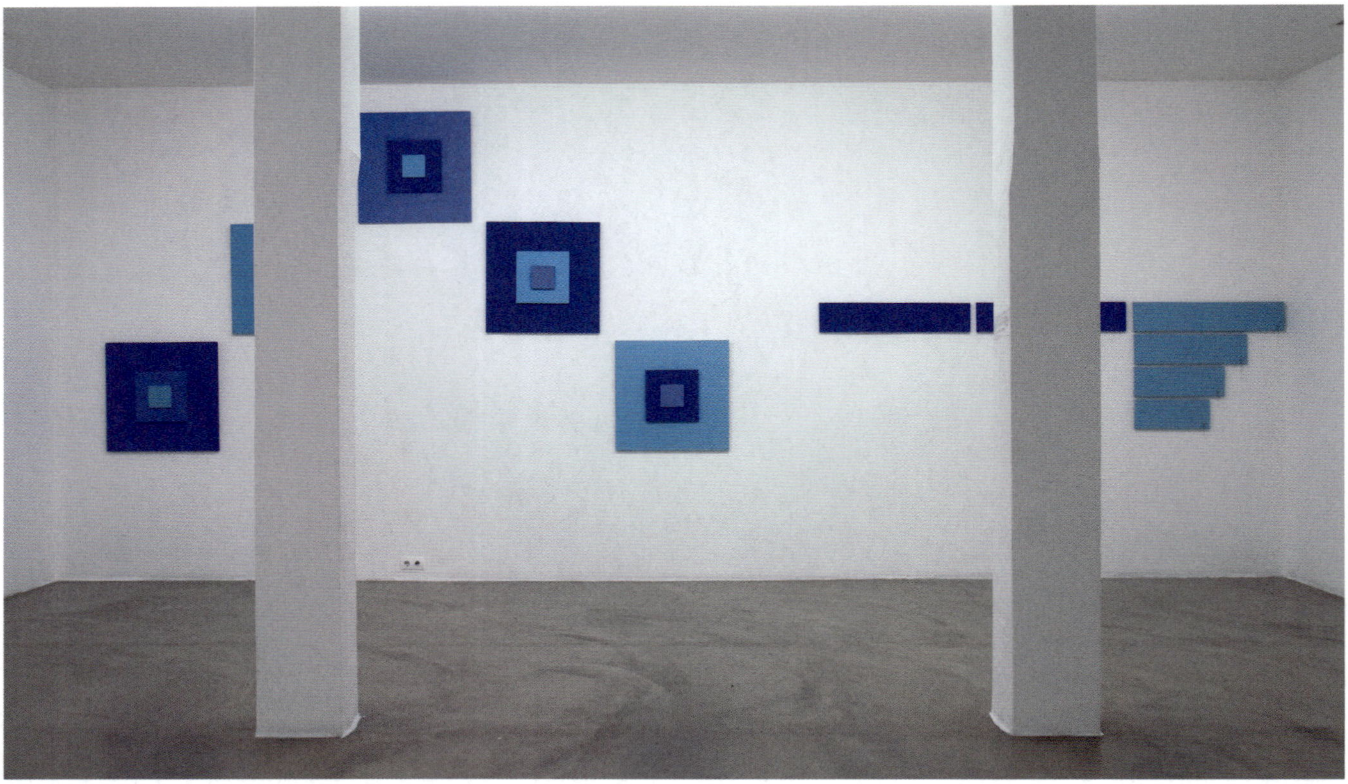

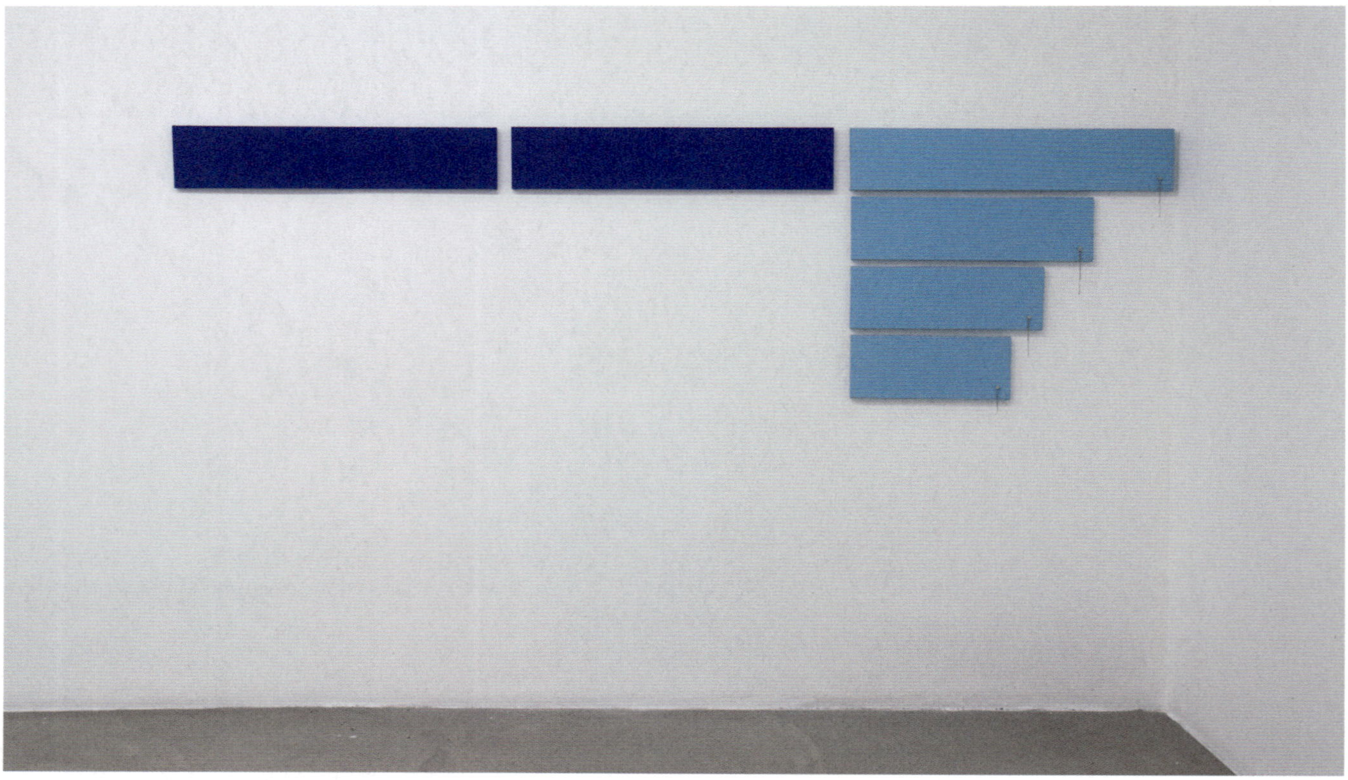

Installation with 11 canvases

Opus II – Variation (2003) is a musical installation consisting of 11 pieces. Füsun Onur composes the pieces, which are made of paint and canvases, and places them on the wall in accordance with the musical rhythms, unifying space and music. Three-piece-canvases, placed on top of one another, are organized with relation to the musical tuning system and the different shades of blue are used as half sound intervals to create the effect of the chromatic scale. The first five square shape canvases are placed with inspiration from orchestral music. This row consisting of five sounds, are arranged in tune with the pentatonic scale used in music, especially in Far Eastern music. These squares strengthen a systematical structure in which music is visualized through. The rectangular canvases arranged horizontally imply a different totality (especially, when the four canvases are below each other, resembling the 4 octaves of the human voice) which is not quite structural but rather natural and spontaneous.

Misal Adnan Yıldız, excerpt from the *Organized Conflict* exhibition catalogue, Proje 4L, Istanbul, 2003.

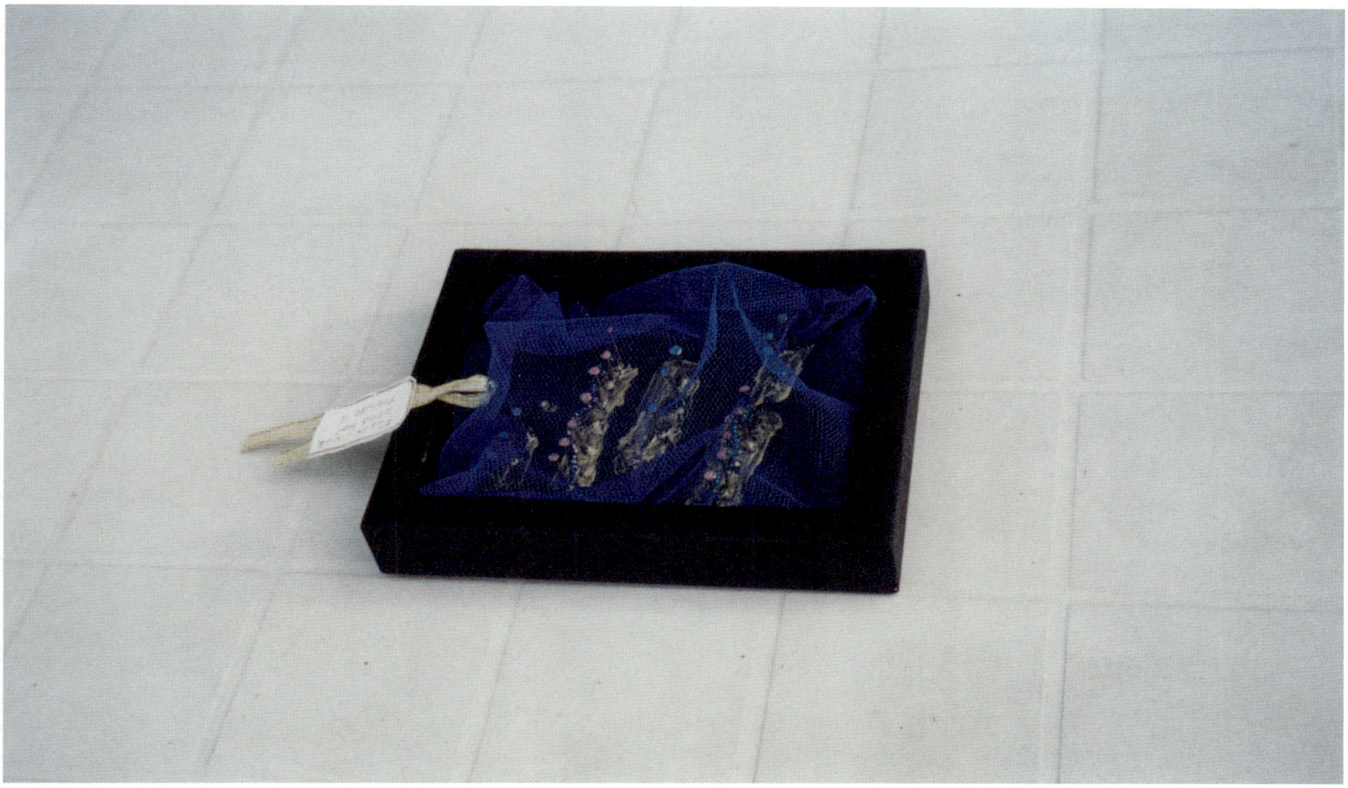

Wooden box, bead, tulle

2004 CALL ME ISTANBUL

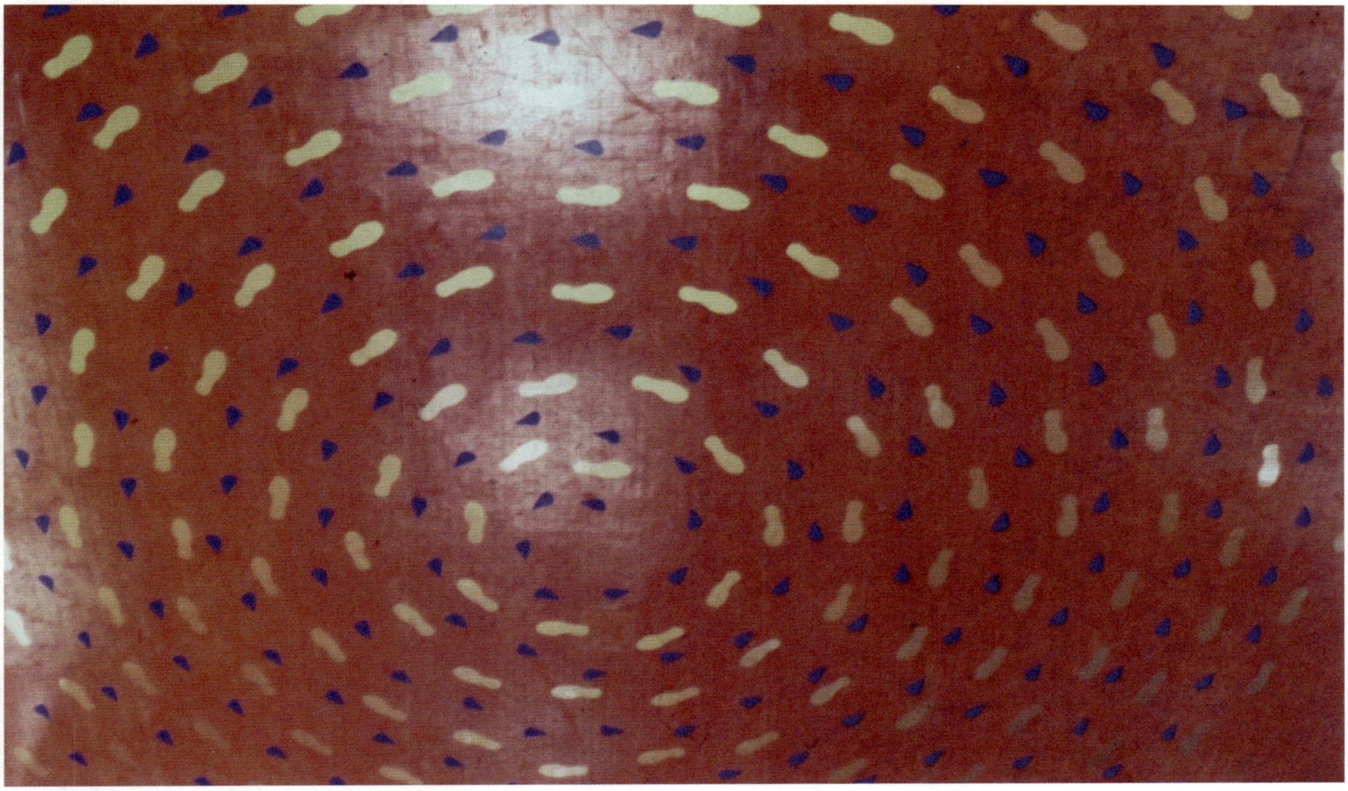

Site-specific installation, footprints applied on the floor, variable dimensions

Her last work *Call Me Istanbul* (2004), a site-specific installation created specifically for this exhibition, embodies the rhythm of walking with the contrasting currents and routes of Istanbul. In this work, Onur articulates the act of walking as our direct, bodily involvement with the city, while taking the challenge of solidifying the sound spatially and temporarily. The work consists of two different types of footprints: male in gold, female in blue colours orienting towards opposite directions. The footprints, which are applied directly onto the floor, allow the audience to step over while proposing a promenade that comes to an end in a spiral form, an abyssal hole. This form together with the rhythmical placement of footprints indicates an infinite movement inward and outward repeating the complexity of Istanbul.

Fulya Erdemci, excerpt from the *Call me ISTANBUL is my name* exhibition catalogue, ZKM, 2004.

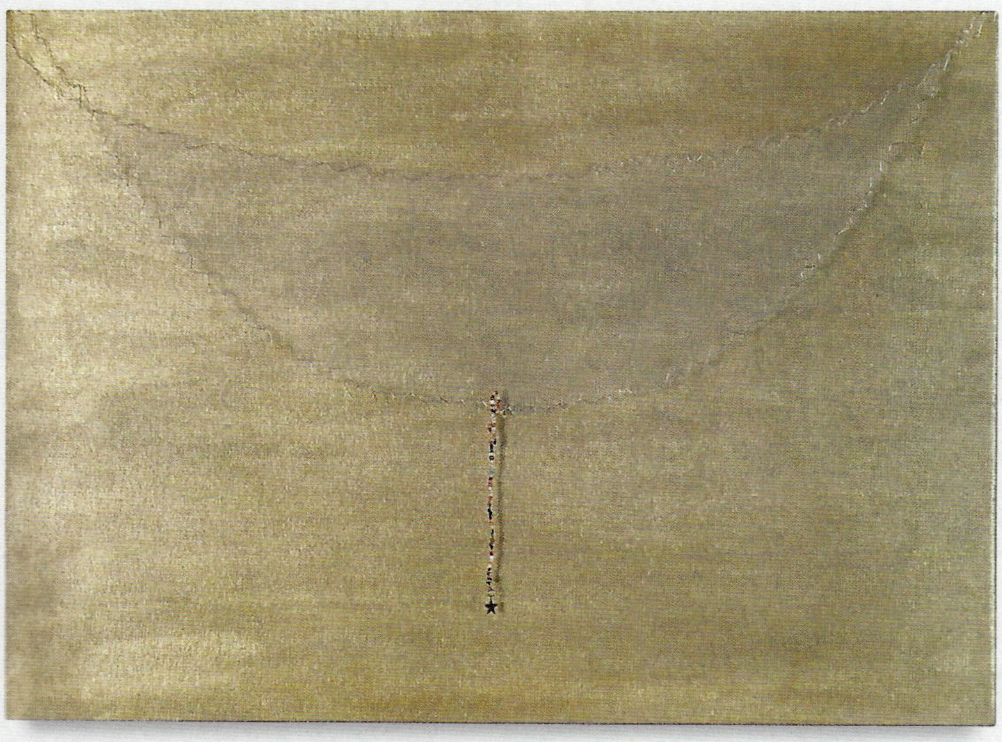

Mixed media on canvas, 45 × 60 cm

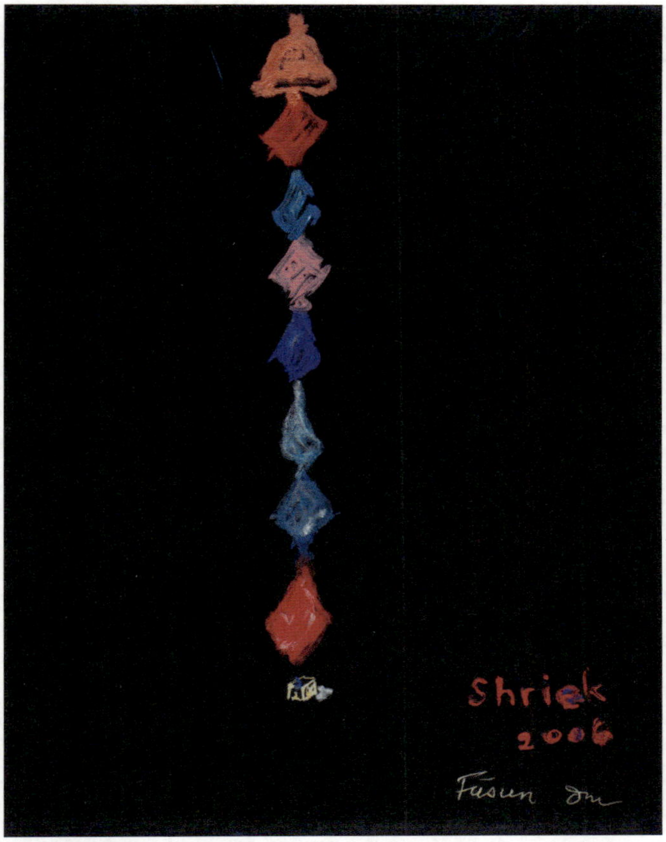

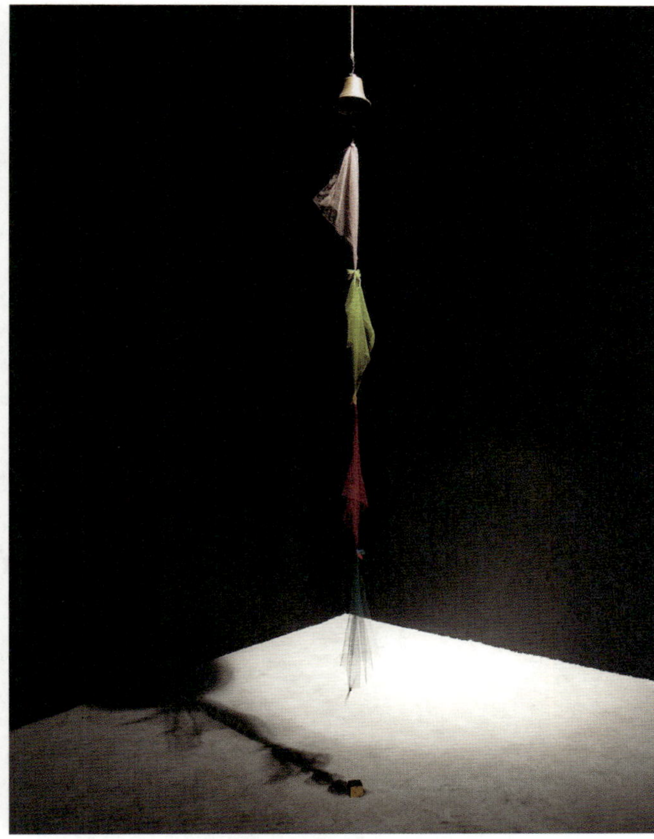

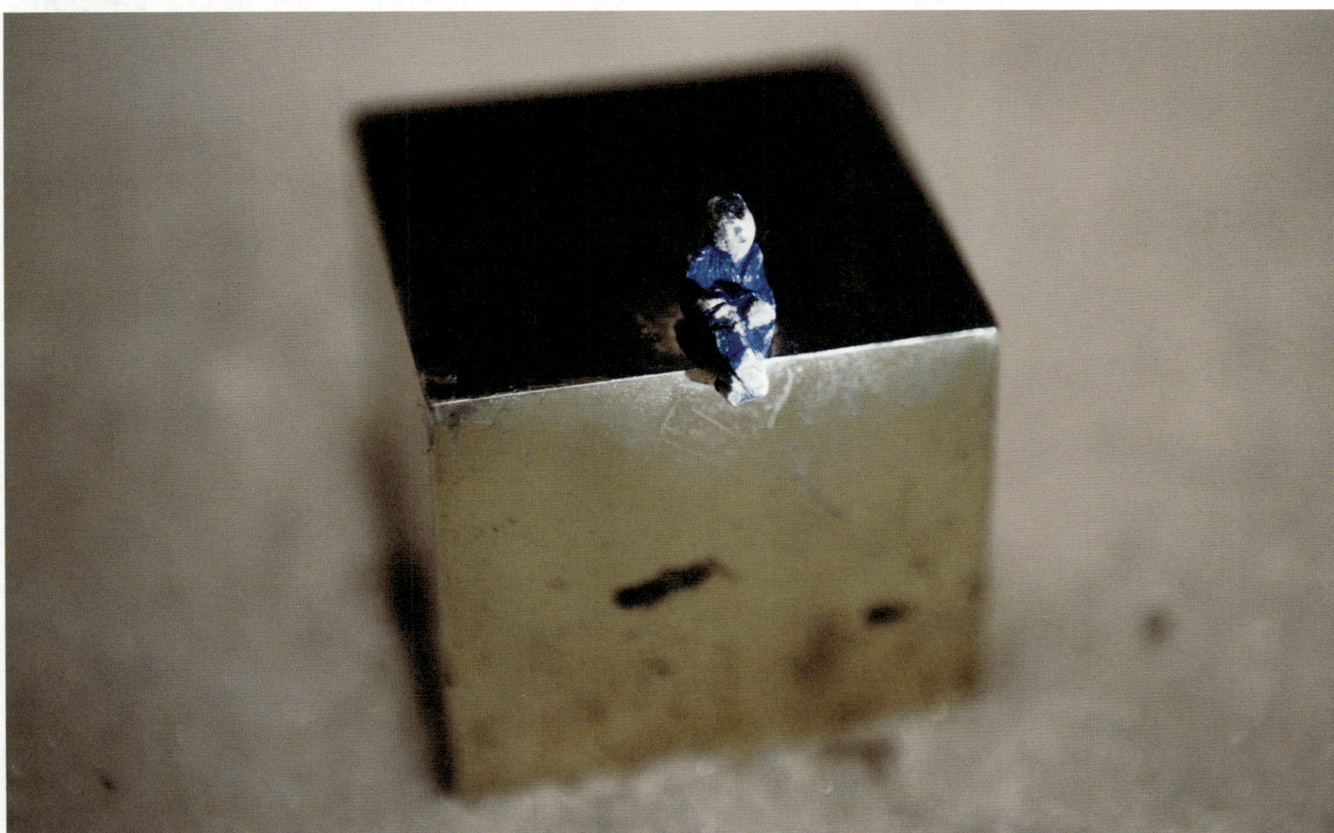

Mixed media, variable dimensions

Meanwhile, in the 2nd Moscow Biennale, there was a huge bell hanging from above, and colourful pieces of tulle the size of napkins were attached to its pendant rope. On the floor, a one-centimetre man was seated on a ten-centimetre yellow metal cube. The man was pensive, anxious. It was part of a metal toy from my childhood. And the cube was given to me by a friend, and I had fallen for it from the get-go. I designed this work as soon as I received the exhibition invite. When you pulled the rope of the bell, the tulles would start waving, and the work's name is *Shriek*.

Excerpt from Füsun Onur's letter to Necmi Sönmez, undated, from artist's archive.

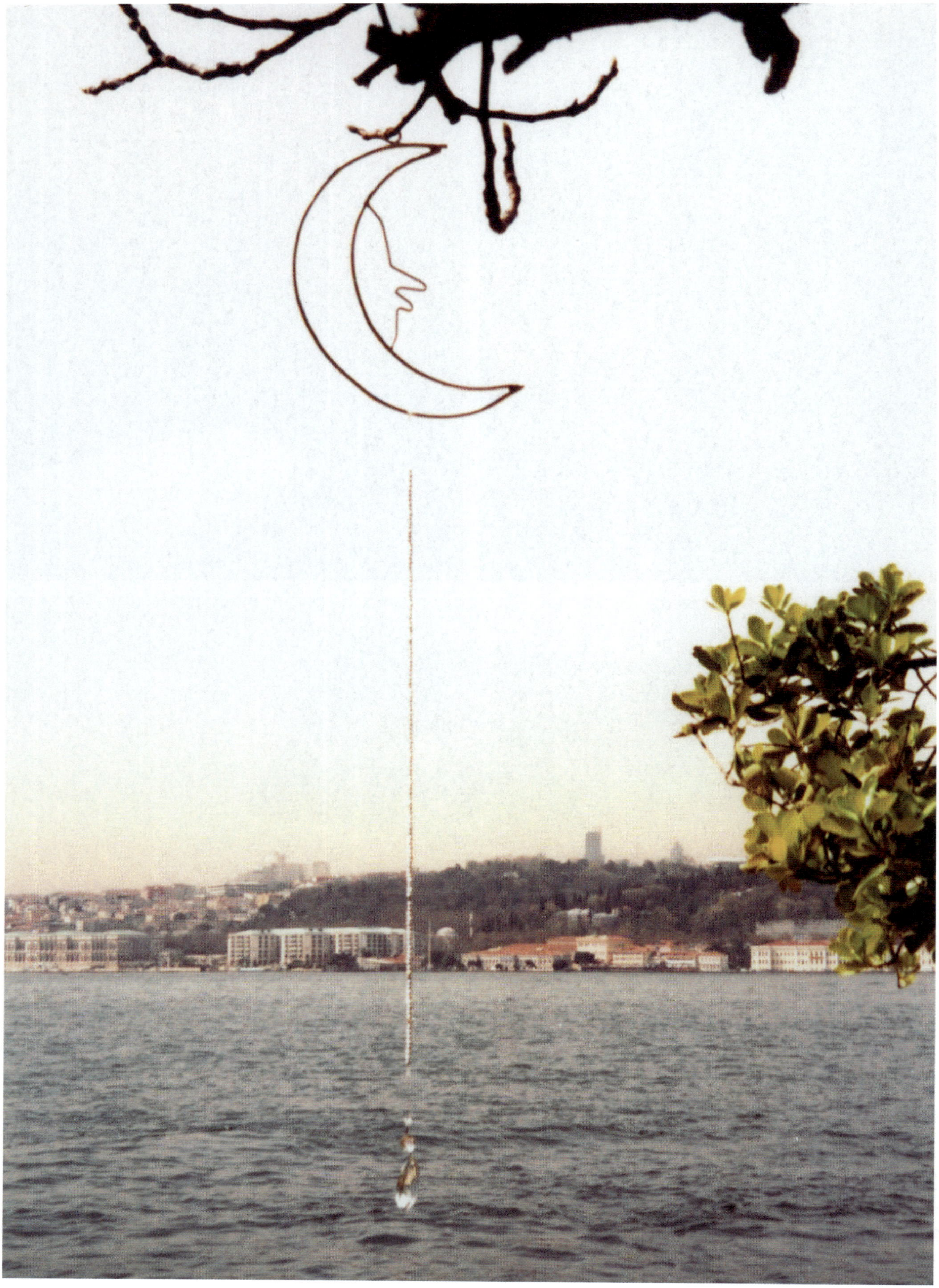

Iron, metal rope and crystal

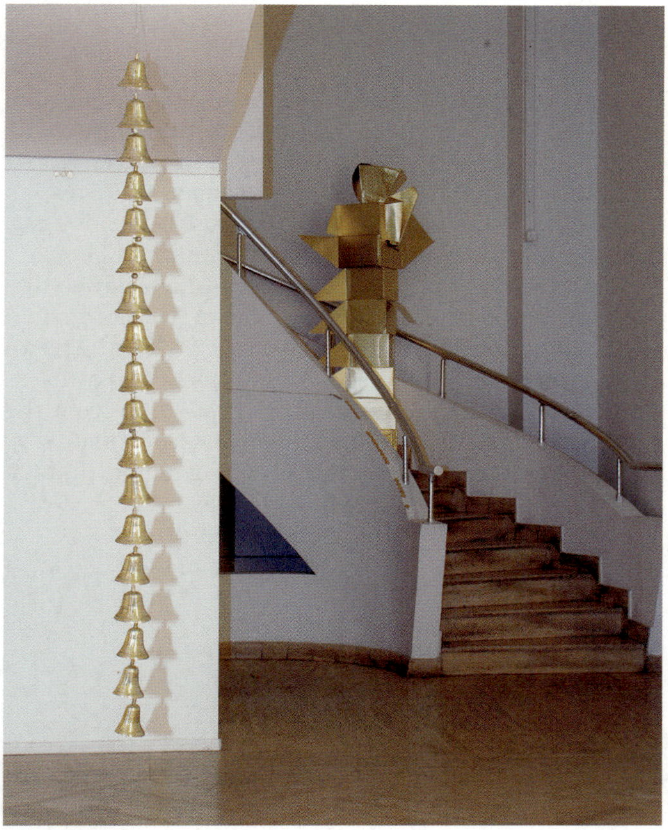

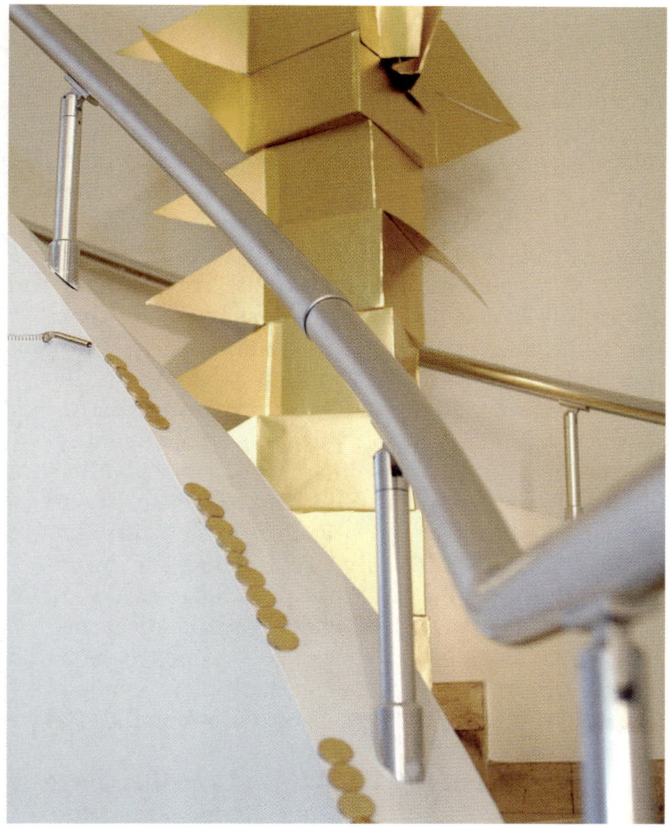

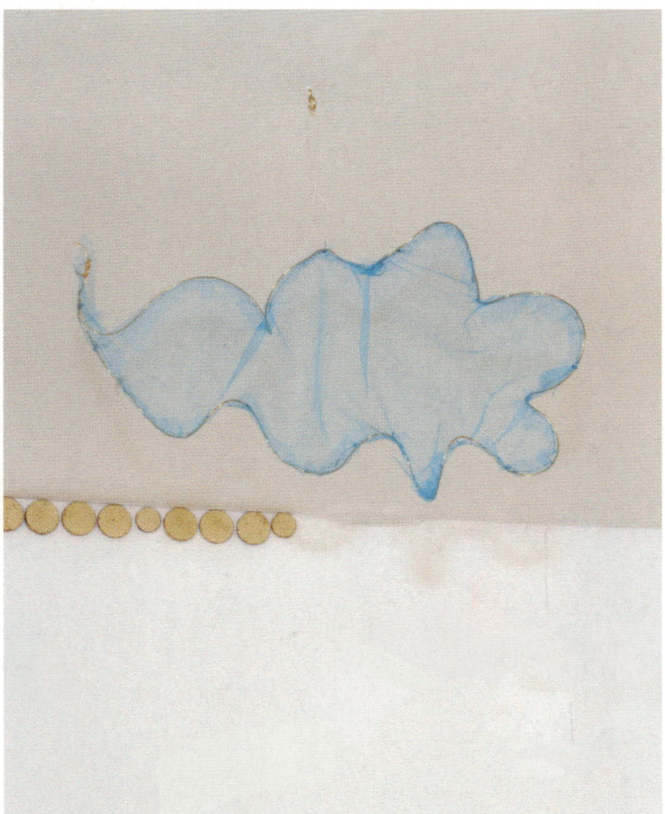

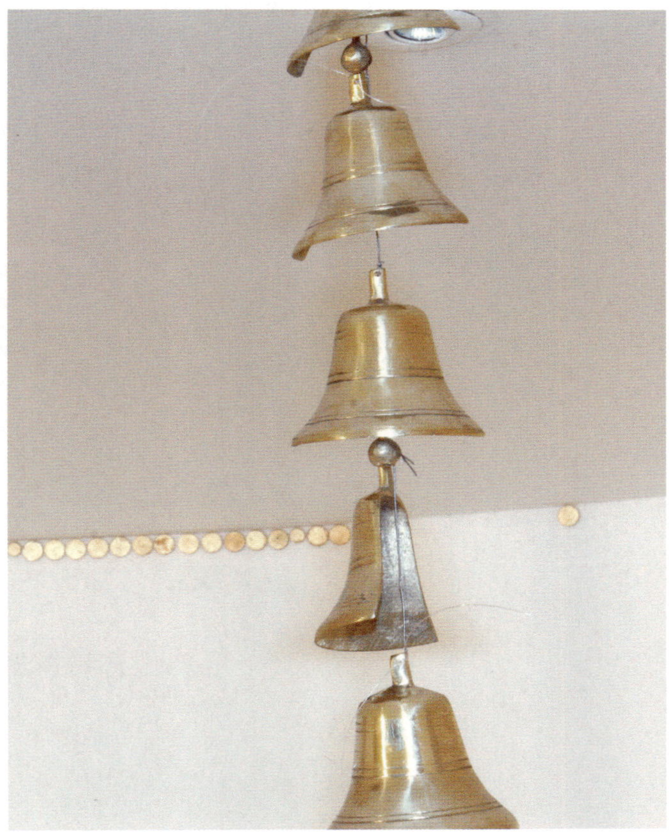

Installation view from the exhibition *Erratum Musicale*, Yapı Kredi Culture and Arts, Istanbul, 2007

Usually, I lay out my elements of musical notation on the floor, in a legible manner [...] As this gallery is two storeys, I wanted to connect it to the top floor by using the stairs. That's why here it gives the impression of notes fluttering in the air. It's essentially dispersing. And on the stairs is the *Kemancı Kadın* [Violinist Woman], a cubic work ... Since the exhibition at large is cubic, there are intersections, and I divided the bells in two as well; notes resembling butterfly wings and round yellow notes scattered about. Finally, I placed the small, coloured cubes on the top floor to represent orchestration. And by tightening the strings, I completed the exhibition setup.

Füsun Onur, excerpt from an interview by F. Candil Çulcu, *Hürriyet Keyif*, 2007.

It is difficult to write about an artist whose work I've never actually seen, except virtually. Füsun and I are roughly from the same generation, and when we studied art, the art world was conservative, male-dominated both in the Middle East and elsewhere. Even in New York City, only one or two female artists were promoted.

I happened to visit Istanbul in the 1960s and eventually I travelled all over Turkey, where there was no organised art world in general. There were neither female artists nor international exhibitions like today's Istanbul Biennial. The ambiance, as in Egypt, was traditional, although there was a movement towards Abstract Expressionism in Cairo, as well as an abstractionist trend in sculpture. However, Füsun was lucky enough to get a Fulbright Scholarship and go to the US to study sculpture. In 1967, she graduated from the Maryland Institute College of Art and at that period she started using dumped and discarded everyday objects in her works. Over time, these found objects began to dominate her sculptures, some of which were shown in the gardens of Dolmabahçe Palace and the Archaeology Museums.

Space, time and light worked together to create her minimal compositions, but at the same time, her strong statements resisted conventional norms. For example, in *Icons of Time* (1990), she uses materials like wood and skin. The mass is weightless and vibrant; light passes through the skin, suggesting violence, the breaking up of social, political and economic systems, the cruelty of the world. There is also a sense of light, transparency and space as immortal or infinite. These frames suggest that Füsun's paintings have flowed like water out of the traditional frame, out of the accepted norms, and become three dimensional. Similarly in *Flamboyant* (2007), the frame contains not a painting, but a scarf, perhaps evoking protection from the wind or femininity. Both works demonstrate Füsun's concise way of expressing herself using simple materials that say a lot about the world today.

2007 FLAMBOYANT

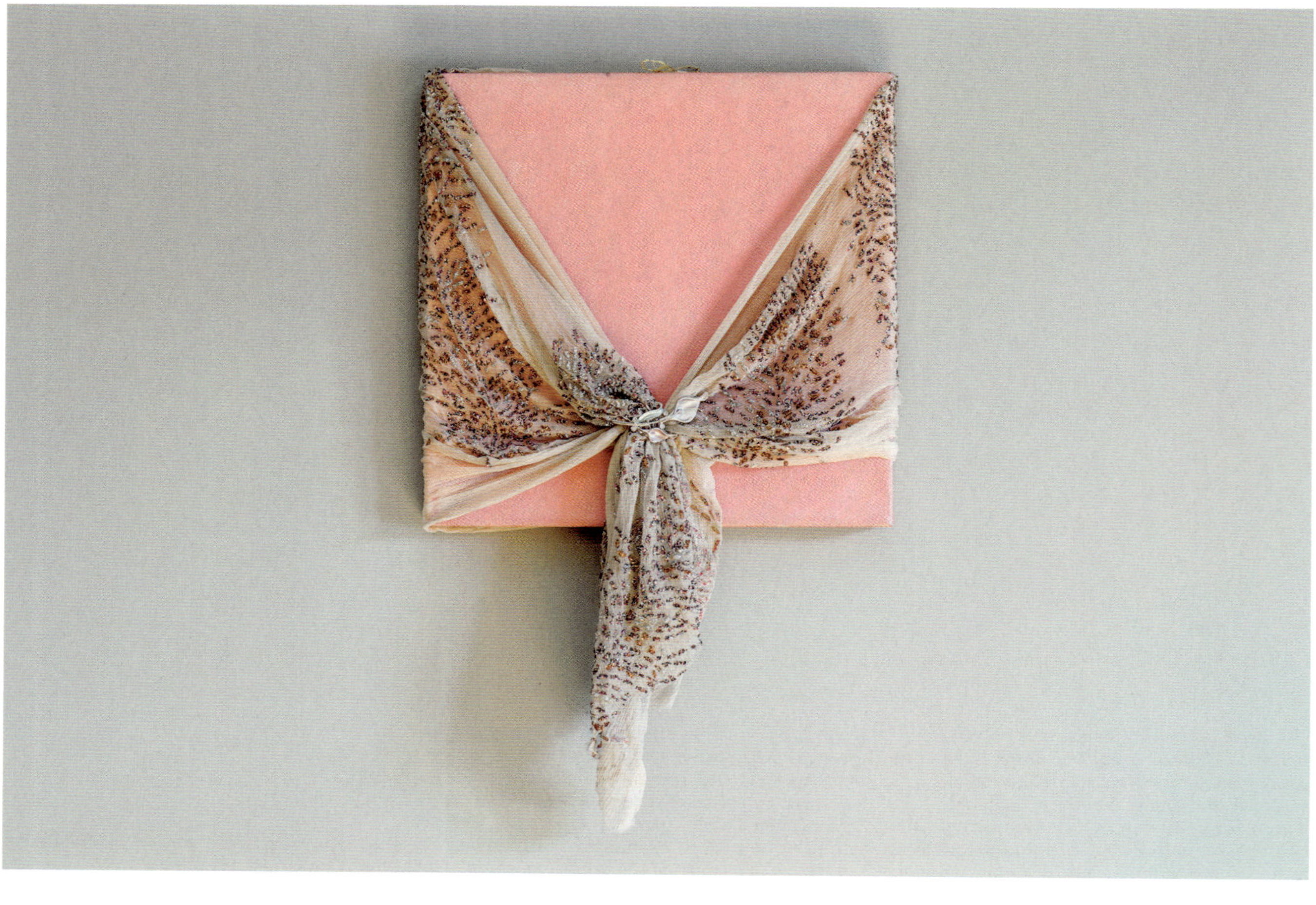

Tulle, beads, canvas, 57 × 35 cm

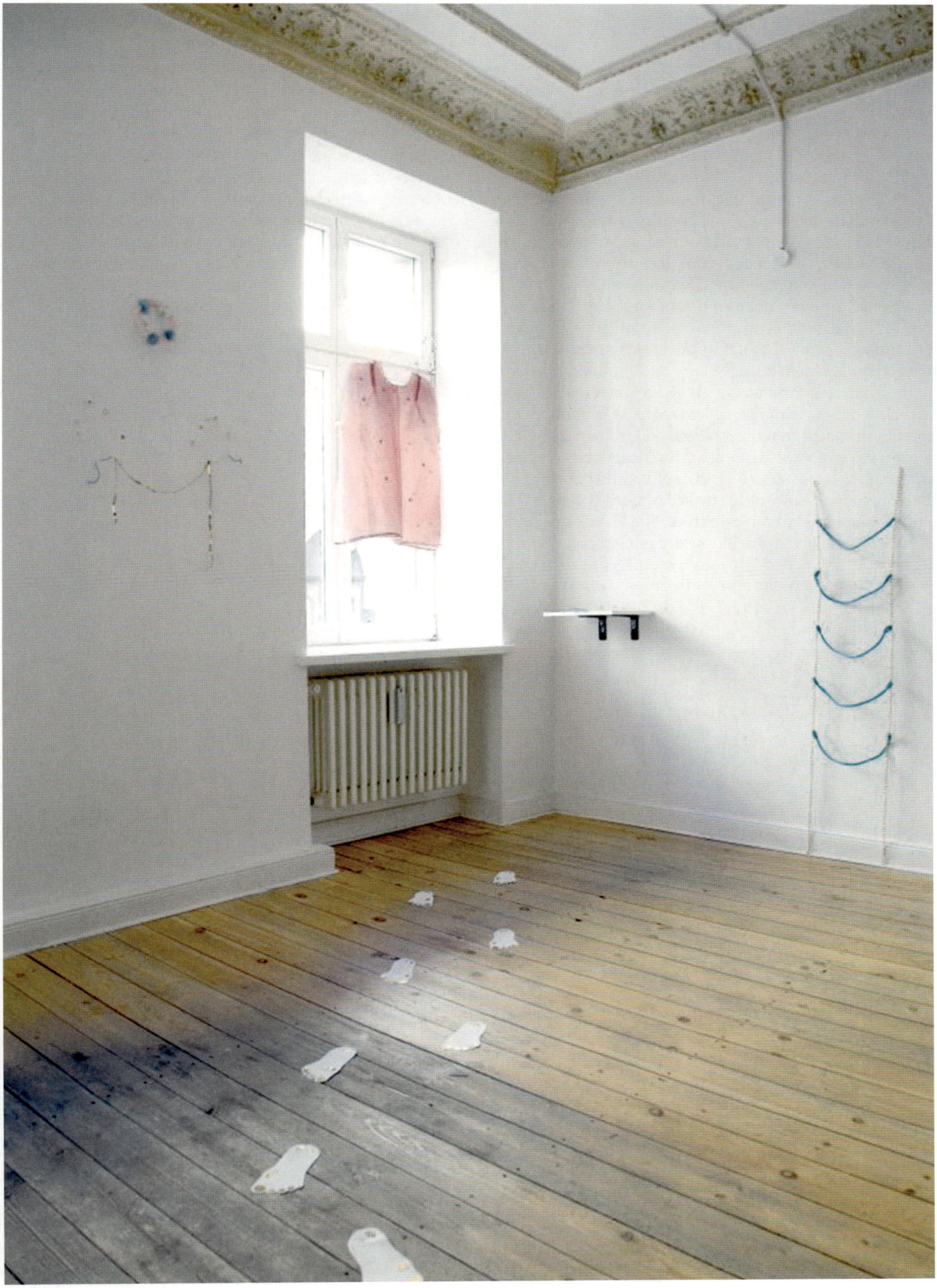

Installation view from the exhibition *She Has Been Here*, Galerie Davide Gallo, Berlin, 2008

A particular conviction I had until I was about eight was that it was quite possible to grow into a dog during puberty. I didn't imagine what the specifics of this future might hold, since a part of me already identified with K, the middle-aged, black cocker spaniel I grew up with. I didn't appear to the world in dog form, but this wasn't a concern, because of the tight knots of attachment I had formed interiorly, my adoration for K, which sat within the realm of eros. That space of longing between human, child and animal was preserved and encouraged by imagination, since it wasn't mirrored, nor reciprocated as expected. Instead, fuelled by obscurity and nonsense, it grew expansive, becoming a central motif in my creative vocabulary long after K's death.

An attachment of this kind, once made, has an afterlife of its own. The reflexive pulse of mourning means that anima treads back and forth on the threads woven through the lifetime of the deceased – catching its paw now, showing a tip of a tail then – in some half-lit space, sending surprise tremors through the path of the lover-survivor-artist. The blown-up shadows of the scattered minutiae and the central, caught figures of Tekir (Old Persian *tigra*, Greek *tigris*) on the walls evoke such spheres of intimacy, longing and play. The five-piece installation stirs the viewer's visceral memory through images of the momentary, familiar postures of the cat Tekir amid household textures. We remember what is lost through the way in which its absence resonates and tickles. In the silent, spectral rise and fall of the textile, the apostrophe becomes audible, not a composition in full, as explored in many of Onur's silent, musical installations, but another kind of accumulation: twists and turns of limber, non-human spines and fragments of the human companion quietly humming the impossibility of mourning, an impossibility in translation.

*Anne Carson, *Eros The Bittersweet: An Essay*, (1986 Princeton University Press), 37.

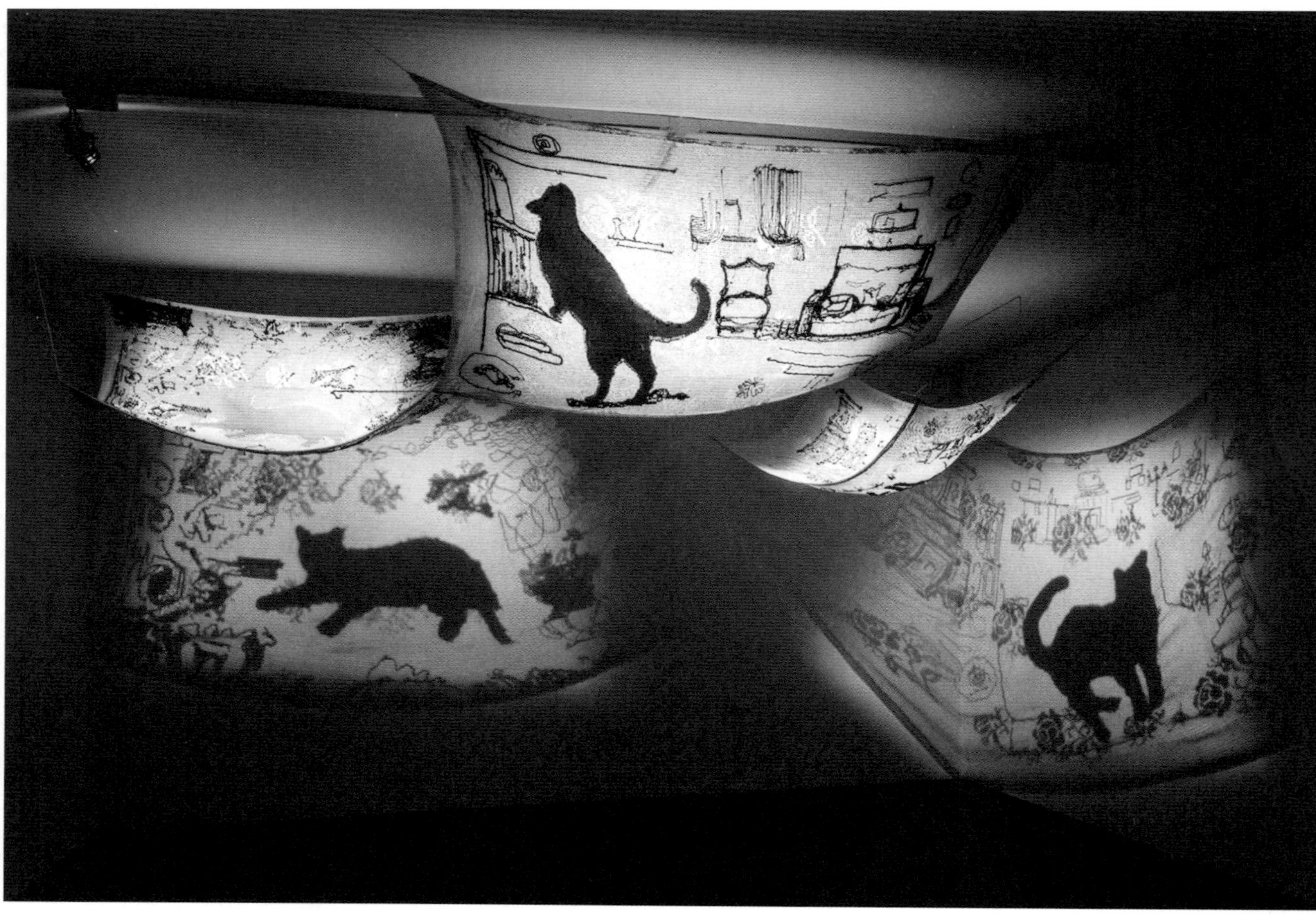

Mixed media on fabric, 5 pieces, 160 × 100 cm, 195 × 90 cm, 200 × 90 cm, 107 × 210 cm, 105 × 200 cm

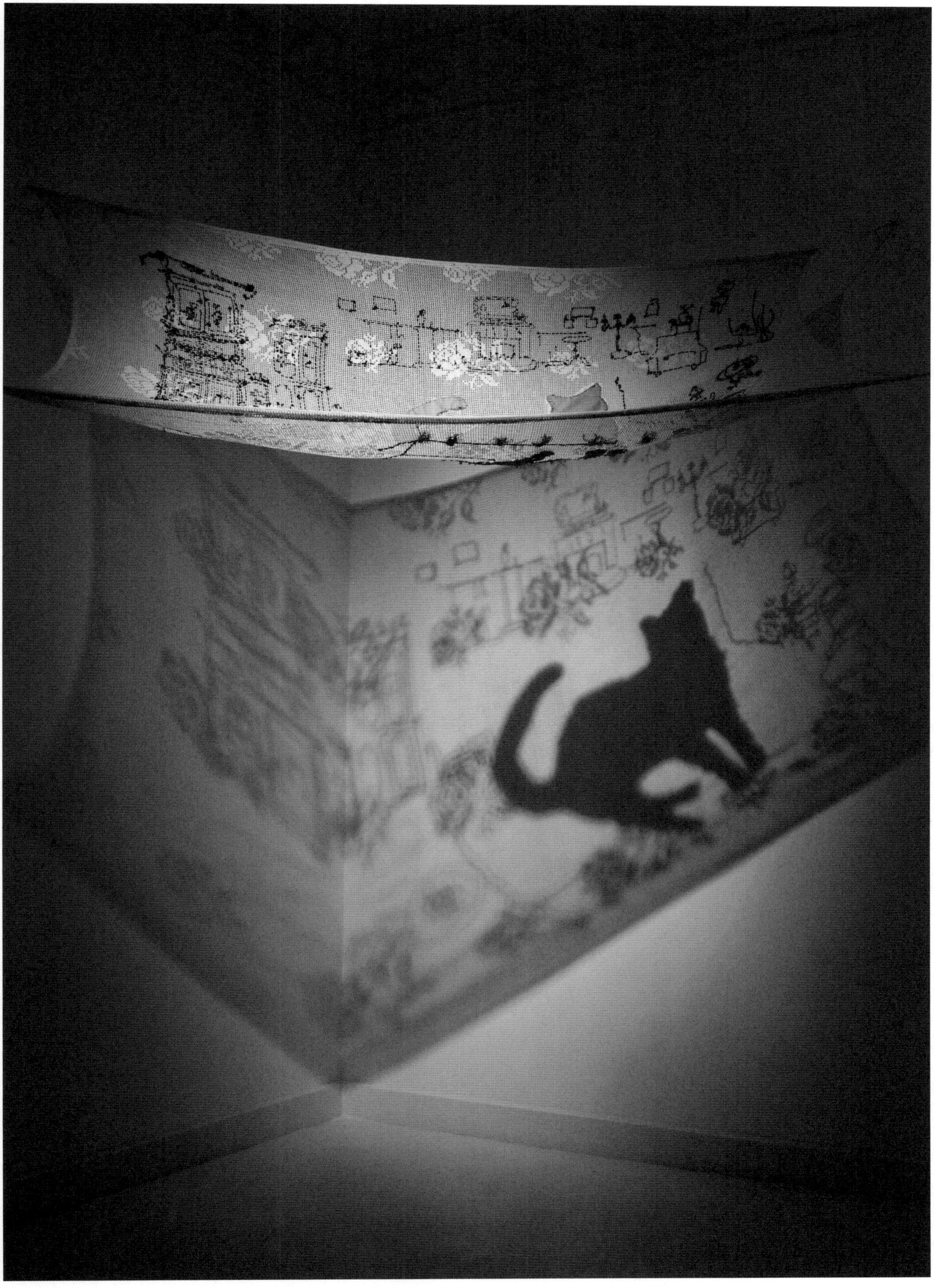

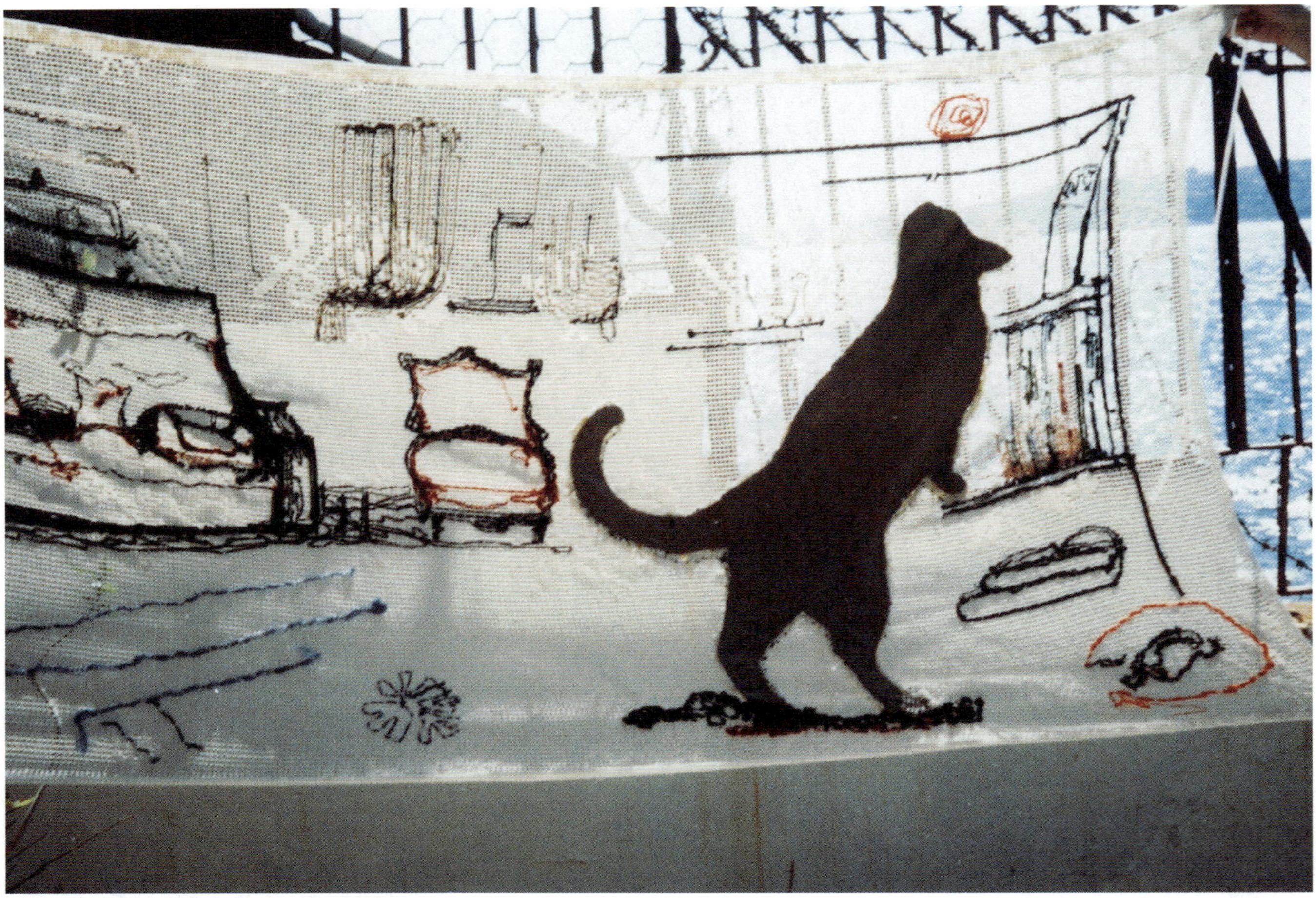

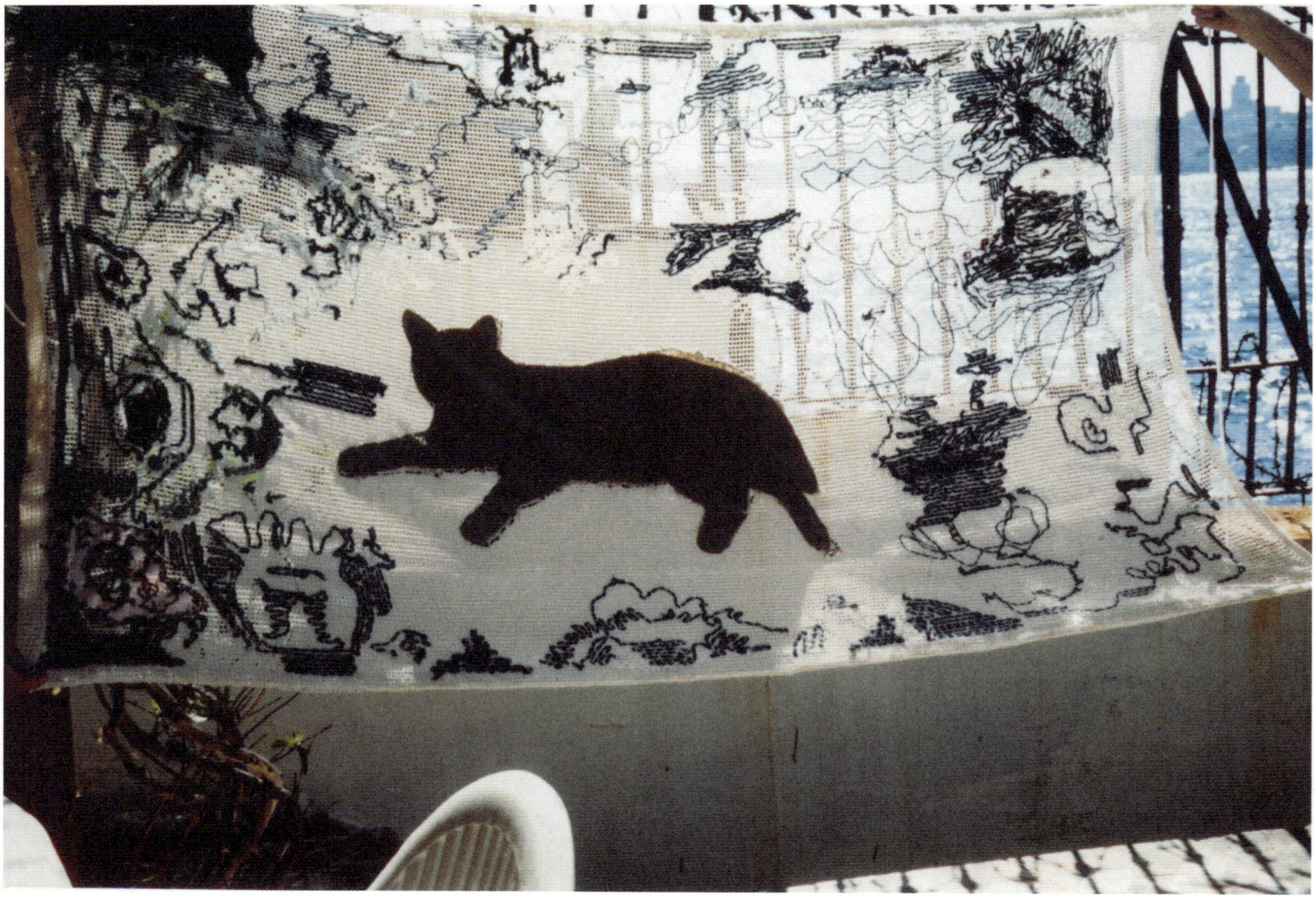

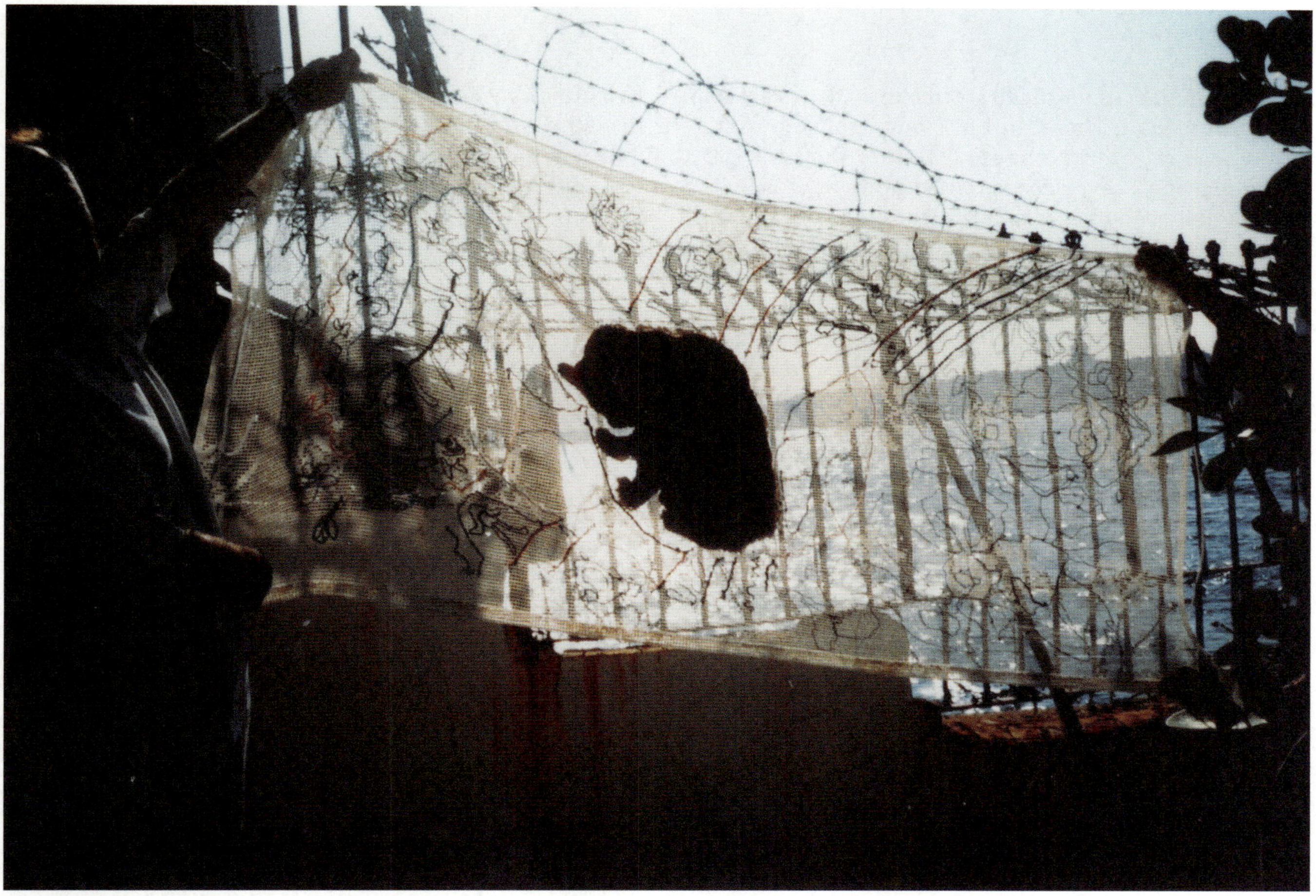

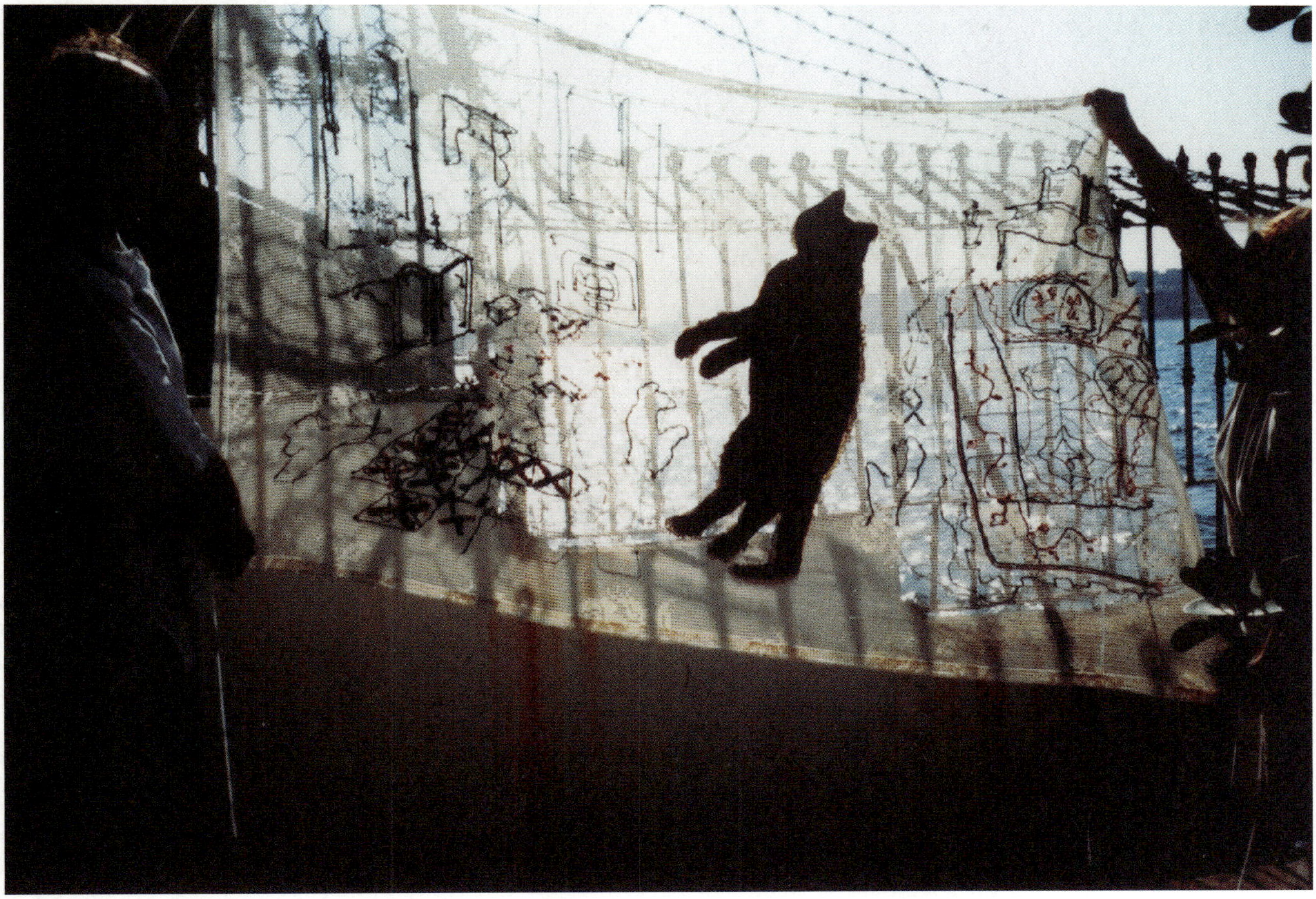

Meeting audiences for the first time in 2010 at Port Izmir 2: International Triennial of Contemporary Art, titled *Silence_Storm*, the installation *Whisper* (2010) is comprised of seven pieces lined up in succession. It is as if a wooden stool or coffee table is being gradually reduced from its original design and abstracted into a visual poem that I look at and imagine the flow of water, the rhythm of the sea, the sound of the waves.

A whisper is the lowest frequency the human ear can hear; to whisper is to utter what you wish to be known, but do not wish to be its utterer. This word, which evokes the feeling of mystery, secrecy, intimacy and privacy, has a depth of meaning that is fitting for Füsun Onur's installation. The elders say, 'What two people know is no longer a secret.' And this form, repeated seven times, is like the gradual diffusion of sound, of word, of utterance; like the undulating rings of water ever receding from the centre and disappearing.

Istanbulites know best how words and water travel.

Wherever it may be exhibited – the Tütün Deposu at Port Izmir, or the Antrepo building in the 12th Istanbul Biennial; the exhibition halls of Arter, or the terrace overlooking the Bosphorus in Onur's home in Kuzguncuk – *Whisper* will titillate its viewers' instinct to listen and hear. The sound of the poem within will never be silenced. The melody of this installation is a song with a refrain that will be forever echoed.

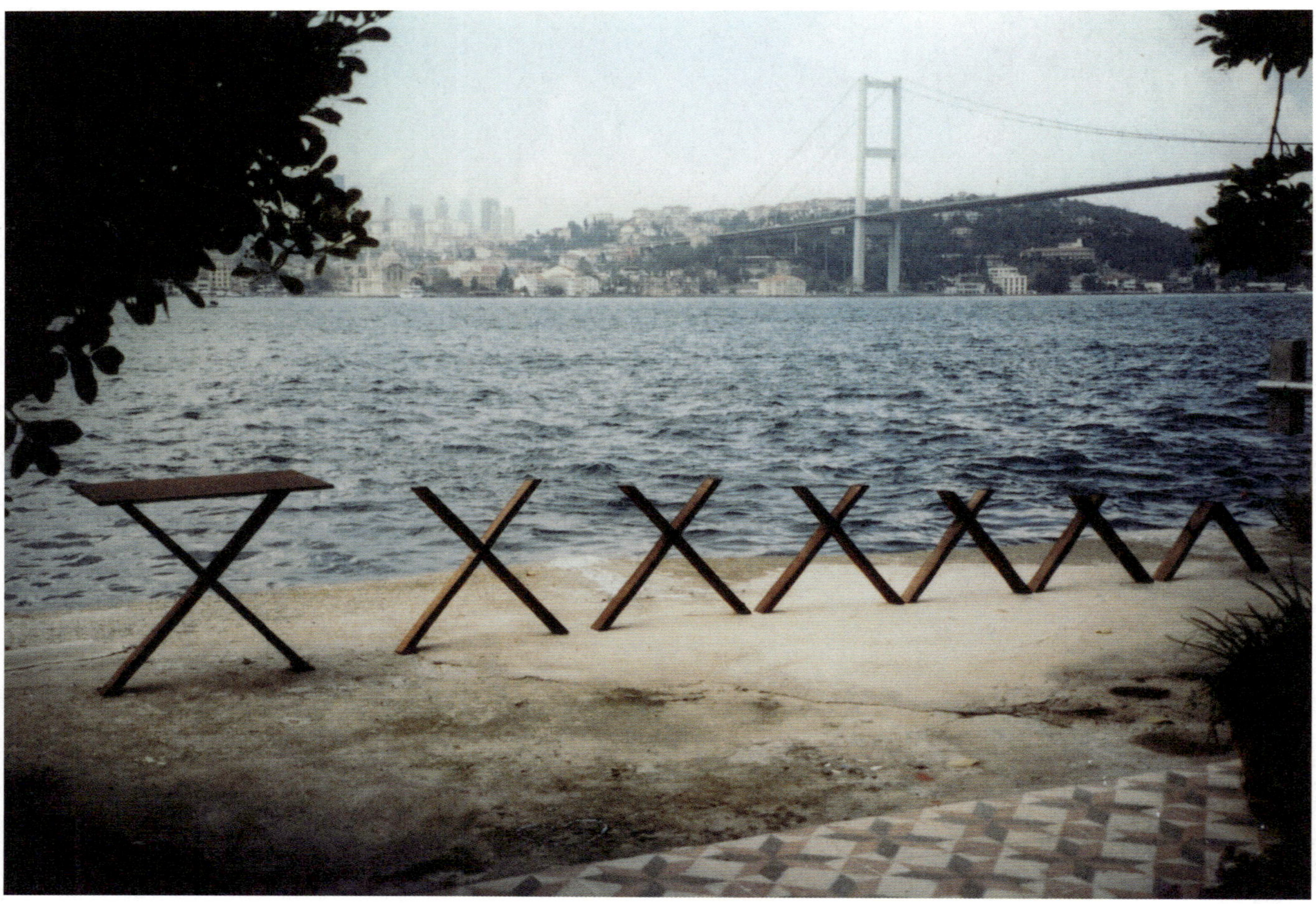

Installation with 7 wooden stools

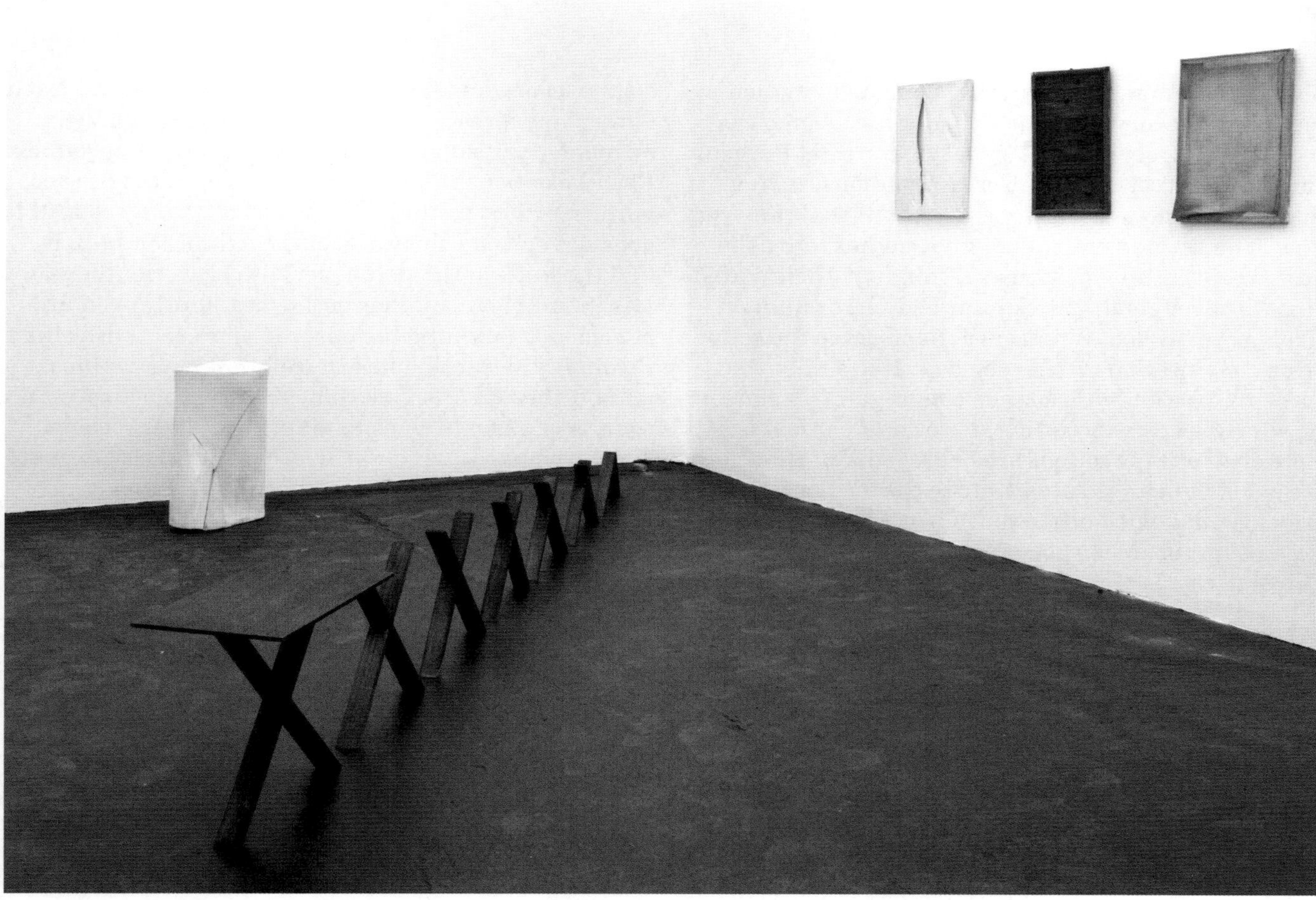

Installation view from *Untitled*, *12th Istanbul Biennial*, 2011

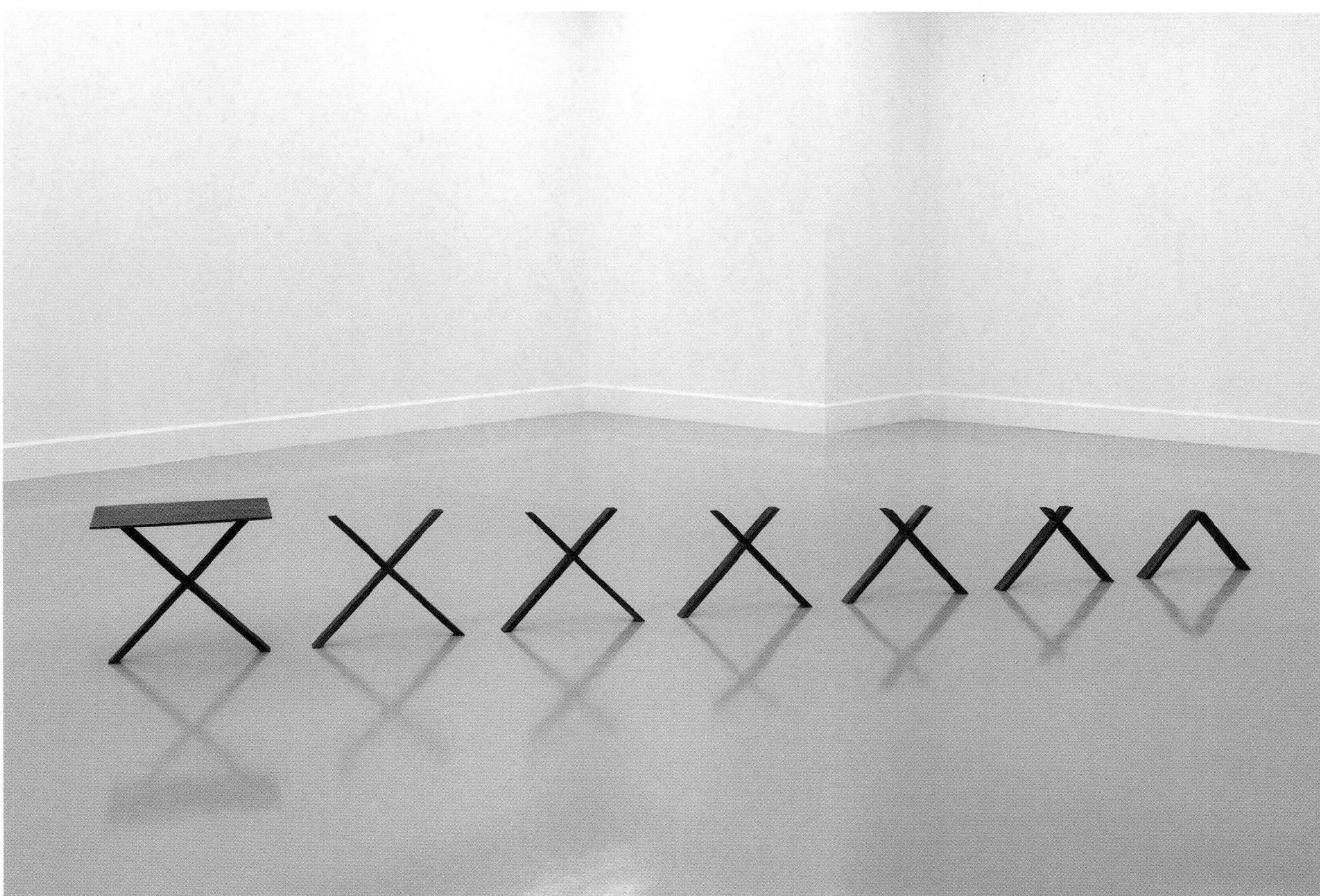

Installation view from *Through the Looking Glass*, Arter, Istanbul, 2014

Flamenco
by Murat Alat

If we concur that every existing thing is in motion, we can say that every thing has a sound. In as much as every moving object vibrates, each material harbours many a sound at its core. Certain motions, such as the internal motion of a stone, are small-scale and very slow. The sounds emitted cannot be heard by the human ear. Other motions are mighty; their sounds pulsate throughout the human body like thunder, jarring every bone. What, then, happens to the sounds after the vibrations strike our body like a flash and leave? Where do these sounds congregate? The memory, which keeps a record of the world in motion, is a plate on which the sounds are engraved. But the sounds are not kept in an isolated state in the memory; they are entwined with other sensory particles, thoughts, states of mind. When you summon a sound, a whole universe comes along with it.

Füsun Onur's *Flamenco*, which she produced in 2011, is a composition constructed from the latent sounds of objects. Some of these sounds are born from the momentary, minimal vibrations of objects. Others are memory-soaked high-frequency undulations, spilling over the depths of the viewer's mind. Like notes on a stave, hammers, ribbons and wires line up side by side and form a composition. The execution of the composition, meanwhile, falls to the audience. Each viewer interprets what their eyes see through their own personal baggage, hearing all manner of sounds. Each execution is different and unique, since it is the performer's own story. The sound of *Flamenco* (2011) does not echo off the walls of the exhibition hall; it fills the halls of the performer's inner world, therefore it is inaudible to another performer. Trails open up at each note, pinning the past to the present, travelling through different bodies in different geographies; and on these trails, one comes across the stories and sounds of various objects, plants, animals, people. This orchestra, which at first you think will create a cacophony, gradually synchronises, achieving a humble harmony.

Flamenco loosely knots together the pieces of the material world discerned by the helpless organ called the eye, which is dominated by the despotic power systems that have laid siege to the world. With delicate touches, it arranges the vibrations whose hazy origins would take a lifetime to enumerate, and releases them back into the universe to be reinterpreted anew by those who seek a music to listen to in life.

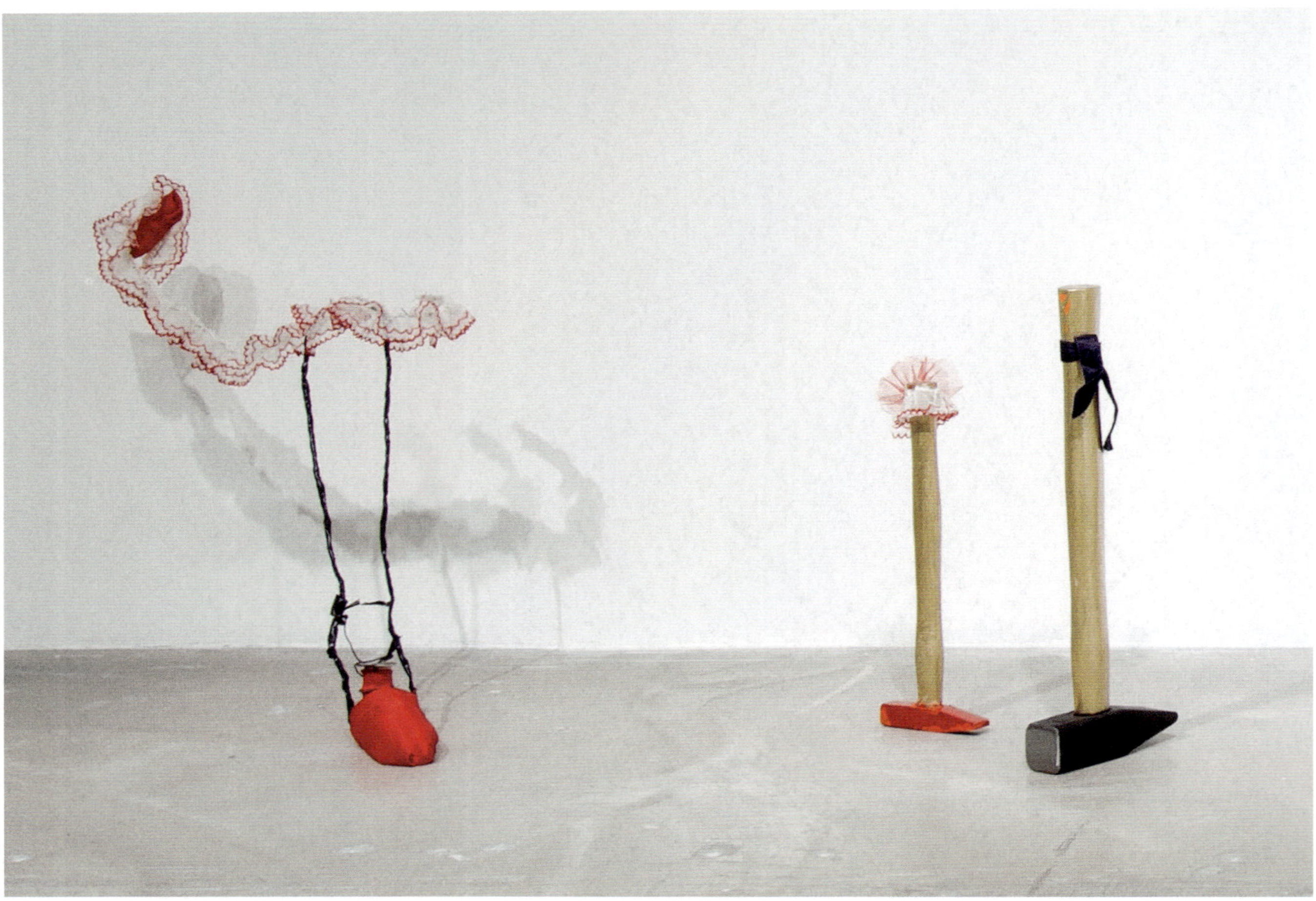

Installation (hammer, tulle, fabric, wire), variable dimensions
Installation view from the exhibition *Continuous Variations*, Akbank Sanat, 2011

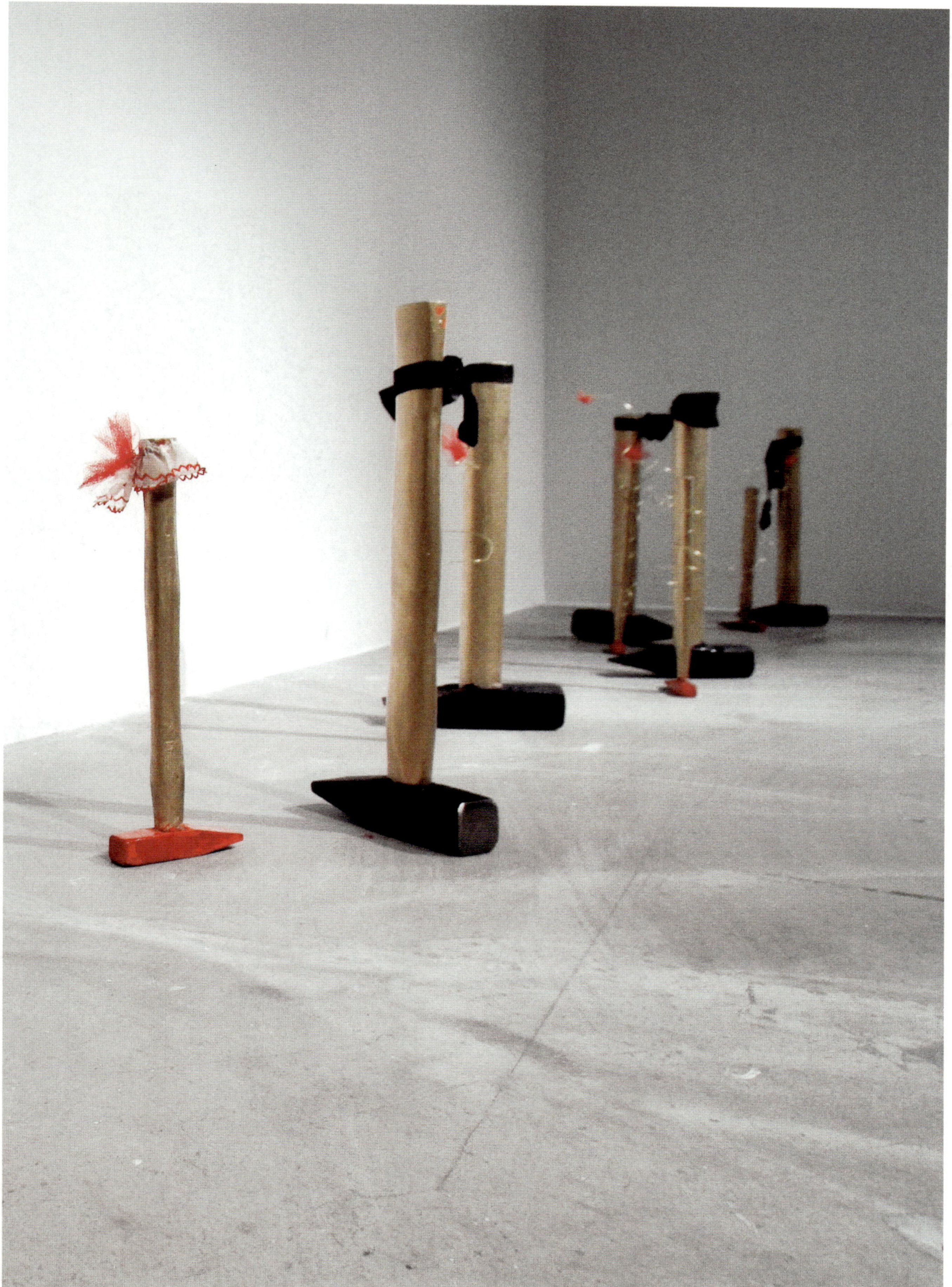

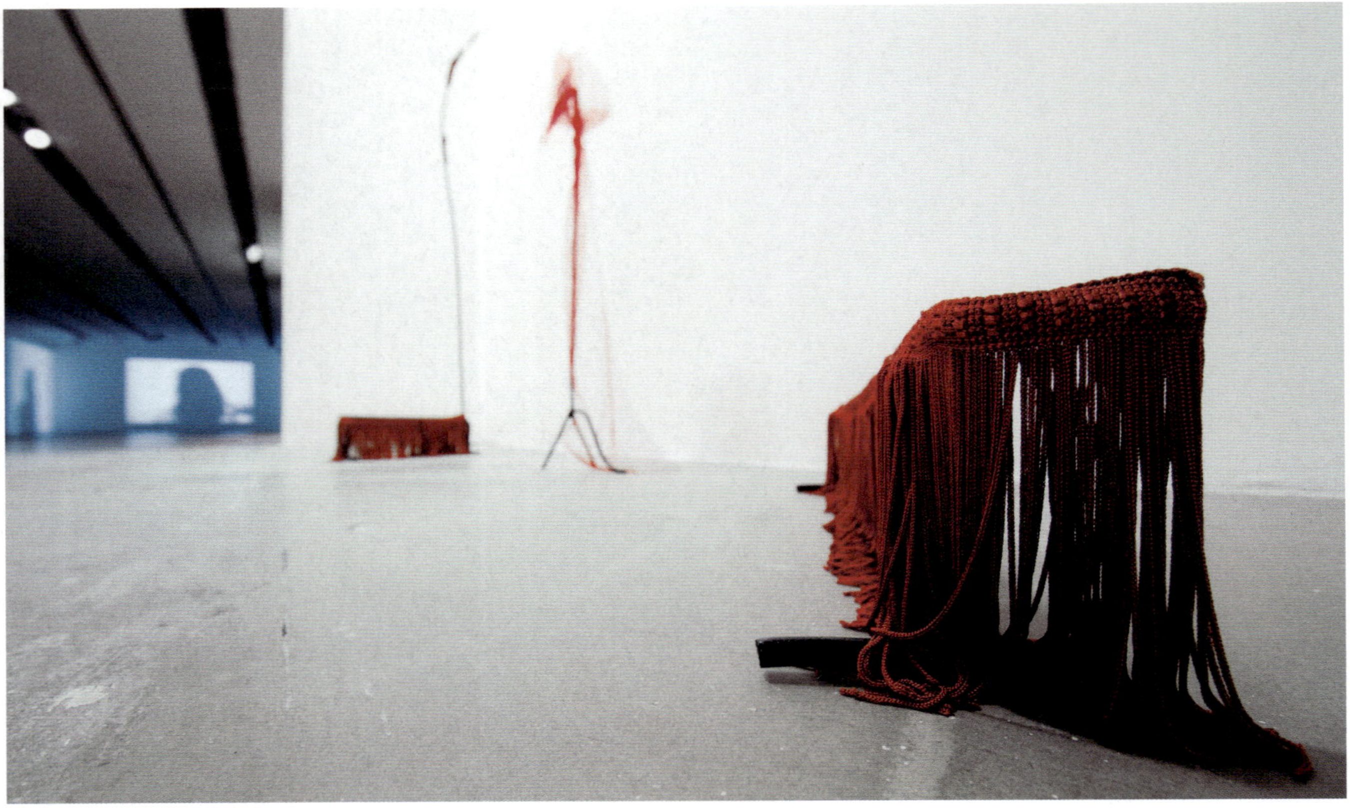

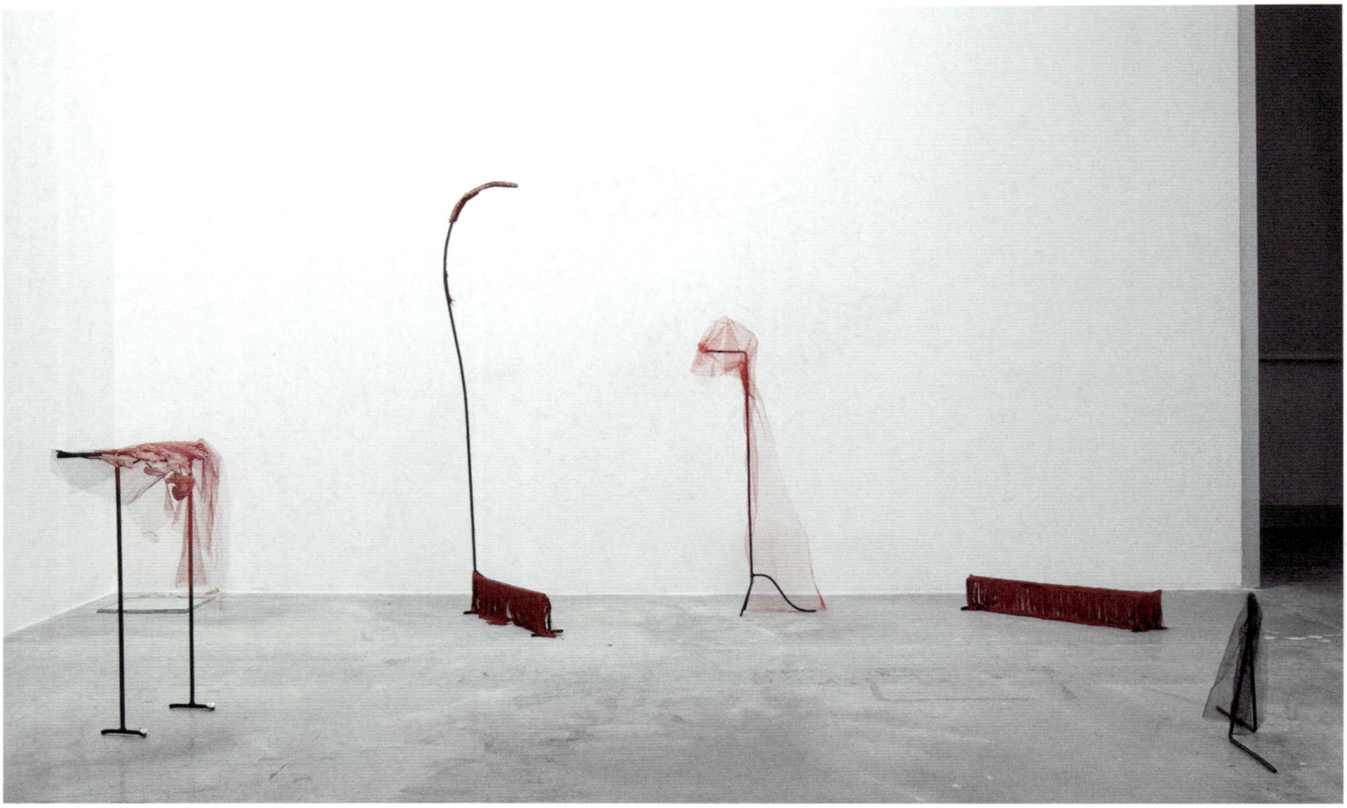

Installation (iron, tulle), variable dimensions

In her work titled *Silence* realised in 2011, reminding us of a room, Füsun Onur mobilises the layers of time in her own language. This installation regarded as a room and referencing a space without walls belong to the artist's world of confiding: it rests on an understanding where silence and sound could simultaneously coexist. Silence somehow indicated a condition of the absence of music, yet the ever presence of sound.

Ali Akay, excerpt from the *Continuous Variations* exhibition catalogue, Akbank Sanat, 2012.

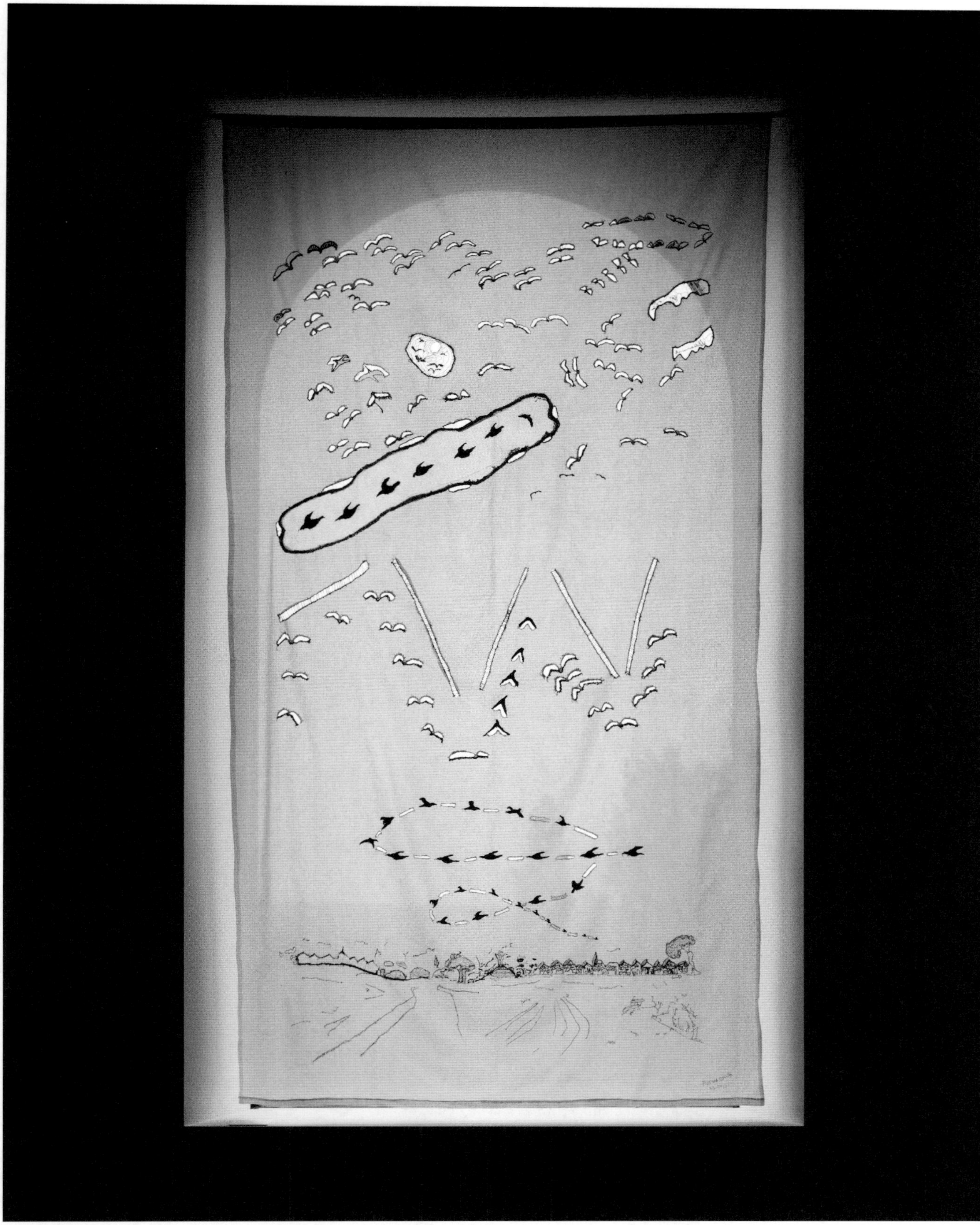

Embroidery on fabric, 267 × 451 cm

For dOCUMENTA (13), Onur furnished the windows of her room in the newly renovated Neue Galerie – now a perfectly white cube – with curtains embroidered with images of birds. Corresponding to the nature outside, her poetic intervention subtly rearranges the light and atmosphere in the otherwise empty room.

dOCUMENTA (13), Guidebook, (Ostfildern: Hatje Cantz, 2012), 168.

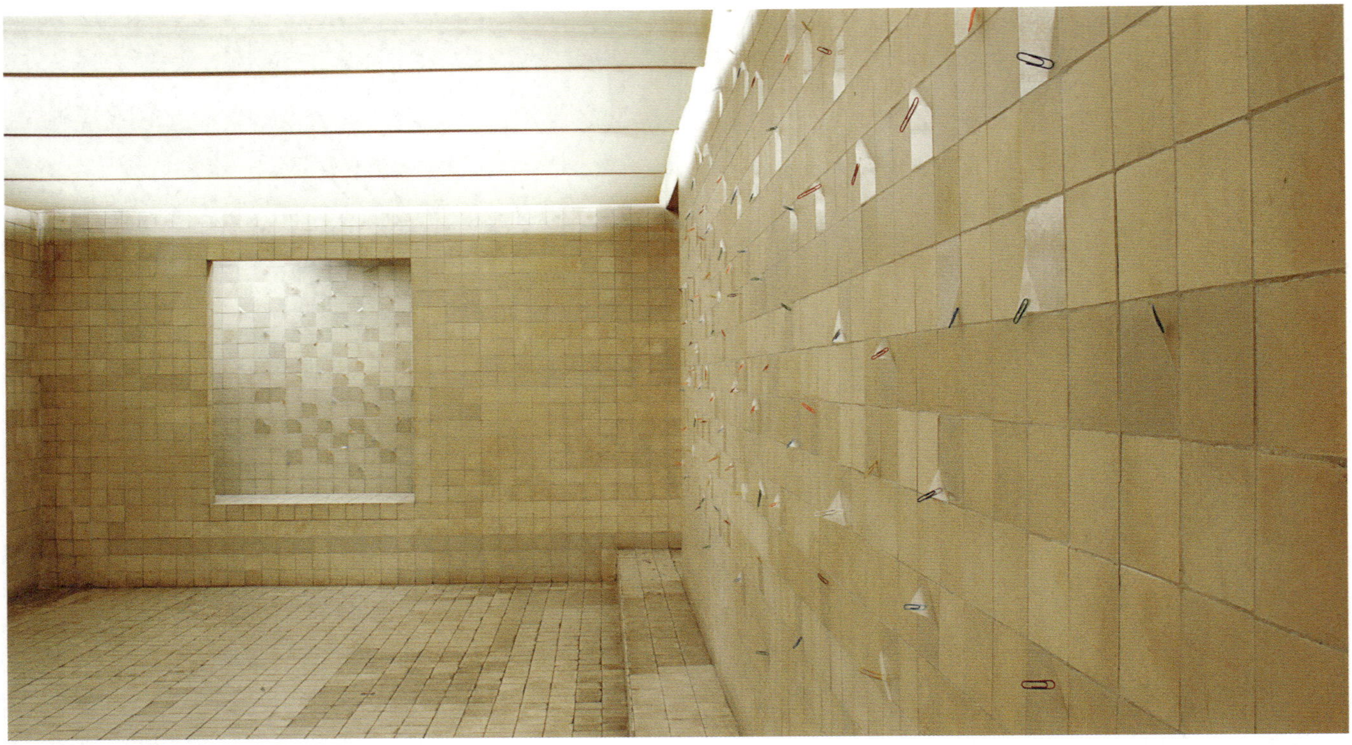

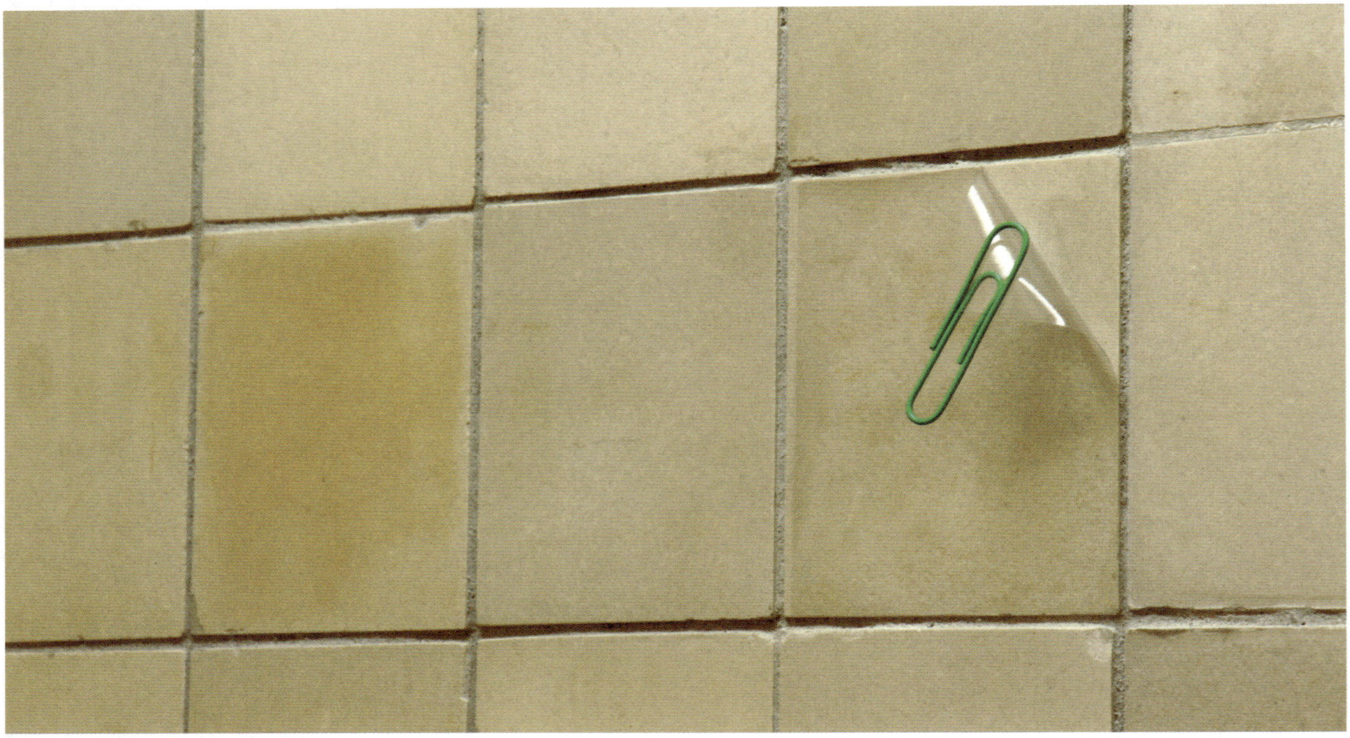

Site-specific installation, variable dimensions

A slightly below ground level storefront, Maçka Sanat Galerisi is covered wall-to-wall in light brown-yellow tiles, from the steps leading to the entrance of the gallery into the gallery itself. Onur has employed the unusual space as both a catalyst and central element for *Variations*, with the muted lighting acting as a subtle deviation from the very particular architecture. The installation in the front room, at first glance, is almost invisible. From a distance, the tiled wall seems to be speckled with colorful dots, but upon closer inspection, the work is revealed as barely but fully three-dimensional. Each tile is covered in sheer plastic that is peeling off on one edge, weighted down by colorful paper clips. Here we find a subtle threat of being dismantled – the fragility of the material in clear contrast to the flawless yet weathered unity of the tiles, suggesting a graphic modernism, self-contained albeit wounded. [...] *Variations* is Onur's markedly respectful de-construction of the venue of an institution with which she shares a long-term affiliation. At the crux of this exhibition is the artist's gentle, playful handling of the gallery's architecture and tricky setting. Once again, she has chosen to treat the space as an accomplice, striking an uneasy alliance with its quirks and limitations. It is an impossible gesture acknowledging the fledgling experimentation that has defined her work from the very beginning.

Merve Ünsal, excerpt from 'Füsun Onur's "Variations" at Maçka Sanat Galerisi, Istanbul,' *art agenda*, November 8, 2012, www.art-agenda.com/criticism/234025/fsun-onur-s-variations-at-maka-sanat-galerisi-istanbul (last accessed: 20 December 2021).

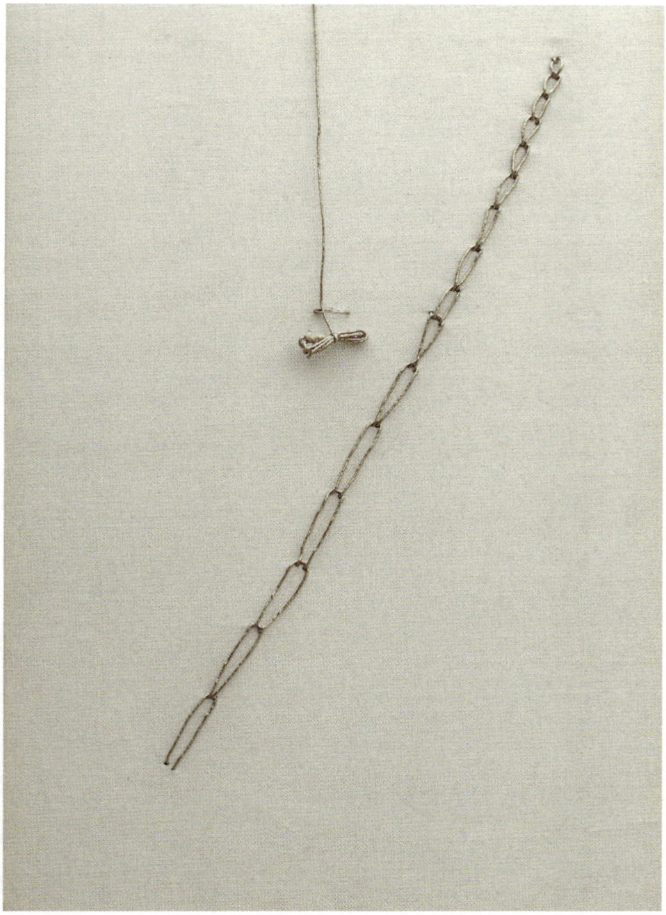

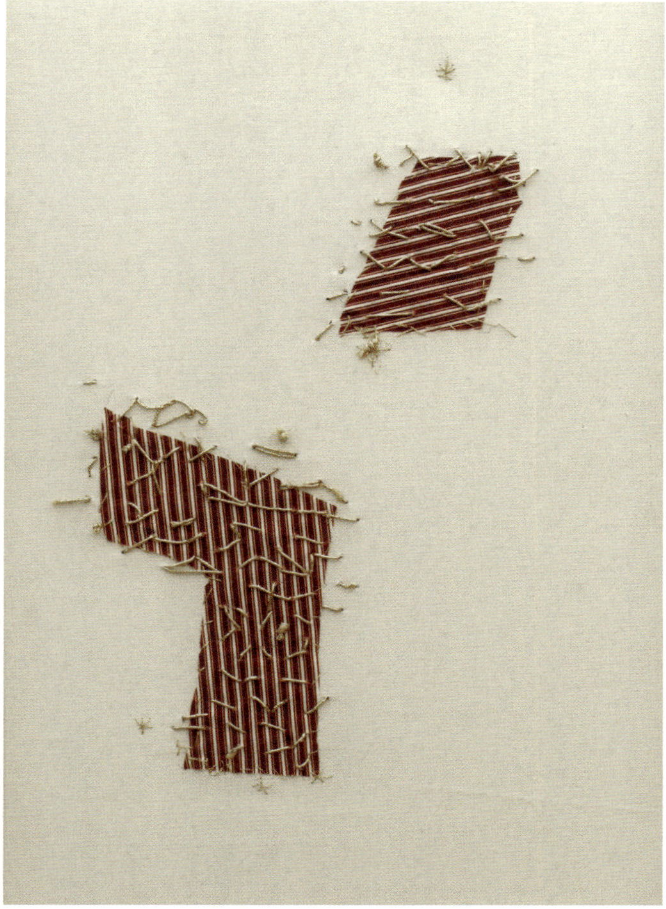

(Left) Mixed media on canvas
(Right) Mixed media on canvas

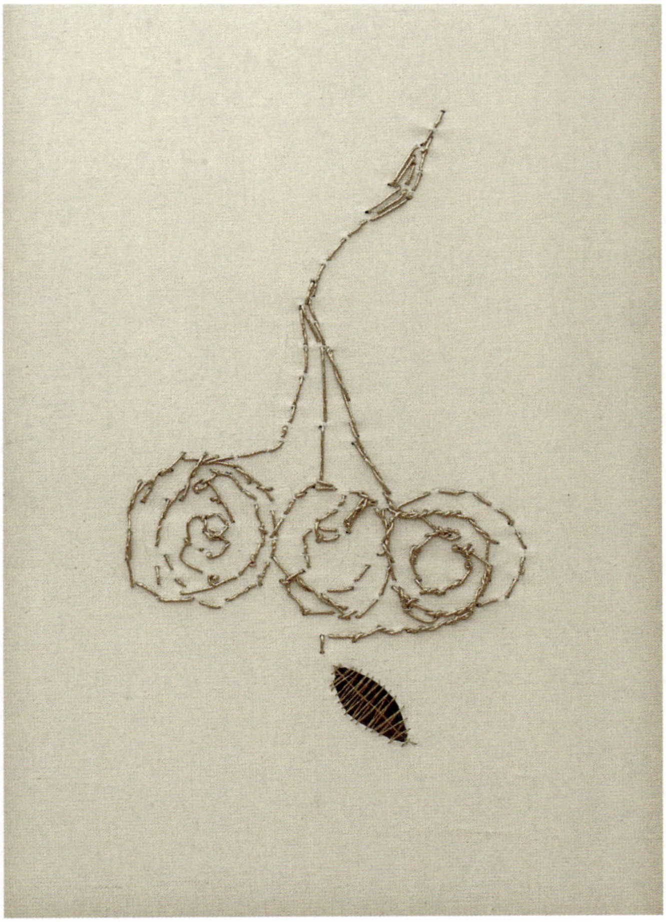

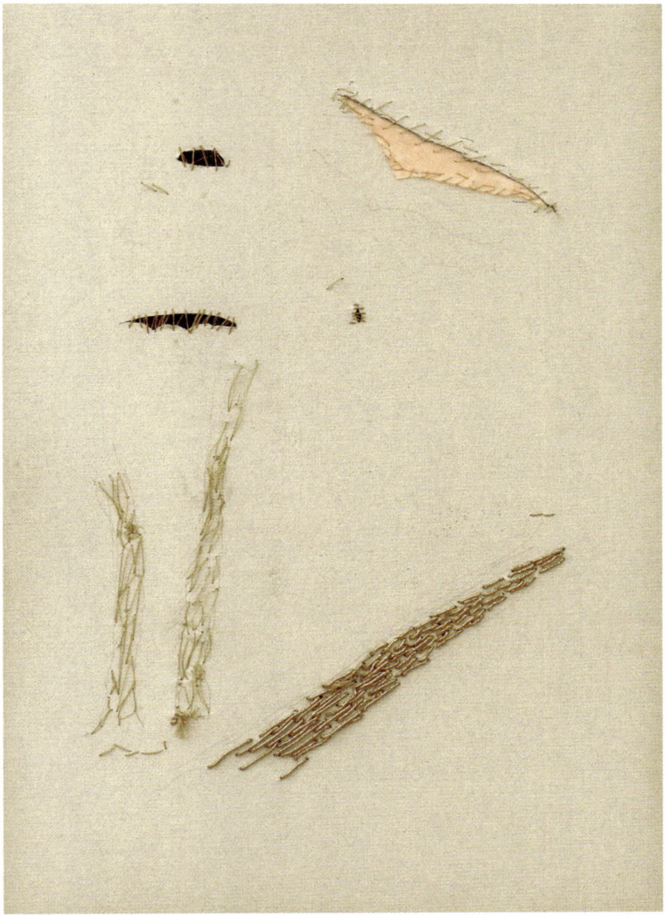

(Left) Mixed media on canvas
(Right) Mixed media on canvas

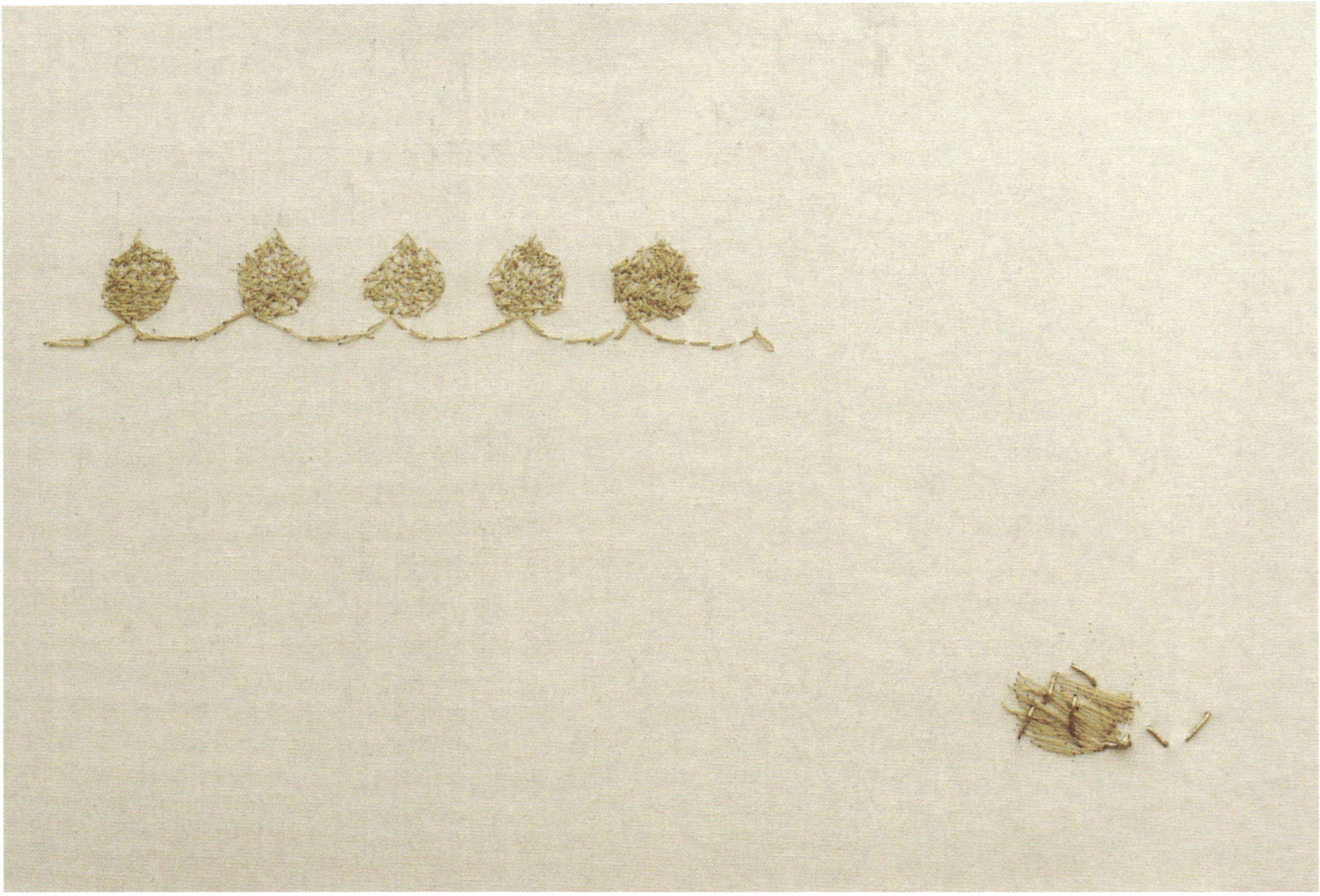

Mixed media on canvas

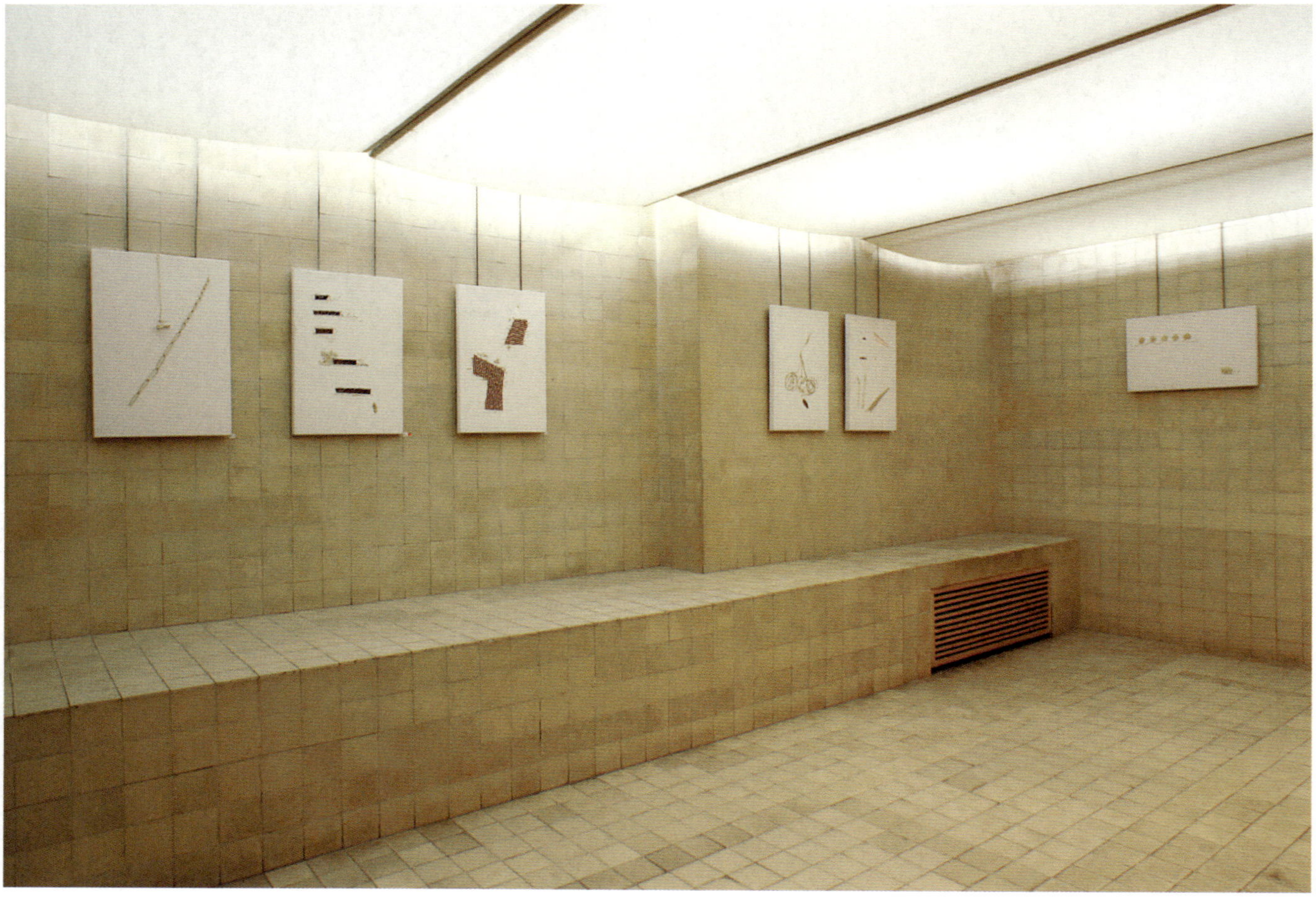

Installation view from the exhibition *Variations*, Maçka Art Gallery, 2012

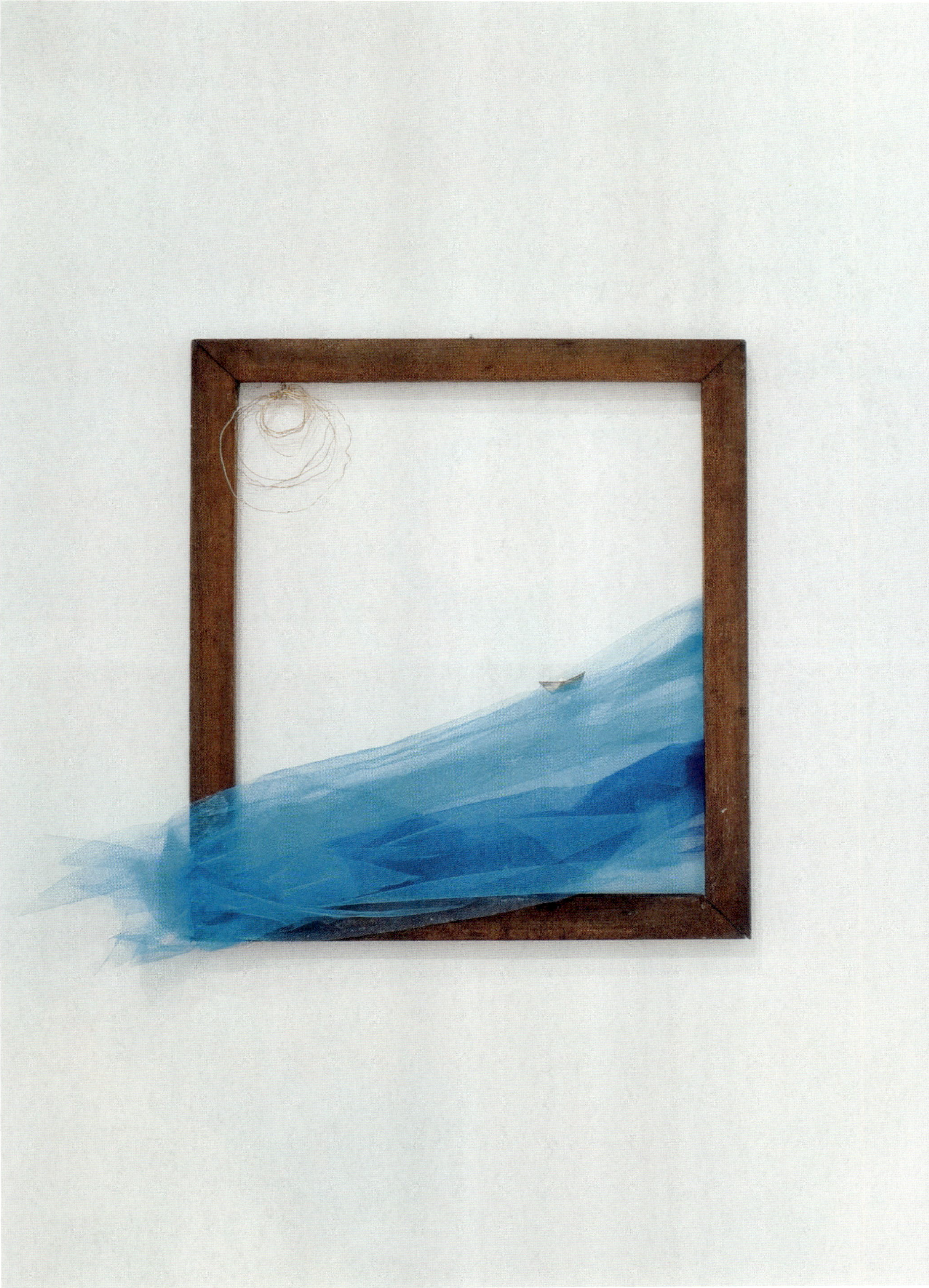

Wood, tulle, wire, 60 × 66 cm

2013 MIRACLE (SYMPHONIC POEM)

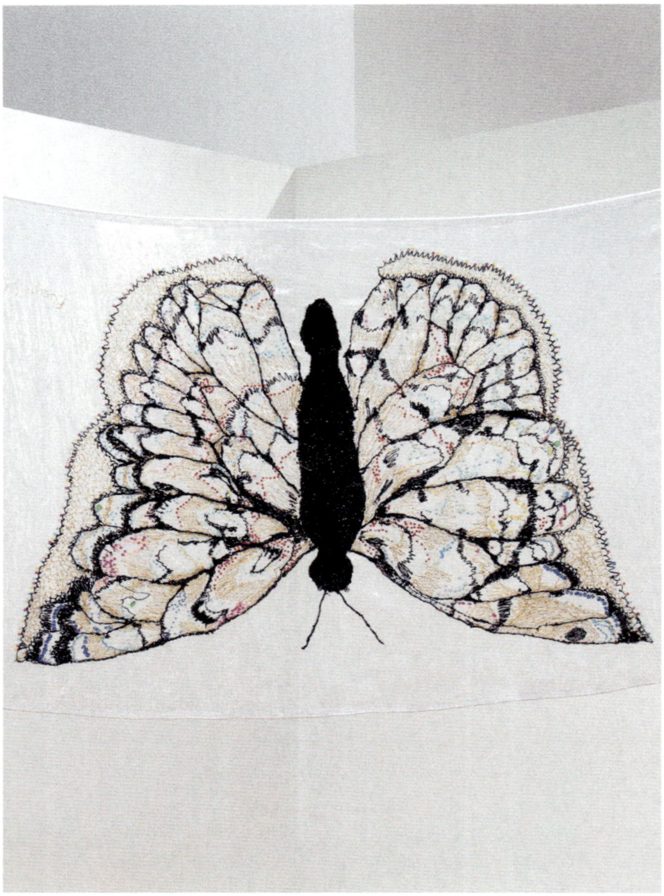

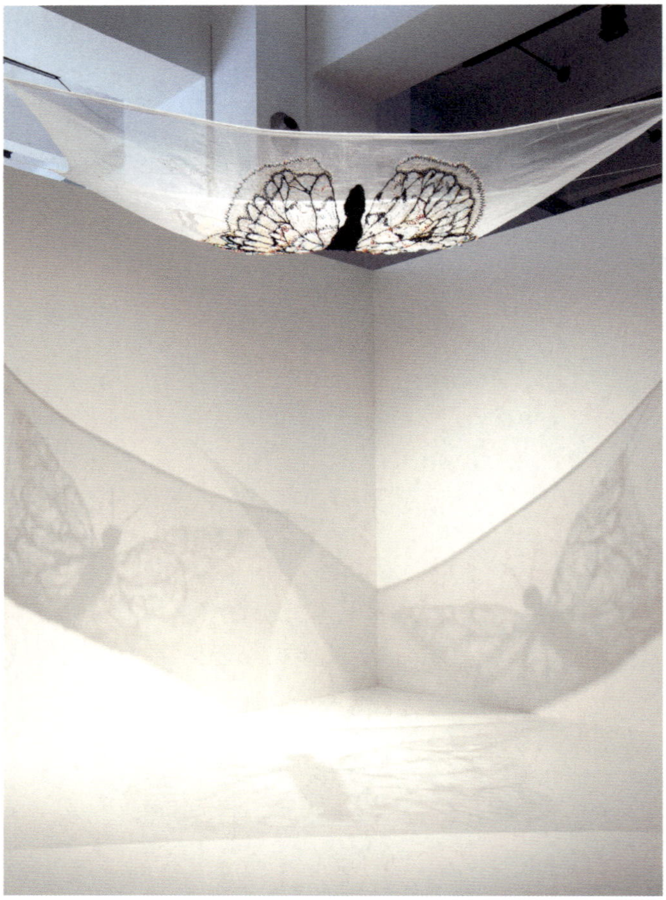

Textile, beads, 300 × 150 cm
Installation view from the exhibition *Signs Taken in Wonder*, MAK Vienna, 2013

2014 INTERVENTION FOR THE MAK COLLECTION TEXTILES AND CARPETS

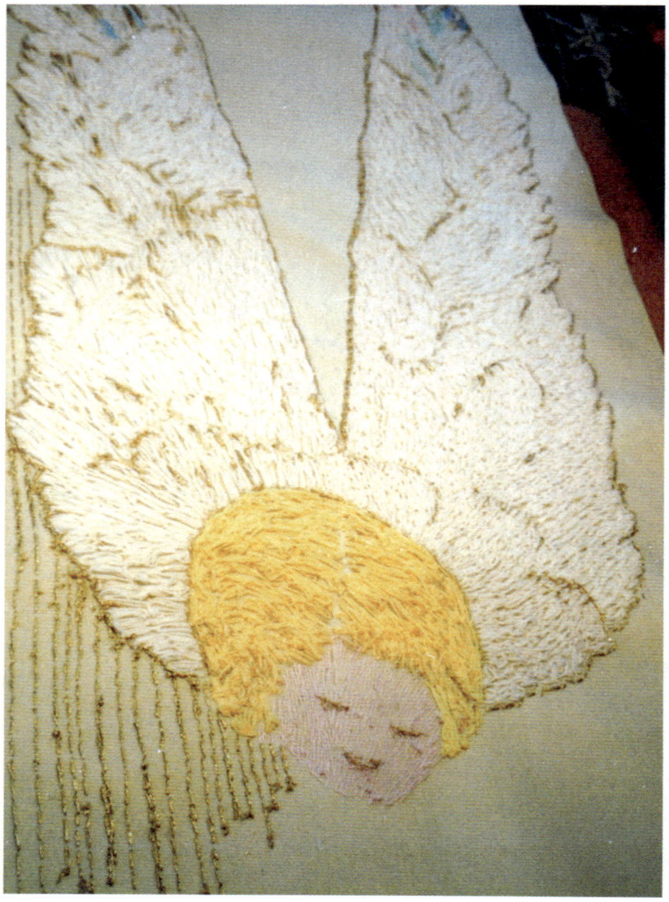

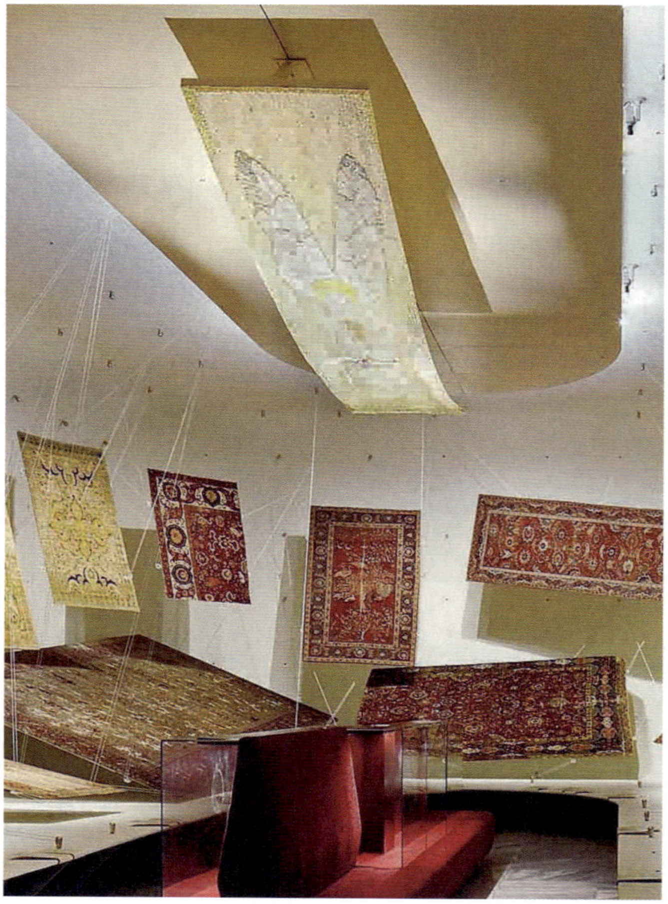

Embroidery, felt, glass, metal, textile, 450 × 100 cm
Installation view from the MAK Vienna Permanent Collection Carpets, 2013

2014 PEGGED

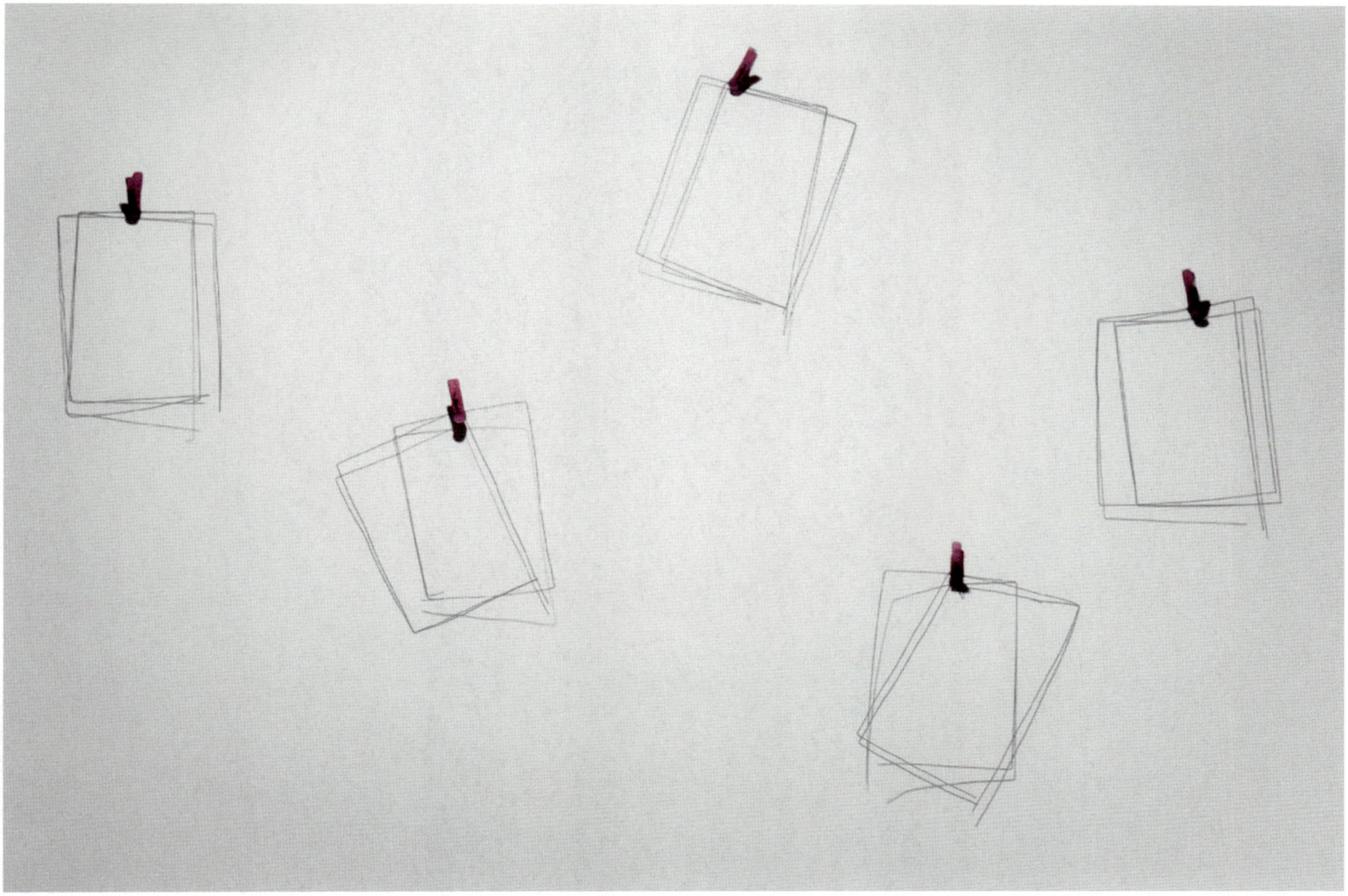

Metal string, plastic pegs

2014 (1972) MIRRORED LABYRINTH

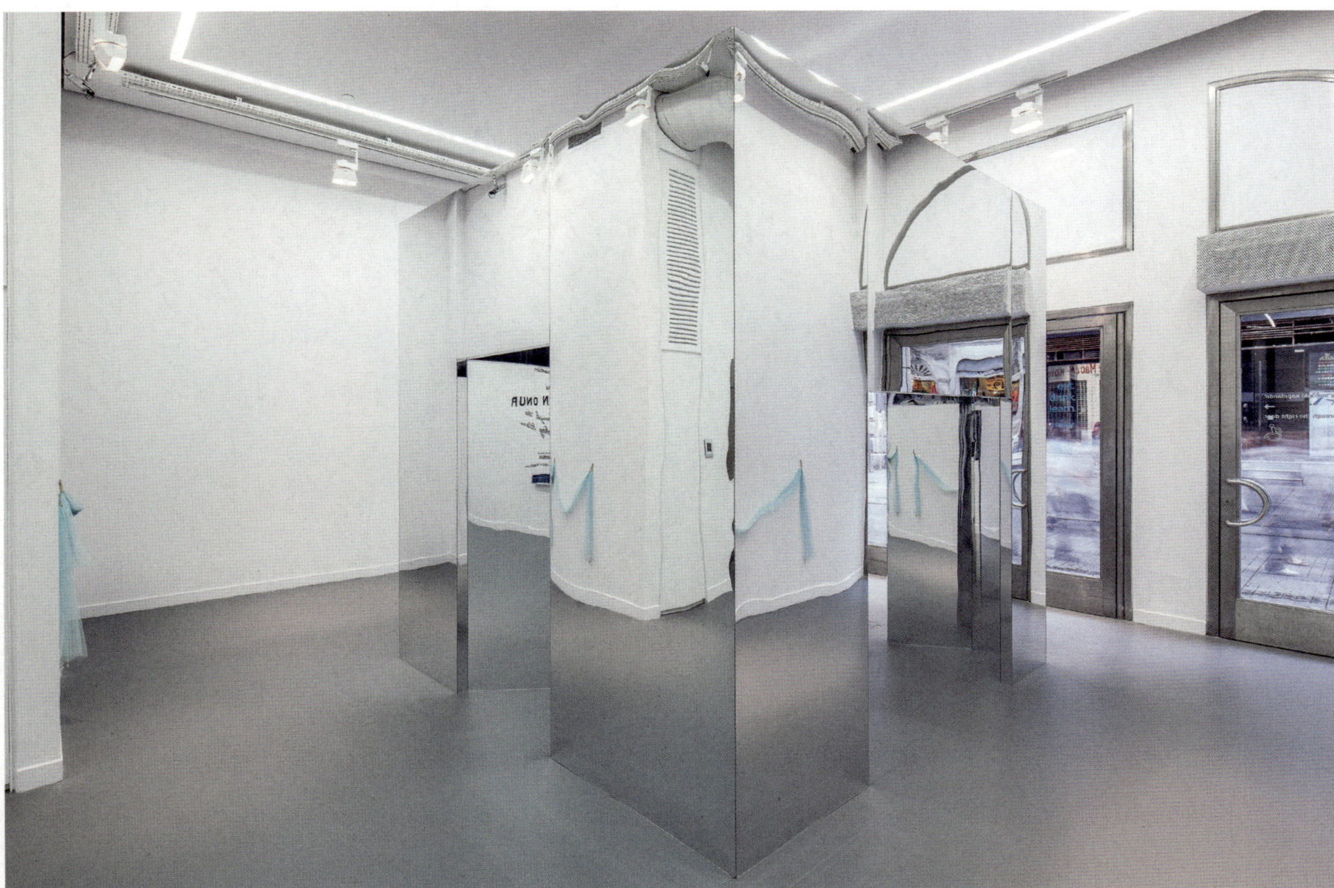

Wood, Plexiglas mirror, 300 × 300 × 300 cm (see *Untitled*, p. 109)

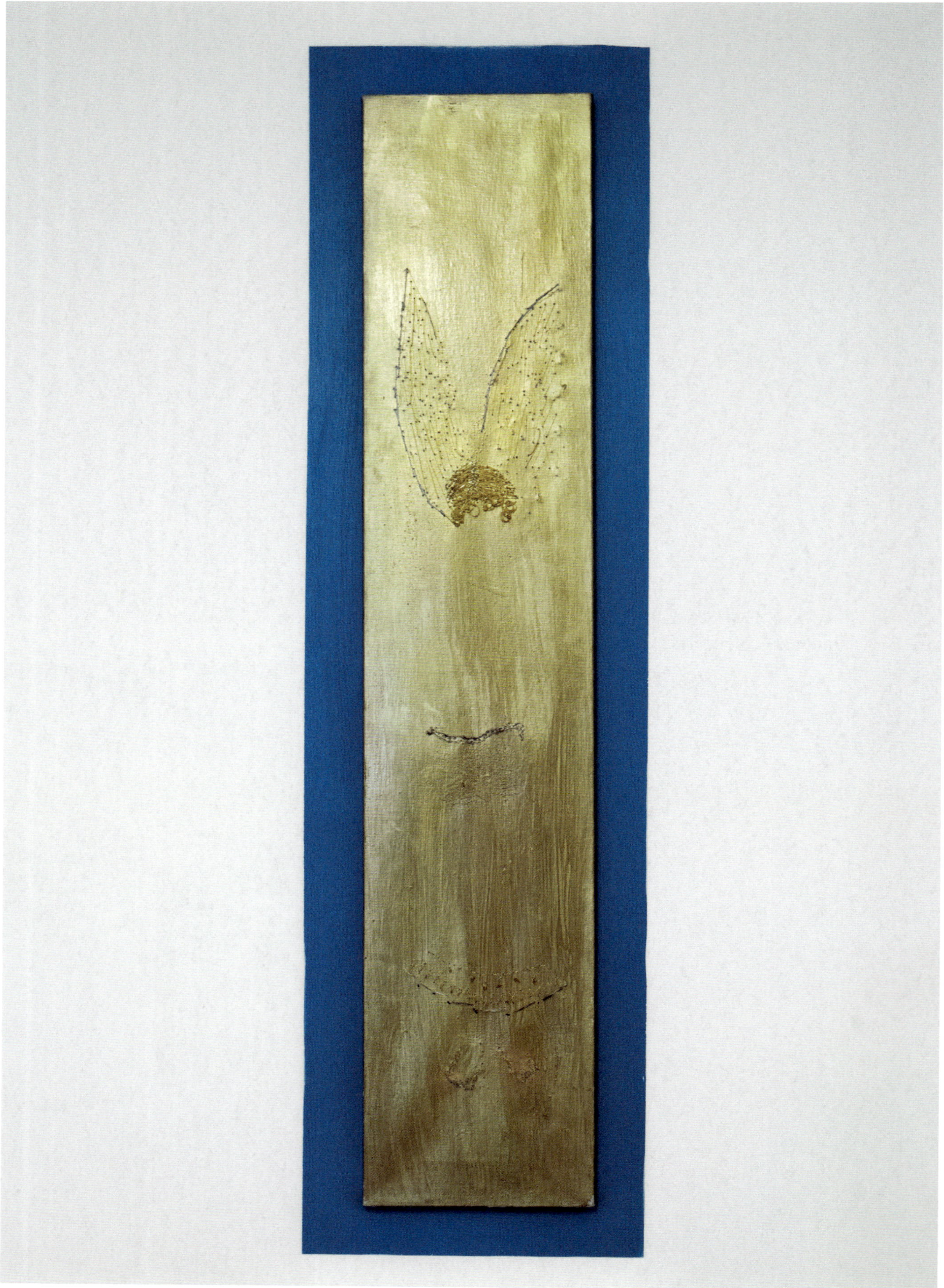

Mixed media on canvas, 20 × 101 cm

And then went down to the ship,
Set keel to breakers, forth on the godly sea, and
We set up mast and sail on that swart ship,
Bore sheep aboard her, and our bodies also
Heavy with weeping, so winds from sternward
Bore us out onward with bellying canvas,
Circe's this craft, the trim-coifed goddess.
Then sat we amidships, wind jamming the tiller,
Thus with stretched sail, we went over sea till day's end.

Canto I by Ezra Pound, part of the audio installation

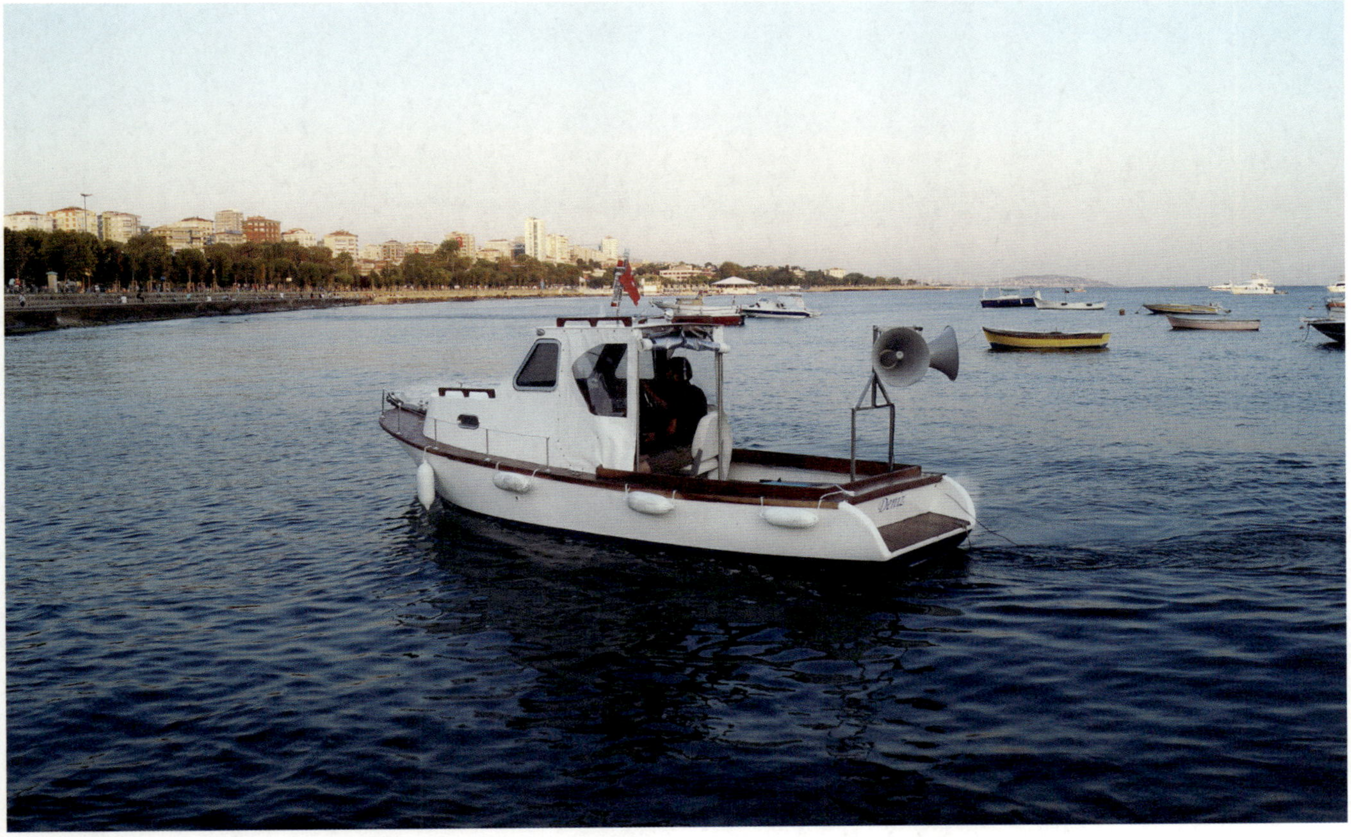

Fishing boat with sound installation

Füsun Onur's artwork is a small white boat with the sound of a poem being read out loud. It travels up and down the Bosphorus.

Excerpt from the 'Introduction,' 14th Istanbul Biennial catalogue

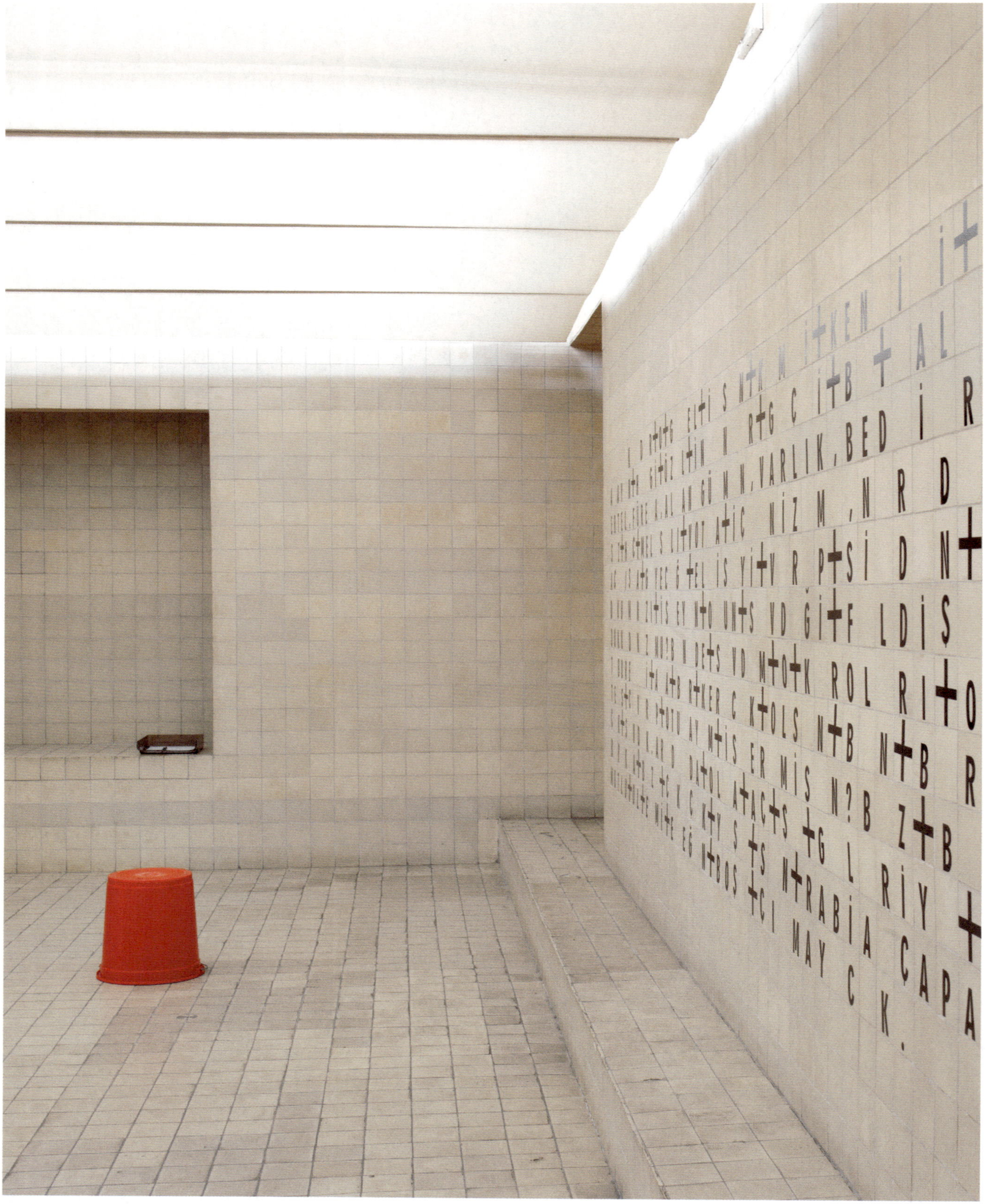

Site-specific installation, dimensions variable

Once we step in through the door, a bundle of (+) s, and bits and pieces of vowels and consonants lie before us. You stand astonished in front of this installation, which for all intents and purposes is clearly a puzzle. Conceptual art is engaged with puzzles. There's a platonic dalliance between them. Blending with the site-specific references to each individual visiting the gallery, the most serious issues signify a very important and never-ending problematic of memory. [...] Over time, precisely like in the other works of Füsun Onur, as you enable empathy, have patience, and surrender yourself to the volatile candidness of this work, you begin to solve that puzzle. That puzzle turns into a timid remnant of the gallery's history and of Füsun Onur and Rabia Çapa's shared destiny.

Evrim Altuğ, excerpt from *The Smile of a Girl of Honour*,* https://www.artfulliving.com.tr/sanat/onurlu-bir-kiz-cocugunun-tebessumu-i-5863 (Last accessed: 20 December 2021).

*In a play on words, the original title alludes to the artist's last name Onur, which means 'honour' in Turkish.

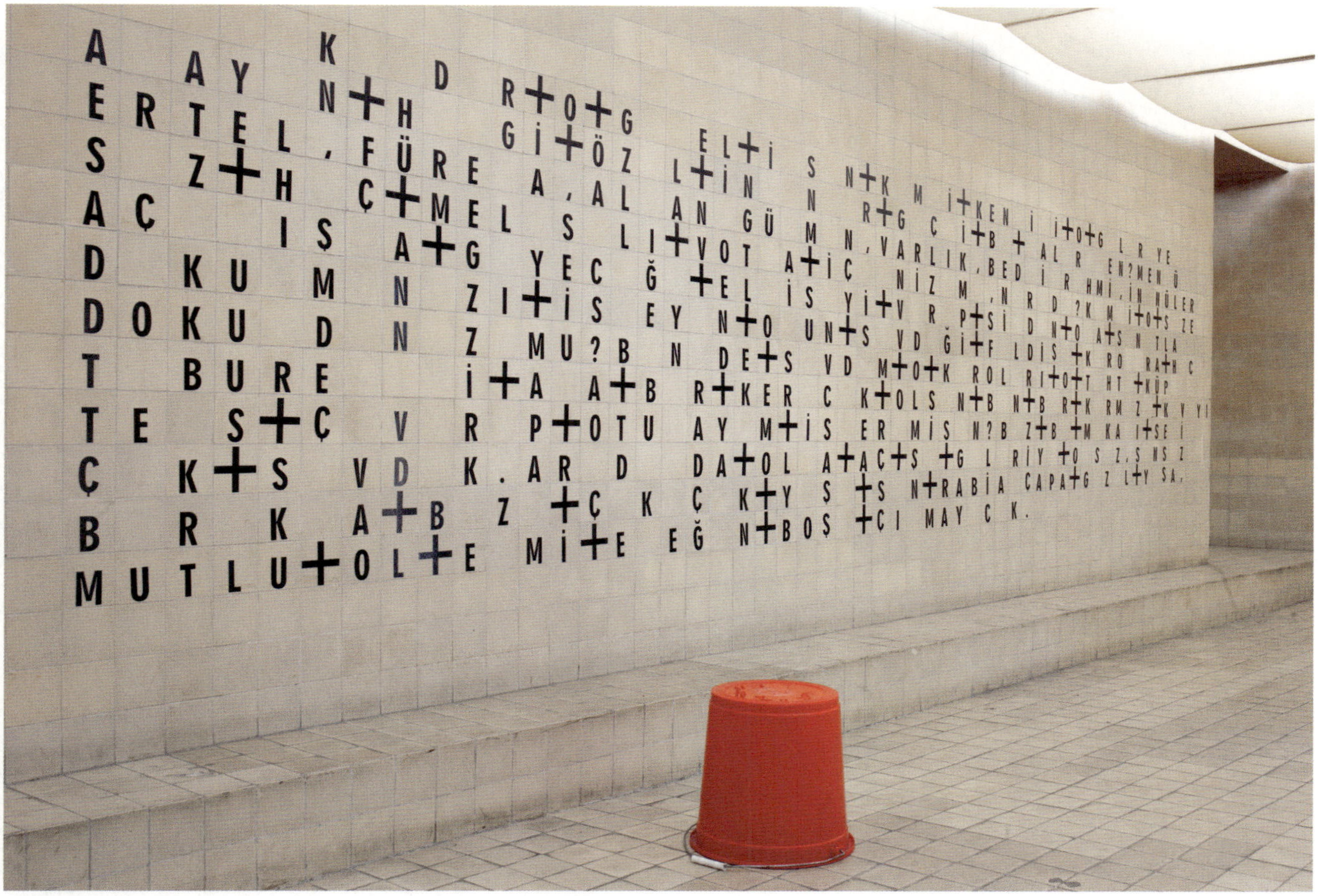

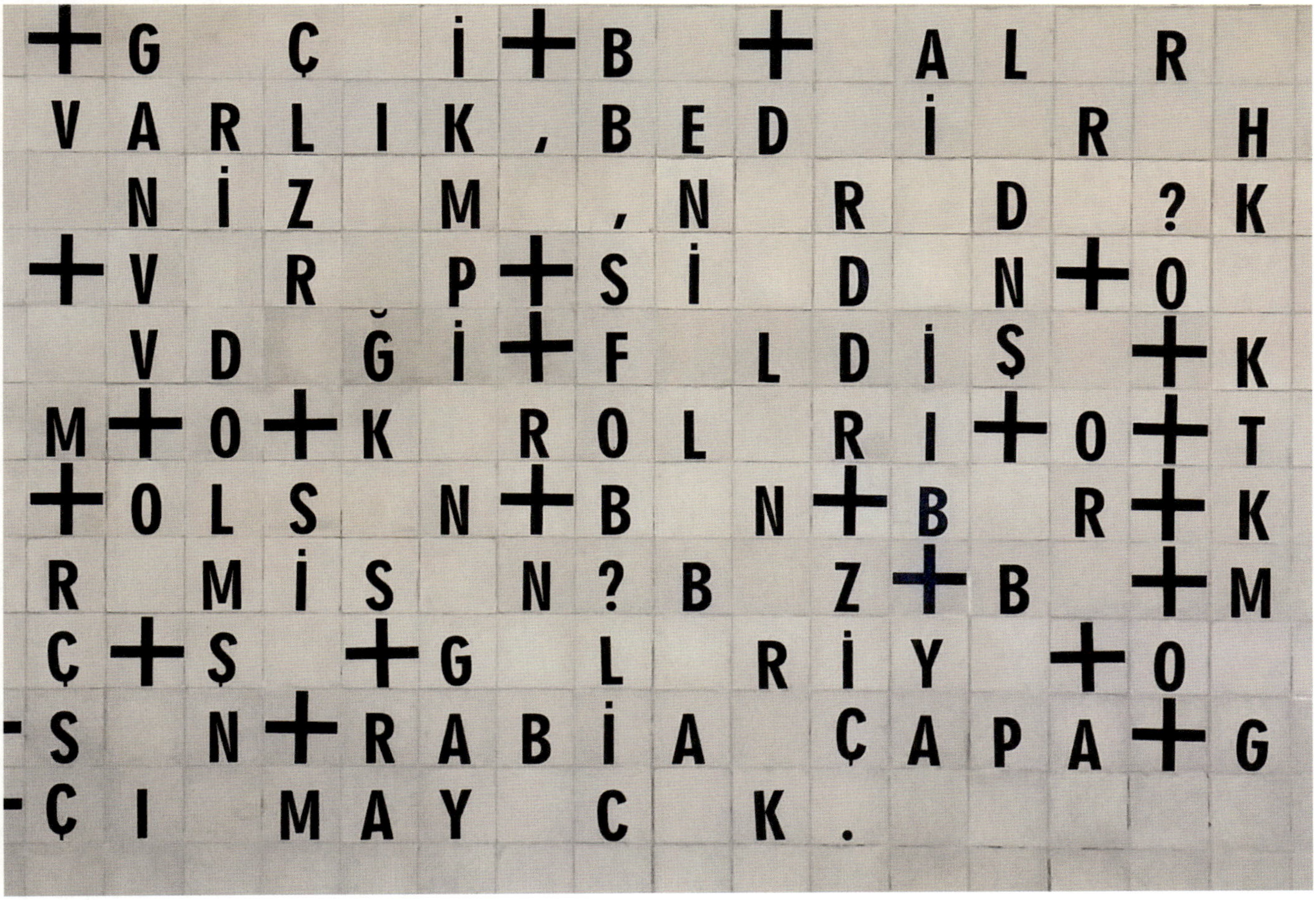
+ G Ç İ + B + A L R
V A R L I K , B E D İ R H
N İ Z M , N R D ? K
+ V R P + S İ D N + O
V D Ğ İ + F L D İ Ş + K
M + O + K R O L R I + O + T
+ O L S N + B N + B R + K
R M İ S N ? B Z + B + M
Ç + Ş + G L R İ Y + O
S N + R A B İ A Ç A P A + G
Ç I M A Y C K .

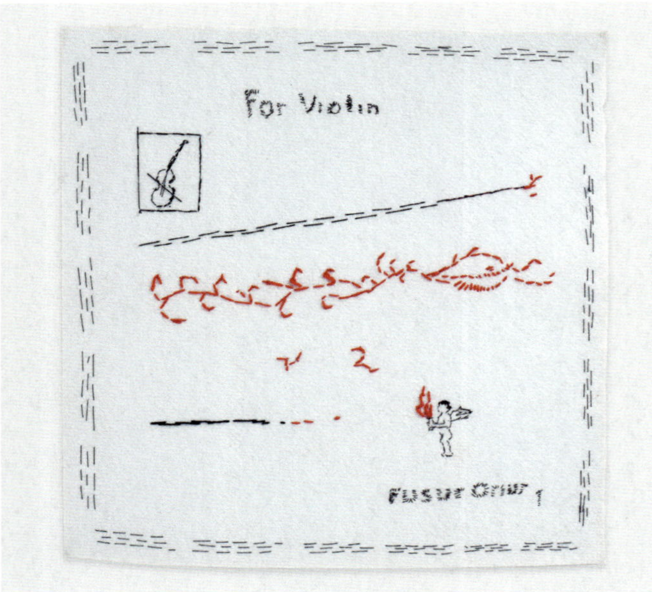

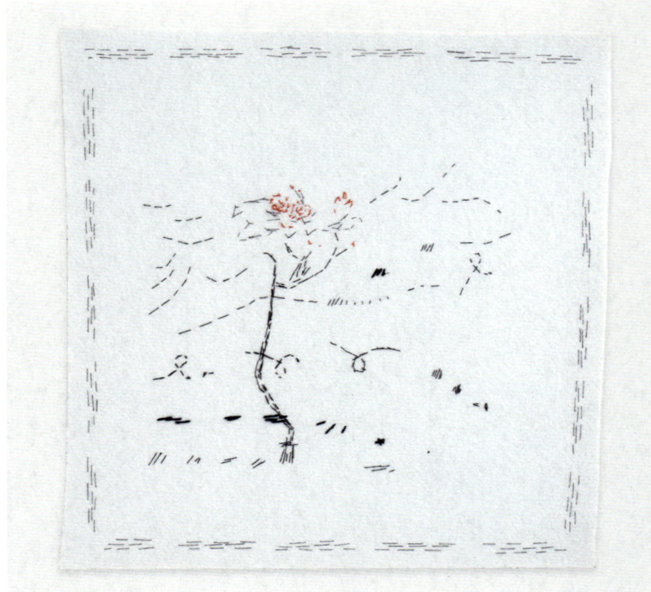

(Left) Embroidery on felt, 51 × 50.5 cm
(Right) Embroidery on felt, 50 × 48 cm

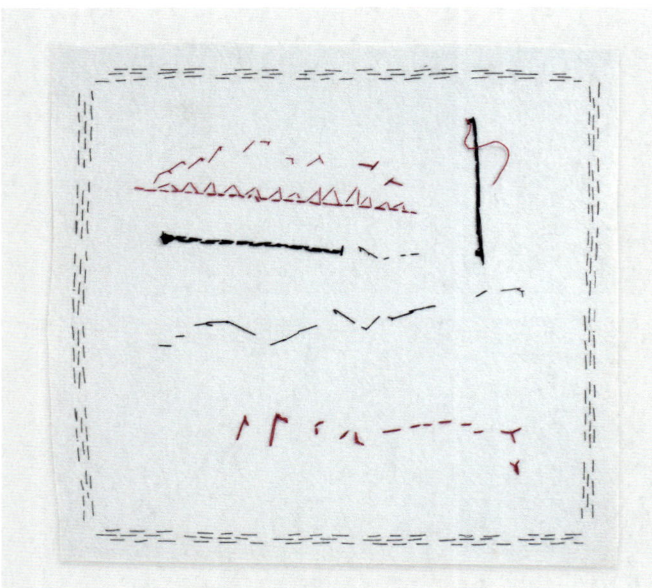

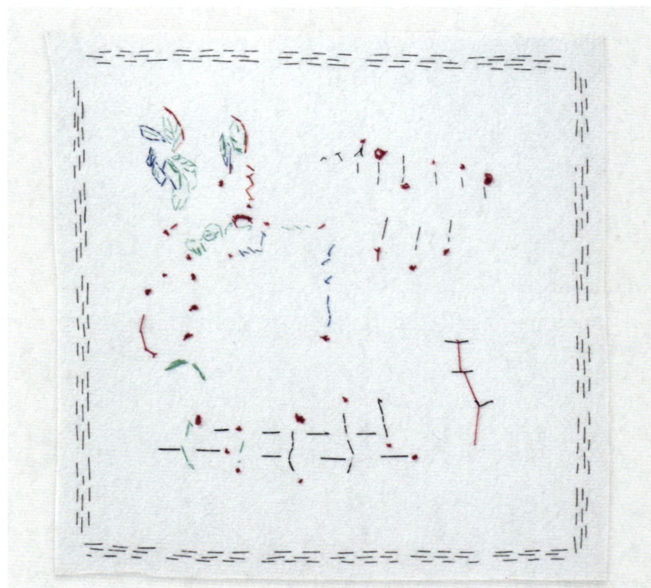

(Left) Embroidery on felt, 50.5 × 53.5 cm
(Right) Embroidery on felt, 51 × 51 cm

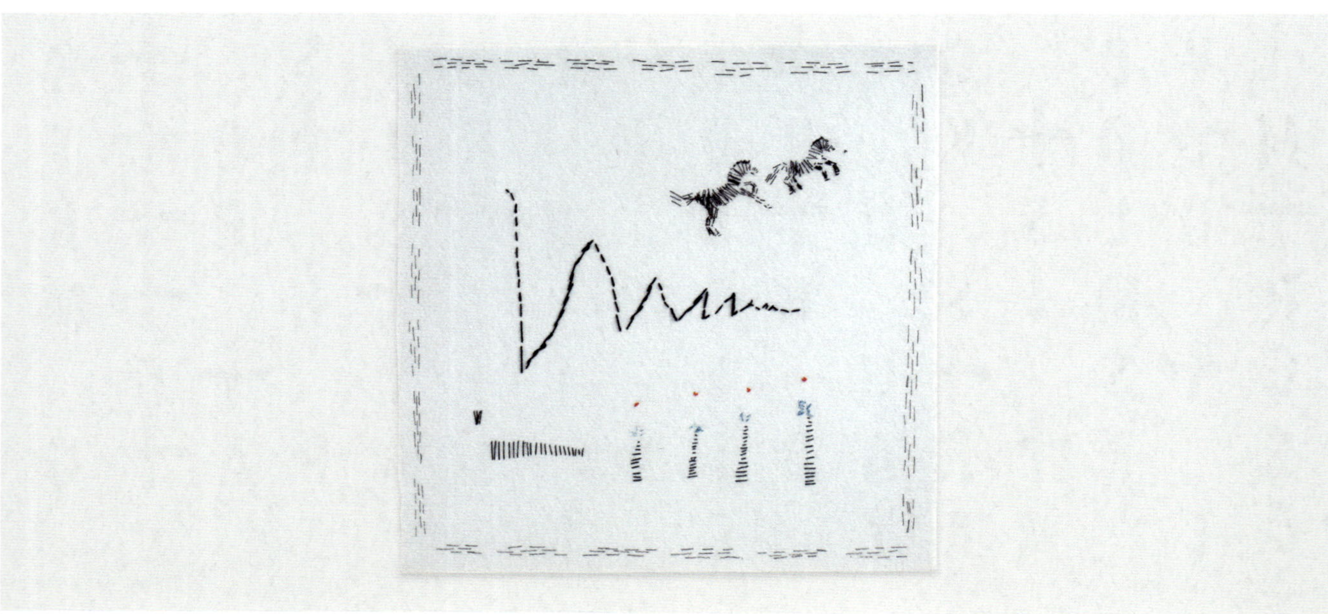

Embroidery on felt, 50 × 50 cm

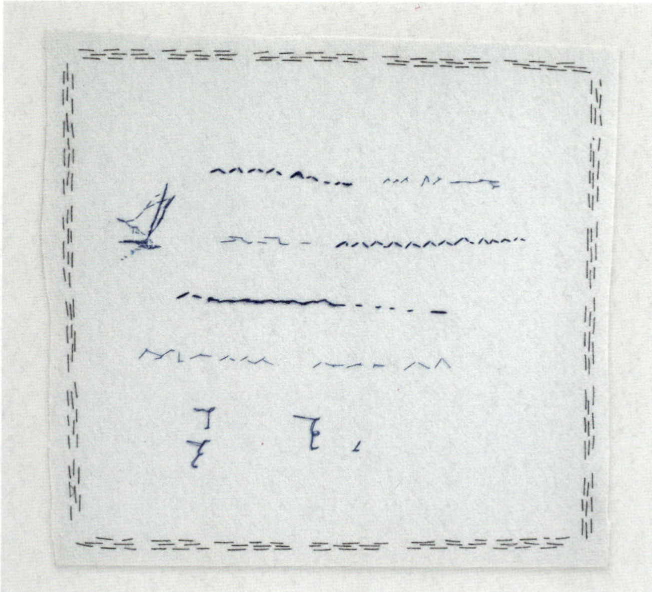

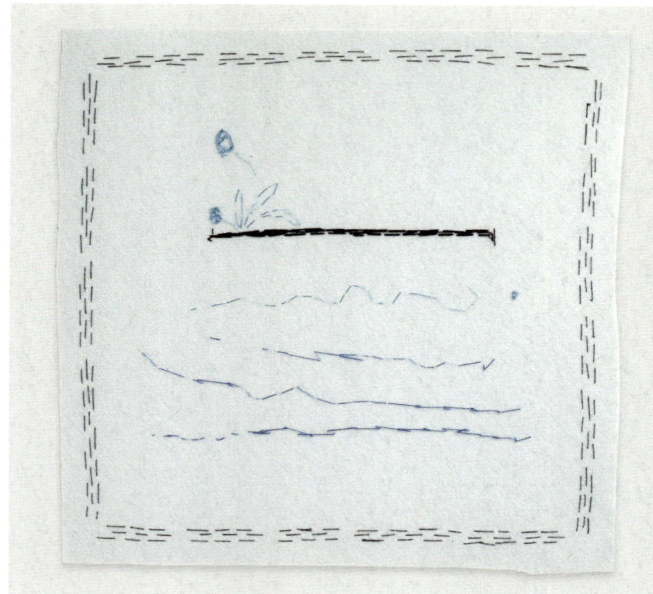

(Left) Embroidery on felt, 49 × 52 cm
(Right) Embroidery on felt, 50 × 49.5 cm

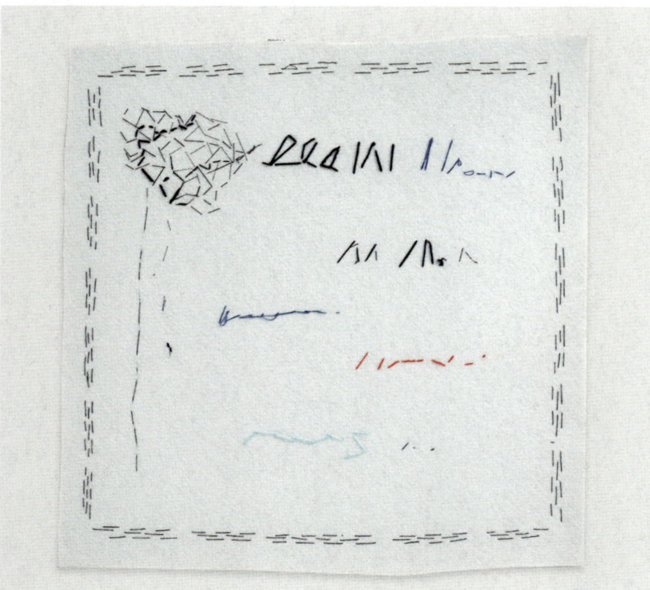

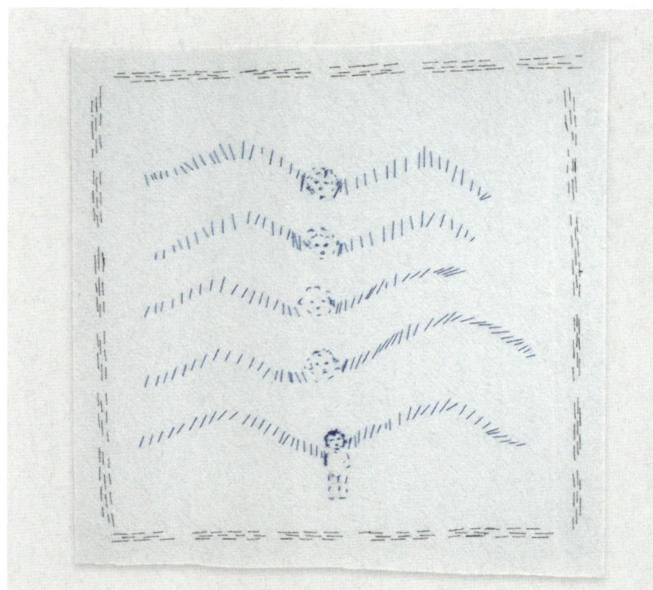

(Left) Embroidery on felt, 52 × 51 cm
(Right) Embroidery on felt, 50 × 50 cm

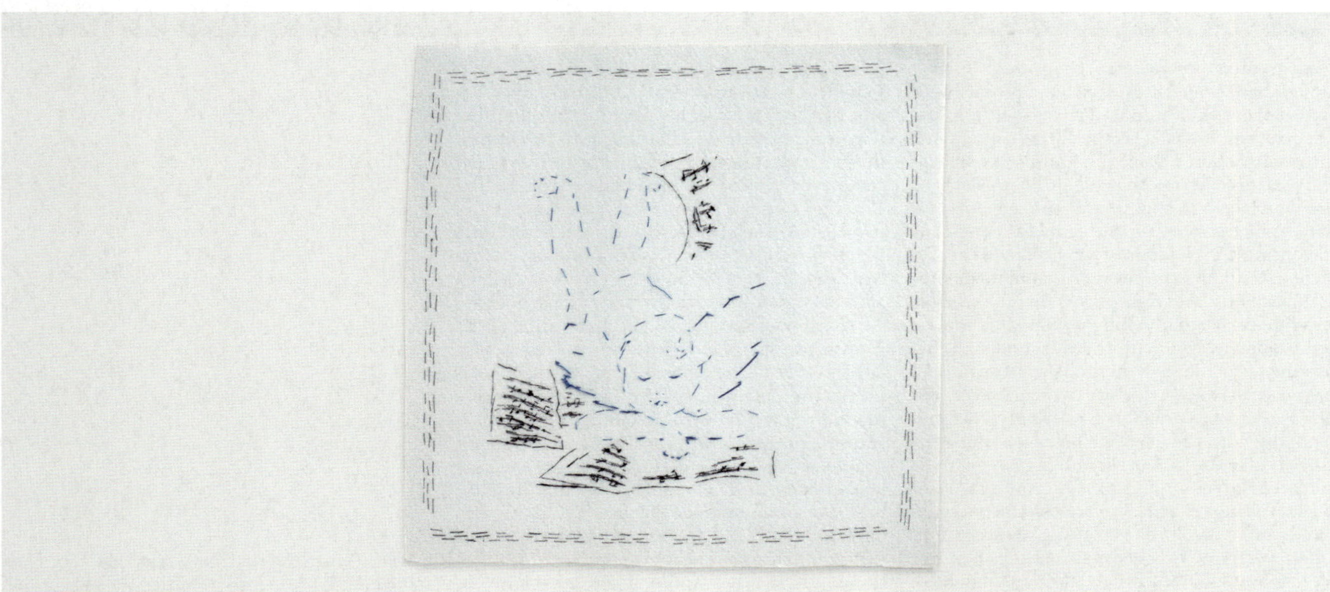

Embroidery on felt, 50 × 50 cm

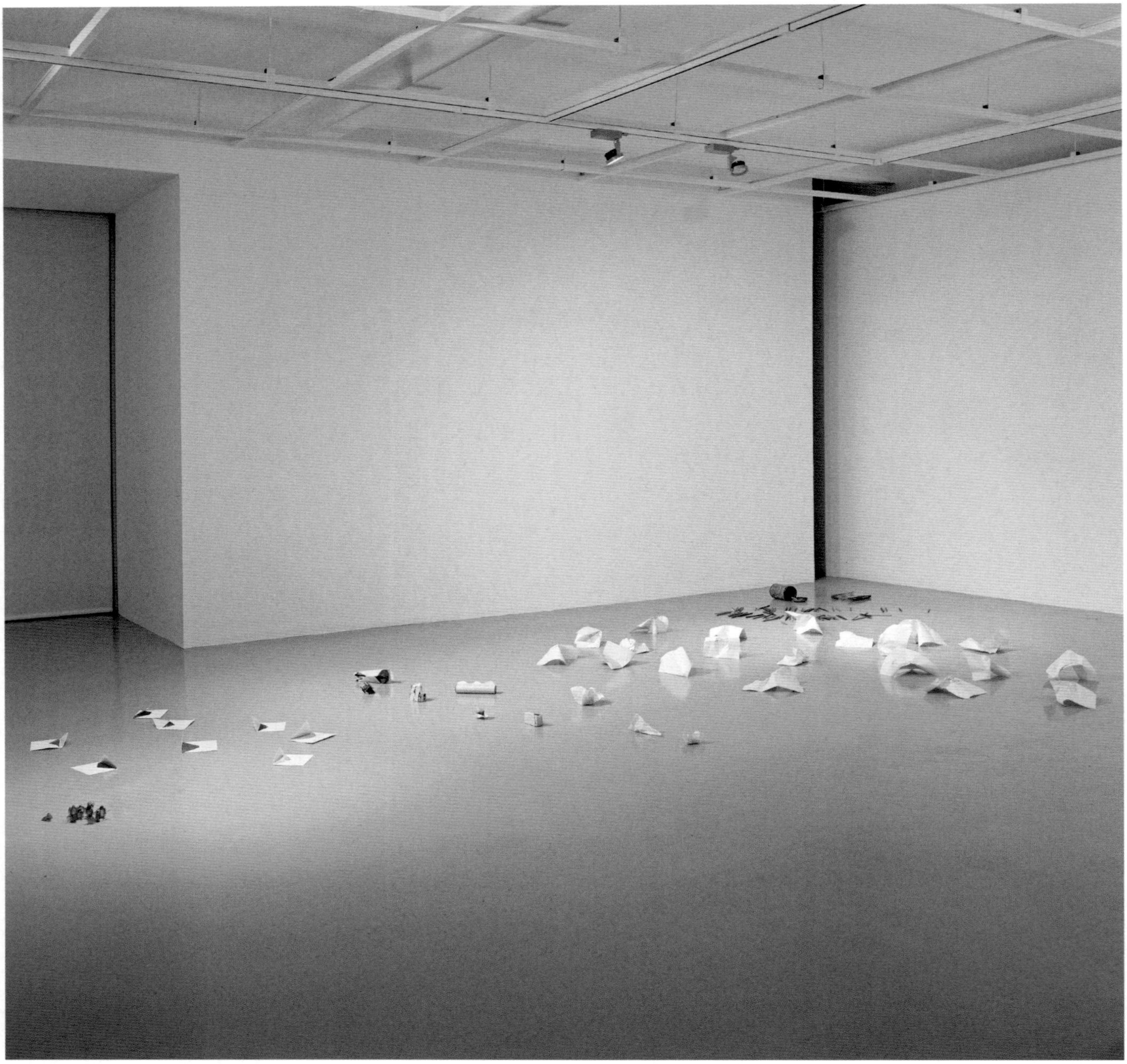

Installation, dimensions variable

I was greeted by objects on the ground which at first glance seemed scattered but closer up were installed over a designated space, set in a specific rhythm. It was as if the entire content of a suitcase snatched from the hand of its bearer had scattered across the gallery floor. As I bent over and began to examine, I realised a procession of objects starting with a metal pencil box disgorging all its coloured pens; followed by discarded, crumbled, or perhaps abandoned notes with scribbles and designs on them; and then toys like tables and violins wrapped in papers; and beads and colourful threads; and right before them the illegible (perhaps written but not posted, or perhaps never written) multicoloured letters that were probably never sent; and finally ending with the perfume bottles wrapped in tulles beside the thread resembling a rope in the colour of the sea in Kuzguncuk. As I got closer to the writings, I began to browse the personal notes that read, 'Zorba is playing a trick on me,' 'I had worn my purple dress at that opening,' 'oh a seagull caught a fish,' 'ten springs have blossomed into roses.' I approached the scents, I expected them to smell but I think they didn't. I smell something or am I making it up, I began to wonder. I was bending further and further and was afraid of falling into the installation. I was telling myself: I think I do smell something. Realising that I had gotten too close I decided to move away. Was I afraid of getting myself too much involved with the work? As I stepped further back wishing to look at this installation from a distance, I drew close to a wall on which I saw the white picture holders. As if the photographs it held had fallen (or as if awaiting the photographs to be taken), only two or three of the holders remained still hinting at the four sides of the frame. Definitely made *For Careful Eyes*. I couldn't figure out if these holders were waiting for the future photographs or were dedicated to the loss of the past ones. It was as if I was seeing the picture in it, just like I had smelled the scent. Later, I understood that I was invited to a play... There is a childlike lightness to this play, but if you feel its weight, in other words, if you see the invisible, then its sediment slowly settles inside you.

Larissa Araz, excerpt from the article *Would You Remember?*, https://www.border-l-e-s-s.com/hatrlar-msn (last accessed: 20 December 2021).

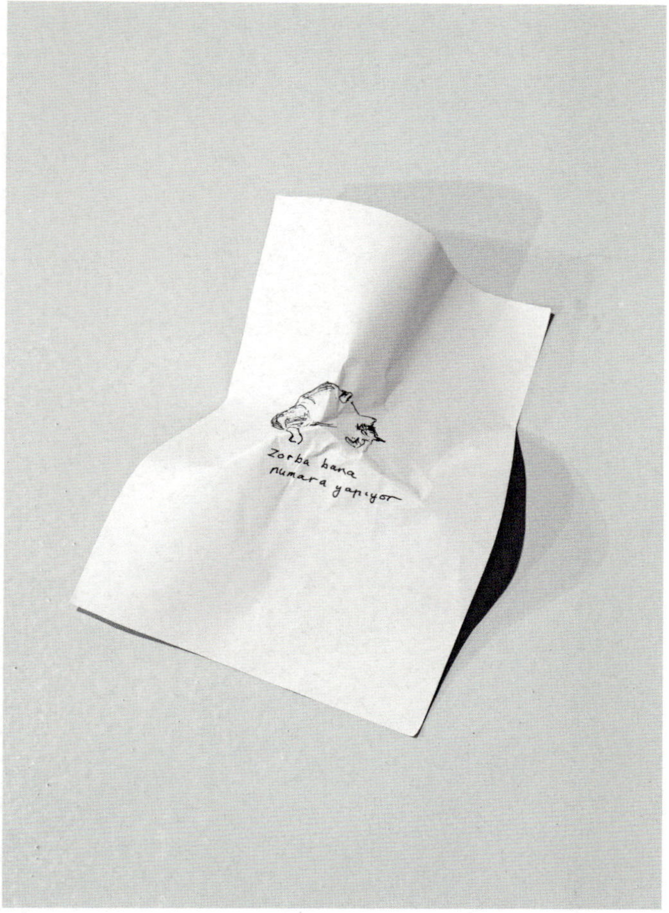

(Left) Installation, dimensions variable
(Right) White gussets for framing space, variable dimensions

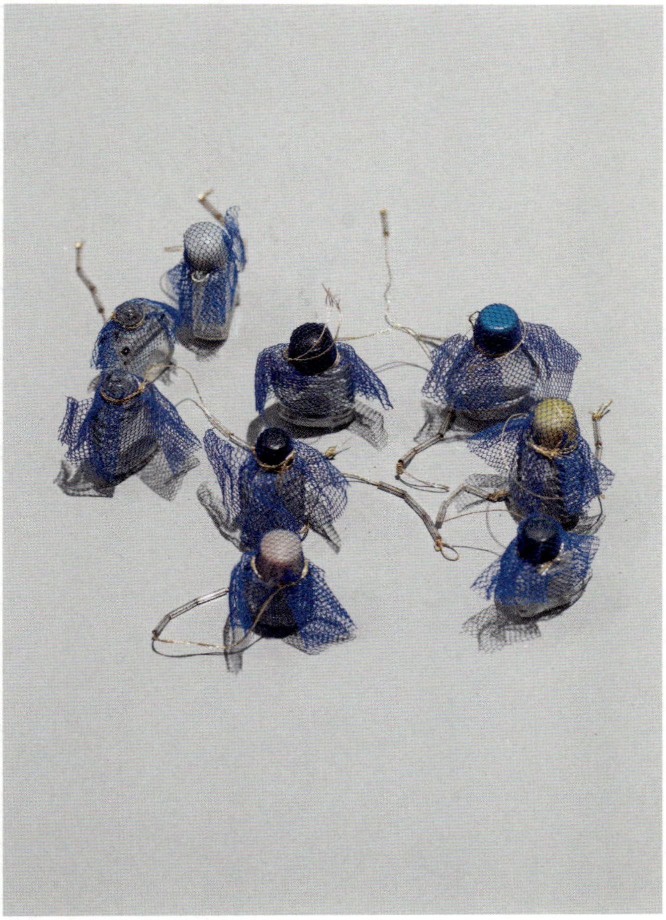

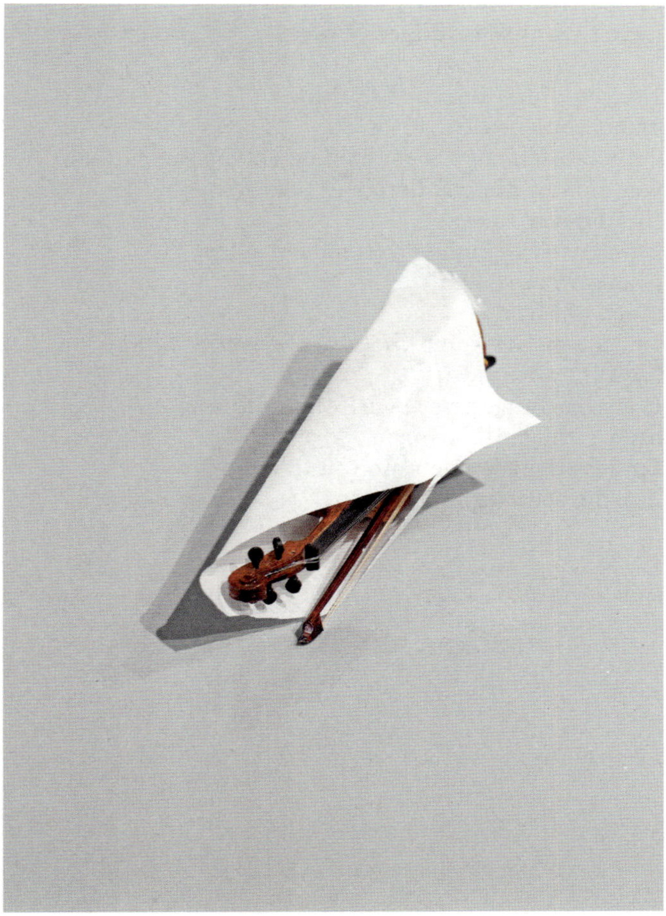

Installation, dimensions variable

I am here! Where are you
are you upstairs
it is very dark, cloudy pouring rainy outside
it is very cozy inside as usual;
this weather reminds me of a day years ago
do you remember
it was a day like this and I was in Berlin for a group show, again
just as I was ready to go out my umbrella was lost.
I was at the door, helpless, hopeless, gloomy
Then I heard: Here is your umbrella madame
May I help you? I was stunned
it was you. My hero, you
wanting to go out, may I accompany you

we walked talked laughed and stopped
Suddenly you broke the silence
May I invite you to my house
to rest, drink a tea
We are just in front of my house
So our story began. So forth…
do you remember too?
What did you say?
It is very dark. I will go upstairs.

Now you are gone forever
nothing left here
Not even a note for me

I hope you have gone away
Didn't want to talk face to face

No, you didn't tell me anything
about your health
Only 3 weeks ago we talked on the phone
you did not die, my hero can not die
I will never know
I am ready to believe you moved away
I hope you are healthy
and went away
I wish you are somewhere in the world, happy
I will never know
It will be buried here with the umbrella
unless the walls whisper.
I'm leaving the perfume you liked here.
Maybe, someday (or one day) you will come back.

Poem by Füsun Onur, part of the audio installation in gallery space

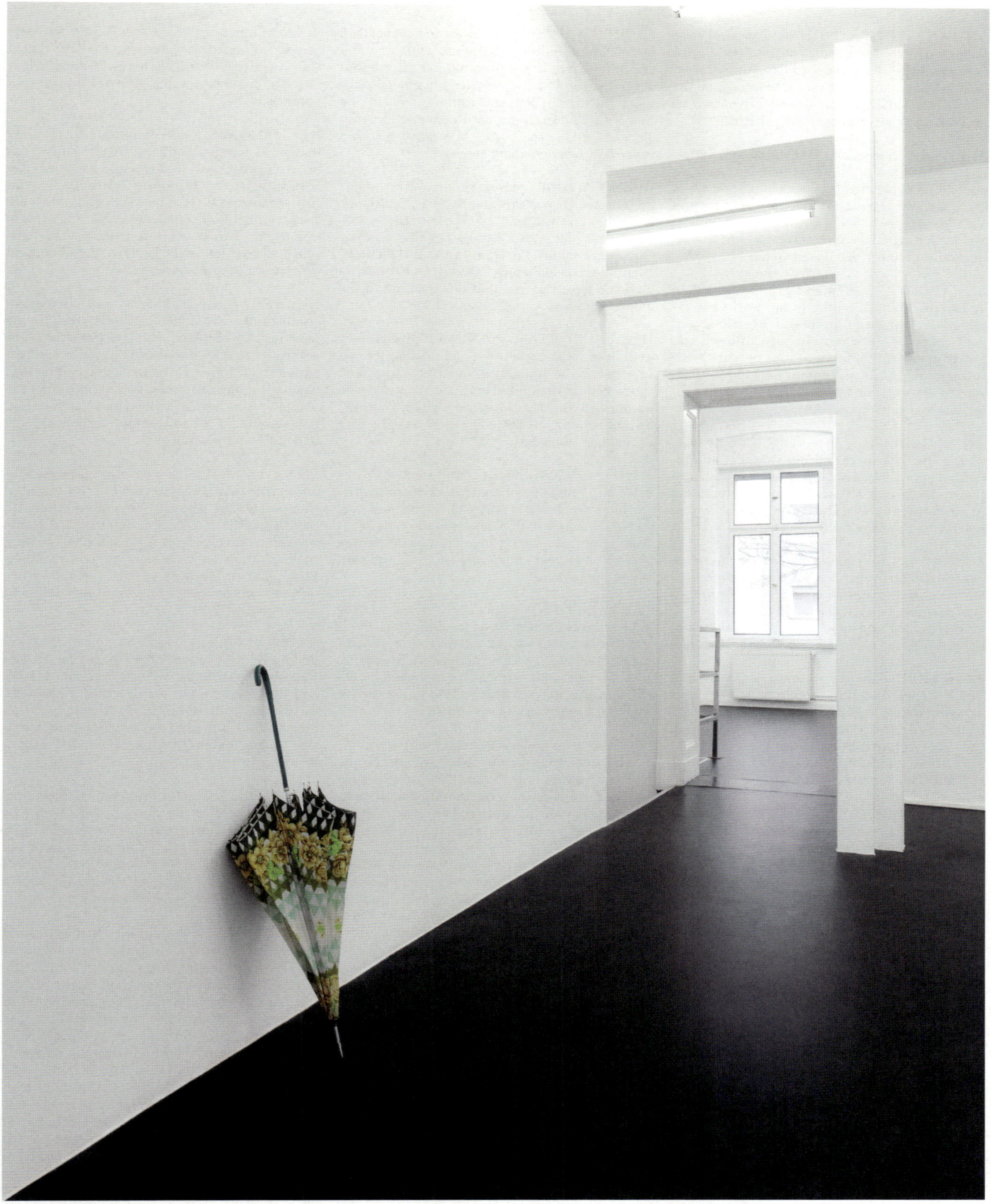

Audio installation, scent produced by Cise Osmanoglu from givaudan & glokal, scent diffusors, umbrella

[...] But despite my request to fill the space, Füsun filled nothing. The gallery I sent her came back empty – devoid of objects, but indeed once more full of memories. She sent a manuscript with words to be pronounced by someone else; a perfume to be spread in the space; and a request 'to find a lost umbrella'– the only object meant to be in the room. Füsun invites us to listen to the voice, breathe in the fragrance, and observe the umbrella, made for accompanying and protecting one's path between one place to another, to shelter from rain or perhaps hail. Left in the room is the memory of all that has been, her personal memories fading into everyone else's, and the promise that this story will continue.

Jennifer Chert, excerpt from the exhibition text *This story will continue*, ChertLüdde Berlin, 2021.

AHU ANTMEN (Prof Dr) is faculty member at Sabancı University Faculty of Arts and Social Sciences, Visual Arts and Visual Communication Design Programme. Her research focuses on the reflections of modernity and gender dynamics in modern and contemporary art practice.

ALEV ERSAN is a poet, translator, and artist. Her recent area of inquiry has been literary, queer, and experimental forms of post-mortem texts and how translation both as a practice and a mode can speak to and within the site of grief and mourning. She is currently working on a bilingual text and video based on her research.

ANNA BOGHIGUIAN is an Egyptian-Canadian artist of Armenian origin. In her works she explores the impact of historical, economic and political events. Boghiguian has exhibited regularly in international museums and art institutions, biennials and major solo exhibitions worldwide, and her works are in important international collections.

ANNE BARLOW is Director of Tate St Ives, where she oversees its programme of exhibitions, displays, residencies, commissions, education and research. She was formerly Director of Art in General, (NY), and Curator of Education and Media Programs at the New Museum, (NY).

ASLI SEVEN is a curator and writer based between Istanbul and Paris. Her research focuses on infrastructure, landscape and performativity of documents, with an emphasis on fieldwork, ficto-criticism and co-creation. She is a member of AICA and C-E-A; a collaborator with ICI.

AYŞE EREK is an art historian and a writer. She has contributed to numerous publications as writer and editor on exhibiting practices, histories of modernity and politics of aesthetics in the urban context. She worked as a researcher in Istanbul and Berlin and is a faculty member at Kadir Has University.

CAROLYN CHRISTOV-BAKARGIEV is an Italian-American writer, art historian and exhibition maker. She was the director of dOCUMENTA (13) in 2012 and curator of the 14th Istanbul Biennial in 2015. Currently, she is the Director of Castello di Rivoli Museo d'Arte Contemporanea and Fondazione Francesco Federico Cerruti in Turin.

CHUS MARTÍNEZ is the head of the Institute of Art Gender Nature of the FHNW Academy of Arts and Design in Basel, Switzerland. She is also the curator of the Ocean Space, Venice and curator at large of The Vuslat Foundation, Istanbul. Previously she has served as curator and artistic director at various art institutions.

DEFNE AYAS has served as a director and curator in several cultural institutions and research initiatives across the world, including the Netherlands, China, the United States and Russia. Ayas was recently the artistic director of 13th Gwangju Biennale (2021).

DENİZ GÜL's artistic practice investigates how language performs as text, sculpture and space. She is known for her novel-like exhibitions featuring installations. Her works have been exhibited in significant institutional exhibitions and museums. Her solo exhibitions to date are *Scratch and Surface* (2021), *Deniz Gül, Meydan* (2020), *Loyelow* (2016), *B.I.M.A.B.K.R.* (2013) and *5 Person Bufet* (2011).

FATİH ÖZGÜVEN is a writer and translator. He worked as editor at İletişim Publishing and taught cinema, literature, and art at Istanbul Bilgi University. His articles have been published in various journals and newspapers; he has translated numerous literary works into Turkish, and is the author of a novel, a collection of essays, and short stories.

GREGORY VOLK is a New York-based art writer and curator. He writes regularly for Hyperallergic and other publications, and contributed a catalogue essay for Ayşe Erkmen's exhibition *Plan B* in the Turkish Pavilion at the 2011 Venice Biennale. His book-length essay on Katharina Grosse's painting installations appears in the monograph *Katharina Grosse* (2020).

HERA BÜYÜKTAŞCIYAN's multidisciplinary artistic practice explores notions of absence and invisibility, the fluid nature of memory, time and space. She has exhibited in institutions and arts events including New Museum, British Museum, Toronto Biennial, 56th Venice Biennale, The Jerusalem Show VII.

H.G. MASTERS is a writer and Deputy Editor & Deputy Publisher of *ArtAsiaPacific* magazine in Hong Kong. He is editor of the annual *ArtAsiaPacific Almanac*, a survey of the year in art from across Asia, and has written numerous catalogue essays on leading modern and contemporary artists.

IWONA BLAZWICK has been Director of the Whitechapel Gallery, London, since 2001 and is a critic, broadcaster and lecturer. She was formerly a curator at Tate Modern and London's ICA, as well as working as an independent curator in Europe and Japan. She was awarded an OBE for services to art in 2007.

İZ ÖZTAT lives and works in Istanbul. Her practice engages with diverse forms and media defined by her research. Since 2010, she has been engaged in an untimely collaboration with Zişan (1894–1970) who appears to her as a ghost, an alter ego, and a historical figure.

KEVSER GÜLER's curatorial research focuses on pondering the conditions and possibilities of artworks and exhibitions. Recent exhibitions for which Güler has undertaken curatorial responsibility include: *This Place*, Yapı Kredi Culture and Arts, 2021–22; *On Celestial Bodies*, Arter, 2020–21; *Coulisse: Hagop Ayvaz, A Chronicler of Theater*, Yapı Kredi Culture and Arts, 2020–21.

LEYLÂ GEDİZ is a graduate of Slade School of Fine Art (UCL) and Goldsmiths, University of London. She has held solo exhibitions in Istanbul, Los Angeles, Zurich, Helsinki, Amsterdam and Lisbon. Her works are included in the collections of Istanbul Modern (TR), Arter (TR), ARCO Foundation (ES) and Van Abbemuseum (NL).

MİSAL ADNAN YILDIZ is a curator, educator and researcher. Currently the Director of the Staatliche Kunsthalle Baden-Baden (DE), a post he shares with Çağla Ilk, he is the former Director of Artspace Aotearoa in Auckland (NZ) and the Artistic Director at Künstlerhaus Stuttgart (DE). He regularly contributes to international art periodicals.

MURAT ALAT attended secondary school at Galatasaray High School. He graduated from Istanbul Bilgi University with a BA in Public Relations and a minor in Cinema-Television. He received his master's degree from the Department of Cultural Studies of the same university. Since 2015, he has been writing on art in different publications.

NECMİ SÖNMEZ completed his PhD in art history at Johann Wolfgang Goethe University on Wolfgang Laib. He worked at Moderner Kunst Stiftung Museum Ludwig Vienna, Kunstmuseum Wiesbaden, Folkwang Museum Essen, Kunstakademie Kassel, FRAC Franche-Comté and Kunstverein Arnsberg. He is currently the curator of the Integration Monument project at Zeche Zollverein, Essen.

NİLÜFER ŞAŞMAZER works as an independent curator and editor. She co-curated Füreya Koral's retrospective exhibition, one of the pioneer ceramic artists in Turkey, and also co-authored and co-edited the accompanying monograph. She took part in the foundation of different art platforms. A member of AICA-Turkey, she has written, translated and edited texts for various printed and online publications.

PAOLO COLOMBO is a painter and a curator based in Athens. He curated the 6th Istanbul Biennial (1999), the 3rd Thessaloniki Biennial (2011), and the 2nd Mardin Biennial (2012). His work is in the collections of the Istanbul Modern, the Benaki Museum (Athens), and the Hammer Museum (LA). His poetry book, *Not in Sleep nor in Water* was published by Kiraathane, Istanbul in September 2021.

RABİA ÇAPA, a gallerist and collector, awarded the Knight of Art and Literature by the French Government in 2012, founded Maçka Art Gallery with her sister Varlık Sadıkoğlu in 1976. In 2016, she retired with a publication marking the 40h anniversary of the gallery titled *Looking at the Invisible* and handed the gallery over to Didem Çapa.

SALLY TALLANT is the President and Executive Director of the Queens Museum, New York. She was previously the Director of Liverpool Biennial (2011–19) and the Head of Programmes at the Serpentine Gallery, London (2001–11). In 2018 she was awarded an OBE for services to the Arts in the Queen's Birthday Honours List.

SEZA PAKER is a conceptual artist living and working in Paris and Istanbul. Characterised by a way of thinking, her practice is fluid, discursive and poetic. Paker employs a wide variety of expressive forms. She participated in the biennials of Gyumri, Thessaloniki, Buenos Aires, São Paulo, Santiago. Her works are in the collections of Arter and Istanbul Modern.

SELİM BİRSEL is a visual artist working with diverse medium. Since 1990, he has opened solo exhibitions and participated in a number of group exhibitions in Turkey and Europe. He has published three books. He's been teaching visual arts at Sabancı University since 1999.

TOLGA TÜZÜN (Prof Dr) works in the fields of sound design, improvisation and electronic music, along with his career in contemporary classical music composition. Since 2007 he has been teaching the philosophy of music, composition and electronic music at Istanbul Bilgi University.

Füsun Onur
Once upon a time...

59th International Art Exhibition
La Biennale di Venezia
Pavilion of Turkey

23 April–27 November 2022

Curator
Bige Örer

Exhibition and Project Manager
Selen Erkal

Business Development and Project Coordinator
Duygu Şengünler

Co-Editors
Bige Örer
Nilüfer Şaşmazer

Visual Identity and Book Design
Marcello Jacopo Biffi

Exhibition Designer
Yelta Köm

Lighting Consultant
Erinç Tepetaş

Assistant
Aslı Esra Kocamaz

International PR Agency
Polskin Arts & Communications Counselors

Web Developer
Kayhan Yalınkılıç

Advisory Board
Serhan Ada
Özalp Birol
İnci Eviner
Milovan Farronato
Fisun Yalçınkaya

Commissioner
Istanbul Foundation for Culture and Arts (İKSV)

General Director
Görgün Taner

Deputy Director General
Dr. Yeşim Gürer Oymak

Deputy Director General (Finance and Administration)
Mustafa Yegen

Director of İKSV Contemporary Art Projects
Bige Örer

Assistant to General Director
Nilay Kartal

Communications Group Director
Ayşe Bulutgil

Editorial Manager
Erim Şerifoğlu

Media Relations
Ayşegül Öneren
Talin Gidici
Coşku Atalay
Gizem Güngör

Archive
Esra Çankaya

Sales and Business Development
Dilan Beyhan
Erim Pala
Begüm Çavuşoğlu

Sponsorship Programme
Zeynep Pekgöz
Zeynep Karaman
Elif Doğan

Salon İKSV
Deniz Kuzuoğlu
Ufuk Şakar

Finance and Administration
Ahmet Buruk
Başak Sucu Yıldız
Kadir Altoprak
Deniz Yılmaz
Özlem Can Yaşar

Human Resources
Beste Kayacan

Services
Aydın Kaya
Şerif Kocaman

ACKNOWLEDGEMENTS

Ali Akay
Angelika Stepken
Aslıhan Altuğ
Ayşe Canan Atlığ
Ayşe Emek
Ayşen Ergene
Behiye Bobaroğlu
Beral Madra
Bilge Uğurlar
Burak Güç
Burcu Pelvanoğlu
Büke Akşehirli
Bülent Erkmen
Cem İleri
Ceyla & Timuçin Okdelen
Christian Oxenius
Çelenk Bafra
Derya Aydoğdu
Derya Bozcuk
Dilara Sezgin
Elif Kamışlı
Emil Nilsson
Emre Baykal
Evrim Altuğ
Ezgi Bakçay
Fulya Erdemci
Füsun Ertuğ
Gamze Öztürk
Goran Risteski
Göksu Aydoğan
Güler Demir
Hadiye Cangökçe
Hasan Karakaya
Helin Soruklu
Ilgın Erarslan Yanmaz
Iris Lenz
Itaru Hirano
İlhan Onur
İpek Elif Milli
Jane Quinn
Jennifer Chert
Katherine Cowan
Kıymet Daştan
Kurulay Ateş
Larissa Araz
Laurence Le Poupon
Leyla Bayrı
Luca Racchini
Margrit Brehm
Marina Verhoeven
Merve Çağlar
Merve Ünsal
Micol Saleri
Monica Fritz
Muammer Yanmaz
Nevzat Sayın
Noyan Ayturan
Nur Koçak
Onur Öztürk
Özge Araslı Yardım
Özge Uzunyayla
Rahmi Eyüboğlu
Rabia Çapa
Sarah-Neel Smith
Serap Kaçmaz
Sevim Sancaktar
Sezin Romi
Silvia Dall'Oca
Simonetta Gorreri
Suzana Milevska
Tamara Chalabi
Thomas Heyden
Tomur Atagök
Tuna Ortaylı
Ümit Mesci
Zeynep Arınç

Archives de la critique d'art
Akbank Sanat
Arter
Artlife for the World
Benice Logistics
Beykoz Kundura
Bursa Nilüfer Municipality
ChertLüdde, Berlin
documenta
Elgiz Museum
Galeri Nev Istanbul
Galerist
Govett Brewster Art Gallery
Istanbul Modern
Istanbul Painting and Sculpture Museum
Karşı Sanat
Kunsthalle Baden-Baden
Lunds Konsthall
Maçka Art Gallery
MAK Vienna
Maryland Institute College of Art, Decker Library
Middelheim Museum Library, Antwerpen
Modern Art Museum Saitama
Musée d'Art et d'Histoire Cholet
Neues Museum Nürnberg
Österreichische Galerie Belvedere
Prilep, Center for Contemporary Arts
Proje 4L
Rodeo London
Ruya Maps
SAHA Association
SALT Research
Städtische Galerie Rastatt
The Turkish Fulbright Commission
Üsküdar American Academy
Van Abbemuseum
Visual Arts Department, ifa Gallery Stuttgart
Yapı Kredi Culture and Arts
Women's Works Library and Information
Centre Foundation, Istanbul
ZKM, Karlsruhe

COMMISSIONER

The Pavilion of Turkey at la Biennale di Venezia is organised by the Istanbul Foundation for Culture and Arts (İKSV).

Istanbul Foundation for Culture and Arts (İKSV) is a non-profit cultural institution. Since 1973, the Foundation continues its efforts to enrich Istanbul's cultural and artistic life. İKSV regularly organises the Istanbul Festivals of Music, Film, Theatre and Jazz, the Istanbul Biennial, the Istanbul Design Biennial, Leyla Gencer Voice Competition, autumn film week Filmekimi and realises one-off events throughout the year. The Foundation hosts cultural and artistic events from various disciplines at its performance venue Salon İKSV, located at the Nejat Eczacıbaşı Building, and offers creative events programme for children and youngsters at İKSV Alt Kat.

İKSV organises the Pavilion of Turkey at the International Art and Architecture Exhibitions of la Biennale di Venezia, conducts studies and drafts reports with the aim of contributing to cultural policy development, and supports artistic and cultural production through presenting awards at its festivals, commissioning works, taking part in international and local co-productions and coordinating an artist residency programme at Cité Internationale des Arts in France, as well as the annual Aydın Gün Encouragement, Talât Sait Halman Translation, and Gülriz Sururi-Engin Cezzar Theatre Encouragement Awards.

İKSV celebrates its 50th anniversary in 2022.

iksv.org

Organised by

ISTANBUL FOUNDATION FOR CULTURE AND ARTS İKSV

SUPPORTERS

With the Contribution of

REPUBLIC OF TÜRKIYE MINISTRY OF CULTURE AND TOURISM

Under the Auspices of

REPUBLIC OF TURKEY MINISTRY OF FOREIGN AFFAIRS

Production and Publication Support

SAHA
SUPPORTING CONTEMPORARY ART FROM TURKEY

Airline Partner

TURKISH AIRLINES

SUPPORTERS

The Istanbul Foundation for Culture and Arts would like to thank the supporters of the Pavilion of Turkey at the 59th International Art Exhibition, La Biennale di Venezia:

Abdi İbrahim
Akbank
Akfen Holding
Mey | Diageo
Sevil Dolmacı
Füsun & Faruk Eczacıbaşı
Oya & Bülent Eczacıbaşı
Ahu & Can Has
Emin Hitay
Vuslat Doğan Sabancı & Ali Sabancı
Rana & Erol Tabanca
Sinan Tara
Z. Yıldırım Family

The Istanbul Foundation for Culture and Arts would like to thank the following individuals and institutions for their contribution towards a long-term venue for the Pavilion of Turkey for the period 2014–2034:

Akbank
Mehveş & Dalınç Arıburnu
Berrak & Nezih Barut
Ali Raif Dinçkök
Vuslat Doğan Sabancı & Ali Sabancı
Füsun & Faruk Eczacıbaşı
Oya & Bülent Eczacıbaşı
Nesrin Esirtgen
Eti Gıda San. ve Tic. AŞ
Garanti BBVA
Ahu & Can Has
Öner Kocabeyoğlu
MAÇAKIZI
Tansa Mermerci Ekşioğlu
SAHA Association
Rana & Erol Tabanca
Sinan Tara
Taha Tatlıcı
Vehbi Koç Foundation
Zafer Yıldırım
Yıldız Holding AŞ

MONOGRAPH

This book is published by the Istanbul Foundation for Culture and Arts (İKSV) and Mousse Publishing on the occasion of the exhibition:

Füsun Onur
Once upon a time...

59th International Art Exhibition
La Biennale di Venezia
Pavilion of Turkey

23 April–27 November 2022

Co-Editors
Bige Örer & Nilüfer Şaşmazer

Publishing Editor
Ilaria Bombelli, Mousse

Graphic Design
Marcello Jacopo Biffi, Mousse

Contributors
Ahu Antmen
Alev Ersan
Anna Boghiguian
Anne Barlow
Aslı Seven
Ayşe Erek
Bige Örer
Carolyn Christov-Bakargiev
Chus Martinez
Defne Ayas
Deniz Gül
Fatih Özgüven
Gregory Volk
HG Masters
Hera Büyüktaşçıyan
Iwona Blazwick
İz Öztat
Kevser Güler
Leyla Gediz
Misal Adnan Yıldız
Murat Alat
Necmi Sönmez
Paolo Colombo
Rabia Çapa
Sally Tallant
Selim Birsel
Seza Paker
Tolga Tüzün

Translation from Turkish
Irazca Geray (unless otherwise stated)
Nicholas Glastonbury (pp. 4–8, 44–61, 74–80)

Proofreading
Melissa Larner

Printing and binding
Ofset Yapımevi, Istanbul

Published and distributed by
Mousse Publishing – Contrappunto s.r.l.
via Pier Candido Decembrio 28
20137 Milan – Italy

Available through
Mousse Publishing, Milan
moussemagazine.it
DAP | Distributed Art Publishers, New York
artbook.com
Les presses du réel, Dijon
lespressesdureel.com
Antenne Books, London
antennebooks.com
Idea Books, Amsterdam
ideabooks.nl

Courtesy
All images are courtesy of Füsun Onur and:
Akbank Sanat (pp. 228–230)
Arter (pp. 98, 117, 122, 129, 131, 133–135, 136, 139–141, 144, 148–149, 156, 157, 164, 175, 183, 205, 207–209, 227 below, 238–239, 242–247)
ChertLüdde Galerie (p. 249)
documenta archiv (p. 231)
Füsun & Faruk Eczacıbaşı (p. 100)
Govett-Brewster Art Gallery (p. 210)
Harvard Art Museums / Fogg Museum, Louise E. Bettens Fund (p. 82)
ifa (p. 179)
Istanbul Modern (p. 178)
İKSV (p. 199)
Lunds Konsthall (pp. 211–213)
Maçka Art Gallery (pp. 152–153, 166, 167, 184, 185, 190–191, 202–203, 232–234)
MAK Vienna (pp. 236, 237)
Proje 4L (p. 216)
Rodeo, London / Piraeus (p. 214)
RUYA MAPS (pp. 100, 115, 162–163, 220)
Van Abbemuseum Archive (p. 192)
Yapı Kredi Culture and Arts (pp. 177, 219)

Photo credits
© Andrea Rossetti (p. 249)
© CNAP (p. 184)
© Esen Karol (p. 145)
© flufoto (pp. 177, 207)
© Hadiye Cangökçe (pp. 10–23, 117, 122, 129, 131, 136, 144, 156, 157, 164, 183, 205, 227 below, 242–247)
© Işık Kaya (pp. 222–223)
© İlhan Onur (pp. 100, 109)
© Katrin Wißkirchen / MAK Vienna (p. 236)
© Murat Germen (pp. 98, 133–135, 139–141, 148–149, 208–209, 238–239)
© Natalie Barki (p. 227 above)
© Pavel Gorshkov (p. 217)
© Peter Cox (p. 192)
© President and Fellows of Harvard College, 1934.182 (p. 82)
© Rıza Ertekin (p. 194)
© Rupert Steiner / MAK Vienna (p. 237)
© Ryszard Kasiewicz (p. 231)
© Sarkis (p. 125)
© Stefano Campo Antico (p. 221)
© Werner Maschmann (p. 142)

The publisher would like to thank all those who have kindly given their permission for the reproduction of material for this book. Every effort has been made to obtain permission to reproduce the images and texts in this catalogue. However, as is standard editorial policy, the publisher is at the disposal of copyright holders and undertakes to correct any omissions or errors in future editions.

ISBN 978-88-6749-513-9
EUR 27 / USD 30

Istanbul Foundation for Culture and Arts
Nejat Eczacıbaşı Binası
Sadi Konuralp Caddesi No: 5
34433 Şişhane, Istanbul, Turkey

iksv.org